[0.3.] WELCOME PAGE

Author at work on early drafts, summer 1993, Univ. of Wis.

← *At left* is the LIAISON PAGE. [It gives the rationale of the whole project, which includes Mind-Play, the "repertoire" of thinking skills, of which Teaching Thinking is the advance-guard component.]

→ *Here below*, is a three-part ORIENTATION to Teaching Thinking:

First: to reveal the two-part structure of this book:

-- → **(1) Main Body**—is all about" the teaching-and-learning of thinking, of course…

-- → **(2) Appendix**—is of two types of valuable material. **(A)** Elaborations on thinking-issues in the Main Body, to supplement. **(B)** "Tool Kits" of generic thinking skills: complete-compact-clear. These are: (1) for direct use, also (2) to show how even complex skills can be stated/taught more explicitly, without becoming rote.

Second: to disclose our own view of the project:

I recognized this project's challenges. The issue is both important and difficult. My standards are high. My abilities though strong are of course finite… I've met these challenges via specific methods (noted later), and dedication. Hence, *those who wish insights, can find them here.*

Third: → to help "navigate" the book:

Suggestions: **(1)** at least, **visit the Introduction**, pp. **5-31** anyhow. (*This may suffice for many readers*). **(2)** **Rely on its "Helpdesk" section**, for orientation into the book. **(3)** **Keep in mind the 3 "pillar"-principles** which throughout we use to elucidate "teaching thinking":

-----**(1) The *overall* GOAL: The true "Content" of a course, is now the Skills.** Education's traditional paradigm has as goal, "what to **"Know, Believe, Do"**. It prioritizes content-knowledge about the subject; skills stayed secondary. The emergent model has as goal "how to **"Think Things Through"**. *This reverses things 180 degrees.* Now the true "content" (=substance, stuff, material) of the course is the concepts, perspectives, thinking skills. Factual-knowledge "content" is ample-enough, but functions to elucidate those skills. [True, stating it thus *is* "extreme," as a 100%-purist "Ideal Type." But only to firmly convey the essence of the approach. It may seem as "new" as "earth circles sun not otherwise," "we came from apes not angels," "the people, not God or King, rule."]

-----**(2) The degree of PRESENCE-and-visibility of thinking is an issue.** Is thinking sufficiently "Embedded" in individual courses … sufficiently "Exhibited" as school-wide goals? [And as noted above, even complex skills can be elucidated more **explicitly without** becoming formulaic **rules**]. [This is an overlooked issue.]

-----**(3) The *specific* END-GOAL is defined.** Learners can "Hit The Ground Running." That is, they possess "ultimate expectable readiness" to think well in *the world after school*. [= Can confront complex issues by competent thinking, on their own in "real-life" after graduation… Civic issues: Abortion Bureaucracy Crime Demographics Energy/Environment Finance Globalization etc.—and Vocational and Personal issues too…'] [This helps "assess outcomes".]

-----And we can add the three basic moves. To **Conceptualize, Transfer, Apply.** [= 1. To move **UP** from domain-specific data to the general-generic concepts within the data…..then 2. to *transfer* these skills **OVER/ACROSS** to the "real world" …..and then 3. apply them **DOWN** upon issues even far-removed from the course subject.] We also call this **AAA** or the Autonomous Application of Abstractions {*not* the American Automobile Association}… [This is known, yet new to some]

→ **The teacher first grasps this approach for self. Then s/he must make sure the students know: are clear not confused.**

EXAMPLE. "Writing, or composition," as subject and skill—specific, but then "C.T.A." to situations in real-world arenas:

The **domain-specific** skills:	The **more general-generic** versions:	Some **uses of them in life:**
Sequence… Categorizing… Syntax… Subject-development… Audience-relating… Rhetorical modes… Prewriting process…	"Proportion, balance"…Right-brain creative plus left-brain logical… Introspection self-expression plus empathy with audience… Making choices f/ the given situation or task…	Applied to task-goal situations in real life after School: in Personal, Vocational, Civic arenas…

[0.4.] TABLE OF CONTENTS

PAGES:	CONTENTS and brief description:

[II] the APPENDICES

[= important supplementary material of two types:

[1.] Expanded treatments of basic concepts in TT introduced earlier. (Such as the three principles of TT (goals, presence, end-goal) #2.2 ... basic conceptualizing itself #2.3 ... indispensable "generic-basic" thinking skills often omitted #2.5 ...)

[2.] "Tool-Kits" [#2.4, 1-7] or instructions on how-to-do certain classic thinking skills. These are for (A) direct use, but also (B) to support our stand concerning explicitness in skill-teaching: Namely, that "Even complex skills can be taught-and-used more explicitly, but without becoming oversimplified; and also more completely, but yet remaining clear-and-accessible and thus usable." *]

[I.] INTRODUCTION

→ TABLE OF CONTENTS [Pp. 7-40]

5

IV. To improve understanding: some "**Lab-Exercises**:"
X Graham, X Letter to Editor. X Rose for Emily {"II"}, X Art Contacts 101 totally redesigned.

3. The "HELP-DESK"—*for orientation* | P. 23

[A] **Definitions:** of thinking, of teaching/learning it.

1. *Overall-**goal*** of education ... 2. **Degree of "presence"** embedded, exhibited?... 3. Specific **end-goal**
Graphics: three visual diagrams

[B] **Directory:** showing where Pillars are discussed further within <u>Teaching Thinking</u>.

4. The BRIDGE to the BOOK" or "*Exit-Platform*" | P. 28

[A] **"Wallet-Card":** the book's whole thrust in a paragraph—well, one page.

[B] **Last "Gallery":**

[X "Staged scuffle in history class"... X *Table* [X Cause-Effect, X Lens-work, X Dualism]... X *Table* "Hit Ground Running"]

[C] **"Farewell-Envoi"...**

5. An "ANNEX" {or "*Supply-Room/Staff Lounge*"} | P. 32

[...to PROFFER BACKGROUND INFO if and as desired ...]

[A] Specific **Paired Assignment-Examples**, "beast and beauty"

[B] **Analogies** second set

[C] **"FAQ's"** 13 Objections

[D] **Personal Story of the Author,** and why...

[{(END of the TABLE OF CONTENTS of the "Introduction" to <u>Teaching Thinking</u>...)}]

|~#+#|+~|+#|+|~+#|+~#|~#+#+#~||~#+|~|#~|~#+|#+|~+#|+~|#+|~#|#|#+|+#|~|+#~|+|~+|#|#~+#|~|+#|~#|+#|~|#|~+#|~+#|~+|#+~|#+|~#||

<table>
<tr><td>

→ **QUESTION, or OBJECTION:**
wait, I've skimmed ahead, and <u>your approach seems *much too self-consciously over-explanatory*</u>.. Too much telling us of what you're doing, how, and why. (Enough *"navel-gazing under the hood"* already!...) Repeating basics, too. Why don't you just <u>get on with it</u> and *tell us how* to teach/learn thinking, *please!*

</td><td>

</td><td>

I hear you. *However,* "the longest way round is the best way there." We are *"confronting complexity (thinking) completely."* We are providing an **overall conceptual framework**, of the **Big-Picture overview** from scratch—to provide people with fullest understandings, plural. [ANALOGY: **"Not just quick verbal directions to downtown, but a printed map of the whole large city for you to take along, use later."**] Plus note that we are *modeling* actual thinking-skills as we go! *Bear with us...*

</td></tr>
</table>

ORIENTATION-BAR:

→ [1.] MAIN INTRO: ["Reception-Room"] Who? Why? What? How? Whoa!	[2.] READINGS: ["Library / Theatre"] 3 Pillars...Issues... Analogies..."Lab"... forthcoming	[3.] HELPDESK [The "Summaries"] 1. Key Definitions 2. Directory to TTh	[4.] BRIDGE to the BOOK: ["Exit-Walkway"] 1. Book in 1 Page! 2. Final Readings	[5.] ANNEX: ["Supply-Room"] 1. Examples 2. Analogies 3. FAQ's {"II"} 4. Author's Story

[I.A.] the INTRO. "PROPER"...

Who we are...   **Why** this book in the first place...   **What** the book does and does not do, f/ Purposes, also f/ Content...   **How** it's done "well or better"...   And **"Whoa!"**: or, questions *and* objections, with our responses...

(A) "WHO wrote this?" [The individual author...]

BIOGRAPHICAL DISCLOSURE. This by BRIAN K. BECK, Ph.D., veteran teacher (college, humanities, freshmen and advanced courses: Wisconsin U.S.A. 1966-94)....   [{ **3 books (satire, poetry/visuals, graphics), 200 articles (35 on social issues, 135 general, 50 on pedagogy); see CV, P. 135** }] --From the start, he sought to practice Teaching Thinking....   At first he did *not* understand this quite-new paradigm (his earlier attempts failed or fell short). So he **(1) researched** the large literature on TT, **(2) implemented** it in classes—slowly..., **(3)** *finally* **comprehended** it (discussed in pedagogical articles). And now **(4)** has at last created what he **offers** here, an **"encoding"** of the **"conceptual topography"** of TT. A guide which he *wishes he had had earlier* while teaching....

   "REASSURANCE": he operates *not* as messianic guru or Reformer, *but* as curator or Steward of a valued tradition and emerging realizations; *admittedly via his own perspective, but* aiming for clarity not persuasion...

   [SEE ALSO: FULL Biography, Intro., **P. 42** and "vita" **P. 135**]

All good. **BUT** is that as candid as you wish to be about your motivations?	Well, also to enrich education, preserve thinking, enhance living... *That* sort of thing, you know...

\=\=|+|+\=\=|+|+\=\=|+|+\=\=\+|+|+\=\=\+|+|+\=\=|+|+\=\=|+|+\=\+|+|+\=\=|+|+\=\=|+|+\=\=\=\+|+|+\=\+|+|\=|+|+|+\=\=|+|+|=\+||

(B) "WHY do we do this?" Basic assumptions, rationale. As stated earlier:

1. Thinking is valuable, four ways: --**pragmatically**-practically (for succeeding better in all task goals) ... --for **principle** (to viewing clear thinking as "moral-ethical") ... --**pedagogically** (for fortifying true education)... --and **pleasurably** for sheer sportive "play of mind" or contest against "foe" of ignorance/confusion (to *enjoy* this, as thinker, and as spectator)...

   "II" FULL View: What we mean by "thinking": 4 key aspects for utter "advanced-beginner" learners:

1. It DOES WHAT?: Thinking = confronting content conceptually. ["**confront**" = to describe, explain, interpret, evaluate, etc. etc. etc., ABCDE Abortion Bureaucracy Crime etc. etc. etc.] ... This is simple enough, except that often, **challenges** exists. As when **1.** the content is **complex**, **2.** the task is **crucial**, "important to do well" ... and maybe **3.** the criteria or standards to meet are high, demanding), **4.** hence **competence** is needed—the thinker/doer must have sufficient "savvy & sweat"...

2. |It is of THREE MAIN TYPES or "MOVES":| Thinking = **1.** <u>Induction;</u> conceptualizing UP from factual data toward the ideas within... **2.** Then <u>deduction</u>: applying concepts DOWNward upon specific subject-matter... Also **3.** <u>Lateral</u> or associative-connective thinking ACROSS to related subject-matters... Basic to know!

3. |It is TRUE OR HIGHER-ORDER THINKING:| Thinking = specifically, "<u>essential</u>" thinking (the higher-order type of true thinking always needed). *Beyond* valuable-but limited "critical thinking." *We identify eleven trait,* including of course higher-order... non-formulaic... supple: flexible ... and others... See below...

4. |It is largely "new/different" in formal EDUCATION:| Traditional ("Old/School") paradigm, **goal** is what to <u>Know Believe or Do</u>, *but* "New-Think" **goal** is how to <u>Think It Through</u>, with the specific end-goal outcome-ability to "<u>Hit The Ground Running</u>" (=think about real-world issues later on, on one's own, and competently)... "AAAAAA": Apply Abstractions Anew, and Ably and Autonomously and with Awareness

2. <u>Complex thinking is needed and is possible.</u>
Complex *content* (and most is) repays indeed requires not simple but complex *thinking*.
(And clear views of complexity are difficult but possible...)

3. <u>But complex thinking ["the very ideas"] may get *shortchanged* today:</u>

A. In <u>actual daily thinking</u> in real-world arenas (personal, vocational, civic life)...

TABLE. To see cases where in real-world tasks, vital **concepts** remain unstated:		
The **Subject** discussed:	Factual **Content** in "real-world" publications:	The key **Concepts** which many texts omit, if their authors even derived them:
MICROWAVE OVENS	This and that recipe	Size, placement of food for best cooking...
"CHINESE STIR-FRY COOKING"	Ingredients:	"Small-Sized Food Pieces, Hot Pan Heat, Oil Added When Pan Hot, Ingredients Added so All are Done Cooking Simultaneously, Constant-Continuous Vigorous Stirring, Very Brief Cooking Time."
"EVALUATING A RESTAURANT MEAL"	specific meals, menus, chefs, restaurants, experiences	1. <u>Historical-Social-Traditional</u> A. Classic vs. Innovation B. Ethnic variations C. Basic Flavor-Balance 2. <u>Personal-Individual</u> A. The Particular Chef B. The Particular Diner/Critic 3. <u>Explicit Ranking-Criteria</u> A. Star-systems B. Severity of Standards?
"TIME-MANAGE-MENT"	this and that technique...	1. **Goal-setting.** 2. <u>Prioritizing</u>; specifically, 3. <u>Ranking tasks</u> in four very important categories: as to whether **"Urgent and Important; Urgent but not Important; Important but not Urgent; neither Urgent nor Important"** 4. <u>Lead-Time Planning</u>: Stages
"CRITERIA FOR PUBLIC-ART DISPLAYS"	unconceptualized opinions, the assumptions not clear	1. Conventional Folk-Familiarity 2. Trendy-Edgy Fashionable 3. Laissez-Faire Relativism 3. Pure Visual Aesthetic Design 4. Meaningful Staying-Power 5. ...at least a half-dozen other concepts
HUMOR: COMEDY, WIT, ETC.	No or vague ideas.	1. <u>Aggression</u>. Malice at others' misfortunes. 2. <u>Repression</u>. Topics taboo to discuss. 3. <u>Anxiety-management</u>. Topic painful to confront, uncontrollable. 4. <u>Surprise; Incongruity</u>.
COMPUTERS	Endless instructions	"<u>Functional Abstraction</u>": hierarchy of parts with well-define one-directional interactions. Some <u>separation of levels</u> from each other... "<u>Linear Sequentiality</u>"
...SOME VARIOUS OTHER FIELDS: KEYSTONE CONCEPTS:		Teaching, "imperturbability"... business, "consistency-of-quality/service"... cinematography, "where to place the camera"...

Well, you **DO** cinch your concept with well-chosen examples: varied, but relevant and convincing... Plus you compare the good-rare, with the bad-prevalent...	Which was our intention... And, both **specificity**, and **comparison/contrast**, are both *key thinking skills*... SEE a Tool-Kits on both, App. 4, **P. 270,** and in App. 5.

B. In current-traditional <u>education</u> in the schools...

The subject taught:	Usual **factual-content**, and lower-level skills: *[insufficient...]*	Higher-order keystone **concepts** of the subject: *[enhanced...]*
algebra	(various formulae)	"combination," "permutation," "association"—the **keystones**
sociology	Institutions, social problems. Often <u>some</u> **concepts** (role, status, norm, deviancy, socialization, etc.)	**Theories**: Functionalism, Conflict, Interactionism... **Perspectives**: Debunking, Unrespectable, Cosmopolitan, Relativism...
art history	Egyptian, Greek, Medieval styles....and so forth.	Composition **principles**: balance, proportion, sequence, unity, a/symmetry, simplicity, contrast! Line, form, value,!
literature	Periods. Authors. Themes.	"Schools of Criticism" as **lenses**: biographical, aesthetic, historical, psychological, social-critical, etc.!
computers	this and that program...	"linear sequentiality"
economics	formulae, data on problems...	"scarcity" "allocation cost," or "cost-benefit ratio"—as immensely-applicable everywhere, always!
Natural Sciences	Biology, etc.: facts of mitosis-meiosis and the like, more...	<u>General Concepts of Science</u>: **Dynamic Equilibrium; Change & Evolution; Scale & Proportion; Causality & Consequence; Energy, Its Sources & Transfer...**
geography	[data, data, data...]	["Why is it like it is, here?"]
political science	[info on government systems]	How to confront the recurrent **Big Issues**: individual freedom vs. group security, etc., etc., etc.
history	"kings, courts, dates..."	[Past-present continuities, dissimilarities, etc.]
math	This and that procedure.....	(*) <u>Generic / Generalist Skills</u>: Problem-solving: Trial and error; "Step backwards"; Simulation; Symbolism; Patterns... Cause-and-Effect...
OTHERS:		
APPLIED:	Business, Engineering, Law, Medicine, Technology, Military, Government, etc...	

...okay, but here I'm **NOT** so sure that all schools fall as short as you suggest...	...not all, but many; but anyway you make your own decisions here...

C. In currently-available resource-materials for learning thinking...

4. <u>Hence this publication</u>. A better orientation plus handbook

["Any new writing on a written-about subject must be justified: new or different or anyhow useful/needed."]

BUT, an objection! Aren't these good ideas *already obvious, known*, and now *practiced* already in education today? Anyhow, more-and-more?.....	<u>No</u>, in that *certain forces currently oppose*: 1. <u>**Decline of standards of quality**</u>—and of peoples' knowing and valuating same. 2. <u>**Anti-generalization**</u>: technical specialization instead of this overall strategic monitoring toward "general overview as a specialty in itself" 3. <u>**Fashionable relativism/nihilism**</u>, idea that "we can't know reality at all, only our images of it, which are always biased by power-concerns," etc. ["True," *but an either-or fallacy: only partially the case...!*] 4. <u>**Within education**</u>, cultural lag or "cake of custom." The "Old-School" paradigm ("what to know") persists, plus good *introductory-orienting* info about "how to think" (the new paradigm) is still rare. 5. Still <u>**other factors**</u>, more obvious ones such as "standardized testing" and external forces... *Thus some challenges to confront...*

\=\=|+|+|+\=\=|+|+|+\=\=|+|+|+\=\=\+|+|+\=\=\+|+|+\=\=|+|+|+\=\+|+|+\=\=|+|+|+\=\=|+|+|=\=\=\+|+|+\=\+|+|\=|+|+|+|+\=\=|+|+|+|=\+||

(C) "WHAT WE DO AND DON'T": our approach is clearly-focused:

[1.] Our CONTENT: what this resource does *not* contain, and *does*:	**[2.] Our PURPOSES:** what we do *not* try to do, and what we *do* seek to offer:

1. We **OMIT** emphasizing what most people imagine is teaching thinking: traditional specialized "**critical thinking.**"

CLARIFICATION. "Logic, reasoning, argument, fallacy-avoidance." All these are important, but (ironically) are sometimes (not inevitably) [1] *too limited-specialized* to cover **essential generic** thinking. Plus, they are [2] *already covered,* well, in many resource-materials on C.T.

2. We **OMIT** emphasizing **other domain-specific subtypes of thinking** (scientific, creative, problem-solving, etc.) (--*Except as they do illustrate general-generic thinking skills.*)

3. We **OMIT** discussing "more **effective teaching**" per se. (--*Except related to teaching thinking.*)

4. We **OMIT** exploring **teaching movements, cycles, trends.** (➔ Including current movements, especially [*ca.* 2007], the *active or student-centered* approach to learning, also critical literacy; etc. (--Except as they *seem* to "teach thinking," *but* do they really?...).

5. We **OMIT** dealing with **integrative, liberal/general-education** learning. (--Again *except as related to higher-order thinking*—connecting, synthesizing, etc.)

[OUR ROLE(S) HERE. As noted above, not "gurus," but "stewards" of an approach ...]

1. We **DON'T argue, persuade, convince, "sell."** (Bible or soapbox manifesto). Our audience is only those interested… [--*Still, we do offer enthusiasm…*]

2. We **DON'T** give simply **Our Personal Story, diary, journal**—how we experienced teaching. Objectivity is better… [--*Still, personal testimony and voice is important.*]

3. We **DON'T** present undigested **Formal Research Reports**… [--*Still, we have distilled much from the vast literature…*]

4. We **DON'T** offer **rote instructions, recipe-rulebook** style. (No "What to do at 9:00 Mon. A.M. in Rm. 212.") Teaching true thinking by rote, would be—ironic! [--*Still, the best formulae do offer both focus plus flexibility, are quite usable thus…*]

CONTENT, continued...

6. …*instead*, we do aim to elucidate **(A) a certain kind of THINKING, and (B) its TEACHING / learning.**

[A] Essential" thinking – that is, "*essential*" in two senses of the word… #1, in principle, it is "of-the-*essence* of true thinking"; and #2 pragmatically, it is *essential*-to-know, in order to think well. (With ten traits: higher-order, meta-formulaic, self-aware, seven others…)

[B] The teaching of thinking: an alternate paradigm… [see below]

PURPOSES, continued...

5. Instead, we **DO** offer an introductory orientation plus resource-guide. A "familiarization tour" of Thinking Territory. **Awareness** of the lay of the land, **Ability** to navigate it.

To do this we use throughout a particular thinking tool. We "mention *all* the key issues, and for *each* issue, all the A-to-Z options." We call this tool "**variables-variation.**"

PRE-VIEW: The alternate paradigm of teaching thinking, in a capsule-nutshell:

(1) Goal #1: GENERAL-OVERALL goal of education—is toward thinking.
Not "Knowing-about" subjects, but Thinking them through to attain goals.

REASSURANCE: yes indeed this is stated 100% purist "Ideal-Type," as if crudely-extremist, but not to dictate, only to clarify a new approach against misunderstanding, (or "backsliding" as into content-coverage as usual, and the like…)

(2) Degree of EXPLICIT "presence" of thinking in a school program—is high.
(A) in specific courses—are thinking-skills "embedded," included solidly?
   (1) quite ABSENT from the course…? (Instructor never selected X and Y skill…)
   (2) are EMBRYONIC (only "suggested, implied, talked-about, etc.)…?

(3) made EXPLICIT (tools are explicitly given)…? → **Students informed clearly about this new approach!**
(4) TAUGHT AND TRANSFERRED (tools are practiced) and TESTED-FOR (as required)?)

(B) in whole <u>school</u> itself—are thinking-goals ”exhibited,” stated overtly?)…..
(1) quite NON-EXISTENT hence of course UNMENTIONED?…
(2) talked-of but only in GENERALITIES…?
(3) *“BILLBOARDED”* or given more attention (whether beyond “lip-service publicity,” or not…)?
(4) created, and then conveyed in explicit, detailed (but non-formulaic) ENCODINGS or STATEMENTS?

(3) GOAL #2: specific end-goal for learner. We’ve phrased this two ways.
--<u>Formally</u>, we say “*Ultimate Expectable Preparedness*”: ability to think through real-world problem-issues on one’s own later on…
--<u>Informally</u>, we phrase it, ability to “*Hit The Ground Running*…” and tackle the issue with tools-at-hand…

\=\=|+|+|+\=\=|+|+|+\=\=|+|+|=\=\+|+|+\=\=\+|+|+\=\=|+|+|+\=\+|+|+\=\=|+|+\=\=|+|=\=\=\+|+|+\=\+|\=|+|+|+\=\=|+|+|=\+||

(D) “HOW” we do it—and, do it “better”?

Okay, **BUT** you claim you offer nothing “new.” <u>But don't enough other introductions to “teaching thinking” exist</u>? So *how is yours* **distinct** <u>enough to be</u> *better*? (As you said, any new book or additional text, in today's overloaded info-glut and data-smog, must be justified: either new, or better…)	Fair question. We’d be more **“elucidating”**: complete *yet also* conceptualized (thought-through) *and also* clear/accessible. This is explained later: here, just get the *sense* of it via **four ANALOGIES employing the subject of** <u>“travel,”</u> and one using <u>“a small machine”</u>: (1) **“Familiarization Tour”**: travel-industry professionals take this to acquaint themselves with a tourist-target region. May lack total depth, *but empowers* with strong overview, orientation… (2) **“Two guidebooks to a foreign region** for the adventurous traveler. Each 200 pages. But **the first, inferior**: unbalanced, thin, incomplete, biased, vague… And then **the second, superior**: bird’s-eye overview plus compact distilled data… all bases covered neither skimpy nor overdone… the reader's needs always attended to… and more!... *And it can be done!* (3) **Purposes: particular vs. principled.** Telling people **information**, recipes, arguments, stories (how to bicycle in Burgundy, you should do social work in Africa, our trip to Japanese museums…) vs. the keystone **issues** in travel: Purposes, Security, Timing, Equipment, Modes of Movement, Rapport with Natives, etc…. The point: *let key concepts provide many options!* (4) <u>Two Maps of a Large Urban Area.</u> **(A)** “How to get from here to your destination downtown,” scrawled on an envelope by a friend, versus **(B)** complete map, showing *all* regions, options, possible detours! *Which would you prefer to gain ultimate empowerment?* Finally, another **ANALOGY**: I often think of the subject to be communicated, as if it were like “a small complex <u>machine</u>.” First **<u>un</u>-elucidated**: [= as if “dirty-&-disassembled in a dark workshop at night”] … But then **elucidated**: [= as if “repaired, set up in a museum on display on eye-level revolving platform under shadowless lighting, all parts labeled, etc.…”]

Okay, impressive goals, **BUT** is it just pie-in-the-sky? Exactly *how* do you **elucidate** better? Don’t just say “good writing”…	See the table right here below. (Also shows **Consciousness** of our own thinking: “meta-cognition.”)

To present difficult material clearly, we employ these “thinking moves”:

1. Overall goal, **“Elucidation”** or a more-competent image of a subject which is *simultaneously* more **Comprehensive** (complete) *but also* more **Comprehended** (conceptualized: understood, interpreted, explained, etc.) and also more **Comprehensible** (compact-clarified for best audience-intelligibility). [ANALOGY: not just the “entrance-lobby,” but “the whole 12-story building,” and in 3-D blueprint!]
2. [*] Especially via <u>correlating contraries</u> [= serving *both* of *two* opposing, conflicting *but* valuable-necessary polar demands]. Especially **Conceptual** (*key ideas more clear*) and **Concrete** (*more, better examples-of*), plus a half-dozen other dialectics…
3. [A] <u>“Essential” Thinking</u> used—higher-order, also Conscious or self-aware. [B] Plus, **“Variables-Variation”**: give not just one provincial position, but state all options, and the pros and cons of each.
4. <u>Varied learning-styles</u>. Exposition. Experiencing actively. Visual or graphic. Interactive argument. Etc. [*As done here already!*]
5. <u>Structure</u>. Material [4A.] <u>staged</u>, in “I” Brief and “II” Full views, for varied readers’ varied needs, also easier gradual absorption. Also [4B.] <u>“hypertexty”: connections, references</u> to related skills, previews, reviews.

6. <u>Formatting layout "encoding."</u> Different types of material (points, examples, references, etc.) given in different styles of type and borders etc., for easier identification.

\=\=|+|+|+\=\=|+|+|+\=\=|+|+|+|=\=\+|+|+\=\=\+|+|+\=\=|+|+|+\+|+|+\=\=|+|+\=\=|+|+|=\=\=\+|+|+\=\+|\=|+|+|+|+\=\=|+|+|+|=\+||

(E) "WHOA…" But readers may still have questions (as they should):

Here, the key FAQ "frequently asked questions"—also FVO, "Frequently Voiced Objections": And Responses …

[1.] *Superfluous?* If nothing "new" here, <u>how is this book needed,</u> since other books discuss thinking?	But we just *explained* this; see [D] above…

[2.] *Overdone?* Your approach seems <u>topheavy:</u> <u>over-elaborated, too complexly-complete.</u> What if we only want a simplified version to use in class "next Monday morning"?	Let me state totally firmly, that we here go for **true thinking**: <u>complete comprehension of the key variables above-and-behind specific actions.</u> [In our jargon: "beyond surface features routinized, the conceptual topography of contours and operations for better orientation and navigation."] This is in itself, ironically, **essential thinking** *itself*! I return to this later, but for now remind you of that best travel ANALOGY. *"Two maps of a large city."* (1) is *"a sketch of where you are now, to the destination you want this afternoon,"* drawn by a friend on an envelope. (2) is *a quality map of the complete city area, all roads, all points.* Which do you prefer—no, scratch that: which will give the traveler much more competence in confronting changing complexities? [Quick how-to recipes on teaching thinking, or the in-depth from-scratch whole picture to let you truly control things?] The first map is *easy but expedient, limited*; the second, *truly empowering. I rest my case; we offer the second map only. Each to one's own; solid completeness is our privilege-and-duty here; for shortcuts, seek elsewhere…*

[3.] *Unnecessary?* I think enough educators generally <u>all already know about</u> teaching thinking and are doing more of it.	*We'd strongly question this.* Few educators (including ourselves earlier) truly comprehend this paradigm-shift: **"Now true course 'content' is no longer the substance, but the skills (content enters to support same). And true course goal, is not to know, but how to think and apply…")**
	--ANALOGY: Most classes' final exams are more like "now, harvest the corn I the teacher gave you in lecture," rather than "now, demonstrate how to grow corn on your own"…
	--EXAMPLE. The assignment on "A Rose For Emily" (to follow) is *grossly embryonic, primitive, inept as true education*—at least via the paradigm of "thinking skills as the goal"]… <u>But</u> not all teachers at first will easily recognize the assignment's *stunted shortcomings*…
	→ I fear the dual hurdle is (1) grasp the new approach <u>oneself</u>, (2) then somehow be sure to explain it to your <u>students</u>, otherwise confusion will remain, not to mention resistance.
	--"CONFESSION": *I myself,* have been *as guilty here* as *anyone else.* Two EXAMPLES. ---(1) I assigned <u>the last theme</u> of the five in English 101 to be done "totally by yourself the student." But the students collapsed in impotent, vexed frustration. I *thought* I had been teaching them CTA <u>c</u>onceptualize <u>t</u>ransfer and <u>a</u>pply skills autonomously. I had *not*… ---(2) I assigned students to <u>rewrite an assignment from another course of theirs, to make it teach thinking better</u>. But, a second disaster! An example from one student, MICHELLE:
	Original question: Political Science 150. "Identify and describe the techniques interest groups use. Why do some groups favor certain techniques over others? Give examples." *Rewritten Question:* "Explain which technique used by interest groups <u>you</u> think is best and why. Give specific examples." *Michelle's Analysis:* "The original question was simply fact-dumping. All I had to do was

12

remember from the textbook and basically rewrite what was in front of me, in my own words. There was no real thought process present.....To make it a thought-provoking question, I had to <u>personalize</u> it and <u>possibly ask for an opinion</u>. <u>Each person may feel different</u> about the different techniques used by interest groups."

--COMMENT: I feel this response is *regrettably-flawed*—it mistakes for true Thinking, mere personal opinion and response. No more "fact-dumping," but only unmonitored "opinion-depositing" instead. Gives reasons why, but does not reflectively critique one's response.

--...and so, as for "teaching thinking already," I rest the case for now...

[4.] Okay, granted it's still new, but it's *superseded!* You're overlooking the new paradigm of **"Active" or "Student-Centered Learning."** It's launched, it's gaining ground to replace memorization and lecture. With respect, we tdon't *need* all your analysis here.

You may err in your thinking, mistaking **Letter and Spirit**, surface Appearance similarity vs. profound difference in the Reality. Admittedly, "Active/Student-Centered Learning" <u>is</u> leagues better than traditional "Sage on Stage: lecturing. <u>But</u> it still lies kilometers short from *explicitly teaching thinking*, because unlike the latter, it does not "embed" skills, does not guarantee showing "exactly how" (short of rigid recipe-rules) one can confront content conceptually!

--Two EXAMPLES only here. (1) <u>An Active Learning unit</u> says, "Look at the subject from three different perspectives." Excellent, but incomplete; by contrast, <u>our 20-p. unit on "Lens-work"</u> shows exactly but not narrowly how to employ plural perspectives... SEE in App. #4, P. 252

(2) Plus <u>this quotation</u> (about "what are museums for?") gives the gist of the case:

"It [new museum interactivities] reminds me of the dispiriting way history is taught in school now where instead of the teacher giving you an idea of what actually happened you're handed a variety of different texts and accounts of the same event and invited to make your own mind up. A nice idea: creating a nation of free-thinking intellectuals. The problem is, it's predicated on the lamentably optimistic notion that our ailing education system has given the nation sufficient intellectual grounding on which to form such subtle judgments. It hasn't." [-- JAMES DELINGPOLE]

--Or permit one more ANALOGY. Active Student Learning risks being *like* "an active class in baking," where, , students actively do roundtable messing-around, better than a teacher lecture-demo <u>but</u> without recipes or the principles solidly "blackboarded" behind them [=ingredients; types of cooking; sequences of operations...] Many educators **(1)** may not *know* basic-advanced thinking skills, **(2)** don't *realize* that such are not explicitly forwarded, and **(3)** *misconceive* that while learning should be active exploration, all explicit skills reduce to rote recipe formulaic rules...

[*SEE* DERZKO touchstone- comment later... *SEE* also M. LIPMAN on six fallacies in teaching for thinking, elsewhere in the module: Keystones and D- Machine...].

[5.] *Unrealistic!* It's good, but <u>too many **barriers** exist</u> to realistically expect teaching of thinking education-wide. <u>Teachers</u> don't understand it. Are not supported in doing it. <u>Students</u> demonstrate massive hostile resistance to it. <u>Administration</u> is unsupportive. The "<u>reward-structure</u>" doesn't—reward it. And <u>more</u>... So why not get real, avoid this Utopian ideal? Let's work on solvable problems, attainable goals...

--First, the **either-or fallacy** here: it's not all-or none. *Although* indeed 100% teaching thinking is Utopian and even excessive, and still 90% of classes don't teach thinking now, *nevertheless* X% of classes could teach Y% of thinking right now."

[EXAMPLES: **"lens-work"** or using multiple viewpoints as a semester-long goal, 5 minutes in every class hour. Or **dispositions** toward thinking." Or "**ways of knowing and evidence.**" And aim toward testable "end-goal" competence during and by the end of the semester...]]

--Second, **a more personal comment.** Isn't it better to know the truth and not be deluded, to know that we fall massively short of something which is nevertheless <u>more valuable</u> than the existing—pragmatically better, truly empowering and respectful of the learners, principled and moral as a way to live, and pleasurable too via the sportive play of mind? And something which is now <u>more approachable</u> than we realize even today?...

[*SEE* later discussion of "how we respond to the Teaching Thinking issue, " as examples of ways to respond to any issue—our **"3-DDD"** model—In the **Gallery**]

```
\=\=|+|+\=\=|+|+\=\=\+|+|=\=\+|+\=\=\+|+\=\=|+|+\=\+|+\=\=|+|+\=\=|+|=\=\=\+|+|=\+|+\=|+|+|+\=\=|+|+|=\+||
\=\=|+|+\=\=|+|+\=\=\+|+\=\=\+|+\=\=\+|+\=\=|+|+\=\+|+\=\=|+|+\=\=|+|=\=\=\+|+|=\+|+\=|+|+|+\=\=|+|+|=\+||
```

[1.]MAIN INTRO:	**→[2.] READINGS:**	**[3.]HELPDESK:**	**4.] BRIDGE to the**	**[5.] ANNEX:**
["Reception-Room"]	*["Library / Theatre"]*	*[The Summaries]*	**BOOK:**	*["Supply-Room"]*
Who?Why?What?		1. Key Definitions	*["Exit-Walkway"]*	1. Examples
How? Whoa!	**[2A] 3 Pillars**	2. Directory to TTh	1. Book in 1	2. Analogies
	[2B] Issues		Page!	3. FAQ's {"II"}
previous	**[2C] Analogies**	forthcoming	2. Final Readings	4. Author's Story
	[2D] A "Lab"			

[2.] The READINGS :
where examples "rehydrate" concepts...

[2.A.] To illustrate the three "Pillars" (keystone concepts) of teaching thinking as we model it:

PILLAR #1: MAIN GOAL: to what extent "what to know, believe, do," versus "how to think things through"?

EXAMPLE. A course-assignment—with what implicit and questionable assumptions?
On the **LEFT** below, the *original*, from college English 101 class ..... on the **RIGHT** below, *reconstructed*:

"The narrators of Faulkner's 'A Rose for Emily' and Gilman's 'The Yellow Wallpaper' are both women who go mad. They go mad in part as a result of the way women in their respective societies are treated. Demonstrate the ways in which their being women affected their lives and led to their madness."	"Feminism, Marxism, Freudianism, New Criticism, and Reader-Response are <u>major ways-of-reading</u> we have practiced so far this semester. Take <u>these three stories assigned but never discussed in class</u>, and *show what you can do* in the skill of "LENSwork" or Plural Perspectives in reading literature. Discuss: (1) Which approaches seem better, and less productive, for which stories and why? And how can you apply this approach of "varying viewpoints" to areas outside literature, in "real life after school"?

ANALYSIS: By the TTh model anyhow, the ***left-hand*** assignment ***grossly falls short of anything resembling "teaching thinking."*** At least by the model we use, It fails in multiple ways; in obvious, also subtle, ways...

   1. **Explicit thinking skill present explicitly or not?**   2. **Purpose, Recall/ Indoctrination vs. Think-through?...**
   3. **Who makes how many and which decisions, teacher or student? 4. And other issues...]**

Let the ***right-hand*** recasting above, suggest thinking-possibilities.;

This is "I" ***BRIEF*** analysis; for "II" ***FULL*** unpacking" treatment, see right below in the Intro. itself, **P. 21**...

MORE EXAMPLES: Two other sets of "before" & "after" assignments. For what to know and believe, vs. how to think things through:

In what ways is Workfare a punitive program?	How would you apply (critically) which feminist
What was the early role of midwives?	perspectives to what important social issues today?

PILLAR #2: Issue of PRESENCE: thinking embedded in courses? exhibited in whole school statements?

EXAMPLES. Six "outcome-statements" (three pairs) about thinking skills. *Note how they contrast in explicitness...*

[1.A.] Liberal Arts Graduates: You have acquired <u>the ability to listen, to assimilate, to learn on your own, to project your own insights, opinions and views.</u> Some faculty members taught you <u>how to think, how to challenge, to have confidence and to be independent.</u> Most of you acquired <u>the ability to analyze and to synthesize.</u> Many acquired a love of learning for its own sake.... In all this time, you also acquired knowledge, most of which is long gone. But ... You learned <u>how to read analytically and critically,</u>... you began to appreciate the role of originality and creativity. You know <u>how to formulate and defend a hypothesis.</u> And you learned <u>how to assimilate the ideas of others and to interact,</u> whether to support or to disagree. [-- *from* INSIDE HIGHER EDUCATION, 2006]	**[1.B.]** Some of the THINKING SKILLS we shall Confront in this course, *Meta-Stenology 101*: Ways of knowing: levels (group, individual)... Synthesis vs. Analysis/categorization. Induction, Deduction and empiricism, idealism... "Field": contextual or system or integrative thinking: comparison-contrast... Structure-order-pattern-arrangement... Veracity: "truth"—and biasses!... The "Objective vs. Personal" tangle... The "Relativism" trap!... Dispositions or attitudes toward good thinking... "Conscious" thinking; reflexive self-awareness or meta-cognition about one's own thinking... Quality, Criteria: thinking vs. *good* thinking... Background: Motivations, Assumptions, World-View... Basic Logic-Argument-Reasoning 101 and fallacies... "Lens-work" or multiple-plural views, **interdisciplinarity**. [-- *from* CAESURA COLLEGE, LACUNA UNIVERSITY, WEST DAKOTA]
BUT I *much* prefer this left-hand side. It's more accessible, performance-oriented, self-contained.	Agreed—*superficially.* **BUT** what about "the black box under the hood"—*exactly how* (short of recipe) might we **produce, achieve** those fine goals? The right-hand version seeks to pinpoint them. (Or do we "pick it up on our own as we go along" sufficiently? We can accelerate learning via the "catalyst" of explicit "moves")

[2.A.] "To apply to other areas than English, the skills learned in the study of languages and literatures." [-- #6 OF "GOALS FOR ENGLISH MAJORS," STATE UNIVERSITY, WISCONSIN]	**[2.B.]** "In <u>every class and every subject</u>, students will learn to ask and to answer these questions: 1. From whose viewpoint are we seeing or reading or hearing? From what angle or perspective? 2. How do we know when we know? What's the evidence, and how reliable is it? 3. How are things events people connected? What is cause, what effect? 4. What's new and what's old? Have we encountered this idea before? 5. So what? What does it matter? What does it all mean?" [-- DEBORAH MEIER, POLICY STATEMENT, THE EAST CENTRAL PARK EAST SCHOOL, NYC]

[3.A.] "<u>Liberal Education:</u> A philosophy of education that empowers individuals, liberates the mind from ignorance, and cultivates social responsibility. Characterized by *challenging encounters with important issues*, and more *a way of studying* than specific content, liberal education can occur at all types of colleges and universities." [-- AACU REPORT]	**[3.B.]** At IU-Purdue, IN, "the desired outcomes of college study are crystal clear. *Six Principles* for Undergraduate Learning summarize <u>what graduates are expected to demonstrate</u>" whether they major in the arts and sciences or in professional fields. "The *principles* are never far from anyone's mind, since the university has distributed thousands of laminated, three-hole punched copies for students and professors to slip into their notebooks." [I wrote for a copy. The skills are 1. core communication and quantitative skills (six), 2. critical thinking (six), 3. intellectual depth breadth adaptiveness, 4. integration and application of knowledge, 5. under standing society and culture, 6. values and ethics.] [-- AACU REPORT, "GREATER EXPECTATIONS," 2002]

15

| Now I agree: **YES**, these six do elucidate your point. Decide on goals, state them clearly, **showcase** them, and "every day" implement them… Especially 2A and 2 B are day-and-night apart: the Park School is explicit yet flexible! | Well, new paradigms take time to absorb. And to really **know** something, means more than just knowing-*about* it; one can employ it as needed… |

|#|+|#+|#+|+#|+#|+#|+#|+#|+#|+#|+#|+#|+#|+#|+#|+#|+#|+#|+#|+#|+#|+#|+#||+#|+#|+#|+#|+#|+#||#+#|+|#|+|+#|+|#+#|#|+#|+#|+#|+#|+#|+#||#+|#+|#+|#+#

Pillar #3: END-GOAL: Ultimate Expectable Readiness, to "Hit The Ground Running" and "confront content conceptually" or "think things through on one's own in the real world after graduation"…

EXAMPLES: Left-hand, two rather-*questionable* instances… right-hand, a more *powerful* instance of my own:	
[1.A.1.] After taking EDWARD DE BONO'S famous course in <u>creative or lateral thinking</u>, A RESPONDENT stated, "Now when having coffee, I open not one but two sugar packets at one time." **[1.A.2.]** A San Diego SCIENCE EDUCATOR I interviewed, praised knowing <u>key principles such as energy, its transfer and conservation</u>. She claimed, "This helps us understand why on a hot day, water condenses on a cool glass." I agreed *but* criticized: "But is this factoid really important, useful, applicable in actual life?" The EDUCATOR was *not* pleased at my objection …	**[1.B.]** I self-studied <u>the economic principle</u> of **allocation cost or cost-benefit ratio (also opportunity cost)** [= "is the cost to achieve something, worth the thing, relative to other possibilities?"]… *I soon found I could use this keystone for better decisions in varied life-arenas*: **(1)** leaving a boring movie without regret… **(2)** taking costly taxi, not slow bus, when in Thailand on a brief expensive trip… **(3)** self-printing a brochure, or having the Copy Shop do it… **(4)** applying (or not) for a grant I probably wouldn't get… **(5)** learning Photoshop to illustrate my book myself, or hiring a graphic artist do the job… **(6)** returning the toner-cartridge for recycling: noble, but worth the time?… **(7)** avoiding the pleasure of sex for a few days, for the reassurance of a more-accurate medical blood-test for the prostate gland…

EXAMPLES. Individual teachers on their students learning thinking…	
[2.A.1.] In a media class, students balked when asked to critique their own favorites, so the teacher resorted to showing her own favorites, "a little hope, a little beauty." Students felt freer to respond. The teacher ends: *"If I'm lucky*, my students will apply their critical skills to their own favorites. In any case, I'm feeling a lot less cranky." [-- MARY S. ALEXANDER, IN CHE] **[2.A.2.]** A history teacher believes in a "student-centered" approach and has "truly embraced the idea of myself as a facilitator. I don't give midterms. I don't give finals. Instead, my students spend four months with me working on *becoming better thinkers*. Sure, participation-based classes skew the bell curve, but I have found that student interest and *retention of the material* soar along with their grades." [-- KELLY MCMICHAEL, in CHE] **…But can either of these teachers have any realistic sense of whether and how well, students learned exactly what skills?…..**	**POLICY. [2.B.]** Alverno College in Wisconsin has an "ability-based" and "outcome-oriented" learning program. (These are "outcome-oriented" and hence related to our goal of real-world competence after graduation. And they involve <u>thinking</u>: "analytical capabilities" and "problem-solving skill." But they also involve "making *value-judgments*" and "facility for *social interaction*" and "*global perspectives*" and "effective *citizenship*" and "*aesthetic responsiveness*." All good major goals of a liberal or general education. All surpassing our goal of "basic" higher-order applied thinking. [-- ALVERNO COLLEGE OF WISCONSIN]

| **BUT** the instances here are *simplistic, straw men*. Few schools are as *sloppily-vague* as the left-hand examples. Plus, few schools really can (or should be?) as densely *over-specified* as the right-hand instances… | That's possible… What's more certain, is that The Real Question here is: ***does* the above gallery help *elucidate* the concepts of teaching thinking, "the very idea"—for those who don't yet fully know, but want to know more?…..** |

|#|+|#+|#+|+#|+#|+#|+#|+#|+#|+#|+#|+#|+#|+#|+#|+#|+#|+#|+#|+#|+#|+#|+#||+#|+#|+#|+#|+#|+#||#+#|+|#|+|+#|+|#+#|#|+#|+#|+#|+#|+#|+#||#+|#+|#+|#+#

Example: Graphic to distinguish Knowing *In* School, *vs.* "Thinking *After* School" …

\=\=|+|+|+\=\=|+|+|+\=\=|+|+|+|=\=\+|+|+\=\=\+|+|+\=\=|+|+|+\=\+|+|+\=\=|+|+|=\=|+|+|=\=\=\+|+|+\=\+|+|\=|+|+|+\=\=|+|+|=\+||

[2.B.] To show **KEY ISSUES** to be confronted in teaching thinking:

EXAMPLES. Now a gallery of classic statements elucidating key concepts of the Pillars:

➔ **Caution: teachers must first (1) comprehend this well __themselves__, but then must (2) somehow clarify to their __students__ what the new approach is. Else, inefficient bafflement and confusion result...**

[1.] The core essence (a day-night reversal): now the **goal** becomes not content but **skills**:

The first goal should be to teach thinking skills. The second is an awareness that they are thinking skills, not content-bound, can be somewhat transferred from one area to another. Third one should teach them via content. And indeed let the content be "interesting, useful, elevating, and inspiring." But *let not the content obscure the first two primary goals*, as it might if it's fascinating, or traditionally accepted as the goal.
[-- RICHARD CREWS, PACIFIC COLLEGE, in CHE; excerpted...]

COMMENT: Might this this "180-degree" shift may be as major (and difficult to grasp) as others in intellectual history?
EXAMPLES: 1. The sun does not go around the earth, but the earth, the sun... 2. power derives not from God or the king, but from the people... 3. we are descended not from the angels, but from the apes... 4. painting does not represent reality, it becomes its own reality... 5. knowledge cannot be given to us objectively as a mirror of the real world, but is constructed in the mind... All these led to "growing pains"...
[**SEE:** facing **Major Change**, Tool-Kit in the Appendix, #4:, **P. 242**]

[2.] But we may still leave thinking skills unstated, __not explicitly named, spotlighted__ as such:

[A.] DERZKO says that we ignore teaching thinking in most schools and corporations, for various reasons—some other teacher will do it, budget cuts prevent doing it, we simply overlook doing it, or we think we can think well enough already. But are we really good-enough thinkers not to need explicit training in thinking skills? DERZKO says: "Consider the paradox. We expect students and staff to be math-literate. So what do we do? Back in grade 1 and 2 we teach everyone *the operancy skills behind* math...the plus, subtract, multiple and divide. Once we master these basic math-related operations we go on to *higher order applications*....Yet when we switch domains from numbers over to fact, ideas, concepts, values, assumptions, and notions (the content for all other subject areas in school and later at work), we totally ignore the thinking operations needed to explore or create new ideas."
[-- W. DERZKO, THE IDEAS BANK]

[B.] [Another EDUCATOR Comments:] Having studied Learning Scholarship for the last five years, I am increasingly uneasy about [an approach] that does not name and teach clearly articulated methods and perspectives to students, and then assess them accordingly,...and then provide some kind of structure to build on those capacities. I do not see how students move from "novice" to "experts" without this, and thus be able to transfer their knowledge beyond their coursework into their communities, vocations and personal lives.
[-- MICHAEL GOLDBERG, Univ. of Washington/Bothell, AIS discussion, 2007]

COMMENT: To fully grasp this key point, **EXAMPLES** may help: what are some higher-order concepts/skills in fields?:
--**Sociocultural** perspective, or "culture as silent school shaping our selves" --**Anthropological** perspective, true cultural relativism as a way of seeing diversity more objectively. --**Psychological** perspective, the drives motivations

etc. of the psyche... **Economic** perspective, "scarce goods and resources" and cost-benefit ratio. --**Geographic** perspective, the importance of place and space for many issues... **Statistical** perspective, at the very least "sampling errors" --**Mathematical** perspective beyond numbers: six strategies for general thinking. --**Literary** perspective: the nuances of a text. --**Artistic-aesthetic** perspective: dynamic dialectic or organic balance with vitality of elements within a frame of form. --**Communication** perspective: the sender-message-receiver chain and all the complexities therein, pesky but perceptible. --**Engineering**: a total-thorough vision of which I wish I knew more!...

These key perspectives are the (or a) true content of a discipline, hence of a course. But how explicitly are they set as GOALS... "embedded" in a course...taught EXPLICITLY... practiced for TRANSFER?...

[3.] Indeed complete content-coverage <u>is</u> impossible anyhow, <u>but</u> what can save us is to know the concepts, perspectives:

[We *cannot* and *could not* be an expert in all the facts in every field related to solving a complex problem—e.g., for abortion: biology, theology, sociology, psychology, ethics, etc. However we don't *have* to be. "What *is* necessary is that the individual has a firm grasp of **the basic concepts and principles of the pertinent fields**, experience thinking within them, and the ability to learn new details and assess relevant details the subjects contribute to understanding the problem." To confront a challengingly-complex issue, one needn't know everything, just enough **background knowledge and skills** to guide one's confronting the issue.]   [-- RICHARD PAUL]

COMMENT: Although abstract, this is lucid. Now to *articulate* these "concepts and principles."

EXAMPLE. A college department moves from fact-coverage to concept-cinching—but almost by chance?

BRYN MAWR found that "you could no longer teach biology as an accretion of information. There was too much information." They shifted from a large body of facts, to "distinctive" ideas and perspectives in biology. E.g., many genes influence sexual behavior—but instead of teaching about it all, they teach students that "their sexual behavior is influenced by genes but not determined by them, and that's the important message to take home." [-- CHE, 2006]

...almost seems it was by accident not design, that they shifted to teaching-for-understanding/comprehension!

[4.] And while covering content is <u>lengthy</u>, gaining *perspectives* can be surprisingly *rapid*:

"While interdisciplinary courses indeed make use of <u>concepts, theories, methods, and factual knowledge</u> from various disciplines, the interdisciplinary understanding they develop is grounded primarily in the <u>perspectives</u> from which these concepts, theories, methods, and facts emerge. It takes <u>many years</u> to learn a discipline; *it takes <u>only a few readings</u> to begin to develop a feel for <u>how</u> that discipline characteristically looks at the world*, its <u>angle of vision</u>, its <u>perspective</u>." [-- WILLIAM NEWELL]

COMMENT: ...a quite new idea , upsetting the "content-first" model or mandate, but perhaps reassuring...

[5.] [Report from a science class.] The <u>key difference</u> between concrete data level, and the great <u>move upward to conceptualize (induct)</u>, or to deduce via using concepts upon the data:

"When presented with a novel problematic situation, students tend to look to the *surface features* for cues as to what learned ideas and procedures to apply: "What other problem have I done that has the features of this one?" In physics, students look for *features like inclined planes or pulleys* rather than for possibly relevant <u>principles</u> such as forces or energy conservation. For example, when two bodies interact, as in a collision, students tend to attend to *features such as which one is moving faster, which is bigger, and which will sustain the greater damage*, rather than considering **equal and opposite action and reaction forces**."   [-- JIM MINSTRELL, "EXPERTISE IN TEACHING"]

COMMENT: More specific, this vividly illustrates the major leap upward often missed: "from Procedures, toward Principles"... One then of course DEducts and applies... [SEE App. #3, Conceptualizing UP, **P. 157**]

[6.] But still, misconceptions do seem to exist about, first, higher-level thinking itself, and

18

second, about teaching it—in relation to teaching content. --First, does "critical thinking" even exist in itself outside of a specific domain, discipline, subject? (See comment **#1** below).....
--And second, can thinking be taught by itself before the learner is immersed in subject-material? (**#2** below).

[#1] [The notion of context-free critical thinking, is vacuous—i.e., mistaken. No such thing exists.] "There are areas of study such as mathematics and geography. Each has its own ideas, problems, and epistemology. The overlap, such as may exist, belongs to philosophy…where we treat problems in the most abstract setting possible… There is no critical thinking that applies to all, or even most, disciplines. The kind of thinking mathematics requires will be quite distinct from that which history may require. The only things we can say about thinking in general are superficial, misleading and platitudinous. These professional educators need a more rigorous schooling in the history and development of ideas." [-- ONLINE REVIEW of Becoming A Critically Reflective Teacher, amazon.com]

COMMENT: I'd really like to reply with derisive denouncing, sardonic ridicule, and hacking laughter—were it not for the pathetic nature of this. This reviewer is truncated. Thinking is higher-order conceptualizing; this person was beheaded. Above domain-specific thinking skills, emerge general-generic ones—the lion's share of this book…

SEE Table at end of Introduction on "dualism, " "lens- work," and "cause- effect" **P. 30**..

Then as for the second issue, that one must cover content first, this depressingly-useful example:

(1) Stated in *colloquial form*, I often hear "Well, you can't think about nothing. You have to think about something. So we have to give students the facts and data first; and then, we can teach them to think via that prior content." [*Of course, this nicely defers actually teaching thinking to—sometime later!*]…

(2) But in *a more sophisticated version* of this stumble, a respected EDUCATOR discusses the shortcomings in knowledge on all fronts of today's students. In this excerpt, history:

[# 2] [An operative contrast exists:] "…a knowledge of historical data versus thinking historically. The one amounts to a storage of facts, the other to a mode of reflection. But do we have any evidence that the latter is possible without a fair measure of the former? 'Thinking historically' is one of those higher-order critical-thinking skills that educators favor, but how can one achieve it without first delving into the details of another time and place is a mystery. The facts are not an end in themselves, of course, but are a starting point for deeper understanding, and the ignorance of them is a fair gauge of deeper deficiencies. "
[-- MARK BAULERLEIN, CHE, 06 Jan 06]

COMMENT: To me this seems well-intentioned, but overlooks the whole other paradigm-shift.
SEE CREWS, PAUL, and NEWELL above as to how keystone concepts and thinking skills can be the "subject" in themselves, quickly illustrated by specific "content" then…]

[7.] What about teaching thinking and the end-goal of "Hitting the Ground Running": the learner is prepared to confront complexities "on one's own in the real world later"?

Content usually wins out over skills. For instance, few schools offer, say, a senior-year capstone course explicitly requiring students to transfer and apply abstractions (thinking skills). E.g., to use "self-selected sample," "functionalism vs. conflict in society," cognitive dissonance," "sampling errors," calibration scale proportion," and others… to confront "immigration policy," or "welfare reform," or "same-sex marriage," or "national security," others… [-- B. K. BECK, 01 AUGUST 2000]

…my own attempt at specifying and applying: specific skills to specific issues, connected…

[8.] Are teachers sometimes misconceived: they honestly *believe* they are teaching thinking, but may well *not* be doing so? The following is a common situation, or so we propose:

--IN A COURSE, <u>CONTENT IS COVERED</u> (e.g., a literary period or movement with authors, texts, interpretations, etc.). <u>Then</u> <u>students are tested,</u> *but* on what they essentially recall (or sometimes, "personally feel or relate to.") *Not* on whether they can **apply domain-specific principles** (of reading), and **general-generic** ones too, to **other new works**—and ultimately to **real-life issues** as well. <u>The teacher never considers this level</u>, or else blithely <u>assumes</u> "students are learning how to think about literature," and even perhaps "they're learning thinking skills applicable to other situations." They may well be doing so—but not explicitly: intuitively, catch-as-catch-can, subliminally? Or, only doing directed and mildly-elaborated—recall?...

--OR IN A COURSE <u>A SKILL IS TAUGHT</u> (e.g., how to write a basic essay). *But* students are never really tested whether they've learned the concept as such...

> | ANECDOTE: | As noted above, my English 101 required "five themes." For the first four, I taught how-to-write skills. Then for the fifth assigned: "Now you yourself design and write an essay from scratch, making all the needed decisions." Result? Meltdown! The class exhibited near-total disarray: panic, hostility, resentment, confusion. I had <u>not</u> taught autonomous application of abstractions. Nor did I <u>realize</u> I had not truly been teaching, they not truly learning...

[9.] The difficult "Rubicon to cross" is indeed in <u>actual transfer-and-application</u>...

A problem in the... [interpretation] category requires the student to know an abstraction well enough that he can correctly demonstrate its use <u>when specifically asked</u> to do so. "Application," however, requires a step beyond this. Given a problem new to the student, he will apply the appropriate abstraction <u>without</u> having to be prompted as to which abstraction is correct or <u>without</u> having to be shown how to use it in that situation." [-- BLOOM, TAXONOMY...]

COMMENT. Those who would say, "but this is old-hat, from the classic Taxonomy of 1956; we know this" are right. But they might ponder whether these principles (in this gold-standard statement) about Transfer, Application), are "embedded" and in place as end-goal today—students "hitting the ground running." Perhaps not fully even now...

[2.C.] To aid awareness by a few ANALOGIES:

Analogies may convey the essence of **Goal #1, "Think Things Through"**

For the TRADITIONAL "OLD-SCHOOL" MODEL:
--*"Banking,"* deposit knowledge in student [PAULO FREIRE] ...
--*Vaccination or Dipstick,* fill up but not too much!
--*Agricultural*: does student simply harvest teacher's crops (in the bushelbasket of the final exam blue book), or learn to grow crops on one's own?...
--*Athletics*: training wheels, water wings *(or solo flight)*?
--*<u>Motivation</u>*: student passively gets their card stamped "requirement satisfied" *(vs. internalize learning: tattoo self?)*...
--The Education *Building*, first floor conventional busyness, second floor "thinking" still vacant...

COMMENT. Analogy is a powerful thinking tool. Do yet other powerful analogies exist?
[*SEE ALSO:* "II" FULL version in Intro ANNEX, below. **P. 39**, also, Tool-Kit "Analogy" **P. 232** in App. #3...]

[2.D.] And to aid understanding via a few "LAB EXERCISES":

[WHAT THINKING SKILL USED HERE?] Our major ploy **"variables-variation."** For completeness, it asks:

[1.] <u>What is the variable-issue involved here, whether named or not?</u>

[CLARIFICATION: **Variable-issues** is our term for labeling or naming "<u>matters which for success of the task-goal must be confronted:</u> <u>handled-managed-attended to-reckoned with-satisfied-employed etc.</u>" EXAMPLES: [1.] in *photography*, "shutter speed," "depth of focus,"

[2.] What are the polar-opposite stands possible on the V/I—that is, the A and Z? And **what are all possible in-between AOCs,** Alternate Optional Choices or stances [B, C, D, etc.]?

[3.] What position does the statement take? [B or C? M?]

[4.] And is that position okay, OR questionable [arguable, problematic, suspect] (by what criteria or way-of-knowing yardstick!) **and if so, should it be altered,** to what other stance, why?

SEE treatment of V-V in detail, at the end of Appendix #6, Pre-View of Mind-Play

---

EXAMPLES # 1 A B. Statements about education to "unpack" for questionable limited assumptions:

(1.A.) DR. GRAHAM: He was "possessed of those rare qualities of greatness as a teacher: impressive knowledge of his subject, a closeness to students, a desire to impart knowledge, and the style and skill requisite to do so in the classroom...."

(1.B.) LETTER TO EDITOR: "What all these movements in education neglect—whether they're the social-progress movement, the related multicultural-diversity movement, the Back to Basics movement, the vocational-emphasis movement, the media and electronic education movement—is the key basic emphasis on mastering knowledge which is the perennial heart of the educational enterprise."

Can we spot the "old-school" paradigm here? Might some teachers and students overlook it, as a fish swims in water but does not know there is air or land?

|#|+|#+|#+|+#|+#|#+|#+|#+|#+|#+|#+|#+|#+|#+|#+|#+|#+|+#|+#|+#|#+|#+|#+|#+|+#||#+#|+|#|+#+|+|#+#|#|+#|+#|#+|+#|+#|#|#+|#+|+#|+#|+#+#

EXAMPLE #2. Now let us thoroughly "unpack" the "Rose for Emily" original assignment, to identify the unstated **variable-issues** present, and the stands taken on each—and other possible stands. **"V-V"** in action.

"The narrators of Faulkner's 'A Rose for Emily' and Gilman's 'The Yellow Wallpaper' are both women who go mad. They go mad in part as a result of the way women in their respective societies are treated. Demonstrate the ways in which their being women affected their lives and led to their madness."

Teacher #1:	Teacher #2: "*Distasteful* assignment, ignobly tells student to repeat course-content and ideology "go and harvest the corn the teacher textbook course planted"! Disempowers the learner…"
"Excellent assignment! It clearly specifies *Exactly What Is Wanted.* It tests *Mastery of the Material.* This will thus truly *Measure Learning.*"	1. **Goal**: Does not teach thinking or how to Think It Through. Teaches only the usual what to Know (memorize material presented and discussed in the course already.) Plus what to Believe—indoctrination into feminist ideology instead of valid exploration of same.
	As for the **"autonomous application of abstractions,"** 2A. no **autonomy**. All decisions already made by the Teacher/Course/Assignment. 2B. **Application** or *transfer* to new material? But no, this story was already discussed in class! 2C. **Abstraction?** What ideas, except "feminism," given…
	And it is 3. **Formulaic**: rote rule not flexible tool. Only one "lens" offered (feminism), not other plural perspectives (aesthetic, historical, Marxist, reader-response, etc.) …
	4. Failure in the whole process (**CTA**—Conceptualize, Transfer, Apply) which might have taught an Explicit, Elevated skill Exported or applied to new material—and taught throughout the course. And set a base for ultimately the student able to achieve
	5. the **end-goal**: apply plural lenses to other subjects in real life later on autonomously and competently!
	(Nor any 6. **Articulation** or self-evaluation of student required either.)
	7. **Criteria** also seem absent: "describe" does not specify how well, etc. Hence this assignment a major *shortfalling* right in our midst, and not recognized as such. (Yes, a blunder only by *our* **Criteria** ; but that's what's on the table here, and no, it's *not* "all relative"…) Can

we say, "major paradigm shift" here with resulting fault-line "disconnects"?

...how about the English 101 course working toward <u>an alternate assignment</u>? For the final exam (or before, for discussion of the results!), how about "Apply whichever of the X or N main lenses upon literature—feminism, aesthetics, psychobiography, etc.—which are appropriate to this short story which we have NOT yet read and discussed." Or even: "apply feminism and other lens X to a real-life situation far removed from literature." Or ultimately: "Specifically how has this course taught you how to—no, make that specifically how have you in this course learned to think better?".........

RESPONSE #1: ...well, I do now *finally* see your big *point*! Whole new paradigm-shift which critiques many variables which the "what to know/believe" paradigm overlooks or values! ... ...**BUT**, in your workshops, *how did fellow-teachers respond to seeing this?*	...largely with understandable defenses against Major **Change**. <u>Resistance, evasion, denial, counter-attack,</u> and a few "<u>oh we do this already</u>." [I wish, some *legitimate* objections, but no—at least as I perceived...] At least the issues were brought up.

RESPONSE #2: ...**NO!** Really, the "alternate assignment" is unrealistically too "vague" for most students today! Complaints would abound...	Hey, how about this one for a true Final Exam: "<u>Show competently, what you've truly learned this semester, period.</u>" I'm sorrrrry, but if students couldn't handle that, Ably Apply Abstractions Autonomously (by the end of the course, that is), they have not learned...

#+|~#+|#+|~+#|~+#|+~|#+|#+~|#+||~+#|+~#|~+#|+#|#~+#|#+|~+#|~+|#+|#~|+#|~#+#|~+#|~+#|+#|~#+|#~~#+|#+|~+#|~|||

EXAMPLE #3 A B C. A "for-instance" revamping of a high school/college course in **"Art Appreciation."** (Plus suggestions for **English**/language-literature, and **Government/Political Science**.) What might a "makeover" look like, if done for "thinking things through"?

[3.A.1.]   ART CONTACTS: *"CURRENT-TRADITIONAL" OR CONVENTIONAL:*

--Goal is what to *know-about*, perhaps believe, not what to "do" let alone how...
-- Study great Western (and world?) traditions. "Cover the material." Approach is content-mastery: "knowledge of" historical, also Great Artists, also schools or periods. [Egyptian, Greek-Roman, medieval, Renaissance, etc.].
--Be able to identify and describe styles, etc., as presented in textbooks and lectures. <u>Final exam</u> to "measure learning-retention." *End of course...*

[3.A.2.] ART CONTACTS: *INNOVATIVE, REVAMPED:* 180-degree change; now neither the very **1. goal**, nor the "content" (substance, material, stuff), of the course, is any longer "knowing information." It is knowing **concepts: keystone issues in artistry**, and "thinking with and through them." The "material covered" is this—concepts not subjects, and the *only* "required information" (periods, schools, artists) brought in is that needed to subserviently illustrate the concepts! We now see as a misconception, the truism to "teach the facts first, then think about them" We can go right to concepts as the true "material" to be "covered"!
--These are the **principles & elements of design**: line, value, composition, proportion, **Organic Form, varied <u>theories</u>. Perspective:** 3-point western, eastern, other. Etc.
--Students would <u>actively learn</u> these concepts. (EXAMPLE: *immerse* in **"composition"** by doing a "lab" by moving six one- inch squares of black paper around one letter-size white paper, *until...*)
<u>Dense application:</u> "how would you re-decorate your college room, your future habitat? Can we see these principles in "non-museum" situations: written literature, hobbies and folk-crafts, sport-games-play, etc.?
End-Goal: in Life After School in real world of Personal, Work, Civic arenas, <u>students could *Hit The Ground Running* (1)</u> appreciating any and all artistic situation they encounter, indeed also **(2)** *even enhancing their own living-quarters themselves: decorating, creating their galleries where they choose and match* VAN GOGH, HIROSHIGE, LONDON TRANSPORT POSTERS, *myriad others*. fortified with the concepts. They can thus pick up needed "knowledge-information" (about artists, periods, etc.) along the way as needed (and will probably do so more efficiently and meaningfully, too...)
<u>Final exam:</u> one would autonomously apply these abstractions in a project: the student decides... *End of course,* **but** if all goes well, only the beginning of lifelong active response fortified with empowering concepts...

[3.B.] LANGUAGE/LITERATURE. Current/Traditional: "survey course" by historical periods, perhaps authors and	Focus on the literary aesthetic stylistic expressive use of language. This is the quintessence of "English." Figures of speech, rhetoric, etc. [Poets: G.M.HOPKINS, many other

themes. Today, most probably social issues: diversity, minorities, etc.	innovators.] **--End-Goal:** to "hit the ground running" and understand, see, and use language more creatively, expressively in the real world…

[3.C.] GOVERNMENT: POLITICAL SCIENCE. Current-Traditional: possible historical plus approaches via schools of thought…	Identify key variable-issues in history and the world regarding power-law-authority etc. (and where such are incommensurate issues also!). Examples: balance between individual and society; the use of how much force; many others. (*) Bring in "content" only to see how many thinkers differed A-to-Z in how they responded to these key variable-issues. **--End-Goal:** learner hits the ground running to spontaneously recognize issues, many possibilities for each, in real-world political matters…

[3.D. .....] …and YOUR OWN OTHER COURSES?	…space here for contributions…

Well, it's paradigm-shift. "Covering content is dethroned in favor of the upstart "mastering content"…	Seeing the "ground-rules" change, takes time and not everyone sees it at first.

```
\=\=|+|+\=\=|+|+\=\=|+|+|=\=\+|+\=\=\+|+\=\=\+|+\=\=|+|+\=\+|+\=\=|+|+\=\=|+|=\=\+|+\=\+|+\|=|+|+|+\=\=|+|+|=\+||
\=\=|+|+\=\=|+|+\=\=|+|+|=\=\+|+\=\=\+|+\=\=\+|+\=\=|+|+\=\+|+\=\=|+|+\=\=|+|=\=\+|+\=\+|+\|=|+|+|+\=\=|+|+|=\+||
```

ORIENTATION - BAR :

[1.]MAIN INTRO: *["Reception-Room"]* Who?Why?What? How? Whoa! previous	**[2.] READINGS:** *["Library / Theatre"]* 3 Pillars…Issues… Analogies…"Lab"… previous	→ **[3.] HELP-DESK:** *["Summaries"]* **1. Key Definitions** **2. Directory to the rest of TTh**	**4.] BRIDGE to the BOOK:** *["Exit-Walkway"* 1. Book in 1 Page! 2. Final Readings forthcoming	**[5.] ANNEX:** *["Supply-Room"]* 1. Examples 2. Analogies 3. FAQ's {"II"} 4. Author's Story

[3.] "HELPDESK"

WHAT THIS IS: "In case you need—well, help. Orientation- ahead, or a summing- up…"

3.A. How do *we* DEFINE/DESCRIBE Thinking, & its Teaching/Learning?

[#1A] "Please, the *briefest possible definition* of **thinking** [as you see it …]" \	Okay: beyond the basic "Confront Content Conceptually," we have: **Ability**: to **(A)** <u>induct</u>, and find the higher-order concepts or ideas "UP" above/behind/within the factual material? And **(B)** to <u>deduct</u>: to employ which thinking tools to bring to bear "DOWN" upon the facts to elucidate them better? And **(C)** <u>connect</u> "ACROSS" one subject with another laterally-associationally.

[# 1B] "…No, make that even *more* clarified"	"[1.] Get ideas (concepts) *from* the facts {"upward"}… [2.] apply ideas (concepts) *to* the facts {"downward"}… [3.] interrelate material {"across"}. And [4.] be able to do this conceptualizing, to [A] *new difficult* material… [B] *later* on… [C] *autonomously*… and [D] *competently*."
	--Some **EXAMPLES** of this: Apply both **psychology** and **sociology** to *terrorism/extremism* … Apply **evolutionary biology** to *family issues*, also *political systems*… Apply "complex **systems**" thinking to *globalization*, also *energy* and *environment* issues… *Etc.* [End-Goal, to *Hit The Ground Running*.]
	--An **ANALOGY** for this: the "Ladder of Abstraction," from Material to Mental. "The thinker can *adroitly ascend UP the Ladder of Abstraction* from data to ideas, using induction (and also can use deduction *deftly descend DOWN to more concrete particulars)*—all as needed." Then the thinker can *swing out on the "trapeze" horizontally OVER-ACROSS* to Real-World situations & plummet *DOWN* to apply those concepts specifically…

Good BUT *narrow*! Unarguably, the above does <u>not</u> describe <u>all</u> major important types of thinking, even!	Admittedly! I aimed for a good indispensable foundation, baseline for all thinking. Then we can build from there …

AN ASIDE. Near the summit of **IN**ductive Conceptualizing, is the skill of **"Reading the Situation."** This means discovering hidden concepts and patterns in complex real-world skills, subjects, situations: idea-systems plus in-the-world happenings. … Some **EXAMPLES**:   [also *SEE* App. #2, "Why The Very Idea"] P. 161

--RICHARD PAUL the philosopher had to grasp **"the logic of medicine"** to read competently about *a family member's illness*.

--JOHN SEARLE was able to find the *unstated-but-prevalent keystone-assumptions* of both **"traditional humanistic study,"** and **"postmodern challenges** to that world-view"…

--R. LAIRD, in his The Boomer Bible, could discover how **today's youth** are driven by **three assumptions** which are *problematic*: **Desire** (you deserve whatever you want), **Certainty** (surely you are right), and **Blame** (your actions are not blameworthy.)

--DAVID PERKINS the educator could sift-and-strain out "the rules of the classic **detective story**."

--Every JOB CANDIDATE needs to be able to read quickly the **"corporate culture"** of the organization s/he is interviewing.

--I MYSELF was able to assemble *ten* definition/descriptions of "what people think **art** is or might be."

--Only the astute OBSERVER at a panel on "sexual orientation" could listen out **the foundational assumptions ("world-views")** of both the traditional-**religious** speakers, and the **gay-liberation** speakers. Few were stated explicitly.

--JOHN OMOHUNDRO says that anthropology can train students in "<u>social agility</u>, seeing **rules of the game**, seeing **patterns**, seeing **larger systems**"

--I MYSELF was able (with help!) to decode the often-unstated differences between **two types of writing**: "formal academic" and "real-world magazine articles" (in **length, tone, visual aids, explicitness** and **location of point, audience,** etc.)

BUT: What please is your *point* in dumping in here, this "assemblage of secret ideas"?	AHA, to show INduction UPward in practical action in challenging circumstances—to read a whole complex situation. The challenge is to comprehend what a mass of material, means. A thinking-skill vital, difficult, possible.

[# 2] "Okay, now exactly <u>how</u> can teachers actually <u>do</u> "the teaching of thinking"? A handhold for	**GUIDELINE:** *Okay: Simply ask and decide:*
	(1) How much do you want to do the traditional <u>Know, Believe, Do</u> == and how much the alternative <u>Think Things Through</u>? *[= Pillar #1: OVERALL GOAL]*
	(2) <u>WHAT</u> thinking skills do you want to teach/learn *[and higher-order "elevated" generic ones?]… [Are they already <u>in</u> the material—or to be added <u>to</u> the material?] and (*) **how pervasively** will you include them?* *[= Pillar #2A: % of PRESENCE or embeddedness in course]*

shirtsleeve educators on Monday mornings (plus education majors and self-teaching learners):	...{ideally, as *few* main ones as possible—Less is More!}... then,
	(3) HOW will you teach, and students learn, them?
	[*explicitly?*] ... [*and "exported" for transfer-application?*] and also decide...
	(4) WHETHER you'll measure if they succeeded? (testing for true transfer...).
	[= Pillar #3: END-GOAL of hitting the ground running...]
	Know facts about racism, women's studies, biology, sociology == *BUT THEN*, be **able** to confront diversity, genetic issues, social policies, etc., with perspectives of these fields...

BUT *NO*, THIS IS *NOT* CLEAR OR HELPFUL. It's like saying in cinematography that good directors always in every scene "*know where to place the camera...*" Or in photography, "*one paints with light.*" Fine, but *how?*	BUT *YES*: THIS **IS** CLEAR. A keystone concept. It's **higher-order** thinking beyond rote formulae... Strategy for navigation, not tactics or Orders. [True, some teachers want a more formulaic approach, or perhaps a looser, laissez-faire mode...]]

PAUSE: Okay fine, but **what is the toughest part of all this** to do for the teacher of thinking?	Glad you asked. It just might be **to foreground thinking in a "three-step tango"** thus.
	(1) First to IDENTIFY (and select!) **what higher-order thinking skills actually lurk in the course material**. (Traditional education overlooks this; the many examples herein will help ...) **Or bring same in...**
	(2) Second is to CONCEPTUALIZE UPward and **identify in the course's subject-specific skills, the general-generic ploys useful more widely for Gen. Ed. purposes.**
	(EXAMPLE: in composition, "calibration proportion balance of parts," but this skill also in Real Life, in personal-life planning, in on-the-job projects, in civic management...)
	(3) Third is to remember to APPLY, **to actually have students use, employ these skills** on actual *new* foreign challenging complex issues, and finally autonomously with minimal instructional "help"... *...TRANSFER! all different many from usual assignments, papers, Final Exams...*

BUT I'm baffled, or even more so now!...	Please: recall "Rose for Emily," "Art Contacts 101" above...

|#|+|#+|+#|+#|#+|#+|#+|#+|#+|#+|#+|#+|#+|#+|#+|#+#|+|+#|+#|+#|+#|#|+#|#+|#+|#+|+|+#||#+#|+|#|+#||+|#+#|#|+#|#+|+#|#+|+|+#|+#||#|+|#+|#+|#+#

[3.B.] DIRECTORY: *Where* (in Teaching Thinking) does one locate <u>discussion</u>/<u>examples</u> of these three "key-pillar" ideas?

[**SEE:** *later,* Thruout the **Body** [Keystones, D-Machine, Gallery] , also **Appendix #2.**
➔ *Now, for "BRIEF" view, just skim* **these cameo-summaries below** *for the gist...]*

1. Goals #1 Prior Overall: <u>Know/Believe, vs. Think Through?</u>

A PRE-VUE only: See the **major table** in Appendix #2, P. 143. Here, a cameo glimpse of the instances:

1. <u>Homosexuality</u> as Social Issue. **Three** *sneakily-indoctrinating* approaches, one *more honestly-empowering* one.
2. <u>Liberation Justice.</u> (Believe) [**X "Effect change," X "teach the conflicts," X "Bill of Rights for Conservatives"** *versus* ➔ OPPOSING VIEWPOINTS: X Four Systems, X Two Central American Films, and untangle them responsibly...]
3. <u>Science</u>: minor vs. key principles ["**Condensation on glass on hot day**" *vs.* ➔ "**Dynamic Equilibrium, change, Scale & Proportion, Causality/Consequence, Energy...**"]
4. <u>Social Sciences</u>: vague vs. vivid. "**Do relate course to life**" *vs.* ➔ "**Exactly how psychology helps in life**"
5. <u>General/Freshman</u> education. [How does **King Lear, particle physics, economy of England, relate to issues in the**

office, dining room, hospital waiting room, voting booth?" – BARBARA MOSSBERG, GODDARD COLLEGE]]

6. <u>Geography</u>: facts vs. concepts. ["Where is Mt. Erebus" <u>vs.</u> ➔ PLACE AND SPACE, its influence on so much else]
7. <u>Mathematics</u>: "patterns in nature," <u>vs.</u> ➔ math and issues: (1) <u>general</u>: trial & error, work backward, modeling, alter variables, etc. and == (2) <u>specific political</u> issues: probability and trials, game theory and balance of power, infinity and abortion, chaos theory and Constitution's survival, etc.
8. <u>Biology</u>: ["meiosis-mitosis" basics <u>vs.</u> ➔ evolutionary insight on *current life-issues*: mate-choice, step-parenting]
9. <u>Diversity Education</u>. [Info & indoctrination == <u>vs.</u> ➔ key CONCEPTS: selective perception, stereotype vs. sociotype, causes of prejudice, stereotype-override, Relativism: moral but also Cultural, Traits of Minority Victimization, Surplus Visibility, etc.]

|#|+|#+|+#|+#|+#|#+|#+|#+|#+|#+|#+|#+|#+|#+|#+|#+|#+|#+|#+|+|+#|+#|+#|#+|#+|#+|#+|+#||#+#|+|#|++#|+|#+#|#|+#|+#|+|+#|+#||#|+#|+#|+|#+#

2. Goals #2: Degrees of PRESENCE: Course-embedded? School-exhibited?:

RECALL: Above, also in other major table in App. #2. There, these specific pairings for learners:

<u>Goals</u>: #6 of an English Dept. VAGUE ["apply to other areas the skills learned in English"]==	== Five goals in Park School SPECIFIC [What viewpoint angle perspective? How do we know we know? Connections? Cause-effect? New and old? So what?]
AACU statement VAGUE ["challenging encounters with important issues, and more a way of studying"] ==	== IUPUI's Six Goals SPECIFIC [1. core communication and quantitative skills (six), 2. critical thinking (six), 3. intellectual depth breadth adaptiveness, 4. integration and application of knowledge, 5. under standing society and culture, 6. values and ethics.]
Two teachers VAGUE: ["if I'm lucky" students will transfer learning, <u>and</u> "interest soars" when I discuss thinking] ==	==Alverno College, eight *SPECIFIC* <u>Outcomes</u> thinking: ["analytical capabilities" and "problem-solving skill." But they also involve "making value-judgments" and "facility for social interaction" and "global perspectives" and "effective citizenship" and "aesthetic responsiveness."]

|#|+|#+|#+|+#|+#|#+|#+|#+|#+|#+|#+|#+|#+|#+|#+|#+|#+|#+|#+#|+|+#|+#|+#|#+|#+|#+|#+|+#||#+#|+|#|++#|+|#+#|#|+#|+#|+|+#|+#||#+|#+|#+|#+#

3. Goal #3: END-GOAL EXIT-OUTCOME desired..."Hit The Ground Running":

PRE-VUE. Again see in Appendix #2: A set of "beast- beauty" contrasts in application::

<u>Statistics</u>. *But this was too easy and obvious.*
"Gay" again.... Ostracism; family relations; the Boy Scouts' policy; social images of. [Lenses, interdisciplinary endeavor, sociocultural perspective, world-views, objectivity...]
<u>Free Speech</u> on Campus.... [SIMPLER "Ban them!" vs. "Free Speech" == but also MORE COMPETENT J.S.MILL, Stereotype vs. Sociotype, Major Change, Listening-ability.
<u>Same-Sex Marriage</u>.... SIMPLER "No!" "Yes!" == MORE CONCEPTUAL: [Philosophy: implications... Psychology... Affinity Group... Normative vs. Behavioral culture.]
<u>Creationism vs. Evolution</u> in schools..... SIMPLER "No!" "Yes!" vs, MORE COMPLETE [Ways of Knowing... Motivations... Lenses... Historical Perspective...]
<u>America</u> the Empire...[LEVELS: group Selfishness... Power... Win-Lose Politics... Religious Right... Pres. Bush]

\=\=|+|+|+\=\=|+|+|+\=\=|+|+|+\=\=\=|+|+|+\=\=\+|+|+\=\=\+|+|+\=\=|+|+|+\=\+|+|+\=\=|+|+\=\=|+|=\=\=\+|+|+\=\+|+|\=|+|+|+\=\=|+|+|=\+||

VISUAL GRAPHICS. A trio of diagrams maps out the concepts:

(1) Base-line View to note <u>the concept</u>. The three areas of (1) School: courses (thinking skills Embedded?), (2) School: statements (thinking goals Exhibited?), and (3) "Real World/Life" after graduation…

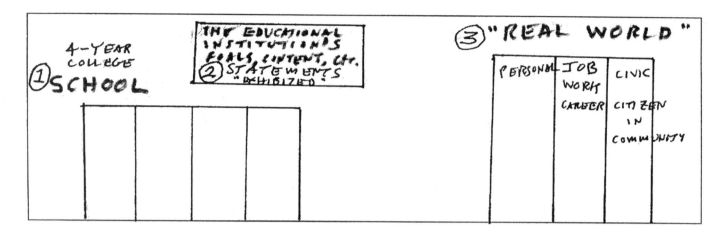

(2) Stereotyped view of perhaps <u>the common situation</u>:
(Major field as job-preparation, skills and statements secondary…)

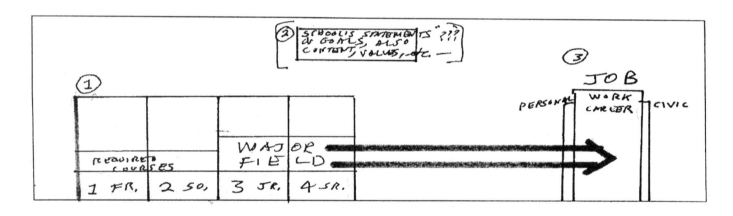

(3) More-"ideal" <u>infusion</u> of thinking; UPward to higher-order concepts, OVER ACROSS transferred and applied DOWNward upon real-world issues in all arenas…

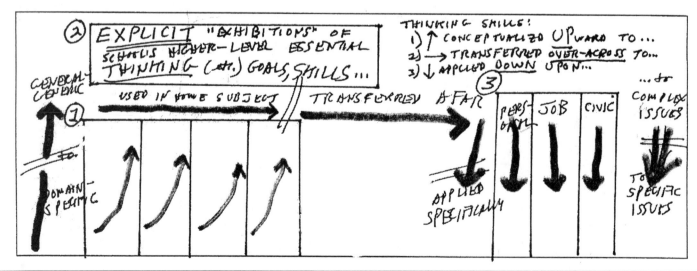

BUT your drawing-quality here is *abysmally sloppy!*	TRUE, BUT I had no in-house artist-person… Do the sketches anyhow help elucidate the key "pillars" via visual literacy?

```
\=\=|+|+|+\=\=|+|+|+\=\=|+|+|+\=\=\+|+|+\=\=\+|+|+\=\=|+|+|+\=\+|+|+\=\=|+|+\=\=|+|+|=\=\=\+|+|+\=\=\+|+\=\=|+|+|+\=\=|+|+|+\=\+||
\=\=|+|+|+\=\=|+|+|+\=\=|+|+|=\=\=|+|+|+\=\=\+|+|+\=\=|+|+|+\=\=|+|+|+\=\+|+|+\=\=|+|+\=\=\+|+|+\=\+|+\=\|+|+|+|+\=\=|+|+|+=\+||
```

O R I E N T A T I O N - B A R :

[1.]MAIN INTRO:	**[2.] READINGS:**	**[3.]HELP DESK:**	**→4.] BRIDGE to BOOK:**	**[5.] ANNEX:**
["Reception-Room"] Who?Why?What? How? Whoa!	*["Library / Theatre"]* 3 Pillars…Issues… Analogies…"Lab"…	*[The "Summries"]* 1. Key Definitions 2. Directory to TTh	*["Exit-Walkway"* **1. Book in 1 Page!** **2. Final Readings**	*["Supply-Room"]* 1. Examples 2. Analogies 3. FAQ's {"II"} 4. Author's Story
previous	previous	previous		

[4.] "BRIDGE…":

--Either "good-bye for good!" (for those who "got this far" but are *exiting* <u>Teaching Thinking</u> after having received the book's essential "gist")…

--Or "fare-well for now" (for those *continuing* on into the Main Part …)

CONTENTS: (1) Checklist for the harried: "The Book In A Page"….. (2) "Litmus-Test" examples test comprehension ….. (3) "Envoi" or "Send-Off / Invitation to the Voyage…..

How about a distilled flow-chart of the major moves a teacher would make to introduce thinking. To "flexibly guide" their doing. Can you provide?	The summarizing-"reminderandum" below is fixed and focused, but also flexible. Taken with the concepts and readings, it may provide a "handhold" for navigation…

[4.A.] "The BOOK-IN-A-PARAGRAPH": Checklist for "Pillar" #2A," "Embedding" thinking into an individual teacher's class. How?...

1. **Decide whether "thinking" will be a considered component of the course.**
   […okay, in <u>my course on "Current Social Issues: vegetarianism, energy, globalization,</u>" I'll aim for not just content-coverage, but thinking skills—specific to these issues, also general-generic…]

2. **Explore "why" (what rationale and goals), "which" kinds of, "how much/many" (fewer is better!), and the like. Set goals: exactly what will prove "Hitting The Ground Running" with competence?**
   *[Let's see: could choose **Lenswork, Dispositions, Ways of Knowing, Value-Clarification**… I guess I'll select **Lenswork**, or multiple-plural perspectives…]*

3. **The movement UPwards. Isolate, recognize, elucidate the thinking skills already inherent in the course's subject-matter or content.**
   […well, "lenses" are Unavoidable… often Subliminal… Useful but limited… Hard to locate the best lenses for the task-goal… Can become outdated, but also wrongly-neglected… wow…]

4. And continuing upwards… perhaps try to move the domain-specific skill, into a general-generic skill, higher-level or anyhow applicable transferred to arenas etc. distant from the domain.

[…Lenses applied not only to the course issue of vegetarianism, but to issues in learners' Personal lives, or on the Job-Vocational, also Civic-Citizen arena… Learners choose, or are given a topic, with or without "instructions to use lenses" etc.]

5. **Plan for transfer ACROSS: within course … to other courses in discipline?… to other disciplines in School… to other issues in life (Personal, Vocational, Civic-Community).**

[Lenses upon "vegetarianism": the Traditional Cultural, the ecological-environmental, the semi-religious….]

6. **The grist: implement how the skills will be taught. Degree of explicitness. Method of presentation. Degree of practice for transfer. → Somehow be sure you inform the <u>students</u> just as clearly as possible of the new approach; this is crucial, overlooked.**

["All the above" used. Different learning-styles, see D-Machine. The heart of pedagogy.]

7. **Decide criteria, standards. Decide testing, measurement, evaluation.**

[Students will do a final project applying these skills to a fourth issue either common, or <u>utterly each individual student's own custom choice</u>—terrorism, environment, minority-diversity issues, aesthetics to enrich personal life…]

Some other Variable-Issues here : 1. To what extent domain-specific, to what extent general-generic?
2. To what extent isolated and taught explicitly as such, apart from the course material subject content?
3. To what extent a "tool-kit" assembled in an interdisciplinary way—integrative, or at least additive?
4. To what extent explicitly formulated, decided-about—then explicitly stated, and distributed?
(*RECALL* **IUPUI's** handout for all three- ring binders… **Park School:** "in every class and subject, students will…")
5. Perhaps, to what extent these issues addressed in a "Senior Capstone" course? To pull together past courses from varied fields, via varied students—then to do real-world application (end-goal), via a project, first communal, then individual?

| …say, you know, the above is pretty obvious by now… | Good for you! *[Arrgghhh…..]* |

|~#+#|+~|+#|+|~+#|+~#|~#++#~||~#+|~|#~|#|#+|+#|~|+#~|+|~+|#~+#|~|+#|~+|#|~+#|~+#|~+|#+~|#+|~#||#+|#+|+#|+#|+#|+#|

[4.B.] The "LITMUS TEST": "test your wrist-strength," or examples to unpack for issues…

EXAMPLE #1: Can one better identify "PITFALLS" (misconceptions, shortfallings, etc.) in actual *practices* in re "teaching thinking—especially, *specific assignments?*

RECALL **Rose for Emily** assignment, **P. 27** …: superficially fine, ultimately questionable…

EXAMPLE #2: Can one better appreciate "POTENTIALITIES" in "good or better" *classroom practices* in teaching thinking? In this case a high school history class activity. An example of x-ray reading for what issues exist, what stand was taken on them…

KEVIN O'REILLY, a Massachusetts teacher, "stages a scuffle" in the corridor outside his classroom, and asks student witnesses to describe what happens. The accounts conflict; he compares this to reports about the Battle of Lexington in 1775. *The goal: the skill* of judging accuracy of information via judging the reliability of the sources. Discussion produces *a checklist of factors* for judging accuracy of information, a checklist "which *they use again and again* in O'REILLY'S classroom, and which enables them to back up their assessment of the accuracy of information with supporting reasons." These involve eyewitnesses, observation, secondary sources—"skills that are very *important in our life outside the classroom*." The students are more able to judge various textbook accounts of the Lexington incident.   [-- ROBERT SWARTZ, NCTT] [*Italics* added]

| Well, this seems pretty good. It is | …*true, BUT this may not be the whole story.* In contrast, O'REILLY'S example |

active learning—no boring lecture here! It involves the students in **experience**. This is one of the main learning-styles beyond lecturing. And this way each student can make up their mind as to what happens. This would show **tolerance of diversity in viewpoints**. Plus the students would feel more entertained and **respond more positively to learning which is enjoyable**.	proffers much to see and say here—many decisions on many subliminal issues. What issues exist? **Goal:** thinking skills! **Method:** dual learning styles of experience plus reflection, and also group discussion. **Explictness:** yes an overt checklist of possible thinking skills results! **Criteria:** important, beyond Authority or mere Personal Opinionation… --At the same time, the question arises of whether transfer was practiced, **Export** of these skills to new situations in actual life (though this End-Goal of Hitting the Ground Running is mentioned). --All in all, (1) the exercise is a refreshingly thought-infused ploy, and (2) we hope our analysis of it here is an example of *elucidation of a complex concern via "variables-variation": how one can unpack statements and versions to identify unmentioned variables and choices made…*

Example #3. An exemplification of the major move "CTA"

(1) To move UPward to Conceptualize the content… then to **(2)** Transfer OVER-ACROSS… and then to **(3)** to APPLY same to real-world issues…

(As "*at 9:00 Monday Morning in Room 212* at ELLIPSIS COLLEGE in HIATUS UNIVERSITY…")

Specific CONTENT (concerns, also domain-specific TTools) of specific courses in varied fields or disciplines:	Perhaps the *general-generic* THINKING SKILLS and issues common to all:	Toward a possible "tool-KIT" (even pocket textbook or "Wallet-Card") for these generic TTools:	…and APPLIED to what real-world areas: (1) now for test, (2) later in Hitting the Ground Running:
The LITERATURE class is discussing reasons why Emily Grierson (in Faulkner's story "A Rose for Emily") went insane..... The BIOLOGY class is studying multiple, interconnected causes, and effects, of diabetes..... The HISTORY class is discussing "three main causes of World War I"…	**[3.A.]** CAUSE-EFFECT analysis.	1. Types of Causes. Philosophy: Aristotle's four causes: formal, efficient, etc.... "Necessary & Sufficient." "Potentiating (=?) & Precipitating." 2. Number of Causes. Science: "parsimony": the fewest explanations possible (Occam's Razor), but see... Psychoanalysis: "over-determination": the more causal strands, the more accurate! One or many causes; one or many effects. "Threshold" Effect: water freezes suddenly. "Butterfly Effect": small cause leads to large result.	?????
The LITERATURE class is discussing "biographical, historical, political, aesthetic" responses to the story "A Rose for Emily"..... SOCIOLOGY is studying the Structural-Functional, the Conflict, and the Symbolic-Interactionist perspectives on social life..... The GEN.-ED. CAPSTONE-COURSE is examining "Freudian, Darwinian, Marxist, Religious, Existential" viewpoints about human nature.....	**[3.B.]** MULTIPLE-PLURAL PERSPEC-TIVES upon one given subject. This book tags this TTool "LENS-work	1. Do lenses exist, or do we in fact see reality directly?! Lenses as inescapable-unavoidable. 2. The central paradox. Lenses are virtually always incomplete/biassed.....yet they are powerful for seeing and understanding..... 3. Origin, source, motivations of lenses: why they're chosen, even if unconsciously? 4. One lens only? One main, several minor lenses? Plural lenses? 5. What of cooperation among lenses—or conflict? Differing world-views?! 6. What of mere mechanical or serial, 1-2-3 separated "multi-disciplinary" work vs. more organic integrated "inter-disciplinary" syntheses?	?????

| LITERATURE is discussing the "subject-matter" vs. the "theme" which may be hidden, implicit; also, irony: statements vs. true meanings.....

SOCIOLOGY is discussing "manifest" functions (results) of something and "latent" ones, those | **[3.C.]** Basically a DUALISM of | ????? | ????? |

30

	"surface vs. reality"		
neither intended, nor recognized, by the doers!..... **PSYCHOLOGY** discusses the "defense-mechanisms." Projection, transference, displacement, etc.—all seek to manage unknown, unconscious compulsions.....			

YES: I finally do see a major point. "True thinking skills often are not isolated from the content, made central, then applied…"	YES! Education as Thinking Things Through. (CTA is not the Chicago Transport Authority, but "conceptualize, transfer, and apply…")

WHOA, your fourth columns, "Applied," are rather sparse. In fact, they're blank. What gives? Can't you Walk the Talk?	Ouch, egg on my face. Maybe Teaching Thinking this way, is very arduous… Well, take any current issue,…

[4.C.] …and the "FARE-WELL" send-off:

I now see your big main idea. Goal to apply thinking in life. Spotlighting the goal but without either overkill or blur. Still, *is* this notion of an "End-Goal" of readiness, really all that defensible—or accepted?	As for the end-goal issue, I think it remains subliminal among educators. But consider *two different affirmations of it—depending on…*:

MILD: by STANTON the Office Clerk…	WILD: by CHESTER the provocateur… This end-goal of "ultimate preparedness later on," seems a great enforcer but also focuser. It buttonholes us and asks:
This "end-goal" is probably helpful, yes. It does focus efforts. It helps us to know what we're aiming for, even if far off and never knowable whether students will really reach it (=skill in life after graduation). Makes education more meaningful, anyhow more "accountable." Of course, this "end-goal" concept of <u>thinking</u>-as-goal, is <u>not</u> the whole picture; <u>other</u> goals do exist in and for education…	--"What I'm doing in class, does it make a difference? Is it a vector toward the goal of <u>intellectually empowering the student to face the complexity and chances, the problem-opportunities, of life, of the ex-student's life itself?</u>" --In fact let <u>every element in the whole course</u> be laser-beam arrowed toward the learner, becoming ex-student, to be able to step out on the path and <u>confront complexities competently</u>. Otherwise what do I think I am doing in class really?

…HMM… your above rant-and-rave, sounds also like a whole philosophy of life, of living more intensely, morally-ethically, pleasurably, fulfillingly, etc.	Oh I'd never say… Couldn't scandalously depart from dour educational duty, after all.. Toward life-enhancement, the pleasure of the thinking game. So, don't tell those others—they would neither care or be jealous, might just cause trouble……

[{(END of the Body of the Introduction; the second part, Annex, follows…)}]

```
\=\=|+|+|+\=\=|+|+|+\=\=|+|+|+\=\=\+|+|+\=\=\+|+|+\=\=|+|+|+\=\+|+|+\=\=|+|+\=\=|+|+|+\=\=\+|+|+\=\+|\=|+|+|+\=\=|+|+|+\=\+||
\=\=|+|+|+\=\=|+|+|+\=\=|+|+|+\=\=\+|+|+\=\=\+|+|+\=\=|+|+|+\=\+|+|+\=\=|+|+\=\=|+|+|+\=\=\+|+|+\=\+|\=|+|+|+\=\=|+|+|+\=\+||
```

O R I E N T A T I O N - B A R :				
[1.]MAIN INTRO: *["Reception-Room"]* Who?Why?What? How? Whoa! previous	**[2.] READINGS:** *["Library / Theatre"]* 3 Pillars…Issues… Analogies…"Lab"…	**[3.]HELPDESK:** *[The Summaries]* 1. Key Definitions 2. Directory to TTh	**[4.] BRIDGE to BOOK:** *["Exit-Walkway"]* 1. Book in 1 Page! 2. Final Readings	**→[5.] ANNEX:** 1. Examples 2. Analogies 3. FAQ's {"II"} 4. the Author

[5.] ANNEX: supplementary...

PURPOSE: This is *only* for those who want more *elaboration plus resources* on our "how and why." [Serious teachers. Serious beginning learners or self/teachers. Also "thinking buffs" for enjoyment...] *["Equipment-Room"---plus, "Staff Lounge": drop in and visit...]*

[5.1.] assignments: earlier [#1] and new [#2]:

EXAMPLE #1: From Women's Studies: [1.] part of a more-traditional final exam ==
.....and [2.] Applying Abstractions Autonomously to a crucial current concern:

[1.] What were women's essential contributions to colonial American households? What did midwives do? Why were they displaced by doctors? What are problems with fetal monitoring? How have estrogens been used to regulate women? In what ways is Learnfare a punitive program?	[2.] 1. Select a significant social issue today. 2. Select perspectives from feminism theory (Big Ideas, lenses, etc.) which apply to that problem. 3. Show how they're vital / valuable to explicate it. 4. Would opponents deny or decry this? Why? 5. Critique feminism theory itself: in what ways might parts of it be irrelevant or even erroneous (or misused) in confronting this problem?

..... #1 as appropriate, or *demeaning*?.. #2 as *over-*ambitious, or fostering true student "empowerment"?

EXAMPLES #2...: MINI-GALLERY. Examples of COURSE EXAM ASSIGNMENTS GIVEN FRESHMEN STUDENTS in various courses at Univ. of Wis. at Whitewater, as reported by my English 101 students, 1990's:

Left-hand: more *current-traditional*:

Right-hand: more *toward thinking*:

---

1. State the Greek contributions to art.
2. Why was *Learnfare* punitive to women?
3. Would *you* choose a F.L.Wright house like "Fallingwater"? Why?
4. Work # 1-5 in section 2 of math book
5. Define "allocation cost" w/ examples.

~#|~+|#|+#~|~+~|#+|~+~|#+|~+|#+~|#+~|~#+~|#+~|~#|~+|

1. What are two reptilian adaptations for a terrestrial environment, and why did they evolve? [Strong support system, harder-shelled eggs.]

2. What marked the beginnings of human civilization? [Food-production, etc., etc.]

3. Evaluate the contributions of the ancient Greeks in science and philosophy, using specific examples. *[Is this true evaluation, or reporting what the course said the contributions were?]*

4. How does the exploitation of the Third World by the First World reflect on the USA? [Shift from pride to embarrassment, etc., etc. ...]

5. How does the classroom teacher identify a child with possible hearing loss?

6. When you speak publicly, how can you control your nervousness, even make it work for you? [Be at physical and mental best; think positively; use visual aids...]

7. Should the electoral college be banned in the United States? *[Did teacher give own opinion on this?]*

8. Would you like to live in a house like Frank Lloyd Wright's "Fallingwater"? Why or why not? *[Does this ask for more than mere Personal Opinionation? Did it seek to teach a skill of "how to evaluate and decide more competently"?]*

9. Explain which technique used by interest groups in trying to influence legislation you think is best, and why. *[persuasion, litigation, rulemaking, election activities, lobbying] [I am confused. By what Way of Knowing? Personal Preference? This criterion and why chosen? AND Transfer:*

---

1. Apply Greek Art "golden section" to your residence-hall decoration.
2. How does feminism help explain issues in your family/school/job?
3. Apply Objective Evaluation pros and cons to Wright's designs.
4. Apply "regression to the mean" to famous celebrities...
5. Explain household economics to your parents.

~#|~+|#|+#~|~+~|#+|~+~|#+|~+|#+~|#+~|~#+~|#+~|~#|~+|

LITERATURE:

1. Write a ten-minute burst of PERSONAL response: *every question you could think to ask* about this group of poems by Walt Whitman.
2. Then, assess the PERSONAL questions OBJECTIVELY.
--Which call for factual knowledge only—which for mere opinion—which for "reasoned judgment"?
--Which can have one right answer—which can validly allow for disagreement?
--Which are convergent and close down—which can stimulate further thinking?
--Which are limited—which may represent a larger **Variable-Issue** about confronting literature itself (oh, such as "continuity vs. change in a writer's output or career"....."importance or not of the biographical"....."topical references vs. more "timeless" appeal.....and others!)
3. [*] --What have you learned about (A) approaching *poetry*, (B) *thinking skills in general?* Can you apply same to a situation in your own Personal life, on the Job, or as Citizen in community?

[...Seems good, to guide convergently toward autonomous divergence. Focussed accurate precise – but also flexible adaptable pragmatic. How to ask which questions. [*] *And how to generalize one's learning of thinking itself...*]

And two from Economics:

"You are talking with your parents, who wish to know what you're learning in ECONOMICS at school. Explain the term **'leakage'** as it relates to the **'circular flow'** concept. Then describe a type of **leakage** taking place in your parents' own household. Be specific, and explain how that example of **leakage** affects **'aggregate demand'**."

"Take this or that major social issue and show how which key concepts from economics can help illuminate it. But also which are less relevant for this particular issue even though probably productive for other issues—and why? Same could be done with a statement someone else makes on an economic issue, and your response to that..."

| *.....No* to all these here! I am *confused.* I do see real differences, but also some potential problems, and in any case, *not how* to re-design assignments... | *...These were Just For Openers.* In Section #3 below, "D-Machine," we present a dozen **Variable-Issues** to help you crowbar and then sculpt your responses. *Stay tuned...* |

|~#+#|+~|+#|+|~+#|+~#|~#++#~||~#+|~|#~|#|#+|+#|~|+#~|+|~+|#|~+#|~|+#|~#|~#|~#|~#|+#|~+#|~+|#+~|#+~|#+~|#+~||#+|#+|+#|+#|+#|+#|

[5.2.] ANALOGIES illuminate [*full* view here]...

RECALL: the earlier comparisons. To orient to a totality with choices, "two maps of a large city: destination- sketch, vs. A- Z complete."….. Old- school education: banking, vaccination, dipstick, harvesting corn.

MINI-GALLERY: To illustrate the difference between the current-traditional, and the emerging "thinking" models: Here, comparisons from 1. **Agriculture.** 2. **Aviation.** 3. **Aquatics.** 4. **Personal Travel.** 5. **Architecture.** 6. **Athletic sports.** 7. **Medicine.** 8. **Identity Card vs. Tattoo.**

1. Agriculture: "The students go and harvest the three rows of corn the teacher/textbook planted, in bushelbaskets of essay-exams (or multiple choice). "Acquiring of the material."	"The students end up able to plant their own corn, confront other cornfields—and apply skills to other crops too, perhaps."
2. Aviation. The students learn about flying, perhaps simulate, ride in the class plane.	The students can **solo flight**, autonomously apply skills on their own and competently.
3. Aquatics. The students can swim the prescribed lane with water wings.	The students can swim open water, or navigate with aids: buoys, lighthouses, on their own...

4. Travel. [4A.] "Facts about Japanese Museums" [information] …"You should do social work in Africa" [indoctrination] …"How to bicycle in Burgundy, 1-2-3" [instruction] (Now take an exam.)	Keystone <u>VARIABLE-ISSUES</u> are: **Purposes; Regions; Safety; Transportation; Equipment; Rapport with Natives; Others** – *Now you plan and decide on your own.*
[4B.] [No travel, or a superficial guided tour, or an in-depth but very narrow travel, or uncontrolled...]	**"Familiarization Tour"** taken by travel professionals, to better Orient them so they can Navigate clients.
[4C.] Purposes: lesser (to instruct how-to, argue that you should do this or that, Tell About Our Trip...)	**Principles** of all Travel! Goals... Security... Movement-alternatives... Rapport with Natives... etc.
[4D.] "Two Maps of a Large Urban Area": (-) the one, a mere *partial sketch* on an envelope of "how to get from right here, to downtown" (useful but grossly-limited)	...the other, *a complete map* of the whole city and outskirts, to show, complete-but-clear, **all** variables, options; roads, sectors of attractons— (overpowering? but really, truly empowering...)

| **5. Education, as "*a Two-Story Building.*"** The first floor is for "education as usual": goal what to know, believe, do. It is finished and occupied busily with people "convering content," "mastering the material," "transmitting and receiving knowledge" ….. | "But <u>the second story is the area for "teaching of thinking"</u> and it is—well, scarcely even finished off; gaping windows, and the like, unfurnished. And unoccupied except by a skeleton crew; a few stray boxes imported but unpacked. Further, any stairway or elevator communication between the busy first floor, and the embryonic second floor, seems nonexistent or hidden, and there is no direct communication lines between the two stories... |

6. "CONTEST" As noted earlier, we see thinking as not only workhorse dutiful, but also as *a pleasurable* SPORT-GAME-PLAY. Higher enjoyment, deeper satisfaction. --The thinker-*athlete* uses savvy and sweat (dedication) to *win, over the Foe* of "ignorance/confusion."
--And it's a *spectator sport*: the reader-listener audience in the grandstands, Thinking Buffs cheer deft moves—but also boo inept foul-outs. Or even gymnastics and artful acrobatics approaching Dance... *Beyond calisthenics!*
So **competence** surely enters in: not just "thinking," but "good or better" thinking.

7. **An analogy from Medicine:** the usual exam of essentially, "what did I say in lecture" or "what is YOUR opinionation on this" or "work these 1-2-3 formulae"... is no more revealing as is early *X-rays* or perhaps even *phrenology*...	The "autonomous-application" exam [write your own paper; apply feminism to something complex; take these twelve new poems; etc.], is *monstrously efficient* as a diagnostic tool to measure what has been truly learned—or rather, what *truly has not* been. Medically speaking, it is *a modern MRI or PET scan*! *It shows up the unpalatable truths hitherto unsuspected: the pervasive presence of, not disease, but of failure to Truly Learn Thinking below surface compliances*....

8. On **Motivation**. Many students stay distant from their education. Too often, students seem simply to (so to speak) attend class but passively, and they just wear a plastic-coated *identification badge* dangling on a cord around their *neck*, on which various stickers are placed to certify they've completed a paper, test, course. The badge is exterior to the student, kept at a distance, useful only as gateways to fulfilling requirements and hence exit. And in re attitude, the students just seem to *sit or wait around*...	Whereas a true learner would *tattoo* learning-material onto his/her very *skin*, to let it permeate in to their personal selves! And in re attitude, the learner would <u>bound into the course like a hunter-and-gatherer, a forager, a poacher even</u>, *grabbing by the double-handful* material of use and interest to the learner him/herself...
BUT how idealistic hence silly. This Active Student is **_not_** the way in which most, or mass, education works today, or ever!	Aha, **BUT** motivation's the *only* way *any real* learning occurs. [*Better we know the truth than not?*]

I have no analogy or comparison to convey the idea of **the how teaching true thinking can positively *ennoble* education.** To mature the classroom, truly empower the students, profoundly satisfy the teacher...

9. While writing up the book, I came to realize that specific thinking/writing skills can be clarified—and focused—by using a "dominant guiding overall" analogy:
Structure: "get *a string for those beads*..."
Adequate Catchment-area of research: "search not just one tree, but the *whole* 40-acre apple-orchard, & the next field over too"
"Colloquializing," or getting other peoples' opinions; "your *own radio* may not pick up the *whole* spectrum"
Ladder of Abstraction, concrete-conceptual: "get an *altimeter* to see how specific or general you are thinking: lowlands, or peak?"
Major Change: "as events recede, a *'fog'* comes in and masks them from us; use *'radar'* to see through it"
Cause-Effect: "a *billiards table* with many types of factors impulsions and results—not simple one-cause, one-effect. Carom!"
Number and Relation: "sometimes *separate* two things with *knife/scissors*, sometimes *connect* them with *tape/glue*"
Prior Basic Thinking Skills: "we may need a *vaccination, remedial vitamins* or *calisthenics*, or a common *Basic Training*"
Concretization, Specific Detailing: over arid abstractions, pour the *warm water* of examples to rehydrate, refresh them!
Analogy itself: to grasp the new unknown idea, provide a *"mirror on the ceiling"* which reflects it to you in your known position...
The **"15-C"** or more-complete checklist for **essay or thesis-and-point thinking**: it is a *"powerful diesel front-loader or fork-lift,"* as against the simplistic "five-paragraph theme," traditional schooling's format for exposition, which is a simple—*"wheelbarrow"*...

Good, **BUT** I think that earlier "corn growing" analogy above is a little **extreme.** Corny (sorry), but really *insulting to education.* Your Strong Personal Opinion. Are things really as bad as that?	I thought so too, but others liked it. Plus education expert JOHN GARDNER himself recently said "Much education today is monumentally ineffective. All too often **we are giving young people cut flowers when we should be teaching them to grow their own plants.",,,**
	--As for *"insulting to education,"* I think that the tradition of rote knowledge transmission (etc.) is indeed itself profoundly insulting—to *true* education, let alone to motivated students.
	--Plus, claiming to **"empower"** students by indoctrinating them that Social Progress is The Goal of Education and they must Work Against Injustices, and the like—is the reverse of true empowering, and a misuse of that word and concept...

SEE ALSO: the "II" *FULL-* dress unit on **Analogy** within Appendix #3, "Why The Very Idea"...

|~#+#|+~|+#|+|~+#|~#|~#++#~||~#+|~|#~|#|#+|+#|~|+#~|+|~+|+|#~+#|~|+#|~#|+#|~|#|~+#|~+|#+~|#+~|#||#+|#+|+#|+#|+#|#+|#+|

[5.3] FREQUENTLY-ASKED QUESTIONS (plus OFTEN-VOICED *OBJECTIONS*)...

This is "II" the FULL version; "I" BRIEF was in Introduction above...

Hey, I don't really have any objections now...	Well, skim these to enjoy the "dramatic conflicts" involved. Plus ways of responding fairmindedly, or at least trying to!...

[1.] Your **goal** for education as "thinking," is **too narrow.** Other important goals exist. Vocational, personal development, moral-ethical, citizen in community, etc.	True, except we take the stand that Essential Thinking is *indispensable base for all else*, plus grossly-shortchanged currently. So, This Is What We Do Here, our focus, our contribution...

[2.] Your claim of need of this stuff, is **outdated.** Already, major reforms advance: "active learning" fosters thinking!	Yes, except beware mistaking surface changes as real ones; as mentioned earlier, note that "active or student-centered" learning does **_not_**, per se, explicitly identify or teach thinking skills.

[3.] Okay, but your **definition** of thinking (conceptualizing upward etc.) is itself **too narrow.**	True by-the-book, but pragmatically we need a solid firm benchmark to orient everyone, build firm base. (*Convergent* common comprehension first, then *divergent* individual-reader development later...)

[4.] In *tone* you're **too personal, subjective, informal**—and in *vision*, you are inescapably **incomplete**, since as you yourself affirm, one correlator can't know it all.	First, "personal" *can* be valid and balanced too. Second, true *but* the "generalist" approach is a possible specialty itself. The key here: is an individual attempting competently, to be fair?

[5.] Okay, but frankly at times you do seem **too— "extreme."** Too **enthusiastic** urging 100% teaching thinking as a kind of— Utopia?	I grant my zeal. But (1) note that *enthusiasm need not mean bias*. Note the distinction between fervent candid obsession with an idea, and fair-minded civil objectivity about it (the thinking skill of **comparison-contrast**). We can **correlate contraries** (another thinking skill) and *I can be both wild and mild.* (2) Also (yet a third thinking skill here), note why I employ the **"Ideal-Type"** or **"100% pure"** model. Not to combat and convince, persuade, bowl over. Instead, to utilize the advantages of this Ideal-type approach:
	Namely, the **"Ideal-Type"** thinking-approach can **(1.)** simply better clarify the new idea (and defend it against misinterpretation)... **(2.)** show its limits and even excesses... **(3.)** allow us to know where we are or stand on a scale of responses to this issue... **(4.)** combat inappropriate resistance-evasion-denial of the new ("hew to the line, no compromises right now")... and **(5.)** help achieve discussion without rancorous argument (as in, "I'm simply using this lens, not arguing it's right for us or you or everyone always")...

[6.] Your intended **audience** is **too general, diverse.** You'll baffle beginners, bore fellow-experts!	One can write simultaneously for novices and for insiders—the trick is to Layer or Level things in stages.
	True, I concede that we do aim only for certain readers—those who are *already interested*... who *value excellence*... who prefer a *considered slow* approach... who are fascinated by *true teaching* of baffled beginners... and who are not out to combat and win but to *consider and work together*... The "flippant care-less" others, can go *elsewhere*...

[7.] Your material is at times **too basic,** "we already know	Too basic? Earlier I thought so, but in today's situation—abysmal lack of teaching thinking, immense need for the new workforce to know "advanced Thinking 101"—I

35

this"—at other times it's **too advanced**, over-elaborted.	*don't think so any more.* **Anyhow I shall steadfastly clarify the very basics of advanced thinking—a duty is to curate material which myopic experts think is "too elementary"**… As for <u>too advanced</u>: we calibrate things, keep the refinements compact-minimal but present…

[8.] Regarding your guidance, sometimes you seem **too narrow and prescriptive**: "this is right, that is wrong, do this, don't do that." Yet at other times you seem **too vague, loose, unfocussed**: "this is the principle and need here" and just give some "guideline to think about using."	[*TO HIMSELF:* "Alas, how some responders misperceive me as the Traditional Teacher indoctrinating them—they misread the dictatorial schoolmarm into every statement…. But then other responders initially welcome the flexibility, but soon when it comes for them to actively engage and do some work, they yearn for more "guidance, truth…]
	--First, I *refuse* to be prescriptive and dictatorial, tell people the Truth to know, the Doctrine to believe, the Procedure to follow. True, I personally believe that "teaching thinking" as described here, is the perfecting of education, truly empowering learners, truly satisfying teachers, and that its opposite—rote didacticism—is a botch and bungle, inefficient, "immoral," and a bore," etc., etc. <u>But so what?</u> Didn't you know that true learning is 100% self-motivated: each reader will decide for oneself where to go on this. (To ask "Which stance should we believe, which option should we select to use?" is juvenile…)
	--But second, <u>I do try to demonstrate objectively, usefully</u> my belief that "practice or belief X is baaaad—incompetent, a shoddy bungle, etc."—but then that "procedure or concept Z is better: more efficient, principled, and robustly playing the game well."
	--The thinking-skill/issue here is **"correlating contraries."** Both sides are important, even if contradictory: I try to give *definite but nuanced* guidance. Beyond just description or observation, etc., i.e., "usable," but short of rote prescriptions or recipes.
	[Thus, both **(1)** "tight and loose"; other **contraries** include **(2)** fervent enthusiasm plus fair-minded objectivity… giving basics for beginners but also advanced points for expertise… **(3)** welcoming everyone (egalitarianism) but also defending standards of quality competence ("good" elitism)… and others.]

[9.] At times your material is **overelaborated**. (1) Too much *repetition* of point, especially (2) too many *examples* of point given (especially in the Gallery).	Granted my tendency to over-clarify! Still, "research confirms" that <u>learners master difficult new concepts (such as here) better</u> if (1) the *concept is repeated* for reinforcement and in different viewpoints, also (2) *examples are given* to illustrate it, but instances numerous and varied in type. Thus to triangulate in… **(So research says…)**

[10.] Your material is ***non*-practical for teachers.** ("We can't apply it Monday Morning in Subject 101 in Room 212…")	[Ouch—shades of the Old-School approach of knowledge given in pre-packaged units?] As noted earlier, we offer **"the whole city map"**: more work for you, but ultimately more empowering than a Bus Tour… One plans one's own route, with aid….

[11.] You are **[A] too idealistic**—this teaching thinking *can't happen.* Plus explicit training in thinking is **[B] unnecessary**—*good* students teach/learn *themselves*!	**[A]** True, "100% teaching thinking" **(1)** *should* not be the Total or Only approach, and admittedly **(2)** *will* not come to pass, not even 50%, due to: **(A)** frank teacher-disinterest, **(B)** fierce student resistance [and negative course-evaluations can torpedo non-tenured instructors…] **(3)** administrative non-support, and **(4)** structural-institutional lag. … *However:* 5% teaching thinking in 5% of almost *any* class, and *every* class-hour, <u>yes</u>… **[B]** As for "unnecessary, "true **but** not totally: give a motivated student the right unit at the right time as catalyst, and see learning accelerate, avoid "re-inventing the wheel."

[12.] <u>You shortchange</u> "holistic synthesizing **integration**" which is vital for liberal-general education.	First things first. First, a basic grasp of the elements. Next we can connect them—at least to the extent possible. Besides, "associative, connective" thinking is one of our basic Trio tools…

[13.] Candidly, what is **the worst, and the best, thing** *you yourself* can say about this manual your offer to us?	*--Worst,* well "earnest embroidery in the dark" for only 37 interested souls nationwide. "Anyone able to understand this, will already know it" [P.S.—this is *not* true...] *--Best,* well, two analogies here. First, a valuable **"cache in the woods"** to sustain those travelers who need clarified material on sportive play of mind... And second, a **"familiarization tour"** of "thinking territory": a resource like no other current material to provide Orientation & Navigation... [P.S.—also a lively account of the Education Wars and all-too-human conflicts between contrary stands, myself included...]

[14.] <u>But does it really matter?</u> Tell me exactly why and how this whole issue here is truly **crucial...is important to attend to?** ...	... Well ... if people ask THAT, then I MUST take space for the following. Below are some major **"connexions"** of essential thinking, with "life as we would know it today":

1. <u>Crucial Pragmatic Life-Skills</u>. The younger generation risks being unable to navigate personal tasks. Coping, life-management...

> A leading professor of pediatrics and specialist in studying "development and learning," says that "The most common learning disorder among undergraduates is incomplete comprehension. Affected students have difficulty understanding concepts, terminology, issues, and procedures." In high school, "rote memory and procedural mimicry" taught them how to manipulate "cosines and tangents" but not to truly know them. Another shortfalling: "abysmal disorganization" in handling "activities with multiple components that must be integrated". [-- MEL LEVINE, CHE, 2005]

2. <u>Vocational</u>: Thinking for a Living? Is it a *cliché* now that today, **workers need to be able to confront complex and ill-structured tasks requiring multiple perspectives,** *and all that...?* A touchstone-comment:

> "Employers have not considered the need for both **critical** (**logical**, judgmental, convergent) cognitive thinking skills for decision-making, problem-solving, system-thinking... and also **creative** (lateral, **exploratory**,) thinking skills needed for *strategic competitive thinking*, pattern recognition, opportunity spotting and creation, etc." [-- W. DERZKO]

3. <u>Education</u>—but for the Guerilla Bands "Still in the Hills"... Especially **to offer resources to the grass-roots, contrarian paradigm still outside the mainstream of education... To help train the trainers.** Education for thinking is still an alternate-paradigm, Johnny-Appleseed endeavor... (And for in-group minority solidarity: to defend and reassure those thinking educators whose good goals are neglected, misunderstood, misrepresented...)

> "Truly new ideas are not retained, any more than is a water-soluble marker used on a porcelain bathroom fixture... If your ideas are truly new, don't worry about people stealing them; you'd have to shove the new stuff down peoples' throats... And anyhow, people don't change their minds on major issues, they die off and the new generation grows up with the new paradigm... [-- CHESTER OBERHAUPTKARTOFFELKOPFE & R.S. WURMAN]]

4. <u>Corrective of Current "Bad Thinking</u>." Thinking goes in cycles, "in" doctrines and "out" ones. We need to help *rebalance* the pendulum-swing. Notorious culprits include (**A**) *excess <u>Postmodernism</u>* or "we really can't know anything about reality-out-there"... Close behind is (**B**) *rampant <u>Relativism</u>* or "who's to say what's true or right after all." (**C**) *Other current orthodoxies* exist to be rebalanced.

[{ A **THINKING SKILL** in itself: "Identify the TTT (Today's Truths & Taboos) and see if the implicit "either/or, A or Z, and Z unthinkable," should be returned to explicit "to what extent both-and or more toward A or more toward Z." }]

5. <u>For "Excellence in Quality</u>." Remember our mantra: "Complex subjects, skills, tasks can be elucidated and performed *more completely plus more clearly* without oversimplification—hence *"better"*—than people know or do or value."

6. <u>"Civilization</u>." *Burnishing the lamp of Intellect in a larger world of darker irrationalities.* Now Islamic-related fundamentalism. (And other mania nearer...) But always others...

A UNESCO report on higher education in developing countries, peril and promise, the importance of general education… The best universities [in Iraq, elsewhere] are becoming interested in "changing the lecture-and-memorization model of instruction to one that encourages students to read, discuss ideas, and think for themselves. In time, the liberation of minds will be the surest guarantor of the liberation of a country…" […wouldn't it be nice…]

7. For <u>Preservation & Conservation</u>. A Resource Access-Center, not a boot camp nor open field, but a cache, a toolshop, though of open access.

"A place that upholds the primacy of **difficult and demanding skills that leak from a culture and are lost unless they are incessantly taught to those who want to have them. And those people are always in a minority.**"   [-- ROBERT HUGHES, ON THE BRITISH ROYAL ACADEMY OF ART])

8. …and <u>Unsuspected Personal Hedonism</u>. In a "post-oil" future of *fewer material resources and downscaled living styles*, **the "life of the mind" and its pursuits could be even more essential to enrich satisfactions in life…** As sport, the athlete out to gain the goal with style. As war, to defeat the Enemy Ignorance… *[Assuming the real enemies, encroaching totalitarianisms, out to re-primitivize the planet, are held at bay…]*

"Only when love and work are one, / And the work is play for mortal stakes, / Is the deed ever fully done, / For Heaven's and the future's sakes." [-- ROBERT FROST]

YES: These "Objections" while so-extensive are better-than not. I see your modeling of an educator candidly anticipating reader-questions, especially criticisms, as you seem to above…	Well we hope this not only "helps," but also models this meta-cognitive **consciousness** of one's own thinking. (Plus also the disposition of **"conscientious"** thinking means Ya Gotta Wanna truly <u>hear the other side</u>, seek valid views opposing your own…)

\=\=|+|+|+\=\=|+|+|+\=\=|+|+|+|=\=\+|+|+\=\=\+|+|+\=\=|+|+|+\=\+|+|+\=\=|+|+\=\=|+|+|=\=\+|+|+\=\+|\=|+|+|+|+\=\=|+|+|+|=\+||

[5.4.] The Author's Personal Story, Journey…

The "personal" can be biased—but also powerful. Even Strong, passionate, motivations are helpful if "cleaned up," sublimated. If the wild stallion of Personal Temperament is harnessed to good workhorse use…

A PREVIEW. See <u>on the "personal" in thinking</u>. App #6 Pre-Vue of Mind-Play] … Also SEE Vita, App. Intro. **P. 135.**

[1.] CAMEO-BIOGRAPHY: My Professional Experience *Personalized* …

--How I <u>struggled for decades to *try* to teach thinking, but</u> only *pseudo*-taught it. (Urged it; discussed it; modeled it, etc…)

--How I persevered, seeing <u>thinking **ennobles** education</u>: can mature classroom, empower students, satisfy teachers …

--How I experienced the issue as <u>a real major-change or paradigm-shift issue</u>, with all the dynamism—and discord and obstacles!—resulting. [The Thinking Teacher as non-understood maverick, with lower course-evaluations…Then s/he attends a conference on Teaching Thinking and finds 200 welcoming cohorts who feel equally alien At Home!…] …

--How I sedulously <u>researched the "critical thinking" movement</u> [R.PAUL, R.ENNIS, M.LIPMAN, B.BEYER, D.SCHWARZ, R.PERKINS, others…] but found this approach too narrow for Big-Picture complexities…

--How <u>I came to feel strongly</u> about some issues—even sounding "100% extremist" perhaps—but offer them *not* as grandstanding or dictating, *but* as stimulants-to-focus…:

--"True teachers enjoy helping beginners comprehend and self-empower, but such true teachers are **rare.**"
--"Teaching/learning thinking could truly **ennoble** education, empower students, gratify teachers."
--"**90% of education today teaches nothing resembling true essential thinking.**"
--"But **100%** teaching thinking would be impossible, impracticable, improbable."
--"We revolutionarily **reverse** Content and Skills. We topple Content-Coverage and put Skill-learning as the goal. Content exists only to support learning higher-order concepts, thinking skills."
--"We teachers both *do too much* for our students (make all the decisions, shortchanging learners' Autonomy), and *don't*

do enough (1. in specific classes, we don't **explicitly** teach or proffer **higher-order thinking skills** ... also 2. in general *institutionally* we do *not* explicitly state skill-goals as if on a Public-Space billboard as a common-resource **tool-BANK**)."
--"**Motivation** comes from 100% within the learner. Not even 99%, with 1% from the teacher. Sorry!"

--How I *finally* realized an ultimate meaning of all this. That "teaching thinking" is ultimately about **Much More** than just "ennobled" formal education. It's about **escaping mechanicality, alienations, inefficiencies, impositions**, and the like—and **approaching integrity, challenge-reward, solidity, validity, and enhancement**. [Nor have I described it well here...] And in so being, it touches toward —*a higher quality of Life itself*...

| ...aha, I see. Your True Religion at last! And we your converts? | Yeah, but it's *totally do-it-yourself*. "All true education is self-education." |

\=\=|+|+|+\=\=|+|+|+\=\=|+|+|+|=\=\+|+|+\=\=\+|+|+\=\=|+|+|+\=\+|+|+\=\=|+|+|+\=\=|+|+|=\=\+|+|+\=\+|+|\=|+|+|+|+\=\=|+|+|

[2.] RETRO TESTIMONY: My *Uncensored* Recollections of "College":

"Heck, FROM COLLEGE I RECALL ACQUIRING *ONLY A FEW* "KEYSTONE PERSPECTIVES" which I could use for confronting challenges in the world, etc... (1) From <u>economics</u>, *nothing at all* (a bunch of graphs—only later did I truly absorb and apply the keystone concept of "allocation cost" (also stated as "**cost-benefit ratio**") to all areas of my life, personal and vocational.... Nothing at all from (2) <u>political science and government</u> (we read Hobbes, Locke, Rousseau, others in an evening seminar).... And from (3) <u>philosophy</u>, only the distinction between Direct and **Representative Realism** (=do we see the world directly, or through "lenses"? This planted seeds).... And from (4) <u>psychology</u>, **learning theory: stimulus-response**, and if a response is not reinforced, it becomes extinguished—people give up doing it if no reward.... And from (5) <u>anthropology</u>, the seminal concept of **cultural relativism**: one understands actions better if one comprehends, let alone judges, them in their own sociocultural context, not in our own. (My anthro prof, DR. ROWE, told us that he was indeed a "murderer." He had indeed killed five men, with a rifle. {In World War II, of course})... Oh of course some other courses, my (6) <u>English</u> major, also (7) *art history* I guess (though *no real appreciation of aesthetics*—my love of **Organic Form** etc. came later...), also vibrant (8) <u>French language and literature</u>...
-----But *THAT SEEMED TO BE IT* FOR MY COLLEGE EDUCATION AS FOR **KEYSTONE CONCEPTS** installed into my Tool-Belt for use later on where they made differences... (No connections of courses to each other or to life—except on that last day of class!) (*) No practice in transferring key concepts to new material)...
Oh, and *no* (9) <u>"senior-year capstone-course" integrating or correlating the perspectives of many disciplines to confront a challenging issue</u>—"What is the Good Life, or Design a Good City Park, or whatever....!"

| Well, you must *not* have been a good student. Or else hindsight is perfectionistic. Perhaps they did all that they could, and you too at the time... | ...true indeed, but maybe I *could* have been offered a more explicit **Exhibiting** or "Billboard" or "Tool-Bank" of ways of thinking... |

\=\=|+|+|+\=\=|+|+|+\=\=|+|+|+\=\+|+|+\=\=\+|+|+\=\=|+|+|+\=\+|+|+\=\=|+|+|+\=\=|+|+|=\=\+|+|+\=\+|+|\=|+|+|+|+\=\=|+|+|

[3.] PERSONAL PROFILE: My "Psychic History" and "Taste-Temperament" (revealed via X-Ray for more than mere Gossip, Confession...)

PERSONAL PSYCHOLOGICAL PROFILE: A disclosure of my taste-temperament and other motivational contours...

As stated above, one's "psychic profile" influences one's thinking. One's mental stances also imbue (even motivate) some Strong Stands I offer on this-and-that issue... I'd rather confront not ignore this dimension, and be up-front about one's "pulsions" (Know Thyself, then disclose same to others as useful; turn one's excesses into controlled focus)?

Origins of Traits:

(1) <u>Early childhood</u>: loving but insecure parents made intelligent child curious to comprehend complex situation.

(2) <u>Later childhood</u>: parents also

Traits themselves:

(1) "Cognitive Voyeur": a (non-erotic) "lust" for **comprehensive completeness,** Big-Picture scanning, integration, synthesis, scrutiny. (Admittedly, this can become overdone for own sake.)

(2) **Competence**: love excellence in quality. (Also can be overdone if not needed by the situation.)

had good values of civility, true class, truly-moral behavior.

(3) Innate intelligence enables pleasure in "thinking complexities."

(4) Temperamentally, prefer holism, synthesis, which includes all its opposites, correlating contraries also.

(3) "**Craft**": interest in method, technique—including awareness of same.

(4) "**Contest**": love the sportive game of play of mind seeking goal of Truth to defeat foe of Ignorance.

(5) **Considerateness.** Prefer fair-minded working cooperatively to warring in combat to win.

(6) "**Classroom**": Love true teaching of beginners.

DISLIKE: "*Sloppy Casual Oversimple Blowoff*" Statements ("Oh, we're already teaching thinking in our classes," etc. – *oh are we now really? Let's discuss.*)

Do you love confessionallly revealing this *dirty laundry*? This narcissistic *navel-gazing* will **bore** readers, *discredit* the *author* too.	…Or *increase* credibility, comprehension, rapport?... Are you stumbling on the basic prior issue of "**Personal vs. Objective Knowledge**"? At 9:00 in **Sci** students may hear "be objective" and then at 11:00 in **Lit** they hear "Tell Your Story." *They should know to determine when each approach is valid, and when each is inappropriate*… **SEE** Appendix #5 "Prior Basics" for "**Personal and Objective Ways of Knowing.**"

\=\=|+|+|+\=\=|+|+|+\=\=|+|+|=\=\+|+|+\=\=\+|+|+\=\=|+|+|+\=\+|+|+\=\=|+|+|=\=\+|+|+\=\+|+|\=|+|+|+|+\=\=|+|+|=\+||
\=\=|+|+|+\=\=|+|+|+\=\=|+|+|=\=\+|+|+\=\=\+|+|+\=\=|+|+|+\=\+|+|+\=\=|+|+|=\=\+|+|+\=\+|+|\=|+|+|+|+\=\=|+|+|=\+||

All this is unfortunately very good-and-useful, even at times interesting, for the most part anyhow... But give me the *gist* of it: what is this type of thinking you label "**essential**"?	See Appendix #6 Pre-Vue, but right below a sneak preview:

1) <u>**Confronts Complexity**</u> (17 aspects of)

A) In movement: holistic panoramic systemic synthesizing integrating etc.

B) In Content: Comprehensive, Complete (enough)

2) <u>**Meta-Formulaic**</u>: (A) "strategic monitoring" as a default ploy (B) in general: "not rules but tools"

3) **Higher-<u>Order</u>** (complex itself)

4) **Higher-<u>Level</u>.** Moves from concrete specifics == to concepts, principles inducting up the Ladder of Abstraction.
   [Note that this is pragmatically our <u>keystone summit</u> skill. Conceptualizing 101: induct UP to get ideas from facts, deduct DOWN to apply ideas to facts, and then interrelate laterally... See Appendix 2.3. devoted to this skill.]

5) "<u>**Supple**</u>" agile adroit: dialectic "both-and": correlates important contrary demands-opportunities. Especially, both Complete-Comprehen*sive* == and Clarified-Comprehen*sible*.

6) **Conscious:** reflexive self-awareness of own thinking, meta-cognition. Describe *and* evaluate own product.

7) "<u>**Considered**</u>": s-l-o-w, reflective, deliberate, re-considering...

8) "<u>**Considerate**</u>": disposition to be not agonistic (combat to win victory), but authentic (cooperate to win validity). Resultant attending to one's own biases, listening truly to the Other Side *"no but really"*.

9) **Competent.** Avoid errors, aim for excellences. Via high **Criteria**, Standards. ["**Command**" = whether win-succeed, or lose-fail, one *did all one or anyone could do toward* success...]

10) "<u>**Contest**</u>": sportive game, play, the thinker-athlete performs to gain goal through obstacles via "savvy & sweat" ... the reader-spectators cheer the deft suave moves—or boo the blunders...

\=\=|+|+|+\=\=|+|+|+\=\=|+|+|=\=\+|+|+\=\=\+|+|+\=\=|+|+|+\=\+|+|+\=\=|+|+|=\=\+|+|+\=\+|+|\=|+|+|+|+\=\=|+|+|=\+||
\=\=|+|+|+\=\=|+|+|+\=\=|+|+|=\=\+|+|+\=\=\+|+|+\=\=|+|+|+\=\+|+|+\=\=|+|+|=\=\+|+|+\=\+|+|\=|+|+|+|+\=\=|+|+|=\+||

[{ **END** of the entire **Introduction** section to <u>Teaching Thinking</u>...}]

2: "KEYSTONE" issues-to-consider

THE ISSUE HERE: **What are the <u>issues to decide about</u> regarding teaching/learning thinking?**
WHY IMPORTANT: Not as easy or obvious a question as it might seem—though central.
OUR SUGGESTION: *This chapter seeks to collect and clarify "all" the <u>important basic matters to confront</u>— [and as completely/clearly as possible—more than many other currently-existing resource-materials].*

Not only the <u>mandatory</u> matters, which one *must* attend to ("handle, manage, satisfy")...
but also <u>optional</u> matters, which one *may* or may not elect to utilize ("employ, utilize")...

ORIENTATION NOTE—this **Keystones** section, deals with *identifying* the issues; the following **D-Machine** section deals with options for *implementing* them...

The **Table of Contents** of *Keystones* :

ISSUE: Causes of objections: legitimate criteria… innate difficulties… "paradigm-shift" pains… other factors?

6. How explicitly-or-indirectly, <u>should</u> one teach thinking? $\boxed{\textbf{P. 54-}}$

A. Whole fields do possess identifiable (but under-stated?) key concepts, skills…

B. These thinking tools are perhaps not "embedded" in class, "exhibited" in schools…

C. Still, how much-or-little to actually instruct thinking skills explicitly?

D. Two Cautions: over-teaching, plus need for active constructivist learning…

7. Is the <u>motivation</u> of learners, a significant issue?… $\boxed{\textbf{P. 59-}}$

|+#|+|+|+|#+|+|+|+|#+|+|+|+|#+|+|+|+|#+|+|+|+|#+|+|+|+|#+|+|+|+|#+|+|+|+|#+|+|+|#+|#+|#+|+|#+|#+#|+#|#+|#+|+#|+||#+|

WHAT THINKING SKILLS USED HERE IN THIS SECTION: Three powerful skills, not always made explicit:

(1) "<u>Personal Stands</u>" strong but fairminded—**_not_** to persuade so much as to "save" key insights…

(2) <u>Variables-Variation</u>. ["Identify *all* issues; then for each, *all* its options; then, the pros *and* cons of *each* option…"]

(3) <u>the "Ideal-Type"</u> of theoretically-complete or purist models. [["**90% of education does not teach thinking**" … "**Only an End-Goal of competence in the world defines and measures true learning of thinking**"…]. _Not_ to argue bias, but in order to 1. clarify the concept, 2. show all possibilities, 3. suggest excesses, 4. prevent rancor and resistance …

|+#|+|+|+|#+|+|+|+|#+|+|+|+|#+|+|+|+|#+|+|+|+|#+|+|+|+|#+|+|+|+|#+|+|+|+|#+|+|+|#+|#+|#+|+|#+|#+#|+#|#+|#+|+#|+||#+|

$\boxed{\textbf{[1.] How interested } \textit{are} \textbf{ educators in teaching?}}$

Disengagement. Frankly dislike teaching…	Minimal-acceptable job- engagement	Other scholarly interests: esp., "advanced research"…	Vivid interests, but in subjects or "ideologies"?…	More dedicated to teaching.	A Passion for truer Teaching. Empowering beginners…

A PERSONAL POSITION: I loved what I called **"true teaching"** or "clarifying 'obvious' [?] material for baffled basic beginners." This fulfilled me more than "doing advanced research with advanced students" and the like.

--It's the difference between saying, "<u>Oh, we already know that, it's basic, hence uninteresting…</u>" ….. VERSUS: …..

"<u>I know that well but an interesting challenge is how to truly convey its nuts-and-bolts, plus spirit, to a basic and baffled beginner? …</u>"

--I surely concede my bias and limitation. Good teaching comprises more than my narrow focus, more than just working to "launch" a learner past a difficult point. But my pursuit helped enrich the "utter basics" in this book…

EXAMPLE. My satisfaction in teaching basic skills to beginners. Writing a précis…

Students in my state-university English 101 could *not* read conceptually, for the *ideas* in a simple student paper. They wrote [1] below as a summary. <u>But</u> after brief instruction, they <u>could</u> "x-ray" for the concepts. They could move to [2] or near, *conceptualizing.* To some, this may be boring, secondary remediation. To me, it was satisfying to offer…

[1] Being a lifeguard is not as easy as it may appear. There are tasks that many do not realize exist, and dealing with the various people is not always a pleasant experience.

[2] The job of lifeguard presents unrecognized problems in two areas. The natural world (including a dirty beach to clean, hot weather, and bad equipment). And the world of people (including rowdy and destructive kid swimmers, over-anxious mothers, uncooperative co-workers, and the absence of attractive personnel).

Perhaps the *hour* of instruction in x-ray reading, *saved them hundreds* of hours in later classes, Real Life…

EXAMPLE. The importance [or *not*...] of "research" in teaching general and introductory courses...
SCENARIO: Assume it's "noon on campus," and two teachers are separately cross the "Quad" to go to lunch. One is a True Bona-Fide Researcher. The other is a Teacher-Scholar or whatever... What might be playing inside their minds?

RESEARCHER: attention to:	TEACHER: "In my 11:00 class, on use of <u>specific detailing in writing</u>,
(1) 18ᵗʰ-century law and the novel Clarissa"... (2) "Dynamics of Nigeria's foreign policy..." (3) "Synthesis of n-alkyl tetrahydroisoquinolines..." (4) "The pricing of thrift conversions..." (5) "Cervical auscultation in swallowing disorders..." (6) "Teacher mentoring in Sweden..." [= all products of UW-Whitewater faculty 2004...]	--(1) I may have spotted an *Amateur Misconception* I had overlooked. Some students seem to feel that "detailing is just decorative filler, padding—not needed proof." *Have to see if they really do believe that...* --(2) Also, an *Amateur Ignorance*: some students didn't seem to know the difference between a concept and an example (this ruined their outlining of texts!)... Egg on my face; *have to clarify...* --(3) And an *Amateur Puzzlement* has arisen: 80% of students asked "But how do we know when we've used enough specifics?" Does this mean that many are still situation-blind, audience-deaf, purpose-numbed? *Have to work on that one...* --*Hmm,* much grist for the mill here.....
BUT are you editorializing *against* "Research," to *favor* Kind Caring teachers?	Sorry. I do question **"Today's Truth"** that "well, a teacher's original *research* helps him/her to *teach* courses, even introductory ones." True if goal is What to Know, and in advanced courses, but not in re basic Thinking Things Through?...

|+#|+|+|+|#+|+|+|+|#+|+|+|+|#+|+|+|+|#+|+|+|+|+#|+|+|+|+#|+|+|+|+|#+|+|+|+|#+|+|+|+|+#|+|+|+|+#|+|#+|#+|#+|+#|+#|+#|+#|+|#+|

[2.] Goals of education: what are the major ones?

ISSUE. Goals may <u>vary</u> significantly. Do other goals *conflict* with liberal general education, critical thinking, our own "essential" thinking?

> **A ROSTER OF GOALS:** Socialization-acculturation?... Indoctrination into ideologies and commitments?... Narrower training?... Teach truths about the world?... Encourage each student's personal potential, individual happiness?... Educate for citizenship?... Inculcate a love of learning?... Produce docile citizens, good workers? [-- H. SIEGEL, K. EGAN, Univ. of Wis.-Madison, R. PAUL]

ISSUE. But don't <u>other</u> *valid* thinking-related goals exist beyond just "thinking" as in the think-things-through model? Conflicting or not?

> **POLICY.** ALVERNO COLLEGE in Wisconsin has an "ability-based" and "outcome-oriented" learning program. These are hence related to our goal of real-world competence after graduation. And they involve <u>thinking</u>: "<u>analytical capabilities</u>" and "<u>problem-solving skill</u>." But they *also* involve "making *value-judgments*" and "facility for *social interaction*" and "*global perspectives*" and "effective *citizenship*" and "*aesthetic responsiveness*." All good major goals of a liberal or general education. All surpassing (or anyhow supplementing) our goal here of "basic" higher-order applied thinking. [-- ALVERNO COLLEGE statements]

ISSUE. Proportionate Prevalences. How much <u>does</u> the traditional model of "Know, Believe, and Do" <u>still</u> predominate, *dominate over* the "Thinking Things Through" model?

> OUR STRONG STAND: "Up to 90% in most classrooms today, still." But we shall see...

Goal I of III [in the "Old-School" model] : "What to Know," or the covering of content...

EXAMPLE. Regarding "knowledge," two statements:

(1) TESTIMONIAL: Dr. Graham was was "possessed of those rare qualities of greatness as a teacher: impressive knowledge of his subject, a closeness to students, a desire to **impart knowledge,** and the style and skill requisite to do so in the classroom...."

(3) LETTER TO EDITOR: "What all these movements in education neglect—whether they're the social-progress movement, the related multicultural-diversity movement, the Back to Basics movement, the vocational-emphasis movement, the media and electronic education movement—is the key basic emphasis on **mastering knowledge** which is the perennial heart of the educational enterprise."

These statements carry implications; can people identify their assumptions? **"Imparting and mastering knowledge"** is education. (Cf. the sign in a park in Singapore during colonial occupation 100 years ago: "NO DOGS OR CHINESE ALLOWED." I'D SAY: not intentional bigotry, simply a taken-for-granted, though questionable, paradigm...)

Goal II of III [in the "Old-School" model] : "What to Believe": (value-clarification, or indoctrination?):

EXAMPLE. Three examples regarding homosexuality, within *diversity-education.* Rich grist-for-the-mill:

(1) A sixth grade class was asked "what might be good about having a gay or lesbian friend?" RESPONSE: Guffaws from the boys, stereotyped comments from the girls. [**Alternate approach:** might be to pause, consider: ask "How do you really feel about the sexual orientation issue and why and so what? Does all this matter? Or the like...]

(2) A high school Lesbian teacher said students should be sure to "call" other students when they make a "slur" or "epithet" regarding sexual orientation. RESPONSES: The students objected. (A) Didn't believe it was wrong to slur. (B) Or that gays/lesbians "just had to deal with it." (C) Or feared guilt by association.)

(3) The "Riddle Scale of Homophobia" proposes we should move to more-"desirable" attitudes:

1. Repulsion. Crime against nature! Gays/lesbians are sick crazy sinful, must be changed.
2. Pity. Heterosexuality is more mature, to be preferred; G/L should be pitied.
3. Tolerance. It's just a phase, those who stay in it should be treated like children in a sense.
4. Acceptance. Still implies there is "something to accept." Fine if it's not flaunted, etc.
5. Support. Approve civil rights for G/L, even if uncomfortable personally with it.
6. Admiration. Realize G/L folk must be strong; willing to re-examine one's attitudes toward them.
7. Appreciation. Values human diversity, with G/L folk a part of that. Become anti-homophobic.
8. Nurturance. G/L folk as *indispensable* in society. View them with "*genuine affection and delight*"; be an ally.

WHOA! So what is wrong with *values* of tolerance plus acceptance and celebration of diversity?	**NO.** It falls short of thinking diversity through—confronting it as an issue. How do I the citizen in the world deal competently with it? Find my own stand, both personal and principled? **"Hit The Ground Running"** confronting my own biases, others' misconceptions also? Come to *the most solid stand possible for me now,* whether ideally-"correct" or not?

[Perhaps come to say, as one of my students did: "The subject still disgusts me plus contradicts my religion, but I now see gays are oppressed multiply and unnecessarily. I would not add to this now..." I see this as valid, moral, true learning. The student himself went as far as he truly was to go at that time, "tattooed" his own response...]

> **SEE** the Tool-KIT #7, on "Diversity Education," in Appendix #4: Tool-KITS. It offers the tools of **Selective Perception, Stereotype vs. Sociotype, Cultural vs. Moral Relativism,** and a dozen more...

[{ Plus this Scale is *grossly unrealistic.* I'm supposed to regard some flaming faggot or screaming queen with "*genuine affection and delight*"? Or feel that some diesel-dyke or butt-pirate is "*indispensable in society*"? Get Real...}]

HEY, I *don't* like that last little statement there. It's *gratuitously* offensive, objectionable because *no* social or educational benefit!	Right as for "social," but **no** educational benefit? Such problematic statements might be **"learnable moments"!** *Why* did a person say it? *How to respond* to it? What if a graduate heard it Afterwards in a Real-Life arena? What to do then?...... (*) Can students **"hit the ground running"** and competently to confront such *cranky, cantankerous"* statements?

EXAMPLE. Regarding **new movements** toward *liberatory education* or *critical pedagogy....*

As seen in the work of HENRY GIROUX, BELL HOOKS, and others, this approach rejects education as "the amassing of information," toward education as "emancipation." Its substance is "diversity, multiculturalism, gender, race and class." The <u>goal</u> is to "understand the effects of power, the social construction of knowledge and identity, the meaning of education, and the need for social and cultural change." A need is to "question and challenge authority," and surely an emergent goal is to "think about making the world a better place."

And from these goals follow the teaching <u>methods</u>. The teacher shares experience with students, recognizing and valuing everyone's presence, and aims toward learning which is no longer competitive, but instead supportively-cooperative. It even welcomes questions for which there is no one easy answer, or even which the teacher cannot answer authoritatively.....

BUT why couldn't one learn to *think* through complex social issues! Especially by truly gaining power, knowledge, identity. And moving away from memorization and authority, also.	*I feel Strongly that::* this seems to remain rank frank Indoctrination into an Ideology which probably demeans learners. It tells them what the issues are, how to think about them, what to do. As against looking at a dozen arenas, this one included, and learning how to think complexities through. To evaluate, prioritize, see biases in the stand itself, etc. Maybe to "save society" in the end but to come to that goal oneself…
	SEE later the examples of <u>Four Systems</u> by CARL COHEN, a book explaining democracy, socialism, communism, fascism. It simply describes and argues for each system in turn. No One Right Answer in an appendix. So, students delve in and discover discuss and decide *on their own*…

<u>Goal III of III</u> [in the "Old-School" model] : Regarding "what to Do": do skills stay formulaic, rote, not strategic?

"Capacity for problem solving is limited by our use of inappropriately simple practice exercises."
[-- LION GARDINER, FROM R. PAUL --]

"Many [students] succeeded admirably in high school through the exclusive use of rote memory and procedural mimicry (known in mathematics as the "extreme algorithmic approach"). So a student may have received an A in trigonometry by knowing how to manipulate cosines and tangents yet without really understanding what they represent. Such underlying deficiencies return to haunt… A young adult may be selling a product without fully understanding it, or preparing a legal brief without perceiving its ramifications." [-- MEL LEVINE, in CHE]

In <u>statistics</u>, most students can easily do problems that are all the same type. All texts put t-test problems in one chapter, chi-square in another, and so on. The difficulty arises when students have to decide for themselves what type of analysis to use, since problems in real life do not come neatly labeled with chapter references. This problem applies in all academic fields beyond statistics—assuming an interest in teaching transfer of skills, of course.
[-- RICHARD PAUL]

And another step: what of the keystone concepts in statistics of use in the real world? As we'll discuss in the **Gallery**, sampling errors, regression to the mean, etc.? P. 117

|+#|+|+|+|#+|+|+|#+|+|+|+|#+|+|+|+|#+|+|+|+|#+|+|+|+|#+|+|+|+|#+|+|+|+|#+|+|+|+|#+|+|#+|#+|#+|+|#+|#+|+|#+|+||#+|

[3.] How should "teaching thinking" be (A) defined and described, then (B) measured?

"REASSURANCE"… Our own formula here (Goal of "Think Things Through" etc.) might seem too simple, even dictatorial. But I only offer it as an **"ideal-type"**: a theoretically 100%-pure concept. Not to be valued-as-good or as a goal—*or even always "true."* But simply to describe better: to clarify what *the concept itself* is. Because, to comprehend this two-paradigm issue, requires a *focused encoding*. (*ANALOGIES*: a device such as a maypole; or Esperanto; or surveyor's benchmark; or yardstick…) A *clarifying base-line for common discussion*. Let us all initially converge on the common concept, then each of us can diverge on our decisions about it … <u>To review, then:</u>

45

[1.] **Traditional Education:** goal, what to **Know, Believe, Do…** Content-mastery, value-clarification, formulaic skills…	[2.] **Thinking Model** (our version): (1) how to **Think Things Through.** (Content is subservient to thinking skills (at least in the Ideal-Type version), a radical 180-degree reversal from traditional education.) (2) Specifically, how to apply concepts to situations in actual life. **CTA.** Conceptualize UPward, Transfer OVER-ACROSS, Apply DOWN UPON…. (3) More specifically, a "6-AAAAAA" model. The "Autonomous Application of Abstractions, Ably, to Arduous material, and Afterward." [In POEP or **Plain Old English Please:** "You can think tough but important things out okay on your own in the world after school."] (4) Finally, an **End-Goal** of ultimate expectable readiness or **"Hit The Ground Running"** on competently confronting challenging complexities in real life. (This at least focuses attention remarkably on "what of value is really getting learned after all or not"…)

COMMENT. The critical-thinking expert RICHARD PAUL on "assessing knowledge":
Memorizing definitions and working drill-exercises is insufficient. Instead, "…proof of knowledge or understanding is found in the students' ability to explain in their own words, with examples, the meaning and significance of the knowledge, why it is so, and to spontaneously recall and use it when relevant."
The underlined portion points to the **end-goal** suggested.

ISSUE: **What is the RELATIONSHIP and RELATIVE POSITION of "CONTENT" AND "SKILLS"? [Perhaps a radical, 180-degree, reversal: "Content" dethroned, skills reign?]…**

MINI-GALLERY. Four classic quotations to illustrate:

[1.] **TOUCHSTONE.** A college president sets radical priorities in core- or general-education:
The first goal should be to teach thinking skills. The second is an awareness that they are thinking skills, not content-bound, can be somewhat transferred from one area to another. Third one should teach them via content which is "interesting, useful, elevating, and inspiring." But *let not the content obscure the first two primary goals*, as it might if it's fascinating, or traditionally accepted as the goal.　　[-- RICHARD CREWS, PACIFIC COLLEGE, IN CHE]

Right, that's radical right in our midst…	An explicit reversal of the usual—and a "brave" statement. Many people might not fully comprehend at first (cf. **"Knowing, vs. really Knowing"**). Agreement is optional anyhow.

[2.] Nor is this thinking-first stance limited to General Education. A HISTORY PROFESSOR claimed:
"I am less interested in teaching students factual information than teaching them a set of thinking skills, a set of reasoning skills—sort of critical inquiry…you constantly have to be looking at alternatives, what's not being told, different perspectives." [--　SOURCE]

Well, that's clear. Would you add anything?	Only to mention *explicitly* that the prof. here uses two identifiable generic thinking skills, **"employing multiple-plural perspective"** and **"identifying background, subliminal information"**… And they could be Transferred and Applied ["Exported"] *outside* of history to other subjects…

[3.] Also speaking about general education, at Stanford Univ., TWO FACULTY SAY:
"The core of humanistic education is not whether you've read the Iliad or Dante. The core is whether you have the skills to read The Iliad or Dante. You can learn the skills to read Shakespeare by reading Sophocles…What we're trying to do is not to show every variety of fish, but to teach people how to go fishing." [-- J. BENDER, AND R. POLHEMUS]

[4.] The "general" approach teaches thinking separately from content. Of course "content" *is* present (political issues, problems at school, or previously-learned subject-matter). But the *purpose* is teaching thinking, using nonschool-subject contexts. Theoretically, *no* content is required. Logic can be taught mathematically as variables. If A then B and so on. However, of course, universally education uses specific examples to illustrate the abstract principles.   [-- ROBERT ENNIS; paraphrased]

ISSUE. (AND POSSIBLE PREVALENT MISCONCEPTION. That "thinking skills take *longer* to learn than content, plus must be taught *after* content..." A RECONSIDERATION:

TOUCHSTONE. WILLIAM NEWELL helpfully shows that perspectives are more available than we may have realized. A vital statement of an overlooked opportunity.

"While interdisciplinary courses indeed make use of concepts, theories, methods, and factual knowledge from various disciplines, the interdisciplinary understanding they develop is grounded primarily in the perspectives from which these concepts, theories, methods, and facts emerge. **It takes many years to learn a discipline;** *it takes only a few readings to begin to develop a feel for how that discipline characteristically looks at the world*, its angle of vision, its perspective."

...For me, less scandalously-revolutionary, than a useful new path-breaking perspective too often *quite* unrealized. I like it because it opens the way to explicit elucidating of thinking skills short of oversimplification...

A PERSONAL POSITION. I am sardonically amused by the "Objection!" #1 which religiously arises at this point like a mantra or chant: "but you can't thinking about nothing, you have to think about something, therefore you need content first, and then you can think about it..."
[I sense here: plural motivations to this objection. Perhaps **Honest Misperception** (math has no content) plus **Internalized Professional Norm** (duty to cover content) plus garden-variety **Defensiveness, Evasion, Resistance** (here today now, acquire Knowledge as usual; tomorrow *perhaps*, start thinking about it, but preferably elsewhere, anyhow NIMC, "not in my course" ...]

|+#|+|+|+|#+|+|+|+|#+|+|+|+|#+|+|+|+|#+|+|+|+|+#|+|+|+|+#|+|+|+|#+|+|+|+|#+|+|+|+|#+|+|#+|#+|#+|+|#+|#+#|+#|#+|#+|#|+||#+|

[4.] *Is* TTh really "shortchanged" today? And <u>if</u> so, perhaps unavoidably? [Is it "Utopian" to teach thinking?]

nonexistent	condemned	embryonic	"sort-of" done	pervasive	"the" practice

FORMULA. Recalling part of our claim-to-be-tested, from our Rationale:

(1) "About <u>90%</u> of classrooms are teaching nothing much resembling true thinking—as *we* see it."

(2) *but also* "<u>100%</u>" teaching thinking is Utopian-impracticable and even too extreme, ...

(3) *further,* "<u>X%</u>" of classes already DO teach thinking here and there (and we bring you their fruits)...

(4) *and* "<u>N%</u>" of classes COULD teach more thinkingly a little every day (and we offer ideas)...]

ISSUE 4.A. But what does "<u>research</u>" and "<u>expert</u>" testimony say?

TOUCHSTONE. W. DERZKO starkly notes the Thinking Took-Chest seems usually *empty* …

DERZKO says that **we ignore teaching thinking** in most schools and corporations, for various reasons—some other teacher will do it, budget cuts prevent doing it, we simply overlook doing it, or we think we can think well enough already. **But are we really good-enough thinkers not to need *explicit* training in thinking skills?** "Consider the paradox. We expect students and staff to be math-literate. So what do we do? Back in grade 1 and 2 we teach everyone *the operancy skills behind* math...the p lus, subtract, multiple and divide. Once we master these basic math-related operations we go on to *higher order applications*....**Yet when we switch domains** from numbers over to fact, ideas, concepts, values, assumptions, and notions (the content for all other subject areas in school and later at work), **we totally ignore the thinking operations needed to explore or create new ideas**."

       [--WALTER DERZKO, from the Ideas-Bank]

[*] *This may be THE key quotation in this entire material.* We may think we "know" this, but awareness keeps on dawning. True, DERZKO *omits specific examples* of "thinking operations," as do many other resources, but in this resource we seek to offer instances (for full sets, see Mind-Play).

GALLERY: FIVE EXAMPLES: suggesting that thinking is not—taught? Learned and practiced?

Also suggesting that learning to "Do," often means *simpler* thinking; tactics, rote rules…

EXAMPLE #1. Math instruction may be atomized, let alone not applied?

Researcher ALAN SCHOENFELD has explored high school and college mathematics teaching. He finds that many college students study calculus, and know some powerful specific mathematics. (Find maxima of complicated functions, determine exponential decay, compute the volumes of surfaces of revolution, etc.) But they can do these only because their exam questions are carbon copies of problems they have seen before; "the students are not being asked to think, but merely to apply well-rehearsed schemata for specific kinds of tasks." (Only 19 of 120 attempts at application-to-the-new, succeeded.) SCHOENFELD concludes incisively:

"In sum, all too often we focus on a narrow collection of well-defined tasks and train students to execute those tasks in a routine, if not algorithmic fashion. Then we test the students on tasks that are very close to the ones they have been taught." If they succeed we feel they know math. But they may only know mechanical application, lacking true understanding and thinking skills. [-- ALAN SCHOENFELD, in R. Paul]

This nicely spotlights **Application** (#2) let alone handling tasks **Autonomously** (#4) and echoing whether the tasks are real-life important (#7 **Acute Arrowed**.) But one might ask how **Abstract** the skills themselves are (1) to begin with, are they more formulaic (algorhythms, rules, tactics) – or higher-level (heuristics tools strategies)… and also whether they are (2) taught and learned as such.

EXAMPLE #2. PIAGET never got from being learned (?), to being used, even when assigned:

REPORT BY A TEACHER: All students in a first course in elementary teacher education have to pass and do well in a developmental or child psychology course as a prerequisite to being admitted to the program. Early in the semester, I assign a two-minute in-class freewrite on the following question. Imagine that [the Swiss educational theorist Jean] PIAGET walks into a second grade classroom. He sees the children sitting quietly in rows, with pencils and worksheets, doing math problems. What would he say? Apparently the students fail to respond fully. "If even half or a third of the students can apply to this question their memorized knowledge about PIAGET'S stages of development, I feel elated, though troubled, because *even those who don't have a clue about PIAGET'S view of that situation claim to have gotten A's in their psychology courses.* So what is—or is not—going on in those courses—and in *our* courses? What should we teach, and how, so that people about to be teachers can have a real working understanding of developmentally appropriate practice, and can, in each unique situation they face, try to think their way through the connections between theory and application?" [-- AARONSEN… CT]

| WHOA. Don't be too hard on the students—or on the | BUT the big issue seems stated here. A regrettable shortfalling? A key goal, **"autonomous application of abstractions,"** has *not* happened here. (Not even non-autonomously!) Nor in many other courses—cf. even or also my own freshman English class where "write that last theme |

system. True and instant use of knowledge takes time to...	on your own" defeated them... Also **"Knowing, vs. Knowing."** The students couldn't access the material when needed. They did not meet the **End-Goal** of **"Hitting The Ground Running"** with ultimate readiness.

EXAMPLE #3. "The long and the short of the story is this: Schools today do not focus on how to introduce children to the logic of the subjects they study. The do not focus on what it is to reason historically, what it is to reason mathematically or scientifically, what it is to reason sociologically, anthropologically, or geographically, what it is to reason philosophically or morally. Hence, disciplined reasoning—which is at the heart of the logic of every academic subject and profession—is largely absent from the classroom of today." [-- RICHARD PAUL]

...PAUL, a critical thinking expert, echoes DERZKO's touchstone comment earlier...

EXAMPLE #4. The Sonoma Study Strongly Suggests **Shortfallings—and Teacher Unawareness**

The Center for Critical Thinking, at the university at Sonoma, CA, directed by RICHARD PAUL, is as major an organization as any in the "teaching thinking" movement today. Recently they released results from a "ground-breaking" study of "professors at 48 public and 38 private colleges and universities."] *Initially*, the report's conclusions—or claims—*do* seem impressive.

Definition, & Practice...Overwhelmingly (80-90%) of the teachers said they valued critical thinking as a goal in their own instruction. *However, "only* 19% could give a clear explanation of what critical thinking is; and *only 9%* of the respondents were clearly teaching for critical thinking on a typical day in class."

As for Criteria and Standards..."*only a very small minority* (8%) could enumerate any intellectual criteria or standards they required of students or could give an intelligible explanation of what those criteria and standards were."

Integration..."77% of the respondents had *little, limited, or no conception* of how to reconcile content coverage with the fostering of critical thinking.

NO: "yeah sure," but PAUL'S probably *biased*. He runs a Center, holds conferences, gives in-service presentations nationwide. He needs a market!	*Ignoring your "reasoning" there* [it might be somewhat-Relevant but not Right-On Related right here now], I can only say that PAUL'S results jibe with my own back-yard shirt-sleeves "research" in interviewing teachers on my home campus..... ...Especially the ultimate Blow-Off Statement which I admit I personally "love to hate": the cheerful, oh-so-assured **"Well, of course we're already teaching thinking in our classes here!!"** ["Oh, *are* you now, and in what ways..."]

EXAMPLE #5. PERSONAL ANECDOTE... The General Education goals emphasized Knowing, but *any* true Thinking? My own response—and their response to that...   At the Univ. of Wis.-Whitewater in 1992, the Core Courses Committee proposed a revision of goals:

Their roster of nine goals included *knowing about* and *appreciating* everything from word historical context to science processes and aesthetic enrichments and so forth and so on. Specifically, *"understand"* the factors in health.
"Appreciate the importance of" fine arts, also world cultures.
"Acquire a base of knowledge" and *"understand how"* knowledge is handled. Somewhat passive! True, the roster did include the mathematical and quantitative *"skills"* plus the *"ability"* to "communicate effectively" and "to make sound ethical and value judgments."

Seeing what to me was an egg-on-face Blunder (a sin of Omission), I wrote a Strong (but Fairminded) letter questioning the *utter omission of higher-order thinking skills*, whether pure or applied......   I received no direct response......
But later I was "amused" to see that the *revised* Goals did include (as #1 at the start!) the statement, **"Think critically and analytically, integrate and synthesize knowledge, and draw conclusions from complex information."**

THREE PERSONAL EXAMPLES—OF MY OWN BLUNDERS. (#1) "That Last Theme" they could *not* do on their own. (#2) "Poetry Probes": they had learned *nothing* really. (#3) and MICHELLE'S bungle even *later*…

[1.] in English 101, I *thought* I had taught **WRITING**, via five themes. For the writing exam, via the sixth and last paper, I said: now, Write. Autonomously apply those abstractions. "*You show you can write. Plan and write a paper all on your own now. Select appropriate (challenging) topic, audience, purpose, genre and arena. Then make the style-decisions necessary. And annotate or report Articulately on what choices you made, why, and was it bad or good.*"

Result? Instant and ***massive upset, hostility, panic*** in the classroom. They had learned how to follow orders, not to **conceptualize** skills, and **transfer** them via their own **Autonomy.** I had not taught them thinking thus, explicitly step by step. *Until then, I thought or assumed that I had…*

[2.] Same for the **POETRY** test in English 102. "Take these 12 poems we have not discussed in class, and show what you've learned about poetry-reading by responding to them…" Again, failure, showing that they had really learned nothing. Admittedly here, motivation plays a part. These required-course students were awaiting their "cards being stamped" instead of going for growing corn by the "double-handful" themselves…

…perhaps many other teachers also *thought* skills were being learned, including ability to transfer. But the teachers never tested for them like this, the acid test of Autonomous Application of Abstractions, the acid test? So, never realized?…

EXAMPLE (#3). This is worse, because later, I was assuming I was teaching thinking. Yet "MICHELLE'S" misstep revealed to me my own stumbling blunder (my foul-out on the Athletic Field) ….

I had added more basic thinking techniques in English 101. Criteria, standards, ways of knowing, evidence, etc. I gave an assignment. "Take an assignment from another course you're taking and reconstruct it so it asks for more and better thinking. Then (2) Design for another course an ideal thinking assignment. In both cases, explain."

Here is the answer of MICHELLE, an average-to-above student in English 101:

(1) THE ACTUAL QUESTION RECONSTRUCTED: Political Science 150.

Original question: "Identify and describe the techniques interest groups use. Why do some groups favor certain techniques over others? Give examples."
Rewritten Question: "Explain which technique used by interest groups you think is best and why. Give specific examples."

Michelle's Analysis: The original question was simply fact-dumping. All I had to do was remember from the textbook and basically rewrite what was in front of me, in my own words. There was no real thought process present.....To make it a thought-provoking question, I had to personalize it and possibly ask for an opinion. Each person may feel different about the different techniques used by interest groups."

MY RESPONSE TO THIS: Omitted was the potential for the generic thinking skill: "why people differ in their preferences," etc. , thus discussing causes, motivations. Omitted was "fact-dumping" but it was replaced by thought-dumping. The student could end up only equating good thinking with merely—"personal opinion" and "different feelings" on the issue…

(2) THE "IDEAL" THINKING QUESTION DESIGNED. Spanish 142.

Michelle's Design: "Why in your opinion, is foreign language learning so necessary in these modern times?"

Michelle's Analysis of her Design: "This question definitely uses higher-level thinking skills. It is an opinionated [*sic*] question that <u>requires you to seriously think</u> about why something is so necessary.....WITH AS MANY FOREIGN PEOPLE AS WE HAVE IN AMERICA TODAY, IT IS VERY IMPORTANT TO LEARN A FOREIGN LANGUAGE. This is <u>my opinion</u>, and with more examples to back it up, it could become a thorough, well-thought-out essay-question answer."

MY RESPONSE: First, this is <u>not</u> the powerful thinking skill of **Objective Evaluation** or assessing both or all sides of a complex issue. (Nor is the issue all that challenging to begin with...) It is **indoctrination**. [As didactic as "Emily in the short story is driven mad by social pressures; show how"... Or "what would be good about having a gay or lesbian friend?"...] Above all, "backing up your opinion with facts" is scarcely **good thinking**; it is garden-variety "**just-thinking**" or uncontrolled unconscious opinionating, and likely is **rationalizing** a prior held position...

.....this incisive "x-ray" showed me the dismal situation within. Nothing gained... Whereas I had assumed something. Maybe conventional tests are about as revealing of true learning (autonomous application etc.) as would be a "phrenological" examination, reading the bumps on the skull...

ISSUE 4.C. Are students not taught (or do not know) the <u>super-basic</u> thinking skill of INDUCTION? CONCEPTUALIZING UPWARD from data and concrete specifics, to conceptual abstractions, generalizations, ideas about the material?

LEVELS. Below is a "I" BRIEF View for right here, of the "II" FULL View, found in **Appendix #3.1.**

The **very concept of a concept**—and is it taught?
1. Do students even know what a concept *is*?
2. ...But no *really*! "Principles" of Snowboarding—*this* is *conceptual*?...
3. Egg On My Own Face: I *assumed* students *knew* about the conceptual...
4.A. Reading 101: simpler texts. X-ray of "Lifeguard Job" student paper to extract its *sort-of*-explicit—ideas...
4.B. Reading 102: *implicit* meanings. Proverbs, also Poetry ...
5. Reading 103: real-world Situations. Finding patterns and ideas in experience.
6. We shortfall from conceptualizing in real life: Personal, Vocational, Civic arenas...
7. We can all improve. Even teachers (R. Paul, M. Taylor, Merrill & Tennyson...)

ISSUE 4.D. How "realistic vs. Utopian" after all, <u>is</u> teaching thinking?

A PERSONAL STAND: "<u>Dubious, yet Do-Able...</u>" "Realistically, the teaching/learning of thinking *100% or pure-extreme-total*, in education generally, in a specific course, does seem *dubious*. Impossible, improbable, inadvisable, impracticable. This due to roadblocks plus other valid educational goals. <u>However</u>, it is also *doable*: *some* teaching of thinking <u>is</u> also much more possible even "every day in every class" than is realized ... "

ELSEWHERE: No need to detail here, the many <u>difficulties, barriers</u> to teaching thinking. Some were mentioned in the "objections!" in the Intro. Annex. A Brief View lies just ahead in the next Section #5, And for the full-dress treatment, see GALLERY, #5, Responses To... **P. 125--**

EXAMPLE. Elementary art classes learned color, but no information—and no thinking...

A teacher reports that students worked weeks creating large Olmec heads (from early Central American history) but upon examination, *remembered only the experience, and not any information* about Olmec society and history. So to the visual art the teachers decided to add writing stories which "had to incorporate information about time, location, and geography instead of just allowing free reign of creativity where opinion and fact can easily become one." [-- SOURCE]

| …I see your point. Even with information added, **not any time at all now for any explicit "thinking" skills also.** At least at that lower level. We admit the problem of implementing "thinking" in a real-world already-crowded syllabus… | …That is my point here. Of course, *something* can be done. **EXAMPLE:** the distinction between **Fact, Opinion, and Reasoned Judgment** (a basic tool, see Prior Basics Appendix) might begin even down in the sixth grade?
 [**F:** "Alaska is the coldest state… **O:** Alaska is the best place for a vacation…**RJ:** Alaska is a good place to start a certain business…"] |

ISSUE 4E. Still, "Might X% of education *already be* teaching thinking, whether strongly, or gently?" The answer does seem "Yes"…

PRE-VIEW: We'll present many of these small and large successes in the **Galleries, #**4 of Main Body.
- - Prof. PAUL HEYNE'S economics: powerful keystone principles amid all the graphs…
- - The PARK SCHOOL: *"every day in every class,"* six key questions to apply to the content…
- - The senior capstone interdisciplinary seminar: "design an urban park" (or similar task- goal) focuses, collects, makes explicit, thinking skills learned less- explicitly in earlier courses…

ISSUE 4.F. "Can Y% of courses *begin* to teach thinking, even if "under the radar screen" of the Required Syllabus and other constraints?" Also "Yes" if implanted deftly…

EXAMPLE. In many (not all) courses, one could select to gently emphasize the thinking skill of **"Lens-work"** or "methodologically applying plural perspectives, multiple frames-of-reference, to an issue."
--One could first make Explicit, the six **variable-issues** concerning **lenses.** [Lenses are: 1. unavoidable; 2. often subliminal/unrecognized; 3. both good and bad (insightful and biased); 4. each lens is probably partial / incomplete; 5. lenses may contradict each other; 6. it's hard to find & use the best lenses)….   --One could then try for light-touch but continuous and progressive training over a semester, and students emerging more ready to Hit The Ground Running on *other* issues later on, Exporting the skill to issues even far removed from the course's subject-matter…*And even if only for 5-7 minutes during each class hour all semester!*   --"Clean Water Supply" and: biology, geography, economics, politics, technology…   --"Human Nature and a Current Problem-Issue": psychoanalysis, socialism, evolutionary biology, existentialism…   --"Same-Sex Marriage:" Functions of an institution, Ways of Knowing, Criteria for deciding, World-Views…
…Infiltrating of the Vital Nutrients of Conceptualizing, to leaven the Concrete of "Content"? Performing "guerilla warfare" under the noses of the existing model? The Trojan Horse deftly entering? Much failure—some success—and anyhow for many teachers (not all), the *Right Thing Being Attempted* in one's teaching career…

|+#|+|+|+|#+|+|+|+|#+|+|+|+|#+|+|+|+|+#|+|+|+|+#|+|+|+|+#|+|+|+|+#|+|+|+|#+|+|+|+|#+|+|#+|#+|#+|+|#+|#+#|+#|#+|#+|+#|+||#+|

[5.] How do Educators Respond to the TTh Issue?:

RESPONSES, "I": Roster of common responses to the issue of "teaching thinking." A "I" *BRIEF* View:
"Students pick up thinking as they go along" … "We're already teaching thinking in our classes" … "Got to cover content first, to give them something to think about!" … "I was not trained to teach thinking, nor was I hired to do so, nor am I rewarded for doing so" … "I have my more-important agendas to share with the students" … "I feel safer delivering information as an authority" … "Teaching thinking is just too much effort" …
These can provoke agreement… alarm… ridicule, mockery… useful discussion… and *more*… Analysis of them can be—*interesting*… For "II" *FULL,* SEE in "Galleries"—Responses of Educators. **P. 125**--

ISSUE. To what extent is "paradigm-shift" or "major change" issues, a cause of problems here? *ALSO RELATED*: See ➔ Tool-KIT on "Major CHANGE" in Appendix, Tool KITS.

LAB-EXERCISE. Teaching thinking does concern major change. How to perceive this? Perhaps give learners the following examples, let them perceive the subliminal assumptions?
1. Sign in a park… 2. Four suspicious comments: (A) on education, (B) on minorities:

One response to the Truly New, can be not just neglect, or outrage and condemnation, but a sort of null or non-response. (As in the feminist charge or plaint, so often well-merited: "You just don't get it, do you?") As if the New is not just not-comprehended, but non-comprehensible. Outside the whole paradigm; off the radar screen. Do we *see* teaching thinking?

[1.] WARM-UP EXAMPLE. A century or more ago, in colonized Singapore, the occupying British placed in a public park, this sign: "NO DOGS OR CHINESE ALLOWED."

Now, was this *conscious intentional recognized* prejudice, stereotyping, bigotry, oppression? *I really wonder…* Not if the then-prevalent <u>world-view</u> (paradigm) was that "the different races are civilized differentially, and if some were (faultlessly) naturally 'lesser breeds,' we must control them but also improve them with beneficent help." *But could the Westerners of that time, even question this belief as a belief not as a fact? Would they react to the Equality model, "a heresy!" or even "…you mean* **what***?...*"

[2.] TEST OR GAME. "SPOT THE IMPLICIT PRESUPPOSITIONS" …
Here are statements concerning education, and also minorities. For five points from our friendly Staff, <u>seek to identify the paradigm or **Implicit Presupposition** or World-View</u> in the statements, and name it.

[2.A.] Four comments on EDUCATION:	**[2.B.]** Four comments on VARIOUS GROUPS:
(1) DR. GRAHAM: He was "possessed of those rare qualities of greatness as a teacher: impressive knowledge of his subject, a closeness to students, a desire to impart knowledge, and the style and skill requisite to do so in the classroom...."	(1) <u>**A passage from Mark Twain's novel**</u> <u>Huckleberry</u> <u>Finn</u>. In it, Huck's aunt is wondering why the boy has been delayed on his riverboat journey to visit them: "We been expecting you a couple of days and more. What's kep' you?—boat get aground?" "It warn't the grounding—that didn't keep us back but a little. We blowed out a cylinder-head." "Good gracious? anybody hurt?" "No'm. Killed a nigger." "Well, it's lucky; because sometimes people do get hurt. Two years ago last Christmas, your uncle Silas was coming up from Newrleans on the old *Lally Rook*, and she blowed out a cylinder-head and crippled a man..."
(2) LETTER TO EDITOR. The perennial cycles of educational "fixes," including trends, fads, and fashions, such as the new math, whole language, competency-based and outcome-based education, mastery-learning. All seem to be "pedagogical quackery," or "a focus on teaching techniques rather than a genuine **transmission of ideas and information.**"	(2) A <u>popular anecdote, or "puzzle,"</u> circulating in the 1970's and later: A young boy is hurt in an accident. His father rushes him to the hospital. In the E.R., the attending surgeon arrives, but takes one look and says, "I cannot operate on this boy; he is my son."
(3) LETTER TO EDITOR: "What all these movements in education neglect—whether they're the social-progress movement, the related multicultural-diversity movement, the Back to Basics movement, the vocational-emphasis movement, the media and electronic education movement—is the key basic emphasis on **mastering knowledge** which is the perennial heart of the educational enterprise."	(3) The <u>sociologist Edward Sagarin</u> tells how language can subtly, insidiously inflict our perception. "We say of a person who drinks too much that he 'is' an alcoholic, and we say of people who think bizarre thoughts that they 'are' schizophrenic. This person is a drug addict and that person is a homosexual. Others are sadomasochists, pedophiliacs, juvenile delinquents....<u>we speak of people being</u> [certain things] <u>when all we know is that they do</u> certain things....<u>That kind of identity is a myth</u>. Admittedly, if a person believes the myth [that he is an addict, alcoholic, schizophrenic, homosexual], the chances rise that he....can result in relinquishing the search for change and becoming imprisoned in the role."

| (4) CAMPUS EVENT. In 1997, students petitioned to be able to _test out of the Core Courses_ if they were able to. (U.S. Experience in a World Context; Global Perspectives; Individual & Society; World of the Arts; Science & Technology in Society; World of Ideas).
--Many students felt the core courses are "a repeat of high school college-prep courses," hence "unnecessary to many students," who have **received similar, if not identical, information** in high school courses."
--Hence these Core courses were "not challenging or stimulating" enough to be required of all. (Plus could delay graduation unnecessarily.)
--"If you already **know the material,** you should be able to go to the next level," a student senator stated. | (4) A _Newsweek_ article about **high school girls** [=young women] **suing for sexual harrassment** from the male students in classes. The concluding paragraph, indeed sentence, from the article is as follows:
[A Ms. Brawdy sued for emotional distress and collected $20,000. So what was seen as "a routine nuisance" may become "a serious disciplinary matter."] ➔ "And, while there may not be a man today who can honestly say he never spent most of a math period staring at the prettiest girl in his class instead of a blackboard...someday there might be." |

| AS FOR THE ABOVE on Education…..

--DR. GRAHAM "imparted knowledge," but did he teach thinking?

--The TWO LETTERS—they mistake "transmission of ideas and information" or even "mastering knowledge" as true Education!

--The STUDENT LETTER remains deluded that "knowing the material" (via "receiving information") vs. being able to use it is the goal!

…is "What to Know," the water in which education often swims?... | THE ABOVE on Diversity… all show how major change is sometimes not just judged un-thinkable, a Heresy, but is utterly overlooked, non-comprehensible...
--First, Twain satirizes treating Blacks as "non-persons" and quite _unknowingly_ too....
--Second, the anecdote (which the early feminists popularized) overlooks that women _can_ be surgeons (and more)..._and shows that we overlook(ed)…_
--Third, the sociologist links homosexuals with criminals and the mentally-ill—utterly overlooked or taken-for-granted Yesterday, open-question arguable Today... _Today we probably spotted this assumption._
--And fourth, the Newsweek article stereotypes young males, as testosteroned (1) Animals instead of perhaps (2) Brains, able to be intellectual after all!... _But we saw this assumption also, right?_...

[…. CAUTION: PITFALL… : In the last example above, perhaps a "(3)"… Sm f th bys mght hv bn lkng x th thr bys n th clssrm… Wx sxxd: Sxmx xf thx bxys mxght hxvx bxxn lxxkxng xt thx _xthxr bxys_ xn thx clxssrxxm…..._bingo?_ How many people would miss the heterocentric (not "homophobic") assumption that all the boys were non-gay, er, ah, straight?..... Don't all deny at once…] |

| HMMM…and what is the exact _point_ of your fascinating little detour into "Change Country" here? (Not to mention your dramatically overstating the case that "we don't get it"…) | To explore whether teaching thinking is all that truly new that it is **unknowingly non-comprehended…** Some might think they understand, but don't know that they don't fully know…

Oh, and to practice upon a specific issue, the general thinking skill of "responding to major change." SEE Tool-Kit on; Not to mention **identifying Backgrounds:** See P. 334 In App. #5. |

**and a couple of issues with which to close the "Keystones"…**

|+#|+|+|+|#+|+|+|+|#+|+|+|+|#+|+|+|+|#+|+|+|+|#+|+|+|+|#+|+|+|+|#+|+|+|+|#+|+|#+|#+|+|#+|+#|#+|#+|+#|+||#+|

[6.] The issue of "explicitness" of skills:

ISSUE: How implicitly-explicitly _should_—and _can_—we (A) identify thinking skills (name, label, mention), and then (B) explicitly teach them, as procedures?

➔ CAUTION: _once again,_ before trying to teach thinking explicitly to the students, surely the teacher must somehow inform the students effectively of what this whole new paradigm is (even as the teacher had to learn). Otherwise student confusion and more resistance…

ANALYSIS: The issue is complex. Below, four **variable-issues** to attend to:

(1) Secondarily, **learning-styles** may enter in here. Some students discover actively, others benefit from exposition. _But_ prior is whether, sooner or later, skills are named explicitly, taught as techniques explicitly.

(2) More primarily, a *pitfall* to avoid: **over-formulizing.** Let us separate *clarity of depiction of thinking skills* (**= using lenses or frames of references, specificity, conceptualizing upward, comparison and categorization, identifying presuppositions, etc., etc.)** from *over-rote rule-like imparting and employing of them...*

(3) Also, **the issue of possibility at all**. Can skills be made all that explicit (without simplification, overelaboration, rigidity)? We may not be aware they can—SEE examples below, Chicken Sexers and Structure. Or we may not agree that they can be—which would be useful grist for the mill for the issue of "why do people differ, diverge, disagree on an issue. [SEE our "3-DDD" model, in Gallery, **P. 127**]

(4) And, **Personal-Preference elements**. I myself relish generous complete scrutinizing of nuts-and-bolts from soup-to-nuts. My Insight here: it is valuable; my Bias, risks excess in it for some people and places...

GALLERY: Examples: **(1)** Training chicken-sexers! **(2)** My own toolkit on generic "structure/organization"

RECOLLECT: W. DERZKO warning how we teach math operations, but fall short of teaching many other skills...)

[1.] TOUCHSTONE-EXAMPLE. How the training period of "chicken sexers" (workers who discern the sex of day-old chicks—important to the poultry industry) was reduced drastically, and by thinking; by skillfully conceptualizing out the subliminal principles (contours and operations, etc.) of the process...From **"six to twelve weeks"** at a special school, to **"one minute"** of glancing at a sheet prepared by interviewing a veteran chicken-sexer. (Which reminds that "better" elucidation of complex skills is indeed possible...)

[This is "I" *BRIEF* Example; for "II" *FULL*, see Appendix #3 (A), "Why, The Very Idea!"] **P. 173**

[2.] OWN EXAMPLES. Our **Tool-KITS** seek to elucidate complex skill-issues Completely, also Concisely-Clearly. See APPENDIX #4 for examples Change, **Structure**, **Cause-Effect**, Lenses, Specifics, the Essay, Diveresity-education. Here below, a "I" BRIEF view of **Structure**, to support claim that skills can be taught explicitly and completely without either confusion or oversimplification... [For FULL, see Tool-Kit #2, **P. 244**]

[1.] Structure: SIMPLER:	**[B.] Structure: ELUCIDATED:** The *concept* and *craft* of organization-arrangement:
The issue of structure is *omitted*. Or it is tightly *formulaic* or loosely *"creative."* Thus: "In your five- paragraph theme, arrange the three points (1) in this or that specific order I tell you to, or (2) however you feel like doing....." [...**The first being** <u>RRR</u> **or "rigid rote rule" given, the second being** <u>OOO</u> **or "only one's own opinion"...might we move toward** <u>TTT</u>**or "thinking technique taught taut?...**]	**(1)** <u>Basic sequentiality or serial structure</u>: *options*: 1. <u>Time</u>... 2. <u>Space</u>... 3. Utterly <u>random</u> by <u>chance</u>… 4. <u>Free</u> association, to "one best felt" order... 5. <u>Writer-based</u> (meaningful to him/her) "vs." <u>reader-based</u> (better for reader-comprehension)... 5. Via some <u>conceptual scheme:</u> (<u>alphabetical</u>, or an <u>ideology</u>, or the <u>modes</u> such as compare-contrast, etc.)... 6. <u>Hierarchy</u>, or "from the most or A to the least or Z"... 7. "<u>Hypertext</u>" or flattened networked associated hierarchy... **(2)** <u>Other issues</u>. --(A) ONE or Unity: Leitmotif, "Organic Form" (theme repeated/varied), "Maypole"... --Perhaps **(B)** DUAL or the "Alpha & Omega" or Out-&-Return or Braided-Intertwined.... --(C) SERIAL vs. PARALLEL, or left-brain linear "vs." right-brain lateral...
YES... I *begin* to see—**elucidated**, or more Complete yet Clarified—a checklist of an "arena of possibilities"—drawn from a larger catchment-area than any one system...	Right. And still perhaps under-practiced in courses?.

ISSUE 6.A. Do <u>whole fields, disciplines, areas of knowledge, possess more</u> elevated (higher-order) basic concepts and skills, than *educators* explicitly elucidate? (More sometimes than actual *practitioners* even conceptualize?)

<table>
<tr>
<td colspan="2">EXAMPLE. Document Design designs documents, but via what explicit direction? A pointed statement…</td>
</tr>
<tr>
<td colspan="2">

--In her solid book <u>Dynamics of Document Design</u>, KAREN SCHREIVER worries about students' learning merely concrete formulae—instead of the principles beyond the "rules," the concepts which can, of course, (1) help designers learn skills faster in the first place, and (2) then help the designers troubleshoot more competently in complex, non-rule-bound situations.

--But the true root problem is <u>not</u> simply that "<u>teachers know the principles explicitly, but don't convey them to the students.</u>" No; worse, the problem is that the profession of "<u>today's design educators</u>" haven't even studied—developed—clarified—say "elucidated"?—the "theory, methods, and research" of the field <u>for themselves, let alone for their students.</u>

--SCHREIVER rather sharply charges her own field with failing to conceptualize. She quotes Levy as saying that although design educators value "fundamental knowledge" of design, an "understanding of the processes of analysis, synthesis, interpretation, creation, evaluation, and judgment," nevertheless this design knowledge "develops tacitly,…based upon the designer's own experience," and is "not written down." SCHREIVER concludes:

--Although outsiders to design may find it hard to imagine that a reliable design education program could be put together without an underlying model of design, [many design programs] have not put their purpose in writing….'often the models exist but rarely, if ever, are they explicit or conscious.' [philosophic beliefs are held tacitly, but of course are crucial in determining practice. however,] If teachers of design and typography can't tell us <u>what designers know and can do</u>, it is hard to imagine their students will do any better. Design educators might help students discern the key features of design models, their strengths and weaknesses. This will help students to reflect on their own developing model of design.   [-- KAREN SCHREIVER, <u>Dynamics of Document Design</u>; selected]

</td>
</tr>
<tr>
<td>

I see the issues clearly stated here… but maybe this problem of subliminality is limited to <u>small specialized technical</u> fields such as this one, document design?

</td>
<td>

Well, many other fields have noticed this lack also. (It echoes at a higher level, DERZKO'S seminal comments about education lacking explicit thinking techniques.)   Perhaps many people in many fields do not seem to realize the embryonic quality of their conceptual schemes… This statement also previews ALVIN KERNAN who in a later section will charge that his **English literature** colleagues lacked an explicit coherent schematic overview of their field… The **GALLERY** proffers examples from other fields: **medical training, the military…** Of course, is this not-elucidating the conceptual "overpinnings," bad, or unimportant after all? This issue itself is sometimes overlooked

</td>
</tr>
</table>

ISSUE 6.B.   How clearly—or vaguely after all—IS a field's key "concept-content" elucidated? How explicitly MIGHT key concepts be given?

<table>
<tr>
<td>PERSONAL EXAMPLE. My Own Disappointing Foray into Conceptualizing <u>Philosophy</u>…</td>
</tr>
<tr>
<td>

Valuing Philosophy but not having studied it well in college, I recently tried to elucidate its keystone thinking skills. I recalled reading articles on my own, on various and "real-world" subjects (sex, food, graffiti, the bicycle) which a "philosophical stance" had enriched, and tried to abstract out (think through!) what those good qualities were. (Listed below.) Concurrently, I tried to research others to augment my own amateur efforts. My results led me from vapid, to vague, to somewhat-more-valid, as follows…

</td>
</tr>
<tr>
<td>

[1.] FIRST FORAY. **"Inanity on the Internet."** First I asked <u>a philosophy discussion website</u> for response on "how does philosophy think?" Here is a response, actually the sole response, but quite sufficiently-astonishing I thought…reproduced verbatim (except for two <u>underlinings</u> I added for focus).

    I am but a meager student of Philo..I'm not sure how to answer your note at this time.. but I would like to say that Philo for me has been impossible to "define." in one word it's <u>ideas</u>, in two words, it's <u>questioning ideas</u>.
    in three words, it's <u>balancing several ideas</u>. so how can you actually define it.
    I'm glad you're writing a book, but try to think of Philo as such an abstraction as, "draw music." different for everyone, not everyone understands it, and nearly impossible to just sit down and "do."
    philo, as I'm, sure you know, is quite abstract, and so i'm not sure how I could answer your question.

</td>
</tr>
</table>

YES! This comment shows things are complex, and thus warns against your attempt to make a foundational (!) definition applicable to everyone!	NO! This above is, while an easy target, a perfect example of current non-intellectualism. It mis-defines "abstract" as "abstruse" (as my students did!). It utterly overlooks "elucidation," the fact that just because a subject is complex, does *not* mean it's non-definable, or that keystone concepts can't be found.

|+#|+|+|+|#+|+|+|+|#+|+|+|+|#+|+|+|+|#+|+|+|+|#+|+|+|+|#+|+|+|+|#+|+|+|+|#+|+|+|+|#+|+|+|+|#+|+|#+|#+|#+|+|#+|#+|#+|+#|#+|#+|+|#|+|#+|

[2.] SECOND FORAY. "Cold Comfort in the Philosophy Department."

Later I then asked <u>the head of the philosophy department at the University of Wisconsin</u> at Madison, essentially the same question. "What are the keystone perspectives-hence-skills of the philosophical approach, as against other fields?" I had ascended to the top floors of White Hall overlooking Lake Mendota…

Well, he seemed "surprised" at my question. He said that in effect philosophy students are an interested, self-selected group of people (I assume he meant upperclass majors?) and they "simply picked up" philosophical ways of thinking as "tacit lore." I must have exhibited alarm at this "subliminal" method, and when I then pushed on for more explicit strategies, I seemed to disconcert the chair. [The brief interview ended cooler than it started, still high above the blue waters of the Lake—which, however, seemed to have become more *chilled*, as it were, in the interlude …]

> Recall: educator MICHAEL GOLDBERG: a call to name and teach clearly- articulated methods and perspectives to students, for structure, to move toward expertise and ability to transfer knowledge to life. **Intro, P. 17.**

|+#|+|+|+|#+|+|+|+|#+|+|+|+|#+|+|+|+|#+|+|+|+|#+|+|+|+|#+|+|+|+|#+|+|+|+|#+|+|+|+|#+|+|+|+|#+|+|#+|#+|#+|+|#+|#+|#+|+#|#+|#+|+|#|+|#+|

[3.] THIRD FORAY. "My Roster I Created from Genteel Desperation, plus Enthusiasm."

Finally <u>I had to assemble what I knew and could</u>… Either my college course in philosophy was non-good, or I was not ready to connect. (All I got out of it was the useful difference between representative and direct realism, which led to my emphasizing the **"lenses"** which represent the world to us indirectly. So recently I researched, and created this <u>roster</u>.

1. <u>Question everything</u>, including the **assumptions** of *one's own* statements and activities. Seek to know the <u>alternatives, options, choices</u>, etc.

2. <u>Identify and then critique</u>, **"background"** elements above-and-behind specific statements-and-positions, especially the **"implicit presuppositions"** and "unexamined assumptions."

3. To test the validity of a claim, <u>seek</u> **"counter-examples"** or contradictory evidence.

4. <u>Consider</u> the **implications, consequences, results** of a statement—or an action or policy proposed as good. Would the outcomes be good or not?

5. <u>Define</u> **key terms** carefully, and with subtleties of language-use.

6. And of course <u>use good</u> **logic**, formal & informal. <u>Avoid fallacies</u> in logic, language, thinking.

NO! Well who are *you* to give your *amateur* roster of ways philosophers think. Why don't you ask the philosophers themselves—*oh wait*, I see, you did try, at least once…	--My Strong view is that it's a *scandal* a Complete-Clarified "ToolKIT" of "<u>philosophical perspective</u>" is not distilled and available to students—that I had to attempt this myself (and that I did not come away from a philosophy course with such…) [Same for "**The Scientific Method: stages, steps & stumbles**" and "**Media Biases**" other crucial thinking clusters… let alone even on current crucial concerns: <u>evolutionary psychobiology, energy/global warming, terrorism</u>…]
	--I feel my amateur effort is better than none—it seeks to show the keystones….And <u>I love what only philosophy does especially well!</u> It can use these six perspectives to enrich daily-arena issues (even such as sex, food, graffiti, bicycles…) Even if the concepts are not mentioned explicitly in the articles…
	--[And <u>even if philosophy has some "warts"</u>: **(1)** may be culture-bound; **(2)** may focus on non-real-world issues; **(3)** may often be example-barren; **(4)** may chop a lot of logic; **(5)** may wearisomely do nay-saying in a series of "no, you can't say or maintain *that, either*"…]

ISSUE 6.C. How much **should** skills be made more explicit—or **not**?

TOUCHSTONE. A WRITING TEACHER pleads explicitly for a "ceiling-bank" of instruments.

"I'm asking simply to be exposed to, and informed about, the full range of compositional possibilities. That I be introduced to all the tools, right now, and not be asked to wait for years and years until I have mastered right-handed affairs before I learn anything about left-handed affairs, that rather, I be introduced to all the grammars / vehicles / tools / compositional possibilities *now* so that even as I 'learn to write' I will have before me as many resources as possible. I'm asking: that all the 'ways' of writing be spread out before me and that my education be devoted to learning how to use them."   [--WINSTON WEATHERS]

This resonates with me personally, given my strong love of method. *Others with different learning-styles will feel the above is unimportant or even mistaken perhaps...* Open Question: but *should* such explicitness at least be *offered*?

ISSUE 6.D. Two *cautions* in re explicit instruction. "Overteaching" skills to overkill. Plus, experiential or active learning: "good, *but*"...

COMMENT. A PSYCHOLOGIST reminds us of the "chicken-sexing" efficiency of light-touch coaching

There is an important difference between playing and practicing, doing an activity and learning that activity. Just doing something does not necessarily lead to learning. The point is well understood in sports instruction. Coaches distinguish between unsupervised play and training. You could play for a *hundred hours* and learn less than from *a half hour* of properly supervised training....
[In "sport, chess, or mathematical recreations," the coach sets the conditions, provides the feedback-guidance which augments the self-reflection upon which players would otherwise have to depend excessively.]   [-- DON NORMAN]

Our point: indeed students do "pick up skills" but supple "Toolkits" as catalysts, might enormously accelerate learning for even *good* students, and be a reference for *all* anyhow. [**Cause-effect, Structure, Diversity-Education...**]

REMINDER: PITFALL...   At the same time **over**-teaching a skill (in detail or in coaching) can be a real **danger**.
[RECOLLECT DON MURRAY'S trenchant warning (repeated now) : See also STERNBERG and MY OWN anecdote.]

Our students need to discover, before graduation, that freedom is the greatest tyrant of all. Too often the composition teacher not only denies his students freedom, he even goes further and performs the key writing tasks for his students. He gives an assignment; he lists sources; he dictates the form; and, by irresponsibly conscientious correcting, he actually revises his students' papers. Is it not surprising that the student does not learn to write when the teacher, with destructive virtue, has done most of his student's writing? [-- DONALD M. MURRAY]

ISSUE 6.E. A caution—from more than this author!—that explicit teaching, *if* formulaic and simplistic, can be quite harmful to thinking.

RESEARCH-REPORT. A study of math instruction via formula-Letter, vs. principle-Spirit. *Surprisingly,...*

In math instruction, a researcher looked at different ways of teaching "equivalence." specifically "step-by-step instructions" ("add up all the numbers on the left side, and then...") versus "the underlying principle" ("the goal of a problem like this is to find..."). No surprises at first. Both methods helped students solve problems just like the initial one. Also, the principle-based approach was much better at helping transfer knowledge to different problems. "Direct instruction of a technique for getting the right answer produced shallow learning." But then some surprises. Why not combine both methods, algorithm and concept? Well, those taught both ways did no better than those taught only the procedure, and far worse than students taught only the principle. "Teaching for understanding *didn't offset the destructive effects of telling them how to get the answer.* Any step-by-step instruction in how to solve such problems put learners at a disadvantage; the absence of such instruction was required for them to understand."
[-- ALFIE KOHN, "Education's Rotten Apples"]

This seems to torpedo my own love of [lust for] elucidating blazingly-explicitly the how-to. I think I see a resolution. First, a problem may be the overly-directive influence of traditional school culture: "the assignment is to work problems 1 thru 4 in section 2." and so forth. This may rigidify method. Second, and more important, perhaps instruction too often remains too algorithmic-rule-based tactical, not flexibly-elaborated as to AOC's alternate optional choices within itself. That is, "one-point provincial" not "continuum of choices." This would rigidify method at least as badly.

EXAMPLE. **Teaching amateur photography**. One variable is shutter speed. Cf. "set the shutter speed at 1/125 second and the film accordingly." Compare this with showing shutter speed can be time, 1 sec., ½ sec., ¼ sec., 1/8 sec., and so forth on to 1/1000 sec. or higher. And each option has functions or uses pro and con (slow shutter to show leaf-blur, or give more depth of field; fast to freeze bird or achieve selective focus).

EXAMPLE. **Writing instruction**. Syntax. "Keep sentences short, long ones are run-on…no, keep sentences long, short ones are choppy." Vs. the pros and cons of different lengths and types. So also with Tone (formal? informal?). And explicitness and location of point. And so forth…

SUGGESTED GUIDELINE: Be quite focused accurate *explicit* about Method Technique Procedure, *but also* quite flexibly adaptable heuristic in approach beyond formula. Don't confuse these two issues: being explicit about how to do the how-to, need not lead to being rigid about how to apply the how-to.

|+#|+|+|+|#+|+|+|+|#+|+|+|+|#+|+|+|+|#+|+|+|+#|+|+|+|+#|+|+|+|#+|+|+|+|#+|+|+|+|#+|+|#+|#+|#+|+|#+|+|#+#|+#|#+|#+|+#|+||#+|

[7.] Motivation & accountability in learning:

ISSUE. The *sources* of motivation to learn—and, the *responsibility* to learn well. To what % the learner—or outside (teacher, other stimuli?)

The A to Z Continuum: Opinions on this vary. The expert scholarly "literature" on "motivation" is "extensive."

A PERSONAL RESPONSE: <u>100% of motivation must come from the learner. Not even 99%.</u> *None* from the teacher course class system etc. I admit this *is* an uncompromising, extreme-purist **Ideal-Type**, but only to be Pragmatic, to try to force the issue of learner-responsibility. To try to hold the line against traditional education's approach of heavy monitoring, spoon-feeding, and the more-recent trend toward "enabling" and non-responsibility (let alone null involvement)… *Of course* a good teacher can "guide by the side" and help students—but whoa, only as catalyst…]

POSSIBLE PREVALENT PITFALL. Perhaps "interesting" has two senses, wrongly conflated. First when many youth today say "interesting," they may mean *continuous absorbing attention* as in a riveting TV drama—must be continuous, or else quickly boring!… Whereas, "interesting" in a major advanced intellectual project would be *a basic drive or momentum* which would sustain one through intermittent rough spots, including T. B. or Temporary Boredom…

EXAMPLES. [1.] One case pro "getting the kids interested." [2., 3.] And two advanced qualifications of "interesting" plus of course also "easy" as an issue… [4.] And the poet speaks…

[1.] Children learn best what they love. We have all been amazed at ten-year-olds who can recite the batting average of every player in the American League or who can discuss and compare minor details in the various Star Trek series. The good teacher needs to inspire love for his subject; then all the rest will follow; children will learn the facts willingly, will read the books eagerly, because they will find them irresistible. [-- MICHAEL DIRDA, Bound To Please]

…this <u>seems</u> "fine"—EXCEPT that <u>TRUE thinking</u> goes farther, "kicks itself up a notch" (or three)—<u>read on</u>:

[2.] "It is not the aim of education to make the student feel good about himself or herself. On the contrary, if anything, a good education should lead to a permanent sense of dissatisfaction. Complacency is the very opposite of the intellectual life. **The dirty secret of intellectual life is that first-rate work requires an enormous amount of effort, anxiety, and even desperation.** The quests for knowledge and truth, as well as depth, insight, and originality, are **not effortless**, and they certainly are **not comfortable**." [-- JOHN SEARLE]

[3.] "Many things in life are <u>wonderful because they are very difficult</u>, as well as being beautiful or interesting or useful, too. Among these are the ballet, playing the solo trumpet as well as MILES DAVIS or WYNTON MARSALIS, and being able to illuminate a play or a novel in the way some literary critics can. They are skills whose exercise leaves the spectator slightly breathless. Good physicists got that sort of frisson from the work of RICHARD FEYNMAN. … I have had half a dozen students in the course of thirty years whose swiftness and acuteness of understanding have done the same to me. <u>Students study</u>

philosophy in part for the sake of the pleasure of seeing people vastly cleverer than themselves engaging with issues that it has taken every intellectual skill they possess to get clear and to see into. To describe KANT'S CRITIQUE OF PURE REASON as a source of pleasure perhaps ought to be avoided, since many students have found it utterly intractable; but if there is pleasure to be had from hanging off a rock face, as there clearly is, there is a pleasure of a not dissimilar kind from venturing a view on what IMMANUEL KANT'S equally vertiginous derivation of the laws of the human mind may have been about.   [-- ALAN RYAN, Oxford University]

[4.] "Only when love and work are one, / And the work is play for mortal stakes, / Is the deed ever really done, / For heaven and the future's sake."   [-- ROBERT FROST]

...this would seem to echo the scandalous suggestion that thinking is **Pleasurable** after all—*but* in the higher senses of deeper satisfaction, more complex enjoyment. "The fascination of what's difficult..." *Let it be one's little secret then...*

PERSONAL ANALOGY. Reflecting upon how students passively resist involvement, go through motions, only, I thought of this comparison, to illustrate passive disengagement vs. active involvement.

--Too often, students seem simply to (so to speak) attend class but passively, and they just **wear a plastic-coated identification badge** on a cord around their neck, on which various stickers are placed to certify they've completed a paper, test, course. The badge is exterior to the student, kept at a distance, useful only as gateways to fulfilling requirements and hence exit. And in re attitude, the students just seem to *sit or wait around...*

--Whereas a true learner would **tattoo learning-material onto his/her very skin,** to let it permeate in to their personal selves! And in re attitude, the learner would bound into the course **like a hunter-and-gatherer, a forager, a poacher even,** *grabbing by the double-handful* material of use and interest to the learner him/herself...

BUT: How silly and idealistic. This Active Student is *not* the person populating education today, at least, if ever!	Aha, but how true about how ANY REAL learning occurs. *Better we know the truth than not...*

EXAMPLE: PERSONAL TESTIMONY. "The Pre-Post Paper: Beneficence *Blown-Away*"
A great TTh assignment (or it *seemed* it would be...) is to **(1)** first, assign a course paper the first week of the course, a do-your-best effort but exploratory-experimental, with no specific directions.

[EXAMPLE: in English composition, "A Job I've Held." In sociology, "The Individual And The Group." In history, "How does the past and present interrelate?" In economics?.. In philosophy?... in biology?... in geography?...]

(2) But, do not grade or even respond to this pre-paper. (You may of course silently examine them, and then return them to the students, or retain safely.) Then *as part of the final exam*, **(3)** assign a re-do of the same paper/assignment.

The Good News: much *Awareness* plus *Appreciation*. Student after student inescapably learn that they've learned much. "Wow, this early version is pathetic, I could do it so much better now!" **The Bad News:** → no *Action. They don't re-do it much better.* Due to non-motivation, they sidestep this great opportunity to cinch their learning, and *hand in disgustingly-minimal touch-ups only.* (At least in my required Freshman English 101 1970-95, anyhow...)
The Modified Good News After All: in advanced classes, with more-motivated students, this *can* work like *magic.....*

COMMENT. RICHARD PAUL *LAYS IT OUT ON THE LINE...*

[The teacher does not have the fundamental responsibility for student learning. Progressively the students must become increasingly responsible.] "Students need to come to see that only they can learn for themselves,... The teacher provides opportunities for students to decide what they need to know and helps them develop strategies for finding or figuring it out."

This comment counters traditional education and teachers' internalized norms that they must help provide motivation and responsibility. Plus public demands on teachers... The comment would disturb many educators let alone students.
RECALL: DON MURRAY'S comment that we do too much for students...

|+#|+|+|+|#+|+|+|+|#+|+|+|+|#+|+|+|+|#+|+|+|+|#+|+|+|+|#+|+|+|+|#+|+|+|+|#+|+|+|+|#+|+|#+|+#|+#|+#|+|#+|+#|#+|+#|#+|+#|+|#|+|+#|

[{ END of "Keystones" section in the Introduction... }]

3: the "D-MACHINE":
useful |options| to deal with:
--delve in; discover; discuss, debate, differ on; decide about; then do...

THE ISSUE; WHY IMPORTANT; OUR OFFERING: How to actually implement in a course, the three "pillars" of teaching thinking? As in all thinking, it helps if the key **variable-issues** to confront, are made explicit. So here follows a checklist of matters to "know of…handle, manage…employ…satisfy" etc. *A-Z options for each…*
> [*This is to be as complete, conceptualized, and concretized, as possible—*
> *at least, more so than many other currently-available resource-materials.*]

So, forward to implementing basic goals, presence in classroom, and end-goal of real-world abilities:

|#+#|+#|+|#+#+|#+#+#+#||+|+#++|#|+#+||+|+#|+|++|#+#++|+|||+#++|+#+#|+|#+|+|#|+#|+||+|#+|+|+#|+#|+#|#+|+|#+||+|#+#+|+#|+|#||

61

(14) <u>Mode of Delivery</u>. Is **T.** taught in freestanding separate course? Infused into existing courses?

(15) <u>Learning-Styles, Teaching-Pedagogy.</u> Are various approaches recognized, used?

(16) <u>Other major **Types of Thinking**.</u> Does our **essential** thinking recognize variety?

|#+#|+#|+|#+#+|#+#+#+#||+|+#++|#|+#+||+|+#|+|++|#+#++|+|||+#++|+#+#|+|#+|+|+|#|+#|+||+|#++|+|+#|+#|+#|#+|+|#+|+|#+|#+|+#|+|#||

[***WHAT THINKING SKILLS USED HERE?:*** Pervasive is the key tool **"variables-variation."** EXAMPLE: *below, an instance analyzed, to refresh awareness of how* **"V-V"** *works to identify all options, critique stands taken on same...*

TEST-CASE EXAMPLE (TO PRIME THE PUMP).... *Where* does this **Letter** stand on *which issues*, although the issues may be *unstated*? Can we identify the issues, critique the letter's choice of stances?
A letter to the <u>New York Times</u> about Harvard University's proposed reform of the undergraduate curriculum. "LAWRENCE H. SUMMERS, Harvard's president, gives the wrong impression about what undergraduates need to learn. Knowing the names of five Shakespeare plays or the difference between a gene and a chromosome prepares one for a trivia contest, but is not education. Students need to *recognize the quality of the poetry and understand how scientists evaluate and explore information.* I recently developed a science-for-nonscientists college course, and my leading aphorism was: We don't want a course in which all test questions consist of What was in bold-face type on Page 257?" [-- RICHARD A. LOCKSHIN, in the NYTIMES]

BUT what is wrong with *this* approach? It moves from your so-hated Facts, on to *understanding* of Criteria and also Method. Sounds like "thinking" to *me*. Are you *never* satisfied?	--**BUT** this comment goes only half way there. Its stand on #1 **Goals of education** and the **definition of learning thinking**? It's still only passive Comprehension, even though "appreciative" of complexities. It notably undermentions **#3Application** or using the skill later on. **#9Explicitness** is implied to be valuable—to an extent. Other variables seem absent let alone unemphasized. --By contrast, the issue of the **End-Goal**. At graduation, can students **"Hit The Ground Running"**? Transfer skills autonomously? Can they <u>appreciate actual new poems</u>, to their own optimal need and interest? [Not to mention whether these skills are explicitly "showcased," we said Billboarded or ideally featured in a Tool-BANK...] --And can students not only <u>critique bad science</u> when perceived, but even ("horrors") actually themselves <u>use the **Scientific Method** itself</u>? Do they not know about, but truly know, the method? Does their Tool-Belt include a Complete but Compact "grip" on the method? Do concepts readily surface as needed, in ultimate accessibility, complete with like **"replicability," "falsifiability," "observer-bias," "sampling errors,"** and more? That would satisfy me. (And yes it is ideal-utopian, impossible and undesirable to attain 100%, but also is being attained here and there, and can be attained much more *than many realize* ...)
Wow, you sure convinced me! [Damed fanatic pushing things beyond proper limits...]...	*Thank you... [...wonder if he really meant that...]*

|#+#|+#|+|#+#+|#+#+#+#||+|+#++|#|+#+||+|+#|+|++|#+#++|+|||+#++|+#+#|+|#+|+|+|#|+#|+||+|#++|+|+#|+#|+#|#+|+|#+|+|#+|#+|+#|+|#||

[1.] Define Ed. Goals	[2.] Essence of TT: AAA	[3.] Presence?	[4.] other Variables

[I.] Overview: "Education" = ? ...

(1) <u>Goals of education</u>. What is decided-upon, as main or other goals generally, and of a specific course?

RECOLLECT: Earlier statements on this: What to Know, Believe, Do:
--**Informational:** DR. GRAHAM "imparted knowledge." [but did he teach using it?]

ISSUE #1.1. How much do <u>individual teachers VARY</u>, as to the GOALS of their courses? Especially in re "teaching thinking"...

MY RESEARCH-RESULTS: Ten Teachers, Not All "Teaching Thinking"—and *Their* Motives Suspect?... A colleague, MARK L., said "but surely all teachers are interested in the teaching of thinking." I could have showed him how my informal research suggested otherwise indeed. Here are the results:

1. MARIE taught short stories dealing with <u>personal development, maturity, growth</u> issues. This was for her students' sake—but also, she affirmed, **for her own personal sake**...

2. GILBERT taught students that <u>America was imperialistic</u> in the Far East and elsewhere. He *fervently believes* that. He stated he intended students would exit the course being quite aware of that. [**I think we call this Indoctrination into Ideologies, or nowadays, "Socially-Committed"?**] By contrast, Carl Cohen described Four Systems (two democracy types, Communism, fascism) and had the students Go At Them and explore, explain, analyze, evaluate—and learn how to do so...

3. JUDY taught about <u>animal rights and anti-hunting stands</u> in classes (in re research reports). She frankly "wants to stop hunting." She "does not give both sides of the cases, because the students already enter class knowing the one, the pro-hunting, side well." [**Do they objectively know their folk-ideologies now, and in thought-out detail? True Thinking involves dispassionately assessing your own stands, their implications, motivations, etc...**]

4. LEO teaches <u>a poetic-creative "alternate style" of writing</u>, even in practical English 101. This involves a collage of imagery, statistics, dry statements, surprises, page-layout. He frankly stated that he did so *to be able to get through the course without tedium and boredom*. The experiments were vivacious...
--But one former student of his said to me that the "alternate style" didn't seem to be real-world practical, for School or for Work. [**Insightful and biassed myself, I could only agree...**]

5. GORDON <u>claims</u> that he indeed "teaches thinking" in his classes. [**He has received student complaints of his intellectually-browbeating them in class, to the point of "soft-core student-abuse" one might phrase it...**]

6., 7., 8. IVAN, NELSON, and GERRY all *attempted* the teaching of thinking, or anyhow more flexible student response. No one of the three found it amenable to <u>their own educational styles</u>, which emphasized *control* (valued for clarity and achievement). After a long discussion with me, GERRY admitted ultimately that he flat-out "did not like *messy* student papers which *experimented*"—the <u>true motivation</u> surfacing? [**Was "thinking" here, confused with OOO or "Only One's Own Opinion"?**]

9. I myself, BRIAN, pursued the teaching of <u>writing</u>: indeed the dreaded "bonehead" <u>Freshman Composition</u>. (Became the department specialist and published 50 articles, in fact...) **But *why?*** Because of (1) dutiful dedication? *Not hardly.* (2) Career-move? *Nope*; that helped, but was secondary. Rather, (3) because **writing**, a complex activity, was perfect grist to "dock" or "hook up" with <u>what I wanted to teach in the first place</u>, and simply because of my own impassioned *Personal-Preference Taste-Temperament* which led to this book. Namely, <u>thinking through complexities competently</u>... (Is this disclosure or confession time? Did I harness poor Writing as the handmaiden to serve my own hobbyhorse desires?...Should this issue even be discussed in a book on Thinking, and why not indeed?)
--Plus, I surely chose <u>TT</u> as goal just as *subjectively* as Colleagues #1 thru #8 above chose *their* own "non-thinking" goals. *So...* So, does everything dissolve into Facile Relativism, "Who's to say who's right after all," eh? [**...Or does it?** That would be a classic Amateur Pitfall; SEE App. #5 for mini-unit on "the **Relativism Trap**"...]

Thus—I taught thinking *not* for moral duty. *But* for intense professional pleasure.

TT respects the students. It matures the classroom. It *ennobles* true education....

WHOA: Why rant against your colleagues? Everyone teaches *differently*—a department's strength. Are those Strong Statements helpful? *Let's get on with the variables …*	--Emotionally, I admit a *Pet Peeve* of mine is unexamined **"blow-off statements"** such as *"Well, we already all teach thinking."* Objectively, I I want only to **Save the Subject**: to defend teaching of thinking. Plus to **Serve the Staff**: to help any educators who might want to re-consider, "do I really teach thinking after all?"... *And now on to the variables…*

|#+#|+#|+|#+#+|#+#+#+#||+|+#++|#|+#+||+|+#|+|++|#+#++|+|||+#++|+#+#|+|#+|+|+|#|+#|+||+|#+|+|+#|+#|+#|#+|+|#+||+|#+|#+|+#|+|#||

ISSUE #1.2. But, how much do assignments teach thinking—in general?

MINI-GALLERY. I asked my English 101 students to gather examples of course exam assignments given freshmen students at Univ. of Wis. at Whitewater. Do they raise the issue of "**inert**-interesting vs. **charged**, useful" **knowledge**?

1. What are two reptilian adaptations for a terrestrial environment, and why did they evolve? [Strong support system, stronger eggs.]

2. What marked the beginnings of human civilization? [Food-production, etc., etc.]

3. Evaluate the contributions of the ancient Greeks in science and philosophy, using specific examples.

4. How does the exploitation of the Third World by the First World reflect on the USA? [Shift from feelings of pride to embarrassment, etc., etc. …]

5. How does the classroom teacher identify a child with possible hearing loss?

6. When you speak publicly, how can you control your nervousness, even make it work for you? [Be at physical and mental best; think positively; use visual aids…]

7. Should the electoral college be banned in the United States? *[Did teacher give own opinion on this?]*

8. Evaluate the contributions of the ancient Greeks in science and philosophy, using specific examples. *[Is this true evaluation, or reporting what the course said the contributions were?]*

9. Would you like to live in a house like Frank Lloyd Wright's "Fallingwater"? Why or why not? *[Does this ask for more than mere Personal Opinionation? Did it seek to teach a skill of "how to evaluate and decide more competently"?]*

10. Explain which technique used by interest groups in trying to influence legislation you think is best, and why. [persuasion, litigation, rulemaking, election activities, lobbying] *[I am confused. By what Way of Knowing? Personal Preference? This criterion or that one and why chosen? AND Transfer:*

"WOW"… "Gosh, your concept has **empowered** me to see dull, boring assignments in a new, elucidated light, via x-ray vision. Pitfalls exposed, potentialities noted…"	Well, *thank you…* {(.I *think*…..)}

|#+#|+#|+|#+#+|#+#+#+#||+|+#++|#|+#+||+|+#|+|++|#+#++|+|||+#++|+#+#|+|#+|+|+|#|+#|+||+|#+|+|+#|+#|+#|#+|+|#+||+|#+|#+|+#|+|#||

ISSUE #1.3. Doesn't some "knowledge" itself, possess "*thought-ful*" qualities? Can't key "information" already be a *thinking* tool *itself*?

Whoa, enough. I can't have this! You become extremist, you throw the baby of Knowledge out with the bathwater, you'd evaporate up to Pure Thinking only—for your Sportive Pleasure! ***This will not do.*** Please remember and respect E. D. HIRSCH'S plea for **"cultural literacy,"** the *facts, data, information* in our heritage we need to navigate, to Confront Complexities!	--Well, I'll agree with you for more Knowledge-as-such—but still from my Thinking position. How about "**CONCEPTUAL Literacy**" then?... Oh, and true knowledge but *not* inert textbook; instead about (1) current crucial issues and (2) new-emerging perspectives plus (3) important but sidelined fields? --In short, *not* "BACK TO THE BASICS," *but* "FORWARD TO THE ADVANCED BASICS OF TRUE THINKING"...

ROSTER. Types of "knowledge" not at all inert, but perhaps crucial for thoughtful education: **[1.]** "Currently Crucial" items and issues. [**EXAMPLES:** Energy. Environment. Globalization? Security? Others?...] And the current new perspectives emerging. [**EXAMPLE:** Evolutionary Biology and Cognitive Science.] What new

discoveries in these volcanically-erupting fields have led to new insights which can illuminate everyday life every day? To elucidate these into (say) a 50-to-100 page unit, presented during one's college years, seems to be an unthanked unrewarded hence neglected task. So students graduate not updated...

[2.] Timelessly-Technical. More subjects pure and applied, salient in real-life living, but out of the mainstream. How about "One-Day Seminars" to grasp the gist of these intellectual actions? For more **conceptual literacy**?

[EXAMPLES: **Architecture**, the principles and issues... **Engineering**, the powerful perspectives beyond the technical formulae... **The Law**, what issues recur over time place and system and what varied responses occur?]

[3.] "Campus Cupola." Is the student offered keystone <u>perspectives</u> of the varied academic disciplines?

[EXAMPLE: in **sociology/anthropology**, <u>**"culture as silent school"**</u>: a system socializing us subliminally into norms, a "required course," helpful but at times 'a standardization of error,' a 'cake of custom' resistant to change...]

And so these are all *higher* forms of "knowledge-about," short of severe practical application but beyond mere inert unconnected lower-level "information-on." These powerful updates consolidations and perspectives do seem valid in the curriculum to "know of and about" indeed...

NOO... You mean well but you've "lost it" and have spiraled out from solidity into a dilettante *overgeneralizing* on a cloud. "The Law in One Day," *reeaallly*!....	**Yes the keystone salient core issues of the Law, in one sitting, as never before done**... We can try to elucidate complexities more-completely and more-clearly, via **conceptualizing** upward. EXAMPLE: in political science: "the **relation of individual freedom and social-group security**"—responses all the way from the authoritarian "this is not even a relevant question," onward, to..... This empowers students to confront the facts and their absence...
Oh all right then? You've softened your Strong Stand that skills are the only real educational content?	Yes except *no* insidious backsliding to "teach the facts first, then how to think about them"...

THREE EXAMPLES. Of cases which do exceed mere "inert" data, become useful:

EXAMPLE #1. A book on <u>human motivation</u>, a biobehavioral approach to it, gives the reader an understanding of why an individual exhibited certain behaviors, the causes of those actions.

Though seemingly "academic" and scholarly, etc., psychology Prof. RODERICK WONG can analyze "motivated behavior such as **sexual activity, parental behavior, food selection, fear, or aggression**." From studies in animal behavior and comparative psychology, the book analyzes "<u>relevant issues in human motivation</u> such as **mate choice, nepotism, attachment and independence, sensation seeking, obesity, and parent-offspring conflict**." Ironically, the introduction concludes that the book will be particularly useful for undergraduate <u>students</u> in psychology or behavioral science who are studying "motivation and emotion, comparative psychology, animal behavior, or biological psychology." [-SOURCE]

...why do you say "ironically"? The book would seem to—well, are you saying that others than pre-professional scientists should read it?	--I am saying "wow," it's relevant to all students and our end-goal of **Hitting The Ground Running** to face complexities in life. Couldn't the knowledge here be not inert but charged with power? *Marriage, parenting, adopted children, addictions of various sorts*—couldn't the book offer, not thinking tools, but informational-packets to "open and sprinkle over a difficult situation to control it"? --Of course, how about also, and primarily, powerful **thinking** tools which let one confront situations even when **information** is absent or outdated?.."I can apply **cognitive dissonance** to our family squabble. Not information. A *theory*..."

EXAMPLE #2. Another book offers "everyday applications from <u>mind-brain research</u>."

It notes "why **blue rooms lower blood pressure and stress**, why men tend to **like food sweeter than women**, why **women have a better sense of smell**, and why men are able to **talk about sports and work on a car at the same time**, while women are able to **combine right and left brain activities**." [-- SOURCE]

Now I am seeing your point. But doesn't this second	I'd say so. The moral? Make sure all materials focus on

example drift away from "charged" powerful usefulness, and more toward a sort of "nice-to-know" information?	empowerment to face larger, more-challenging issues.

EXAMPLE #3. From a cognitive scientist, revelations and relevancies...

--In all social species, **relatives are more likely to help each other**, and nonrelatives are more likely to hurt each other. (Relatives share genes, so any gene that biases an organism to help a close relative will also often be helping a copy of itself, hence increase its own chances of prevailing.) Result: having a stepparent is the largest risk factor for child abuse ever examined.

--Our **tastes for sugar and fat** as nutrients were adaptive earlier, when in short supply, but are no good now when cheap and available.

--**We prefer physically-attractive marriage partners.** This makes no *current* sense regarding goals of compatibility or happiness, but it made *earlier* sense because physical beauty is correlated with health and fertility, which was important for species-survival earlier.

--Perhaps **a universal thirst for revenge** was adaptive earlier when one couldn't dial "911" for help if threatened; but such belligerence is now maladaptive.

[-- STEPHEN PINKER]

...these "facts," could easily become strong thinking tools, for better managing of conflicts, making decisions...

EXAMPLE #4., The lost chord! I saw a book on **evolutionary biology and larger political and social issues.** It seemed vital, offering comment on such crucial issues as "what are certain limits of effectiveness of certain proposed social systems, given apparent hard-wired or basic human evolutionary natures?" But I lost the source.

SUGGESTED RULE-OF-THUMB GUIDELINE. **Avoid the pitfall of mistaking merely Knowing information, for using it, thinking it through to get ideas FROM it, or applying concepts TO it...** *However,* some "factualities" do seem to empower daily thinking: evolution and people...

|#+#|+#|+|#+#+|#+#+#+#||+|+#++|#|+#||+|+#|+|++|#+#++|+|||+#++|+#+#|+|#+|+|#|+#|+||+|#+|+|#+#|+#|#++|+|#+||+|#+|#+|+#|+|#||

[II.] The core-essence. The central skills:

→ We repeat the CAUTION: *before* teaching in the new way, the teacher must somehow <u>clarify to the (unaware) students that this is a new approach</u>, and *what* it is, at least basically!

(2) ABSTRACTION. Do classes sufficiently move from Facts upward to Concepts, to "Elevate" to higher-order skills?

ISSUE #2.1.   <u>Do learners know</u> the ladder of abstraction? INducting UPward

--**The Concept:** the vertical-level range of thinking skills? From concrete operations and observations == to generalizations == to hypotheses == to theories, first of the middle range == then to larger Principles == and on to keystone summit concepts, even "laws"?

--**Competence** in it: can we locate any given statement or example, accurately on the Ladder of being specific, half-general, general? Can we estimate: too specific or general? And alter as needed and desired?

--Cruciality of it: and *does it matter*, whether "we" have a sound sense of this so-called "LADDER OF ABSTRACTION"?

SEE: here a "I" **BRIEF** version; a "II" **FULL** version is in Appendix **# 3A and B**, "Conceptualizing 101"

GALLERY: EXAMPLES. The "Ladder of Abstraction" moves upward to higher-order thinking. *Of all thinking skills, could not "conceptualizing 101" or <u>induction</u> be reinforced "every day in every class"?...* This sequence below starts at the top general and descends to specifics...

---

(1) RECOMMENDATION. The curriculum of a subject should seek fundamental understanding of "the underlying principles that give structure to a subject"... Teaching specific topics or skills without connecting them to "the broader fundamental structure" impedes transfer of learning, which requires "fundamental principles and ideas." "<u>To understand something as a specific instance of a more general case</u>—which is what understanding a more fundamental structure means—is to have learned not only a specific thing but also a model for understanding other things like it that may encounter.]

[-- JEROME BRUNER, Process of Education]

> **...of course this is great but still *vague*. *What* specific principles, structures, ideas? And so this:**

(2) ROSTER. The "laws of thought" illuminates "all conscious endeavor." In "all good thinking and feeling" are seen "the **three great ideas** underlying both logic and mathematics, namely, **Generality; Form** (something that can be handled when its type is recognized); and **Variability**." They vary in appearance, but "they rule thinking about art as well as politics, business as well as science." [-- JACQUES BARZUN]

> **...but this moves *only one millimeter* down the Ladder.**
> **Great "northstars" or "standpoints" here, but *what to <u>teach</u> <u>students</u>*? And so,...**

(3) PROPOSAL. The General Education committee recommended that science courses introduce "the following *COMMON, GENERAL CONCEPTS*": Dynamic Equilibrium; Change & Evolution; Scale & Proportion; Causality & Consequences; and, Energy: Its Sources and Transfer.

[-- Regarding the Gen. Ed. course "STS" or Science & Technology in Society, UNIV. OF WIS.-WHITEWATER]

> **...well, this gets *some*where: both marvelously Principled, and also able to be Particularized...**
> **Can we move even lower while still remaining Conceptual above the Concrete subject-data?**

(4) EXAMPLE. Math can be more than rote routine algorhythms far from real life...

<u>Mathematical</u> thinking-skills: 1. Number sense. 2. Numerical ability. 3. Spatial-reasoning ability. 4, 5. A sense of cause and effect. 6. Algorhythmic ability. 7. Ability to abstract! 8, 9. Logical, and Relational, reasoning ability.

[-- KEITH DEVLIN, CHE]

> **...a gratifying start toward hammering math ploys into "human" usable concepts. *Better than:***

(5) EXAMPLE. <u>ALGEBRA</u> key concepts include: "combination, permutation, association..."

> **...*none* of which I *ever* heard of or imagined or sensed throughout my formula-filled courses...**
> **But maybe this trio could be "Elevated" to more-generic thinking skills?...**

(6) EXAMPLE. SOCIOLOGY, the discipline. Levels from the top down to the bottom:

(A) *Largest perspectives, paradigms or frames of reference or keystone concepts*:

   1. **Debunking**—values questioning traditional conventional "common-sense" explanations of things, of "what everybody knows."
   2. **Unrespectable**—can examine non-elite, discredited, non-mainstream, "deviant" subjects.
   3. **Cosmopolitan**—values being non-provincial (non-ethnocentric, non-xenophobic), also world-wide in scope.
   4. **Relativistic**—questions absolutes, one-standard-only or monistic views, static not dynamic views; is sensitive to context.
      [-- PETER BERGER, INVITATION TO SOCIOLOGY: A HUMANISTIC PERSPECTIVE]

(B) Then key *theories*: **Functionalism; Conflict; Symbolic Interactionism; etc.**

(C) Then keystone *concepts*: "Culture," as learned behavior for social interaction. Inevitably learned; largely tacit perhaps; has force of norms and mores; may be counterproductive; etc.

(D) Then working *mid-range* concepts: statistics, "class, stratification, institutions, conformity and deviance, role and status, the family, cultural lag, differential life-chances, latent and manifest functions, ROLE: reversal, strain or conflict, distance, exit, etc. etc."

(E) Then *specific studies*: *field-research*, etc.… on down to *data and information*…

… rich higher-order concepts, useful mid-range concepts …

(7) EXAMPLE. **BIOLOGY,** the discipline. Levels from the top on down to the bottom?

(A) **"Big Ideas,"** or ways of arranging the field. Be it **"levels"** from cell to organism to individual population community on up to ecology. Or from **Energy** to **Nutrients** to **Information**? (Lists exist of a dozen key concepts in biology…)

(B) **Facts**. "Stimulus receptors," "meiosis and mitosis," "enzymes," "photosynthesis," "five types of tissues in plants and animals (muscle, connective, etc.)"….

…I'd like to see more Keystone Perspectives of biology. Of which, of course, "evolution" a kingpin…

NO!: Did you enjoy your *dizzying, self-indulgent whirl* up and down the Ladder of Abstraction? (Plus, you really *fall short* on Biology there!)	Enjoyed it more than *you* did, it seems… <u>Pleasurably</u>, since powerful conceptual principles nourish, mere facts only are not full-filling… Best is to combine the Conceptual and the concrete. <u>Pragmatically</u>, it reminds about identifying higher-order concepts in a course. Do students learn to distinguish them from concrete operations? It's anyhow better than the ROSE FOR EMILY assignment asking for ideology… (Oh and as for biology, yes indeed regrettably *I know nothing—but* why haven't the *biology teachers* proffered us the powerful keystones of their field? I can't locate them in research…)
Yeah, it's good. **BUT** I still want to know the *practical shirtsleeves difference this makes* in classes, even in Room 212 at 9:00 on Monday morning…	Glad you asked. Consider the following example from a master teacher of science, JIM MINSTRELL. This shows both the pervasive pitfall—and the instantly-available potentiality to remedy it (namely, "at all times, seek the idea in and behind the specific facts"):

REPORT FROM CLASSES. "When presented with a novel problematic situation, students tend to look to the *surface features* for cues as to what learned ideas and procedures to apply: "What other problem have I done that has the features of this one?" In physics, students look for *features like inclined planes or pulleys* rather than for possibly relevant <u>principles</u> such as forces or energy conservation. For example, when two bodies interact, as in a collision, students tend to attend to *features such as which one is moving faster, which is bigger, and which will sustain the greater damage*, rather than considering **equal and opposite action and reaction forces**."
[-- JIM MINSTRELL, "EXPERTISE IN TEACHING"]

ISSUE #2.2. Is the variable of FORMULA vs. FLEXIBILITY addressed? Especially the pitfall/potentiality of "RULES VS. TOOLS"?

THE ISSUE. **"Letter vs. Spirit,"** including Correct Form vs. Effective Function, and Rules vs. Tools—this cluster is a major issue in thinking well… (**Rules**: "must do, success will ensue" or **Tools**: use or not, depending")

WHY IMPORTANT? <u>Traditional education</u> (goal what to Know, Believe—and Do) may still present most or all processes and procedures (skills, moves) as rules, not tools. Beginning learners in the classroom context may thus need "re-programming." This may involve two levels.
(1) First <u>to clarify the basic distinction</u>. (Otherwise, learners too often will **"rule-monger,"** for instance take a dozen probe-questions for poetry and apply them all mechanically to the same poem whether they are all relevant in that instance or not!)
(2) And second <u>to speed advanced expertise</u> in selecting and applying flexibly, dexterously, effectively larger techniques in larger more complex issues. (Not easy.)

A SUGGESTION: The following material. ["I" BRIEF; for "II" FULL, see Prior Basics, Appendix #5.]

"MINI-TOOL-KIT":   Some of the components of Formula-Flexibility thinking:

(1) **"Rules"** are methods or procedures more pre-set and less altered by the user. They may be Necessary & Sufficient: *"This you must do, then success will ensue…"*

"Tools" are more complex, more selective in use, and manipulated by the user.
"Use this or not, depending, whether it gets desired ending."

Related concepts and terms are:

(2) Intermediate Type: **"Rule of Thumb"** or **"Guideline"** (These often depend upon **Operating Principles Behind**, or objective reasons why the ROT/G is usually or often "good"…..)

EXAMPLE. **(1) Specific Detailing** in writing: why needed? Well, needed to *"rehydrate the abstractions* we arrived at in our own minds when we forgot the details which produced the ideas vividly." ["Horrible," vs. "car upside down on the median."]

Ditto for **(2) parallelism:** *"Similar ideas, need similar style-expression, to relate them in the reader's mind":* ["Fred likes skiing, to fish, and he dances" = "Fred likes skiing, fishing, and dancing."]

(3) Also syntax: *"Order of information for best reader-understanding: new important information at end and in main clause."* … ["Breaking my arm, I slipped on the dock" = "Slipping on the dock, I broke my arm."]

(3) **"algorhythm"** vs. **"heuristic,"**

(4) **"tactics"** vs. **"strategy,"**

(5) **"Letter (or literal) vs. Spirit (or figurative),"**

(6) **"Form"** contour or shape vs. **"Function"** operation effect purpose result

(7) **"correct vs. effective"** [including technically incorrect but functionally effective, let alone correct by-the-book but a botch-blunder-bungle in the result…] and

(8) *In Vitro* (="under glass" or by-the-book) vs. *In Vivo* (="live" in the field, in operation).

(9) **"Appearance"** *surface* vs. **"Reality"** underneath-behind-beyond…

(10) **Conceptualizing 101**: concrete **Particular** instance, and conceptual **Principle** above-and-behind it.

…a cameo-attempt to begin a Tool-KIT of a major skill.

Suggested Rule-of-Thumb [!] GUIDELINE

(1) **Awareness:** *"Know of* the very concept of "aRt=hTs." The distinction between algorhythm, Rule, tactic == and heuristic, Tool, strategy. *Know* the pros and cons (powers, and pitfalls) of both rote rules, and flexible tools."

(2) Then, Ability: in a situation, *be able to* decide competently, about implementation. WWWWW or "what to do, when-where, and why.": That is, *which* techniques to employ (and which *not* to); how (as, whether as a fixed rule, or as a flexible tool). And for all the above, knowing "why" indeed you decided as you did, amid options…

EXAMPLES. Five good comments on **"rules vs. tools"** in the complex skill of **writing**. For Schoolwriting, for writing elsewhere. And for teaching writing. *Piitfalls to avoid, potentials to aim for…*

---

(1) The power of the **Variables-Variation** approach.   SEE Kit at the end of MP Preview, **App. #6**

I'd say that **"teaching writing"** too often suffers from provincial half-true rules. Better might be continua of A to Z possibilities and the pros and cons of each position depending on purpose.

"Different tasks and situations demand flexible choices, adjustments!" [A paper for English class… An on-the-job letter, memo, report… A scientific report… A letter-to-the-editor… A pamphlet or brochure… A creative family memoir… a feature-article for a popular magazine… the minutes of a meeting… a recipe for cooking… a technical instruction-manual… What of "tone, length, specificity," etc., in each genre?

Sentence Length: "keep short, longs can get run-on" NO "make long, shorts are too choppy"
Tone: "keep impersonal, don't use pronoun I" NO "put your self on the page"
Length: "one page limit, tops" NO "write at least 1,500 words on..."
Visuals: "don't use any pictures charts diagrams" NO "tables graphs etc. can help"
Thesis-Revelation: "announce your point at the start" NO "gradually reveal, build up to, your idea"
Stance: "write to discover, express yourself" NO "write to reach and serve a specific reader-audience"

I asked students: in what skill or work or hobby etc. of yours, do Rules exist, but also Tools?....

(2) EXAMPLE. In a well-written paragraph itself (I like the parallelism, specifics, categorization), A WRITING TEACHER shows how his students arthritically **"rule-monger."** They went for the *Letter* and ignored the *Spirit*; did not see the *Function* behind/beyond the *Form*; fell for *Correct* instead of pursuing *Effective*...

Student comments on my papers often seemed like handbook generalizations unskillfully applied.

--Thus, the students, or some of them, said *my use of contractions was inappropriate.* (But I wanted conversational tone.)

--They warned me against *repeating "I" so often.* (But this was autobiographical; would passive voice verbs have been better?)

--They complained about some *very long sentences.* (But I was describing terrain and trying to suggest how spaces and objects adjoin and connect in long vistas.)

--They admonished me against *rambling.* (But I wanted to sound like an old man reminiscing.)

--They gleefully schooled me for a *shift in point of view.* (But I thought I had the old man describing a childhood experience vividly enough to become the child again.)

--They groused about *inconsistencies in style* such as big words popping up in simple stories. (But that old man was a career English professor and word-lover.) [-- FROM TE2YC]

By the way, good use of multiple vivid varied effective specifics, of mindless rule-applications, contrasted with real intent.

(3) EXAMPLE. A TEACHER shows how different writing arenas demand unspoken changes. Especially the transition from School-writing (across disciplines), to Vocational venues:

1. Length: in school, "at least 500 words"; outside, "one-page minimum" or the like.
2. Tone: in school, often formal-impersonal; outside, usually a person on the page.
3. Structure: in school, sometimes lead up to the point; outside, announce the conclusion first.
4. Audience: in school, a vacuum—the professor is the reader; outside, rhetorical tuning.
5. Graphics: in school, just prose on the page; outside, often charts-tables-diagrams, etc.

So what's so hot about this roster? Surely once they're out there on the job, graduates will "pick up" on what to do differently...	*You hope and wish,* and so did I. But **"pattern recognition and technique-altering in new situations"** is a *difficult thinking*-task, it doesn't happen automatically. (Not when I started doing journalism...)

(4) ROSTER. This Reads the Situation to uncover the tacit code, the folk-wisdom, of "Schoolwriting."

1. Generally avoid the personal except in certain English courses.
2. If there is a choice between being abstract and being concrete, be concrete.
3. Use a propositional rather than an oppositional structure.
4. Avoid metaphors and figurative language.
5. Generally avoid using graphic signals such as underlining, subheads...except in science and mathematics.
6. Focus on the content rather than on making the reader feel comfortable.
7. Select a single aspect of your subject. Also, have a thesis and announce it as early as possible.
8. Make sure the surface appearance of the text is attractive. Check spelling, punctuation, and grammar.
9. Use complex or embedded sentences.
10. Avoid humor. [-- ALLAN PURVES]

.....a classic case of the Provincial Position, "one way or choice only and that prescriptive in a vacuum," instead of **Variables-Variation**: name the issue here ("sentence length"), show all options A to Z, pros and cons, plus also the **contextual** approach, a thinking skill in itself. "What range of variation is needed or preferred (or forbidden) in which situations: diaries, letters to the editor, academic writing, brochures, etc.?"...

(5) PERSONAL TESTIMONY. <u>When I myself began to write</u> not just academic articles and research [520-page doctoral dissertation], but <u>popular magazine articles</u> [130 pieces in 12 outlets], I had to *wrench and twist my Germanic style* toward one more *brief, personal, specific, and flowing*. <u>It was arduous</u>.

--[CHARLES MASON, then the editor of <u>Sail</u> magazine, helpfully told me: "You spend too much time circling around your point, which is to tell beginning sailors how to sense changing wind velocity and direction"...]

--I had to post notes above my desk to remind me: Structure, Tone, Specifics, Audience etc. I wish I had then, the A-to-Z checklists I did develop later.

---

(6) COURSE-RESEARCH.   <u>My own student's failure</u>—and <u>a better student succeeds in the issue</u>..

--[A] On the **LEFT**-hand side is testimony of one of <u>my students</u> from English 101. I would say that *this tested **me***
the teacher of thinking, and that **I *failed*** to bring him up to competence...

--[B] On the **RIGHT**-hand side, a comment from <u>a student at my alma mater</u>, a liberal-arts college. I'd say he
succeeded, is airborne, or can Hit The Ground Running...

[A] We are told to use the form of the five-paragraph theme but to expand it as needed. But how and when is it right to do so? I feel I am supposed to use it to be correct, but it doesn't always feel right. And when should I depart from the form totally, if ever? And also I don't know when to use more specifics and fewer. I have no confidence in knowing how to make the decisions you said we should learn to make. Who is to say? [-- A FRESHMAN STUDENT, my Eng. 101, Univ. of Wis.-Whitewater, paraphrased]	[B] Whether in liberal inquiry, harmony in music (is jazz rule-free or different?), and modern democracy, "the uncritical acceptance of any set of rules, whether of musical harmony, liberal inquiry, or modern democracy, risks leading to a numb society incapable of change, progress, expression. We must ask where rules come from, over what situations they apply, are they ethical and relevant or merely codified practices or customs, or inherent in nature." [-- STUDENT, DOUG SCHNEIDER, of Lawrence Univ. of Wis.] [... and to think that a *mere undergraduate **student***, could write the above *mature, competent* position-statement! ***Astonishing***...]
...Don't be too hard on yourself as a teacher. The existing paradigm trains students for 12 years to follow orders, at least mainly!...	...*at least I tried*. Some teachers teach fixed forms," procedural mimicry," and *never seem to realize at all* that the students know them, but not why and when to use vs. to vary. [Nor did I, until assigning "that last theme to be done all on your own"—and, Crash...] It's like "here's the pottery shop, and only one mold to use for a bowl or vase..."

|#+#|+#|+|#+#+|#+#+#+#||+|+#++|#|+#||+|++|#+#++|+|||+#++|+#+#|+|#+|+|#|+#||+||#+|+|+#|+#|+#|#+|+|#+||+|#+|#+|+#|+|#||

ISSUE #2.3. Does the learning distinguish between "<u>Domain-Specific</u>" and "<u>General-Generic</u>" Thinking? And move toward the latter?

This is an issue. Some educators have written about it. I find little true clarification...
Thinking skills can be "domain-specific," limited to a particular discipline... or general-generic, applicable perhaps to other disciplines, surely to larger issues in life-arenas.

WHAT THINKING SKILLS USED HERE? IN DISCUSSING THIS ISSUE; **(1)** Comparison-contrast... **(2)** Also our own **"CCC==DDD"** or "should we emphasize the Connections/Correlations or more the Distinctions/Differences?" ... Plus **(3)** the meta-dualistic ploy of moving from "either/or, "is it A or is it Z," toward the **"to-what-extent"**: "for any particular instance, is it *more toward* A, or *more toward* Z?"...

First, consider the differences, the contrasts.

Mathematics has different criteria for good reasons from other fields, because it <u>accepts only deductive</u> proof, unlike most fields which do not even seek it for a conclusion.
In the *social sciences*, <u>statistical significance</u> is important, but in many branches of *physics* it is largely ignored.
In the *arts*, <u>subjectivity</u> is acceptable and often welcomed, whereas in the sciences it is usually shunned.
[-- ROBERT ENNIS]

But also, consider whether SPECIFIC discipline skills, can RISE UP to become GENERAL-generic skills?

EXAMPLES: [1.] "The law," also [2.] my examples of **Dualism**…and of [3.] "essay-writing" conceptualized…

[1.] STATEMENT. Does studying the law, comprise both specific thinking skills but which also easily-enough could blend into general good thinking skills for other fields?

"Although MUDD suggests that there is little consensus in the profession about the meaning of 'thinking like a lawyer,' he was able to delineate thinking processes to be learned in first-year courses. These include, in addition to briefing cases, the ability to analyze facts and appreciate the shifting legal results produced by factual nuances (evaluation), to separate a problem into its component parts (analysis), to assemble facts into a meaningful whole (synthesis), and to find the features in a problem situation relevant to its resolution (description and selection). MUDD argues that thinking like a lawyer can be seen within a more general framework of thinking clearly and precisely, as in any field."
[-- JANET DONALD, Learning to Think: Disciplinary Perspectives, P. 185]

…marvelously connecting the specific and generic. But of course do the lawyers know **Explicitly** what they've learned? Recall DR. HAYES saying that psychology majors know much about perception skills, but don't know how well they really do know such. And DR. OMOHUNDRO spelled out **explicitly** skills learned in anthropology—for once…

[2.] PERSONAL RESEARCH. I wondered whether disciplines have some common thinking styles.

I then noted a similarity in different fields' thinking…

--Psychology studies a sort of *dualism*: defense mechanisms, what we say vs. what's really there, what the motivation is underneath, or the avoidance of same… [= Projection, Transference, Reaction Formation, Intellectualization, Sublimation…]

--Sociology studies *dualism*: its concept of ideal-normative vs. real-behavioral culture [=what people say and believe they do, vs. what actually is believed and done], also HOWARD BECKER'S concept of the "latent vs. manifest functions" of a social action [= what was intended and recognized, vs. what actually happened, desired and perceived or not! Missionaries' giving African tribes clothing intended modesty, but increased disease…] …

--Literature studies dualism: subject-matter vs. theme [=a poem is about an automobile simply, or it is about an automobile and also freedom/loss/people/etc.] , also ironies: verbal, dramatic, etc. [=saying one thing and meaning another: Yes, he's a splendid fellow, for sure]…

….. Do all these DOMAIN-SPECIFIC dualisms, lead Upward to a GENERAL-GENERIC thinking skill? A sort of "dualistic perspective"? "Different forms in Letter or concrete surface *appearance,* but arising to a common concept in Spirit?" And then the skill to be applied to issues beyond even psychology, sociology, literature—perhaps to engineering, finance, life-goals (my examples here are not good, but…) [- B.K.BECK]

[3.] IN-CLASS RESEARCH. The "Expository Essay"—and, 'Life'?…" A sort of bravura attempt, but productive.

I tried to **Elevate** humble principles of composition, to a general-generic altitude and then to **Export** their spirit out afar to actual real-life situations having *nothing to do* with writing skills. To sportively "push the envelope" of "applying to other situations, the skills learned in English studies, " as the English Department's statement of goals declared…

Below, some of the skills in my "15-C" model	Some of the applications my students could produce as

of advanced essay-writing, Expository Elucidation of thesis-points-discussion:	possible in real life far from writing (dutifully, when I "asked" them to…):
1. **Conceptualizing**, or thinking facts through to arrive at ideas, thesis.	1. Thoroughly thinking through a puzzling <u>local social conflict</u> to see the *issues behind* the data.
2. **Con-Vergent**, or do all points support the unified thesis? (And 13. "Crisp" brief-concise!)	2. To *focus* better, one's <u>speech</u> tonight… (And 13. Less is More, KISS or Keep It Simple Stupid!)
3. **Categorization**: divide into subpart components as much as advisable.	3. We have KEITH'S example of his organizing his points 1-2-3 in <u>everyday conversations</u>…
6. **Calibration**: scale and proportion: emphasize major points, downplay minors.	6. Which parts of a <u>recreational project</u> are more important, which less vital?
9. **Con-Sequent.** What structure order sequence arrangement for the several points?	9. In planning <u>a project at work</u>, should I re-think the order in which I schedule elements?
BUT you are "pushing" more than the Envelope here! You are riding your Hobbyhorse of *Thinking Above All Else*! You hijack content! Whoever heard of *writing rules* becoming *Philosophies of Life*?…..	…I grant you that it *is* unusual to **Elevate** a specific skill to its general perspective, and also to **Export** same to supposedly-*unrelated* areas. Unusual, infrequent, hence a major change. [Might that cause *some* people to feel—well, *uneasy* here?...]

SUGGESTED RULE OF THUMB OR GUIDELINE. Consider whether the domain-specific skills are also general-generic… If so, "elevate" them to *explicit* status… And consider "exporting" them to subject-matter even removed from the course issues, in arenas of life…

|#+#|+#|+|#+#+|#+#+#+#||+|+#++|#|+#+||+|+#|+|++|#+#++|+|||+#++|+#+#|+|#+|+|+|#|+#|+||+|#+|+|+#|+#|+#|#+|+|#+|+|+#|#+|+#|+|#||

(3) APPLICATION. Will the skill be "Exported"; Transferred to new situation, applied there?

KEY QUOTATION: "The test of understanding involves neither repetition of information learned, nor performance of practices mastered. Rather, it involves the appropriate application of concepts and principles to questions or problems that are newly-posed." [--JOHN GARDNER, 1991]

ISSUE #3.1. What about <u>variables concerning TRANSFER?</u>

(1) Transfer <u>varies in "length."</u> There would be short-distance transfer only to material or arenas which are <u>Near, Familiar, Related, Old</u> (though not identical with the home material) == and also to <u>Far Foreign New</u> areas (in a different church altogether?). Foreign both from the home-base subject-matter, and even perhaps from the learner's experience and expertise? The latter tests true Liberal or General Education skills…..

(2) Transfer <u>does not occur automatically,</u> usually has to be taught. And yes, "Explicitly" we presume. (Not to teach explicitly for transfer, may be a subtle Pitfall of Unawareness let alone Sin of Omission…)

(3) A Possible Prevalent Pitfall? **"Pseudo Bogus Phoney Non-Transfer"** This is my rather-impolite label for when teachers give an assignment and *believe* (or *assume*, or *neglect to consider whether*) that it is teaching thinking, use, transfer, creativity, when it is really simply testing information mastered.

EXAMPLE. "Discuss <u>nature and culture in the works of American writers Dickinson, Emerson, Whitman.</u>" And myriad others. [**Recall:** Greek culture, causes of <u>World War I, electoral system</u>…]

EXAMPLES. Three assignments on "cause-effect." One is ridiculously over-explained (the answers given in the question!) – next is probable simple Recall (the answers to be remembered from the course) == and the last one seeking true Transfer (answers generated by the student, focused but flexible).

1. "Causes of the first World War. First, explain the indirect causes (imperialism, nationalism) which facilitated the appearance of European networks of alliances. Briefly, describe these networks. Next, tell how the crisis at Sarajevo was directly responsible for the First World War."
[-- EXAM IN THE FRENCH NATIONAL SCHOOL SYSTEM; QUOTED BY A. SHANKER, HEAD OF THE AFT]

2. "What was the effect of World War I on Europe?" [Expected answer: the war transformed Europe mentally, politically, and economically"]   [--UNIV. OF WIS. AT WHITEWATER]

3. "Attempt to analyze competently the causes and effects of an issue. Of course, draw upon the menu of cause-effect models we learned in our ToolKit on the subject. And of course practice non-Formulaic thinking: select only those which are relevant... Then, Articulate: analyze what you did and why, and how yourself and others might critique it. (Did you Hit The Ground Running in terms of ultimate reasonable preparedness?)"

SUBJECT-ISSUES: *terrorism... crime... the fall of Rome... popularity of exercise recently... (etc.)*

C-E TOOLS: Linear vs. network....   One or more causes, effects....   As few as possible vs. overdetermined.....   Necessary and sufficient causes.... Aristotle's Four..... Enabling, initiating, precipitating..... Threshhold or tipping-point or "lily-pond" and "butterfly" models..... Manifest, and latent, causes, and effects....

.....a progression from the simplistic recital, toward autonomous application of abstractions...

|#+#|+#|+|#+#+|#+#+#+#||+|+#++|#|+#||+|+#|+|++|#+#+|+|||+#++|+#+#|+|#+|+|#|+#||+|#+|+|+#|+#|+#|#+|+|#+|+|#+|#+|+#|+|#||

(4) "AUTONOMY" Did the learner...
(A) Make some decisions? (B) Move to independent doing?

ISSUE # 4.1. In an assignment, "decisions, decisions—who makes which and how many?" How many by the *teacher/ course*? How many by *student-learner*?

--The following proceeds from Tight "boot-camp" guidance == toward Loose "open-field" or rather self-structured work.
--Some teachers will (1) disagree. They might start from pure open-ended "chaos" at first and work toward clarification... They might have found that, once given Rules and Systems, students will then never let them go, especially unmotivated students...
--Other teachers will either (2) not confront the matter at all really, or will
--(3) *assume* that students are gradually attaining autonomy.
   (This may be a pitfall; RECALL my own experience with "That Last Theme of Five, " in which I suddenly
   pulled the scaffolding and told students to "do it on their own now." And discovered that they could not, were
   paralyzed. It turned out that I had taught them—to Follow Orders, it seemed...)

[In any case, different **learning-styles** can be used, just so that Thinking and Doing, acting and reflecting, do alternate. See V-I #14, below here in the D- Machine...]

First, DURING the course, actual instructions: "Decisions, Decisions"
To what extent was autonomy fostered earlier?

No. Teacher tells do this 1-2-3 this way. (Formulaic rules.)	**Somewhat:** "Select any 3 items from this 6-item roster."	**More:** "Use course materials to help you."	**Near-Total:** "Write a paper on your own now. But make	**Total:** "To show what you learned in this course, *design*

			it good."	*your own*
(Recall the "Rose for Emily" assignment—all decisions made by Teacher, about message, about method…)	Balancing direction overall, flexibility within.	Pointing more generally to resources as Tools…	[In a writing or composition course]	*assignment and do it.*" "Surely unfair and confusing"—but not if Autonomy was taught…

Second, AFTER the course, was End-Goal reached of "Hitting The Ground Running"

Does learner possess *ultimate expectable readiness*, **autonomy** of knowing what to do on one's own?

Paralyzed outside of class	Still formulaic	Some rigidity, some flexibility	More autonomy	Hits ground running autonomous able agile etc.

TOUCHSTONE. BLOOM'S Taxonomy provides the *classic* clarification of this issue:

"A problem in the . . . [Interpretation] category requires the student to know an abstraction well enough so that he can correctly demonstrate its use *when specifically asked to do so.* 'Application,' however, requires a step beyond this. Given a problem *new* to the student, he will apply the appropriate abstraction *without having to be prompted as to which abstraction is correct or without having to be shown how to use it in that situation.*"
[--BENJAMIN BLOOM ET AL., TAXONOMY OF EDUCATIONAL OBJECTIVES, 1956, P. 120]

…written way back in 1956 (complete with masculine pronoun…). "We all know this…" And yet, still shortchanged—recall the differences between **"Knowing, vs. *really* Knowing"**…

TOUCHSTONE. Veteran writing teacher DONALD MURRAY *radically* urges student decision-making.

Our students need to discover, before graduation, that freedom is the greatest tyrant of all. Too often the composition teacher not only denies his students freedom, he even goes further and performs the key writing tasks for his students. He gives an assignment; he lists sources; he dictates the form; and, by irresponsibly conscientious correcting, he actually revises his students' papers. Is it not surprising that the student does not learn to write when the teacher, with destructive virtue, has done most of his student's writing?

I know you'll say this truly **ennobles** the classroom because it can truly empower the students (even while mightily alarming them at first, irritating them later on…) But *what were your colleagues' responses* when you quoted MURRAY to them at that conference?	Well… (1) DALE said: "too advanced for freshmen, they can do this in later classes" [I said: *They can start to try, right now.*] (2) ED said: "whoa, don't you have to correct their grammar?" [I said: *I mark their errors in green ink, they find them and correct.*] And (3) GENEVA said, rather acerbic-accusatory: "But <u>no</u>, students <u>Need</u> Structure!" [I didn't reply that *what students truly need,* is to be shown the very *concept* of structure, the multiple *options*, and thus how to create it themselves, #4**Autonomously** in real-world-life. Not to be given the Five-Paragraph Theme as "The Only Pottery Mold in the Studio"…]

EXAMPLE. A somewhat more sober version of MURRAY in re autonomy in learning—yet equally usefully uncompromising! An EDUCATOR names some <u>fallacies in teaching thinking</u>.

Fallacy #8 is **"The job of a course in thinking is to teach thinking."**

This sounds plausible, but it is fallacious. If students learn to think, it is not because we taught them ultimately. "<u>In a very real sense, they must teach themselves,</u> and all teachers can do is to provide every possible means to enable this self-instruction to take place." <u>Nothing is more pathetic than a teacher over-teaching.</u> Saying what the problem is, how to pose it, the way (rarely ways) to solve it, and then letting the student—solve the problem, or complete the assignment "only in the most trivial and impoverished ways. The teacher has done the most important thinking for the student and has left the student with only the most routine aspects of problem solving to complete. The teacher

will probably be surprised later, when the skill that was supposedly learned does not transfer to other situations.
[-- ROBERT STERNBERG]

| I see the **ennobling** of education possible in this self-learning approach. **BUT** how do you get the student to do it? How did you do it, in your 23 years teaching college? | I largely did **NOT**, for too long, until later on.
--The teacher-barriers were (1) my not fully comprehending "teaching thinking" as I finally did... And (2) striking the difficult balance between direction short of prescription; guidance short of imposition—as STERNBERG so vividly notes...
--The two student-barriers seem to be (2) eternal ur-sloth or terminal **non-motivation** (in Freshman English anyhow), but also first (1) **culture-conflict or paradigm-shift bruises**. After learning the new approach of acquiring tools on your own, *some students go for it, many others let it go*. But clearly a teacher's task is to explain to students how it's a new culture now. Irony—I did not comprehend the paradigm enough to conceptually clarify it. |

PERSONAL ANECDOTE.   The teacher "helps" the student...

Entering my classroom early, I observed last hour's teacher still conferring with a student about her paper's revision. On and on the teacher went about how and what to change and how to do it. "Alter this, substitute that, emphasize this, rearrange the other thing." And near the end the teacher said "And I think **we agreed** that..." *But the student had been standing there taciturn all along.* Was anything being taught there other than how to follow orders, or instructions? [-- PERSONAL ANECDOTE]

...perhaps "with help (or friends) like *this*"... [makes me think of "training wheels welded on"...]

MINI-GALLERY. EXAMPLES.   What varieties are possible in re guidance vs. autonomy in teaching, especially in assignment-design and in feedback to students? What balances in "Decisions, Decisions"?

EXAMPLE #1.   *RECOLLECT:* The English 101 assignment regarding FAULKNER'S short story. The issue of **"Decisions, Decisions"** may illuminate that assignment which in turn illustrates the issue.

| "The narrators of Faulkner's 'A Rose for Emily' and Gilman's 'The Yellow Wallpaper' are both women who go mad. They go mad in part as a result of the way women in their respective societies are treated. Demonstrate the ways in which their being women affected their lives and led to their madness."

[All decisions made by the teacher...] | (1) [Lower Level of C.T.A.:]
"Feminism, Marxism, Freudianism, New Criticism, and Reader-Response were major ways-of-reading we practiced this semester. Take the three stories assigned but never discussed in class, and show what you can do in re the skill of **"Lensmanship"** or Plural Perspectives in reading literature. Discuss: (1) Which approaches seem better, and less productive, for which stories and why? | (2) [*Way*-Higher Level of C.T.A.—*yet not the highest theoretically possible!* A two-parter, thus:]
(I) "Using three of the six stories assigned but never discussed in class, show what you've learned this semester.
(II) Select a topic-question-problem-issue in '*real life,*' far removed from '*reading literature.*' Can you confront *it* more competently after this course? If so, how—do it! If not, and/or if problems—explore this, and create conclusions about *education, learning, preparation for life, thinking*, etc." |

EXAMPLE #2.   Did DR. LAURENT'S Silence, Shortchange or Stimulate?

In his introductory economics class at my school, DR. JEROME LAURENT, on every quiz or exam, and from the course's start, assigns a problem-issue which is "messy, obscure, ambiguous, open-ended, complex." He gives them NO techniques or instructions as to how to confront it. (And the issue has NOT been discussed earlier in the class.) Dr. Laurent does this repeatedly throughout the semester. Students enter class apprehensive—they've heard he does this. But during the semester, the students become gradually more conversant with, confident about, confronting such issues.   [-- PERSONAL COMMUNICATION FROM COLLEAGUE]

My personal **strong feeling** for **explicit tools**, objects to this. However, I fairmindedly recognize it as an alternative—

indeed as a basic element in any case! And it surely supports DON MURRAY'S challenge that we do too much for the students. I would only hope that some feedback was given on how to respond to the issue after the exam was returned. But even then...

EXAMPLE #3. DR. ROSENBERG'S "Helpful Hints"... Slack, or Subtle?

At my alma mater, Lawrence University of Wisconsin—a select small private liberal-arts school—DR. ROBERT ROSENBERG taught chemistry. Upon his retirement, the alumni magazine recognized his teaching. Dr. ROSENBERG emphasized "interaction" with the students. "Rather than give formal lectures, I try to entice questions with my contributions to get the students to participate." ASHLEY HAASE, former student, said "It's not an easy trick to get students to learn to think," but ROSENBERG was excellent at this. "He teaches you to *find the answers for yourself*, which is exactly what we all have to do." Revisiting Lawrence, HAASE observed ROSENBERG "with a confused-looking student in front of him. He wanted the answer to a problem. BOB *gave him a few hints and told him to think about it some more, then come back*." ROSENBERG thus sought to help students "anticipate problems and to creatively find solutions."

Well, this seems good. Nudge students to find the "arena of possibilities" on their own, the only way truly to learn…	A complex issue. Is it near-**"100% impossible-impracticable"** in large public schools? (ANECDOTE. I visited a public high school class. I saw a desperate didacticism. Discussing the upcoming exam, the teacher virtually read off the textbook-subjects which would be covered, and gave the students the "exam" in advance.) Was it only a casual hint, or a superbly-tailormade catalyst focused to guide but not to reveal, Dr. R. knowing each student? Fascinating issue here.

|#+#|+#|+|#+#+|#+#+#+#||+|+#++|#|+#+||+|+#+|+++|#+#++|+|||+#++|+#+#|+|#+|+|+|#|+#|+||+|#+|+|+#|+#|+#+|#+|+#+||+|#+|#+|+#|+|#||

(5) ["ARTICULATION"]: Is learner *aware* of own thinking process, and its result—and can *assess* it also?

ISSUE #5. Can learner **explain** what s/he did & why? And **evaluate** the choices?

<u>This point is complex.</u> Studies show that many thinkers can perform operations but not explain explicitly what and how they did. For grading purposes, however, I stress that ability. Annotating one's paper is a part of writing each paper. What did I do, how, why, and how well? This is the **Consciousness** or "reflexive meta-cognitive self-awareness" element of **Essential** thinking.

A Personal Stand: I cheer student self-awareness, it is truly empowering, and I boo (or sigh at) helplessness such as "Gee I just don't know what I did," etc. or the facile "Punctuation could have used some work and the flow was not good." Or "couldn't the teacher see what I did?" Or, "Well, it got its point across." Or, "It needed more examples [because I know the teacher Likes Examples, so why didn't I put them in, oh well...] These approach the "Blow-Off Statements" I especially dislike—inarticulate, if not intentionally-evasive...

EXAMPLE. Minimal "thinking" content—and how my advanced students fell short.

I asked an advanced class ("Stylistics," English 400) of motivated juniors and seniors, "What is your typical recurrent personal thinking style?" But, this question *nonplussed* these able, serious upperclasspersons... In 1,500 class hours needed for a B.A. degree, apparently not 60 minutes' attention to "How do you think?"

But some courses already do seek meta-cognition. Two admirable examples:

EXAMPLE #1. "Young Adult Reflection."

77

A colleague, MARY PINKERTON., taught a course in YA literature. Her exam question (offered at a seminar I gave on teaching thinking):

"Using the criteria we have evolved thus far in class, evaluate at least two of the novels we have read. Be specific about the literary and developmental criteria you are using. Indicate what you see as the appropriate level of this book and the way in which you have reached your decision."

You'll likely like this one?...	**YES**, it seems deftly balanced in re **Decisions, Decisions**... (that is, *assuming* the novels had <u>not</u> already been class-discussed on this point, which risks Sham Transfer). The teacher donates the Criteria, but the student applies them. I would also have asked the student to say whether their decision was secure and good, or doubtful. This more-thorough **self-evaluation** is illustrated in the next example.....

EXAMPLE #2. Solving the problem was only half of the assignment!...

"In seventh grade pre-algebra, my daughter's math grade depended, in part, on the cover design for her Problem of the Week write-up. Solving the problem wasn't enough. Solving it *and explaining how you solved it and why you approached it that particular way and how else you might have solved it and why you think you're right and how you felt about the problem...* <u>All that wasn't enough.</u> It had to look pretty to get a top grade....
[-- JOANNE JACOBS, in THE SUBSTANCE OF STYLE]

BUT what's wrong with *this*? Look at all the thinking skills that were required. What's wrong with teaching multiple, plural skills in any given subject? (Here, weaving in visual-aesthetic communication along with math?)	**WHOA**. Good point, but ***look at <u>the thinking-skills richness</u>*** in this supposed assignment—*if all this was also indeed required.* **--[1] Articulation**: reflexive self-awareness of one's approaches and methods? (I could add *"where you know or feel that you are or might be wrong not right also..."*) --Also, [2] **complexity beyond rote formula**: multiple-plural alternate optional choices, and judgment-calls perhaps. --Even [3] **personal-emotional** aspects: how you felt beyond touchie-feelie. And my Personal Point: I wager that <u>not ten per cent of classes</u> offer-and-require of students that they practice such definable true thinking skills of **Articulation**... (How many education-major students reading this description above, would automatically appreciate the important qualities mentioned in it all too frequently absent in education?)

EXAMPLE. A definition of critical thinking, which *really* emphasizes reflexive self-awareness...

Critical thinking is defined as "thought evaluating thought...the articulated judgment of an intellectual product arrived at on the basis of plus-minus considerations of the product in terms of appropriate standards for criteria."
[-- JOHNSON]

If you translate this out of the Academic-ese, to POEP or **Plain Old English Please**, *it works.* "<u>You got your intellectual product or piece of thinking responding to something, and you judge the product, your own thinking.</u>"

Plus, did you exhibit **command** (cover all bases, miss no chances, make no blunders...?)

Still, do students always fully know what they have been learning?

STATEMENT. Psychology thinking skills as internalized, but *not yet realized*, by the student.

Psychological skills [not just literacies, but also interpersonal awareness, multiple perspectives, ability to see patterns and principles in situations] have a tendency to become very deeply internalized, so that they often *feel* just like "common sense." Moreover, the style of thinking one acquires on a psychology degree is one which feels *intuitively* obvious— so much so that people who have it are often *unaware* of what they have acquired. Psychology graduates have <u>distinctive ways of looking at social and interpersonal problems, which make them valuable in just about any job which involves dealing with people.</u> Yet they often believe that they do not see anything more than other people, and when they venture into the outside world <u>they are often surprised at how other people appear to overlook the obvious.</u>   [-- NICKI HAYES]

MINI-TOOL-KIT. The whole issue of **"Knowing vs. Knowing"** or kinds and degrees of knowing, is richly subdivided into components. ["I" BRIEF View, for "II" FULL, **SEE** Appendix, Prior Basics]

(1) <u>Declarative, procedural, conditional</u> knowledge: knowing *about*, *how* to do, *when* to use.

(2) <u>Four Stages</u>: --**"Known Known"** (you know it)... --**"Known Unknown"** (you know you don't know—medical student "wow I screwed up there"!)... --**"Unknown Known"** (as in psychology example above: you know more than you know you know)... --**"Unknown Unknown"** One may not even be aware that an area exists about which one does not know (a strict religionist cannot *conceive* of "non-Biblical history"—*whaat?*,,,). Or anyhow one may know area but be unaware they missed something within it—medical student "well I guess I did fine on that ...")

(3) <u>Degrees of social knowledge</u>. "Oh *everyone* knows that," or "*relatively fewer* people also know," down to "*only the expert specialist insiders* etc. know."
--SAFER SEX TECHNOLOGY: pitfalls with some condom materials and also lubricants; "nonoxynol-9" *is* desirable...
--WATER PURIFICATION chemicals: chlorine *but* often filters are inadequate *and* sometimes iodine not chlorine; why?...
--HEALTH: red wine against heart disease *but also* green tea against lung cancer...
--SUNBLOCKS & SUNSCREENS: screen out UVA rays *but also* UVB...   --TEACHING THINKING: {*aha*}.....

(4) Knowledge and <u>the **End-Goal of education**</u>: "ultimate expectable readiness." You know it well enough that (A) it *automatically intuitively arises* to help you when you need it and (B) in *"far foreign"* circumstances of use where many others might not see it applies and is needed!

(5) <u>Fuller Emotional **Knowledge**</u> and <u>Connection With Total Self</u>. (Approaches "wisdom"...)

.... embryonic version of this keystone concept...

STATEMENT. RICHARD PAUL notes that truly knowing, involves awareness thus:

[Adequate assessment is not simply answering questions correctly, providing definitions, and applying formulae while taking tests. Students may succeed but lack understanding. Proof of knowing is found when students can "explain in their own words, with examples, with examples, the meaning and significance of the knowledge, why it is so, and to *spontaneously* recall and use it when relevant."]   [-- RICHARD PAUL, "CRITICAL THINKING IN NORTH AMERICA"]

Again, **"Knowing, vs. *really* Knowing."**

AN OBJECTION. An expert friend warns ME of a pitfall in my own mania for explicit explication...

Dr. HADLEY, a friend—and a superb psychoanalyst and general brain-mind expert—strongly cautions me against a mania for articulation. "Many people can intuitively achieve high performances, yet cannot trace explicitly how they did it. Maybe you better allow this and not say learners don't know how..."

...I allow this—*except in my class.* See, for course-accountability, I tell the student, "You will <u>not</u> claim simply that in your paper, you "improved the flow" and "related better to the reader," etc. You <u>will</u> state exactly what you did, how, why, whether appropriate, and how well. This is because **articulation** or Consciousness of one's own thinking is one of the ten traits we establish for true, **Essential**, Thinking..." Plus, some things are to be known by-the-book, others more flexibly.

[*SEE below*, "In Vitro By-The-Book Perfect, vs. In Vivo Adapted for the Context" a component in Quality...]

|#+#|+#|+|#+#+|#+#+#+#||+|+#++|#|+#||+|+#|+||++#+|+#++|||++#++|+#+#|+#+|+|#|+#|+||+|#+|+|+#||#+|+||+|#+|+||+|#+|#+|+#|+#+#|+|#+||+|#+#+|#|+|#||

(6) Actual ABILITY, ACHIEVEMENT ... Did learner *acquire* skill?
(A) *How* is success in thinking <u>defined</u>? (B) *How* is it <u>measured</u>?
(C) ...and *was* it measured?

ISSUE #6A. How can one "define" success in learning thinking?

SUGGESTION. Central the ability to <u>autonomously</u> <u>apply</u> <u>abstractions</u> (ably to arduous material after school). We follow up with the **End-Goal of "Hitting The Ground Running"** or "ultimate expectable readiness" to **think things through** thus.

A PERSONAL RESPONSE. I liked focusing the course to a lean economical point, thus: <u>"Any portion of any class—</u> <u>is it directly fortifying the learner to "Hit The Ground Running"</u> later on in dealing with real-world complexities? *If not, why not, and what is it doing in the course*, and why are we not focusing toward such "solo-flight" ability to "grow corn on one's own." What with "course requirements," this arrowing is hard to do sometimes!

|#+#|+#|+|#+#+|#+#+#+#||+|#++|#|+#|+|+#|+|++|#+#+|+|||+#++|+#+#|+|#+|+|#|+#|+||+|#+|+|+#|+#|+#+|#+|+#||+|#+|#+|+#|+|#||

ISSUE #6.B. How do we actually *measure* the result?

NO: I object. You *can't* measure now, what students will do later on, on their own, in unknown situations!	But we can (1) <u>Test for transfer</u>. Give students a "validly-vague" assignment: self-structured. Or more directive, right on up to "How can you better confront this issue X having been in this course?" (2) Also as an admittedly-lesser measure, <u>test via the "In Vitro By-The-Book Perfect"</u> approach, see below…

ISSUE #6.C. How much *do* teachers test for true mastery—or not?

EXAMPLES: MINI-GALLERY. A quartet of examples suggesting a shortfalling here…

RECOLLECT: **Two earlier examples:**
- -- In the math class, students <u>worked calculus, but could not transfer skills</u> to problems on their own.
- -- In the elementary education class, <u>students could not apply the Piaget viewpoint</u> (which they had studied in psychology) to a problem assigned, *even when asked explicitly* to do so.

EXAMPLE #3. Is it difficult to sense how students really think? Does this teacher know?

A history teacher believes in a "student-centered" approach and has "truly embraced the idea of myself as a facilitator. I don't give midterms. I don't give finals. Instead, my students spend four months with me working on *becoming better thinkers*. Sure, participation-based classes skew the bell curve, but I have found that student interest and *retention of the material* soar along with their grades." [-- KELLY MCMICHAEL, in CHE]

BUT surely something rubbed off in this post-lecture pedagogy of dynamic interpersonal interaction. So many students report they learned to think better in active learning…	Undoubtedly true somewhat. **BUT** first, the issue of measurement. [#6B **Achievement**.] To what extent *did* they learn to think better? Seems only assumed or hoped for or predicted—instead of planned-for and monitored… (Oh, and incidentally look what comes in at the end—*"retention of the material."* Or, what to Know [#1 Goal])

EXAMPLE #4. A teacher of communication has students develop critical thinking skills through analyzing media: newpapers, TV news, films, speeches, comedies.

Students balked when asked to critique their own favorites, so the teacher resorted to showing her own favorites, "a little hope, a little beauty." Students felt freer to respond. The teacher ends:
"*If I'm lucky*, my students will apply their critical skills to their own favorites. In any case, I'm feeling a lot less cranky." [-- MARY S. ALEXANDER, IN CHE] [italics added]

Didn't the teacher test for it? Of course it may be *realistically impossible given time-constraints*. "100% teaching thinking is Utopian or anyhow improbable and impracticable." Still, transfer *was not* tested.

MINI-TEXTBOOK: The ploy of **"In Vitro versus In Vivo"** can measure deftly...

I found success in asking students to demonstrate advanced writing skills *both* "textbook-perfect" (truly formulaic, rules or 1-2-3 tactical moves) *as well as* applied to some writing situation where Flexibility was required: heuristics, tools, strategies "whether or not and how and why depending on the context-variables—purpose, audience, arena, etc.

I called it **"In Vitro"** as in under glass in the laboratory, as against **"In Vivo"** or alive and moving in the "field" out there. Both tested **competence.** One the no-argument *"do you know how to do the moves perfectly or not."* The other the judgment-call *"which moves did you choose to do, how, and why?"*

The result was a win-win situation. **"In Vivo"** (= write to this or that audience, etc) tested the *ultimate* goal of *pragmatic power*: their ability to vary the variable-issues: length, tone, use of visuals, structure, modification of essay form, explicitness and positioning of stating main point, etc... I could test their supple adaptability....

But first, **"In Vitro"** tested the *building-block* goal of *underlying competence*: "scales" or "finger exercises"— and much more. Their "going through the paces." Advantages were ability to say "you know this or you don't" as a firm base of skill.

A side-benefit for all was reducing classroom conflict and friction, by banishing grade-grubbing argument. **EXAMPLE:** (1) "Frank likes fishing, to ski, and he dances." *Hey, you either* spotted that this sentence needed parallelism, *or you didn't! No argument* about varying style to be relaxed, etc. The correct version is (2) "Frank likes fishing, skiing, and dancing." Even as **In Vivo**, one might well say (3) "Frank likes fishing and skiing. And as Marie knows, he likes to dance also."

EXAMPLE. **A letter to an inflight magazine** praising airline personnel, then two rewrites of same. *Proposal:* there exists an *unarguable* "wrong and right" version here (via **In Vitro** by-the-book anyhow) *but* without mechanical rigid authoritarianism! *Let's see...*

ORIGINAL LETTER, from an in-flight magazine, late 1980's:	MY REWRITE: *[More in Less, and more vivid too...]*	A STUDENT'S REWRITE: shift from Essay to Story.
As a frequent traveler I have found that some of your staff are very helpful and accommodating which is extremely appreciated. Two of your staff members whom I have encountered numerous times are Ellen Lui and Carrie Law. I have found them to be extremely pleasant, helpful and accommodating. Although I have no specific incident to recount to you I just thought it was important for an airline to recognize those who excel in their positions and to give them the praise they deserve. --DL, Hong Kong	I really appreciate the excellence of your flight crews—especially Ellen Lui and Carrie Law. They're "basically" helpful. (The reassurance about my luggage...then that extra pillow and blanket.) They're "advanced" accommodating. (The change to a better vacant seat...then the third bottle of water.) And they're "world-class" pleasant. (Their smiles throughout a flight tossed by turbulence and babbling babies...and while finding me the gate number of my connecting flight in case of delay!...) Thanks to them and the whole crew.	Boarding my flight, I was anxious. Would all go well—would the attendants be good? Things started well—Ellen Lui reassured me about my luggage storage. Things continued well—feeling cramped, I requested a vacant seat. Carrie Law accommodated me, and with a smile with the extra service too. Airborne, I became cold. Once again "no problem"—Ellen returned with an extra blanket and still a smile. But would they become vexed when I asked for a fourth glass of water? Once again no, despite crying babies all around plus mid-flight turbulence. Again worried that weather-delay would make me miss my connection, I asked Carrie, and she told me the gate number ahead of time. And still smiling, ever helpful and accommodating. Exiting the flight, I was not anxious but admirable. Thanks.

81

MILD CIVIL RESPONSE: "The original writer Got His Point Across *just fine*! Oh, he might have been a little more detailed to really reach the reader better with fewer words. But, perfectly adequate for that context!"	WILD CANDID RESPONSE: "Foul-up and foul-out! Egg on the face of the original writer! He starts his drift down the page and *only babbles dilutedly* instead of using prose style to tighten, arrow, aim, and cut cleanly to the finish line! We (or I) have to gently *ridicule* this naïve Amateur Communication!" (And yes adequate for that context, but how many would realize *unenjoyably sub-minimal* also?) --So also your own response to the left, "loses" too. Or else I'm just tired of students' responding to a text by saying "it gets its point across." Lowest common denominator. ANALOGY: as a TAB (temporarily-able-bodied) person, I can easily "hit the wall of my office with a tennis ball." But what achievement there? What challenge, cruciality, satisfaction?

Specifically can learners note the differences in the letters?

--I saw that the original author neglected some **variable-issues**:

(1) Conceptualization plus **Categorization** (=discovering and grouping the ideas under the thesis),

(2) "Concretization" or **specific detailing** (and using six subtypes thereof...), then

(3) Cohesion through **parallelism** (state related ideas in related style for easier reading), not to mention

(4) Conciseness: reducing diluted **wordiness**.

--And the student who rewrote, discovered another option, that of **(5) Essay "vs." Story** (=expository-vs.-dramatic)!

BUT aren't you steering us down the "retro" path to Rule-Mongering, getting the One Right Answer without judgment? *Ironic!*	Good point, always a danger. **BUT**, perhaps more-complex technical skills need "suave letter-perfect ability" as a desirable mid-range goal...

EXAMPLE #2. A letter to the editor of a college newspaper: **critiquing the paper's "police blotter" column.** The beauty-beast pair here, the amateur text and the (by-the-book) better revision, may speak volumes, about pitfalls and potentialities—if you already know the issues, that is...

ORIGINAL	REVISION

Dear Editor,
    While I have not had the distinction of having my name appear in your police reports, I nonetheless feel compelled to question the need for them.
    Thought there may be some merit to an informed public, is, indeed, this argument applicable now? Before answering, please examine the following:
    1.) You are dealing with accusations only. Since you print only accusations and not acquittals or defense replies, you, in essence, allow only the police department to speak. If you feel you must continue, then at least print those names exonerated of charges to facilitate full disclosure.
    2.) There is a distinct lack of relevancy. Of what benefit is it to us, your readers, to know of those arrested who are totally independent of UW-Whitewater?
    3.) Do you have the right to further humiliate those arrested? Since it is already a matter of local, public record, of what purpose is there for additional reporting?
    4.) Your sensationalized reporting is fostering police disrespect. Perhaps you should fully examine the consequences of informing the public. By letting us know of Johnny Doe's arrest for urinating all over a fire hydrant, you are, at the same time, feeding a contempt for the local law officials.
    Because of these reasons I feel you should discontinue your police reports. If nothing else, at least reconsider your reasons for a continued effort.   Mark McNally
	Dear Editor,
	    Do you really need to print the Police Blotter column, that record of public peccadillos and pratfalls?
	    (1) It doesn't seem fair or complete to the arrestees. Why print only those names accused, and not those exonerated of the charges in future weeks?
	    (2) It doesn't seem just or genteel to the arrestees either. Why further humiliate those who are already in the public record anyhow?
	    (3) It doesn't seem relevant to our readers specifically. Who cares if non-UW personnel were arrested?
	    (4) It doesn't even seem beneficial for norms and morale generally. Doesn't reporting a urination all over a fire hydrant, foster contempt for law and order, for local law officials?
	    It's not that my own name has appeared in the Blotter. It's just that I question the Blotter itself.
	    Millicent Offenbach

This time, I **DO** see your point. In terms of your **15-C** model for better essay writing, the original writer *bungled* several of the "C's" (wordiness, lack of crystal point-stating, utter neglect of possibilities of parallelism, even structure...)! These are	...Yes, and *it even took me, a writing teacher, more than one pass* to spot all pitfalls/potentialities. But the **15-C** rubric, helped ... Oh, and *you forgot to mention (or did not spot)* 9Con-Sequence, or structure. I seem to have

| specifically **5Crystallized** (the points not crisply labeled), relatedly **11Co-hesion** (monstrously no parallelism), and **13Condensed** (the rewrite trimly slims the bloated verbiage)... | reversed original points #2 and #3 for better logical flow or **10Co-herence...** |

RELATE TO: The **In Vitro/In Vivo** ploy seems to affirm Criteria short of Authority, against three obstacles:

(1) the pesky current obstacle of Rampant **Relativism** or who's to say who's right after all *plus*

(2) the *downsizing* of **Quality** or high **standards**—in Awareness and Appreciation itself, let alone Acceptability & Ability-to-do, *plus*

(3) the more formidable issue of **Context**, namely formally correct in theory doesn't always mean functionally effective in practice. (To break students of the habit of **"rule-mongering,"** of taking every given technique, as a rule one must apply, rather than a tool one uses, or not, this time...)

|#+#|+#|+|#+#+|#+#+#+#||+|+#++|#|+#+||+|+#|+|++|#+#++|+|||+#++|+#+#|+|#+|+|+|#|+#|+||+|#+|+|+#|+#|+#|+#|+#+|+#+||+|#+|#+|+#|+|#||

ISSUE #6.D. Full Meaning Of *Really* "Knowing": What does it mean to "know" something? (What might End-Goal Readiness (etc.) look like in specific practice?)

GALLERY. Two examples of truly knowing two keystone thinking skills (from economics, and statistics) well enough to Hit The Ground Running in agile application of them when needed.

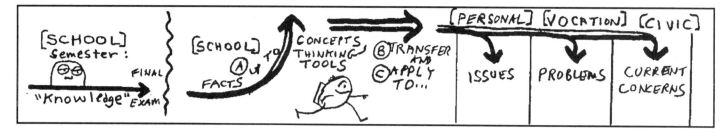

SKILL #1. First, the keystone issue in economics called **ALLOCATION COST** or **COST-BENEFIT RATIO**. Also **OPPORTUNITY COST**.... Resources are scarce, limited. To obtain a desired good or service (etc.,), a cost exists in obtaining it. *Is the cost worth the benefit?*

School	Personal	Vocational	Civic Citizen	Other Enterprise
(N) *RECOLLECT*: NISBET reported that economists may be more likely to depart early from a boring movie... (N) Add up your time vs. income on your part-time work-study job, is it worth it? (N) I have to print off and mail out a 16-page handout. Benefit if I print double-sided (reduce	(N) On my Asian trip, taxi from Bangkok airport costs $20, takes 20 minutes. Bus costs $5, takes an hour or more. I practiced pathetic false economy in waiting for bus, when each hour of trip to Thailand costs so much anyhow! (N) A male should avoid sex for a few days before having	(N) Getting this grant is doubtful; is it worth the cost in time needed to fill out the long application? [*Sub-issue of probability here...*] (N) To put the illustrations in my book, should I: 1. cut-and-paste [takes time] , 2. try to learn Photoshop [takes time, money] , or 3. pay a student to do the picture-pages [takes money]? [Possibly, learning P.shop myself	(N) Returning the toner cartridge for recycling is noble, but worth my time? (N) To save five minutes time in commuting traffic jams, saves X amount of time and gas money in a year!	(N) I badly need for my article, the quotation from this library book, but it is due back, no copy machine, should I rip out the page? (Possibly if I judge that my readers will need the quotation more than the book's readers will...) In another case, cut out a color picture to duplicate it and tape it back in; a compromise... [*Sub-issue of morality or*

postage costs), but my printer jams on double-sized jobs (time-cost to clear it). Decide: double-sided printing not worth the postage savings).	blood drawn for a prostate exam. (The "cost" of "deprivation," vs. the benefit of accuracy, also of increased "peace of mind"...)	is economical: then I could use it for future projects.]		greatest good here...]

Skill #2. Then the keystone issue in statistics, called **SAMPLING ERRORS**, including **INSUFFICIENT, UNREPRESENTATIVE, SELF-SELECTED SAMPLES**. _Is the sample from which we draw a conclusion, adequate—or too small or biased?_

SUB-ISSUES: --[1.] Proportion of the distribution: even, or skewed? ["90% of the Volvos made in the last ten years are still on the road"—but perhaps only the very newest ones?...] ["A box of strawberries"—but with the biggest best ones on the top...]
--[2.] Completeness of response: ["Madame Claire Voyant the medium made three accurate predictions!"—but how many inaccurate ones, and how did other mediums do?]

School	Personal	Vocational	Civic Citizen	Other Enterprise
(N) Are homosexuals psychologically sick? Early studies relied on samples drawn from—*psychiatric patients*! BUT early study claiming gays were just as healthy as average, drew their samples from—the *gay liberation groups* of the time! [With all due respect to "diversity," neither of these two subgroups seems safely representative of the general minority group of sexual variants...]	(N) Those former schoolmates of mine who did attend our class reunion, may not be a representative sample of *all* my classmates now. [Hard to tell what differences, though: maybe more energetic?...]	(N) As NISBET said, judge the job candidate on more than just the (often "flashy" or lively) interview. See other materials also (references, etc.). [For a more sufficient and representative sampling of his/her suitabilities...]	(N) Newspaper columnist says "I personally have never witnessed a car accident due to a cell phone." [Hideously insufficient sample of one person as a research source...] \=\+|+\=\=|+|+\ (N) Five out of five letters-to-the-editor violently objected to an earlier anti-gay guest-column by a conservative religious group. [But was this representative of all sentiment, or just vocal minority? "Self-selected" sample of those who chose to write in. Or, did editors choose only the more-"lively" letters?...]	(N) Do "all" Asians strongly emphasize education for their children? [But those who emigrated to America in 1970's to escape problems in their countries, were more educated (immigration policies favored trained people) and they'd pass those values on to their children...]

NO! Really, this is overdone in two ways. First, content. I think that *most of us already know* this, about cost tradeoffs in life. Second, style. I	My Mild Response: But the Above might help students practice relating ideas to life. [My Wilder Response: *Arrggghhh.* "Of Course We All Already Know And Do This Already..." *Do* we really know, now? Only *gradually* did I come to make **CBRatio** and **Sampling** two of my favorite internalized tools. Only *slowly* did I come to *intuitively* Hit The Ground Running using those two powerful tactics *almost daily now*. Only *now*, do I truly fully **Know** them. Meaning *use them appropriately and spontaneously* (as RICHARD PAUL stipulated...)] ....so the points here are

think most readers don't need *so many examples* stating the obvious! Thorough, but tedious…	--**(1)** the <u>concept</u> of **"Knowing, vs. Really Knowing."** --**(2)** the fact that **Applicability** of a concept can vary, being limited, or as here, in *many* instances or arenas… --**(3) Concretization**: the confession that I do give too many examples, but the defense (not of me, of examples) that multiple, varied, effective instances efficiently cinch a point for learners… --And **(4)** the <u>motivation</u> of **Pleasure**. It's enjoyable to think well to gain goals…

|#+#|+#|+|#+#+|#+#+#+#||+|+#++|#|+#||+|+#|+|++|#+#++|+|||+#++|+#+#|+|#+|+|#|+#||+|#++|+|#|+#|+#|#++|+#+||+|#+|#+|+#|+|#||

(7) *Does* course apply thinking to "important" issues not just "textbook" ones? [Cf.: "current crucial concerns"]

ISSUE #7.1.   …*Should* course emphasize *transferring* skills to "charged" issues (significant "meaningful" vital), not "inert" (pro-forma material?)

OPENING EXAMPLE. From the **family cartoon "Sally Forth."** The parents of the daughter are talking:

"So, you were able to convince Hilary that <u>piano lessons</u> are worth her efforts?" …
                                        "Yes, we finally came to an 'understanding.'" …
   "Great! What did you do?" …
              "I simply explained to her that playing piano develops *skills she'll find useful in other areas of her life.*" …
"That's surprising. She's not usually open to such a general idea." …
              "Actually, I told her it would improve her timing and dexterity on that <u>video game</u> she's been trying to beat."

TWO PERSONAL EXAMPLES. I myself **reacted strongly against** these two, as not really **"crucialized"**

(1) After taking E. DEBONO'S world-famous course in creative or "lateral" thinking, A RESPONDENT stated: "As a result, among other things, now when having coffee, I open not one but two sugar packets at one time."
         (…..**Down-to-earth arrowed-in indeed**, *but still*…**can we not learn concepts more powerful for larger issues?…**)
 	
(2) I was asking A SAN DIEGO SCIENCE EDUCATOR about key principles in life-sciences. She mentioned **energy**, and its transfer and conservation. This could help us understand why on a hot day, water condenses on the outside of a cool glass of beverage. I opined that this was true but not of crucial significance it seemed to me.
         (…..THE EDUCATOR **seemed "a little disappointed" with my response, to say the least. In fact, she was royally vexed. Just possibly, embarrassed?…**)

…two small and obvious examples of a large and often-overlooked issue…

EXAMPLE: skills fleshed out in real-world situations—and relevant ones?…
Harvard University will apply <u>mathematics</u> more. Teach quantitative reasoning not only via elementary **number theory**, but also via *health economics*, plus *demography* or counting people. Calculus topics such as **change** and **accumulation** may be taught not as such, but in computer-modelling courses. Math courses may tackle real-world problems. 1. How long before *fish in mercury-poisoned water* would be safe to eat? 2. How to calculate the *health benefits* of exercising. 3. Probability of *an STD being transmitted* by a condom-user. [-- CHE, JAN 2000]
One would certainly *hope so*…   Ah, the gap between "Shakespeare and the waiting room"…

EXAMPLE. A Call to Relevance—but *house repair*, are you *serious*?
Begin to help change our education policy to create students who prepare for the real world they will inhabit by learning how to **wire their houses** instead of quoting **Ohm's law** or how and when to **refinance their house** rather

than learning Euclidean Geometry. I would create more curricula in science and other subjects that emphasized everyday reasoning issues like the use of **stem cells** or **waste cleanup** or **snow removal** or **alternative energy sources**. Why can't science be about real issues in real people's lives? [-- EDGE, WORLD QUESTION CTR 2003]

This is bad and good. Reduces things to vocational education. But also forces needed relevance…	Look at the variables here. Surely it champions **Arrowing** toward relevant, Crucial or important issues. --However, in terms of **Goals [#1]**, does it slide a bit toward the old What to Do in the sense of rote formula rules and lower-level technical skills? (Still, wiring and refinancing could be taught with their principles too!) --But then it returns to more complex issues where indeed "reasoning" or **Abstraction [#2]** to higher-order skills would be needed. --Of course also the issue: is Transfer being taught **[#3 Application]**? That is, a set of generic scientific thinking skills which can confront varying diverse changing concerns later on?…

EXAMPLE. *__The last and the best:__* A college president urges us to Connect! Connect! Connect!…

[We must ask] "…how each discipline can help us live more *wisely, ethically, responsibly, and productively…* living a life that has *more meaning* to oneself and the world. Is not the purpose of a liberal-arts education to equip us to make better choices through out our lives as we confront problems [that confront our personal lives]? …that freshman mystery: How is *King Lear, particle physics,* or *the economic history of England…* related to the complexity of issues with which one must deal in the *office,* the *dining room,* the *hospital waiting room,* and the *voting booth*?"
[-- BARBARA MOSSBERG, President, Goddard College, Vermont]

WHOA, *wait* a minute. This *reduces* general liberal-arts education to a higher kind of "vocational training"!	Oh **NO.** (Or, life as a vocation…) *A superb comment.* Focuses on the **Crucial,** important, issues—of real life in Personal arenas. I feel the strong thrust (and painful difficulty) of trying to **Export** or Transfer of **Application** all the long way **across [#3A]**— *whaaat,* all the way from *lofty Shakespeare,* to the *grubby waiting room*? A noble foray….

RECOLLECT. Earlier, the writings on **"evolutionary biology"** *usefully* mentioned mate-selection, step-parenting, the ingroup-outgroup issue, even "are humans basically peace-seeking or war-like," plus social policies which may go with or against the grain of the heritage of "hunter-gatherer tribes in the savannah"…

|#+#|+#|+|#+#+|#+#+#+#||+|+#++|#|+#+||+|+#|+|++|#+#++|+|||+#++|+#+#|+|#+|+|+|#|+#|+||+|#+|+#|+#|+#|#++|+|#+||+|#+#+|+#|+|#||

(8) "ATTITUDE": Was issue present of thinking "morally-ethically" (honestly, fairmindedly reason-ably etc.) *vs.* manipulatively (biased agonistic exploiting etc.). (Cf. "Considerate" thinking, "Dispositions")

THE ISSUE, WHY IMPORTANT: …in the **Critical Thinking** movement especially. CLARIFICATIONS: **(1)** This does *not* mean thinking on moral and ethical topics. **(2)** And it does *not* equate with sheer raw skill in thinking as such. RICHARD PAUL most usefully points out that the 1930's book Mein Kampf ("My Struggle") contains adroit reasoning—but its author was ADOLPH HITLER, its purpose neither seeking the Truth, nor treating his opponents fairly… **(3)** But presumably this *can* include argument reasoning persuasion—*if* the standards are to "win" only fairly, not by just any selfish means…

TOOL-KIT SUMMARY. The "critical thinking" movement calls this issue, **"dispositions"** in thinking. We attempted to elucidate this keystone issue. We also touch on the related issue of **"personal thinking,"** relatedly also one's **"psyche or self"** in thinking…

1. Decide first your basic prior goal: to Win or to Win-Win? Is it ACV or ACV? That is, is it Argumentative, to Combat to win Victory over your side, defeat your opponent, anyhow persuade-and-convince? (This is the common "Agonistic" tradition or argument, from "Medieval debating days" onward, as the sociolinguist DEBORAH TANNEN notes in her writings) …. Or is it more Authentic, to Cooperate and work with others to achieve Veracity or Truth, or anyhow Validity for all? (This is rare, possible, satisfying…)

EXAMPLE. An educator spent an entire day in a meeting at a group-oriented company. He was astonished at the success. More good ideas emerged in that one day than in any other meeting. This was because of the "healthy group mentality." "No one cared about who had which ideas. The goal was to produce the very best possible collective product." [-- ROBERT STERNBERG]

A PERSONAL STAND: all parties involved have to decide and agree on this, it usually doesn't get settled clearly, if it is not only chaos and tangle results, and yes this is "idealistic," but it is the civil fair-minded mature way to go, and you can do it if all parties want to, but Ya Gotta Wanna.....

2. If to Cooperate, then avoid Selfish thinking, aim for Fairminded thinking. Selfish thinking may be skillful but still biased. Recall RICHARD PAUL on Adolph Hitler's adroit reasoning.
   (My *analogy* is automotive. Selfish thinking is a powerful sports car driven to endanger other drivers. Fairminded thinking respects the road, gets to the destination safely...)
--**Fairminded** thinking seeks to (1) **identify and disclose one's own "biases" to oneself and work with them** (cf. our **Personal Profile** of our motivations and strong stands!). Then also (2) **listen to "the other side," but *"no, really!"*** That is, truly listen without needing either to agree (groupspeak) or disagree (defend self), but simply *to come to know the other side so well that you can phrase its argument and have them say "Yes, this is indeed exactly what we mean and feel!"*

A PERSONAL STAND: Technically this DISPOSITIONS element in thinking, is Indoctrination into an Ideology: "we must be fair-minded." But I value it greatly. Due to subjective personal temperament etc. Others do not value such. But objectively I believe (not just to rationalize my preference) fairmindedness has three good reasons for it: pragmatic, principled, pleasurable...

PERSONAL EXPERIENCE. At <u>a campus debate between Biblical fundamentalists condemning homosexuality as a sin, and a group for sexual-orientation rights,</u> *few students listened* to the religious folk. I did. I felt strongly that suppressing one's true sexual nature was a sin in itself, a distortion—and bad not only for a gay man but for his wife and children especially. *But I listened,* and found <u>they felt that a man with gay tendencies who wished to stay with his wife and church could feel more rewarded that way.</u> Neither trying to *accept* or *critique* their point of view, I finally truly *grasped* it. This helped communication, also my sense of power over the situation—not at the mercy of my own ideas or out to win. To open up and truly comprehend without either pressure to agree, or drive to disagree—it was suave thinking...

I came to see <u>three advantages</u> to taking this empathetic unthreatened/unthreatening openness to The Other Side.
(1) Pragmatic: Agonistic. If you want to defeat them after all, heck, "Know Your Enemy"!
(2) Principled: ethical-moral maturity. Mature it seems to truly admit, relate to, acknowledge, generously donate attention to, the Other...
(3) Principled, plus Pleasurable: Psychological. Wow, the non-egotistic ego-gain in my being able to control myself, not to have to rush to condemn or defend or submit to the Other!...

Our attempt to distill "dispositions" into the most complete but most compact elucidation...

|#+#|+#|+|#+#+|#+#+#+#||+|+#++|#|+#+||+|+#|+|++|#+#++|+|||+#++|+#+#|+|#+|+|+|#|+#|+||+|#++|+|+#|+#+#|#+|#+||+|#+|#++|+#|+|#||

| [1.] Define Ed. Goals | [2.] Essence of TT: AAA | [3.]Presence? | [4.] other Variables |

[III.] Issues of TRUE "PRESENCE" of thinking:
I EMBEDDEDNESS in a *specific* course,
II EXHIBITION of skills by the *whole* institution... Three variables on this:

(9) "EXPLICITNESS": of thinking skills in a course.

If then thinking is a goal of the course, how present is it in the course?
(A) "TAGGED": are the skills named, labeled, identified as such?
(B) "TAUGHT": are the skills taught *explicitly* (but short of rote didacticism)?

➔ And *again* the [caution]. Before teaching conceptual skills explicitly and for autonomous transfer, <u>make sure the students know that this is a new paradigm</u>, different from "old-school" rote-learning—and what its ground rules are. Otherwise, confusion: "what do you want?"

VOCABULARY. I would like to say "liminality" to mean degree of explicit presence. Starting from the *familiar* **"subliminal"** meaning literally "below the *limen* or doorstep in Latin" but covert not overt, latent not manifest, stated not tacit, implicit not explicit. Thus, are the thinking skills ***"liminal," "liminalized"***? And even ending up with "<u>superliminal</u>." (The thinking skills in neon? On a billboard? In blaze orange? And the like....) *But, enough of terminology.* <u>On to the issue</u>: once thinking skills Exist in a course, ***are they Explicit enough in two phases***...

A PERSONAL STAND: I confess that I <u>intellectually lust for total **Elucidation**, for seeing the subject just as completely-clearly as if "a machine on a museum stand, all parts labeled,"</u> etc. *I cannot justify this objectively; it is Personal Preference Taste-Temperament and more.*

--And indeed, **surely a a thinking skill could be <u>too</u> explicitly [and extensively!] named, also described, and—to** *some* **degree—taught?** <u>Seems excessive, *if*</u> (1) more than situationally-needed, or (2) (and especially) if it slips into being taught as formula, rote rule, etc. or (3) with no active student learning participation, of course. <u>But short of this</u>...

--I'd say: <u>at the least, consider letting the relevant thinking skills be located, distilled, elucidated, made "accessible but unobtrusive" to learners who want to use them</u>, in ToolKIT form. **Cause-Effect, Structure, Lenses, Categorization, Change, Induction-Deduction,** and more. Analogy: a "pegboard" of varied tools... [For samples, see ToolKits in Appendix #4...] --If skills are not made accessible thus, is the course perhaps *shortchanging*?

RECOLLECT: W. DERZKO'S charge that <u>most skills beyond math are not taught as such</u>.
E. D. HIRSCH <u>training chicken-sexers</u>: skills can be conceptualized and thus clarified and efficiently-abbreviated, at least somewhat...
And WINSTON WEATHERS' <u>plea that he have available all the skills at once</u> if he should desire them...

Still, alternate approaches do exist:

The approach of **infusion** of thinking uses subject-matter and "general principles of critical thinking dispositions and abilities are made explicit. Whereas in the **immersion** approach, "general critical thinking principles are *not made explicit.*" [-- R. ENNIS]

ISSUE #9.A. Does one first <u>identify, name, label</u> *explicitly* the skills (even or especially if complex, higher-order?)

EXAMPLES. College English courses: two instances of *fairly-explicit* (but still domain-specific) definition of course goals, anyhow, with skills implied...

EXAMPLE #1. First, HEDDA FISH at S.D.S.U. spotlights "a number of characteristics common to all literature":
1. Conventions of genres—novels, character.
2. Conflict, with action and suspense.
3. Specific examples provide general inferences.
4. Ambiguity can be rich, not inexact.
5. Form and feeling combine; structure and emotions.
6. Organic Unity: theme plus repetition with variation.
7. Literary elements: plot character, imagery, diction, tone, voice, style, pace, figurative language.

EXAMPLE #2. Second, EDMUND WHITE the novelist speaks against the idea of a pre-set "canon" of Great Books which all should read:

> Literature courses should teach students *how* to read, not *what* to read. Students can acquire from teachers the rigorous pleasure of close reading, of comparison and analysis, of broadened sympathies and finer moral discrimination. Students can be *taught to be skeptical, to label rhetorical strategies, to uncover political subtexts, to spot allusions, to recognize the anxiety of influence and to detect the function of such fictional structures as mystery, suspense and characterization.* They can't be taught to like or even finish *The Nicomachean Ethics.* Our reading lists should be long, heterodox, seductive...."

Maybe this does support your point that **"100% teaching thinking would be impracticable."** Also, the *difficulty* of **Elevating** and **Exporting.** True, WHITE'S toolkit suggests some *General* Thinking Skills (skepticism, naming strategies, reading—text, or situation—for many subliminal elements). So we could hijack this rich stuff, yank it out and impose it to do service upon subjects far from literature, subjects in the workplace, dinner table, "hospital waiting room." **But that would impoverish reading literature as such—***no time to do both...*	True, hard to fit everything in, skills and content (if content is still a major goal, as it often must be). Plus, a "wrenching" to impose general skills onto course-foreign subjects… Still, WHITE is helpful to show #9**Explicitly** stating some possible thinking-goals *within* the subject of literature. Not just "learn to read and appreciate better" Explicit—and yet not oversimple or reductionistic…] P.S. – *were* students given these key principles on a Wallet-Card handout? (Like IU- Purdue's principles on the 3- ring binder insert given to all students and faculty?...) And *should* they have been?

ISSUE #9.B. [1.] At what level of abstraction are skills stated—more-specific or more-generic? ..... [2.] And to what degree of elaboration, exactness, detail—more general once-over, or more 1-2-3 operational? [And what level and degree are desirable?...]

TWO PITFALLS. –(1) Some education doesn't **Elevate** the skills to generic, applicable levels. They remain domain-specialized. **"Concrete Shortfalling."**
--(2) Other education may ascend to higher-order skills, but leave them described vaguely not precisely.
"Conceptual Stratosphering."
--To distinguish between these two bungles, try the following examples:

MINI-GALLERY. Examples which remain high-order general, but move to more elaboration or specificity.

EXAMPLE #1. *Too General?* Liberal Education beats narrow vocational training?:
As for "liberal education," narrow vocational training is limited. More capable are students "who can work analogically with a broad number of models derived from fields at times remote from their own and can relate their work to a variety of contexts—social, economic, geographical, and political." [Article in COLLEGE ENGLISH]
…once more: rather *high-level*, but not **Explicit.** Plus, does this **Exporting** happen automatically? is it ever discussed with students?

EXAMPLE #2. *Too Vague?* Goal #6 for English majors at Univ. of Wis.-Whitewater
"To apply to areas other than English, and to real life, the thinking skills derived from the study of languages-and-literatures." [-- Departmental Statement, 1990's]

HMMM… You think this is stratospherically vague (which I guess it is). Plus probably never explicitly practiced by teachers. *Or are you just trying to slam your own unresponsive department*??	NO; I'm too mature, plus why even bother to try? ☺)... I only say the statement is depressingly-*embryonic* in terms of what *can* be done, not necessarily what always *should* be done.

EXAMPLE #3. "Science & Technology in Society," some *great generic* concepts emerging...

Introduce the following common, general concepts: Dynamic Equilibrium... Change and Evolution... Scale and Proportion... Causality and Consequence... Energy: Sources & Transfer...	
What's the matter, you hate scientific *facts* and *data*?	I hate "data-*only*." I would love to see these made **Explicit**, then **Exported** to use in #3**Application** to #7**Acute** issues in so-called real life. These are big rich **Salient Ideas** which could **ennoble** specific scientific content... Billboard seems vague...

EXAMPLE #4. **Anthropology** can teach *more-specific* thinking and interpersonal skills.

Anthropology can teach students Social Agility & Sensitivity & Perspective; Observation; Planning; Accuracy in Interpreting Behavior, plus other generic-scientific skills such as Interpreting Info, Critiquing Conclusions, Contextualizing Details, Problem-Solving.   [-- JOHN OMOHUNDRO, SUNY-Potsdam]
This I like *better*. Generic skills arising from a specific subject. True, still somewhat high-level. (But were they mentioned and taught explicitly during courses? OMOHUNDRO suggested no; students were unaware they might have been "picking up" these skills, they did not #5**Articulate** them!)

EXAMPLE #5. **Psychology** can teach *the summit* generic skill, Conceptualizing UP 101"!

First, of course psych grads are skilled in (1) Literacy, Numeracy, Computer Literacy, Information-Finding and Research and Measurement Skills..... Then also in (2) Interpersonal and Environmental Awareness plus Perspectives or "the ability to look at issues from several different points of view" as being "a skill in which psychology graduates are directly trained….. But also, in (3) "The ability to extract *general principles* from immediate or concrete situations. Psychology graduates tend to be better than most people at spotting *recurrent patterns or similarities* between situations, and at looking at issues in terms of their *underlying principles* rather than becoming bogged down with the details of the immediate situation." [*italics added*]
     [--DR. NICKI HAYES, psychology teacher]

EXAMPLES #6A, B. **Math** can be more than rote routine algorhythms far from real life...

[A.] Mathematical thinking-skills: 1. Number sense. 2. Numerical ability. 3. Spatial-reasoning ability. 4, 5. A sense of cause and effect. 6. Algorhythmic ability. 7. Ability to abstract! 8, 9. Logical, and Relational, reasoning ability.   [-- KEITH DEVLIN, CHRONICLE OF HIGHER EDUCATION]

[B.] 1. Use Trial and Error. Via feedback loops, refine guesses (auto mechanic).
2. Use Symbolism: write it in a different mode.
3. Perceive Patterns (physician and upset stomach).
4. "Step Back." Solve an invented simpler problem.
5. Work Backwards to Solve a Problem (retire at 65, how to start now?)
6. Simulation (run with different potential majors, salaries).
[-- DR. JEFF BARNETT, SCHOOL OF EDUCATION, UNIV. OF WIS.-WHITEWATER]

...a gratifying start toward hammering math procedures into "human" usable concepts... But unfortunately rare, or so it seems...Is DR. BARNETT'S example here quite conceptual, but also more specific, and ripe for transfer or Exporting to the world?...*Would that I had had some of these skills* **Embedded Explicitly** *amid my Math 141 formulae.*
Though not all math teachers agree; *RECALL* "TITU'S Math Column"...

ISSUE #9.C. **Then does one *actually teach* those skills very explicitly—or at least make them available...?**

Here we rest the case without *repeating* it, though one can recall earlier comments:

RECOLLECT: -- WINSTON WEATHERS' pleaded for having all the writing tools <u>laid out for him</u> at the outset (not everyone's learning-style, but still...) ....

-- I MYSELF tried to learn <u>philosophy's keystone concepts</u>—higher-order, but stated more explicitly than usual. (I experienced how a Philosophy Department Chair's retreated into "tacit lore" which interested major students "pick up as they go along"...)

-- I MYSELF *strongly suggested* that indeed while 100% explicit teaching thinking skills may well be inadvisable and worse in many cases, nevertheless *not to offer Tool-KITS, elucidating completely but compactly and clearly basic-essential thinking skills, seems educational malpractice* and a terrible shortfalling...

SUB-ISSUE. How *early* may we have to start teaching basic conceptualizing?

RECOLLECT: -- In "KEYSTONES" the unit on "<u>the very concept of a concept</u>." Snowboarding, other examples *not conceptualized enough.* ("Computer," but not linear sequentiality, parallel and serial processing... "Tax-sheltered annuity," but not asset-allocation, diversification. "Forehand serve," but not position, readiness, timing...

[For "II" FULL-dress version, see unit in Appendix 3.1., Why The Very Idea" or Conceptualizing 101

COLLEAGUE COMMENT. A friend and dedicated teacher, TOM DRUCKER, in math, says perhaps college teachers don't teach thinking because we know how to think, and we assume students do, or that they are picking thinking up from us. Or that we were not trained in teaching thinking—and were not hired to do so via any job description...

(Or perhaps some teachers never consider the issue...) (Or do all teachers really **know** Consciously how they think, indeed—how to think? In the next section, a high school science teacher feels that he knew only formulae, not true understanding...

|#+#|+#|+|#+#+|#+#+#+#||+|+#++|#|+#+||+|+#|+|++|#+#++|+|||+#++|+#+#|+|#+|+|#|+#|+||+|#++|+|+#|+#|+#|#+|+#+||+|#+|#+|+#|+|#||

(10) How "EMBEDDED" *is* a given <u>course</u> with thinking goals and material? How Existent, Explicit, Elevated, Exported, Entered

Absent	Embryonic	Modest	Substantial	Predominant	to "Total"?

ISSUE #10.A. Educators' Stances Today. How many teachers are "where" in re the two conflicting paradigms? ["what to Know Believe Do," *vs.* how to "Think Things Through"]

MINI-GALLERY: Four cautionary vignettes, not to prove our claim, just to illustrate the concept:...

EXAMPLE #1. The teacher wanted to be taught rote rule, not flexible tool?

An educator presented to high school administrators an hour-long program on "principles of choosing programs for teaching thinking." Goal, to enable intelligent choice. But during the questions, the inevitable arose. "All this is nice, but let's get down to nuts and bolts. Which program should we use?" The educator felt this was somewhat *ironic indeed...* [-- R. STERNBERG]

EXAMPLE #2. The flexible toolbook, taken as a rigid rulebook.

John Dewey wrote <u>How We Think</u> to attack rote learning of fixed bodies of truths, to promote whatever skills helped solve problems. It was given to trainee teachers to memorize and recite, as if it were the fixed truth its author deplored. One orthodoxy was replaced with another... [-- ALAN RYAN]

91

EXAMPLE #3. Personal Anecdote. Even the teacher mistook tools, for rules?

I visited the the Diversity & Multiculturalism/Minority Center at the University of Wisconsin at Madison. The head of the Center *objected* to my notion of <u>empowering</u> majority students to better confront challenging situations of diversity via knowing key explanatory <u>concepts</u> as "tools."

(Selective perception; stereotype vs. sociotype; relativism cultural vs. moral; aversive racism; others.)

¡[**SEE** "Diversity Education," in Appendix, Toolkits... **P. 296**]¡

She felt this would be simplistic, like giving students a "tool kit" to carry around and open and use mechanically. Further talk revealed (or suggested) to me that she seemed to envision method? all method?? as rote tactics not as heuristic strategies? Odd, since the antonym opposite word for *tools* is, after all, *rules*... Hmmm....

NO. You're misinterpreting this innocent person's response to forward your own agenda—*and you so fair-minded*!	Possible indeed, he said **Fairmindedly**... But my neutral point was that the traditional rote-learning paradigm seems truly "embedded" into education today... Most thinkers do know to use rules, formulas, rubrics with a grain of salt—but perhaps others including even educators at times revert to rule-ritual?

EXAMPLE #4. "Titu's Math Column" [**Warning: may be—ahh, er, "entertaining"...**]

--Recently, my school's student newspaper took to giving 9 or 10 column inches each week to a column setting a dense, technical math problem to be solved for a prize. (=Dissect into N squares, for all n.5, or 'n ones, written in base 9, is a triangular number for some integer...) Tiring of this disproportionate specialist-technicality, I wrote the math department chair suggesting that this project fell short of general liberal education. How about, instead, setting math concepts to be applied to complex issues in real life? CTA: Conceptualize, Transfer, Apply! (=Cause-effect, relational-reasoning, step and work backwards, symbolism, simulation...)

--The Chair's reply to me was "noteworthy": "<u>The column was not for education but for entertainment, and to interest people in math. Do you also write to newspapers who offer crossword puzzles and the like, and chide them for not being educational? Surely you are wasting the time of us both here...</u>"

NO. See, the chair *did* have a point. Why *not* take a lighter touch, make math *fun* to review? You're too serious and heavy!	The Chair's **profoundly anti-intellectual** response (not to say <u>sneeringly dismissive</u> hence demeaning, but not to me, to a noble cause) tells all it has to—to those who can *hear* it, that is... The emperor had no clothing, plus a three-egg omelet on his face. (But as usual, who realized? For, "If a tree—or a Scandal—falls in the forest and people think it's either neutral or a Good Thing, then is it a Scandal really?....)

CHECKLIST-TABLE. An "ideal-type" continuum to estimate where a course lies in re embeddedness of thinking.

Has even (1) the *field or discipline or subject-area itself*, been <u>clarifying</u> its own keystone concepts?

Then does (2) the individual *teacher* even <u>know</u> the thinking skills? Know them well, clarified and usable?

(0) → Has the teacher <u>first</u> helped the students understand this whole new approach to education?

(A) Does teacher <u>decide "whether"</u> to include thinking as a goal, specific skills as means?

(B) Does teacher explicitly <u>define and select specific</u> (but not rote-mechanical) thinking skills?

(C) Does teacher explicitly <u>signpost</u> them: name and label: to him/her*self*? to the *students*?

(D) Does teacher explicitly <u>teach</u> them (infusion) or just leave them implicit (immersion)?

(E) And does teacher explicitly <u>practice transfer</u>, and then <u>assess</u> abilities?)

THE COURSE STAGES:	1. Planning the course: goals, content.	2. Statement on the syllabus, to the students.	3. Teaching: actual implementation?	4. Repetition for reinforcement?	5. Practice in Transfer & Application?	6. Assessment: testing for true learning?

MODEL #1 **TRADITIONAL?** [To "KNOW, BELIEVE, DO"]	"Thinking" not a part of course-construction. (In fact, teacher never considers the issue in his/her mind.)	No formal statements (or just vague comment). (Teacher may "assume" some "thinking" will be learned...)	(*) Shortfallings: --*Encourage* T. --Talk *about* T. --*Tacit model* T --Drill in skills. --Teach subject "thinkingly"	None. If anything taught, it's in a one-shot deal, not followed up.	None. Or **"bogus" transfer**: asks students to discuss "old" course material as if that is thinking about new material!	None. Or **"bogus" testing**: give students "old" content, ask them to "think about" it...
MODEL #2 **"THINKING"?** ["THINK THINGS THROUGH"]	"Thinking" skills explicitly identified in instructor's mind. Then installed in course as goal and as content.	"Thruout, we shall emphasize these specific thinking skills 1,2,3..."	(*) **Actual teaching** of specific higher-order thinking skills! [Cause-effect; multiple viewpoints; categorization; *whichever*...]	Careful repetition for reinforcement.	1. Transfer to new **course** material. 2. To **other** courses in SCHOOL? 3. To issues in **outside** areas in PERSONAL, JOB, CIVIC arenas?	(*) **"Acid Test."** Can they transfer concepts to new material autonomously? (Cf. AAAA scheme)

[*THINKING SKILLS USED HERE:* the **Conceptual Continuum**, A to Z, all possibilities sought, for **elucidation** of the **ideal-type** totality...]

ISSUES-GALLERY. Below, a cluster of sub-issues on the issue of embeddedness of thinking elements. We seem to have to *ask some **pointed, poignant, penetrating** questions* here, even though Fairmindedly not in Combat...:

ISSUE # 10.B. First, in some <u>disciplines/fields</u> themselves, are their key concepts currently *not* yet explicitly thought-out, elucidated?

RECOLLECT. K. SCHREIVER: the field of <u>document design</u> has principles, but they remain *subliminal, not articulated*...

EXAMPLE. The Lack of Literary "System"...

The English scholar ALVIN KERNAN valued *a solid foundation for viewing reality, some consistent overview*—what Thomas Kuhn would later call a paradigm—however provisional, of the order of things." Here is his interesting report of his stealth research among his collegues:

> On one occasion I distributed to a number of very distinguished colleagues a list of a hundred basic literary terms— comedy, novel, symbol, plot, meter, and so forth—and asked them to *put them in some systematic order*. The results were ludicrous, not only helter-skelter but inept, not because the professors were stupid—quite the contrary—but because <u>they simply had never thought of their subject in this structured fashion</u>. They were for the most part historical and 'practical' critics who interpreted this or that text, or investigated one author or period, without ever really worrying about whether their interpretations followed from *<u>some larger theoretical structure</u>*. Terms like symbol and image were used interchangeably, and the novel could be treated as a myth like comedy or a formal mode like poetry." [KERNAN noted that when "*this theoretical chaos*" was revealed, "no one was bothered much," and a psychiatrist even said that his own field seemed "crippled by a surplus of fraudulent theory."]

[-- Alvin Kernan, IN PLATO'S CAVE]

Well, **WAIT.** KERNAN is *violating one of your goals*, which is to confront reality's complexity—but not to simplistically reduce it, not to seek so much for coherence and unity as to risk oversimplification!	Agreed. **YET** it simply points up a **shortfalling**. A lack of **Elevation** into larger principles even *within* the **domain** of literature, let alone moving on to any **Generic** thinking skills which might emerge! (As in "literary irony" perhaps leading to "a dualistic way of seeing appearance/reality," which is also seen in psychology's defense-mechanisms, sociology's ideal vs. real culture...) ...but **Personally** I can't throw stones. To be properly **candid**, it took me *two decades* to explore and comprehend Teaching Thinking to the extent we offer here— imperfect, but clarified... See elsewhere, some of my earlier bungles...

ISSUE #10.C. And how well *do* teachers themselves, think—or *not*, after all?

EXAMPLE: A TEACHER finds out he may have *not* learned truer thinking in his field:
I came to realize that I head learned physics by rote, and that I really did not *understand,* all that I *knew,* about physics. My thinking students asked me questions for which I had the standard textbook answers. But this made me start thinking by myself. And I realized that these canned answers were not justified by, or produced by, my own thinking. My training made me memorize the thoughts (and skills?) of others, but I had never learned or been encouraged to learn to think for myself.   [-- A TEACHER with a M.A. in physics and math and 20 years high school teaching in physics: paraphrase, quoted by R. PAUL]

...yeah **BUT** wait, this is just more of R. PAUL'S (and your own) Special Pleading. It's a sampling-error; this teacher is unrepresentative! It's propaganda! No specific examples to support his claim, either...	Thanks for your example of Bad Thinking, A/K/A Resistance-Defense-Evasion-Denial #17... I *did* warn that the truly-New may appear to be—"Threatening," to *some...*

ISSUE #10.D. Then, *do* teachers infuse thinking goals explicitly? *Seemingly, but...*

ANECDOTE. A COLLEAGUE did list thinking goals, *but still...*
I was on an English Department committee surveying syllabi of courses. Of all the 50 instructors, *only* "GEORGE S." stated higher-level thinking goals explicitly on his syllabus. (I myself did not do so at that time.) Later I commended "George" personally for doing that. He responded: "I did it because the week before doing the syllabus, I read an article suggesting that we do that..."

ISSUE #10.E. "Timing" [I]: Does a course start out initiating concepts to be "exported" and applied to life? Options here do exist...

EXAMPLE: Economic Concepts *At Once...*
A friend of the family, BILL BRANDL, taught secondary-level economics. The very first hour of the course, he opened by defining some key economic terms, concepts, perspectives—and then assigning the students to go forth and locate examples, instances, illustrations, applications of the same in the daily press, their own lives, etc.

ANECDOTE: Statistical Concepts *Disgustingly-Deferred ...*
--By contrast, I myself recall the first hour of a basic graduate class in statistics. (Required for the M.A. in anthropology I was pursuing at the time.) The first hour, the instructor started right off—with *standard distribution:* mean, median, and mode. And went on from there right into the technical minutiae of statistics. There was no pause first for any preview-orientation to either *higher keystone concepts* in statistics, nor to *its uses and advantages, what statistics can do or mean in the real worlds,* academic and non-academic...   I am sure that to "liberalize" and "think about" statistics, would have been a warp, a torsion, a wrench, a real unthinkable action, for the conventional instructor...   --Nor, for as long as I continued in the course, were any applications offered.

ISSUE #10.F. "Timing" [II]: Does a course continue to reinforce a skill over the whole semester? Often not?

Many core competencies can be built into required courses. (This via writing and speaking assignments, and small-group problem-solving work.) But the sequence of instruction must be carefully orchestrated, and pedagogy must change. "To *learn* a problem-solving technique is one thing; to *apply it throughout the semester* in a political-

science or sociology course is a far more effective learning strategy, but one that requires ingenuity on the part of faculty members."   [-- CHRONICLE OF HIGHER EDUCATION, forum]

--This is the key issue of *repetition and reinforcement* of a complex skill. Not simply *mentioning once* of mterial to know...
--This also suggest that while teaching thinking is difficult, nevertheless "Y% of courses could begin teaching thinking "*right now every day*"—by selecting one or a few key skills—**lens-work, knowing vs. knowing, singularity / dualism / multiple-plurality**, etc.—and reinforcing them each class hour, for some mastery by seme3ster's end...

ISSUE #10.G. Is Transferring/Applying concepts, sometimes merely *suggested* not practiced—and "too late" also?

ANECDOTE. "Be Sure to Relate your Knowledge"—*but* That Came *Much Too Late*...

This is a true story; I Am Not Making This Up (& I wish I were...)
--On the last day of the class, my college <u>history</u> teacher said: "Be sure to relate history to your *other courses*."
--That very same day, my <u>psychology</u> professor also advised us to "Be sure to relate psychology to *life*."
[-- ANECDOTE from MY OWN college career]

Arrgghhh......

|#+#|+#|+|#+#+|#+#+#+#||+|+#++|#|+#+||+|+#|+|++|#+#++|+|||+#++|+#+#|+|#+|+|#|+#|+|+|#+|+|+#|+|+#|+#+|+|#++||+|#+|#++|+#|+|#||

(11) Shortfallings "II": *subtleties*... Are there *non-obvious* ways in which "thinking" courses may *shortchange* thinking?

WHOA, you're simply repeating that <u>90% of courses</u> don't teach thinking, etc. Why be *redundant*?	No, some subtle sneaky shortfallings here...

ISSUE. *Have* specific but "under-the-radar" shortfallings been identified in research?

ASSESSMENT. M ATTHEW LIPMAN'S X-Ray Report on *Subtle Shortfallings*.
Employing good thinking himself (comprehensive but clarified), DR. LIPMAN (a philosopher-educator) pinpoints overlooked shortfallings, also perhaps misconceptions.

1. "Teaching for thinking is equivalent to teaching for *critical* thinking." Mr. A shoots questions at students to challenge them. (But do the questions embody thinking skills? And what of the students' responses to them?)

2. "Critical *teaching* will necessarily result in critical thinking." Mrs. B. knows her subject well, down to the assumptions. But presenting this settled end-product may not trickle down and create the thinking skills embodied.

3. "Teaching *about* critical thinking, is equivalent to teaching *for* critical thinking." Ms. C knows the research, but informing students of this without their actively participating, will not impart thinking skills.

4. "Teaching for critical thinking involves tight drill in specific thinking skills." Mr. D. believes we learn by practice (swimming, dancing, skating). He drills students in specific operations. But this can be artificial. One also needs dialog in the classroom, knowing criteria to avoid bad or "just" thinking, and clustering more than one skill at a time.

5. "Teaching for logical thinking equals teaching for critical thinking." Ms. E. decries sloppy thinking, gives formal logic. But this may be insufficient without practice in application to messy real-world complexities.

6. "Teaching for learning is just as effective as teaching for critical thinking." Mrs. F. knows her subject, teaches it traditionally. But knowledge-based tests fall short of judgment-based skills.

[-- MATTHEW LIPMAN, <u>Thinking in Education</u>, 1989]

95

--P.S. – I would note two other pitfalls.

(1) ➔ The repeated caution : failing to inform the students clearly of what this new approach *is*!

(2) A current assumption that "Reducing lecture-course instruction and favoring **'Active Learning'** and **'Student-Centered Learning** and **'Interactive/Collaborative Learning'** and the like, will increase students' abilities to think better"..... Related is the **Constructivist** stance of not absorbing, but creating, knowledge...

--Surely these are 99% better than traditional lecture, but with a potential major pitfall? Is there a **Questionable Implicit Presupposition** here that although students may experience more discussion, diversity of opinions, and the like, will this approach automatically insure clear acquiring of specific thinking skills—let alone testing of them later in the course?"

[EXAMPLE: "Look at the subject from three different perspectives." But this only says What to do, not How to do it. Consider: Which perspectives to choose—and how to find them? Why was each one chosen--subjectively? What are their presuppositions, assumptions? The strengths of, but also the biases in, each? How many perspectives to use—more than three? One main and several secondary? Do the perspectives merely add up, or do they interrelate—or do they conflict with each other? And more...]

| OUCH: all this hurts my brain. All these subtle distinctions! And what do you want, isn't enough enough? | I never said "100% teaching thinking" was probable.....But *LIPMAN can deftly elucidate subtle* **shortfallings** *I myself* might never have suspected... Maybe the acid test is <u>does the teaching enable the learner to **Hit The Ground Running**</u> and competently think through a challenging complexity in real life later on? If so, fine... |

MINI-GALLERY: EXAMPLES:

--First, two instances of, perhaps, *pseudo*-teaching of thinking: <u>subtle blunders</u> perhaps overlooked...

--And then two instances of <u>brave, blunt, overt, "plunge-ins"</u> toward teaching how to assess complexities objectively and competently ...(And with **Autonomy**: students making most decisions, with guidance.)

EXAMPLE #1. During the "culture wars" between political correct liberalism and traditional-conservative forces on campus, GERALD GRAFF proposed that WE "*teach the conflicts.*" That is, in class discuss, explore, these two different and charged points of view.

Fine, *but* would also be taught, critical thinking or how to competently comprehend and evaluate them? (As against covert persuasion or simple relativism, "plural systems, who's to say who's right"?) And after studying the conflicts, did students possess **Explicit** analytical skills for any similar complex issue, **Elevated** to generality, and could they **Export** said skills (on their own later on) to new problems? *A possible shortfalling here...*

EXAMPLE # 2. Ca. 2003, ex-radical DAVID HOROWITZ proposed legal mandates requiring schools to "*hire more conservative professors*" to redress the supposed imbalance of too many liberals causing a monopoly of ideology.

Fine, *but* what might result but a "Band-Aid" fix only? More Agonistic shouting, or talking, matches—or again, rampant relativism? Missing would be a dedication to train students in—well, you know. "Confronting complexities conceptually..."

EXAMPLE #3. RICHARD PAUL'S assignment: *two contrasting films* on Central American politics.
He showed the class two films. One was in defense of the rebels, a liberatory viewpoint. The other was conservative, religious. He asked the students to identify the "philosophies" of each—world-views, key paradigms, assumptions, reasoning. And then to assess each competently. And to conclude by comparing-and-contrasting them—again objectively.

...**Good**: excellently non-Indoctrinating. A truly "liberating" approach, truly "empowering" the student. An ennobling of education. (Here comes again my boring refrain, my tedious themesong: <u>make thinking explicit, conceptualize "up" to the backgrounds of statements, identify the larger "lenses" which are usually selected subjectively...</u>)

EXAMPLES #4, 5. [4.] CARL COHEN'S book Four Systems *described four political systems.* Democracy, Individualistic. Democracy, collective. Fascism. And Communism. Each system was simply described, plus defended or advocated—COHEN gave the supposed advantages for each. (As a tour de force...) COHEN did not evaluate the stances for the students.

[5.] And an astute teacher, DENNIS DUTTON, had students encounter the book. Similar to PAUL'S two films above, he made them confront this complexity and seek to know how to respond to these conflicting claims, competently.

…again, true brave stuff, rare, invaluable for the **end-goal** of Hitting The Goal Running confronting confusing contested concerns later on…rare in education? ["Well, we have to Cover Content," and etc. …..]

|#+#|+#|+|#+#+|#+#+#+#||+|+#++|#|+#+||+|+#|+|++|#+#++|+|||+#++|+#+#|+|#+|+|+|#|+#|+||+|#+|+|+#|+#|+#|#+|+|#+|+||+|#+|#+|+#|+|#||

[1.] Define Ed. Goals	[2.] Essence of TT: AAA	[3.]Presence?	**[4.] other Variables**

[IV.] *Secondary* variable-issues regarding TTh:

[{ This quickly becomes a grab-bag, or rather a hamper or in-box to save items less important or related but important nevertheless. "You" will omit some, add others of "your" own… }]

|#+#|+#|+|#+#+|#+#+#+#||+|+#++|#|+#+||+|+#|+|++|#+#++|+|||+#++|+#+#|+|#+|+|+|#|+#|+||+|#+|+|+#|+#|+#|#+|+|#+|+||+|#+|#+|+#|+|#||

(12) Number of Skills. *How many or few* thinking skills shall a course include?

RECOMMENDATION. *An issue indeed!* RICHARD PAUL thinks that "less but deeper is more"…

#4. Focus on fundamental and powerful concepts with high generalizability. Don't cover more than 50 basic concepts in any one course. Spend the time usually spent introducing more concepts applying and analyzing the basic ones while engaged in problem-solving and reasoned application.

…down with coverage, even of skills let alone content… up with in-depth practice toward use…

|#+#|+#|+|#+#+|#+#+#+#||+|+#++|#|+#+||+|+#|+|++|#+#++|+|||+#++|+#+#|+|#+|+|+|#|+#|+||+|#+|+|+#|+#|+#|#+|+|#+|+||+|#+|#+|+#|+|#||

(13) When, in student's education sequence, should which skills be taught?

|#+#|+#|+|#+#+|#+#+#+#||+|+#++|#|+#+||+|+#|+|++|#+#++|+|||+#++|+#+#|+|#+|+|+|#|+#|+||+|#+|+|+#|+#|+#|#+|+|#+|+||+|#+|#+|+#|+|#||

(14) Location of Thinking Skills.
In separate freestanding course—or infused in existing courses?

STATEMENT. The general approach teaches thinking separately from content. Of course "content" is present (political issues, problems at school, or previously-learned subject-matter). But the purpose is teaching thinking, using nonschool-subject contexts. Theoretically no content is required. Logic can be taught mathematically as variables. If A then B and so on. However, of course, universally education uses specific examples to illustrate the abstract principles.   [-- ROBERT ENNIS]

|#+#|+#|+|#+#+|#+#+#+#||+|+#++|#|+#+||+|+#|+|++|#+#++|+|||+#++|+#+#|+|#+|+|+|#|+#|+||+|#++|+|+#|+#|+#|#+|+|#++|+|#++||+|#+|#+|+#|+|#||

(15) Correlation with different LEARNING-STYLES?

ISSUE. **In teaching/learning thinking, how important *is* the matter of varied LEARNING-STYLES?**

SUMMARY-GLIMPSE. The literature on "styles" is immense…

--(1) Grasp experience or take in information: more via concretely, or more via abstractly.

Then (2) process, transform that experience or information: more via reflective observation, or more via active experimentation…

--Alternate reflection and practice, practice and reflection: Think-Do-Think, Do-Think-Do….

--Holistic lumping, analytic splitting. Analytical or field-independent (isolated) and relational or field-dependent (context).

WHAT THINKING SKILLS USED HERE?: The issue of degrees of **"Knowing vs. Knowing."** "We all know of-or-about" learning-styles, but many fewer of us (myself earlier—and even now) *truly know richly and "autonomously apply as appropriate."* End-Goal of "ultimate expectable readiness"…

TABLE: For teachers even more than learners, the concepts of **(1) WHAT is the TRUE "CONTENT" (SUBSTANCE)** of a course—traditional Content-knowledge? And/or Concepts?
Plus also **(2) ORDER OR SEQUENCE.** Options as to how idea and illustration can sequence and interrelate…..
(1) **True content?** The difference between "<u>covering content</u>" (as in subtypes-of, historical time periods, great individuals, etc.) and "<u>conveying concepts</u>."
(2) **Material to know, or also to use?** Awareness, or also transferring or Exporting it to apply in actual situations?
(3) **Order or sequence of both Content and Skills, also Theory and Application**? Think-Do-Think, vs. Do-Think-Do, just so all is included…

The course:	Traditional content coverage approach:	Altered concept-conveying approach:	Increased use not just knowing:

"Visual Art(s)-Appreciation"	Historical, also Schools, also Great Artists: Egyptian, Greek, then Renaissance schools, Rembrandt, Impressionism...	The Principles and Elements of Design: balance symmetry proportion line texture value color etc.	"Re-design your living quarters"... "
Philosophy	(1) Historical Schools: Greeks (Plato), on to Renaissance. Idealism, realism, materialism, empiricism. Modern: existentialism etc. Also (2) Great Questions ("how we know," etc., etc.)	Six key perspectives: Questioning, Definition of terms, Implications, Consequences, Consistencies, Logic-Reasoning.	"Philosophy of" applied to (1) current controversies, also (2) the "daily": sex, food, the bicycle, graffiti, more!
Economics	Traditional: much theory, and perhaps little practice beyond "textbook exercises"	[Prof. L. J. MALONE at Hartwick College:] start with theory first half, like "supply and demand, pricing, decision making, and the laws of returns," but then... [But also Prof. PAUL HEYNE: start with felt problem-issues, then learn the theory to explore them...] INDUCTIVE?	...apply to current issues of **"Immigration," "File-Sharing," and "Drugs"**... DEDUCTIVE?
HOWARD GARDNER'S proposed General Education core course:	[Traditional: Great Issues without theory?]	Examine three topics in detail: **evolution, Mozart's The Marrige of Figaro, and the Holocaust.** (Presumably with intellectual apparatus...)	[Ideally then apply on own to other current issues as ultimate test of end-goal readiness. E.g., **"the longitude problem, Shakespeare, the Native American issue"**]

...Okay, I guess that this time, I **DO** concur. Relatively few courses do emphasize both theory (tools) but also then application to the content, which is selected to support the theory. Plus you can go either way, theory or examples first...	...that was my recent realization of the Teaching Revolution which is *not occurring except it is*, here and there.

RECOLLECT:. Variations in learning economics...
BILL BRANDL gave students concepts the first day of class, asked to find real-world examples of them at once.
PROF. HAYES held to starting with problem-situations, real-world concerns, and then applying the concepts.
PROF. MALONE'S first half of the semester was theory. But then, application to "immigration, file-sharing, drugs."

PROCEDURE. Prof. BARRY BEYER teaches skill-first...

1. Introduce the skill. 2. Explain it. 3. Demonstrate, model it. 4. Review what was done. 5. Apply the skill (guided practice). 6. Reflect on the skill

...I personally like this, but **could also go with "do-then-think"**: a problem-situation first, experientially, then the **skill to "rescue" students' perplexities**. *Just so the end-goal is to Hit The Ground Running...*

ANECDOTAL EXAMPLE. "Oh How We Differ On Balance of Didacticism and Experiment..."

I wrote an article on teaching writing. "Predrafting," or "having students learn to write before we teach them how." The tactic offered was that I would simply mention and illustrate a skill (parallelism, specific detailing, sentence-variety) and then have students do an exploratory practice draft, a "mistake" or "learning"-draft, free from worry about correctness, to freely find out how much they already knew about the skill personally. Then sample model answers were shown. This tactic, of course, to blend in personal prior knowledge with formal instruction...
I submitted the article to the leading journal College Composition and Communication. Its then-editor was *alarmed*. He wrote back, "*By having students try to apply a skill which you have not yet taught them, you are surely setting them up for failure!*" I re-explained my rationale as above. The editor responded by simply rejecting the article without any further comment of his own... [-- PERSONAL ANECDOTE]

...stellar instance of an expert (the editor) ***utterly unaware of*** a differing major paradigm, it seems...

EXPERIENTIAL LEARNING. A great roster of possibilities—but note a **PITFALL**: failing to *conceptualize about* the experience later... Here are varied instances of using experience educationally, in various courses, fields:

1. "M & M Walk": must walk *this far*... to work off a handful of candy. (dieting, health).

2. A day in a wheelchair on campus. (Awareness of disability minority issues.)

3. Wear a "Gay Pride" button for 24 hours. (Self-experience of minority feelings.)

4. "Stage a scuffle in the corridor." (History: how we perceive the same event differently)

5. Instructor composes a poem just like Rod McKuehn's on the spot. (To question those students impressed by that poet's *supposed* subtlety, quality. But the instructor could just "dash it off"...)

6. "Here is your personal astrology profile." (Students thought it reflected them, then exchanged profiles; all were the same... Questions pseudoscience.)

7. Fl)uroridation: two texts against it, a ranting letter to the editor, a supposedly-good pamphlet. Students "bought" the latter. Then a third: Consumer Union article devastating the (politically-motivated) pamphlet. (Again, self-esteem threatened; students didn't like to get fooled. Motivating...)

8. Philosophy professor Monday discusses Plato. Wednesday, tells class he gave them Plato's wrong name, true name was XXXXX. Friday, tells them to cross out their notes, Plato's real name was YYYYY. Students are irritated, questioned the prof thereafter. (Issue of "how do you know something is true?")

ANECDOTE. ROGER L. and I *disagreed* on heart in the street, head in the study...

In re "diversity education," an administrator recommended experience: sharing our stories, etc. I said that the concepts in the book Black And White Styles in Conflict helped me enormously to understand that Black students conversing loudly in the cafeteria, were less rowdy than naturally-communicative via their own styles. Roger condemned this. We neither fought, agreed, or discussed further...

A Personal Stand: I seem to favor concepts as potentially emotional, empowering after all. "Know why you feel or do thus, and you paradoxically reduce self-blame, have a better chance for freer choice now..." "Therapeutic"...

--EXAMPLE: JANE ELLIOT, who produces the talk "Blue Eyes and Brown Eyes," goes for scenarios to raise anger hence awareness, and the only handhold tool she could offer was "Always ask, is it the race, or is it the case?" Is a trait racial, or that of an individual?

--And our **Tool-Kit** for **Diversity / Multicultural / Minority Education** (see Appendix) is heavily conceptual. Tools such as **Selective Perception, Stereotype vs. Sociotype, Relativism: Cultural vs. Moral**, and others replace mere information (or diversity-"celebration"), and may help students hit the ground running later on in the arena...

GALLERY. Some choice assignments *interbalancing* the **Think** and **Do** polarities of concrete experience, conceptual reflection.

Again, *both* the personal-experiential, *and* the objective-decentering, moves have drawbacks *and* benefits. PITFALL: students may be informed only one or the other is better...

Personal (+) **ORCHIDS**: for motivation, for indispensable truth-source, for relevance...	Impersonal (+) **ORCHIDS**: for powerful "decentering," empathy, accuracy...
Personal (-) **ONIONS**: if experience remains unanalyzed, egocentric.	Impersonal (-) **ONIONS**: if detached from self and whole response, of course.

Following is the "cream of the crop" (of two decades of collecting assignments). These *correlate two important contraries* of **learning-styles**. The **personal-experiential**, and the **expository-informational**. "*Do,*

> *then think and be told," or "Be told then try out," and in dynamic oscillation.*
> *They also correlate **three other important contraries**:*
> **(1) Personal** experiential exploration, but also **Objective** explicit thinking criteria.
> **(2) Tight** guidance but also **Loose** flexibility.
> **(3) Group** Convergence/Divergence and **Solo** Divergence. "Collaborative learning" is present, but again, not to the *pitfall* of "groupthink," but to open out to diverse responses as each being valuable.

PITFALL: But do even *advanced* assignments always densely embed thinking?

GALLERY. A set of *selected* assignments *deftly* interweaving learning-styles:

> But note that <u>they fell short</u>… to all of them <u>I had to add the following three last steps</u>, which are key to our TThinking approach and which were largely absent from the assignments themselves: We recall the elements of **EMBEDDEDNESS:** *EXISTENT, EXPLICIT, ELEVATED, EXPORTED* …
>
> In re the D-Machine variable-issues:
>
> **(#1) Goals** of Education: include thinking, or not?
> **(#9) "Liminality."** How **Explicit**?
> **(#2) Abstraction.** How far **Elevated** up to higher-order not rote-rule thinking level? To generic, not domain-specific, thinking?
> **(#3) Application:** how much **Exported** or transferred to new and foreign or far material.
>
> In re the Embedded model:
>
> **[0. → Were students first informed explicitly about this new approach to education?]**
> **1.** Were thinking skills EXISTENT at all?
> **2.** What EXPLICIT thinking skills were explicitly identified and taught to the students?
> **3.** "What did this assignment tell you about (A) the specific subject [as sociology, biology, etc.], but also (B) about thinking skills: both (1) in the subject-field, and also (2) ELEVATED or generic ones?
> **4.** "Transfer or EXPORT those skills, to (A) something else within the field [=a different story or poem, a different psychological case-history, etc.], and then (B) to real life: personal, vocational, citizen-in-community"

> **(1) HIGH SCHOOL SOCIAL STUDIES.** The subject is, say, "*capital punishment*" (or another current contested controversy of common concern—*security, immigration policy, welfare reform*, the *drug problem*...)
>
> 1. <u>First</u>, write down all your opinions for and against the practice. For each one, decide what the opposing argument might be.
> 2. <u>Next</u>, write a short paper making your own stand on the practice.
> 3. <u>Then</u>, read the reserve material in the Media Center and find other arguments.
> 4. <u>Next</u>, in small groups, assess what you've found.
> 5. <u>Next</u>, rewrite your original paper—and articulate it (annotate, gloss, etc.) as to how you improved it in **Competence** along the way.
> 6. [*] Finally, briefly assess: what have you learned about **better *thinking in general*** from this?
>
> That's potentially <u>powerful</u>. That assignment blends the personal and the more scholarly-objective. It properly starts with the "me first" approach of splashing in and thinking it through for yourself as a baseline. Then also it nicely compares/contrasts not only the personal, and the more professional or objective, but also it Com-Munes with other learners to try to resolve complexities. Oh, and it surely urges Consciousness or meta-cognition about one's own thinking. <u>Of course, all this presumes</u> *the course will furnish EXPLICIT thinking tools and criteria, standards...*

(2) ART HISTORY:

1. Describe your <u>personal impressions</u> of a painting or other work of art about which you now have no background information. (I.e., personally like or dislike, and why? Opinion/judgment, good or bad art and why?)
2. Then <u>learn more</u> about the work--research the work or read the textbook and hear the lecture.
3. Then <u>analyze</u> how your new knowledge affected your initial impression. Did it *reinforce, modify, alter* your original views?
4. [*] What did you learn from this about ***better thinking generally***? Derive the techniques, state explicitly!

Again, <u>blends</u> the *Personal-Discovery*, and then the *Objective-Delivery*, methods nicely...

---

(3) SAFETY EDUCATION—but this would work in any specific-skills course, people-oriented, technical, social, whatever:

1. <u>Read</u> this description of an accident.
2. Then <u>write</u>, quickly, to analyze the problem and recommend course of action.
3. Then, <u>discuss</u> your response with your peers, sharing and evaluating differing responses. *Make explicit the criteria you are employing*.
4. Then, after discussion, <u>re-evaluate your response</u>. "What is the correct solution here—if any? And what judgments are legitimately-arguable? And if you still differ, why is this—**incompetence, personal taste, judgment-call, legitimate conflicts, bias?**"
5. [*] <u>Assess learning on two levels</u>. What have you learned from this about not only (A) better Safety Education procedure, ***but also*** (B) ***generic thinking skills***—how to observe carefully, and how to deal with group disagreements and differences?

This anyhow gets into Competence and "<u>one right answer</u>" vs. "<u>judgment-call</u>" because of different specific factors—prior belief-system, estimations, situationality.....A nice progress away from either Ground Zero—the one right answer the course gives—and also away from Ground One—"naïve relativism," who's to say who's right after all, let alone Thinking as mere Personal Opinionation or what do *you* think!...

---

(4) LITERATURE:

1. <u>Write</u> a ten-minute burst of *every question you can ask* about this group of <u>poems by Walt Whitman</u>.
2. Then, <u>assess the questions</u>.
--Which call for factual knowledge only—which for mere opinion—which for "reasoned judgment"?
--Which can have one right answer—which can validly allow for disagreement?
--Which are convergent and close down—which can stimulate further thinking?
--Which are limited—and which may represent a larger **Variable-Issue** about confronting <u>literature itself</u> (oh, such as "**continuity vs. change in a writer's output or career**".....**"importance or not of the biographical**".....**"topical references vs. more "timeless" appeal.....and others!**)
3. [*] --What have you learned about (A) approaching *poetry*, (B) ***thinking skills in general?***

Seems self-explanatory in its explicit, guided-convergent training in autonomous divergence! Focussed accurate precise – but also flexible adaptable pragmatic. How to ask which questions. [*] *And how to generalize one's learning of thinking itself...*

SEE LATER: Teaching **music appreciation**, DOUG OVENS starts in the sea of raw experience (*clank, ding, thud, bonk*) and proceeds to the mountaintop of concepts. (See in the Gallery, #5)

(16) The issue of *other major* "types of thinking."

Creative, right-brain associative. **"Emotional intelligence" including empathy, sympathy, rapport, de-centering. "Women's Ways of Knowing."**

RECOLLECT: ALVERNO COLLEGE'S roster including citizenship, aesthetics, ethics…

QUOTATION. A favorite one of mine suggesting **"GUT FEEL"** as a non-intellectual but very powerful "knowing" which can help thinking via awareness and judgment, etc.

"If you have really learned what <u>calculus</u> means, you have a gut feel for the behavior of billiard balls, automobiles, electric currents, servomechanisms, space vehicles, and all the other objects of engineering which no amount of practical experience alone can provide." [ON ENGINEERING EDUCATION]

…points the way to this whole element of "intelligences" *beyond* explicit **Conceptualizing UPward 101**… But glad that we have here concentrated on that as <u>the bedrock standpoint for **all** thinking</u>…

[{(**END** of "D-MACHINE" component of <u>Teaching Thinking</u>…)}]

|#+#|+#|+|#+#+|#+#+#+#||+|+#++|#|+#+||+|+#|+|++|#+#++|+|||+#++|+#+#|+|#+|+|+|#|+#|+||+|#+|+|+#|+#|+#|#+|+|#+||+|#+|#+|+#|+|#||
|#+#|+#|+|#+#+|#+#+#+#||+|+#++|#|+#+||+|+#|+|++|#+#++|+|||+#++|+#+#|+|#+|+|+|#|+#|+||+|#+|+|+#|+#|+#|#+|+|#+||+|#+|#+|+#|+|#||

103

(4) Gallery of EXAMPLES :

Experts' <u>statements-about</u> teaching thinking… actual course <u>assignments</u>
teaching thinking… and, educators' *varied* <u>responses</u> to the issue…

--THE ISSUE AND OUR RESPONSE: "The Material illustrates the Mental: concrete specific examples, help clarify conceptual generalities." <u>Therefore this gallery of illustrative quotations</u> to help "solidify" the concepts (and problem-issues) about teaching/learning/doing thinking. [*ANALOGY*: descend from the Peak of Principles, to the Pond of Particulars to "rehydrate the abstractions."] [The "opposite sin" from having Ideas Only: having Information Only, or only unanalyzed specifics, a flood of mere data-information, facts, and Stories, without the distilling-out of thought-ful conceptualizing, inducting upward to harvest the concepts therein…]

WHAT THINKING SKILLS USED HERE?: **Concrete-Conceptual balance**. The right mix of generalities and specifics is needed, plus enough of varied examples but not too many… Plus examples should be commented upon, explicated.

#+||#|+#|+|+|#+|||#+||+#|+||#|+#|++|+#+|||#+|+#+|+||#|#+|#|+|+#|+#||#|+|||#|+#|+|+|#+|#+|+#|+#|+#||+|+#||##|+|#+|#+||+|#+||

TABLE OF CONTENTS of these readings:

(5) Responses of educators to the teaching-thinking issue: *(And, ours to theirs…)* **P. 125-**

(5.A.) First Survey, of 18 typical responses to the idea.

Not needed… not possible… too many formidable barriers: institutional, etc… the "reward system" doesn't reward it… Not the job I was hired for!… A better educational goal is [indoctrination… technical training… etc.]… I wouldn't know how to!... I'm the "Sage on the Stage"… Too much work… *And more…* }]

(5.B.) Why do people disagree on an issue? The "3-DDD" model.

(1) Roster #1, Brief   **(2)** Three examples of *"wild-wide"* faculty responses to student papers   **(3)** Roster #2, Full

(5.C.) Eight key responses explicated in detail.

#+||#|+#|+|+|#+|||#+||+#||+||#|+#||++|+#+|||#+|+#+|+||#|#+|#|+|+#||#|+|||#|+#|+|+|#+|#+|+#|#+|#|+#|+#|+#|+|+#||#+#|+|#+|#+||+|#+||

WHAT THINKING SKILLS USED HERE?:   **(1)** __Variables-Variation__. We (1) identify what variable-issues the examples discuss: (and students by now can identify them— *yes, even if the writer left them unnamed, subliminal*) … and then we (2) critique the particular choices made as valid or not (and students by now also know of more options A to Z—*yes, even more, probably, than some of the writers themselves did* …)

(2) Also **"3-DDD":** people will diverge, differ, disagree on the same issue. *Why?* See the varieties of responses. [= Legitimate objections; misconceptions; conflicting values; biases; evasions, resistances…or so we thought…] It seems useful to discern, plus pleasurable to spot blunders and successes…

"WARM-UP" EXAMPLE: Here is how one can *respond to someone else's response* to an issue.
The text is by STANLEY FISH, literary critic. Its gist: "The university should not try to do everything, including moral education." *Can learners discern "x-ray" style,* WHAT STANDS HE TAKES ON WHAT ISSUES—WHAT OPTIONS ARE POSSIBLE—WHAT OTHER ISSUES HE MAY NOT BE CONFRONTING?

In Aristotle, the Gospel, Plato, Kant, William James, etc., moral concerns do arise, but the students are *not* to learn morality, they are to learn "the ways in which poets, philosophers and political theorists structure their inquiries and reflections. These authors are worth studying *not* because of their answers or stands, but "the verbal, architectonic, or argumentative skills they display" in their thinking and writing. So the goal for the student is to inquire, *not* "about what sort of person they should be, but an inquiry about what kind of person Plato or Hobbes or Rawls or Milton thought they should be, and for what reasons, and with what poetic or philosophical force." The exam is *not* "in a given situation, what should you do," but rather "in a given situation, what would Plato, Hobbes Rawls, and Kant tell you to do, and what are the different assumptions and investments that would generate their different recommendations?"… Now, *"somewhere down the line"* your learning may factor into the moral response you give to a situation, but down the line is a long distance away," and *meanwhile, one should stick to the proper academic enterprise…*   [-- STANLEY FISH, in CHE]

This approach takes stands on many important issues. The issues are not named explicitly by FISH., Nor are alternate stands often given also. But can we identify the text's issues present but unstated; know of other issues not even mentioned; know of all options within an issue not just the one the writer chooses?…

--First, FISH __does echo our model__ of Thinking Things Through. **Goals of education #1?** FISH __surpasses the current-traditional model__; for him, not Indoctrination in What to Believe or how to act, but rather, **#2 Abstraction**, learning *how* moralists think not *what* they think. [Bravo…] And the goal being also to **Apply #3**…

--But then FISH __stops short of our model__. One does *not* **Export** to a far-off real-world situation, Hitting The Ground Running for sure when faced with a bank scandal, a sexual issue, an ethical dilemma … Nor is **Autonomy #4** sought: the teacher chooses or sets the issue to be examined on, not the student…

…..Thus we scrutinize a statement for its **variables** and the **variation** of stands possible on them.

#+||#|+#|+|+|#+|||#+||+#||+||#|+#||++|+#+|||#+|+#+|+||#|#+|#|+|+#||#|+|||#|+#|+|+|#+|#+|+#|#+|#|+#|+#|+#|+|+#||#+#|+|#+|#+||+|#+||

O R I E N T A T I O N - B A R

1. G. Gallery	2. Advanced	3. Leisurely Lab	4. Transformed	5. Responses

[1.] Gorgeous gallery of "Orchids"

ISSUE: Explicit "Presence" of Thinking Goals—"Embedded" in courses, "Exhibited" schoolwide?

[1.1] EXAMPLE. A policy-statement from a secondary school in New York City.

"In <u>every class and every subject</u>, students will learn to ask and to answer these questions:
1. From whose viewpoint are we seeing or reading or hearing? From what angle or perspective?
2. How do we know when we know? What's the evidence, and how reliable is it?
3. How are things events people connected? What is cause, what effect?
4. What's new and what's old? Have we encountered this idea before?
5. So what? What does it matter? What does it all mean?"
[-- DEBORAH MEIER, CENTRAL PARK EAST SCHOOL]

Good, **BUT** who's to say that this will actually *happen*? That these fine questions *will* get posed and faced on "Monday mornings"?	--Right, **BUT** irrelevant to this statement, which I see as *amazingly good, anyhow a classic example* of both #10.**Embeddedness** (these Explicit and Elevated skills shall be present in *every course*) and also of **Exhibiting** (we the *whole school* are Billboard-announcing that this shall be so—which sets the stage for actually Walking the Talk with a Tool-BANK...) --Also the skills seem both **2.Abstract** or conceptual, but also **accessible** for younger students. --*Overall, a dignified fostering of—thought-full thinking amid the info-glut and data-smog or fact-blitz of "content-coverage".* Surely this school is **ennobled** by their "billboarding" this quintet of queries. And if not taught every day, as you suggest, anyhow a start...

#+||#|+#|+|+|#+|||#+||+#|+||#|+#|++|+#+|||#+|+#+|+||#|#+|#|+|+#|+#||#|+|||#|+#|+|+|#+|#+|+#|#+|#|+#|+#|+|+#||#+#|+|#+|#+||+|#+||

ISSUE: **Explicit Naming of High-Order Concepts/Skills—Interdisciplinary, Also...**

[1.2] EXAMPLE. A first semester freshman social science course that examines what kind of control the students have over their own lives":

"They learn a portion of each social science discipline dealing with individual freedom, which means they learn everything from the theory of *consumer behavior* in economics, to *operant conditioning* in psychology, to *the socialization process* in sociology. [Also *cognitive dissonance* theory in social psychology, and the *existential psychology* of R. MAY and the *humanistic sociology* of P. BERGER.] The theories are treated in their full academic rigor..."   [-- WILLIAM NEWELL, interdisciplinary specialist]

This short description also *repays scrutiny*. ---It is unusually **2.Abstract**, concept-heavy, rich with powerful thinking tools. ---While **Elevated** and conceptual-general, the theories are also obviously **3.Applicable**. ---And **7.Acute** relevance exists, between theory and students' lives—but without using mere raw Personal Experience and Opinionations (my student MICHELLE re-designed an assignment for better thinking, by "giving my own opinion and asking others"...) ---Plus, there's the chance for ultimate transfer, of <u>using these same concepts not only for the freedom-control issue, but for *other* questions</u>. ---And of course *learning how to use theories*. This course seems to offer quite an arsenal of tools for the Ceiling-Bank for students to use to Hit The Ground Running later...

Well now <u>wait</u>. Wouldn't *any* good course in social science, present the keystone theories, the Big Ideas, the salient concepts, as well as the factual information? Textbooks mention these frequently!	First, <u>no.</u> At least not always as here, UP to **explicitness**, then ACROSS to be **Exported** and **applied**, as this course seems bravely to seek to do... (From my psychology course I learned nothing Applicable, except bits of behaviorism theory on my own—if *a response is not rewarded it is extinguished, so "praise people when they do well,"* etc.) (*SEE* The three textbooks I saw, two in anthro and geography, which stayed earthbound, lacked keystones.) Plus I like the interdisciplinary or **integrative** scope here. All or many of the social sciences are represented, for less partiality, more power...

ISSUE: Subject-Matter ["coverage"] now Secondary to Thinking Skills for Future Use...

[1.3.] EXAMPLE. HOWARD GARDNER'S proposal for "more with less"...

In a recent book, The Disciplined Mind, the famous Harvard researcher of "multiple intelligences" urges that schools quit attempting to teach encyclopedic coverage of material (which is forgotten and which changes anyhow). Instead, schools should focus students' abilities (and even young children can and do "reason") on "a much reduced but deeper curriculum." For EXAMPLE, close examination of three topics: evolution, Mozart's "The Marriage of Figaro," and the Holocaust. By *"scrutinizing levels, examining evidence, analyzing texts, and proposing alternate theories approaches and solutions,"* students may develop the *"critical reasoning skills they need to figure out any sort of problem,"* plus will "learn the bases for truth, beauty and morality in our society." (Topics are variable. Americans could also study "the longitude problem, Shakespeare, and the Native American issue." Japan or Bolivia would find other issues seminal to them.)   [-- BILL CAMPBELL, review, in Milwaukee Journal Sentinel]

You may well like this one. You implied other teachers might not. The ten teachers at your home school...	**YES,** this seems as good a "touchstone" as NEWELL'S social science course above, and even more **comprehensive** in scope for general thinking. (Analogically, this seems like water and nutrients added to the soil of knowledge-information, to grow thinking power.) Here "covering content" is harnessed to "thinking through" that content. And ultimate **3.Application**, skills **Exported** to figure out *"any sort of problem."* Could be a suave model for re-designing many courses...

Half of the Course Applies Theory to "Hit The Ground Running" in the Real World...

[1.4.] EXAMPLE. Not "Economics 254." Instead, Economics: **Immigrants, File Sharing, and Drugs**."

At Hartwick College, Prof. L. J. MALONE quit cramming theory into his introductory economics course. Instead, he now balances: first half, theory; second half, "current controversies" to which the theory is applied. <u>First</u> half, "basics like <u>supply and demand, pricing, decision making, and the laws of returns</u>." But in the <u>second</u> half, "students use what they have learned to examine <u>government policies on immigration, file sharing, and illegal drugs</u>. MR. MALONE purposely selects topics on which students are likely to have strong opinions."
He also steers clear of "chalk and talk," letting students drive the discussion, including in interactive small groups which cooperate and then present results to the class. But the point here is the teacher's "whole learning objective," which is "to push the learning outside the classroom, which in my mind is where learning happens in college."
[-- CHE, Oct. 2004]

--Seems lively, articulate, brilliant. It anyhow takes a stand on **learning-styles** plus the **essence of teaching thinking**: Conceptualize, Transfer, Apply. First Exposition, but then quickly heavy Transfer or Exporting. [*Personally, it makes me "sad and mad" that my own economics course wasn't more like this. I know I took one; I recall endless graphs, period...*] Surely these Hartwick College students Hit The Ground Running.

--Might <u>this notion of *"half-and-half"* course balance help re-design other courses</u>? --**(1) Literature**: first stylistics etc.--*then* weeks of shirtsleeves-explication of genres from A to Z. Graffiti, letters-to-the-editor, Found Poetry, and more...
--**(2) Art Appreciation:** first the principles and elements of design (no historical or Great Artist approach, please) – *then* re-design the campus landscape, or an interior hallway...
--**(3) Philosophy:** first the six key principles (see elsewhere) (no Great Issues, please)—*then* weeks of scrutinizing the nicely-mundane philosophically. *Sex, food and cuisine, bicycles, graffiti*, and more. And so forth...

...I expected you to yap your yawning yawp about "But of course the thinking skills must be made **Expli-cit**" {blah blah, nag nag}... Like in a Tool-KIT...	Hmmm...*forgot to remind the world.* <u>But</u> this course-design seems to get **explicit conscious application** *halfway there already*. The lively topics would probably draw recalled techniques to them like magnets?...

#+||#|+#|+|+|#+||#+||+#||+|#|+#|++|+#+|||#+|+#+|+||#+|#|+|+#|+#||#|+|||#|+#|+|+|#+|#+|+#|+|#|+#|+#||+|+#||#+#|+|#+|#+||+|#+||
#+||#|+#|+|+|#+||#+||+#||+|#|+#|++|+#+|||#+|+#+|+||#+|#|+|+#|+#||#|+|||#|+#|+|+|#+|#+|+#|+|#|+#|+#||+|+#||#+#|+|#+|#+||+|#+||

107

[2.] ADVANCED SEMINAR: subtle points, nuances...

... *Will* these cases help learners grasp finer points more easily? ...

"Astonishing" confirmation that the disciplines teach facts—but also thinking...

[2.1.] **RESEARCH.** Social psychologist ROBERT NISBET finds that—**the disciplines *do* teach thinking**...

He studied whether people's [current, personal] reasoning skills could be improved by teaching them new rules for thinking." He had *assumed* that it would be difficult if not impossible to change [existing and/or conventional] reasoning-patterns, even if the change-agent was significant college-level study in fields such as, for instance, statistics and economics.

"But to my surprise, I found substantial training effects. For example, people who have taken a few statistics courses avoid lots of errors in daily life. They're more likely to see that the 'sophomore slump' in baseball could be due to statistical regression to the mean rather than to some mystical curse, and more likely to realize that an interview should be regarded as a small sample of a person's behavior and, therefore, that a wise hiring decision should be based on the larger sample of information in the application folder. Economists, it turns out, think differently about all sorts of things than the rest of us do—from deciding whether to remain at a boring movie to reasoning about foreign policy."

[NISBETT also found that he could train people briefly and change their thinking habits and even behavior when tested outside the lab.]

"MILD" response: Well, this shows that people do "pick up" thinking skills as they go along after all. Heck, maybe we don't have to teach thinking all so "explicitly" after all, (as you laboriously keep asserting)...

"WILD" response: Well, "duh!" as current slang phrased it! *If NISBET's original idea was right—that we can't change reasoning even through college study—then what the heck is general or liberal education for?* Here is the true reason for studying all those courses and "gaining knowledge." Here is the Conceptualize, Transfer, and Apply of a discipline's thinking tools to actual new situation. Here is the keystone skill-issue of **"allocation cost"** or **"cost-benefit ratio"** (the movie: don't waste time as well as money). Also the skill of **"sampling:** insufficient or unrepresentative data" in cycle too. Here is modestly stated the strong call to thinking skills as the crown and crop of true higher education. *But how often do teachers attend to these results as NISBET briefly mentions here? Rarely, especially as explicit goals, trained for...*

RECOLLECT: J. OMOHUNDRO noting skills from anthropology—observation, etc. –and NICKI HAYES claiming that psychology trains to exact principles, patterns from situations:

Social Agility—adds to sizing up quickly the "rules of the game," getting accepted easier.
Observation—interview as a participant.
Planning—see patterns in a cultural group, generalize, then predict what might happen.
Social Sensitivity—as in "cultural relativism."
Accuracy in Interpreting Behavior—knowing ranges of behavior, cultural causes.
Social Perspective—seeing individual and group actions as cause and effect of larger sociocultural systems.

[The other skills are more generic-scientific: Challenging Conclusions scientifically; Interpreting, and Simplifying, Information; Contextualizing details; and Problem-Solving.....] [-- JOHN OMONUNDRO, anthropologist, SUNY]

#+||#|+#|+|+|#+|||#+||+#|+||#|+#|++|+#+|||#+|+#+|+||#|#+|#|+|+#|+#||#|+|||#|+#|+|+|#+|#+|+#|#+|#|+#|+#|+#|+|+#||#+#|+|#+|#+||+|#+||

Maybe the "best single" case of radical course-revision for "empowered" THINKING...

[2.2.] COURSE PROCEDURE. Economic-textbook author PAUL HEYNE explores: **"What is the 'true content' of the economics course?** Is it information... technique... issues... or the key concepts themselves?" (He also takes a definite stand on the **variable-issue** of "Specific issue first or general concept first?") He asks:

[...but first, A Personal Response: I'm greatly biased in favor of this one. I cannot think economically myself (I or my course failed), and furthermore, I found no fellow teacher in economics who could or would help me with this!]

"What should be the learning goal in the beginning economics course?" HEYNE rejects "the usual learning goal: introducing the student to bits and pieces of technique. Why have beginning students know "*average variable, average total, marginal cost, downward and upward shapes*" and so on and so forth? Well, to learn theory, for its "predictive or clarifying power." But theory is difficult to communicate.

So a second usual goal is the "problems and issues" course. But this can dissolve into naïve relativism: pro and con "*guaranteed incomes, planned obsolescence, free enterprise, unregulated competition, nuclear power, uncontrolled economic growth.*" Too often, students end up feeling "opinions abound, with data to support every one of them, 'it's all relative,' every American is entitled to an opinion, and economics is not a science and is probably a waste of time."

HEYNE therefore opts for the following goal, which seems to echo our approach of thinking as CTA, AAA...

"I want beginning students to master a set of concepts that will help them think more coherently and consistently about the wide range of social problems that economic theory illuminates. The principles of economics make sense out of buzzing confusion. They clarify, systematize, and correct the daily assertions of *newspapers, political figures, ax grinders*, and *barroom pontiffs*. And the applicability of the economist's thought tools is practically unlimited. Students should come to appreciate all of this in a beginning course.

"But they won't unless we, the teachers and textbook writers, persuade them. And we can persuade them only by showing them. *The principles of economics must therefore be taught as tools of analysis.* The teaching of a concept must take place in the context of application. Better, the potential application should be taught first, then the tool. There is so much evidence from pedagogy to support this approach that it's hard at first to understand how any other approach could ever have conquered the field.

"Here is a problem. You recognize it as a problem. What can we say about it?" That's step one.

"Here is how economists think about the problem. They employ the concept of such and such." Step two entails the exposition of some concept of economic theory."

"After the applicability of the concept to the original problem has been demonstrated and some of the implications examined, the concept should be applied to additional problems. That's step three...."

...Masterful. **Ennobling of the classroom,** enriching via Explicit thinking concepts which are Elevated to general complex levels, and then Exported and used. CTA with a vengeance: conceptualize, transfer, apply. And covering a wide range of daily life. How much more empowering than many usual approaches...

#+||#|+#|+|+|#+|||#+||+#|+||#|+#|++|+#+|||#+|+#+|+||#|#+|#|+|+#|+#||#|+|||#|+#|+|+|#+|#+|+#|#+|#|+#|+#|+#|+|+#||#+#|+|#+|#+||+|#+||

Do course textbooks infuse thinking skills with content? If not, could they...?

[2.3.] PERSONAL EXPERIENCE. Recently I was perusing three discarded recent textbooks from my University's introductory courses in anthropology, biology, and geography.

--I saw in them things—actually, the absence of potential things—that I would not have noticed before I started researching this issue of TT....

--Take the single important, generic thinking skill of "Cause-Effect Analysis." What factors cause something, what are its effects?" Surely an important thinking skill also in economics, politics, history, and even... Real Life.....

--Well, these three textbooks were laden with EXAMPLES which *implicitly* involved causalities. (Whether causes of group-conflict in New Guinea due to norms vs. technological changes, or the causes of the enormous human population increase (agricultural, industrial, medical), or the many, varied causes of migration—these issues *tacitly, covertly* involved such CAUSAL MECHANISMS as we'll discuss in Ch. 5, Elucidation of a subject.....The threshhold effect—gradual change, then sudden alteration (water suddenly freezes). One main and several minor contributing causes. A sort of complex network of concurrent causes (as in psychoanalysis and in diabetes). Necessary vs. sufficient causes. And more.....

--But I noted that <u>not one</u> of the three textbooks exploited this possibility in the material. <u>Not one</u> tried to not only convey *explicitly*, to *intertwine*, the FACTUAL CONTENT (and an understanding of it indeed), but also WAYS OF THINKING ABOUT IT and related complex problems, simultaneously!.....<u>and a year ago I would not have perceived this lack, this possible pitfall, anyhow this potentiality not explored...</u>

| NO, you become too strong here, too impractical. How are you going to *stuff or wedge* thinking skills in with the content which undeniably has to be covered? You would *pervert* every course from bio & anthro & geog & sociology & history etc. into a Thinking Skills course... | BUT I *conceded* that "<u>**100%** teaching thinking is indeed</u> <u>impracticable, improbable, even undesirable</u>," So there. It's just that I also said that <u>**N%** of thinking *could* be infused into</u> <u>any course more than it currently is</u>..... |

#+||#|+#|+|+|#+|||#+||+#|+||#|+#|++|+#+|||#+|+#+|+||#|#+|#|+|+#|+#||#|+||#|+#|+|+|#+|#+|+#|+|#|+#|+#|+#|+|+#||#+#|+|#+|#+||+|#+||

<u>Issue:</u> Major reforms in teaching currently include "ACTIVE" or "STUDENT-CENTERED" learning (also "COLLABORATIVE" learning). And "CONSTRUCTIVIST" learning. These *admirably* exceed traditional lecturing. But may they subtly, insidiously *fall short* from teaching thinking explicitly-enough?...

A PERSONAL RESPONSE to spotlight an often-overlooked point:

1. **Competence is not addressed,** this may be the Prevalent Pitfall or misconception of confusing "Just-Thinking," with Good Thinking." [As in MICHELLE'S examples, see the Touchstones, where the personal opinionations of "what do you and others think about it" was supposedly—better thinking!]

2. More to the point, **explicit thinking technique,** let alone teaching (or offering!) them explicitly, **is not addressed.** Take #4 above, look at something "from three different perspectives." This is the great, basic, prior, generic **thinking skill** of "<u>confronting a complexity from *multiple, plural perspectives*—world-views, paradigms, theories, systems, ideologies, schools of thought,</u> etc. [Darwinian evolution (or creationism), behaviorism, democracy, situation-ethics, Natural Law, existentialism, postmodernism, Organic Form in art, liberationism, "camp" or Decadence, whatever...] Especially, *plural and competing schools of thought within* a discipline: theories of literature, anthropology, psychology, sociology, etc. " We call this **"lenswork."**

3. **And again, ➔ what the new education-style *is*, might not have been clarified first!**

[2.4.] EXAMPLE #1. A CONFERENCE PRESENTATION. Here are some of the suggested activities from a Madison, WI seminar on **Active Learning**, late 1990's. At first it surely does *sound* good:

1. "Identify a problem unclear to you" in the material.
2. "Say where you stand on a continuum of positions on the material, and why."
3. Formulate "burning questions" about the material.
4. <u>Look at</u> a case-study of the material **"from three different perspectives."**
5. Decide "which answers on multiple-choice questions are best and why."
6. Critique the lecture's thesis as to its "strongest and weakest supporting points."
7. Identify some important "unstated presuppositions" which lie behind the lecture or textbook material.
...initially this surely seems superior to Straight Lecture. However, I wondered about #4 above..

BUT simply to say THAT one should "look using plural perspectives," does *not at all* tell HOW to do so. I had to create a Tool-KIT on perspectives. I called it **"lenses,"** i.e., systems, frames of reference, etc., for seeing the world. I found its unstated variables to be many.

---

1. Lenses and "reality, the world out there" are <u>different, distinct</u>. "The map is not the territory"!
2. Lenses are <u>inevitable, inescapable</u>. (Though some would deny or not realize this.)
3. Lenses are often <u>subliminal</u>: invisible, tacit-covert-latent, not recognized (or even intended!)
4. Lenses are not "cleanly pure," they come <u>freighted</u> with world-views: presuppositions, implications!
5. Lenses are "<u>double-edged</u>": (+) very powerfully-insightful, <u>but</u> (-) also *surely* limited, *perhaps* biassed too.
6. Lenses <u>over time</u> can become (A) *outdated*—<u>or</u>, (B) wrongfully *neglected* due to thinking fashions. Beware both.
7. Using <u>multiple</u> lenses raises many issues. –Which ones? –Are some primary, some secondary? --Cooperate or conflict? -- Integrate or not finally? --Purposes?
8. The <u>selection</u> of lenses. (A) they may be chosen not at all or subjectively, (B) needed other lenses may be overlooked...

Well, **OKAY**, I do see your point that generic thinking skills and "moves" exist which are not made explicit to the student. But which can be without either overelaboration or oversimplification—or obtrusiveness. **STILL**, I don't think perspectives are all that <u>difficult to find and use</u> once you have been prompted to seek plural ones...	Oh? Lenses always "on tap"? See the example right below. From English 101, the short story "Baseball in July." "Four different perspectives" were all relevant. However, three were *not* automatically seen by students! Nor even by the instructor at first...

[2.5.] EXAMPLE #2. A quality **short story**, "Baseball In July," by PATRICK HOCHTEL, describes what happens when a gay son attends a family christening—and brings along his *male* partner.

Specifically, *various relatives respond variously.* (The half-aware kid brother remains indifferent... The older brother is utterly relaxed about it... The older aunt is puzzled but clueless... The uneasy father painfully attempts to "understand"... And, the disgusted mother exhibits tight-lipped, toxic disdain...)

The Issue: "Definition of the Problem" here. How to locate its cause(s)? **Four useful "lenses"** were:

1. *Natural Law*: unnatural and abnormal, homosexuality *itself* is the problem.
2. A *traditionalism* of sorts. The *over-assertive gay son* was the problem in being too non-assimilationist.
3. *Bigotry & Prejudice*: the *anti-gay* relatives were the problem.
4. *Homophobia*: also "*Heterosexism*." A *socially-learned "ism"* was the problem, like white racism, male chauvinism, ablism.

The Point Here: I doubt students (or myself) could have easily gathered all these four and more useful lenses *on their own*. [The 12:05 class, always a bit "slower" (because either they had eaten lunch, or they hadn't), got stuck on "natural law: unnatural, abnormal gayness was The Problem." They had to be helped to see the other three possibilities.] **PITFALL:** to find all and the right lenses is challenging. *I myself found it difficult to assemble* these four differing, but all productive, lenses. And surely all four are necessary—even though "politically-correct" or "diversity-education" courses might use #4 *only*, risk Indoctrination thus...

#+||#|+#|+|+|#+|||#+||+#|+||#|+#|++|+#+|||#+|+#+|+||#|+#|+#|+|+#|+#||#|+|||#|+#|+|+#+|#+|+#|+#|+#|+#|+#|+|+#||#+#|+|#+|#+||+|#+||

ISSUE. Learning and Life -- Exposition and Experience. How to skilful blend the two methods, and move from concrete experiences to conceptual elucidation...

[2.6.] COURSE DESCRIPTION. DOUG OVENS' "Intro to Music Composition" at Muhlenberg College

--In essence, he offers "studio sessions" to complement lecture-discussion in "fine-arts appreciation" courses—the exact counterpart of labs in science courses. Many of the students in the course are there to satisfy the fine-arts requirement....

--The course opens by students bringing "<u>found instruments</u>" to class and just plain experimenting with them. Dustpan, jar lid, cookie tin, saw, alarm clock, plastic zipper, pencil sharpener—and especially the so-resonant stainless-steel kitchen bowl....

--"I'm trying to find hooks, to get them excited about pushing notes around, without saying, 'First you have to have 15 hours of theory,'" says MR. OVENS.

--The students first compose <u>a 30-second "sound sculpture"</u> attempting "a design of timbres or sound colors" based on the found instruments. They devise their own notational system.

--By Week #4 or #5, the conventional signature-and-stave system replaces the homegrown one, and the "found instruments" give way to vibraphones, drums, marimbas. More important, speedily the students learn "<u>the

<u>rudiments</u> of reading music, of scales, intervals, chord progressions, harmonies...improvisation and <u>the basics of musical form</u>."

--Not so incidentally, students who arrive with a background in music, profit unexpectedly. Despite music lessons, they haven't considered "how pieces are put together." They "have musical experience, but they *haven't thought at all about the issues we're covering in class*." Nor is perfection attained—students won't leave the course "knowing all the reasons" why a particular piece of music works. "But they'll know there *is* a reason. It's not arbitrary. This works. This doesn't."

--This, the summary of DOUG OVENS' "experiential-immersion" course, quite unlike most, and illustrating vividly this Variable-Issue.... [--CHRONICLE OF HIGHER EDUCATION, 1999]

Marvelously correlates the contraries of Personal Experience also Conceptual Guidance. Helps illuminate this Variable-Issue. Dense concrete activity, builds toward objective competence. "To what extent do we use experience, to what extent do we use formal instruction?" Or, "In what sequence and by what methods, and in what proportion-balance, do we use experience vs. conceptual mastery of concepts?" Done carefully, a "hotbox" for creating *true* **knowing**.

#+||#|+#|+|+|#+|||#+||+#|+||#|+#|++|+#+|||#+|+#+|+||#|+#+|#|+|+#|+#||#|+|||#|+#|+|+|#+|#+|+#|+#|+#|+||#|+#|+|+#||#+#|+|#+|#+||+|#+||

#+||#|+#|+|+|#+|||#+||+#|+||#|+#|++|+#+|||#+|+#+|+||#|+#+|#|+|+#|+#||#|+|||#|+#|+|+|#+|#+|+#|+#|+#|+||#|+#|+|+#||#+#|+|#+|#+||+|#+||

O R I E N T A T I O N - B A R

| 1. G. Gallery | 2. Advanced | **3. Leisurely Lab** | 4. Transformed | 5. Responses |

[3.] "LEISURELY LAB":
Self-Test; Discussion-Board; "Game Room"...

INTRODUCTION. The pace now slows, to ponder these easy, simple—or suspect?—examples. For profit: can learners do so? For "fun": identify their presuppositions, stands, excellences, errors...

Even "wayward minor" issues, may benefit from a tool-BANK of varied thinking ploys:

[3.1.] EXERCISE. Trying to explain a mildly-"scandalous" social sub-issue—but, competently...

| ...didn't you also do something *else* on your Favorite Subject of HOMO-SEXUALITY? Something about **"gay men being sex maniacs"**? | ...well not exactly but yes. I pondered, "**Why is it that** homosexual males, **gay men**—*some big-city acquaintances when I visit them, anyhow*—**seem so obsessed with sex?** With performing it, with discussing it?" Then I found emerging, an **interestingly-varied "tool-set" of possible responses**. Which became *interdisciplinary* as well as suspect bad-thinking on my part...

(1) In re "diversity studies": (A) a **stereotype.** Plus (B) **"selective perception."** Plus even (C) our disgust with overt gay sexuality as a component of **"homophobia,"** one of the isms like chauvinism, racism, even if not our fault... That is, do we *over*-perceive gays' *sexual* comments, and over*look* their many comments on *other* subjects such as politics, religion, art, interior decoration, and the like? (Admittedly, *not* usually on sports or cars—or is that Selective Perception on my part?...)

(2) In re minority groups: perhaps in public gays can't talk about sex as openly as straights usually can today. So when gays gather, they use that chance to discuss sexuality more. Perhaps a sort of "psychological demography" thus?

(3) In re psychiatry: do some gay men indeed copiously use sex as a way of dealing with psychogenic issues in their own past, sociogenic oppression in their lives now?

(4) In re psychobiology: is it that gay men are *men, males*? The male of the species approaches sexuality more directly and forthrightly than women do. And so when you get men-and-men and |

112

	sexuality, without the balance of women, eroticism gets ramped up?
	(5) In re <u>communication</u>: does our culture mis-define "sexual orientation" as sex only, not also emotion, affection, love? Another reason we'd mis-perceive gays as "sexual" only?
	(6) In re <u>ethics, morality</u>: does our over-concern with this have a Puritan tinge? *Who cares* if gay men talk or do sex?... Are we still hung up on sexuality?
	(7) ... and <u>more</u>. *The whole point being:* <u>**to competently confront complexities, we need to survey a wide catchment-area of possible and ill-labelled thinking ploys**</u>. This mastering of a larger "tool-bank" is a keystone of true education for thinking, but seems under-developed. *That's* all... [Now let's go talk about fine art, and even lustily if you like; I do...]
...well, good. **BUT** still, I think you emphasize this subject of homosexuality too much in this module...	[Now we can either combat, or cooperate to unpack and examine your statement... And I can cooperate falsely, or actually truly... It's would all be about **Considerate** thinking, the **dispositions** thereof...] **(*)** The main point of the above "queered" example: **complexity of subject repays, requires competently-complex thinking.** *But how to know of <u>all</u> lenses to apply?*

#+||#|+#|+|+|#+|||#+|+#|+||#|+#|++|+#+|||#+|+#+|+||#|#+|#|+|+#|+#||#|+|||#|+#|+|+|#+|#+|+|+#|#+|#|+#|+|#|+#||#+#|+|#+|#+||+|#+||

Connecting learning and life—but beyond superficiality?

[3.2.] EXAMPLE. The <u>course-evaluation</u> feedback comment about my own freshman English 101 course by student KEITH KOSLOWSKI, Univ. of Wis.-Whitewater, 1991:

Another skill I often use is **categorization**, relating ideas into groups. It has helped in school; before this class I dreaded making outlines for papers, but now it is simple. It also helps when speaking with parents or friends. Calling home, I used to say just anything that popped into my mind, jumping around whether about fishing, school, work, or basketball. My parents couldn't follow my train of thought and reply to my questions, but now I break the talk down into separate subjects, and stay on one subject and ask the questions I want answered.

[KEITH then continued and mentioned the skill of **concretization** or using specific detail and examples. He is now less vague and more vivid both in work on the yearbook, and in telling friends about what he does on the yearbook staff.]

WOW! How *ridiculous*. This apple-polishing student dutifully would have us believe he **Categorizes** in talking or writing home! *Give us a break.* This is mechanical, and not appropriate or significant, either—it's trivial. He's telling the teacher what he knows the teacher wants to hear. It's hollow, sham... And anyhow in terms of **Transfer**, it's to some pretty trivial, Lower-level applications, isn't it, even if in the arena of his personal life...Not "hitting the ground running," just tapping...	**WHOA.** You're right, or at least, the other students also said they felt KEITH was brown-nosing. *But I just don't care.* Because between KEITH'S lines I sense a true **Knowing** of the skills of **Categorizing, Concretizing,** (and also **Con-sequencing** or structure organization arrangement and yet others). What they are, and how to use them. KEITH has **Awareness**, and also **Ability**—If he wishes can clearly **Apply** these skills in real-life Arenas. This plus **Articulation** is what counts. He is **Hitting The Ground Running** here, even if with basic skills in easy or lower-level situations. This is education! ...And as for it being a trivial application—I rather like on the other hand the launch, the trajectory, the soaring across, and the arrival or delivery. A skill from the classroom, used in real life—again, Shakespeare and the waiting room? ***Not*** *crammed for an exam and forgotten,* **not** *learned by rote and unused.* I'll buy and celebrate *that.*

#+||#|+#|+|+|#+|||#+|+#|+||#|+#|++|+#+|||#+|+#+|+||#|#+|#|+|+#|+#||#|+|||#|+#|+|+|#+|#+|+|+#|#+|#|+#|+|#|+#||#+#|+|#+|#+||+|#+||

Even the "Library Research Paper" can be infused with thinking?

[3.3.] ASSIGNMENT. Fortifying the traditional library research assignment...

In my mid-career teaching, I realized how the research-paper assignment (at least in a more-general course such as English 101) could be ramped up from Information (plus at times Indoctrination or also mere Personal Opinion) toward more competent thinking-through an issue. Below, briefly but quite adequately, a roster of some term-paper <u>subjects</u> ... and some obvious types of thinking <u>skills</u> which could be infused, imbued, learned:

SUBJECTS:	SKILLS:
History of Alcoholics Anonymous. Development of Color Television, History of Snowmobiles. Current Concerns: Abortion, Capital Punishment, Euthanasia, Gun Control, etc. Compare and contrast Christmas and Hanukkah. The Chicago fire; the San Francisco earthquake. UFO's and Atlantis: do they exist?	Causes and effects, of social movements. Difficulties in innovation. Why we differ on contended issues. Criteria, standards, "lenses" we use. Evaluation of functions of an institution. Social problems: prevention, recovery. Why we believe folk traditions.
NO, once again, impractical! The research assignment is to teach technical research skills. You can't crowd in thinking on top of it. Maybe not just 100% but even 50% of thinking is impossible in a course, as you say!	Think of the **pitfall** of merely researching facts with no (or intuitive) structuring! And the **power** (and the potential **pleasure**) of framing a flood of facts, by conceptual constraints! Of shaping guiding working raw material via deft suave thinking it through! I rest my case for ennobling education, also preparing students to **Hit The Ground Running** when facing issues alone later… *P.S.—One of the best ploys I happened upon, was to "prime the students' pumps" before research by having them think through what questions to search about.*

#+||#|+#|+|+|#+|||#+||+#|||#|+#|++|+#+|||#+|+#+|+||#|+#|+#|+|+#|+#||#|+|||#|+#|+|+|#+|#+|+#|+#|+#|+#|+#|+|+#||#+#|+|#+|#+||+|#+||

Decisions which one school made. Which variable-issues chosen?

[3.4.] PROGRAM. STANFORD UNIVERSITY'S current system for **General Education**
In the first quarter, a team taught three or four texts. Students were immersed for two to three weeks in <u>a single book</u>, examining it via lenses literary historical philosophical. Goal was to "teach how humanists think by exposing them to <u>the kinds of questions</u> such scholars ask and <u>the methodological approaches</u> they use to find answers." Then the classes moved from general to particular, examined specific themes and disciplines. REVOLUTION, LOVE, MEDITERRANEAN BASIN, for example. Not a survey but it "would allow students to apply the skills they had developed in the first quarters." Teachers preferred in-depth thus instead of a "peep show" of great texts flickering by. Having no theme, risked incoherence. [-- CHRONICLE OF HIGHER EDUCATION…]
…by now we hope students of "teaching thinking" easily identify the **variables** confronted by Stanford, the **choices** Stanford made, and other options not selected, roads not travelled.

#+||#|+#|+|+|#+|||#+||+#|||#|+#|++|+#+|||#+|+#+|+||#|+#|+#|+|+#|+#||#|+|||#|+#|+|+|#+|#+|+#|+#|+#|+#|+#|+|+#||#+#|+|#+|#+||+|#+||

What, explicit conceptualization and as early as in the fifth grade?...

[3.5.] EXAMPLE: How Explicit and Elevated concepts enrich a course—and in *elementary* school, already:
One fifth grade teacher who skillfully has students use "manipulatives" in collaborative groups for math finds each year that his kids do better on the math sections of the mastery tests than they used to, before he began to use either manipulatives or cooperative learning. The point he makes is that <u>by the time the test comes, although they may not *remember* formulae or functions, they can *figure out* what needs to happen to solve any problem</u>. It is mathematical thinking, asking and talking through problem-solving questions—not memorizing content or right answers—that matters in the real world of actually *using* mathematics. [-- AARONSEN]

| This time I think I **DO** see your point—and agree. Enrichment by the **strategic keystone principles** behind the specifics, not just the tactical rules used in specific instances. Knowing these higher-order concepts can almost-magically help one | Exactly. The prize, the treasure, the indispensable resource of the concept above-and-behind the specific instances—a Swiss-Army-knife too indeed, multi-adaptable. Note that this conceptual approach exceeds What To Know & Do: beyond "content," also "right answers," and beyond "formulae or functions" or rote rules. But again this thinkingesque approach seems absent in 90% of classes…
Strongly and personally, I feel the true empowering of the students here, as against keeping them puerile or juvenile with handy but limited little formulae with governors on them or safety-grade scissors only! |

<table>
<tr>
<td>

master new situations…

Oh, and I'm beginning to like your use of examples to convey the difficult new concepts. They are high-quality, plus you explicate them to show the concepts within them.

</td>
<td>

Oh, and as for the use of examples—don't thank me, thank the major thinking/communication skill of **"concretization"** or deft interrelating of Specifics and Generalities… [How many other educational resources either use bad nonproductive examples, or more often few at all, and remain with abstract generalities?…] SEE Tool- Kit on **Specific Detailing, P. 270.**.

</td>
</tr>
</table>

#+||#|+#|+|+|#+|||#+||+#|+||#|+#|++|+#+|||#+|+#+|+||#|#+|#|+|+#|+#||#|+|||#|+#|+|+|#+|#+|+#|+#|+|#|+#|+#|+#|+|+#||#+#|+|#+|#+||+|#+||

True Test: can "liberal education" help confront real-life complexities better?

<table>
<tr>
<td colspan="2">

[3.6.] EXAMPLE. A History/Philosophy Major, Exports Expertise into the Far Field of *Metallurgy*?

</td>
</tr>
<tr>
<td colspan="2">

A BUSINESS EXECUTIVE reported to an EDUCATOR: My company took a contract to extract beryllium from a mine in Arizona. I called in several consulting engineers and asked, "Can you furnish a chemical or electrolytic process that can be used at the mine site to refine directly from the ore?" Back came a report saying that *I was asking for the impossible*—a search of the computer tapes had indicated that *no such process existed.*

I paid the engineers for their report. Then I hired *a student from Stanford University* who was home for the summer. He was *majoring in Latin American history with a minor in philosophy.* I gave him an airplane ticket and a credit card and told him, "Go to Denver and research the Bureau of Mines archives and locate a chemical process for the recovery of beryllium." He left on Monday. I forgot to tell him that *I was sending him for the impossible.* He came back on Friday. He handed me a pack of notes and booklets and said, "Here is the process. It was developed 33 years ago at a government research station at Rolla, Mo." He then continued, "And here also are other processes for the recovery of mica, strontium, columbium, and yttrium, which also exist as residual ores that contain beryllium." After one week of research, he was making sounds like a metallurgical expert. [-- RICHARD PAUL]

</td>
</tr>
<tr>
<td>

BUT what's so hot about *this*? This guy just got lucky in his library-science searching skills! (Or perhaps **Comprehensiveness** of **strategic** searching, I *will* grant that as a higher-level thinking skill.,,) But you can't Export philosophy skills to metallurgy!

</td>
<td>

Ah **BUT** this *does* illustrate (1) the great *potential* of **Exporting** skills to Far-Foreign fields. But also (2) a *pitfall*, not being somewhat explicit about what one is learning. (Is the school's "Exhibition"-Space empty, or just a billboard, or an actual tool-bank of resources?)

</td>
</tr>
</table>

#+||#|+#|+|+|#+|||#+||+#|+||#|+#|++|+#+|||#+|+#+|+||#|#+|#|+|+#|+#||#|+|||#|+#|+|+|#+|#+|+#|+#|+|#|+#|+#|+#|+|+#||#+#|+|#+|#+||+|#+||

Possible pitfall: too-narrow a subject used to practice End-Goal Readiness?

<table>
<tr>
<td colspan="2">

[3.7.] EXAMPLES. Two senior-year general-education capstone courses: the *elitist* **"The Good Life,"** but also the *earthy* **"How to Design A City Park"**…   [The differences if any?…]

</td>
</tr>
<tr>
<td>

GOOD LIFE: A "capstone course" at my University was the senior-year-level "The World of Ideas." To be taken after Science in Society, and the other core-courses…. The "focal issue" varied, one time "Community," another time—the syllabus I obtained—"The Good Life."

--The readings for that section did seem to me to be *richly-wide.* They included the Bible, the Tao Te Ching, PLATO'S Symposium, FREUD, SARTRE, THOREAU, the Romantic poets, ANDREW CARNEGIE, URSULA LeGUIN, CAROL GILLIGAN on feminist perspective….

--The objectives stated seemed to me similarly-*impressive.* Among them: to show how ideas shape perceptions….to see how ideas were formed historically and remain influential….to know of diverse intellectual traditions, and their common and differing points….to note continuing human issues, questions,

</td>
<td>

CITY PARK: I particularly recommend a year-long course in Interdisciplinary Critical/Creative Thinking. In such a course students would learn the genetic/chemical/environmental bases of how humans think and the evolution of human intelligence. More importantly, they would learn to think in a variety of ways—mythically, analogically, behaviorally, empirically, and spatially and to use the interdisciplinary technique of think tanks. In the course, students would be trained to use multiple problem-solving strategies—visual, verbal and mathematical, brainstorming, synectics, and each of the disciplines' own methods. Each is a tool, and they need to see that no problem is really "solved," until many thinking languages have been applied to it. Students should be assigned practical and theoretical problems demanding multidisciplinary

</td>
</tr>
</table>

and problems....to interpret difficult literary works....to appreciate the humanities as education....oh, and "to further cultivate students' critical and analytical thinking skills," as well as "abilities to deal with ethics and values...."

--The final exam also seemed to me *supple*. It required a 4-page essay on one topic such as Material Possession, Pleasure, Competition, Love, Freedom, Seeking and Finding, The Mind....For example, on "Material Possessions": Discuss Carnegie, the Bible, Thoreau on materialism. Then, "evaluate these perspectives and articulate your own sense of the importance of material possession in relation to a good life."

goals. For example, "Design a plan for a beautiful, economical, ecologically diverse, and socially inviting, park on campus." That's the kind of problem they'll face after graduation; let's prepare them now. The new social science or engineering graduate who is asked in his job to work on a housing development problem will soon learn that s/he has not been given just an economic, sociological, and numbers problem, but also a psychological, environmental, historical, and artistic one as well....
  [-- M. GARRETT BAUMAN, Phi Kappa Phi Journal, spring 1989]

MY CRITIQUE: An "onion" seems to "sour" the *GOOD LIFE* here… Problem is, --(1) seems too limited in true interdisciplinary scope, not complex enough.
--(2) Plus, not Connected, the concepts not **Exported**: very few of the resulting papers made any references to either the Arenas of Civic or Work or other real life, let alone the Personal life of the student-writer.
(3) Not to mention whether it was covert Knowledge-acquiring or Indoctrination? *Because how was it true Thinking?* **Conscious Competence** was not stressed. The instructions permit merely Personal Opinionating about the issue. Like my student Michelle's supposedly- thinking assignment about special interest groups, the importance of foreign language study?.....
…and an "orchid" seems to "bloom" in the *PARK* here… Although predictably dismissed by some of my (haughty or politicized?) fellow humanists, this assignment seems more powerfully complex to better confront complexities. **Interdisciplinary** *perspectives* (not just facts or data!) almost across the spectrum from the soup of aesthetics to the nuts of physics…

#+||#|+#|+|+|#+|||#+||+#|+||#|+#|++|+#+|||#+|+#+|+||#|#+|#|+|+#|+#||#|+|||#|+#|+|+|#+|#+|+#|+|#|+#|+#|+#|+#|+|+#||#+#|+|#+|#+||+|#+||

What is the teacher's stand here on teaching thinking? Is it "problematic"?

[3.8.] EXAMPLE. A chemistry PROFESSOR vividly praises but finally critiques the whole movement (and mandate) of **"interactive learning"** as against the traditional "passive learning."

(In a nutshell: it is indeed a good method—but can be sabotaged.) If the goal is "getting information to students" better, and (as he says) "I have to **present a body of information to cover all the fundamental concepts** in my field," then admittedly "the lecture given by a professor using chalk and a blackboard has certainly been an effective way of transmitting information for nearly 200 years." *However "I",* the newer may be better (or at least theoretically…)

The new approach of "interactive learning" is that "students work in small groups, ask and answer questions throughout a lecture, teach a small portion of the subject themselves, or do extensive out-of-class work in libraries or on the World-Wide Web." And, both anecdotal evidence and studies suggest that "interactive learning *is far more effective* than the old system of lectures and passive learning." In one example, research has shown that people retain more information when they try to explain it to somebody else."

However "II," the professor's incisive critical point is that "interactive learning *requires more effort and more thought from both the teacher and the learner.* That is where the problem lies. Many professors are willing, but too many students don't care and aren't willing. This wastes the approach, and causes student resentment also. Hence an important caution about a pitfall in "interactive learning" despite its proven theoretical benefits to increase—learning.   [MARK BENVENUTO, IN CHE—QUOTED AND PARAPHRASED]

By now I know what you're going to say. You're going to *trash* this perfectly-valid critique because it doesn't climb aboard your own hobby-horse. You're going to craftily point out the irony that the professor critiqued a new bottle—but is still presenting the old wine. Namely, **the goal of education as What to Know**, or *"getting information to students"* so

Right. Of course here I emphasize chemistry for General, Liberal Education—not for vocational training of chemistry majors… Ultimate goal being to **Hit The Ground Running** by thinking chemically in a world of complex problems. (Even as calculus "gives one a feel for" this, that, the other thing—as in that earlier

116

that *they "retain more" of it*, including *to "cover"* the "fundamental concepts." You're going to ask: but beyond Knowing or memorizing, what can students do thinkingly with the information and especially the concepts? Can they **Autonomously Apply** chemical **Abstractions** (or charged information anyhow) in advanced chemistry, more important for true education in the real world? Right? You show your purist, even extremist, idealism.

example.) This-here does not move high Upward or anyhow Out over-across-down to use the material. Once again a pause halfway on the journey, it seems to me... *[And yes this is an idealistic purist even extremist stand. But only to defend the concept of teaching thinking against* wrongful *neglect or misunderstanding. Not to "convert." It's "Up To You"...]*

#+||#|+#|+|+#+|||#+||+#|+||#|+#|++|+#+|||#+|+#+|+||#+|#|+|+#|+#||#|+|||#|+#|+|+|#+|#+|+#|+#||#|+|+#|+#|+#||#+#|+#|++|+#||#+#|+|#+|#+||+|#+||

Statistics. But, giving only formal facts, "vs." noting transferred tactics?

[3.9.] PERSONAL EXPERIENCE. [I] I myself recall the first hour of a graduate class in statistics.

(Required for the M.A. in anthropology I was pursuing at the time.) The first hour, the instructor dove right in—with standard distribution: mean, median, and mode. And ploughed on from there right into the technical minutiae of statistics. There was <u>no</u> pause first for any preview-orientation to either *higher keystone concepts* in statistics, <u>nor</u> to *its uses and advantages, what statistics can do or mean in the real worlds*, academic and non-academic... Nor, for as long as I continued in the course, were any applications offered. (It was a required course for upperclass and graduate social science students...)

Well, the course was simply a requirement, perhaps for familiarization? Why do you expect the teacher to try to "sell" the subject? Each student would decide later what portion of statistics he or she would need for...	**WHOA.** Again a Scandal experienced. Profoundly non-intellectual. But <u>so different is the paradigm</u> of "thinking things through" from "what to know and do," that probably the teacher would have found it incomprehensible, or ludicrous, to pause for the Big Picture of "so what and why this material after all." Pitfalls avoided with competent statistics, potentialities approached, applications in myriad arenas... *Regression to the Mean—* and sports and business cycles. *Sampling Errors.* That would be *a truly liberal-arts or general-education approach as well as a vocational-technical one*. And I again rest my case.

PERSONAL EXPERIENCE [II] Concepts corralled at last...

But long after that bad experience, I came across a book <u>Statistics You Can't Trust</u>, by a STEVE CAMPBELL, PH.D. Although "simply" about fallacies, it was accessible and I was inspired to *try to discover how to think statistically*. That is, <u>to derive the unstated **statistical-thinking** concepts behind the explicit technical concepts</u> (such as mean-median-mode; standard distribution; contingency table; causation vs. correlation; etc., etc.). I got the following—better than I thought I could do. (Again, why can't things like the **scientific method**, or **listening** or **oral interpretation** skills in communication, or psychological **defense-mechanisms**, be made clear? *Of course many are. But then sometimes the bigger, higher-level concepts are not elucidated.* As when I had to try to derive my roster of six key strategies of **philosophy**...)

(1) "<u>Don't take a too-limited or too-unrepresentative sample of a whole situation and then try to generalize from that.</u>"

(EXAMPLE: Women who seek psychotherapy, and "women in general." Or, survey people who owned cars and telephones in 1936 to predict who would be elected president—they overwhelmingly predicted the Republican Alf Landon instead of the triumphant Franklin Roosevelt...)

Then, and related, (2) "<u>Beware that the ingredients of the whole situation may be unevenly-distributed; that could cause unrepresentative sample.</u>"

(EXAMPLE: the largest four strawberries in the carton had been placed on top. Or, "90% of Volvos made in the last eleven years are still on the road," but maybe they're all only a few years old...)

And, (3) "<u>Beware taking seriously only one or a few similar actions by somebody. Examine all their actions, which may be dissimilar. And also, examine the actions of others doing the same thing.</u>"

(EXAMPLE: "Madame Claire Voyant made three successful predictions!" Great, but how many inaccurate ones did she make, and also were the track records of other such practitioners better than hers was?...) I think this is called the Contingency Table, but it's a way of thinking per se, surely....

Finally **(4)**, "Beware relying on a sample taken at one point in a chronological series, because ups and downs can cyclically occur."

(EXAMPLE: "When an athlete gets on magazine covers, his/her fame starts to decline," but whoa—cause, or result of cycles?...) I think this is called "regression to the mean," but again, it's a real way of thinking....

I guess I **DO** see your point—thinking skills, applicable, stated clearly, with examples. And applicable.	This gave me a handgrip onto the maze of numbers in a statistics textbook... The start of a "Tool-Kit," or brief but solid techniques "to go"... Plus the whole flavor of #3A&B **Application** to the real world, to items large and small. Indeed also #7**Acute-Arrowed**, important crucial issues... To **"Hit The Ground Running"** indeed.

#+||#|+#|+|+|#+|||#+||+#|+|#|+#|++|+#+|||#+|+#+|+|#|#+|#|+|+#|+#||#|+|||#|+#|+|+|#+|#+|+#|#+|#|+#|+#|+#|+|+#||#+#|+|#+|#+||+|#+||

Relatedly, two forays to Conceptualize mathematics, Export skills to real life.

[3.10.] EXAMPLE. Math can be more than rote routine algorhythms far from real life...
Mathematical thinking-skills can include: 1. Number sense. 2. Numerical ability. 3. Spatial-reasoning ability. 4, 5. A sense of cause and effect. 6. Algorhythmic ability. 7. Ability to abstract! 8, 9. Logical, and Relational, reasoning ability. [-- KEITH DEVLIN, CHRONICLE OF HIGHER EDUCATION]
...this does conceptualize the math skills—but do they remain somewhat Domain-Specific, not General-Generic?... so, see the next example...

EXAMPLE. Dean of Education (and math education specialist) JEFFREY BARNETT offers Explicit and Elevated skills teachable in mathematics—and Exportable to real-life reality without doubt...

1. Trial and Error. Solving a math problem, one tries a possible solution, tries again via feedback loops, refines guesses, not arbitrarily. Rational action means modifying future behavior accordingly. (In real life: an automobile mechanic suspects five causes of an ailing car, eliminates the variables....)

2. Symbolism: take a situation and write it in a different mode. Enactive mode of real objects; ikonic mode of pictures; symbolic mode, like x-y-z.

3. Patterns. Ability to perceive something repeated in a logical structure. Theorems are patterns. (In real life: a physician treating an upset stomach will look for patterns in how, when, etc., the complaint recurs.....)

4. "Step Back." To solve a more complex problem upon which one is blocked, solve an invented simpler problem.

5. Work Backwards to Solve a Problem. In math: in a plane theorem, the base angles of an isoceles triangle are equal, so.....(In Real Life: A student exhibits problem-misbehavior. Look back: did the mother not feed, did the father beat, etc.....A teacher wants to retire on full salary at age 65. How to get there? Start earlier.....A dinner party at 6:00 P.M., it is now 5 P.M., four things to do before leaving, how to proceed?.....)

6. Simulation. Simulate versions of a real situation, to discover cause-effect patterns. (In Real Life: Atomic reactors—manipulate engineering variables in a model to see if we explode it if we do this, and so forth.....A Department chair hires a new teacher at what salary? "Run it at 25K, at 30 K," see what that would do to total faculty salary distribution in five years? in 10 years?.....A student plans for a major: "suppose this major X, that minor Y, now what is needed? Run it with five different minors, see the differences....."

The above **(1)** conceptually isolates and identifies EXPLICITLY, "**higher**-level generic thinking-skills" from mathematics (and, not just too-narrow math-operations, but not just too-cloudy statements such as "think analytically" either). It can then **(2) Connect** them with real-world examples. What a justification for math as a required course—*at last*...

#+||#|+#|+|+|#+|||#+||+#|+|#|+#|++|+#+|||#+|+#+|+|#|#+|#|+|+#|+#||#|+|||#|+#|+|+|#+|#+|+#|#+|#|+#|+#|+#|+|+#||#+#|+|#+|#+||+|#+||

Even when "exhibited," are keystones truly Embedded, Present and Taught?

[3.11.] EXAMPLE. . At a university, the General Education committee recommended that <u>science courses</u> (especially "Science & Technology in Society") introduce "the following common, general concepts": Dynamic Equilibrium; Change & Evolution; Scale & Proportion; Causality & Consequences; and, Energy: Its Sources and Transfer. [-- UNIV. OF WIS.-WHITEWATER]

--Two-fifths of the way there?... On the good side, high-level concepts *are* **Existent**, *have* been "invited in" to the course. They *are* also satisfyingly-**Elevated**, higher-order, generic, and powerful for real-world issues.
--But then, they are also **Explicit**—*or are they?* They *are* named, but ***will*** they be taught, *as skills not just ideas, explicitly?* [For **EXAMPLE**, "Causality & Consequence": see Appendix for our Tool- KIT "Cause-Effect" with a half-dozen or more major tactics: **multiple causality, latent vs. manifest effects, threshold and butterfly effect, etc**....] Furthermore, will the skills then be **Exported**, transferred to issues—and **Embedded** in crucial real-world issues?
.....True, "100% teaching thinking would be impracticable," *but* also "Thinking could truly empower students," to comprehend the World After College so to speak.

BUT are you sure that teachers don't already teach, and students don't already acquire, these potent-fecund concepts and their applications?	Well…in March of 2005, in Wisconsin, I talked with a dedicated biology teacher about these five fine concepts above. While quite sympathetic to the cause, she was *unable* to produce for me, on the spot, vivid crucial applications of the concepts… --**Change & Evolution**: true, she <u>did</u> say *how bacteria become resistant to antibiotics and why* --**Scale & Proportion**: she <u>did</u> mention **"order of magnitude"** as a useful tool to grasp large complex variations (*a seed of corn grows to a mature plant through two orders of magnitude*)… But she then said she would have to try to think of other examples for **Equilibrium, Cause-Consequence,** and **Energy**… Thus the whole idea of **Exporting** of **Explicit Elevated** concepts, still seems sidelined, if not embryonic, anyhow off of many radar screens.

#+||#|+#|+|+|#+|||#+||+#|+||#|+#|++|+#+|||#+|+#+|+||#|#+|#|+|+#|+#||#|+|||#|+#||+|+#+|#+|+#|+#+|#|+#|+#|+#|+|+#||#+#|+|#+|#+||+|#+||

Are even some future views of education, falling short of true thinking?

[3.12.] EXAMPLE. I also recall a memo from a colleague on an email list. This is worth quoting; in it, four stages of education are discussed (I added the **boldface** emphasis):

"Here are actually four modes of learning in my model but I emphasize the first three because *the fourth won't appear until the middle of the next century* and I don't want to confuse people too much.
"1. Transmission—purposeful <u>instruction</u> (traditional education today).
"2. Acquisition—purposeful <u>learning on one's own or by doing</u> (current educational reform efforts).
"3. Inheritance—learning that <u>addresses our cultural, social, and personal experiences along with our genetic and neurological inheritance</u> (used in non-mainstream education such as AODA programs, equity education—race and gender, environmental ed, and media literacy education).
"4. Emergence—learning that <u>promotes creativity, accommodates for change, and promotes thinking that evolves or in which new ideas emerge</u> (seen in non-academic programs such as Odyssey of the Mind, science fairs, gifted and talented programs, and arts classes.) *By the middle of the next century* this will be the primary mode of education.)"

Well, I guess this surely shows that *your own* model of Thinking Things Through, via CTA and AAA (apply abstractions autonomously to new real issues) is *not the only* model, or conception, or vision, of teaching thinking! (Of course you do concede that, fairmindedly).	Well **NO**, this shows to me, that "my" [?] model of TTT (actually my distillation of the essence of the "teaching thinking" movement), is still truly "new-and-different." Because note that even # 4 above does not arrive. (1) Could sharpen the "creativity, change, evolving" statement into simply: ability to Think Difficult Things Through Well (competently confront challenging crucial content). (2) Could also focus on the End-Goal. **Hitting The Ground Running.** *Does* the learner have Ultimate Competence to confront real-world complexities competently with a tool-set of thinking skills?

#+||#|+#|+|+|#+|||#+||+#|+||#|+#|++|+#+|||#+|+#+|+||#|#+|#|+|+#|+#||#|+|||#|+#||+|+#+|#+|+#|+#+|#|+#|+#|+#|+|+#||#+#|+|#+|#+||+|#+||

And, "dessert": Conflict (&blunder?) on teaching method "vs." content…

[3.13.] JAMES TREFIL, Prof. of Physics, concedes that citizens cannot make technical judgments about specialized scientific issues (nor can scientists in other specialties). But he defends teaching scientific informational knowledge. He refutes an objection. (His account seems rich grist…)

--TREFIL notes that some educators object that "merely teaching scientific facts and concepts will fail to convey the nature of scientific method." But he responds by critiquing "method fetishism." "To claim that <u>the paramount goal of teaching basic science is to convey the scientific method</u>" is as mistaken as "to claim that the main goal of reading instruction is to teach reading strategies. <u>You cannot study scientific method in the abstract; you can only study scientific methods in specific instances</u>, and in order to understand those instances you need to know the scientific facts and concepts represented in our list. Can anyone seriously argue that a student can understand how scientific method operates in nuclear physics if he or she doesn't know that the atom has a nucleus?"

--TREFIL concludes that "instrumental utility" of scientific knowledge may be less important than knowing science "as one of the great expressions of the human spirit." It is "one of the noblest achievements of mankind," "on a par with great achievements in art, literature, political institutions…"

SEE! This does reinforce that we need to ground a course solidly in factual disciplinary content. We can get too fancy about high-level, high-flying "ideas."	**--Via my Personal "Insight/Bias," NO.** This is an **atrocity**. A **headless decapitation**. The poor **Conceptual** level has been lopped off. We seem stalled on the **Concrete** factual-data level. This statement seems to "erase" the "other" of the <u>Skills</u> of Science, as against the <u>Content</u> of a specific issue. --For instance: such rich satisfying powerful essential matters of science as a skill, as **Falsifiability, Replicability, values** of objectivity and tentativeness, let alone more specific confusion of **Hypothesis and Theory, Observer-bias**, influence of the **Zeitgeist or schools of thought**, **sampling** errors: insufficient, unrepresentative, self-selected…the *meat and gist and pith* of science! --For, **the true "Content" is the "Skills."** And it ends with a little curlique of evasion, or Resistance. "No, not know if not know atom…" Who ever would claim that. And it ends setting the stage for the good old response against TThinking. Well, Facts First! Let's give them the facts, and then they can Think about them later (=*much* later, and not in *my* class or course…) --Finally, TREFIL ends by almost insulting science, by soaring into the dreamy stratosphere in re "noble achievement of the human spirit." How seemingly dismissive of (if not denigrating to) a marvelous thinking method with which students can **Hit The Ground Running** to confront complex issues, and others' statements about them, in the real world! To evaluate media reports on smoking, environment, technology, To perform their own better thinking on various subjects.

#+||#|+#|+|+|#+|||#+||+#|+||#|+#|++|+#+|||#+|+#+|+||#|#+|#|+|+#|+#||#|+|||#|+#|+|+|#+|#+|+#|#+|#|+#|+#|+#|+|+#||+#+|#+|#+|#+||+|#+||
#+||#|+#|+|+|#+|||#+||+#|+||#|+#|++|+#+|||#+|+#+|+||#|#+|#|+|+#|+#||#|+|||#|+#|+|+|#+|#+|+#|#+|#|+#|+#|+#|+|+#||+#+|#+|#+|#+||+|#+||

ORIENTATION-BAR				
1. G. Gallery	2. Advanced	3. Leisurely Lab	**4. Transformed**	5. Responses

[4.] "TRANSFORMED" Assignments :

GALLERY: A series of before-and-after versions, from teaching "Knowledge," toward "Thinking"…

THINKING TECHNIQUES USED HERE: "Comparison–Contrast" as a tool powerful, but often underutilized. SEE unit on same in Mind-Play Pre-Vue, Appendix 6…

RECOLLECT: The "Rose for Emily" assignment is maybe clearer now.

[4.0.] LITERATURE:	LITERATURE: Many variations possible.
["College freshman English 101"]: "The narrators of Faulkner's 'A Rose for Emily' and Gilman's 'The Yellow Wallpaper' are both women who go mad. They go mad in part as a result of the way women in their respective societies are treated. Demonstrate the ways in which their being women affected their lives and led to their madness."	(1) [Lower Level of C.T.A.:] "Feminism, Marxism, Freudianism, New Criticism, and Reader-Response were major ways-of-reading we practiced this semester. Take the three stories assigned but never discussed in class, and show what you can do in re the skill of "**Lensmanship**" or **Plural Perspectives** in reading literature. Discuss: (1) Which approaches seem better, and less productive, for which stories and why? (2) [*Way*-Higher Level of C.T.A.—*yet not the highest theoretically possible!* A two-parter, thus:] (I) "Using three of the six stories assigned but never discussed in class, show what you've learned this semester. (II) Select a topic-question-problem-issue in '*real life,*' *far removed from 'reading literature.*' Can you confront *it* more competently after this course? If so, how—do it! If not, and/or if problems—explore this, and create conclusions about *education, learning, preparation for life, thinking,* etc."
You're beating a solo horse. Surely other assignments were better…	Hmmm… Okay, <u>another one by the same teacher, same exam.</u> "Show how SHIRLEY JACKSON in "The Lottery" and WILLIAM FAULKNER in "A Rose for Emily" mislead the reader." How many student-decisions to make, there?.

[4.1.] ART HISTORY:	"VISUAL-AESTHETIC APPRECIATION":
[A Western-HISTORICAL approach: learn about the PERIOD-STYLES of Egypt, then Greek changes, the Medieval, then Renaissance perspective, on to Impressionism, the moderns…..Goal, "what to know/believe"; testing is on content-mastery as per usual procedure…..]	*Jettison ANY pre-scribed Content-coverage whatsoever. Learner may exit knowing* **nothing** *of Egypt,……Modern.* Instead, immerse in Principles of **Composition / Design** (a-symmetry, balance, etc.) and **Organic Form** (="the complex balance between symmetrical pattern-repetition and dynamic asymmetrical variation"). But then <u>import plenty of content, Egypt onward</u>—*but,* to cinch the concepts… Method: Active-Laboratory type (cf. "*play with six one-inch squares of black paper on a piece of white paper, over and over and over, to learn about Composition…..*") Goal: learner can **Transfer-Apply** these **Concepts** to enrich all aspects of life. Can design <u>own home's</u> interior décor, wall art, etc., with satisfaction…..Can appreciate and critique <u>public projects</u>, architecture, etc. And has base (and motivation?) for <u>later learning more </u>about any historical period/style, as need and interest arise…

[4.2.] ECONOMICS:	ECONOMICS:
"You are talking with your parents, who wish to know what you're learning at school. Explain the term '**leakage**' as it relates to the '**circular flow**' concept. Then describe a type of **leakage** taking place in your parents' own household. Be specific, and explain how that example of **leakage** affects '**aggregate demand**'." [Disclaimer: This does already seem more than rote memory, it does seem to ask for Application of an Abstraction, even if not Autonomously—directed by the teacher. So, it <u>is</u> a "thinking" question.]	(N) "Take this or that <u>major social issue</u> and show how which key concepts from economics can help illuminate it. But also which are less relevant for this particular issue even though probably productive for other issues—and why?" [Which issue? <u>Either</u> the "TTT" or Teacher Tells To do: *welfare reform, or immigration, or energy sources, or…*<u>or</u> "OOO" the learner On One's Own (A) selects from a given list or (B) selects from his/her own list] (N) "Take this <u>statement (opinion, judgment, etc.) about</u> this major social issue (made by a *politician, or columnist, or talk-show person, or "citizen" in a letter-to-the-editor venue, or whoever*). Can your economic perspective from this course, help you Confront and evaluatively respond to it, better—more **Competently**—than someone would who lacked these perspectives?"

[4.3.] BIOLOGY / SCIENCES CORE:	BIOLOGY / SCIENCES CORE
	(N) Show how the two schemes of viewing biology (levels from cell to organism to population

(N) "Define and give an example of 'stimulus receptors,' 'meiosis and mitosis,' 'enzymes,' 'photosynthesis,' and five types of tissues in plants and animals...."	community to ecology) (and from Energy to Nutrients to Information) are examples of **"lenses"** or plural perspectives onto a subject. [*Assumes knowledge of the basic TT or "moves" regarding Plural Perception...*] (N) Show how **critical mass; lily-pond example; order of magnitude; and self-selected sample** [*or even other salient concepts in natural science*] can be used to confront competently, **a current social problem-issue**. (From a given list, or from learner's own choice—this option would confront the issue of #4**Autonomy**: who makes which decisions, teacher or student?) (N) How would you explain to a learner two grade-levels below you, the significance of the key concepts **Dynamic Equilibrium.....Change & Evolution.....Scale & Proportion.....Causality & Consequence**.....and, **Energy: Its Sources & Transfer**?

[4.4.] Political Science/Government: "Questions—Variables for a course focussing on <u>the U.S. Constitution</u>": 1. Is there too much or too little national power (are Constitutional limits realistic and enforceable)? 2. Does federalism work—is national and state power balanced? 3. Is the judicial branch too powerful? 4. Can liberty and security be balanced? 5. "All men are created equal"—what kinds of equality should be protected, and how? 6. Does the president have adequate, or too much, power over foreign policy and war? 7. Does the U.S. government have too many checks-and-balances?	"Questions—Variables for a course focussing on "<u>Contemporary Political Ideologies</u>": 1. How does human nature effect the political system? 2. What is origin and development of government or the state in society? 3. Political obligation—duty, responsibility, law. Why do people obey, should they ever disobey, revolt? 4. What is law? Should society be regulated by individual decisions, or the rule of law? Should a constitution be unchangeable by ordinary legislation? 5. Freedom and liberty. Are, should, people be free in re the government? If so, what freedoms, what limitations, who limits? 6. Equality. Are, should, people be naturally equal? If so, is equality absolute or relative, and via what criteria, how established, how enforced? 7. Community. Should group-bond ties exceed individuals' needs and wishes? If so, how encouraged—and vice versa? 8. Power, authority. Should any person or individual hold it over others? Qualifications? 9. Justice. Individual, or social? Who decides, enforces its characteristics? 10. Goal of society/government? What purposes—and who says via what criteria? 11. Structure of government. What's best or best-possible form? Are alternate forms equally good?

Seems that the right-hand side gets more **higher-order**, general-generic on **big questions** to ask: a good example of degree of **conceptuality** in the course. <u>Personally,</u> I felt my own education often <u>failed</u> me here. Oh heck, we "covered" LOCKE, HOBBES, ROUSSEAU in an evening "Political Theory" course. But, it <u>didn't</u> train me with TT or <u>how to think</u> in **Political-Governmental Perspective**. Let alone how to respond to the **Big Issues** so well delineated in the right-hand column above,

[4.5.] Social Studies and Big Issues. RICHARD PAUL offers this useful roster of **Big Issues** which students should be able to confront competently after their social studies courses.
The point here? Not thinking tools, but **Elevated variable-issues** in the field—not low and picky, but high and significant. Plus as usual, the **explicit thinking concepts** which can lead to **Ways of Knowing** beyond "authority's answer" or "relativism" or "personal opinion" to better thinking on the issue...)

1. What are people like? How do people come to be the way they are? How does society shape the individual, how does the individual shape society?
2. Why do people disagree? Where do people—where do I—get my points of view from?
3. Are some people more important than others?
4. How do people and groups solve problems; how can we evaluate their solutions?
5. What are our biggest problems? Their causes? The best approaches to them?

6. "Interdisciplinary Endeavor." What are the relationships between politics, economics, culture, psychology, history, and geography? How does each influence the others?

This would be a *tall order*—to get learners able to competently-confront these **complexities**. Could they be made a key part of a social studies course, *the truer "content"* after all, and taught *explicitly*? And in the combination here of high Conceptuality but also lower Clarity and accessibility, PAUL'S six-pak here seems to echo the Park School's Deborah Meier's five Embedded questions...

ISSUE: "Does course starts off with course subject-matter == or with real-world problem-issues?" Chemistry, also other courses...

[4.6.] Chem istry:	(N) At <u>Columbia College in Chicago, Prof. Zafra Lerman</u> no longer teaches chemistry "as it had been for decades, beginning with the structure of the atom." In fact *20 years ago*, she "turned that approach inside out," and "developed a model science course for non-majors that was designed to capture their interest with subject matter like *nuclear power, acid rain*, and *ozone depletion*. Once she had their attention, she was able to move more easily from the broader picture to the minute and abstract." [--<u>Chronicle of Higher Education</u>, 16 June 2000, P. B2] (N) **Statement from the program ChemLinks, a consortium for teaching college-level chemistry**: "<u>What Do We Do</u>? We are developing and testing topical modules for the first two years of the college chemistry curriculum. These 2-4 week modules *start with relevant real-world questions and develop the chemistry needed to answer them*. In the process, students model how chemistry is actually done and discover connections between chemistry and other sciences, technology, and society. In order to develop critical thinking skills as well as cover chemical content, modules feature student-centered active and collaborative classroom activities and inquiry-based laboratory and media projects, rather than relying primarily on traditional lectures, exams, and verification laboratories. This approach is based on <u>research showing that</u> students learn best when they build on past experience, relate what they are learning to things that are relevant to them, have direct 'hands-on' experience, construct their own knowledge in collaboration with other students and faculty, and communicate their results effectively. By providing a model for students preparing for careers in teaching, we also have an impact on teacher preparation programs." [--from an Internet website on ChemLinks, *ca.* 1999]
	...this does echo Prof. HEYNE'S approach to economics: start with a real and relevant problem-issue, then tape or staple the theory to that... Although recall "immigration, file-sharing, and drugs" which reversed the order, put theory first... but did get to real-world application anyhow...

[4.7.] EXAMPLES. Two **college freshman English 101** assignments on the subject of **"work."**

--Write an essay of 500-700 words on working. You should refer to any three of these sources: 1. "Work in an Alienated Society, 2. "The Hopes of a Hard-Working Man," 3. "Counterparts," 4. "A. & P.," 5. your own work experiences. Use the sources equally. --First choose a topic narrow enough to treat in detail. You might want to discuss an idea from the FROMM article such as "alienating work" and show how this operates in specific lives (LEFEVRE, FARRINGTON, YOURSELF). The body should be three or four well-developed paragraphs. --Organize the paper into standard essay form: introduction with thesis statement, body, and conclusion. Unify the paragraphs around good topic sentences and then developed with specifics....	Write a paper which is <u>good writing</u>, and which deals somehow with the topic of "<u>a job you've held</u>." "Good writing" refers to **Challenge**, the task should involve some difficulty and plans for surmounting the obstacles... and relatedly **Cruciality**, how important was it that this be written and communicate well and why... and **Competence**, specifically **command** or the writer whether succeeding or failing "doing all that savvy and sweat can do toward success." **Consciousness** also enters in; you will annotate your paper in the standard way (explaining all decisions: what you choose to do and how and why and how well or not for sure plus questionable). I have not mentioned **Craft** or the techniques for writing let alone the Variable-Issues to confront and decide about. You will know what to do by now... [-- B. K. BECK, INSTRUCTOR]

[-- JOHN F., INSTRUCTOR]	

Roadmap for success on the left; recipe for "open-field" disaster on the right!	By now you know *my* stand. The left-hand example is "training wheels welded on." The right-hand is— *quite pursuable over the whole semester if* one teaches strategic tool-use (not tactical rule-following) from the start or soon enough. (As I assuredly did <u>not</u> do soon enough; remember my disaster of "That Last Theme"…) Admittedly, I do know what happens in Freshman English. Massive blow-off of the assignment, due to <u>gross lack</u>, not a lack of knowing "Exactly What Is Expected," but a lack of <u>**motivation**</u> to do well … This, **even when the new approach to learning has been explained…**

[4.8.] EXAMPLE. Yet other fields… Might even <u>**medical education,**</u> sidestep "conceptual frameworks"?

The 3-year study by an 18-member panel recommended, among other things, a shift from mainly content-mastery of "current information and techniques," toward "the ability to identify, formulate, and solve problems; *to grasp and use basic concepts and principles*; and to gather and assess data rigorously and critically."

The report said that the approach of "memorizing facts" was actually "folly, because much of the information students learn now may be outdated in even five years. It is far more important for students to be able to relate factors to problems and to obtain the relevant information *and put it into a conceptual framework*."

Specifically, the panel recommended that "Medical faculties must limit the amount of factual information that students are expected to memorize while increasing the time spent teaching how to solve problems…." [I added the *italics* above.]   [-- From CHE, ca. 1985…]

…why do you keep on repeating, redundantly reiterating, the same point? By now, we *get* it! Like, "facts vs. concepts in education"! Also, applying not just knowing. Also. "conceptual framework" as tool.	I see your point about my over-pointing. But *examples from different arenas*, can help different readers, grasp that point. Especially, that **conceptual shortfalling** seems *pervasive indeed…* [P.S. – This article is dated <u>1985</u>, this year is <u>2007</u>. Have things changed? But just the other week I read that a DR. CROSKERRY says, "<u>Currently, in medical training, we fail to recognize the importance of critical thinking</u> and critical reasoning. <u>The implicit assumption in medicine is that we know how to think. But we don't</u>." (He was speaking to DR. JEROME GROOPMAN, who wrote in the New Yorker and is publishing *How Doctors Think* in 2007…)

[4.9.] EXAM QUESTION. Spring 2005 Univ. of Wis.-Whitewater "History 124 **American History**"

"Two of the following questions will appear on the midterm exam. You should be able to answer one of those two. Use specific examples to support your answer."

1. Was technology (a driving force in American history) a unifying or dividing force between 1800 and 1840?

2. Was territorial expansion (another theme) positive or negative for the nation-state and it s people between 1800 and 1840?

3. The War of 1812 ("the war nobody wanted and everybody won")—what were its causes, how were those issues resolved? What was its most lasting impact?

4. Explain the process by which slavery took hold and became a central feature in American society. Why was it largely limited to certain regions and how did the North American example differ from the historic varieties of the institution?

Okay, I get it now—**BUT** *I already did earlier*! You think this is 100% traditional Knowledge-Transmission. And therefore a "scandal," not "empowering" the student at all. {**But what of content-coverage? No time to teach thinking also!**} Okay, I do see your point. *But it's obvious by now, you practice overkill, why do you keep on reiterating your examples and lengthening this bulging module anyhow?*	True, but "repeated examples, significantly varied, and exlicated help to cinch a new complex concept…" [Psychologically, many people (unnecessarily) hate to admit either ignorance or inferiority. (Some dedicated Thinkers prefer to affirm it and smilingly continue—feeling less threatened by imperfection, than if they had defended themselves…). The above questions seem knowing about, not thinking-through. … Description, not interpretation; no concepts (hence of course neither **EXPLICIT** nor **ELEVATED**)… It's old material, not transfer (**no EXPORTING**). No learner-decisions, hence no **AUTONOMY**…

#+||#|+#|+|+|#+||#+||+#|+||#|+#|+|+#|||#+|+#+|+|#|#+#|+|#|+|+#|#||#|+|||#|+#|+|+#+|#+|+#+|#|+#|+#|+#|+|+#||#+#|+|#+|#+||+|#+||
#+||#|+#|+|+#||#+||+#|+||#|+#|+|+#+||#+|+#+|+|#|#+#|+|+#+|#||#|+|||#|+#|+|+#+|#+|+#+|#|+#|+#|+#|+|+#||#+#|+|#+|#+||+|#+||

[5.] RESPONSES to issue—
{ and our responses to the responses... }

OTHER OPINIONS HEARD FROM"—VARIED (and *disagreeing*) RESPONSES
of educators to "the very **idea**" of..... TEACHING THINKING [*or, indeed, not doing so, and why-not*]:

RATIONALE. "But *why* would we want to consider (or spend much time on) these largely-__negative__ comments on teaching thinking?..."

Serves pragmatic and pleasurable goals. And demonstrates some generic thinking tools.

(1) To be not argumentative but fair-minded (**"Considerate"** thinking)—to critique *specifically* the very *idea* of teaching thinking openly, not defensively. This includes spotting biases in our own positions, hearing the other side openly...

(2) To explore more *generally* **the generic thinking-issue** of "why people think as they do—their motivations in a sense—and why therefore they differ and disagree.

(3) To confirm value of **"colloquializing,"** group-discussing for *as many different responses to something as possible*.

(4) And secondarily, to study peoples' reactions to **major change, the new and different.** How they sometimes accept, but also can resist, evade, become defensive, and anxious, feel threatened—realistically or not....

(5) Finally **"contest."** Thinking as sport-game-play. We specator-readers in the bleachers cheer deft moves of the thinker-athlete on the field—but also boo their incompetences: oversights, omissions, biasses, etc. ..... [*"Illegal" but permitted here, this motive is unproductive, not pragmatically-useful—but quite satisfying, enjoyable, pleasurable...*]

Perhaps you badly overelaborate here. *Still*, this navel- (or cerebral)-gazing *does* model **Consciousness** of one's thinking and the optional alternate methods...	...YES, all part of **strategic comprehensiveness**: to monitor the Big and Complex Picture and identify all the applicable **variable-issues**... ...

#+||#|+#|+|+|#+|||#+||+#|+||#|+#|++|+#|||#+|+#+|+||#|#+|#|+|+#|+#||#|+||#|+#|+|+|#+|#+|+#|+|#|+#|+#|+#|+#|+|+#||#+#|+|#+|#+||+|#+||

[5.A.] First Stage. Full-Dress summary "I": BRIEF view
of responses to, comments on, "teaching thinking":

---

(1) --**"Students pick up thinking as they go along"**... [True, but while this is both desirable and realistic, it may also be incomplete, even incompetently-haphazard...]

(2) --**"Well, we already all teach thinking in our classes!"**... [Monstrous blundering misconception—or evasion?]

(3) --**"Students can't and won't learn thinking—due to inability plus non-motivation"**... [Inability, true and significant, __but__ not totally blocking; motivation, unfortunately *all too true*...]

(4) --**"Superior students don't need this, average and inferior students can't benefit from**

125

this"... [Big grain of truth except becomes superficial, overgeneral, incompetent shortfalling from a potentiality. Even eggheads can grow faster; even midrange students can "get something out of it"]

(5) --"We have to cover content, plus you can't think about nothing, you have to get a knowledge-base first and then you can think about it"...
[As we've said, a marvelous combination of traditional mandate in the profession... conventional-paradigm ideology... utter unawareness... and very soon, a handy dandy little resistance-technique, defense against. "Yes, let's teach thinking—but later on somewhere else"...]

(6) --Students need structure, and need to be told *Exactly What Is Expected* on assignments!"... [Hideous presupposition of conventional-traditional Didactic education. Of course, to be Fairminded, quite true and proper—*according to the credo of that paradigm*, that *lens*...]

(7) --"*Student resistance* to teaching active thinking anew, is *massive*. Teachers who try to teach thinking receive *lower student evaluations, more complaints*—let alone is not compensated for in the so-called reward structure"...
[Astute sociocultural factor operating. True, due to (1) paradigm-shift growing-pains, plus (2) T.N. or Terminal Non-Motivation on the part of at leas many students...]

(8) --At this point in time, TT in one course is *not reinforced in the other courses* students are taking" ... [Also astute sociocultural factor]

(9) --"Anyhow, massive institutional inertia or lag will prevent TT: textbook publishers, standardized testing, and more"... [Admitted major prevalent obstacle...]

(10) --"Teaching thinking is just another educational fad or fashion"... [Well it was, and is out of the floodlight now, but it remains much more, indeed the centerpiece, even though subliminally]

(11) --"I like being the expert authority: delivering true facts is safer"...
[Candid statement of psychological propulsion plus political or professional convention]

(12) --"I don't like messy, experimental student work"...
[A valid personal-preference taste-temperament response against this system]

(13) --"The reward-system of the institution, values research and service over teaching. Also, values traditional teaching over this experimental sort of approach"...
[Again, on-target. Of course, A.T. {After Tenure}, why would not a True Teacher proceed for the intrinsic rewards of truer teaching?...]

(14) --"I was neither trained in, or hired for, the teaching of thinking (as against teaching subject-matter plus specific skills, and doing research...)"
[Another astute sociocultural and historical factor]

(15) --"I know of many other legitimate educational goals. The transmission of information. Values-clarification or indoctrination into moral ideologies. Self-development. Social adjustment. Etc." [Legitimate recognition of Pluralism 101. TTh is not the only educational goal...]

(16) --"I definitely have my own personal subjects skills beliefs concerns I want to transmit to or share with students. An ideology, a method, personal exploration, etc."...

RECOLLECT: --"Marie" taught personal self-discovery in fiction because that was her personal interest...
--"Greg" taught students to "see" how America is imperialistic overseas...
--"Leo" taught students the alternate A-style way of creative writing, because that made the course much less boring for him, himself a creative writer...
--"Victor" and "Gerald" abhorred experimental reaches, "messy" work, and wanted student performance to be corralled within safer, even if smaller, channels."

(17) --"Frankly (but off the record), teaching thinking is simply too much work: covering factual content is much easier"... [Candid but usually-unspoken Fact of Life. But "True Teachers" would enjoy TThinking as the naissance of the classroom, truly empowering the student, both moral and pleasurable, and enriching the teacher's professional satisfaction...]

(18...) --"..... [... plus here *the ones we incompetently Overlooked...*]

BUT what are we supposed to *do* with all this? Just a warmup for the issue of attitudes?...	I saw this "academic" issue of Teaching Thinking thus become dynamic. Grist for the thinking mill—plus almost human drama ...

#+||#|+#|+|+|#+|||#+||+#|+||#|+#|++|+#+|||#+|+#+|+||#|#+|#|+|+#|+#||#|+|||#|+#|+|+|#+|#+|+#|#|+|+#|+#|+|+#||#+#|+|#+|#+||+|#+||

[5.B.] Second Stage.
"3-DDD" roster of differing motivations:

Why do people disagree on an issue, or on a statement/claim about it? Disagree when trying to be reasonable, and even using the same criteria? Or when acting all-too-humanly via other motivations?
SEE ALSO: "The Relativism Tangle" in Appendix: Prior Basics for RICHARD RORTY and others on this.
Until then, this here below, on the issue of varied responses to "teaching thinking"...

"I" *BRIEF* View: MINI-ROSTER. Possible types of varying responses to a challenging concern:

(I) EXplicit (Stated, Voiced) Responses (largely objections, dismissals, qualifications, etc.)

SUCH AS: need content first.....no time to do it.....we're already doing it.....not necessary.....can't teach it anyhow.....average students can't learn it.....younger students can't learn it.....

(II) IMplicit (Probable; anyhow Tacit) Reasons for dismissing, etc., **TT.** SUCH AS:

(1) "Paradigm-Dissonance": stems from the reality that the "New Paradigm" of **Education Two** (goal: *how to think through the subject, and others later on*) is quite different from, indeed conflictingly dissonant with, hence perhaps obscure to, and hence de-valued and resisted defensively by, those teachers who were first socialized, later trained professionally, in the "Old Paradigm" of **Education One** (goal: *what to know and believe about the subject*)—which includes many teachers, of course.

(2) Institutional reasons, pragmatic roadblocks there.

(3) More-**personal** reasons: *course goals*.

(4) Even-more-personal reasons: psycho-political *temperament*, etc.

(5) Psycho-genic: being the "*Expert*"

(6) Non-Motivation: or, the four-letter word: "work".....

A PERSONAL RESPONSE: ...and one can "Export" these, to discuss statements on *other* subjects, on *any* subject, **not** just "teaching thinking." That would be learning these motivations as **thinking tools**...

|+#|+|#+|+#|+|+|+ #|+|+|+|+#|+|#+|+#|+#+#+#||+#+|+#+#+#+#|#||#||++#+#+#+|+#+|#+|#+|#+|#+|#||||#+|+#|+#|#|+|#||#|+#|||

GALLERY: APPETIZER, PLUS REFRESHER... Here I share the results of <u>three faculty evaluations of student papers for the Superior Student Writing Contest</u>. I give the comments of the members of the committee.
--Their numerical *scorings* range from (0) "bad, forget it" on up to (3) "excellent."

--Their written *comments* are more relevant indeed…..

The point of this? The **wild variety** of responses, *seems to torpedo any claim that we can arrive at a consensus of agreement.* **Fascinating**, at least to some of us (also initially **amazing** and then **discouraging** plus **challenging…**)

PAPER #1. "A Trip North." The paper condemned big-city deer hunters who boorishly mistreat in many ways (noise, pollution, bad hunting skills) the environment of small northern Wisconsin towns during deer hunting season in the autumn. [My own response was #10 below]

1	The structure of "you" makes for a difficult and strained reading. Too chronological, perhaps. **(0)**
2	O.K., but I've read far too many essays on this. **(1)**
3	Interesting point of view, with the I persona dogging the "you," but the constant reference to "you" and "your" get monotonous and heavy-handed; needs editing. **(1)**
4	Good force of personal anger behind this one. Nice use of cliches: "it's Miller time," "promised land," etc. **(1)**
5	Interesting use of point of view. A bit picky in complaints in places. **(2)**
6	Writing has energy. Good strong verbs. Some shifts in person at the start. Your/you're error. Very effective writing. **(2)**
7	I like the point; seems too polarized. **(2)**
8	Fine tight writing—cross between story and editorial—a little too didactic. **(3)**
9	Excellent technique to nail bad guy, teach lesson. **(3)**
10	Tone is controlled: intense but understated, superior in this way. Also, writer's thesis—claim that hunters are boorish—is exhaustively shown, proved, achieved, not just stated. **(3)**
11	Fervent anger under taut control. Beautifully done. Tight but not constipated sentence structure, word choice just right. **(3)**

|+#|+|+|#+|#+|+#|#+|#|+#|+#|#+|+|+#||#+#|+|#+|#+||+|#+||

PAPER #2. "Education in Singapore." The paper rather straightforwardly described education in that country, by a student native. [My own response was #2 below]

1	Quite formal—lost interest in this essay because of formal writing. **(0)**
2	Good, competent—but no real self of writer present, nor any evident specific audience who needed/wanted to know these things or be told them. No strong purpose either; no thrust. **(1)**
4	A bit heavy and abstract in style, but highly competent. **(1)**
5	Good content and detail, but the writing is stiff and "unnatural." **(2)**
7	The level of emotional and personal feeling is high, and well worked into the argumentative structure. **(2)**
9	Solid. Missing only illustrative detail. **(3)**
11	This is the kind of cool, controlled writing that I especially like. **(3)**

#|+#|+|+|#+|#+|+#|#+|#|+#|+#|#+|+|+#||#+#|+|#+|#+||+|#+||

ESSAY #3. "Coping with Stress." The paper was a blended personal story & research-report. [My response: #8]

1	Couldn't get past first paragraph. Obvious and embarrassing errors. **(-1)**
2	Rambling—had a hard time maintaining my attention. **(1)**
6	…all this detail…[is] altogether too much for my tastes. Still, it's clear. **(2)**
8	Needs editing, especially in early long anecdotal part. However, a fine example of blending both personal experience and formal research—too many students can't do this seamlessly. **(2+)**
9	Good examples—and I like the opening leading in to the how-to. **(3)**
10	The build-up of stress in the style of the beginning is excellent. Gripping, well-argued, the narrative style perfectly fits topic. **(3)**
11	AN ABSOLUTELY FINE ESSAY! I urge Sherry to publish this in the student newspaper. Make it happen! **(3+)**

I guess I **DO** sort of see your point about the problem here. Myriad criteria applied, some contradictory. Surely personal-preference taste-temperament involved inevitably. No attention to challenge or degree of difficulty in chosen task? Hmmm….. *BUT what could be done otherwise? Mechanical consensus? Again, your passion for "elucidation" etc. is unrealistic!*	Or at least to know the **criteria** upon which we are judging, made explicit. The varied subliminal **motivations** make for great "**lens**-hunting"… This may enable more valid consensus *if* desired…

"II" FULL View ROSTER. Varied factors leading to *differing responses on the same issue…*

[1.] Frankly-Considerable Criticisms: "Legitimate, Valid, Important" Statements Critiquing ("Attacking," Denying, Objecting To, Questioning, etc., etc.) a prior Statement or Position

[2.] Frankly-"Wrong" Statements: simply Mistaken-Uninformed, simply Inaccurate-Incorrect Statement (or response to a prior Statement)

[3.] Group Values: Deeply-Internalized & Fondly-Held Norms, Mores, Mandates, etc. (of any group: professional, social, other) [Perhaps on thinking: socialized to "cover content," also "be the authority"?]

[4.] *Individual* Insight/Bias: Sheerly-*Personal* Temperament Taste-Preference of a Solo-Operator Thinker

[5.] Overgeneralization, Oversimplification—whether simply mild, or deviously-deceptive

[6.] Implicit Presuppositions (unexamined assumptions, individual or perhaps of one's group, etc.)

[7.] *Bias:* Emotional Content of varied sorts (Psychogenic: Defense-Mechanisms, Unconscious Repetition-Compulsions, Other Syndromes—cf. "Authoritarian Personality Type," etc.) (Sociogenic: Prejudice, Stereotype, Ethnocentrism, other "Isms," etc.) .)

> ("…the major obstacles or blocks to rational thinking: prejudice, bias, self-deception, desire, fear, vested interest, delusion, illusion, egocentrism, sociocentrism, and ethnocentrism.") [-- RICHARD PAUL]

[8.] Motivations: ("Sometimes reason, but also prejudices, superstitions, social and antisocial affections, envy jealousy arrogance contemptuousness, class interests and feelings of superiority, but always our desires and fears for ourselves, our legitimate or illegitimate self-interest…") [-- JOHN STUART MILL]

[9.] "Change-Challenge": Resistance to the New-Different-Threatening (actual or perceived); Defense Against Change

[10.] Rationalizing a prior (even if unconscious) "Root-Reason" for Belief: such as Just-Personal Pet Peeve-or-Preference; Extremist Position; Psycho-Political Stance; Sociocultural Convention; Vested Interests; etc.

[11.] "Naïve Innocent Benign Enthusiasm" (a tunnel-vision of intense focus which makes one overlook "the other side" but not militantly, simply due to this blind spot) [MY OWN: why, wouldn't *everyone* enjoy thinking?…]

[12.] Vastly-Diverse **"Lenses"** (ideologies; "schools of thought"; paradigms; value-systems; subject-fields or disciplines; "isms"; etc.)—as for instance, Freudian, Darwinian, Existentialist, Supernatural, Pragmatic, but many more types of Lenses exist, and in all arenas of discussion) [Example: TTool of # "16-L" or no fewer than sixteen lenses suggested for how we respond to general varied written texts. And even more, surely...]

[13.] Certain Varying Basic Philosophical Presuppositions. I.e., epistemology, as in "monism," or "absolutism," "essentialism".....or then "dualism," on to sheer "relativism" ("pluralism"), or back to "qualified relativism." This echoes the "Perry Scheme of Intellectual Development"; but of course many other contradictory philosophical systems may be in use in one group-setting.....)

[14.] Variations in stances on **"Excellence-in-Quality"**: specifically, conflicting **Criteria** to be applied ("by what yardsticks shall we decide failure-or-success"), and varying **Standards** to be attained ("just how good is

good-enough, good, superior, excelling, etc.?")
[E.g., unawareness of the issue of Competence-Quality-Excellence, that a piece of writing could have been much better than it was, hence says it is "okay" and others disagree, on quality-level not other criteria as in 16-L such as PPTT, morality, minimal satisfactory effectiveness in situation, etc.]

[15.] **"Competent Judgment-Calls"** in Situations Difficult & Unclear: cf. "Even The Current Recognized Experts Disagree," etc.

[16.] [*] **Dispositions.** One person wants to Combat or win his/her case or side, the other discussant wants to Cooperate and together seek "The Truth or a some better truth" or the like.

Well, this is good material: more **Comprehensive** than other rosters. However, this is also Imperfect Thinking—or Communicating. It seems more *disorganized*: jumbled, with no *categorization* of the points, and unorganized, with no real *structure* or sequential arrangement, it seems to me...	Yes it **is** imperfect in categorization and structuring. **BUT** take it as a working checklist— and more complete perhaps than other studies of disagreement?

RELATIONSHIPS: <u>Connections of the above 3-DDD issue to other thinking tools/issues.</u> As noted, (1) **Dispositions**; shall we combat or cooperate?... And also, (2) **"Relativism"**: See ➔ Appendix X, "Prior Basics" Also (3) our **"7-RRRRRR"** model: is a response Right- on Relevant? or Related somewhat? or merely Random, Ricochet, ...? SEE IN Prior Basics module...

#+||#|+#|+|+|#+|||#+||+#|+||#|+#|++|+#+|||#+|+#+|+||#|#+|#|+|+#|+#||#|+|||#|+#|+|+|#+|#+|+#|+#||#|+#|+#|+|+#||#+#|+|#+|#+||+|#+||

[5.C.] Third Stage: Key responses analyzed in detail:

[LEFT-HAND SIDE BELOW] **Some Educators' Responses** to the very idea of Teaching Thinking (garnered via discussion with colleagues, in the corridors, on committees, at panel-discussions, and at conferences—plus reading the research-literature):	*[RIGHT-HAND SIDE BELOW]* **Our attempt to identify the *type* of Response** to a topic (be it to a general subject, or a specific statement about that subject, such as "Homosexuality is caused by tiny springing bugs" [AKA the "cootie theory of inversion" as one student phrased it] or "Marijuana causes baldness in mice"—or even more important issues...
[1.A.] "Well, teaching for thinking is a nice idea, but heck, **you've got to have something to think about. You can't think about just nothing. Therefore students have to learn the factual Content material first. Yes; and then they can think about it....**" [Heard as often as any negative response. Usually delivered in a cheerful, final, and totally-certain tone....]	This seems as "beautifully"-overdetermined (=complexly-motivated) as any response...] --*Probably* a reflection of the **Traditional Subgroup Norm-Value** (of the culture of education): we are socialized into valorizing "content-coverage" as proper..... --*Possibly* an **Over-Simple Un-Thought-Through Generalization** reflecting **Incomplete Knowledge of / Comprehension** of an Issue.....For one thing, unawareness of the Variable of "interbraiding" factual content and skills thinking about same; see above. Let alone overlooking the more radical stand that "All true learning involves thinking about the subject all along." --*Eventually* (if held on to), a great (if unconsious!) **little Defensive Resistance against New-Major Change:** "business as usual with covering the content, then at some unspecified time in the future, students can learn to think about it—hence, Not Our Problem...."
[1.B.] "Well, surely thinking in a specific field or domain, academic discipline, or the like, requires a solid base of facts before one can think like a biologist, or an economist, or an engineer, or the like..."	An astonishing but prevalent **Misconception** or also **Unawareness!** In that crucial paragraph, WILLIAM NEWELL pointed out that although <u>factual</u> mastery of a field *takes a long time*, nevertheless acquiring (at least a solid operating **awareness** of, if not advanced **ability** in) the field's perspectives—including thus <u>thinking</u> strategies—*can be done much more speedily*. And again "facts" would be necessary only to illustrate the skills...
[2.] "But there's no time for teaching thinking; we have to cover the material, the subject-	Surely too often a realistic and **Legitimate Objection**, based on real constraints such as mandated syllabi, standardized tests, etc...... Often, of course (as above), a vindicating of **"Internalized, Deeply-Held In-Group Norm or Value,"** violating which might threaten the person's self-esteem.

matter, the facts!"	

[3.] "Well, of course we're already teaching thinking in most all of our courses!"	Although I feel biased as well as insightful here, I peg this as too often **a Monumental, Major, Non-Comprehension** of a large issue—a different paradigm. I unfairly reply: a **Sloppy-Superficial Blow-Off Response**. As in, "Well, do you *have* two hours for me to begin to explain thinking??" (**SEE** elsewhere, M. LIPMAN'S six misconceptions in teaching thinking. The true goals of ten of my university COLLEAGUES. R. PAUL'S study of teachers. And more in the Shortfallings sections...)

[4.] "T.T. as such, is not necessary; students develop it, absorb it, pick it up on their own as they go along."	How about Quite Probably a **"Grain Of Truth There But,"** (yes, one learns by doing, and also the more-able students especially will "osmose" higher-order thinking "as they go on). However, this response seems to overlook the issues of **Competence** and of how explicitly to teach concepts. (As in, wouldn't explicit instruction in thinking—but deftly not by rote—accelerate the progress of the more *able* students *also* and especially!) Hence this response is perhaps at the least, **a Hotly-Contested Issue**, or (as LIPMAN would say) a **Dangerous Misconception?** (Also perhaps a **Pitfall:** sure students learn thinking, but do they learn good/better-quality thinking and **Criteria?** See Variable #8, Quality, above....) And so, most probably an **Over-Simplification**.

[5.] "You really can't teach higher-order thinking."	**Oversimplification**—and/or **Unsupported (and Dismissive) Claim?** What would the "C.E.C." (= "current experts' consensus") be on this issue?

[6.] "The only-average students cannot learn higher-order thinking, Conceptualizing 101 and the rest! At least, too many of the median learners cannot!"	Most probably—and, sadly—(1) **Legitimate Valid Objection, To Be Considered**. Perhaps a rather-high minimal sheer I.Q. level *is* required to enjoy, even to do well, higher-order conceptualizing? (*However*, from my own experience in English 101—cf. "Biltmore Beach" etc. in App. #3—I would say—almost surely too much an **Over-Generalization**.....)

[7.] "Learner-age matters here. Younger students can't grasp higher-order thinking. It should be done in higher, later grades."	A complex one. I'd say surely a **"Legitimately-Debated Issue: Even Current Experts Disagree"!** And yet also most probably an **"Older Orthodoxy But Now-Questionable Viewpoint."** JEAN PIAGET is being revised, and the like..... (Anecdotally, colleague "DALE" felt this conceptualizing was "too much for Freshman English 101 students," and "they come to do it in the higher grades." However I had succeeded in conceptualizing with my freshmen, as noted.)

[8.] "*All* thinking-skills are DOMAIN-SPECIFIC. We think biologically, historically, sociologically, etc. So we can't teach thinking as such."	Ah—a great instance of "Legitimate Professional Debate." But possibly **"C.E.C."** (= **Current Expert Consensus**) says that *some* thinking skills are GENERIC, exist in all fields. (Cf. **Comparison-Contrast, Categorization**, and more.)

#+||#|+#|+|+|#+|||#+||+#|+||#|+#|++|+#+|||#+|+#+|+||#|#+|#|+|+#+|#||#|+|||#|+#|+|+|#+|#+|+#|#+|#|+#|+#|+#|+|+#||#+#|+|#+|#+||+|#+||

[{(END of "Galleries" section. END of the MAIN BODY of Teaching Thinking)}]

#+||#|+#|+|+|#+|||#+||+#|+||#|+#|++|+#+|||#+|+#+|+||#|#+|#|+|+#+|#||#|+|||#|+#|+|+|#+|#+|+#|#+|#|+#|+#|+#|+|+#||#+#|+|#+|#+||+|#+||
#+||#|+#|+|+|#+|||#+||+#|+||#|+#|++|+#+|||#+|+#+|+||#|#+|#|+|+#+|#||#|+|||#|+#|+|+|#+|#+|+#|#+|#|+#|+#|+#|+|+#||#+#|+|#+|#+||+|#+||
#+||#|+#|+|+|#+|||#+||+#|+||#|+#|++|+#+|||#+|+#+|+||#|#+|#|+|+#+|#||#|+|||#|+#|+|+|#+|#+|+#|#+|#|+#|+#|+#|+|+#||#+#|+|#+|#+||+|#+||

[1.E.] Our Current GAPS... CALLS for Further Needed Work...

<u>Teaching Thinking</u> offers many good "tools," but of course can be neither "perfect," nor complete. One solo operator can't do it all; complex skill-issues require **"colloquializing"** or the input of many minds. --Here are some suggestions for input from the community of other interested workers in this vineyard...

(1) <u>To generate generating Tool-KITS for complex thinking.</u> Competent kits; "elucidated" (complete-comprehensive, plus compact-clear, accessible...conceptual indeed, but also with concrete particulars...and so forth). Above all, to be complete enough, use or strategic monitoring of the totality" to survey the subject well via "catchment" and "colloquializing." That is, cast a wide enough net to research and discover/recover from diverse contexts, arenas, milieux, venues. All key variable-issues to consider, for each "all possible and more" AOC's or alternate optional choices. Survey a wide space: all the academic disciplines, and more... *All this is assuming that the above methods have worked well and sufficiently in our kits...*

(2) <u>To estimate what seems still needed, whether vital, or simply valuable:</u>

Cause-Effect analysis: the treatment here surveys fairly well, but does not elucidate *and* interconnect.

Interdisciplinary methodology is emerging from other quarters [ca. 2007].

"Systems" approach.   Perhaps out of official fashion, but still relevant...

Capstone Concepts from the Disciplines, please. I've gathered from mathematics, biology, history, political science—but improvements (toward conceptuality) are needed. Plus other fields: geography...

And please, relatedly, **Statistics** perfected from beyond the treatment here, **P. 117.**

And especially, **"Science as a Way of Thinking":** Please to get the key perspectives in elucidated order: falsifiability, replicability, etc. The steps of the method(s)—and the stumbles possible along the way: observer-bias, etc. One could say "this can't be done" (dubious), or " it has been done" (if so, where located)?

(3) <u>On individual campuses, more on "presence" of thinking?</u>

(A) Curate the "billboards"? Work toward defining focused-flexible goals, principles?
Is truly terra incognita, sometimes Blank Slate also...

(B) Move toward a Senior Capstone Seminar which bookends the college work, etc.?
For applying which generic thinking, to which real-world issues, how consciously and completely?

(C) Other **informationals about key fields and issues?** X Engineering X Law X Evolutionary Bio-Psychology with Cognitive Science etc. X Energy   As noted in D-Machine, **P. 64.**

+#|~+#~#+#|+~|#+|#+|#~+|#~+|#+#~|#+~|#+|#~+|#~+#|~+#|~+#|~+|#+~|#+|~#+|~+#|~+#|~+#|~+#|~+#||#+~|#+~#|+|~+#|~+#~|#+||~+||

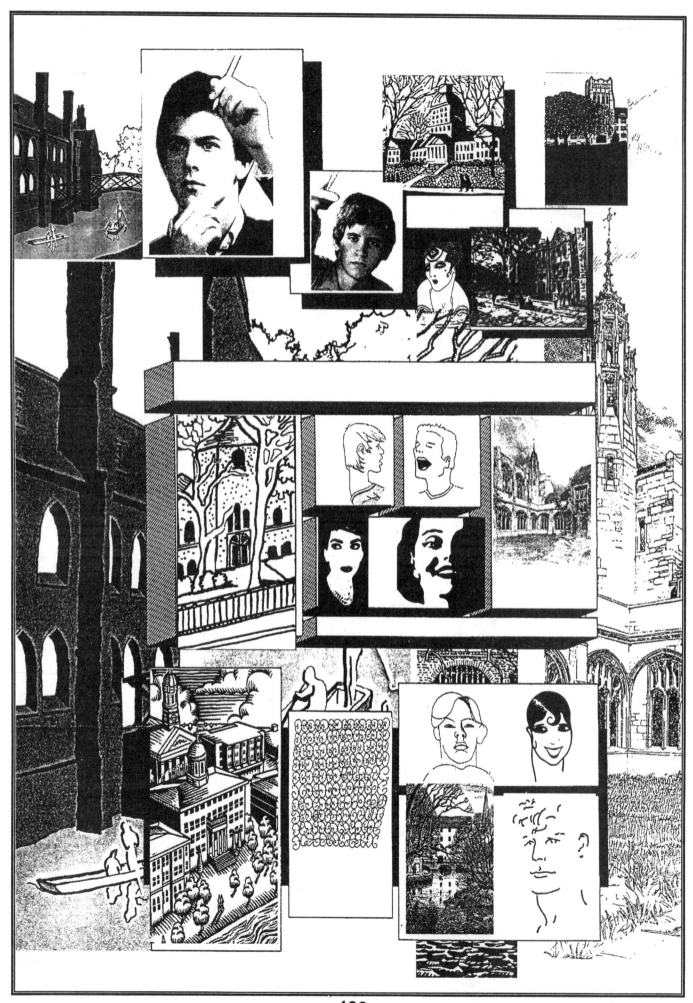

← back this way to the

MAIN BODY

...a focused-flexible model to aid the teaching of thinking

[{(the **Boundary-Page**)}]

"Continental Divide"...   Scenic Ridge...

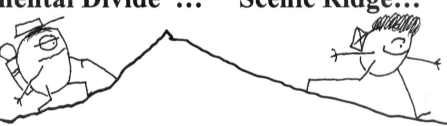

... onward to the →

APPENDICES

GENERIC THINKING SKILLS, formulated explicitly *yet* non-simplistically... "completely" *yet* clearly-accessibly...

BRIAN KEVIN BECK, Ph.D.

[1.] TEACHER: Professor of English, Univ. of Wis.-Whitewater, 1966-1994.
[*Specialties*: **teaching thinking... teaching writing... "interdisciplinary" endeavor...**]

[2.] WRITER: {2.A.} -- GENDER-role-identity liberation: 53 articles in GPU News (1972-78)

(2.B.} -- SAILBOATING, TRAVEL, NATURE: 135 freelance *magazine* articles (1975-1990)
[Cruising World; Sail; Yachting; Lakeland Boating; Canadian Yachting; Pacific Skipper; Small Boat Journal; others]

{2.C.} -- pedagogy in LANGUAGE-ARTS EDUCATION: 50 articles in *professional journals* (1970-90) [College English, English Journal, Journal of Advanced Composition, Technical Writing Teacher, Arizona and Ohio and Wisconsin English Bulletins, College Composition & Communication, others]

{2.D.} -- POETRY: 8 poems (plus one haiku-sequence):

"On Making One's Permanent Home Aboard A Commercial Jet Airliner"   Friends Of Poetry #1 (1979)
"Broken Furnace"   Poet Lore (1980)
"Time & Motion Studies"   FOP #2 (1980)   Two Dozen Haiku   Gay Literature, ca. 1980
"Solo Residence"   FOP #3 (1981)   "Gay Male Pornography as Puritan & Repressed "   Empathy (1992)
"The Child-Eater"   Windfall #5 (1983)   "Back-Road Byways of the S.W. Wis. Uplands"   Wis. Poets' Calendar (1998)
"Field Notes"   Journal of General Education (1987)

{5.} -- book REVIEWING: ca. 40 varied reviews on www.amazon.com   ["Reviewer Rank, *ca.* # 4014"...]

{6.} -- LARGER, BOOK-LENGTH WORKS:

--The **Poison-Pen Personnel-Portrait Portfolio** [satirical and humorous essays on "higher" "education"] [ISBN 0-9645402-9-0 ... 146 pp. ... 2002]

--**But So Did Her Brother!** [--Words-*and*-images on views of "gay male," minority, the human...]   [ISBN 0-9645402-7-4 ... 336 pp. ... 2006]

--**The Potato Kronikles**   *Cartoons*... [--The tuber-tales of "Chester" and his frondly spud-buds...]   [ISBN 0-9645402-6-6 ... 80 pp. ... 2006]

➔ --**Teaching Thinking**   [--Advance-guard version of Mind-Play; orientation-resource...] [ISBN 0-9645402-8-2 ... 400 pp. ... 2007]

{7.} -- ➔ Ongoing WORK-IN-PROGRESS.....: 5 major projects:

--**"Mind-Play"**   { BOOK, emerging as DISCRETE "MODULES" IN PAMPHLET-FORMAT }
[--Resource-collection of the essential techniques for **better** "higher-order" **thinking**; for teachers, students, "thinking buffs"...]

--**Micro-Stories** { Small BOOK, *also* Website PDF file } [--"You know You're X (or It's X) When": a comprehensive, conceptual collection]

--**Operation Art-UP NOW!**   { BROCHURE-PAMPHLET-MANUAL ... *also* on CD-ROM }
[--"We mount good art publicly, to (1) embellish environment, (2) honor artists, (3) advance art-education. *That*'s **Why**; *Here's the HOW*..."]

[3.] SPEAKER: ACADEMIC CONVENTION-CONFERENCES, PRESENTATIONS -WORKSHOPS: a dozen nationwide, 1970-85. [Writing as a Liberal Art.....Humanistic Look at Social Sciences.....Overlooked Types of Feature-Article Writing.....Writing as Complex Decision-Making....."Interdisciplinarity" in 1 Hr.]

[4.] VISUAL ARTIST: 1. Photographs: 350 pub.with the boating/travel/nature articles. Five covers.

2. Copier-Art: Exhibition "Photocopier-Art Collages"   [Janesville WI Library, Mar. 1995]
[{("Petits Desastres della Monde" ... "Restaurant Menu Plaisirs" ... "Hot & Cool Climates" ... "Paris Blurred & Blended" ... Eight others...)}]

3. Conference Presentation: "Copier Art: How to Create/Control"   [Wis. Art Educ. Assoc., 1996]

4. Article: "Two Busts, Four Seasons, Many Shootings"   [Wisconsin Photographer, June 1979]

5. Multi-Media *(slides/poetry):* "Living Close-r to Nature in a Mobile Home"   [*An Experiment in Green*, 1994]

6. Displays ["Operation Art-UP NOW" – Reproductions of good art, to garnish public spaces, foster art-appreciation:
[{("*THREE COLORISTS*": Van Gogh & Hiroshige/Hokusai & London Transport posters ||| the "*4 SEASONS*" in Woodcuts |||
"*FOUR AMERICAN SILENT SPACES*": W.Homer, A.Wyeth, E.Hopper, G.O'Keefe ||| "*ONE SUBJECT, VARIED ARTISTS & MEDIA*": Bicycles,
Venice, Baseball, Bridges, Cable-Cars ... ||| "*GRAPHIC DESIGN*": Stamps, Money, Maps, Book Pages, Ads |||)}]

Table of Contents of the **APPENDIX**
of supplementary-supportive resources: Pp. 136-401

#|+#|+#|+|#+|#+|#+|#+|+#|#|+|#+||#+|+#|+#|+|+#|+#|+#|+|#+||+#|+|#+|+#|+|+#|+|#+|+#|+#|+|+#|+#|+#|#+|#+|#+|+#|+#|+#|+|#+|#+|#+|+#|+#|+#|+#|#|+#|+#|+#|+|#||

NAME of unit:	**DESCRIPTION:**	**READERSHIP:**
#1Touchstones P.137	Seminal quotations by experts to examine for better-knowing…	**All.** (Especially teachers and advanced students.)
# 2 "Explicit" Thinking: the 3 pillar-principles **P. 143**	In-depth on the three keystones of the Teaching Thinking paradigm. Is thinking (1) a *general main* goal… Is it (2) present, embedded in courses, exhibited in whole-school statements… (3) Is it a *specific exit*-goal ["hit the ground running"]…	Especially **teachers** *and* school **administrators**… (Also, motivated and self-teaching **learners**...)
# 3 Conceptualizing 101: INducting UPward **A.** Why, the Very Idea! **B.** Pedagogical Basics **C.** Four Applications **P.157**	Moving from Material to Mental: this is perhaps "the" basic-advanced skill: This 3-part unit sedulously *"nails it to the wall intact for once and all"*…	(**A**) is for **those who truly want to know** essential thinking… (**B**) is for **teachers** to reach *beginning* learners… (**C**) is for **all** thinkers…
# 4 Tool-KITS **P. 239**	All-in-small "wallet cards" of basic generic thinking skills… **(1) Change (2) Structure (3) Cause-Effect (4) "Lens-work" (5) Specific Detailing (6) 15-C Exposition (7) "Diversity"**	**(1) Teachers** seeking compact-complete summaries of skills. **(2) "Everyone":** anyone who thinks, teaches, or learns, thinking.
# 5 "Prior-Basic Background-Thinking" **P.302**	Default or "remedial" or entry-level stuff **[Truth, Knowledge, Authority, Relativism, etc.]**	**Teachers**, to banish Unawarenesses, Misconceptions among *beginning* learners
# 6 Mind-Play: preview of the REPERTOIRE **P. 351**	Digest-version of the major "essential" generic higher-order thinking skills, from parent-product Mind-Play.	**Teachers**, to plan. *Very* **advanced students**, as checklist.
# 7 INTEGRATIVE P.394	Pre-views **interdisciplinary** endeavor …	**Teachers.** *Especially* for "liberal arts / general education"…
# 8 GREENprint **P. 395**	Checklist for **elucidating** complex subjects better.	**All…**

#|+#|+#|+|#+|#+|#+|#+|+#|#|+|#+||#+|+#|+#|+|+#|+#|+#|+|#+||+#|+|#+|+#|+|+#|+|#+|+#|+#|+|+#|+#|+#|#+|#+|#+|+#|+#|+#|+|#+|#+|#+|+#|+#|+#|+#|#|+#|+#|+#|+|#||

App. #1: "TOUCHSTONES"

THE ISSUE: Often, **certain "salient" quotations can embody the essence of a difficult concept.**

WHY IMPORTANT: I for one have found these distilled nuggets to crystallize perspectives. They've repayed re-reading—again, for me and the approach of this whole book.

OUR OFFERING: Space-limitations dictated leaving many rich quotations elsewhere in <u>Teaching Thinking</u>, Here, **[1.]** <u>**the cream of the cream**</u>: to orient toward the book's major hence complex perspectives.
[Plus **[2.]** **a one-page cameo of quotations from the book's <u>author</u>**—at least it helps focus our stance]

|#+|#+|#+#|+|#+|#+#|+#|+#|+#|#+|#|+#|+|#+|+#|#+|#+|+#|+|#+|+|#+|+|+|#++#+##+#|+#|+|#|+#|+#|+#|+#|+#|+|#+|#+|#+|#+#|+#|||

[1.] Essence of EDUCATION: know vs. think through, plus explicitly...

"The real content (substance, material, stuff—and, goal) of true education is not content in the sense of factual informational knowledge, but concepts: keystone thinking-strategies of the material and the discipline. One brings in content of course but which and how much is determined not by coverage, but for supporting the goal of concept-skills." [-- RICHARD CREWS, Pacific Univ.]

[{ ...this neatly states the **paradigm-shift** aspect of Teaching Thinking. Goal not what to Know, Believe, Do, but How to Think Things Through. *Perhaps* this 180-degree shift is as fundamental as "earth orbits sun not reverse" ... "we come from apes not angels" ... "power and authority to come from the people not the deity or the king" ... "visual art represents not reality but its own version" ... "not conscious reason but unconscious emotion propels us" ... and similar ground-rules shiftings... Or *perhaps* not ... }]

#+

DERZKO says that <u>we ignore teaching thinking</u> in most schools and corporations, for various reasons—some other teacher will do it, budget cuts prevent doing it, we simply overlook doing it, or we think we can think well enough already. <u>But are we really good-enough thinkers not to need explicit training in thinking skills?</u> DERZKO says: "Consider the paradox. We expect students and staff to be <u>math</u>-literate. So what do we do? Back in grade 1 and 2 we teach everyone *the operancy skills behind* math...the plus, subtract, multiple and divide. Once we master these basic math-related operations we go on to *higher order applications*....<u>Yet when we switch domains</u> from <u>numbers</u> over to <u>fact, ideas, concepts, values, assumptions, and notions</u> (the content for <u>all other subject areas in school and later at work</u>), <u>we totally ignore the thinking operations needed to explore or create new ideas</u>." [-- W. DERZKO, THE IDEAS BANK]

[{ Leading on from CREWS above, this seems key to confirm how in education, ***thinking* skills may remain subliminal**.... It does lack specific examples of non-math skills [but <u>Teaching Thinking</u> supplies same]. I had to read and re-read this statement, to fully grasp, to "really **know**," how pervasive—outside of mathematics—is this shortfalling is in education, since "content-coverage" remains king... **How many educators fully realize this?** The issue may be way off the awareness-screen. For some people, it is <u>not</u> simply "Terra Incognita," on the map but as "unknown territory" (as in, "we know there's a Thinking Region out there but know that we know nothing about it.") It is further out, not on the map or off of it in any awareness; utterly un-conceived of... }]

#+

[E. D. Hirsch reports on a significant revolution in the training of "chicken sexers." These are invaluable to the poultry industry, which apparently needs to determine the sex of day-old chicks. Now *traditionally the training takes six to twelve weeks, with an accuracy-rate of only 80%.* However, cognitive scientists interviewed a veteran sexer, a MR. CARLSON, who in 50 years had sexed 55 million chicks. From a set of 18 photos of the different chick types, MR. CARLSON identified "the range of critical features distinctive to ech sex." From this, the scientists created a single-page instructional leaflet, and experimented with novice students. The astonishing outcome: people who received no training in sexing, had a success rate of 50% or chance, to be expected. But, people who glanced at the leaflet for only one minute, had a success rate of 84%, even better than the scores achieved by some professional chick-sexers... The psychologist ALAN BADDELEY concluded that "one minute of explicit learning can be more effective than a month of implicit learning." But it was MR. CARLSON'S experience—but also perhaps intelligence?—which allowed him to isolate the protosexual traits of chicks into an analytical chart that could be learned in 60 seconds. E. D. HIRSCH JR. says this feat is analogous in form to that of ancient scholars in isolating the phonemic structure of speech into an alphabet of 26 letters, "one of the great intellectual feats of human history." And so, concludes HIRSCH, explicit instruction with clearly defined goals is superior for beginners, rather than the implicit learning via completely natural, real-world projects (though a combination of the two is ultimately essential). [-- E. D. HIRSCH JR.]

[{ Okay, *here I admit I throw in everybody's face* this lengthy instance which I admit does not prove my pet point about voyeuristic explicitness. But it does illustrate the concept. Namely, that **"Even complex skills (and concepts) can be elucidated (described-comprehended-conveyed) much more than we 1. realize, 2. do, 3. teach how to, 4. value, etc., and without either the twin dangers of A. too-tight oversimple formulaic reduction to rules, or B. too-loose overgeneral vagueness."**

--Cf. again the ANALOGY on travel: a for-instance of "Two guidebooks for independent travelers to a foreign region." Each 200 pages in length. BUT the first one non-conceptual, unbalanced-disproportionate, fact-thin, with irrelevancies, perhaps inaccuracies... AND the second one fortified with the key issues to ponder and their options, many often overlooked; vivid but brief examples; all in balanced proportion, and easily-applicable... }]

|#+|#+|#+#|+|#+|#+|+#|+|#+|+#|#+|#+|+#|+|#+|+|#+|+|+|#++#+##+#|+#|+|#|+#|+#|+#|+#|+#|+|#+|#+|#+|#+#|+#|||

[2.] "Thinking 101" may well be the MOVE of Conceptualizing UPward, INducting from Material content to the Mental: concepts...

Although details are very often critically important, an inability to stand back and chunk facts leads to a myopic favoring of *minutiae* over **ideas** in many contexts. As I've mentioned,
--*computation* is valued about conceptual understanding in mathematics;
--in politics, *smart tactics* bring greater rewards than wise policies;
--*technical hocus-pocus* in the stock market attracts more attention than does analysis of fundamentals;
--for those with a religious temperament, *rules, rites and rituals* obscure wonder, awe, and mystery;
--in sex, *lust and fetishism* are mistaken for love.
I grant that the first element in each of these oppositions does sometimes rightfully take precedence over the second but generally too little stress is placed on the second. It's much easier to put the jigsaw puzzle together after you've seen the whole picture (assuming there's one to see). [-- JOHN ALLEN PAULOS]

{[*A needed and refreshing breath of "oxygen"...* To me it powerfully affirms both "why, the very Idea" (not just information) is important, and how this vision leads to the bird's-eye view of the Whole Bit Picture or forest. A saving grace, a measure of safety perhaps. Yes we do need both levels; of course "concrete and conceptual must be blended, principles and examples," yes yes—(that's why *every page* of Teaching Thinking sports *vivid instances, illustrations, cases...*) Still, PAULOS celebrates (and with a rounded ensemble of five specific arenas) the salvation of synoptic synthesis, of elucidating "why, what is The Very IDEA Here Anyhow!"...
--The ballplayer said, "If you really know what's going on, you don't have to know what's going on, in order to know what's going on." Anyhow, great statement that **if you know the principles above and behind something, you need not know all the details, you are empowered**...And by implication, if you know all the concrete-operation facts but not the concepts above-behind them, you may be clueless!

138

--<u>My other analogy via travel</u>: true thinking about travel is **not** exemplified by *"rote instruction, argument, personal story,"* etc. ["How to bicycle in Burgundy," "You should do social work in India," "Our visits to museums in Japan"], **but** in *the keystone concepts and variable-issues about Travel as such.* **Purposes... Safety... Destinations... Transportation... Morality and ethics... Equipment... Rapport with natives... Timing...** etc. This little instance, may contain a lot about Thinking-as-such... }]

#+

Recently...I got into a lengthy disagreement with an acquaintance on the putative <u>justification of the U. S. invasion of Grenada.</u> Before long we were discussing *questions of* morality, the appropriate interpretation of international law, supposed rights of countries to defend their interests, spheres of influence, the character of U.S. and Soviet foreign policies, the history of the two countries, the nature and history of the C.I.A., the nature of democracy, whether it can exist without elections, who has credibility and how to judge it, the nature of the media and how to assess it, whether it reflects an 'American' party line, sociocentrism, our own personalities, consistency, etc. ..."
[-- RICHARD PAUL, expert teacher of "critical thinking"]

[{ This clear example nicely elucidates what usually does *not* happen—and which is a central thinking thrust. **Seek to know "why, the very Idea" above-behind-beyond the specifics.** Specifically here the subvariety, the **backgrounds** of a surface statement-or claim (with all its "reasonings and arguments"—perhaps **rationalizations**.) This is the thinker's motivations, implicit assumptions, "lenses" or viewpoint-perspectives. These are often subliminal, left unstated; perhaps even unaware to the thinker...To look for the concepts behind, is Pragmatically necessary, a Pleasurable challenge. Is such x-ray vision taught explicitly?... }]

|#+|#+|#+#|+|#+|#+|+#|+|#+|#+|+#|+|#+|+|#+|+|+|#++#+##+#|+#|+|#|+#|+#|+#|+#|+#|+|#+|#+|#+|#+#|+#|||

[3.] Default Skill: "Monitor the Big Picture." The THINKING-MOVE: Survey all elements, to avoid pitfalls of partiality, aim for potentialities of comprehensiveness:

[Imagine <u>you are touring a large old traditional city</u> in Africa, Asia, Europe. Amid the interest and excitement you become lost. One promising maze of alleys becomes another. But then you can climb to the top of a tall tower, look over the streets, and make sense of it all.] "You see where you should have turned one way but went another; you realize that the little shop you walked past, with the cat in the window, was only yards away from the garden in the next street, which you found hours later. And when you get back down into the maze you find your way easily. Now you know your way about."   [-- SOURCE: Introduction to a book on the philosophy of morality]

[{ This little analogy FIRST shows how **Synoptic Monitoring of the Totality**, "safeguards" any task. Admittedly many learning-styles prefer particular-to-general, but it's a matter of *competence over complexity*... }]

#+

[<u>We clearly need</u> both technical-expert specialists (for solid basic knowledge and technology) <u>but also generalists</u> to seek to see the whole picture and then integrate or anyhow interrelate its parts. But we distrust generalists, so why not create new "specialties" in "synthesis and systems." The "genius of integration" required for this is a specialization as all creative effort is, but this time, <u>the person "will be specializing in the construction of the whole."</u>]   [-- VARTAN GREGORIAN, quoting JOSE ORTEGA Y GASSET]

[{ And SECOND, this uncompromising statement (although scandalous heresy to **Today's Truth** that "specialized research" is king) defends **careful generalizing as not dilettantism, but a specialty in itself.** Increasingly needed to deal with increasing complexity. Besides, *"90%" of what we have to encounter in daily life, is outside our own little bailiwick...* }]

#+

139

SHERLOCK HOLMES' brother MYCROFT works for the British government. He is indispensable. His brain is tidy, orderly, can store facts better than anyone else. "The conclusions of every department are passed to him, and he is the central exchange, the clearing-house, which makes out the balance. <u>All other men are specialists, but his specialism is omniscience.</u> We will supposed that a Minister needs information as to a point which involves the Navy, India, Canada and the bimetallic question: he could get his separate advices from various departments upon it, but <u>only MYCROFT can focus them all, and say off-hand how each factor would affect the other.</u> They began by using him as a short-cut, a convenience; now he has made himself an essential. In that great brain of his everything is pigeon-holed, and can be handed out in an instant. Again and again his word has decided the national policy. He lives in it. He thinks of nothing else..." [-- A. C. DOYLE]

[{ ...and THIRD, this little-known passage affirms with its example [!], the "switchboard" or "clearing-house" function of **not only surveying all, but synthesizing within the complete System**. This sort of generalizing is not amateurism, but a powerful "specialty" of its own... }]

#+

An office manager had to decide which of two workers to promote to an important position. One of the candidates was male, the other female. The manager "gave both candidates a vexing business puzzle with three potential solutions, A, B, and C." He told both aspirants to see him next morning with their response.
First, the MAN said <u>he had thought it over, considered all aspects, and selected solution B.</u> But then the young WOMAN thoughtfully said, "<u>Well solution A would be the best if Issues One or Two can be solved first. Solution B would be most appropriate if issue X gets solved instead. Solution C is definitely the best alternative if...</u>"
But the boss looked at her in dismay, and said "I think you should try another line of work." [-- THE FIRST SEX]

[{ ...And finally FOURTH, here I do affirm *my mania for elucidating complexity.* Insight but also bias; I also with egg on my face, concede the <u>downside</u> of complexity-pursuing. It may well <u>exceed any real need at the time</u> (hence be wasteful, or off-putting, as here). But see the **power** of the second candidate... I rest my case; I'd rather "know too much," unlike the myopic MANAGER in the story... }]

|#+|#+|#+#|+|#+|#+|+#|+|#+|+#|#+|#+|+#|+|#+|+|#+|+|+|#+-+#+##+#|+#|+|#|+#|+#|+#|+#|+|#+|#+|#+|#+#|+#|||

[4.] Objectivity. The THINKING-MOVE: try to decenter, empathize, take the role of the other, see "it as it is" not always egocentrically...

In a study, <u>people were asked "to describe their living quarters to somebody."</u> Well, 90% plunged right in with the worm's-eye specific ego-centric viewpoint. "Well, you come in the front door, and then there's the living room. To the left,..." And so forth. Only 3% paused and gave a more comprehensive, synoptic eagle's-eye view of the proportionate whole. "The apartment is long, like a shoebox. In front the living room, in the back, two bedrooms. Now,..."
[-- WRITER BASED VS. READER BASED PROSE]

[{ I love this vivid, telling little report; I know of no better single vivid example, to show the very idea of decentering. The difference between **the pitfall of ego-centric (writer-based) or subject-based perspective—and the power of decentered "reader-based" perspective.** *Especially important in an age of rampant relativism, subjectivity, ego-centrism...* Such other-based viewpoint is (1) regrettably-rare among us self-centric humans, (2) of moral value itself, being generous and empathetic, and (3) a real satisfaction if not Pleasure to achieve ... }]

|#+|#+|#+#|+|#+|#+|+#|+|#+|+#|#+|#+|+#|+|#+|+|#+|+|+|#+-+#+##+#|+#|+|#|+#|+#|+#|+#|+|#+|#+|#+|#+#|+#|||

[5.] Excellence in Quality: thinking as sportive game and play—and more: "CAPTIVATING CONTEST"…

It is not the aim of education to make the student feel good about himself or herself. On the contrary, if anything, a good education should lead to a permanent sense of dissatisfaction. Complacency is the very opposite of the intellectual life. **The dirty secret of intellectual life is that first-rate work requires an enormous amount of effort, anxiety, and even desperation.** The quests for knowledge and truth, as well as depth, insight, and originality, are not effortless, and they certainly are not comfortable." [-- JOHN SEARLE]

"Many things in life are <u>wonderful because they are very difficult</u>, as well as being beautiful or interesting or useful, too. <u>Students study philosophy in part</u> for the sake of **the pleasure of seeing people vastly cleverer than themselves** engaging with issues that it has taken every intellectual skill they possess to get clear and to see into. [-- ALAN RYAN, Oxford University]

[A journalism teacher critiques the "motivational" or "feel-good" movement.] "…<u>real accomplishment</u> is something rarely glamorous or ecstasy-filled: It comes from **steady, reliable effort over time**; a never-ending fight **against ignorance and laziness**; the cultivation of **productive habits** (like reading quietly at home instead of going to noisy conferences); and the building up of **skill and experience by constant effort.** (**Luck** helps, too.) [-- STEVE SALERNO]

"EVAN CONNELL said once that he knew he was finished with a short story when he found himself going through it and taking out commas and then going through the story again and putting commas back in the same places. [I like that way of working, I respect that kind of care.]… I have friends who've told me they had to hurry a book because they needed the money, their editor or their wife was leaning on them or leaving them—something, some apology for the writing not being very good. "It would have been better if I'd taken the time." I was dumbfounded when I heard a novelist friend say this…if the writing can't be made as good as it is within us to make it, then why do it? **In the end, the satisfaction of having done our best, and the proof of that labour, is the one thing we can take into the grave.…"** [-- RAYMOND CARVER, American writer]

"Only when love and work are one, / And the work is play for mortal stakes, / Is the deed ever really done / For heaven and the future's sakes." [-- ROBERT FROST]

[{ Okay, *I could anticipate the skirls of derisive laughter here*: as in, "YOU PROPOSE THAT WE TRY TO GET ENGLISH AND OTHER 101 STUDENTS TODAY, TO COMMIT TO EXCELLENCE? BUT GET REAL! ": *And one would be very right so to ridicule*… I simply feel (mildly) that that **"It's better to know an ideal than not,"** but also (wildly) that **"For gosh sake, didn't you know that Thinking Well (and Working toward significance…) is profoundly attractive: ultimately pleasurable, maturely enjoyable? Because of a better way to live life**… }]

|#+|#+|#+#|+|#+|#+|+#|+|#+|+|#|#+|#+|+#|+|#+|+|#+|+|+|#++#+##+#|+#|+|#|+#|+#|+#|+|#+|#+|#+|#+#|+#|||

[6.] "My Own Page": *self*-grown slogans, *personal* proverbs…:

NOTE. All the following do seem to echo intuitively our **three "Pillars" of teaching thinking.** (1) Goal of thinking-through, not just know-and-believe. (2) Presence of thinking, in courses, in whole school. (3) And end-goal of learners being able to Hit The Ground Running to confront complexities conceptually…

#+

[**1.**] --SOCRATES said that "<u>the **unexamined life** is not worth *living*</u>." "WE" might say that in education, "<u>the **unconceptualized course** is not worth *giving or taking*</u>"… [Yes we could indeed *say* that anyhow…]

#+

[2.] --***Fifteen hundred hours*** *of seat time* for a B.A. college degree, and of that, ***not one single hour*** devoted to asking students," How do you think? What is your personal thinking style? The tools in your personal toolbelt?"... Or at least so it would seem in many cases...

#+

[3.] --*The famous **parable** widely **mis**understood?* The parable said, "Give a man a fish and you feed him for a day. Teach him how to fish and you feed him for a lifetime." *Alas this remains rote; the true skill is* "teach him how to fish beyond formula: how to adapt and adjust to changes in fish supply, even alter to agriculture if needed..." (Thus far is traditional education rampant, teaching-for-thinking embryonic? Well not really but...)

#+

[4.] --*Liberal and general education is **profoundly "vocational"*** in the sense of not just a job to earn grub, but a calling to significant actions or life-activities... It is how to succeed out of School, in the arenas of one's Personal life, on the Job, as Citizen in Community, and in other Enterprises. (This is rather obvious...)

#+

[5.] --We know of the popular self-help series of books, "Subject or Skill X for *Dummies, Imbeciles, Morons, or The Rest of Us.*" From computers to cooking to finance to gardening to statistics to wine and in between, but ***why no simple title: "Thinking for Dummies"?.....*** (this makes one "think," about—the difficulty, but the shortfalling...)

#+

[6.] --Perhaps, **every postsecondary textbook**, in any course supposedly teaching to provide *Liberal or General Education*, **should contain within it:**

[...not as rigid law or rule but as strong **Guideline** {as in "well okay but if not why not"}]:

--**(1) EXPLICIT identification of THINKING skills**, both those germane or specific to the discipline or field at hand, and also general-generic ones. [EXAMPLE: in *composition*, Unity Coherence Emphasis etc. both as rhetorical ploys and perhaps applicable to "life"—proportion, etc.].

--Also **(2)** a dimension of **INTERDISCIPLINARY endeavor:** the subject looked at via the lenses of whichever disciplines help elucidate it. [EXAMPLE: "*physical education*" but via biology, sociology, psychology, aesthetics, etc.]. Also and admittedly as a corollary of #2, **(3)** H.P. and A.P. That is, **HISTORICAL perspective** on the subject, plus especially **ANTHROPOLOGICAL OR CROSS-CULTURAL perspective** to leaven or complicate any generalizations about the subject, which may remain "time-bound" and especially "culture-bound" otherwise. [EXAMPLE: "interpersonal communication," "music," etc. often remain "chrono-centric" and "ethno-centric"]

--But few if any textbooks seem to contain these enriching dimensions; they "cover the material." [EXAMPLE: my *statistics course* which at the start did <u>not</u> overview key concepts in statistics let alone show their powerful potentials, even vital uses. No; it plunged right in to mean, median, mode...]

|#+|#+|#+#|+|#+|#+#|+#|+#|+#|+#||#|+#|+|#+|+#|#+|#+|+#|+|#+|+|#+|+|+|#+#+#+#|+#|+|#|+#|+#|+#|+#|+#|+|#+|#+|#+|#+#|+#|||
|#+|#+|#+#|+|#+|#+#|+#|+#|+#|+#||#|+#|+|#+|+#|#+|#+|+#|+|#+|+|#+|+|+|#+#+#+#|+#|+|#|+#|+#|+#|+#|+#|+|#+|#+|#+|#+#|+#|||

[{ END of Appendix #1, *"potent-fecund"* quotations ... }]

APPENDIX # 2. THE **THREE PRINCIPLES**
of the "teaching-thinking" model—clarified:

PURPOSE. To elaborate further the three "pillar-principles" (the "conceptual topography") of our model for confronting the teaching-and-learning of thinking.

[1.] <u>Goal of education #1: OVERALL, PRIOR:</u>
The two conflicting versions: current-traditional "Old-School": "what to know-believe-do."
versus emergent-alternative "Think-Thru": "how to competently think things through," and "on one's own later…"

> Three informal ways of envisioning our alternative approach:
> --Our <u>CTA</u> formula: not the "Chicago Transit Authority," but "conceptualize UP, transfer ACROSS, apply DOWN."
> --Our <u>AAA</u> formula: not the "Armenian Automobile Associatioin," but <u>A</u>utonomous <u>A</u>pplication of <u>A</u>bstractions."
> --Or go whole-hog to our <u>AAAAAAA</u> formula. (After school in life, to <u>A</u>pply (transfer) <u>A</u>bstractions (thinking skills) to <u>A</u>cute (crucial, important issues), <u>A</u>utonomously (on one's own), <u>A</u>ware (consciously-reflexive with "meta-cognition") and <u>A</u>bly (competently!), thus confronting challenging content competently…

[2.] <u>Issue of PRESENCE (or not!) of teaching thinking.</u> **[A.]** how much "**Embedded**" in individual courses (for this, see esp. "D-Machine"), then **[B.]** how much "**Exhibited**" overall in whole-school environment…

[3.] Also <u>Goal of education #2: SPECIFIC OUTCOME sought. End-Goal desired.</u>
To *"Hit The Ground Running":* to actually implement the AAAAA formula above. *Ultimate desirable-or-expectable readiness* to confront complex, challenging issues "on one's own later on and able and aware too"…

THE ISSUE, and **WHY IMPORTANT:** How to best elucidate this different paradigm of teaching? Never easy; we trust our three-part model helps.

OUR SUGGESTION. "Rx, use as needed…" To help education majors and other interested educators *enormously accelerate their true knowing-of* these new-foreign and complex-difficult issues here.

/~#|+#~|#+|~+#+~|#+|~#|+#|+|##|##|~+|+#+~#|+++#|~+|~#|+|#+|+#|+#|+~|#~|#+|+#|~#|~+#+~|+#|~+|#+|#~+|+#|+~|+#|~+#|~+|+|#~#||

☰TABLE OF CONTENTS☰ of the "PILLARS":

```
|+|#+|#+|#+|#+|#+|#+|+|#+|+#|+#|+|#+|#+|+|#+|#+|+|#+|#+|+|#+|+|+|#+|+#|+#|+|#+|#+|+#|+#|+|+#+|+|+#++||#|++||#+|+#|+|+#|+#|+|#+#|+||
/~#|+#~|#+|~+#+|~|#+|~#|+#|+|##|##|~+|+#+|~#|#++#|~+|+~#|+|#+|+#|+#|+|+~|#~|+#|+|#~|+#|~|~#+~|+#|~|+#+|#~+|+#|+~|+#|~+#|~+|+|#~#||
```

---

1. Pillar #1: two *CONFLICTING* GOALS of Education:
"Know, Believe, Do" *vs.* "Think Things Through"...

TABLE #1. **"CONTENT VS. SKILLS."** A basic beginning table, two elements only not a continuum of many stages. But also is rather complete. A cluster of A to Z disciplines. *A checklist for educators? An alerter for learners—"this is what we mean by concepts"?*

Subject taught:	Usual **factual-content**, and lower-level skills:	Higher-order keystone **concepts** of the subject:
algebra	(various formulae)	"combination," "permutation," "association"—the **keystones**
sociology	Institutions, social problems. Often <u>some</u> **concepts** (role, status, norm, deviancy, socialization, etc.)	**Theories:** Functionalism, Conflict, Interactionism... **Perspectives:** Debunking, Unrespectable, Cosmopolitan, Relativism...
art history	Egyptian, Greek, Medieval styles....Schools, Great Artists.	Composition **principles:** balance, proportion, sequence, unity, a/symmetry, simplicity, contrast! Line, form, value. **Elements.**
literature	Periods. Authors. Themes.	"Schools of Criticism" as **lenses:** bio, aes, hist, psych, social-critical, etc.! (*) Key Questions Asked of Lit....
computers	[this and that program...]	Linear sequentiality. Hierarchy of repeated parts. Interactions one-directional, defined. Functional abstraction: independence of levels.
economics	formulae, data on problems...	"scarcity" "allocation cost," or "cost-benefit ratio"—as immensely-applicable everywhere, always...
Natural Sciences	Biology, etc.: facts of mitosis-meiosis and the like, more...	<u>General Concepts of Science</u>: Dynamic Equilibrium; Change & Evolution; Scale & Proportion; Causality & Consequence; Energy, Its Sources & Transfer...
geography	[data, data, data...]	["Why is it like it is, here? The effects of space?"]
Political science	[info on government systems]	How to confront the recurrent Big Issues: (individual freedom vs. group security, etc., etc., etc.)
history	["kings, courts, dates..."]	Past-present continuities, dissimilarities? "Evidence"?
math	[Formulae, formulae, formulae...]	(1) Problem-solving: Trial and error; "Step backwards"; Simulation; Symbolism; Patterns... Cause-and-Effect... (2) spatial reasoning, cause-effect and causal chain, ability to abstract, to reason logically and relationally
philosophy	[Great thinkers and schools, historically...]	Questioning... Presuppositions... Consequences... Definition of Terms... Logic... [the power-tools]
OTHERS:		
APPLIEDS:	Business, Engineering, Law, Medicine, Technology, Military, Government, etc...	

So **WHAT?** You are just listing what everyone knows. Factual data, plus key ideas, in various fields...	**BUT** do courses always honor the difference? True goal and content is not knowledge but keystone perspectives...

TABLE #2:   LEVELS: LOWER AND HIGHER variation in both skills, and also how applied. To see how one moves from concrete specific particular (could still be complex not simple—cell structure in biology!) ===== on up to large sprawling/unwieldy "ill-structured" complex and the like…..

> GUIDELINE/GOAL. [I.] The learner is Aware of, knows, various levels for three various actions. (1) Response: Observation, conjecture, hypothesis, theory, law, paradigm, world-view… (2) Subject: object, action, recurrent event, issue, larger concept. (3) Skills: rote rule or recipe, then also flexible adaptable tool, heuristic, also general guideline… [II.] And the learner is Able to locate one's confronting of a subject, on the appropriate lower or higher level.

(1) Of course, **thinking skills (which *include* concepts) will be variously specific-general.** Will be at various levels on the Ladder of Abstraction.   (Rules… Tools, heuristics… Generalizations… "Salient Concepts" or "Big Ideas"… Larger Theories, Paradigms… "Theories of Everything?")

(2) So also **content—subjects, issues, etc.—will be variously leveled.** (Simpler-specific (simpler—but usually also complex themselves!)… to more conceptual and complicated…)

(3) This is "obvious." **But note interestingly that skills of different levels, can be applied to content of different levels…** Two "vectors" or directions exist:
(A) LEVEL or ACROSS:
Lower-order skill to lower-order content. (EXAMPLES)
Mid-range skill to mid-range content. (EXAMPLES)
Higher-level skill to higher-level content. (EXAMPLES)
(B) But also DOWNWARD or UPWARD on a vector. (EXAMPLES)

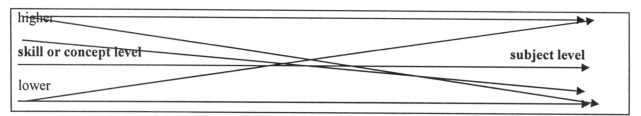

Perhaps sometimes high concepts are applied to *too-low* content?
"The creative-thinking course taught me to open two not just one sugar packets at once for my coffee…"
"The Energy Transformation concept told me why condensation forms on a cold glass on a hot day…"

(4) And for "dessert," note that **the home-base discipline of the skill, can be near to or far and foreign from the application-area of the content.** Applied "right next-door" to an obviously related subject == *or* to an area distant, *seemingly* unrelated but in fact relevant…
   --NEAR: *Ex.:* **sociology**'s tools (cultural relativism, in-group/outgroup, stereotype) == applied to Diversity Education, basically an **applied-social-science** issue…
   --FAR: *Ex.:* **evolutionary biology**'s theory of "prospect and refuge" (what we as Pleistocene hunters sought in a landscape, for survival) == **aesthetics and art criticism and architecture** (what landscapes and shelters we find pleasing now—views of expanses but from protected areas…) (This new field is already helpful for more-familiar issues: ingroup/outgroup conflict, marriage choices, stepparenting…)
   Ex.: Chemistry == cooking… But enough for now!

ARENA OF POSSIBILITIES. Perhaps we can see the complex levels possible…	
The skill applied is higher-order, a perspective?..	The content applied-to is challengingly-complex?
The skill applied is simpler, specialized?...	The content applied-to is simpler, limited?

Arena of SCHOOL	Arenas of PERSONAL, WORK, CITIZEN:
HIGHEST RANGE: ➔ ➔ ["Generality, Form, X" in *all* thought—J. BARZUN]	LARGE COMPLEX perennial issue? ["homeostasis" ➔*why education can't reform*]

HIGH-order generic thinking skill ➔ ➔ [SOCIO: Functionalism vs. Conflict Perspectives.]	MID-range current concern? ["stimulus-response" ➔ *why the group failed*]
"MID-range" concept, theory? ➔ ➔ [ECON: Allocation Cost. STATISTICS: Sampling.]	SMALLER question, problem, issue? ["cognitive dissonance" ➔*why we disagreed*] ["sampling errors: many examples: *are gays mentally ill? do all Asians value education? etc.!*]
LOWER-order rule, formula? ➔ ➔ [SOC. PSYCH: "80/20 Rule"]	
FACT but not inert, instead "charged"? ➔ ➔ [BIO: evolutionary biology: in- and out-groups, hierarchies]	SMALLER technical specific limited subject? ["allocation cost" ➔ *take cab not bus from airport !]*

…well, this **DOES** nicely point out levels… I can see that some learners may not have this "map of the mountain"… And suggest **linkages** … Still, it's somewhat messy or unclear…	… yes, a Map to *Identify parameters usually left subliminal*… Messy a start toward a "pegboard" or mental map of the issue … (To connect Shakespeare and the waiting room…)

+#|~+|+~#|+|#+|+#|+#|+~|#~|#+|+#|~#|~+#+~|+#|~+|#+|#~+|+#|+~|+#|~+|~#|~+#|~+|+|#~#||

~~Table of Contents~~ of the Gallery of examples, for #1, "overall goals":

THE GALLERY itself: goals, "knowledge"/"thinking":

[1.] EXAMPLES. [LEFT SIDE]: Merely factual or indoctrinating stands on **a challenging social issue,** "HOMOSEXUALITY in society today" == vs. [RIGHT SIDE] more-conceptual (hence empowered?) outcomes:

EXAMPLE. **[1A.]** A high school teacher tells her students to critique people making anti-gay slurs, and tell them that "Ms. X wouldn't like it because she is a lesbian and feels demeaned."

EXAMPLE. **[1B.]** A sixth-grade class is asked, among other questions, "What would be good about having a gay or lesbian friend?"

EXAMPLE. **[1C.]** The Riddle Scale of Homophobia runs as follows, describing a move to "desirable" attitudes:

1. Repulsion. Crime against nature! Gays/lesbians are sick crazy sinful, must be changed.
2. Pity. Heterosexuality is more mature, to be preferred; G/L should be pitied.
3. Tolerance. It's just a phase, those who stay in it should be treated like children in a sense.
4. Acceptance. Still implies there is "something to accept." Fine if it's not flaunted, etc.

[1D.]A male college freshman student responds that "After this unit on sexual orientation as a thinking-issue, I still feel personally disgusted by it. And my religion condemns it. Nor am I inclined to "accept and celebrate" that diversity. But, I now see that gays and lesbians are discriminated against in many ways I didn't realize before (and I would never accept for myself!). And wrongly, because they are no real danger. And I would not continue that, and so I support their efforts for equality short of 'special rights' which

5. Support. Approve civil rights for G/L, even if uncomfortable personally with it.
6. Admiration. Realize G/L folk must be strong; willing to re-examine one's attitudes toward them.
7. Appreciation. Values human diversity, with G/L folk a part of that. Become anti-homophobic.
8. Nurturance. G/L folk as indispensable in society. View them with "genuine affection and delight"; be an ally.

[How much of the above is valid socialization—or do items #5 onward become ineffective even intrusive indoctrination?...]

probably is a non-issue anyhow."

[Does this show active learning, true empowerment, incorporating concepts, distinguishing between public responsibility as citizen and private rights-of-belief as person?]

[2.] EXAMPLES. [LEFT SIDE] More vague or ideological, *versus* [RIGHT SIDE] more objective-thoughtful, approaches to OTHER SOCIOPOLITICAL ISSUES:

[2.A.] A stand that says studying social issues requires students to "study social change and social organizing skills and effect change in their community as part of the curriculum." That such social action, exceeding mere learning-about social problems, is "the only truly democratic education for democracy."
[-- MULTICULTURAL AND DIVERSITY EDUCATION

[2.B.] GERALD GRAFF suggested that we "teach the conflicts." When the culture wars and political correctness was rampant, we should not ignore, but teach about, those conflicts...

[2.C.] DAVID HOROWITZ proposes an Academic Bill of Rights whereby conservative or right-wing or traditional viewpoints would be mandated equal time on college campuses along with supposedly liberal and left-wing viewpoints.

[The first here seems rampant indoctrination. But would even the second and third effectively teach how to objectively confront complexity—or not, after all?]

[2.D.] Students view two films about Central America: a right-wing charge of Communist control, a church group defending the rebels. Students must discover for themselves the world-views of the opposing sides. And then critique each. And then propose which is right, but identifying their own world-view as they do. [-- RICHARD PAUL, critical-thinking expert]

[2.E.] Students read Four Systems by CARL COHEN. This simply describes and then argues for two kinds of democracy; Communism; and fascism. Students then must sort out, work through, comprehend, evaluate these competing systems competently—learn how to confront any such complexity competently... [-- ARTS & LETTERS DAILY webmaster]

[If taught skills "explicitly, though short of formulas," learners might emerge with END-GOAL readiness, able to Hit The Ground Running in confronting other complexities in real life later on their own...]

[3., 4., 5., 6., 7., 8., 9.] [GALLERY, CONTINUING: Quotations to elucidate AAA **applying abstractions autonomously** and CTA **transferring concepts to actual situations** real-world and crucial:

[3.A.] "After the course in creative thinking, I now open not one but two sugar packets for my coffee at once."

[3.B.] "After studying energy transformation, I know why moisture condenses on a cool glass on a hot day."

[Seems good at first **BUT** is the reach upward and across, sufficient?]

[3.C.] The General Education committee recommended that the course "Science & Technology in Society" introduce "the following *COMMON, GENERAL CONCEPTS*": **Dynamic Equilibrium; Change & Evolution; Scale & Proportion; Causality & Consequences; and, Energy: Its Sources and Transfer.** [-- UNIV. OF WIS.-WHITEWATER]

[... and then if these powerful concepts were applied to specific issues in real life...]

[4.A.] "Be sure to relate psychology to life" (comment by my college teacher *on the last day of the course*).

[4.B.] "Be sure to relate history to your other courses" (comment by my college teacher *on the last day of the course*).

[This actually happened in my undergraduate education years ago. Does such disconnection still continue?...]

[4.C.] Anthropology can teach students Social Agility & Sensitivity & Perspective; Observation; Planning; Accuracy in Interpreting Behavior, plus other generic-scientific skills such as Interpreting Info, Critiquing Conclusions, Contextualizing Details, Problem-Solving. [-- JOHN OMOHUNDRO, SUNY-POTSDAM]

[... and then if these key tools were made explicit, and then practiced in class each week... !]

[5.] [Yet other similar approaches…]	[We must ask] "…how each discipline can help us live more *wisely, ethically, responsibly, and productively*… living a life that has *more meaning* to oneself and the world. Is not the purpose of a liberal-arts education to equip us to make better choices through out our lives as we confront problems [that confront our personal lives]? …that <u>freshman mystery</u>: How is *King Lear, particle physics*, or *the economic history of England*… related to the complexity of issues with which one must deal in the *office*, the *dining room*, the *hospital waiting room*, and the *voting booth*?" [-- BARBARA MOSSBERG, PRESIDENT, GODDARD COLLEGE] [… a *classic* statement of the (infrequent) Conceptualizing, Connecting of with non-school arenas.]

[6.A.] GEOGRAPHY: the usual take. <u>Information</u> about locating countries, cities, rivers, typical crops. Which is the second tallest mountain, second largest island? Where is Mt. Erebus, which country has the most islands, which is the most populous English-speaking country? And so forth… [… but see next panel…]	[6.B.] GEOGRAPHY. <u>Key concepts</u> of "place and space." "Why is it like it is here," and then "so what, what difference does this make in large issues? Patterns, processes, events, action and change—and interrelations, connections. <u>Real subjects</u>: Chernobyl, narcotics routes, acid rain, El Nino, drought, famine… Example: <u>coastlines</u>. The significance of the river Thames to London and England (narrow, defensible)… Africa and China not having natural ports… Even, geography and <u>sociology/philosophy</u>: China's inland farmland (cooperation) and early Greek mountains and seaports (cosmopolitanism)… Even the N-S or E-W <u>orientation of continents</u> (see Guns Germs & Steel, by Jared Diamond)… [… I was not taught to "think geographically"; I could have been…]

[7.A.] MATHEMATICS. DAN ROCKMORE, professor, in an interview about mathematicians' view of the world. 1. In a café's wine bins, he sees "circles and polyhedra"… 2. In a florist's shop, a sunflower illustrates Fibonacci numbers, a special sequence of natural numbers, 1,2,3,5,8,13,21,34, etc. Found in nature: flower petals, pine cones, seed-head of a sunflower… 3. At a produce stand, layers of tomatoes are staked neatly in efficient "face-centered cubic packing"… 4. An online dating service uses "factor analyses, multiple regression, and discriminant analyses"… [Article in WASH. POST] [All fine **BUT** informational only, not empowering?]	[7.B.] MATHEMATICS. A book <u>Political Numeracy</u> by MICHAEL MEYERSON is subtitled "Mathematical Perspectives on Our Chaotic Constitution." He suggests parallels can clarify legal-political issues. 1. The principle of probability influencing the outcomes of the O. J. Simpson trials… 2. The electoral college as having "mathematical virtues"… 3. Game theory as explaining the federal government's shifting balance of power… 4. The concept of infinity as related to the heated abortion debate… 5. Topology and chaos theory explaining how the Constitution has survived social and political change. [Review from DAEDALUS BOOKS] [Marvelous pole-vaulting over from School to Real Life, and a high-jump up to key concepts too…]

[8.A.] BIOLOGY. Usual information as about meiosis-mitosos, and the like…	[8.B.] BIOLOGY. Push to apply new findings in "evolutionary biology" to key issues personal and civic. [Mate-choice and step-parenting, in/out groups, fear of homosexuality among males—pecking order etc., more……..]

[9.A.] "DIVERSITY / MULTICULTURALISM,: Merely give information-about[what to Know], also maybe indoctrinate in "tolerance acceptance Celebration" of Diversity … ["Band-Aid" or stamping the student's ID card rather than his/her tattooing the perspectives into one's self]	[9.B.] Truly "empower" via providing **thinking tools** such as Selective Perception… Stereotype Override… Causes of Prejudice… Stereotype vs. Sociotype… Relativism: Moral but also Cultural… Traits of Minority Victimization… Surplus Visibility… and others… [To "hit the ground running" able to competently handle tangly real-life conflicts]

```
|+|#+|#+|#+|#+|#+|#+|#+|#+|#+|+#|+|#+|#+|#+|+|#+|#+|+#|+|+|#+|+|#+|+#|+#|+|#+|+#|+|+#|+|#+|+|#+#|+||#|++||#+|+#|+|+#|+#|+#|+||
|+|#+|#+|#+|#+|#+|#+|#+|#+|#+|+#|+|#+|#+|#+|+|#+|#+|+#|+|+|#+|+|#+|+#|+#|+|#+|+#|+|+#|+|#+|+|#+#|+||#|++||#+|+#|+|+#|+#|+#|+||
```

ORIENTATION BAR:		
[1.] #1, Prior Goals	**[2.] # 2, Presence**	[3.] #3 End-Goal

2. Pillar #2, Degree of "PRESENCE" of Skills.

In specific *courses*, how much "EMBEDDED" (absent to core-central)?
In whole *institutions*, how much "EXHIBITED" (embryonic to signposted?

Table of Contents of this Gallery:

[1A.] <u>Goals: #6 of an English Dept.</u> **VAGUE** ["apply to other areas the skills learned in English"]==	**[1.B.]** == <u>Five goals in Park School</u> **SPECIFIC** [What viewpoint angle perspective? How do we know we know? Connections? Cause-effect? New and old? So what?]
[2.A.] <u>AACU statement</u> **VAGUE** ["challenging encounters with important issues, and more a way of studying"] ==	**[2.B.]** == <u>IUPUI's Six Goals</u> **SPECIFIC** [1. core communication and quantitative skills (six), 2. critical thinking (six), 3. intellectual depth breadth adaptiveness, 4. integration and application of knowledge, 5. under standing society and culture, 6. values and ethics.]
[3.A.] <u>Two teachers</u> **VAGUE:** ["if I'm lucky" students will transfer learning, <u>and</u> "interest soars" when I discuss thinking] ==	**[3.B.]** ==<u>Alverno College, eight *SPECIFIC*</u> Outcomes <u>thinking:</u> ["analytical capabilities" and "problem-solving skill." But they also involve "making value-judgments" and "facility for social interaction" and "global perspectives" and "effective citizenship" and "aesthetic responsiveness."]

THE GALLERY itself: degree of "presence" of thinking:

[1.A.] ONION: "To apply to other areas than English, the skills learned in the study of languages and literatures." [-- #6 OF "GOALS FOR ENGLISH MAJORS," STATE UNIVERSITY, WISCONSIN]	**[1.B.] ORCHID:** "In <u>every class and every subject</u>, students will learn to ask and to answer these questions: 1. From whose viewpoint are we seeing or reading or hearing? From what angle or perspective? 2. How do we know when we know? What's the evidence, and how reliable is it? 3. How are things events people connected? What is cause, what effect? 4. What's new and what's old? Have we encountered this idea before? 5. So what? What does it matter? What does it all mean?" [-- DEBORAH MEIER, POLICY STATEMENT, THE EAST CENTRAL PARK EAST SCHOOL, NYC]
[2.A.] "A philosophy of education that empowers individuals, liberates the mind from ignorance, and cultivates social responsibility. Characterized by *challenging encounters with important issues*, and more *a way of studying* than specific content, liberal education can occur at all types of colleges and universities."	**[2.B.]** At IU-Purdue, IN, "the desired outcomes of college study are crystal clear. *Six Principles* for Undergraduate Learning summarize <u>what graduates are expected to demonstrate</u>" whether they major in the arts and sciences or in professional fields. "The *principles* are never far from anyone's mind, since the university has distributed thousands of laminated, three-hole punched copies for students and professors to slip into their notebooks." [*I wrote for a copy.* It arrived, and stated the skills are 1. core communication and quantitative skills (six), 2. critical thinking (six), 3. intellectual depth breadth adaptiveness, 4. integration and application of knowledge, 5. under standing society and culture, 6. values and ethics.]

[3.A.] EXAMPLES. Individual teachers on their students learning thinking...

In a media class, students balked when asked to critique their own favorites, so the teacher resorted to showing her own favorites, "a little hope, a little beauty." Students felt freer to respond. The teacher ends:
"*If I'm lucky*, my students will apply their critical skills to their own favorites. In any case, I'm feeling a lot less cranky."
[-- MARY S. ALEXANDER, IN CHE]

A history teacher believes in a "student-centered" approach and has "truly embraced the idea of myself as a facilitator. I don't give midterms. I don't give finals. Instead, my students spend four months with me working on *becoming better thinkers*. Sure, participation-based classes skew the bell curve, but I have found that student interest and *retention of the material* soar along with their grades."
[-- KELLY MCMICHAEL, in CHE]

...BUT do __either__ of these teachers exhibit any realistic sense of whether and how well, students learned exactly what skills?.....

[3.B.] POLICY. Alverno College in Wisconsin has an "ability-based" and "outcome-oriented" learning program. (These are "outcome-oriented" and hence related to our goal of real-world competence after graduation. And they involve <u>thinking: "analytical capabilities" and "problem-solving skill</u>." But they also involve "making *value-judgments*" and "facility for *social interaction*" and "*global perspectives*" and "effective *citizenship*" and "*aesthetic responsiveness*." All good major goals of a liberal or general education. All surpassing our goal of "basic" higher-order applied thinking.

[-- ALVERNO COLLEGE OF WISCONSIN]

We hope the right-hand examples illuminate the issue of fuller **"Exhibition"** or statement of goals/skills in the Open Space of the institution... Our own **Billboard** pre-viewing the more-**explicit Tool-BANK** perhaps...

NO, I really think you push this Explicit Presence too much. Many courses and schools may wish to modify your stand which seems very-purist, very intense...	Whoa. *Do what you will once you comprehend!* We only offer Awareness of perhaps-new options; the rest is up to individual responders...["active learning," you know, heh heh...]

VISUAL GRAPHIC.   And on the next page, behold <u>the personnel of OFFENBACH UNIVERSITY</u>... excitedly debating (fairmindedly, of *course*) as to what thinking and <u>issue elements to "billboard"</u>—to post and prefer as key thinking goals. [**Personal Stance:** But it's okay after all. For, over in the nearby town of Hiatus, CAESURA COLLEGE in Lacuna University is *not even awake* that a problem-opportunity might exist, in re "<u>what thinking goals shall we select..., then foreground... then value and pursue</u>."   The Faulty Senate there recently affirmed that such selective favoring of some skills, amounts to discrimination," hence violating the anti-hierarchical <u>egalitarianism</u> which is one of **Today's Truths**, the belief that "its all relative anyhow" and "how can you say whats right after all," which (like a breathe of fresh air) has replaced the old repressive exclusionary <u>elitism</u> of selective admission that some skills might be better, then others, now one of **Today's Taboos...**]

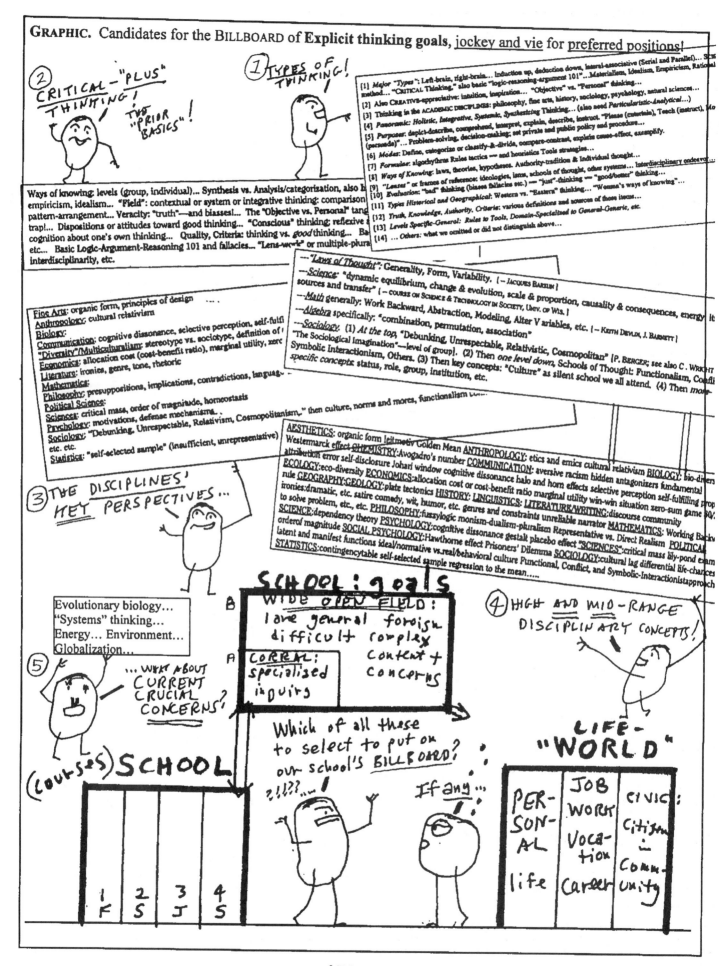

GRAPHIC. Candidates for the BILLBOARD of **Explicit thinking goals**, <u>jockey and vie</u> for <u>preferred positions!</u>

② CRITICAL— "PLUS" THINKING! TWO "PRIOR BASICS"!

① TYPES OF THINKING!

[1] *Major "Types":* Left-brain, right-brain... induction up, deduction down, lateral-associative (Serial and Parallel)... Sci method... "CRITICAL Thinking," also basic "logic-reasoning-argument 101"... "Objective" vs. "Personal" thinking...
[2] Also CREATIVE-appreciative: intuition, inspiration... "Objective" vs. "Personal" thinking...
[3] Thinking in the ACADEMIC DISCIPLINES: philosophy, fine arts, history, sociology, psychology, natural sciences... (also need *Particularistic-Analytical*...)
[4] *Panoramic:* Holistic, Integrative, Systemic, Synthesizing Thinking... (also need *Particularistic-Analytical*...)
[5] *Purpose:* depict-describe, comprehend, interpret, explain, describe, instruct. "Please (entertain), Teach (instruct), Mo (persuade)"... Problem-solving, decision-making: set private and public policy and procedure...
[6] *Modes:* Define, categorize or classify-&-divide, compare-contrast, explain cause-effect, exemplify.
[7] *Formulae:* algorhythms Rules tactics — and heuristics Tools strategies...
[8] *Ways of Knowing:* laws, theories, hypotheses. Authority-tradition & Individual thought... Interdisciplinary endeavo...
[9] *"Lenses" or frames of reference:* ideologies, isms, schools of thought, other systems... — "just"-thinking — "good/better" thinking...
[10] *Evaluation:* "bad" thinking (biases fallacies etc.) — "just"-thinking — "good/better" thinking...
[11] *Types Historical and Geographical:* Western vs. "Eastern" thinking... "Wemma's ways of knowing"...
[12] *Truth, Knowledge, Authority. Criteria:* various definitions and sources of those items...
[13] *Levels Specific-General:* Rules to Tools, Domain-Specialized to General-Generic, etc.
[14] ... *Others:* what we omitted or did not distinguish above...

Ways of knowing: levels (group, individual)... Synthesis vs. Analysis/categorization, also b empiricism, idealism... "Field": contextual or system or integrative thinking: comparison pattern-arrangement... Veracity: "truth"—and biasses!... The "Objective vs. Personal" tang trap!... Dispositions or attitudes toward good thinking... "Conscious" thinking: reflexive a cognition about one's own thinking... Quality, Criteria: thinking vs. *good* thinking... Ba etc... Basic Logic-Argument-Reasoning 101 and fallacies... "Lens-work" or multiple-plura interdisciplinarity, etc.

—*"Laws of Thought":* Generality, Form, Variability. [— JACQUES BARZUN]
—*Science:* "dynamic equilibrium, change & evolution, scale & proportion, causality & consequences, energy li sources and transfer" [— COURSE ON SCIENCE & TECHNOLOGY IN SOCIETY, UNIV. OF WIS.]
—*Math* generally: Work Backward, Abstraction, Modeling, Alter Variables, etc. [— KEITH DEVLIN, J. BARNETT]
—*Algebra* specifically: "combination, permutation, association"
—*Sociology.* (1) *At the top,* "Debunking, Unrespectable, Relativistic, Cosmopolitan" [P. BERGER; see also C. WRIGHT "The Sociological Imagination"—level of group]. (2) Then *one level down,* Schools of Thought: Functionalism, Confli Symbolic Interactionism, Others. (3) Then key concepts: "Culture" as silent school we all attend. (4) Then *more* specific concepts: status, role, group, institution, etc.

Fine Arts: organic form, principles of design ...
Anthropology: cultural relativism
Biology:
Communication: cognitive dissonance, selective perception, self-fulfi
"Diversity"/Multiculturalism: stereotype vs. sociotype, definition of
Economics: allocation cost (cost-benefit ratio), marginal utility, zero
Literature: ironies, genre, tone, rhetoric
Mathematics:
Philosophy: presuppositions, implications, contradictions, languag...
Political Science:
Sciences: critical mass, order of magnitude, homeostasis
Psychology: motivations, defense mechanisms...
Sociology: "Debunking, Unrespectable, Relativism, Cosmopolitanism," then culture, norms and mores, functionalism c...
etc. etc.
Statistics: "self-selected sample" (insufficient, unrepresentative)

③ THE DISCIPLINES' KEY PERSPECTIVES...

AESTHETICS: organic form leitmotiv Golden Mean ANTHROPOLOGY: etics and emics cultural relativism BIOLOGY: bio-diver Westermarck effect CHEMISTRY: Avogadro's number COMMUNICATION: aversive racism hidden antagonizers fundamental attribution error self-disclosure Johari window cognitive dissonance halo and horn effects selective perception self-fulfilling ECOLOGY: eco-diversity ECONOMICS: allocation cost or cost-benefit ratio marginal utility win-win situation zero-sum game 50/ rule GEOGRAPHY:GEOLOGY: plate tectonics HISTORY: LINGUISTICS: discourse community ironies:dramatic, etc. satire comedy, wit, humor, etc. genres and constraints unreliable narrator MATHEMATICS: Working Back to solve problem, etc., etc. PHILOSOPHY: fuzzylogic monism-dualism-pluralism Representative vs. Direct Realism SCIENCE: dependency theory PSYCHOLOGY: cognitive dissonance gestalt placebo effect "SCIENCES": critical mass lily-pond exam orderof magnitude SOCIAL PSYCHOLOGY: Hawthorne effect Prisoners' Dilemma POLITICAL latent and manifest functions ideal/normative vs.real/behavioral culture Functional, Conflict, and Symbolic-Interactionistapproach STATISTICS: contingencytable self-selected sample regression to the mean.....

Evolutionary biology...
"Systems" thinking...
Energy... Environment...
Globalization...

⑤ ... WHAT ABOUT CURRENT CRUCIAL CONCERNS?

SCHOOL: goals

B WIDE OPEN FIELD: lave general foreign difficult complex content + concepts

A CORRAL: specialized inquiry

④ HIGH AND MID-RANGE DISCIPLINARY CONCEPTS!

Which of all these to select to put on our school's BILLBOARD? ?!!??... !

If any...

(COURSES) SCHOOL

1 F	2 S	3 J	4 S

LIFE- "WORLD"

PER-SON-AL life	JOB WORK VOCA-tion Career	CIVIC: citizen = Comm-unity

3. Pillar #3, Goal #2: END-goal OUTCOMES...

"Hit The Ground Running" with prepared to confront concerns competently...

TWO LEVELS. Perhaps "content to be confronted," divides into **easier-more familiar,** and then **more complex-foreign-challenging.** That is, major-subject training involves *more-specific, focused* major-subject skills and content (solving an economic problem, etc.)—the "closed corral of the career"? But liberal-general education may bring in issues that are *larger, new, difficult, foreign to our expertise*—the "wide, wild, open-field."

SEE ALSO: the book's **back cover.** "Chester the scholarly potato" hitting the path to conquer Ignorance...

Table of Contents for Pillar #3:

THE GALLERY: end-goal outcomes:

[1.] EXAMPLE OF END-GOAL. A book review of JARED DIAMOND'S influential book <u>Guns, Germs, and Steel</u>, which discussed **statistics in the rise of human civilization** in broad view:

Was the origin of so many domesticates in Eurasia a matter of mere good fortune? I calculate (from his Table 9.2) the probability of 13 animal species suitable for domestication occurring in Eurasia, and none in Africa, by chance alone as being around 0.003. If we accept conventional levels of statistical inference, Diamond's hypothesis is falsified; the disparity must have some other explanation." [-- REVIEWER UNKNOWN]

| NO! This is much too limited, simple, specialized an example. The reviewer would have known statistics. Give us a better example of going farther afield, | Well, take **"Lensmanship"** or using multiple-plural perspectives on an issue. And also a keystone of the social sciences, **"culture"** as Silent School training in the norms and mores which we pick up unconsciously. Then apply them to the pesky social issue of **"homosexuality"**..... |

[2.] Essentially, **"free speech on campus."** But more... Frequent but unaddressed.

EVENTS TO RESPOND TO: = = =	COMMON BUT OVER-SIMPLE RE-SPON-SES: = = =	POSSIBLE THINKING SKILLS TO ACCESS AND APPLY: = = =
(N) WARD CHURCHILL to speak on Native American rights, but made a speech comparing Twin Tower employees (of Sept. 11) to Adolph Eichmann, a bureaucrat of the Nazis—they being Capitalist lackeys… *--Much outrage, death-threats, speech almost cancelled; state legislator calls for investigation into campuses...*	"Ban these people from speaking!" "Politically-insulting!" "No, Free Speech always!" (Etc.)	(N) **J.S. Mill's classic statement in On Liberty, British, 19th century.** "Any and all opinions even or especially if thought bad (wrong, immoral, bizarre, mistaken, dangerous, etc.) MUST be given FULL hearing, to 1. find their dangers clearly, 2. see any good points about them, 3. keep open the spirit of free inquiry both in public and in private." **[{ An absolutely-vital resource. But never mentioned in 95% of these cases! Perhaps other models exist too; but, Hello Out There, professors of Political Philosophy? }]** (N) From **Education.** Let these hot moments be grist for cool "teachable/learnable moments." To show students how to think, not what to think (amid Liberal vs. Conservative agonistic combat-to-win…). An educational opportunity rarely seized on campuses…
(N) President L. SUMMERS of Harvard suggests informally whether women doing less math, is partly a result of genetic differences. *--A firestorm erupts nationwide; feminists fume (and almost faint); calls for resignation; etc.*	**(-) The Pitfall:** *…and no thinking, principled, controlled, chosen ploy or tactic of dealing competently, seems to emerge other than the two polar-opposite gut-level responses…*	(N) **The concept of Stereotype vs. Sociotype of groups.** RESEARCH: (1.) Differences: males more for "Systems": explore and construct them, extract their working rules (and do well on rotating shapes, map-reading). **Females more for "Empathizing":** identify other person's emotions, relate with care, sensitivity. (2.) Degrees of this, do correlate with hormone levels. (3.) Distribution: 6 of 10 men have S. brain, 2 balanced, 2 an E. brain… and 4 of 10 women have E. brain, 4 balanced, 2 S. brain.
(N) Accounting professor suggests on his weblog that homosexual males are pedophiles. *--Mild explosions...*		Sociotype: *an objectively-existing trait of a group.* [Jewish scholarly achievement… West African success in long-distance running… Swedish talent for orderly precision, enumeration… Etc.] Stereotype: *inaccurate bias* ["Pushy Jews," "Blacks and Dancing," "Dour Scandanavians," etc.] An invaluable distinction. Vital to protect seeking knowledge. We must scrutinize stereotypes. But we must not let Political Correctness deny any differences among groups. The thinking skill of **"connect/distinguish,"** or knowing when to compare for similarities, when to distinguish differences. Very practical: EXAMPLE: races differ in their tolerance of different medicines, physicians had better know this.
(N) Harvard Prof. H. MANSFIELD is against gay rights. "seemed abnormal," etc. *--No protest noted...*		(N) **"Major Change."** [See our Tool-Kit on same.] Movement of new ideas from Heresy, to Orthodoxy, to Commonplace. And Today's Truths and Taboos swing in pendulum-style, often prohibit the other side (currently out of fashion) to even be thought of, let alone heard… ["What, women may be genetically different regarding mathematical thinking?"]
(N) LUTHERAN STUDENT GROUP wrote campus newspaper saying gays/lesbians were sinners, could and should repent. *--Readers wrote back*		(N) **Learn How To Read The Document! Learn Accurate Objective Reading!** WARD CHURCHILL, *only one* teacher pointed out "he's not trashing Americans, he's critiquing harmful world capitalism (albeit awkwardly)." And as for THE ANTI-LUTHERAN LETTERS, *only I* said "Please read that the religious students do not hate gays, their beloved religion (misguided or not…) says it is a sin, we risk damnation, we can be saved—their intent is more humane than you perceived (even if debatable)…

153

with firestorm of charges of bigotry. X Lawrence College invited J. L. ROCKWELL, head of American Nazi Party, to speak. Objections; they rescinded the offer. *--Nobody was alarmed or disgusted by the rescinding except myself, student newspaper editor at the time...*		**(N) Learn Dispassionate Interpersonal Listening!** Learn how to comprehend "the other side" fully without either believing or condemning just so you can state it accurately enough so that the other side can say "yes that is exactly what we do feel!" Marvelous for better communication plus ego-gain for individual... .....but *none* of the above Thinking Strategies was brought to the fore (except of course I spotlit MILL'S mantra in a letter to the editor). "Learnable Moments" were lost... *Were* students being trained in—or offered—these potent-fecund Concepts along with "knowledge" or what to Know?.....And think of at least half-dozen *other* Lenses which could have been used here but which I myself am surely overlooking right here right now!... Methods of which I myself the great "expert" in all this End-Goal Competence, am quite <u>unaware</u>!...

I see (and for once agree)... Things get challenging here. A *tremendously* large and varied "toolbank" of thinking strategies *may well* be needed to *adequately* confront really-complex issues especially those Civic ones outside each individual's Job-expertise or Personal-knowing...	...**YES, AND** how much must things simply take their course (students Pick Skills Up on their own as they go along) ... or how much might we proffer some powerful tools?...

[3:A.B.C.D.] EXAMPLES. Homosexuality, "I": various issues in. Four tiny tiffs about the dread subject. Done via "Conventional, *vs.* more "thinkingesque" via "multiple-plural **lenses**" and also "**sociology**: norms and mores as puppetmasters"...***Do learners need these non-rote perspectives?***

[3.A.] A son or daughter "comes out" as gay or lesbian, and the parent(s) actually throw the child out of the home, virtually disown him/her, banish or ostracize them. *Surely the parent is a bigot*, both oppressive and discriminatory! It is a <u>psychological</u> failing!	➜ Well yes but perhaps the explanation is more <u>sociogenic</u>. Culture is a script we learn to follow. That knee-jerk reaction is currently and conventionally sort of What One Does if a child were to "rebel and choose to be a deviant" blah blah etc. (If a child is alcoholic, currently much easier to "talk about it and get help" etc.) Doesn't make the parent right (or a good parent), but this perspective can help The power of a key concept: culture as "silent school" in which we learn... Also, INTERDISCIPLINARY perspective; many perhaps most complex subjects require more than just one perspective or field for full elucidation...

[3.B.] In the story "Baseball in July," a gay son brings his lover home to a family reunion, and many reactions are negative. Surely this is due to the fact that (1) homosexuality itself is wrong, is the problem, is both abnormal and unnatural. Or else (2) the son is the problem, being too assertive and rebellious. Or (3) the relatives are wrong, are bigoted.	➜ Yes but again, (4) heterosexism and homophobia are learned cultural behaviors. Doesn't make them right, but helps add perspective. A vital but overlooked lens...

[3.C.] The Boy Scouts of America excludes gay personnel: scouts, staff. Surely this is wrong: again, bigoted or discriminatory for no valid reason!	➜ Well yes but that's by <u>your "lens" of liberal tolerance</u> of everything that is not objectively harmful to society generally or others specifically. Whereas by the "lens" of the BSA, namely <u>current-traditional American norms</u>, which include gays as dangerous or at least distasteful deviants, they were indeed *right*... Lensmanship can help us see *why* we disagree with each other...

[3.D.] [And now for a thinking-competent instance:] <u>The father of a gay son</u> stated: "On reflecting about homosexuality, I've learned that: my *religious* tradition taught me to believe that my son was a sinner; my *medical* support system...that my son was sick; my *educational* system...that my son was abnormal; my *legal* system views my son and his partner in an unsanctioned relationship without legal rights and protection that are afforded my married daughter; my *family*, immediate and extended, provided no	➜ ...a winner! This perceptive parent exhibited "lensmanship," being explicitly aware of the many (and here all negative) perspectives possible, for a broader view...

acknowledgement or support for having a gay relative in its midst [*sociocultural* lens...]; my major *communications* sources treated homosexuality as deviant." [-- SOURCE UNKNOWN]	

...well, this does show the **End-Goal** of adroitly, confronting complexities later on, with a great range of thinking tools (a "ceiling-bank" of potentially hundreds?)... **BUT**, who chooses *which* tools to offer to students—by what criteria? Or *does* or *can* anyone choose?...	As to who chooses, a prior question is whether anyone chooses. In many schools, the public space seems empty. *The issue itself has not been dealt with...*

[4.] Homosexuality "II": Same-Sex Marriage...

THE EVENTS TO RESPOND TO: Same-Sex Marriage... (an emerging social issue forced ahead-of-its-time into the general news etc. around 2003...) We could ponder... Why the great support of this major change? And why the great objections to this basic move?

COMMON BUT OVER-SIMPLIFIED RESPONSES: <u>NO</u>: "Marriage Is Between A Man And A Woman, *Period*"... <u>YES</u>: "Denying Marriage Violates Basic Civil Rights of Equality, *Period*"......*and largely no more comment than just these elbow-jerk emissions?...*

POSSIBLE THINKING SKILLS TO ACCESS, APPLY:

(1) From **(A)** <u>PHILOSOPHY</u>, what are the **Variable-Issues** to identify and consider? **(B)** Relatedly, from <u>PSYCHOLOGY</u>, what are peoples' **"Background Stands"** on general matters, influence how they believe on specific issues.
--How do we decide social policy? Morals? Principles? Chaos?
--What are all options available to people—enough exist now?
--Do we decide on things objectively—or by personal feelings?
--What part do our fears play? Our mis- or non-information?
--Is Form or Letter more important—or Function and Spirit?
--What are all available AOC's alternate optional choices to consider?
--What is "marriage"? More religious? Private-personal? Civic-political?

(2) From <u>ANTHROPOLOGY</u>. The concept of **Affinity-Group.** "Minority/Outsider People seen (unconsciously) as Down-&-Out-Group Less Than 100% Fully Human or Citizens" (Blacks 3/5 of a white, women unworthy of the vote, etc.—*so*, are gay/lesbian folk still seen as if not deviant and disgusting, still as somewhat "lesser"?)

(3) From <u>MY OWN ANALYSIS of</u> **Major Social Change** and confronting it.....
1. Incomplete view of marriage as only religious, not civil and more.
2. Factual unawareness of the many benefits of marriage unavailable to the unmarriageable even via legal instruments...
3. Tendency to see people hierarchically. In-group vs. Outgroup. Complete upper rank vs. incomplete lower-down.
3. Sociocultural attitude beyond overt homophobia: "bedrock disgust."
4. Current anxieties; use an issue (marriage) as scapegoat...
...an attempt at powerful thinking tools and concepts and issues which might be accessed for more-competent confronting...

(4) <u>SOCIOLOGY'S</u> concept of **Normative vs. Behaviorial, Ideal vs. Real,** reasons given. A sort of Rationalization. See SCOTT BIDSTRUP'S analyses:
A. **"Homophobia":** the fear behind the hatred?
<u>Reasons given</u> for homophobia: 1. It's not natural, 2. It's a perversion, 3. It's against God's law, 4. It's disgusting.
The <u>real reasons</u> behind their hatred: 1. Us vs. them, 2. loss of control, 3. threat to one's world-view, 4. Fear of being homosexual oneself.
B. **Same-Sex Marriage:** the Arguments, and the Motives.
Reasons given against gay marriage: marriage is: 1. It's between men and women, 2. It's for procreation, 3. It's wrong for raising children, 4. It's immoral, 5. It's for continuing the species, 6. It's threatened by same-sex version, 7. It's traditionally heterosexual, 8. It's an untried social experiment, 9. SSM may lead down to polygamy etc., etc., 10. SSM would be a special right, 11. Sodomy is illegal.
The real reasons behind their opposition: 1. Just uncomfortable with the idea, 2. It offends much of "religion," 3. Marriage

is sacred, 4. Gay sex is unnatural, 5. Male lovemaking betrays masculinity, 6. Gay sex seems repulsive, 7. Gays might recruit, 8. SSM would undermine sodomy laws.

[*SEE ALSO:* the "total" roster of root-reasons why people oppose SSM, and continue to do so even after discussion of the issue as a civil right simply. In **Appendix #5, "Prior Basics,"** section on "Backgrounds" to a statement.. PPPPP]	

The skill: to distinguish two types of reasons given for belierfs:**Ideal/Normative** (overt) vs. **Real/Behavioral** (though covert).

...whoa, you fall short! You have **NOT** exhausted the "arena of possible tools"—indeed, relevant and need tools—to bring to bear on this many-faceted (and contested) concern!	...well, exactly my point. How can one person do so? Here's where **collaborative learning communities**, a "new' approach, *is* useful, even necessary. Yet not sufficient: in full flow, the **solo** thinker has to be able to access an *arsenal* of actions...

[5.] Evolution vs. "Intelligent Design," and teaching about it in the schools...

Unknown, perhaps-not-competent responses... Probably rationalizing a prior larger but unstated viewpoint or world-view... Perhaps combating to win, not cooperating toward wisdom...	1. Ways of Knowing; what's afoot here? 2. Motivations, including background ones. 3. Lenses or multiple-plural ways of knowing. 4. Historical perspective on major controversies.

.....perhaps the right-hand side suggests thinking tools applicable to this and other controversies...

[6.] How one thinker custom-selected thinking perspectives to confront the difficult problem of America's problematic status, position, behavior in the world today.

--Author STEPHEN DAMOURS in his recent [2004] book <u>America the Almighty</u>, argues against our superpower domination and for international cooperation. This, his goal-perspective. But how does he causally explain why America is as ruthlessly-dominating as he claims we are?

--He says that <u>much thought and reading</u> drove him to his answer: "a synergism between <u>three closely related psychological forces</u>." 1. Group selfishness, as the negative side of tribalism whose positives are group solidarity and patriotism. 2. Arrogance of power, using coercion covered with the fig leaf of noble causes. 3. A strong cultural habit of practicing win-lose games instead of win-win strategies. In conversation MR. DAMOURS also mentioned 4. Greed especially of the already-wealthy corporations, also 5. the current Religious Right movement and perhaps even, biographically, 6. President Bush himself.

How did Mr. DAMOURS select his tools, from what ceiling-bank or arena of possibilities? His **background logic or ultimate assumptions** he admits are tinged with United Nations and World Federalist type thinking. <u>My point</u>: here is a thinker out on a large path toward a large target. Did he have agile access to enough of sociology, politics, psychology, anthropology? Did he select the right perspectives for explanation? Would which other type of thinker approach the issue differently? Should a school train toward, <u>not</u> One Right Answer to be either given to or found by the learner, <u>but</u> how to best confront such complexities—and for more than just Vocationally for budding Political History majors too...

BUT, when one thinker takes on a complex issue not his specialty—as we often have to do—is it hit or miss, or... Well, no neat checklist exists for these skills... *Are you being too idealistic* about your recommended Tool-BANK for all learners?	...Only in urging its existence not its perfection. "<u>What higher-order concepts should all graduates have had a chance to encounter?</u>" When I heard Mr. DAMOURS speak, I felt he demonstrated superior End-Goal competence amid complexity...

...You know, you did well in some of these above, **BUT** overall, you know, *you're not that great a thinker*? Is this here the best you can do? Couldn't people have done better—used more tools, lesser-known ones, more effectively?	...I did better than some can or would do, but not as well as many other of you can do. <u>But I tried to do it</u>, to experiment explicitly what *true education* might mean—confronting complexities competently. An educational challenge still too often overlooked? That "Senior Capstone Integrative" course left unconstructed, the billboard vacant?... In summary: there lies a Path: rough, but worthy, but still untrodden...

SEE ALSO: On "why do gay men seem [to some observers...] to emphasize sexuality but not relationship?", **see** the **Gallery,** Main Part #1-D... Our misperception of it... Minority-group emphasis... Gender-role: males?... residual Puritanism? And so forth...	

[{ END of Appendix #2, Three Pillars... }]

This Appendix #3, **"Thinking 101, or INducting UPward to Conceptualize the Content"** is devoted entirely to that very basic—but unexplored—thinking skill/issue…

SECTION #1: "Why, The Very IDEA!" – the **Concept of a** [higher-order] **Concept**…
SECTION #2: *"Basic Pedagogy"*—to *teach* INduction UPward in *"English (etc.,) 101 Monday Morning"*…
SECTION #3: **4 Key Thinking Skills: Letter/Spirit, Definition, Analogy, Creativity**—how they aid conceptualizing.

--THE ISSUE. As basic a thinking skill as any, is **conceptualizing**. Also known as **inducting** UPward, and to an extent **generalizing.** That is, examining Material concrete evidence—information, experience, etc.— and discovering / creating Mental concepts, ideas, generalizations about that specific content.

> **--"We survey vegetarianism and find many motives for, or anyhow reasons given for; varied subtypes or categories of; and more…"**

Yes, very simple and basic. And one of **the "trio of moves" of basic thinking, [1.] "derive ideas *from* facts,"** the second being **deduction** or **[2.] "apply ideas *to* facts,"** DOWNward.

> **--"We apply the criteria of morality, health, ecology, etc., to the issue of vegetarianism."**

And the third move is **lateral-or-associative** thinking ACROSS, **[3.] "inter*relate* two realms."**

> **--"We consider vegetarianism's lesser impact on the environment, then think of the issue of "less is more," both aesthetically and also pragmatically and even ethically; then Zen Buddhism or Native Americans perhaps; then capitalism and 'sustainable growth' plus globalization, and…"**

--WHY IMPORTANT: "…indeed simple and basic, so why teach conceptualizing so extensively as in this appendix here? Surely everyone knows how to induct at some level or another, to get ideas from information…" But the (ironical) misconception here is that many thinkers may not *truly* **"know"** the skill. There's **"Knowing, vs. Knowing."** That is, "of course we all know" that one can and should induct about material, "thinking things through" to ideas. Thus we may know (1) of-or-about thinking for concepts behind the concrete, but not actually (2) really-how-to-do, and the pitfalls-and-potentialities. Very few beginning learners know how to conceptualize basically, but even advanced thinkers find it a challenge to conceptualize thoroughly (to induct from surface specifics to grasp a situation)…

--OUR SUGGESTION. *…therefore this Appendix. Nowhere else have we seen educational resource-materials which (again irony) conceptualize conceptualizing in as elucidated a fashion as we have attempted here, and have largely succeeded in doing—even if overdone for some advanced learners!* We seem to *cover more bases* or arenas, areas of application (see table below, right-hand column)… and *offer clearer conceptualizing* of the subtypes of conceptualizing… plus *provide more vivid examples*. In terms of thinking as a "contest," we've sought to "retrieve from the wild," **the concept of the concept, why the very idea of an idea**, and place it elucidated on a pedestal in the Museum. *Onward…*

|#+#~|+|#+|~+#|~#+|+|#~|~+#~|+##|~#+|~|+#|+~#|~+|#+|~+#|~|#~|+~|#~+|#+#~|+#|~+#|+~|#+|~+#~|#+|~+#|~#+|~+#|~+#|~+||

The PREVIEW "ORIENTATION-MAP" to Help Navigate this Appendix of 3 Sections:

NOTE: formulated "GUIDELINES" (perhaps to become End-Goal Skills) are marked with a ➔

---

1. TEXTS: Basic Reading and Writing.
1A. *Read* the written text of *another* person, to extract the points.
➔ **Can write conceptual précis & outline.** (Of simple clear texts, also of badly-written or implicit texts.)

1B. *Write* one's *own* text, with points identified and made explicit.
➔ **Can write *one's own* text and A. discover, and B. express, the concepts clearly.**

2. RESPONSES: "Scrutinizing a *statement-claim* made by another (or by oneself!)"...
➔ **Can find the background concepts etc. in another person's (or one's own) response to/claim about a subject or situation.**

3. Actual SITUATION. "Reading a 'situation.'"
➔ **Can find the subliminal conceptual patterns in an actual real world observed situation:**
(= group culture, ideology or school of thought, theory, etc.)

4. OTHER CONCEPTUALITIES *advanced, subtle, difficult* ... ➔ **Can use conceptually:**
(A) The "**Big Ideas**" *permeating* an academic discipline or field.....
(B) The "**Operating Concepts**" *behind* procedures, skills.....
(C) "**Variable-Issues**" or matters to consider for success in the task-goal at hand.....
(D) A subject's "**Conceptual Topography**": structure & function (blueprint-flowchart etc.) of a situation.....

5. ➔ **Can also use conceptually, these OTHER MAJOR, BASIC SKILLS:**
(A) "**Letter vs. Spirit**"..... (B) "**Definition**"..... (C) "**Analogy**"..... (D) "**Creativity**" in daily life....

|#+#~|+|#+|~+#|~#+|+|#~|+#~|+##|~#+|~|+#|~+#|~+|#+|~+#|~|#~|+~|#~+|#+#~|+#|~+#|+~|#+|~+#|~#+|~+#|~#+|~+#|~+#|~+||

The **component sub-skill** of **conceptualizing**: (And where used in which Arenas of application)	**Where found** in which section of this Appendix?:	**Examples** given within, to illustrate the issue:
1. To basically [A] Read and [B] Write, TEXTS: GUIDELINE-GOAL: READ: Learner can read the **written text** of another, and *create* a competent précis (summary) and outline of *the ideas not just the factual plot.* (A) Simple easier texts (B) More challenging (difficult) texts: (B1) Because written badly (B2) Because intentionally "implicit" WRITE: Learner can create a text of one's own which is conceptual not just concrete.	**Section II, "Pedagogical Basics"** A "ready-to-wear" or "drive-away" unit for the classroom teacher of "English 101" or the equivalent.	*READING:* X Lifeguard Job at Biltmore Beach X Fast-food Noon-Hour Rowdiness X Brookfield High Needs an Auditorium X The Knee XX Proverbs, and Poetry... *WRITING:* X "A Job I've Held" (teaching 2nd grade art... nursing home... fast-food crew...)

2. To "Scrutinize" someone's "RESPONSE-Statement"…

GUIDELINE-GOAL: Learner can confront someone's response to a subject/issue (a statement, claim, etc.) and can "unpack" _the patterns and background to it beyond the surface claims._
[= Motivations, implicit presuppositions, world-view]

Sec. I, Why The Very Idea: (#4-B, "Responses")

Sec. II, Basic Pedagogy:

SEE ALSO: "Backgrounds, " in **Prior Basics** (Appendix #5)

X The U.S. Invasion of Grenada

X Socarides, Wolverton, Nicolosi on sexual orientation, reorientation

X

---

3. To "read" a "Social SITUATION" itself for its conceptual patterns.

["Situation" here means = _complex clusters of subliminal patterns in some system or other_. (Specific social-group codes, and general cultural norms mores folkways… Schools of thought, ideologies… Systems…)]

GUIDELINE-GOAL: **Learner can confront a situation and derive out (discover / create) the key ideas,** _concepts within-behind-above-beyond the concrete material elements._

Sec. I, Why The Very Idea.

Sec. II: within "Pedagogical Basics"

X Traditional Humanism _versus_ "Postmodernism"

X World-views of humanities, social sciences, nat. scis.

X The logic of medicine—has to be grasped by a non-specialist patient!

X Traditional American culture: norms, mores, folkways

X The Sixties Generation

X Boomer-generation youth today

X Education: "Old-School" vs. "New-Think" paradigms

X Writing and Reading in School

X East vs. West (Europe-Asia)

X Writing: school, job, journalism, etc.

X The _tacit_ "Corporate culture" of one's workplace!

X Sexuality: traditional religion, liberationist or diversity

X Art: ten facets of!

X Cookery: six criteria for!

X The Detective Story's formula

---

4. To know and use, FOUR OTHER TYPES OF CONCEPTUALITIES which are _advanced, subtle, difficult._
--"Big Ideas" in a field
--Operating Concepts in a skill
--Variable-Issues in a task-goal
--Conceptual Topography of any subject (content, skill, issue, etc.)

GUIDELINE-GOAL:
Learner can identify these more-complex variables in a task-goal situation and employ them profitably.

Sec. I: within "Why The Very Idea" (Sec. #4-D 1 2 3 4)

"Big Ideas":
X in Biology [Evolution, etc.]
X in Political Sci./Government
X others…

Operating Concepts:
X Cinematography: "camera-placement"
X Writing: Syntax… Parallelism… Specific Detailing…
X Time-Management: [Goals, Priorities, Lead-Time]
X Business: ["consistency" for customers]
X Education: [a teacher's "imperturbability"…]
X Computers: ["linear sequentiality," "levels," others]
X Algebra: ["combination, permutation, association"]

Variable-Issues:
X Alternative Medicine
X Book Reviewing
X I. Q. Measurement

		X Logistics
		X Poetry-appreciation
		Conceptual Topography:
		X Lens-work: 12 issues
		X Verticalities: 4 mega-issues
		X 15-C or Essay-Writing: 15 points

5. To know and use FOUR TYPES OF "CONCEPT-ORIENTED" THINKING SKILLS which are concept-oriented. --"Letter" *vs.* "Spirit" --Definition --Analogy --"Creativity" in daily life They aid confronting subjects, comprehending them, then also communicating-about them to others): GUIDELINE-GOAL: **Learner can use these skills not just by literal rule but conceptually, for thinking-goals…**	**_All_ of Sec. III, "Appendix of Four Skills for Conceptualizing"**	**"Letter vs. Spirit":** [literal-figurative, form-function, correct-effective, appearance-reality, change or not, rule-tool, etc.] X "No eating, or doing laundry, in the hotel room" (but why okay to do after all?) X An effeminate gay man, is not a real—"man"? X "My anthro prof was a murderer, had shot five men with a rifle" X "Public nudity"—always obscene etc.? X A Sex Act: moral, immoral, etc.?" X Eskimos kill grandparents, Hindus revere cows—is this barbaric and superstitious? X Boy Scouts bars gay personnel: moral, immoral? **Definition:** XX: Religion… Wealth… Pornography, Obscenity… Capital, Property… Literacies… what is a "Map"?… a "Game"?… Sexual Orientation, Home, News, Advertising, Art, Music, Literature, a Minority Group? **Analogy:** X Grief, mourning in bereavement is like… X Good psychoanalytic therapy is like… X An over-sensitive "friend" is like… X Teaching Thinking is like: [cache, route-map, open-access safe-box, vaccination…] X Various thinking skills are like! **"Creativity" in daily life** X What will work as a bird-feeder? X It's raining, no raincoat—aha, a bag… X Bike breakdown, no tools—aha, use… X Clean mud off self downtown—aha, car wash! X Must safeguard manuscripts—aha, old fridge! X To clean carpet, no vacuum—aha, tape!

|#+#~|+|#+|~+#|~#+|+|#~|+#~|+##|~#+|~|+#|+~#|~+|#+|~+#|~|#~|+~|#~+|#+#~|+#|~+#|+~|#+|~+#~|#+|~+#|~#+|~+#|~#+|~+#|~+||

#3, CONCEPTUALIZING 101: SEC. 1, "WHY, THE VERY IDEA—...OF AN IDEA !..."

--The crucial importance of **principles** not just *particulars*—their shortage, their difficulty, but the real possibility of thinking better about *material content* via **mental concepts**...
In school, in real-world life; for profit, for pleasure...

  --<u>Algebra</u>: manipulations, *but also* "combination, permutation, association"
  --<u>Science in Society</u>: facts, issues, *but also* Dynamic Equilibrium; Change & Evolution; Scale & Proportion; Causality & Consequences; and, Energy: Its Sources and Transfer..."
  --<u>Time-Management</u>: procedures, *but esp.* "(1) goal-setting, then (2) prioritizing, then (3) lead-time planning"...
  --<u>Philosophy</u>: figures, schools, *but* "Question all... Spot assumptions, implications... Give counter-examples...Define terms..."
  --<u>Humor</u>: examples, ha-ha, *but beyond,* "aggression; repression; anxiety-management; surprise/incongruity"...

--**Inducting** upward to the **abstractions** beyond-behind the *specific subjects*, (**generalizations; viewpoints**; etc.) is (1) NECESSARY for competent thinking-and-doing ... But it is (2) UNDER-DONE; we too often fall short (in doing; in teaching-about)... True, this **conceptualizing** is (3) quite DIFFICULT... But it is (4) more POSSIBLE than we might realize ...

--So this entire section is devoted to elucidating this one move: "**conceptualizing** *content*." To do this well, we discuss several subtypes / arenas / venues/ etc. of this keystone ploy...

--So, how would learners best understand how to move from the "Pond of *Particulars*," to the "Peak of **Principles**" (and back down again to DEduct or apply said **concepts** to the *content* again...)?

A TOUCHSTONE-QUOTATION: Conceptualizing UP, and Holistic Synthesizing:

Although details are very often critically important, an inability to stand back and chunk facts leads to a myopic favoring of *minutiae* over **ideas** in <u>many contexts</u>. As I've mentioned,
--*computation* is valued about **conceptual understanding** in <u>mathematics</u>;
--in <u>politics</u>, *smart tactics* bring greater rewards than **wise policies**;
--*technical hocus-pocus* in the <u>stock market</u> attracts more attention than does **analysis of fundamentals**;
--for those with a <u>religious</u> temperament, *rules, rites and rituals* obscure **wonder, awe, and mystery**;
--in <u>sex</u>, *lust and fetishism* are mistaken for **love**.
I grant that the first element in each of these oppositions does sometimes rightfully take precedence over the second but generally too little stress is placed on the second. It's much easier to put the jigsaw puzzle together after you've seen the whole picture (assuming there's one to see).

[-- JOHN ALLEN PAULOS]

WAIT. I've skimmed this whole unit. It is *overkill. We all know already*, that **induction** is	→ *Because* I want this fiendishly-difficult, valuable, possible, and satisfying, but under-discussed, skill, to be as accessible as possible to

+|#||+#++||#+|#+||#+|+|+#|+|#|+|#+|++#|+|+|#+|+|+|#+||+#|#+|+#||+#|+|#+|#+|+#|+#|+#+|+#|+|#+|+#|+|#+|#+|#+|#+|#+|+#|+|#+#||
+|#||+#++||#+|#+||#+|+|+#|+|#|+|#+|++#|+|+|#+|+|+|#+||+#|#+|+#||+#|+|#+|#+|+#|+#|+#+|+#|+|#+|+#|+|#+|#+|#+|#+|#+|+#|+|#+#||

[1.] Intro.	[2.] Table of Contents	[3.] Body of Claims	[4.] "Reading"-Situations	[5.] Annex: Examples

[1.] INTRODUCTION: the rationale:

CONCEPT/ISSUE. On the vertical ladder of abstraction, two poles exist. "Specifics, and generalities." That is, the lower-down Material concrete specific content (data, information, etc.), a "pond of particulars" == and the higher-up Mental conceptual abstractions or ideas-concerning that content, a "peak of principles." We INduct UPward from the specifics to make generalities, find principles, use lenses.

[True, **[1.]** INduction is only one of the three main movements in thinking. **[2.]** We also DEduct DOWNward and apply mental models to material situations, **[3.]** plus move ACROSS in associative, lateral thinking to connect elements. All three are needed. But, to induct upward to the **principles *above/behind* the particulars**, is *valuable*. It lets us confront better, two kinds of situations: both (1) standard easier ones with known simpler issues, but also (2) those which are more-challenging new, foreign, changing, obscure, ill-defined.

CRUCIALITY. However, <u>people often fall short of inducting</u>, in life, in education (and induction is difficult). But we can do and teach better. How to formulate generalities, principles, perspectives more explicitly than we thought, but without the oversimplification or formulizing we rightly fear. *How* to do so? Know the principles, elucidated; which this unit seeks to do.

OUR SUGGESTION. We try here to explicitly conceptualize—well, conceptualization! The very idea of an idea. Our goal in this module is to do a better job of elucidating "the very idea of an Idea," than any other educational resource-materials have done to date (otherwise why would we attempt it…).

GOALS: The teacher and learner… This supports the three "pillar" keystone goals of teaching thinking. **1.** Goal is how to think via concepts, not know facts… **2.** Thinking-skills are explicitly present in classes, whole school… and **3.** End-Goal (to be taught-toward and measured?) is Hitting the Ground Running with ultimate preparedness to conceptualize situations in the real world life after graduation…

GUIDELINE-SKILL: Be able to discover and employ the <u>principles behind</u> *specific facts, events, procedures*. The concepts which summarize and explain the *particulars*. Use these <u>keystone abstractions</u> to better confront *content*: to simply comprehend and explain, also to "do to or with," perform a skilled *action*. Not only in (1) routine known simpler moves, but especially to more competently handle (2) advanced, unfamiliar, complex, foreign situations.

BACKGROUND-KNOWLEDGE NEEDED; OTHER SKILLS RELATED-TO:

> SEE The other two units of this Appendix. #2 Pedagogy and #3 the four Letter-Spirit, Definition, Analogy, Creativity.

CONNEXIONS: w/ other tools: Complexity… Essential Thinking Eleven… Verticalities… Lenswork… Elucidation… Knowing vs. Really Knowing… 5-AAAAA: first Awareness but then also Ability… and others.

DEFINITION: An EDUCATOR expands the very concept of "reading," indeed of "literacy":

[During the last century, "literacy" has meant <u>learning to *read printed words* in a text</u>. But more recently, research suggests that "the reading of words is but a subset of <u>a much more general human activity which includes *symbol decoding, information integration, and organization*</u> …. Indeed, reading—in the most general sense—can be thought of as a form of perceptual activity. The reading of words is one manifestation of this activity; but there are many others— the reading of *pictures, maps, circuit diagrams, musical notes...*"   [-- TOM WOLFE, HARVARD EDUCATIONAL REVIEW]

And we can extend this reading—decoding, sense-making, pattern-recognition, concept-cinching—beyond the above existing human-made systems (books, visuals, blueprints, etc.), to situations themselves. Here things get challenging…

```
+|#||+#++||#+|#+||#+|+|+#|+|#|+|#+|++#|+|+|#+|+|+#||+#|+|+#||+#|+|#+|+|#|+#|+#|+|#+|+|#+|+|#+|#+|#+|+|#+|+|#+#||
+|#||+#++||#+|#+||#+|+|+#|+|#|+|#+|++#|+|+|#+|+|+#||+#|+|+#||+#|+|#+|+|#|+#|+#|+|#+|+|#+|+|#+|#+|#+|+|#+|+|#+#||
```

[2.] **Table of Contents** of this module.

[3.A.] *We shortfall in conceptualizing…:*

1. **In the real world** (personal, vocational, civic). TABLE: cookery, time mgmt., art, humor, etc.

2. **In school or education arena**

i., ii.: TABLES showing content vs. concepts in various disciplines.

iii. STATEMENTS show the goal, but not always achieved.

iv. **"Big Ideas"** in a field: useful, but not always clearly-conceptualized?

[3.B.] *…and true Conceptualizing UPward 101, is 1. difficult. But 2. can be done well—at least better!*

[3B.1] Defining "Reading the Situation"

[3B.2.] "Expertise": [1] Elucidated: principles, examples. [2] Expedited: snowboarding, handball, chicken-sexing

A. **Written Texts.** "Write a competent précis and outline"

B. **Responses** to a Situation: **Statements/Claims about it:** know the motivations, lenses, assumptions"

C. Complex Situations Themselves: **"Reading the Situation"** (pattern-recognition of complex systems).

D. Three other types, more complex or specialized:.

1. **Operating Concepts** or "The Hidden Why Behind" a subject or skill. "Know why you do what you do."

2. **Variable-Issues:** "Identify the matters one must or should confront for optimum task-goal success."

3. **"Conceptual Topography"** or the lay of the land (structure, function) of a complex content or craft.

[5.A.] TABLE OF EXAMPLES of **"Reading the Situations"** of various systems (= "pattern-recognition")…

[The "corporate culture" of a business one hopes will hire you… Humanism vs. Postmodernism… The Sixties… Boomer-generation… Education: know vs. think!... Writing: in School, in the Real World… Western vs. Eastern (Asian) basic

+|#||+#++||#+|#+||#+|+|+#|+|#|+|#+|++#|+|+|#|+|+|#||+#|#+|+#||+#|+|#+|#+|+#|+|#+|+#|+|#+|+#|+|#+|#+|#+|#+|#+|+#|+|#+#||
+|#||+#++||#+|#+||#+|+|+#|+|#|+|#+|++#|+|+|#|+|+|#||+#|#+|+#||+#|+|#+|#+|+#|+|#+|+#|+|#+|+#|+|#+|#+|#+|#+|#+|+#|+|#+#||

[1.] Intro.	[2.] Table of Contents	**[3.] Body of Claims**	[4.] "Reading"-Situations	[5.] Annex: Examples

[3.] the body: *opportunities* :

[3.A.] We SHORTFALL in *using* Ideas...

[3.A.1.] IN THE "REAL WORLD": "We too often don't conceptualize UP in real-life situations: in *Personal* life, on-the-job *Vocational*, and *Civic-Community* endeavors."

The **Subject** discussed:	Factual **Content** present in "real-world" publications:	The key **Concepts** which many texts omit, if their authors even derived them:
"CHINESE STIR-FRY COOKING"	Ingredients: vegetables, meat. Soy, ginger, garlic, flour. Etc.	"Small-Sized Food Pieces, Hot Pan Heat, Oil Added Only When Pan Hot, Ingredients Added so All are Done Cooking Simultaneously, Constant-Continuous Vigorous Stirring, and Very Brief Cooking Time."
"EVALUATING A RESTAURANT MEAL"	[from the book Dining Out, about restaurant cooking, meals, reviewing, etc... *I myself had to abstract out the right-hand column of concepts buried in the book's descriptions...*]	1. Historical-Social-Traditional A. Classic vs. Innovation B. Ethnic variations C. Basic Flavor-Balance 2. Personal-Individual A. The Particular Chef B. The Particular Diner/Critic 3. Explicit Ranking-Criteria A. Star-systems B. Severity of Standards?
"CRITERIA FOR PUBLIC-ART DISPLAYS"	unconceptualized opinions, the assumptions not clear [from Letters to the Editor of the Milwaukee Journal]	1. Conventional Folk-Familiarity 2. Trendy-Edgy Fashionable 3. Laissez-Faire Relativism 3. Pure Visual Aesthetic Design 4. Meaningful Staying-Power 5. ...at least a half-dozen other concepts...
"TIME-MANAGEMENT"	this and that technique [...various accounts of Time M. are variously-conceptual; too many lack the ideas as in the right-hand column...]	1. Goal-setting. 2. Prioritizing; specifically, 3. Ranking tasks in four very important categories: as to whether **"Urgent and Important; Urgent but not Important; Important but not Urgent; neither Urgent nor Important"** 4. Lead-Time Planning: Stages
HUMOR, WIT	No or vague ideas.	1. Aggression. Malice at others' misfortunes. 2. Repression. Topics taboo to discuss. 3. Anxiety-management. Topic painful to confront, uncontrollable. 4. Surprise; Incongruity. "The collapse of a strained expectation into

		nothing."
MICROWAVE OVENS	This and that recipe	Size, placement of food for best cooking…
COMPUTERS	Endless instructions…	"Functional Abstraction": a hierarchy of parts, with well-define one-directional interactions. Some separation of levels from each other… "Linear Sequentiality"…
PARALLELISM (IN WRITING)	"Avoid faulty parallelism at the sentence-level"	# If a series of ideas are related logically, then phrase them in related language-style, so the reader sees the relationship."
SPECIFICITY (IN WRITING)	"Support your ideas with specific examples."	# "Our ideas and emotions come from specific—experiences, evidence. So put in to your writing not only your ideas, but the evidence, to re-create them in the reader more powerfully."
SYNTAX (IN WRITING)	This and that rule…	"Place important info in main clauses, secondary information in subordinate clauses. Place old and secondary and orienting info early in the sentence, place new and important info at the sentence's—end." [The mind processes better via this style.]

…SOME VARIOUS OTHER FIELDS: KEYSTONE CONCEPTS:	Teaching, "imperturbability"… business, "consistency-of-quality/service"… cinematography, "where to place the camera"…

Even, some fields may lack explicit elucidation of their "foundational/keystone" concepts:

"Every day we encounter a vast and relentless array of <u>information designs</u>—charts, illustrations, diagrams, icons, pages and screens of text, and legions of others. These designs are saturated with visual conventions with many different profiles…. [But] Not surprisingly, the **structure** of information design as a language has remained elusive, its study largely ignored or focused on *surface features*, rather than sounded for its **underlying system** of conventional codes and the processes that shape and sustain them." [-- SOURCE]

The **same** problem has been found in the **military**, in **literature**-studies, in **advertising**, in yet **other** fields…

[3.A.2.] …AND IN SCHOOL: "We may also shortchange conceptualizing in education. Do many courses remain with concrete information?

i. Table #1: COURSE:	Traditional content coverage approach:	Altered concept-conveying approach:	Increased use not just knowing:
"Visual Art(s)-Appreciation"	Historical, also Schools, also Great Artists: Egyptian, Greek, then Renaissance schools, Rembrandt, Impressionism…	The Principles and Elements of Design: balance symmetry proportion line texture value color etc.	"Re-design your living quarters"… "
Philosophy	(1) Historical Schools: Greeks (Plato), on to Renaissance. Idealism, realism, materialism, empiricism. Modern: existentialism etc. Also (2) Great Questions ("how we know," etc., etc.)	Six key perspectives: Questioning, Definition of terms, Implications, Consequences, Consistencies, Logic-Reasoning.	"Philosophy of" applied to (1) current controversies, also (2) the "daily": sex, food, the bicycle, graffiti, more!
Economics	Traditional: much theory, and perhaps little practice beyond "textbook exercises"	[Prof. L. J. MALONE at Hartwick College:] <u>start with theory first half</u>, like *"supply and demand, pricing, decision making, and the laws of returns,"* but <u>then</u>… [But also Prof. PAUL HEYNE: <u>start with felt problem-issues</u>, then learn the theory to explore them…] INDUCTIVE?	…<u>apply</u> to current issues of **"Immigration," "File-Sharing," and "Drugs"**… DEDUCTIVE?
Howard Gardner's proposed Gen. Ed. core	[Traditional: Great Issues without theory?]	Examine three topics in detail: **evolution, Mozart's The Marrige of Figaro, and the**	[Ideally then apply on own to other current issues as ultimate test of end-goal

165

course:		Holocaust. (Presumably with intellectual apparatus…)	readiness. E.g., "the longitude problem, Shakespeare, the Native American issue"]

|+|+|+|+|++|+|+|+++|||+|+|+|+|+|+|+|+|+||+|+|+|+|+||+|+|+|+|+|+|+|+|+|+|+|+|+|+|+|+|+|+|+|+|+|+|+|+|+||+|+|+|+|+++||+|+|+|+|+|+|+|+||+|+|+|+|+|||

ii. Table #2: **SUBJECT:**	Usual **factual-content**, and lower-level skills:	Higher-order keystone **concepts** of the subject:
Algebra	(various formulae)	"combination," "permutation," "association"—the **keystones**
Sociology	Institutions, social problems. Often <u>some</u> **concepts** (role, status, norm, deviancy, socialization, etc.)	**Theories**: Functionalism, Conflict, Interactionism… **Perspectives**: Debunking, Unrespectable, Cosmopolitan, Relativism…
art history	Egyptian, Greek, Medieval styles….and so forth.	Composition **principles**: balance, proportion, sequence, unity, a/symmetry, simplicity, contrast! Line, form, value,!
Literature	Periods. Authors. Themes.	"Schools of Criticism" as **lenses**: biographical, aesthetic, historical, psychological, social-critical, etc.!
Computers	this and that program…	"linear sequentiality"
economics	formulae, data on problems…	"scarcity" "allocation cost," or "cost-benefit ratio"—as immensely-applicable everywhere, always!
Natural Sciences	Biology, etc.: facts of mitosis-meiosis and the like, more…	<u>General Concepts of Science</u>: Dynamic Equilibrium; Change & Evolution; Scale & Proportion; Causality & Consequence; Energy, Its Sources & Transfer…
geography	[data, data, data…]	["Why is it like it is, here?"]
political science	[info on government systems]	How to confront the recurrent Big Issues: individual freedom vs. group security, etc., etc., etc.
history	"kings, courts, dates…"	[Past-present continuities, dissimilarities, etc.]
math		Problem-solving: Trial and error; "Step backwards"; Simulation; Symbolism; Patterns… Cause-and-Effect…
OTHERS:		
APPLIEDS:	Business, Engineering, Law, Medicine, Technology, Military, Government, etc…	

|+|+|+|+|++|+|+|+++|||+|+|+|+|+|+|+|+|+||+|+|+|+|+||+|+|+|+|+|+|+|+|+|+|+|+|+|+|+|+|+|+|+|+|+|+|+|+|+||+|+|+|+|+++||+|+|+|+|+|+|+|+||+|+|+|+|+|||

iii. "Educational THEORY": it perhaps 'knows about' conceptualizing, but actual <u>teaching</u> does not always apply it."

GALLERY. A set of classic educators' statements, from general to particular instances:

The curriculum of a subject should be determined by the most fundamental understanding that can be achieved of the <u>underlying principles</u> that give structure to a subject….Teaching *specific topics or skills* without making clear their context in the <u>broader fundamental structure</u> of a field of knowledge is uneconomical… An understanding of <u>fundamental principles and ideas</u> appears to be the main road to adequate transfer of training. To understanding something as *a specific instance of a more general case—*which is what understanding a more fundamental structure means—is to have learned not only a specific thing but also a model for understanding other things like it that one may encounter.   [-- JEROME BRUNER, Process of Education]

Digging into the laws of thought illuminates not controversy merely, but all conscious endeavor. For in all good thinking and feeling are to be found <u>the three great ideas underlying both logic and mathematics</u>, namely, **Generality**; **Form** (something that can be handled when its type is recognized); and **Variability**. They appear in different guises fitting the subject matter but they rule thinking about art as well as politics, business as well as science. [-- J. BARZUN]

At the Univ. of Wis.-Whitewater, the General Education Committee recommended that the science courses introduce

> "the following <u>common, general concepts</u>": Dynamic Equilibrium; Change & Evolution; Scale & Proportion; Causality & Consequences; and, Energy: Its Sources and Transfer. [-- GEN ED COMM.]

I would love this. These seem to be <u>true powerful, potent/fecund, keystones</u>... **Dynamic equilibrium** or the difficult balance between symmetry and asymmetry appears in *visual art* also, I know; and, is "*homeostasis*" involved?... Then, **Change** has a dozen variables in it, from many fields: resistance to major change, stages or phases from *heresy-to-orthodoxy-to-commonplace*, and the like... **Scale and Proportion** figure in our own schemes of "*Calibration*" or balance, over- or under-emphasis, skewing of view of a subject, over- or under-valuation, and the like... As for **Cause-Effect**, this is majorly major, it draws a dozen variables from many fields, You have the obvious, *one or many*, causes—and effects. *Speed*: sudden tip-over points. And the like. And then differing models: *number* of causes: from economy and efficiency (the fewer causes used to explain, the better), to overdetermination (in psychiatry, the more and interwoven causes, the more likely the explanation is correct)... And **Energy** is crucial to discuss the hydrocarbon crisis and the like.

> Grasping the structure of a subject is understanding it in a way that permits many other things to be related to it meaningfully. To learn structure, in short, is to learn how things are related. . . . To take an example from mathematics, <u>algebra</u> is a way of arranging knowns and unknowns in equations so that the unknowns are made knowable. The <u>three fundamentals</u> involved . . . are **commutation, distribution,** and **association.** Once a student grasps the ideas embodied by these three fundamentals, he is in a position to recognize wherein "new" equations to be solved are not new at all. Whether the student knows the formal names of these operations is less important for transfer than whether he is able to use them. [-- BRUNER, The Process of Education, 1960]

This reads "neat," it could not be stated a great deal better than it was, to *cinch the concept* of—a "corralling" **concept**...

|+|+|+|+|++|+|+|+|+|++|||+|+|+|+|+|+|+|+|+|+|+|+|+|+||+|+|+|+|+|+|+|+|+|+|+|+|+|+|+|+|+|+|+|+|+|+|+|+|+|+|+|+|+|+|+|+|+|+|+|+|+|+|+|+|+|+|+|+|+|+|+|+|+|+|++||+||+|+|+|+|+|+|+|+|+||+||+|+|+|||

However in <u>practice</u> perhaps education sometimes falls short from this understanding above and <u>theory</u>:

> **EXAMPLES.** The first, more simple and evident. The second, very complex in re conceptualizing.

> *Courses should present general principles rather than individual cases.* I have visited business schools where an introductory 13-week course in entrepreneurship consisted of 26 successful alumni entrepreneurs telling their life stories. These accounts are often inspirational, but the implicit message to students is that there are no **common features of success,** no **typical mistakes** to be avoided, no **predictable moments** when a new organization must make **critical transitions.** In schools of law and medicine, the case method has a proper role. But in business schools, professors need to be more careful to *articulate the principles* that cases illustrate. [-- CARL J. SCHRAMM, CHE]

| **NO,** this is shortsighted. "Telling our stories" is a powerful way of communicating and learning. | This is *excellent*. Your comment is "either/or" (plus either uninformed or defensive). The key is the **keystone idea or issue,** here (1) types of errors and excellences, (2) phases in sequences of progress. Let stories then illustrate these **concepts**... |

> WATSON: "although it is widely accepted that <u>the point of the casebook method is to teach students how to argue about the law,</u> students appear to learn to argue *without thinking about the law.* "<u>The problem</u> lies in the use of a few cases when in fact the law is not contained in a few cases but is usually *distilled from many cases,* so that if only a few are studied they appear out of context. Without a *general framework,* students do not get the big picture. They cannot tell to what extent a case reflects *general propositions* or whether it stands at the edge of a doctrine. It is often impossible to see which facts in the case are relevant. Watson's solution is *to set out briefly the concepts and propositions developed in hundreds of cases,* then follow this with a discussion of a few cases selected to illustrate the rules, their parameters, and issues raised by borderline situations.
> [-- LEARNING TO THINK: DISCIPLINARY PERSPECTIVES: LAW PRECEDENT AND REASON]

| Well, this might seem obvious. "Of course," one looks at a range of examples and then generalizes from them... | Oh, does one now, and always? The point here: law school at times *may well grievously fall short of conceptualizing.* Re-read this excerpt carefully. It charges *non*-thinking because the "general concepts and propositions" have *not* been derived, distilled, and made explicit! Prof. WATSON would **conceptualize the content** thus. It shows the way to go: survey the *whole* arena of content (examples, instances, evidence), and carefully INduct UPward to the Generalities resulting, for a *better* conclusion. |

And the results of not conceptualizing UP from surface to spirit, can be significantly <u>bad</u>.

> REPORT FROM CLASSES. "When presented with a novel problematic situation, students tend to look to the *surface features* for cues as to what learned ideas and procedures to apply: "What other problem have I done that has the features of this one?" In physics, students look for *features like inclined planes or pulleys* rather than for possibly relevant <u>principles</u> such as forces or energy conservation. For example, when two bodies interact, as in a collision,

students tend to attend to *features such as which one is moving faster, which is bigger, and which will sustain the greater damage*, rather than considering equal and opposite action and reaction forces."
[-- JIM MINSTRELL, "EXPERTISE IN TEACHING"]

"Capacity for problem solving is limited by our use of inappropriately simple practice exercises." [-- LION GARDINER]

"Many [students] succeeded admirably in high school through the exclusive use of rote memory and procedural mimicry (known in mathematics as the "extreme algorithmic approach"). So a student may have received an A in trigonometry by knowing how to manipulate cosines and tangents *yet without really understanding what they represent.* Such underlying deficiencies return to haunt... A young adult may be selling a product without fully understanding it, or preparing a legal brief without perceiving its ramifications." [-- MEL LEVINE, IN CHE]

In statistics, most students can easily do problems that are all the same type. All texts put t-test problems in one chapter, chi-square in another, and so on. The difficulty arises when students have to decide for themselves what type of analysis to use, since problems in real life do not come neatly labeled with chapter references. This problem applies in all academic fields beyond statistics—assuming an interest in teaching transfer of skills, of course. [-- RICHARD PAUL]

And another step: what of the keystone concepts in statistics of use in the real world? As we'll discuss in the Gallery, sampling errors, regression to the mean, etc.?

iv. So-called "BIG IDEAS" in a field:
important, but not always conceptualized explicitly?

GALLERY. examples of elucidating salient ideas. *Conceptual enough?*

HISTORY: --What is the purpose of this history—objectivity, persuasion, improvement?
--Does this story have forward movement, linear advancement, or not? Upward, downward, the same level?
--What does this history see as human? Freedom, education, individuality, what roles, what qualities?
--Why do things go wrong? Explanation of evil, wrongdoing, injustice, ineptness, well-meaning but pushed by natural forces? Deadly sins?
--What place does free will vs. fate have? What of "agency"? Fortune or initiative?
--Does this history attend to social problems, improvements, etc.?
--What is the end or goal of history? See above time
--How is this history similar to or different from other histories earlier?
--Do other possible explanations exist than those of this history, from the same facts?   [-- RICHARD PAUL]

BIOLOGY "I": 1. Life builds from the bottom up. 2. Life assembles itself into chains. 3. Life needs an inside and an outside. 4. Life uses a few themes to generate many variations. 5. Life organizes with information. 6. Life encourages variety by reshuffling information. 7. Life creates with mistakes. 8. Life occurs in water. 9. Life runs on sugar. 10. Life works in cycles. 11. Life recycles everything it uses. 12. Life maintains itself by turnover. 13. Life tends to optimize rather than maximize. 14. Life is opportunistic. 15. Life competes within a cooperative framework. 16. Life is interconnected and interdependent. [-- SOURCE]

BIOLOGY "II": 1. Biological knowledge grows through observation and experimentation within the philosophical framework which defines scientific knowing.

2. [Life is based in the physical nature of matter and energy]

3. ...living order is increased as a result of the selective filtering of large quantities of energy over time (development, succession, and evolution).

b Structure and function are complexly and predictably correlated forming a system. If one part of the system is changed, others must change for the system to continue to function (systems theory).

168

5. Life is controlled through the structural isolation of processes (within organelles, cells, systems, organisms) and the specific nature of molecular activity (enzymes).

6. ...the genetic code suggest a common ancestry for all living things.

7. Life demonstrates continuity by the controlled passage of information molecules (DNA) from generation to generation.

8. Life adjusts to short term change thru negative feedback and homeostatic regulation which expend energy to maintain internal conditions within survivable limits.

9. Life adjusts to long-term change thru evolution by natural selection which results in each population having a set of tolerance limits and requirements within which it can exist and reproduce successfully (niche).

10. Living systems can heal minor or brief damage or injury. [-- PROF. HAYES]

GENERAL "BIG IDEAS"... "Involve larger concepts principles processes beyond discrete facts or skills, hence applicable to new situations within or beyond the subject." *But do these fit this stated bill here?...*

1. Impressionism was an attempt to paint scenes in light realistically, not abstractly or by feeling.
2. "The phases of the moon depend upon the relative position of the earth, sun, and moon, so that we see the part of the moon that is not lit by the sun. Ongoing lunar eclipses are not the cause of the phases."
3. Correlation is not causation. Modern science, economics, and medicine deal more with the former as the latter.
4. Fractions when multiplied yield a smaller answer, and when divided, a larger answer. Do we know why?
5. A historian is a storyteller, not a scientist.
6. Two light beams intersecting at crest and trough can cancel each other out and cause darkness—light as waves.
7. The theory of natural selection is what is controversial. Theories of evolution predated Darwin by centuries.
8. The American revolutionaries held that individuals, not governments, had a natural right to property and wages gained through labor. Thus, in one sense, they were "conservatives," not "liberals."
9. Irony is not mere coincidence.
10. The Magna Carta's larger idea was the rule of law, written laws limit the government's power, establish the rights of individuals. [-- SOURCE]

QUOTATION. Affirmation of perspectives not just facts in the social sciences:

"The **perspectives and modes of thoughtful judgment** derived from the study of history are many, and they ought to be its **principal aim.** [Courses in history, geography, and GOVERNMENT should be designed to take students well beyond formal skills of critical thinking, [let alone what they leave unsaid, well beyond mere fact-acquisition to even formal thinking skills!] to help them through their own active learning [to think through complex issues via historical, geographical, governmental perspectives....] [-- SOURCE]

STATEMENT. Higher goals of studying history:

1. Understand the significance of the past to their own lives, both private and public, and to their society.
[I could use many Categories or sub-types of "significance" here, as well as of course examples which are both specific, and also "Crucial" or answer the "but-so-what-why-bother" question!]
2. Distinguish between the important and the inconsequential, to develop the "discriminatory memory" needed for a discerning judgment in public and personal life.
3. Perceive past events and issues as they were experienced by people at the time, to develop historical empathy as opposed to present-mindedness.
4. Comprehend the interplay of change and continuity, and avoid assuming that either is somehow more natural, or more to be expected, than the other. [And perhaps pragmatically how to confront rapid required change?!]
5. Prepare to live with uncertainties and exasperating, even perilous, unfinished business, realizing that not all problems have solutions. [Also a more generic skill or issue here....]
6. Grasp the complexity of historical causation, respect particularity, and avoid excessively abstract generalizations.
7. Appreciate the often tentative nature of judgments about the past, and thereby avoid the temptation to seize upon particular "lessons" of history as cures for present ills.
8. Appreciate the force of the nonrational, the irrational, [and] the accidental in history and human affairs.

9. Read widely and critically in order to recognize the difference between fact and conjecture, between evidence and assertion, and thereby to frame useful questions. [-- SOURCE]

"ESSENTIAL QUESTIONS" embody <u>the key inquiries and core ideas</u> of a discipline...
Is there enough to go around: food, clothes, water? ... Is history, a history of progress? ... Does art reflect culture, or shape it? ... Are mathematical ideas, inventions or discoveries? ... Must a story have a beginning, middle, and end? ... When is a law unjust? ... Is gravity, a fact or a theory? ... What do we fear? ... Who owns what, and why? ... Is biology, destiny? [-- R. PAUL ET AL]   [Query: are these perhaps too general?...]

CIVICS, GOVERNMENT, U.S. HISTORY:

1. Is there too much or too little national power? (Are Constitutional limits, realistic and enforceable?)
2. Does federalism work? (Does the C. balance national and state power efficiently, realistically?)
3. Is the judicial branch too powerful? (Courts interpret C., shape public policy.)
4. Can liberty and security be balanced? (A republican government provided for national security but also protect civil liberties.)
5. "All men are created equal," what does that mean? What kinds of equality are, should be, protected by the C. and by what means?
6. Are the rights of women and minorities adequately safeguarded?
7. Does the president possess adequate, or too much, power over war making and foreign policy?
8. Does the U.S. government have too many C. checks and balances? Separation of powers among the 3 branches can "create a deadlock in governance"?

Well, good: beyond just the facts, and no indoctrination.	True; **BUT** does it attain the highest recurrent Big Ideas in the discipline of Government / Political Science?...

Whoa. Okay, all these examples of Big Ideas—**BUT I'm somehow not impressed...** They're too varied? Are they really the best, productive, seminal/ovular, central keystone ideas?	*I am not satisfied either.* Therefore in the **CALL FOR FURTHER WORK**, I suggest that other educators formulate better, more-conceptual/crucial, Big Ideas...

|+|+|+|++|+|+|+|+++|||+|+|+|+|+|+|+|+|+|+|+|||+|+|+|+|+|+|+|+|||+|+|+|+|+|+|+|+|+|+|+|+|+|+|+|+|+|+|+|+|+|+|+|+|+|+|+|+|||+|+|+|+|++||+|+|+|+|+|+|+|||+|+|+|||

[3.B.] CONCEPTUALIZING UPward, is difficult, but important, plus possible to do better...

[3.B.1.] "READING THE SITUATION" = ?

OVERVIEW. Deriving the very *ideas* from material, falls into several aspects. We can call it in general **"Reading a Situation."** Passively spotting ideas existing, and then actively discovering/creating ideas ourselves. <u>We have categorized "situations" into the following subtypes,</u> "all together here at once for the first time in intellectual or anyhow pedagogical history..."

1. **A written text.** [Give a competent précis and outline...] SEE "II" FULL-dress unit in Sec. #1, Pedagogical Basics...

2. **A Response to a subject/issue, made by another: a Statement/Claim.** [What is its "background"?

3. **Actual "Situations" in social reality.** [EXAMPLES: Social Codes ("corporate culture" of a business)... Cultural norms mores folkways... Schools of Thought, Ideologies... Systems... Literary-artistic genres and conventions... and more...]

4. **Other Types of,** more specialized:

A. **"Operating Concepts"** "The *True Reasons Behind*" a skill/ploy: *Why*-at-all, and so exactly-*How*...

B. **"Variable-Issues":** matters that for task-goal success, must be confronted [= handled managed satisfied etc.]

C. **"Conceptual Topography"** (the "lay-of-the-land" of a complex skill-field—*often "unsurveyed"*!)

5. **Four major moves** toward idea-lizing: (A) **Letter vs. Spirit**, (B) **Definition**, (C) **Analogy**, (D) **"Daily Creativity"**

Truly, real conceptualizing of complex situations is quite difficult. Call it READING THE SITUATION. Describe/define it as "recognizing patterns in systems but the patterns are *multiple—plus subliminal*"

QUOTATIONS. HALL'S is a touchstone classic. ANDERSON'S emphasizes deep structure over surface.

"Reading the behavior of well-known friends and relatives is like covering thoroughly familiar ground without a mental map or talking before writing systems had ever been heard of. One does not need a writing system to talk (or technical awareness of the rules governing speech either). [However,] To abstract such a system from the living data where none existed before, however, is a formidable task, an intellectual achievement that can equal the great accomplishments in chemistry, physics, and astronomy." [-- E. T. HALL, ANTHROPOLOGIST]

NOAM CHOMSKY'S Syntactic Structures was technical on mathematical properties of some grammatical constructions. "But the book's message was that in order to get anywhere in describing the *external facts* of a language, you had to pay close attention to the nature, and not just the *result*, of the rules in your description. That, in turn, means that the object of inquiry in the study of language can't be *words and sentences* in themselves ("verbal behavior") but rather has to be the nature of the knowledge speakers have, by virtue of which they produce and understand those words and sentences.... the point was: Look at the rules, not at their *products*, if you want to understand what language really is." [-- STEPHEN R. ANDERSON, IN CHE]

|+|+|+|++|+|+|||++|||+|+|+|+|+|+|+|+|+|+||+|+|+|+||+|+|+||+|+|+|+|+|+|+|+|+|+|+|+|+|+|+|+|+|+|+|+|+|+|+|+|+|+|+|+|+|+|+|+|+|+|+|+|+|+|+||+|+|+|+|+++||+|+|+|+|+|+|+|+|+|+||+|+|+|+|||

[3.B.2.] The arena of "EXPERTISE"

"In fact, EXPERTISE in skills seems to involve conceptual systems. True *experts* (chess, medicine, electronics, etc.) regularly do conceptualize better than *amateurs or novices* seem to do."

[A.] EXPERTISE in GENERAL: How skilled practitioners do better ...

Pocket Descriptions of EXPERTISE and its Issues:

--Expertise involves "functional, **abstracted representations** of presented *information*."

--Experts have "rich internal **representations** of how *things* work in their domain of practice." These "**mental models**" allow them to learn and understand *situations* more rapidly."

This may include a **cognitive package** that includes the type of situation this is, what to expect from the situation, suitable goals, typical courses of action, and relevant cues.

--Of course experts even are fallible; they may become overconfident, rigid, narrow-visioned within their expertise!

--Still, "Experts see and represent a problem in their domain at a **deeper (more principled)** level than novices; notices tend to represent a problem at a *superficial* level."

--"Expert physicists represent their domain more in terms of **principles**, whereas novices represent it more in terms of the *situation* itself, or *formulae*."

--Also the functional view extends to better views of time and space. To representing entire activities or events not just parts, and the updating of a mental model of the current *situation*. [See below, X Fire, X Surgery...]

[-- CAMBRIDGE HANDBOOK OF EXPERTISE AND EXPERT PERFORMANCE, 2006]

CONCEPTS: "Chunking" of skills, and **"Repertoires"** of Patterns. Two VERSIONS of:

HELEN FISHER, in her book The First Sex, states this. A paraphrase: Essentially, in any skill, one sees quirks, regularities, patterns, details, segments, ploys—but the good players can relate or "chunk" them into larger clusters, concepts, perhaps like our "toolkit" or "toolbelt" analogy of skills accessible-but-unobtrusive. This is true for analyzing the stock market, running a publishing company, diagnosing an illness, playing professional bridge, and surely playing chess.

As for chess, the educational researcher DAVID PERKINS echoes this, with his concept of "**repertoire**." In any skilled performance, "one develops a repertoire of paradigms and patterns of thinking and organizes one's problem solving in terms of those paradigms and patterns." Thus the chess master knows 50,000 configurations, by which he can memorize the board, and search out lines of attack and defense, better than the novice can.

EXAMPLES. How *novices or amateurs*, and *experts*, represent problem-issues cognitively:

The subject, its domain:	Amateur-novice image of:	Expert image of:
The card game of BRIDGE: depictions of four-handed deals:	Via "order of card rank within hands" (not useful for supporting strategic aspects)	Via "suit across hands; recalled cards of the same suit from three hands and inferred the fourth" (useful).
ELECTRONICS: the diagram of an electronic circuit:	Organized via "spatial proximity of symbols appearing in the diagram"	Organized via "major electronic components (e.g., amplifiers, filters, rectifiers)."
BASEBALL: a colorful description of a half-inning.	Via "less integral components," such as observations about the weather and the crowd mood."	Via "major goal-related sequences of the game, such as advancing runners, scoring runs, and preventing scoring."
COMPUTER PROGRAMMING: a list of 21 commands in the ALGOL language. Solution algorithm vs. areas of applications. Experts novices.	Students after one ALGOL course: via surface features (commands with same beginning letter or length of command name) and groups of commands forming natural language segments ("string is null bits") which however have no conceptual meaning.	ALGOL experts: grouped together, components which formed mini-ALGOL algorithms (formation of loops) or which constituted types of ALGOL data structures.
PHYSICS: groups of problems: task, to organize f/ "those you would solve in a similar manner": (Some sets had the same surface features but different deep principles, or different surface features but the same deep principles—an important issue!)	Beginning Students: via "salient objects" (e.g., springs, inclined planes) and features contained in the problem-statement itself. Literal surface features such as presence of inclined plains or concepts such as friction.	Professors, Advanced Graduate Students: via the major physics principles which were applicable there (e.g., conservation and force laws). Second Law or laws of thermodynamics such as conservation of energy.
MEDICINE: task, to diagnose an issue in a subspecialty:	Novices: isolated, dependent on particular patient cues.	Experts: via the major patho-physiological issue relevant in a case (reasonable alternatives, e.g., "lesions involving right-sided heart volume overload")
FIREFIGHTING: analysis of the whole scene of a fire:	Novices: via "perceptually salient" characteristics (such as color and intensity).	Experts: via whole process, "what likely preceded it and how it will likely evolve"
SURGERY: what actions done	Novices: …..	Experts: some actions with no immediate value but may make some later move more efficient or effective.
CHESS: moves made	Novices: …..	Experts: extensively plan and evaluate consequences of alternative move sequences.

PSYCHOLOGICAL COUNSELORS: to organize (categorize, then relate) a client's statements:	Novice Counselors: via superficial details such as the temporal order of the statements.	Expert Counselors: via "more abstract, therapeutically relevant information" (principles, theories?).

FISHES: to sort "marine creatures":	Undergraduates: via the appearances of the creatures.	Commercial Fishermen: via "commercial, ecological, or behavioral factors"

So what is your *point* of all this? We can't all suddenly become experts just by reading this table…	The "point" [*sigh*…]: In your own arenas, *reach **upward** to try to grasp the principles behind the particulars as guidelines, especially in new-foreign-difficult situations*…

|+|+|+|++|+|+|++++|||+|+|+|+|+|+|+||+|+|+||+|+|+|+|+|+|+|+|+|+|+|+|+|+|+|+|+|+|+|+|+|+|+|+|+|+||+|+|+|++||+|+|+|+|+|+||+|+|+|||

[B.] EXPERTISE *EXPEDITED*: A trio of amazing accelerations… snowboarding, handball, and—"chicken-sexing."

EXAMPLES. The three classic instances of how complex skills can be captured more completely-compactly:

[1.] THE SPORT OF SNOWBOARDING. [Usually this sport takes a whole day to learn, but A STUDENT learned almost instantly.] "That's because my FRIEND explained to me the relevant concepts of snowboarding. These are: for steering, one torques the body; for stopping, the back leg is your anchor; for slowing, the edges of the board are used. I realized that most students do not realize that concepts are important in learning. *In fact, I think that most students don't know what concepts are. I certainly didn't.*" [-- from R. PAUL]

[2.] THE SPORT OF HANDBALL. An anthropology professor reported that being taught a simple move—play to the wall not the sides, or something like that—improved his game 600% in thirty seconds! [-- RICHARD SCHWEDER]

[3.] THE SKILL OF SEXING DAY-OLD CHICKS FOR THE POULTRY INDUSTRY. --The astonishing "point" here: *training* in doing a complex task could be cut from the usual *six to 12 weeks*, to *one single minute*, and the *same* degree of success in the task achieved (80 per cent)… And so *by what means?*… [-- E. D. HIRSCH]

…not that all skills could be so accelerated; just to vividly illustrate the concept, and the possibility… As DON NORMAN says, a half-hour of explicit guided-learning instruction can exceed hours of sheer individual experience…

TOUCHSTONE-EXAMPLE. HOW THE TRAINING PERIOD OF "CHICKEN SEXERS" (workers who discern the sex of day-old chicks—important to the poultry industry) WAS REDUCED *DRASTICALLY*, AND BY *THINKING*; by skillfully conceptualizing out the subliminal principles (contours and operations, etc.) of the process…*From "six to twelve weeks" to "one minute."* (Which reminds that "better" elucidation of complex skills is indeed possible…)

--The activity was training chicken-sexers for their work. "The protosexual characteristics are extremely subtle and variable, and even after weeks of guidance from a mentor, trainees rarely attain a correctness rate of more than 80 per cent." Schools exist for this important skill. The training involves "implicit learning from real-world live chicks" and lasts *from six to 12 weeks*. But then cognitive scientists sought to "construct a more efficient learning program." They worked with a veteran sexer MR. CARLSON who in 50 years had sexed 55 million chicks. From a set of 18 photographs of the different chick types, MR. CARLSON identified "the range of critical features distinctive to each sex." From this, the scientists created a *single-page* instructional leaflet. They then ran an experiment. People with no chick-sexing experience were divided randomly into two groups. One group looked at the leaflet, for *only one minute*. The other did not. Then both groups were tested. The untrained scored about 50 percent, the level of pure chance. The leaflet-glancers scored 84 percent, which was even better than the scores achieved by professional chick-sexers…

--The psychologist ALAN BADDELEY concluded that "**one minute of explicit learning can be more effective than a month of implicit learning.**"

--But it was MR. CARLSON'S experience—but also perhaps intelligence?—which allowed him to isolate the protosexual traits of chicks into an analytical chart that could be learned in 60 seconds. E. D. HIRSCH JR. says this feat is an astonishing achievement, analogous in form to that of ancient scholars in isolating the phonemic structure of speech into an alphabet of 26 letters, "one of the great intellectual feats of human history." And so, concludes HIRSCH, explicit instruction with clearly defined goals is superior for beginners, rather than the implicit learning via completely natural, real-world projects (though a combination of the two is ultimately essential). Our point here is of course that explicit instruction which is massively more efficient than usual or imagined, and yet supple and non-formulaic, is more possible than one imagines, or trains or works toward...

[-- from E. D. HIRSCH JR., "Educational Research and Cargo Cults"]

This is biased. One learns *tennis* by being shown—and then by doing, and repeating! *Complex* skills need more active doing. Sexing chicks while useful work is a false analogy for the advanced thinking skills you are promoting! You have a mania for explicitness... --Oh, and you probably think your own Tool Kits here are achievements as great as deciphering the alphabet, ehh?...	--Not that everything can be done streamlined, just that via conceptualizing **we can do astonishingly better** in making complexities (concepts, techniques) much more explicit hence much more elucidated hence effective. (Can be more Complete but also Compact-Condensed hence Clear...) --To support our Strong Claim here? To put our manuals where our mouth is? So *yes* then, case in point: our Tool Kits. They walk our talk here—or try to... See Appendix **"TOOL KITS"** for a shelf-full, collected from various disciplines more widely than usual. More complete, more "channeled"... -----On **Concretization or Specific Detailing**, with more elements ever mentioned anywhere else. -----On **Structure/Organization** (with a larger menu of alternate optional choices than anywhere else in one place.) -----On **"Lensmanship"** or multiple-plural perspectives (with its six vital variable-issues rarely explicitly mentioned—inevitable, subliminal, useful but partial, incomplete and dissonant, hard to locate, ultimately arbitrary). -----On the difficult **Cause-Effect explanation**: not perfect, but "more in one compact place" than anywhere else. -----And **others**... -----Ohh, and as to any egotistic opinion of my own Tool-Kits... All I can say is that (1) their keystone-points are not obvious. It took me years of sedulous exploration to isolate out the keystone Principles-behind the skills. (2) Further, and that no other educational resource-materials I've seen, have presented them also (or else why would I have arduously worked them up to present...)

+|#||+#++||#+|#+||#+|+|+#|+|#|+|#+|++#|+|+|#+|+|+#+||+#|#+|+#||+#|+|#+|#+|+#|+#|+#+|+#|+|#+|#+|+#|+#+|#+|#+|#+|#+|+#|+|#+#||
+|#||+#++||#+|#+||#+|+|+#|+|#|+|#+|++#|+|+|#+|+|+#+||+#|#+|+#||+#|+|#+|#+|+#|+#|+#+|+#|+|#+|#+|+#|+#+|#+|#+|#+|#+|+#|+|#+#||

[1.] Intro.	[2.] Table of Contents	[3.] Body of Claims	**[4.] "Reading"- Situations**	[5.] Annex: Examples

[4.] TYPES of "Situations" to decode conceptually for their very—Ideas:

1. A written text. *[{ Comparatively simple, basic... }]* By another; we can passively read it, write précis and outline of the ideas not just the facts.
By ourselves: we can write ideas not just data into a text, and make those ideas explicit.

 [SEE section in second part of this module. **READINGS:** Biltmore Beach, Fast-Food Rowdiness, "The Knee," a Job I've Held, Brookfield High Auditorium... Bad and good précis, outlines.]

2. A response to a subject/issue, made by another: a statement/claim. We can detect the "background" of it: the motivations of the responder... the world-view and lenses used... the Implicit Presuppositions present...

 [SEE section on Background in Prior Basics] [See here below, **READINGS:** Grenada, Socarides, Wolverton.]

3. Actual situations in reality. *[{ now these get comparatively complex, advanced, difficult... }]*

 [SEE: **EXAMPLES:** Social Codes ("corporate culture" of a business)... Cultural norms mores folkways... Schools of Thought, Ideologies... Systems... Literary-artistic genres and conventions... and more...]

4. Other Types of, more specialized:

A. **"Operating Concepts,"** Solo or Complex Keystones or "The True Reasons Behind" a skill/ploy.
B. **"Variable-Issues":** matters that for task-goal success, must be confronted [= handled managed satisfied etc.]
C. **"Conceptual Topography"** (the "lay-of-the-land" of a complex skill-field: principles always present, quite often subliminal and not codified explicitly: an advanced Read Situation, with V/I's and O.C. also in there; a complex skill-field…) *[{ these also get comparatively challenging indeed… }]*

|+|+|+|+|+|+|+|+|+++|||+|+|+|+|+|+|+|+|+|+||+|+|+|+||+|+|+|+|+|+|+|+|+|+|+|+|+|+|+|+|+|+|+|+|+|+|+|+|+|+|+|+|+|+|+|+|+|+|+|+|+|+||+|+|+|+|+++||+|+|+|+|+|+|+|+||+||+|+|+|||

(4.A.) WRITTEN TEXTS. Those of others, one's own. Can one read skillfully: derive the Gist. Both précis, and outline.

> **SEE:** **#2 of this three-part appendix, Pedagogy.** Biltmore Beach Lifeguard Job. Brookfield Needs An Auditorium. Work at Jobs (fast food, nursing home, 2nd grade). "The Knee" (about physicians and patients).

|+|+|+|+|+|+|+|+|+++|||+|+|+|+|+|+|+|+|+|+||+|+|+|+||+|+|+|+|+|+|+|+|+|+|+|+|+|+|+|+|+|+|+|+|+|+|+|+|+|+|+|+|+|+|+|+|+|+|+|+|+|+||+|+|+|+|+++||+|+|+|+|+|+|+|+||+||+|+|+|||

(4.B.) RESPONSES TO AN ISSUE: Statements/Claims, about a subject or situation. Other peoples,' one's own…

> **SEE:** Unit on "Backgrounds" to a statement: motivations, implicit presuppositions, world-views… in Appendix #5

ISSUE. To identify motivations which "lie above and behind" a response to a complex situation.

EXAMPLE. A well-known TEACHER of critical thinking reports a discussion involving two different responses to a political issue. His report remarkably affirms that above-and-behind the "facts and arguments" given, perhaps merely to rationalize prior stands, lie background elements, a sort of Situation to be Read.

"…recently…I got into a lengthy disagreement with an acquaintance on the [supposed] *justification of the U.S. invasion of Grenada.* Before long we were discussing questions of morality, the appropriate interpretation of international law, supposed rights of countries to defend their interests, spheres of influence, the character of U.S. and Soviet foreign policies, the history of the two countries, the nature and history of the C.I.A., the nature of democracy, whether it can exist without elections, who has credibility and how to judge it, the nature of the media and how to access it, whether it reflects an 'American' party line, sociocentrism, our own personalities, consistency, etc."
[-- RICHARD PAUL, in "McPeck's Mistakes"]

PAUL then goes on to note that he and the other person held differing **"lenses":** world views, global perspectives, points of view, views of human nature (background logic). These influence "subliminally," the different responses he and his acquaintance gave to the explicit "questions" mentioned above. This *divergence* in basic backgrounds—not "the facts in the case"—is why Paul and his acquaintance could not agree regarding *invasion of Grenada.* And this issue of basic Background-differences, occurs on other difficult social issues ("crucial currently-contested concerns"). *Poverty, wealth, welfare, military-industrial complex, welfare, capitalism, racism and sexism, communism and socialism.*

This instance seems rich. What I have bordered in dotted lines in PAUL's comment, seem to hover halfway between subject-relevance, and *even larger* subjective issues. [Might these be such as: **psycho-political stances, "conservative-traditional" "versus" "liberal-radical"** to be overgeneral? **Personality-types: authoritarian vs. tolerant-of-ambiguity** and so forth? And others? …] ***It seems therefore important for learners to begin to sense "background elements" to all issues… to all statement-claims and position-stands on issues… to be "backdrop-savvy"…***

GALLERY. Four statements which show "background elements": motivations, root-stands. (In the first two, the background elements seem hidden; in the second two, they emerge more clearly.) The subject is sexual identity and orientation—*at least on the surface.* (From A CONSERVATIVE PSYCHIATRIST, and AN EDITOR OF A GAY ANTHOLOGY.) The first two writers leave "the very ideas," subliminal: unstated, perhaps not fully known to the writers *themselves*. So, truly **"Reading the Situation"** here is therefore difficult—but instructive…

EXAMPLE #1. Statement by **a psychiatrist**-leader of the position that homosexuality is *a deviancy, an abnormality*—psychologically, also (or because!) in even more basic, bio-historical ways…
The statement was in sharp response to "socio-political activist" movements (in the 1970's) which changed the psychological diagnosis of homosexuality from psychiatric disorder to "normal" behavior or condition per se…

A movement within the American Psychiatric Association has eroded "heterosexuality as the single acceptable sexual pattern in our culture." Although benevolently intended to combat injustice and persecution, this movement resulted in "a full approval of homosexuality and an encouragement to aberrancy by those who should have known better, both in the scientific sense and in the sense of the social consequences of such removal…. This movement has accomplished what every other society, with rare exceptions, would have trembled to tamper with, a revision of a basic code and concept of life and biology: that men and women normally mate with the opposite sex and not with each other…."

"Our sexual patterns are a product of our biological past, a result of man's collective experience and his long biological and social evolutionary march….Not all cultures survive; the majority have not, and anthropologists tell us that serious flaws in sexual codes and institutions have undoubtedly played a significant role in many a culture's demise….

"No society has accepted adult preferential homosexuality. Nowhere is homosexuality or so-called bisexuality a desired end in itself. Nowhere do parents say: 'It's all the same to me if my child is heterosexual or homosexual.' Nowhere are homosexuals more than a small minority at the present time. Nowhere does homosexuality per se place on e in an enviable position."

"Some behaviors are universally deviant, and every society thinks them disruptive. Incest rape, psychopathic (apparently unmotivated) violence are considered taboo in all societies. So is predominant or exclusive homosexuality or even bisexuality."

"…heterosexuality has self-evident adaptive values….[with] thousands of years of evolutionary selection and programming. Man is not only a sexual animal but a care-bonding, group-bonding, and child-rearing animal. The male-female design is taught to the child from birth and culturally ingrained through the marital order. This design is anatomically determined, as it derives from cells which in the evolutionary scale underwent changes into organ systems and finally into individuals reciprocally adapted to each other. The male-female design is thus perpetually maintained and only overwhelming fear or man's false pride and misdirected individual enterprise can disturb or divert it."
[- CHARLES SOCARIDES, "Sexual Politics and Scientific Logic: the Politics of Homosexuality" 1995]

My Response to Socarides: As I "read this situation," behind the text lies the stand of **Natural Law**? True, some of SOCARIDES' statements sound impressive—no society has affirmed exclusive adult homosexuality, etc. But his "root-stance" *seems* to be the **Natural Law** one. Namely, that <u>in nature and human nature, there is one centerline, main-line natural-normal default situation (of anatomy or structure, of physiology or function)… and that variation or deviation from it (even in a kind of pluralism) is unnatural and abnormal… and furthermore is, somehow, positively harmful, both to individuals themselves, and to other individuals and society in general</u>. This position of an essential, unchanging, natural nature of the human, would apply to many issues. Here it is to sexual identity and behavior. But does SOCARIDES therefore ***do violence to the whole truth about homosexuality and well-adjusted gay/lesbian individuals***? Not from the viewpoint of "hyper-liberal/liberationist Political Correctness," but from basic <u>veracities</u>…

The point is that this M.D. claimed he was a *scientist*, but is rather (according to our view here—perhaps our own "insight/bias"!), an individual drawn to a need to accept the Natural Law position *due to the motivations of his own psychic economy*. [Possibly psychogenic elements of "the *conservative stance*" are also seen: an absolutism, a disrespect for change, a hierarchical authority along with a kind of elitism or even disdain, and other such non-savory elements…] SOCARIDES founded NARTH, the "National Association for Research and Therapy of Homosexuality," an organization espousing his views and seeking to treat and change ("cure") individuals seeking to change from homosexuality. (The organization *claims* to be a scientific one, but its publications and participants are shot through with very traditionally religious elements—the "Thomas Aquinas Clinic," and many others. I do not intend this as mud-slinging, only identification.)

…well aren't *you* the Politically Correct Party-Member to object to SOCARIDES' questioning of the dominant li-be-ral position. I thought you said, "question today's Truths" and be open-minded, too!	…ah **BUT** here we are "equal-opportunity critiquers." Next we scrutinize (and skewer) a *pro*-"gay" stance:

EXAMPLE #2. Statement by the **editor** of an anthology of **current gay and lesbian** short stories and writings:

"<u>I'm not much given to fixed categories</u>. Novel excerpts bump up against short stories; science fiction jostles beside literary fiction; punk sensibility elbows its way next to high camp and classically constructed stories. The end of the 20th century has been about <u>the breaking down of fixed categories</u>—of art forms, of culture, of gender, of *SEXUAL ORIENTATION*—the blurring of borders <u>to allow an infinite variety of options for identity and expression</u>. This dissolution brings excitement and possibility but also confusion, frustration, a certain anxiety. *My students, for example, want me to tell them definitively how a short story is different from a personal essay; their foreheads pucker with worry when I say that those forms are moving closer and closer together.* Especially in the United States, we want to *know*, and fixed categories allow us the illusion—however false—that we do.

How long we can float in this sea of suspended definitions is difficult to predict, and in part dependent on the culture's tolerance for ambiguity. Will the millennium see a move back to rigid definitions and the certainty they promise, or will we continue to dissolve categories until we humans understand ourselves quite differently, until SEXUAL ORIENTATION as identity seems a quaint and archaic notion?"   [-- TERRY WOLVERTON]

My Response to Wolverton: One person said "This seems good, it recognizes both complexity and also change, plus valuing pluralism." But to me, **her statement does violence to separate categories** (essay, story) in the service of her desire to break down barriers between people including minority groups (including sexual orientation) wrongly excluded. A noble aim, but why should not the students' foreheads pucker when she ignores their question? See, it can be said that an *essay* has some kind of point, developed through subpoints, formally or informally—and that this technique is valuable; and it can be said that a *story* is an event, a plot with characters and settings, dramatized via narration and ideally conflict, action, suspense—and that this ploy is valuable! Shame on WOLVERTON for this sloppiness! I would say to distort artistic differences and distinctions, in the service of her goal of social over-sameness... rather *ironic*, too, her "oppression" of these distinct genres when she's centrally against "oppressions" supposedly...

EXAMPLES #3, #4: Two *more-balanced* statements regarding "sexual reorientation therapy." I could include many Gay-Liberation/radical statements somewhat formulaically condemning this therapy as "oppressive," etc. I would rather include two others which seem *more revelatory of the true concepts and motivations operating:*

[3.] A major "reparative" therapist notes that "a difference in beliefs exists about the source of moral value that separates clients who seek sexual reorientation from those who seek gay-affirming therapy." The latter's "sexual morality" sees "the individual as his own autonomous source of truth." Sex is moral as long as it is consensual. In contrast, the reorienters approach more from a "moral domain emphasizing the ethic of divinity and/or ethic of community, both of which assume a universal moral order grounded in religious values given by God or community. The act of giving one's consent...does not make a sexual act moral. [Indeed,] Some expressions of sexuality...convey an intrinsic harm to personhood—whether or not this harm is measurable by psychology or actually perceived by the person." [-- JOSEPH NICOLOSI, in Drescher & Zucker, eds.]"

RESPONSE: At least this clears the clouds to largely reveal the contours of the keystone belief system. This largely echoes Natural Law as seen above, and describes the **world-view**, no longer tacit or subliminal. [Not all clear sailing; the notion of "intrinsic harm to personhood" even if scientifically and personally invisible," is a fascinating example of "magical thinking" which however cannot detain us here...]

[4.] In the same volume, a psychiatrist validates "reorientation therapy" (currently as of 2007 under disrepute in the psychiatric community at least on the face of it) as appropriate in two cases. The patient wants to save or improve a marriage which s/he considers more important than satisfying homosexual desires. Or an individual's deeply-held convictions whether religious, social-belonging, or moral conflict severely with homosexual desires, and the patient strongly values these convictions more important than the desires. [-- JEROME C. WAKEFIELD, in Drescher & Zucker, eds.]

RESPONSE: *Learners can benefit by seeing the power of penetrating to the Background of statements... Not easy. Not impossible... And ultimately pleasurable as well as empowering...*

General summary in re SOCARIDES, WOLVERTON: the point, for grasping the very ideas...

If the above analysis is true, it shows how at times, the competent examiner of people's responses to things (SOCARIDES, WOLVERTON, others) can illuminate why people believe, better or more accurately than the people who believe those stands themselves. (Whether we examiners then mock, jeer, and declare victory—or simply fairmindedly share our viewpoint—depends on our stand toward dispositions or moral-ethical attitudes toward good thinking!)

Our view is that SOCARIDES distorts apparent well-adjusted homosexuals in the service of his moral-ethical philosophy. And that WOLVERTON overemphasizes blurring of genres to "all alike" instead of useful separate distinctions in the service of her well-intentioned goal of liberation of minorities from outsider and stigmatized status.

The larger lenses are usually subjectively selected." Why choose, among general systems, Freudianism, or Marxism, or Christianity, or capitalism, or sociobiology and/or evolutionary psychobiology, or existentialism, or...? Because of some subliminal motivation, as much as the evidence of the system itself—or, often, even its appropriateness for a task-goal (unless the task-goal is satisfying the believer's motivations...)

But the point in re WOLVERTON and SOCARIDES here, is less to trump psychic power over them, than to resolutely penetrate to identify the true background motivations for a response, and the distortions from "truth" which may result. In responses of others, as here...and in our own responses, fairmindedly! And all of this a part of seeking, why, the very Idea! The keystone concept, here not above but beneath; hidden, but very real...

(4.C.) "SITUATIONS" IN WORLD REALITY? "Reading the Situation" = recognizing
the elements (usually subliminal, unstated) in systems of many components: be they social groups, ideological schools, literary genres, other principles and practices…

GALLERY OF EXAMPLES. [[{The "I" or BRIEF listing. For "II" FULL View, *SEE* below in this section's Annex…}]]
Showing how many systems exist, systems of **thought, ideologies, world-views** (etc., etc.)—all **conceptual schemes** reflecting the *surface content*—and in many areas. And how only a competent thinker can **Read the Situation**, discover/derive the **principles** behind the *particulars*…

Ideologies, Schools of Thought, Systems. (Lenses: viewpoints perspectives etc.)	*(1) Traditional humanism…* *(2) The ideology of "Extreme Diversity"…*

The academic fields or disciplines.	*(1) World-views of humanities, social sciences, natural sciences…* *(2) Pure, and applied: "the logic of medicine" to be grasped by a citizen non-physician, a patient's relative.*

Historical Sociology: periods in culture.	*(1) traditional American ideologies…* *(2) the" countercultural" Sixties…* *(3) Boomer-generation youth "values"today…* *(4) Traditional versus Postmodern assumptions in the humanities.* *(5) Education Wars: "Old-School" vs. "New-Think" paradigms…*

Space: Changes over different situations, fields:	*(1) East versus West generally…* *(2) Writing: Writing differently even within English studies… General School or academic writing, versus writing in the world: Personal, especially Vocational on the Job, Civic-Community… Freelance Journalism… (3) When job-hunting, "read" the unstated Corporate Culture of specific employers' organizations!…*

Groups, Varied:	*(1) "Sexuality," root-views of (A) traditional religion, versus root-views of (B) liberationist or diversity-minority studies. **The implicit world-views clarified.***

Literary and Artistic Genres:	*(1) "Art," ten separate assumptions-about…* *(2) Detective story: classic rules, formula of…* *(3) "School-writing," "school-reading"….*

|+|+|+|+++|+|+|+|+++|||+|+|+|+|+|+|+|+|+|+||+|+|+|+|+|+|+||+|+|+|+|+|+|+|+|+|+|+|+|+|+|+|+|+|+|+|+|+|+|+|+|+|+|+|+|+|+|+|+|+|+|+|+|+|+|+|+|+|+|+|+|+|+|+|+|+|+|+|+|+|+|+|+|+||+||+|+|+|+|+|+|+|+||+|+|+|||

(4.D.) OTHER TYPES:
[1.] OPERATING CONCEPTS,   [2.], VARIABLE-ISSUES,   [3.] CONCEPTUAL TOPOGRAPHY…

[4.D.1.] Operating Concepts:

THE IDEA. I am labeling **"operating concepts,"** those principles (etc., etc., etc.) which seem to identify the *"central why and how"* of a skilled action (procedure, process …) or even a subject (the content). They are a "black box under the hood" in that they may identify the situation-in-reality to be dealt with—why do we need such a procedure? And how, and why, does it therefore work?
But do such keystones exist? ***And is it pedagogically useful to elucidate them?***
Perhaps these are of two types. More solo or proverbial… and more complex.

EXAMPLES. Perhaps some <u>**solo,**</u> "keystone" principles exist in some fields of endeavor. Not the only ones, but a focal point or "maypole" around which much revolves—which are "northstars" to steer by…
Organization of Workplaces and Residences. "One must balance the demands of **Accessibility** of materials,

with their *Size and Fragility*, and also the **Relationship** of them to other materials they operate with."

Time-Management: "First, explicit **Goal**-Identifying; then, **Prioritizing**; then, **Lead-Time** Planning"

International Business: does the seller adapt to the buyer, or vice versa? (cultural differences are involved)

Business, Customer Relations: **"consistency,"** of product and service

Education: quality of a Teacher: a certain **"imperturbability"**

Sociology: power, and affinity, as two keystones in interpersonal relationships

Computers: **"linear sequentiality"** (of course others…)

Psychology: motivations; defenses; habituated comfort with the familiar even if negative; etc.

Algebra: **"combination, permutation, association"**

EXAMPLE: How <u>one</u> principle in a field might be a <u>pivotal</u> one: **Cinematography:**

"To judge from their work, it seems that the great directors, know immediately and without thinking <u>where the best place is to put the camera</u>. They seem to see it as clearly as we can see that leaves are green. A good director will choose one of several goodish positions. A bad director won't know, and will move the camera about, fidgeting with the angles, trying all sorts of tricky shots or fancy ways of telling the story, and forgetting that the function of the camera is not to draw attention to itself, but to show something else—the subject—with as much clarity as it can manage." [-- PHILIP PULLMAN]

What good is this example? We're not training to be movie-makers…	[{*Argghhh…*}] But, a good example of a single conceptual skill which is "keystone, maypole, central," eh…

EXAMPLE: A whole set of rich concepts—here, about **"critical thinking."** Selected ideas of A LEADING TEACHER OF BETTER THINKING, which have (to me) proven useful over the years:

1. Background Logic. (In discussing any statement-or-claim, we need to identify the Purpose, Question, PointofViewFrameofReference, Empirical, "Conceptual, Assumptions, Inferences, Interpretations, Implications, Conclusions.)

2. Fact vs. Opinion vs. Reasoned Judgment. (This reminds us of three ways of knowing, not just fact vs. opinion or taste or preference, but also of good reasoning. EXAMPLE. "Alaska" is: 1. the coldest state? 2. the best place for a vacation? 3. a good place to set up a certain kind of business now? …)

3. Monological vs. Multilogical Issues. (Issues needing only one approach, vs. those complex ones needing many disciplines to confront well.)

4. Dialectical vs. Dialogical Thinking. (The great need to exceed one's own catchment-area for information. Seek the responses of other people in group interchange. No one approach can know it all.)

5. Intellectual Standards. (It's not enough to learn how to "think"; one must apply **criteria** to think well, **competently**....) [Our own formulation of this is the Continuum of Competence: NON vs. BAD vs. "JUST-" vs. GOOD vs. BETTER/BEST-possible Thinking.]

6. Weak vs. Strong Sense Thinking. (**Selfish** thinking to attain your goals with technical skill but not fairness perhaps vs. **fair-minded** thinking: admit, control your own biases, truly hear the others side fairly.) Perhaps seek Truth not victory.

7. At the same time, **a "Generosity" to *All* Responses**. There is almost no ["bona fide or legitimate"] point of view or statement (etc.) which, when looked at competently, would not yield some sort of considerable or valuable insight or import.

8. And **Thinking, IS Natural (for humans to do); BUT, Thinking WELL, is "UN-Natural"**—takes conscious effort, discipline, decentering, etc.! (Makes me feel better when I foul up thought-fully....) [-- RICHARD PAUL]

…I **DON'T** really see why you're dumping in this list of statements by this one thinker and teacher…	…to help grasp the concept of keystone principles of great power. These have been "maypoles" or "northstars" to me for years…

EXAMPLES. WRITING INSTRUCTION. Capturing the **Operating Concepts Behind** three skills. **Syntax** or sentence-writing… **Parallelism** in structure… and **Specific Detailing**…

EXAMPLES. SENTENCES: varied versions of a real **Operating Concept** behind the skill:

[1.] "A writer of emphatic and interesting prose…is careful to **place his** <u>emphatic</u> **materials in** <u>independent</u> **clauses and his** <u>less emphatic</u> **materials in** <u>dependent</u> **ones: he knows that independent clauses…transmit an illusion of greater strength and weight.** Thus instead of writing, '*He was strolling along the deck when a wave washed him overboard,*' he writes,' *While he was strolling along the deck, a wave washed him overboard.' This is an elementary principle, but it is amazing how many aspirant prose writers are innocent of it.*
In the same way, a writer of effective prose has mastered *a general principle governing all events which occur in time*, whether athletic contests, seductions, or sentences. The principle is that **the** <u>middle</u> **of the event is the** <u>least</u> **interesting part, the** <u>beginning</u> **the** <u>next</u> **most interesting, and the** <u>end</u> **the** <u>most</u> **interesting.** The pattern of natural emphasis in a sentence…looks like this: _____ 2 ____ | ____ 3 ____ | ____ 1 ____, with '1' representing the most interesting moment and '3' the least. The skilled prose writer cooperates with this fact of life and makes it work on his behalf….*Instead of saying, 'He is a fool, in my opinion,' he says, 'He is, in my opinion, a fool.'"*
[-- PAUL FUSSELL, in <u>Poetic Meter and Poetic Form</u>] [*emphasis* added]

[2.] In sentence writing, emphasis and cohesion must be served. Two complementary principles of order and emphasis exist. One of them is: "Whenever possible, express at the beginning of a sentence already stated, referred to, implied, safely assumed, familiar—whatever we might call old, repeated, relatively predictable, less important, readily accessible information, especially metadiscourse." the other principle; "Express at the end of a sentence the least predictable, the least accessible, the newest, the most significant and striking information." The logical outcome is this: "The beginning of a sentence should orient a reader toward new information, should provide a context for him to move from the known to the unknown, from the predictable to the unpredictable." [-- JOSEPH WILLIAMS, Style]

[3.] "Understanding…requires integrating the fragments gleaned from a sentence…speakers cannot just toss one fact after another into a listener's head…When a series of facts comes in succession,…the language must be structured so that the listener can place each fact into an existing framework. **Thus information about the old, the given, the understood, the topic, should go early in the sentence, usually as the subject, and information about the new, the focus, the comment, should go at the end."** [-- STEVEN PINKER, The Language Instinct]

[4.] Here is <u>my own</u> proposed version of it: "The reader wants to know **which ideas are major and which are minor;** and needs to know **some information before other information,** for clarity. Therefore, in sentence-writing, **secondary** (introductory, background, etc.) elements go in **subordinate** clauses and at the sentence's **beginning or middle;** whereas **primary** (more important) elements go in **main clauses** and at the sentence's **end.** " As follows:
"(1) "*Breaking his arm, he slipped on the dock.*" (2) "*He slipped on the dock, breaking his arm.*"
(3) "*He broke his arm, slipping on the dock.*" (4) "*Slipping on the dock, he broke his arm.*" [-- BRIAN BECK]

And I suppose you think *your* example is the *best*?	[*Sigh…*] **All I Am Saying Is,** "keystone principles of a skill often *can* be elucidated **better than they usually are, and need to be."** For pragmatics, principle, and pleasure."

EXAMPLES. The same <u>lucid encoding</u> for SENTENCES, can be done for other writing skills:
<u>PARALLELISM:</u> **"Parallel style helps reader recognize parallel ideas."** "If a series of items are related logically, to help the reader perceive this, the writer can relate the items stylistically, phrasing them in related or parallel language."
[Ex.: "Fred likes skiing, to fish, and he dances."   "Fred likes skiing, fishing, and dancing."]

<u>SPECIFIC DETAILING:</u> **"Remember to re-hydrate our dry ideas—with just-enough, but varied, examples…"** **[1.]** "We often have experiences which give us responses, as of knowledge, emotion, etc. But when we write about our responses, we too often merely state them. We omit the specific experiences (instances, examples, particulars) which created the response in us. Therefore the reader does not experience our response vividly. Therefore, remember to rehydrate the abstractions by including the particulars which helped create it in us." **[2.]** And, we want the right mix of concepts and concrete illustrations. And enough and varied, diverse specifics to round out the concept, not too many of the same type. [-- thanks to E. D. HIRSCH JR.]
EXAMPLE: (1) The automobile accident was quite depressing. It affected us all greatly. (Etc.)
(2) The station wagon was upside down on the median strip with childrens' toys scattered about. None of us said anything as we drove along for the next five minutes.

<u>COMPARISON / CONTRAST:</u>   The concept of "apperception." **"We learn the new in terms of the old."** This is "the process of understanding something perceived, in terms of previous experience." This

underlies the power of C/C. "One who knows nothing of a foreign country, knows nothing of one's own country." "How big is an acre? About the size of a football field…" [SEE Unit on C/C in App. #6, Pre-Vue.]

VISUAL LITERACY: diagrams, charts, graphs, etc. The keystone principles here are (1) **the eye can much faster than the brain, perceive (A) sheer number of items, (B) the interrelationships (special hence conceptual) of those relationships**. Hence "map showing population distribution changes" is more effective, etc.

| …I don't know; I think I knew all these background-principles already… | [{Oh yeah *sure* you did… }] Ah, but are *students* offered these "northstar" guidelines explicitly?… |

|+|+|+|++|+|+|||++|||+|+|+|+|+|+|+|+|||+|+|||+|+|+|+|||+|+|+|+|+|+|+|+|+|+|+|+|+|+|+|+|+|+|+|+|+|+|+|+|+|||+|+|+|+|++|||+|+|+|+|+|+|+|||+|+|+|+|||

[4.D.2.] "Variable-Issues":

THE IDEA. What I label "variable-issues," are matters of subject-content, not thinking-concepts.

The central point being, **variable-issues** are what I call "**matters which**—for the successful achieving of the particular task-goal at hand—must be **confronted, meaning "handled managed reckoned-with exploited considered satisfied"** and the like.

[EXAMPLE: Vegetarianism: *but not* factual data about, not personal experiences or opinions of, etc., *instead* issues such as Nutrition… Social Image of … Moral-Ethical dimensions of… Gastronomy or aesthetics of… Technology of (pressure-cookers for legumes?)… and the like.]

And once again, Level "I" Basics here seems quite simple: "what do you have to discuss here now?" Isn't it always obvious and known? But Level "II" sees that *uncovering, generating the needed, powerful variable-issues can be a complex challenging task!*

GUIDELINE. Know to discover what matters (issues) one either must or might confront, to succeed in the current task-goal, whatever it is. Here, "confront" means such as "*handle manage satisfy explore exploit reckon-with utilize*" and the like. Some issues seem mandatory, by default—they somehow *must* be "*satisfied*"; others seem more elective, enriching—they *might well or should* be "*utilized.*"

| **NO,** this seems too obvious. We all know to ask "what to discuss about the subject." Once more, *overkill*! | Aha, **BUT** "what questions to ask?" is a major thinking ploy. Easy initially—but see below, *difficult also*! |

GALLERY. Examples [in a "I" BRIEF view] of some above-average **Variable-Issues** for varied subjects. Does this collection help "cinch the concept" that V/I's are difficult to find, valuable to employ?

[1.] Alternative Medicine. Powerful issues, if one is considering non-Western (etc.) approaches…
1. Key principles. 2. Variations within tradition. 3. Procedures, techniques. 4. Scientific support, evidence? 5. Strengths and limitations. 6. Practitioner-patient relationship. 7. Evaluating of results? 8. Relationship to other medicine: exclude, conflict, integrate? 9. Costs. 10. Choosing a practitioner. [-- AHHA GUIDE]

[2.] The skill of "book-reviewing"… A fertile subject to show many possible variables to confront. Including alternate optional choices to consider—and pitfalls to avoid, blunders to beware…
[1.] Overall Purposes of the Review: (A) To help reader decide to read the book or not… (B) To give capsule-summary for those not reading it… (C) To critique the book, *but* to do so fairly, according to (1) what the book tried to do (*not* what the reviewer wanted it to do—*but* also (2) what the book perhaps should also, or instead, have tried to do, *and*

always state the specific criteria or standards you're applying!... (4) Also perhaps, was the book "worth doing in the first place or not?"... (D) To state which different kinds of *readers* might like it or not... (E) To state how different *viewpoints* would respond, differently, to this same book.)"... (F) Perhaps to place the book in its context or "canon" of related tradition, how it compares-contrasts with others, including any classics.

2. <u>Pitfalls to Avoid in Writing the Review</u>: **(A)** blurred image of the book, no clear sense of its content... **(B)** Unfairness, the reviewer's axe-grinding, etc. ... **(C)** Too-personal: just the reviewer's own response" digression... **(D)** just plain bad writing: wordy without clarity, etc.

MY OWN summary, assembled from almost a dozen sources from two decades: *more complete than usual*, I hope.

[3.] I.Q., "Intelligence Quotient"... What are the key issues which remain "salient," even crucial, are still unresolved, upon which we should therefore focus? Three similar formulations:

<u>**Two problems relevant to philosophy and education:**</u>
"1.Are human abilities unitary or diverse? 2. Are they determined by heredity, environment or a mixture of both?"
[-- WINCH & GINGELL]

<u>**Three unresolved issues in intelligence:**</u>
1. Whether intelligence is one thing or many things; 2. whether intelligence is inherited, and 3. whether any of its elements can be accurately measured. [-- HOWARD GARDNER, the Atlantic, Feb. '99]

<u>**Two salient questions about intelligence supposedly unexplored by scientist S. PINKER:**</u>
"1. Is intelligence a single trait that can be simply measured? 2. And, if we could gauge it reliably, can we sensibly parcel out its genetic and experiential components?" [-- RICHART, N.Y. Times, 2002]

[4.] Logistics, especially military. EXAMPLE: "you are inviting 1,000 of your close friends to a game at the large stadium." From this, THE RETIRED ARMY GENERAL derived the following "key logistical questions."

(1) What are the supply and transport issues?... (2) Where are the potential bottlenecks?... (3) Must these issues be addressed in a certain sequence, or can-should-must they be addressed simultaneously?... (4) When if at all does the strategy get modified to accommodate logistical realities?.. (5) What kind of experts need to get involved, and when?.. (6) What can you assume about the situation ("virtually nothing; attack assumptions!") [-- GUS PAGONIS]

We're not military officers, but these six seem <u>good examples of true</u> **variable-issues**, and their importance. As is becoming clear, they identify powerful matters to *handle, manage, reckon with, satisfy*—in short, to *confront for success...*

[5.] "Probes" for Poetry... My roster of salient variable-issues which apply variously to varied specific poems. Less mandatory, than here-and-there enriching. (For college freshman English 101.)

1. Is the subject-matter of the poem, in fact theme-or-idea? Or is (Old car in a field in Maine, is it about that alone indeed, or "more"—some idea?)
2. Is there structurally a "fulcrum" or turning, tipping-point pivot somewhere in the poem? (From JOHN CIARDI)
3. Is the "meaning" (theme, idea—if any) stated explicitly anywhere; or implied, left unspoken for us to feel?
4. How much is the poem a report—or the poet's response to an event?
5. Does the style (in various aspects: diction, structure, etc.) support or even create, the meaning?
6. ...and other issues...

Perhaps shows the probing-power of V/I/s. P.S.—a pedagogical precaution. At first, too many college-freshmen students took these as rigid Rules to "apply" all of them to each poem, until I recognized this error in Formula-vs.-Flexibility and said, "Not rules, but tools... It Depends!"

+|#||+#++||#+|#+||#+|+|+#|+|#|+|#+|++#|+|+|#+|+|+|#+||+#||#+|+#||+#|+|#+|#+|+#|#+|+#|+|#+|+|#+|#+|#+|#+|#+|#+|#+||#|+|#+||

[4.D.3.] The "CONCEPTUAL TOPOGRAPHY" of a "Field" of Subject-and-Skills:

182

THE IDEA. Here we mean <u>the "lay of the land"</u> of a skill-area (in thinking: using multiple perspectives... the issue of verticality or the Ladder of Abstaction... Exposition, in the sense of thinking-and-writing via "thesis-and-point-with-development"...). In a two-part sense of <u>**structure and function, anatomy and physiology, the features of the territory, and the events within it**</u>. And beyond mere surface features!

> [*ANALOGY:* obviously, the subject/skill as if <u>a geographical region</u>, "*terra incognita*," unknown but existing terrain describable and where events or operations occur, but whose major contours and operations remain existent but uncharted, uncoded. We the "<u>explorers</u>" visit the area (with pith helmet and butterfly net?) and seek to map it...]

THE SO-WHAT CRUCIALITY HERE. Why do this? To provide better pathways, blazed trails, identification of features, for future travelers—for thinkers.

These contours and operations are like foundation-stones, pillars, roofbeams, keystones. They are structural, how things are arranged, plus functional, how things work or operate. They exist but usually remain subliminal. But they are important to help us in <u>orientation</u>, knowing the "terrain" of the subject. But also for <u>navigation</u>, how to navigate the terrain. If only because they often become in a sense **"variable-issues"** themselves [=matters which for task-goal success it is Vital or anyhow Valuable to confront: handle manage reckon with satisfy etc. etc.]. They are of course <u>complex, conceptual, higher-order</u>: almost like the "essential skeleton" of the subject... Therefore *often overlooked, plus usually difficult to ascertain.*

| ...Whoa, this is impossibly *vague, general,* ironically <u>not</u> a clarification of the very idea of "contours & operations"! Egg on your face; you didn't Walk the Talk! | True, **BUT** we need Abstract Conceptual <u>Exposition</u> of a concept. Now we can offer an <u>Analogy</u>: "the subject is like *unknown geographic terrain,* the thinker explores it and *maps the topography and reports the movements* for future travelers..." And then on to Examples... |

GALLERY. I here share <u>my own work</u> [here in <u>Teaching Thinking</u>; forthcoming in <u>Mind-Play</u>], in trying to elucidate the contours and operations, of the very thinking skills we're viewing. It is <u>difficult</u>: <u>my early versions were sparse, vague.</u> **EXAMPLE:** the *original* checklist for writing, was only **"4-S":** Substance or subject... Structure... Style of writing... and Support, via specific detailing. A *rough sketch*-map only!

> SEE ALSO: These three skills—**lenswork, verticalities,** and **specific detailing**—all are discussed further in Teaching Thinking; two in **tool-kits,** verticalities in App. #6, Pre-View of Mind-Play.

These aspects of the **"conceptual topography"** of a field or skill, can be sort of <u>default-or-mandatory</u>, one can't avoid dealing with this issue—or it can be <u>optional-elective</u>, one may benefit by choosing to deal with this issue but one need not do so. [**EXAMPLE:** in <u>writing</u>, **structure** is *inevitable*, there will be one or the other unavoidably. However, **concretization** is *optional*; one could omit any and all examples, illustrations, evidence...]

(1) "LENSwork" It's one thing to just tell a student "Try looking at this subject from three different perspectives." It's another to proffer (as appropriate) some of the **"contours and operations"** of **lenswork** (as we call *the major thinking skill of competently employing multiple-plural viewpoints* upon an issue.) Perhaps **competence** in **lens-work** is <u>powerfully accelerated by</u> full truer **knowledge**-of/about <u>the following issues</u> about multiple-plural perspectives and the implications of these issues:

1. Full awareness that lenses exist, we see through them.
2. Lenses are inevitable, inescapable.
3. Specific lenses are often subliminal: unnamed, even unrecognized.
4. Lenses are not "cleanly pure/descriptive only" they come freighted with world-views:
5. Lenses are "double-edged": powerfully-insightful, but limited/incomplete, maybe "biased" also.
6. "All Lenses Are 'Good' (or at lest 'Logical')—In A Certain Sense."
7. Over time, lenses can become (A) outdated, also can become (B) wrongfully neglected
8. Number of lenses to use: multiple, for complex tasks. But, what about Priorities? about Cooperation-or-

9. Lens-Selection: How to identify and critique those (perhaps-dubious) lenses already-present, also how to choose objectively and locate those (probably-needed) lenses still-to-import.

[10.] …And that other variable you'll be listing…

Objection! I just think this last bit, Conceptual Terrain or whatever, is sheer flagrant *overkill. Too much!!* Very abstract. Of what pragmatic use? Beyond most students. I never see these lofty matters listed in *other* pedagogical materials. It's enough to say simply, *"Look at the subject through multiple and differing viewpoints."* Or, simply, *"Be specific, mid-range, or general, as needed."* Or, simply *"Give an example to support your idea."* And let it go at that! Again, your well-intentioned "complex response to complexity," has become *over-*complex, topheavy!

…listen, for years, I used lenses. I wrote specific-and-general statements. I wrote essays in effect (thesis-and-points, whether a school paper—or a letter-to-the-editor or business memo or instructions etc.)….. but without fully knowing these fields, their *deeper topography* thus as elucidated here. My work was—well, *"adequate"*… But, gradually I "discovered and derived out," the keystone pillars here. E.g., of Verticality. True, no other educational resources go as far as I do here, and state these contour-components explicitly. ***But by knowing these principles-behind, by knowing the "lay of the land" thus, I have VASTLY IMPROVED my command of specificity-generality in thinking and writing…*** *I'll leave it right there for now …*

---

(2) "Verticalities": The "Ladder of Abstraction": Key variables on this major issue:

(1) We can and do perceive and state a subject on varying levels of specificity-generality. This "ladder of abstraction" means between lower-level Material tangible specific and higher-level Mental conceptual idea. [Example: "vegetarianism": legume recipe, the Green Café,] [Be able to phrase a response at all levels from down-dirty snapshot, to stratospheric meta-generality.]

(2) The ladder is tall and deep, plus has many rungs. (We can be more specific, and more general, than one might think, and with many gradations between "Mark flung mashed potatoes," and "food-service misbehavior."

3. Pros and cons: both specifics, and generalities, have their powerful uses, and their limitations. [Know how to avoid shortcomings or excesses of each position.]

4. Written texts vary in their amount, proportion, arrangement of concrete-specific, and conceptual-abstract, segments. (All conceptual, all concrete; or idea-then-examples; or introductory story and then analysis; or, parable and then conceptual moral given from it; or rollercoaster inter-blending of Material and Mental…)

5. (A) **Three types of thinking here are: Induction** upward, **Deduction** downward, Lateral-**associative** across. (B) **Two types of locus of knowledge** here are **Idealism** and **Realism.** (C) **Two methods of gaining knowledge** here are **Empiricism** and **Rationalism.**

---

(3) "15-C": Expository Elucidation. Our model for fullest elucidation of thinking and writing in, roughly, the mode of "Thesis and points with development and conclusion."

1. <u>Complete and Complex</u> (subject is covered). <u>Collected and Continued</u> (enough material is present).
2. <u>Conceptualized</u>: information is worked for the ideas within it.
3. <u>Con-Vergent</u>: an overall unity is sought.
4. <u>Categorized</u>: subject's component sub-parts, elements are discovered.
5. <u>Crystallized</u>: main points are stated in explicit clear fashion, not left subliminal or implied.
6. <u>Calibrated</u>: main matters treated generously, secondary matters downplayed, in proportion.
7. <u>Concretized</u>: ideas are illustrated by specific concrete examples illustrations evidence etc. etc.
8. <u>Contoured</u>: whole text is divided into chunks, segments, etc., as needed.
9. <u>Con-Sequent</u>: material is structured, arranged, ordered in effective sequence.
10. <u>Co-herent</u>: if points interrelate, this relationship is made clear.
11. <u>Co-hesive</u>: #10's integration is shown by style, especially parallelism.
12. <u>Concatenation</u>: syntax (sentence-structure) skillfully "packages" the content.

13. <u>Condensed</u>: text is free of wordiness, distilled to just-right compactness-conciseness.
14. <u>Camera</u>; visual techniques are used as needed (charts, graphs, diagrams, etc.)
15. <u>Correct</u>: text is error-free, conventions are followed, constraints obeyed.

I see these keystone **operating principles** are vital (and under-featured), **BUT** how do they differ from **"Reading the Situation"**?	"Two different pews in the Church of The Most Very Idea," I'd say… See, **R. the S.** is the <u>process</u> whereby these <u>principles</u> (and others) are discovered…

+|#||+#++||#+|#+||#+|+|+#|+|#|+|#+|+#|+|#+|+|#+||+#|+|+#||+#|+|#+|+#|+#+|+#|+|#+|+#|+#+|#+|+#|+#|+|#+#||
+|#||+#++||#+|#+||#+|+|+#|+|#|+|#+|+#|+|#+|+|#+||+#|+|+#||+#|+|#+|+#|+#+|+#|+|#+|+#|+#+|#+|+#|+#|+|#+#||

[1.] Intro.	[2.] Table of Contents	[3.] Body of Claims	[4.] "Reading"- Situations	**[5.] Annex: Examples**

[5.] ANNEX: "reading *situations*"...

TABLE OF CONTENTS. Summary of major types of Situations to read, with examples to follow:

[1.] <u>Ideologies, Schools of Thought, Systems.</u> (<u>Lenses: perspectives</u> etc.) **[1A]** *Traditional humanism..* **[1B]** *Extreme diversity.*

[2.] <u>The academic fields or disciplines.</u> **[2A]** *World-views of humanities, social sciences, natural sciences…* **[2B]** *Pure, and applied: "the logic of medicine" to be grasped by a citizen non-physician, a patient's relative.*

[3.] <u>Historical Sociology: periods in culture.</u> …. **[3A]** *American traditional culture…* **[3B]** *The Sixties …* **[3C]** *Boomer-generation youth today., …* **[3D]** *Traditional versus Postmodern assumptions in the humanities…* **[3E]** *Education: "Old-School" vs. "New-Think" paradigms…*

[4.] <u>Space, Changes:</u> **[4A]** *East versus West generally…* **[4B]** *Writing:* **(i.)** *Writing differently even within English studies…* **(ii.)** *General School or academic writing, versus writing in the world: Personal, especially Vocational on the Job, Civic-Community…* **(iii.)** *Freelance Journalism…* **[4C]** *When job-interviewing, specific businesses' "corporate cultures…"*

[5.] <u>Groups, Varied:</u> **[5A]** *"Sexuality:" views of traditional religion, versus views of liberationist or diversity-minority studies.*

[6.] <u>Literary Artistic Genres:</u> **[6A]** *Art, 10 facets of…* **[6B]** *Detective story formula…* **[6.C]** *Schoolwriting, schoolreading… .*

QUOTATIONS: A PRIMER. Two statements on the overall goal—difficult, valuable. Plus, how two disciplines supposedly encourage this goal of "reading the situation":
Then only a few quotations from the above Table: SEE "II" FULL catalog in Mind- Play…

[1] "<u>Reading the behavior of well-known friends and relatives</u> is like covering thoroughly familiar ground without a mental map or talking before writing systems had ever been heard of. One does not need a writing system to talk (or technical awareness of the rules governing speech either). <u>To abstract such a system from the living data where none existed before</u>, however, is a formidable task, an intellectual achievement that can equal the great accomplishments in chemistry, physics, and astronomy." [-- E. T. HALL, ANTHROPOLOGIST]

[2] RE◄View Reminder: **"Chicken Sexers,"** this feat is an astonishing achievement, analogous in form to that of ancient scholars in isolating the phonemic structure of speech into an alphabet of 26 letters, **"one of the great intellectual feats of human history."**

[3] The ability to extract *general principles* from immediate or concrete situations. <u>Psychology</u> graduates tend to be better than most people at spotting *recurrent patterns or similarities* between situations, and at looking at issues in terms of their *underlying principles* rather than becoming bogged down with the details of the immediate situation." [*italics added*] [--DR. BETH HAYES, psychology teacher]

[4] <u>Anthropology</u> majors tend to acquire certain skills—usually unstated explicitly—which lets them them **"abstract out" social patterns** better: Social Agility—sizing up quickly the "rules of the game," hence getting accepted easier.... Planning—see patterns in a cultural group, generalize, then predict what might happen... Social Perspective—seeing individual and group actions as cause and effect of larger sociocultural systems. [-- JOHN OMOHUNDRO, SUNY]

[2.B.] The critical-thinking teacher RICHARD PAUL showed how "reading the situation" **helped him make sense of the foreign world of medicine,** a complexly-different, new situation in the Personal arena of life:

--I spent three days reading technical articles in medical journals at the U.C. Medical School Library to help a family member evaluate the status of research on his medical problem. I had virtually none of the background knowledge of the typical readers (doctors), but I did know how to use a dictionary and the resources of my own mind.

--With effort and struggle and some conceptual puzzlement, I was able to identify three distinguishable therapeutic approaches to the medical problems I was researching. I was also able to identify arguments that advocates of each were using in support of their own and in opposition to the other proposed treatments. I was then able to hold my own in subsequent discussions with medical proponents of those approaches.

--This **ability to determine the basic logic of a text in the absence of the standard background knowledge of those it was written for** is *one of the hallmarks of critically literate readers*. It enabled me to read technical articles by cognitive psychologists, anthropologists, economists, and others even though they each presupposed background knowledge within their fields that I lacked.

...a classic, even without specific illustration, of the need and value of decoding "foreign" patterns...

[3.B.] "**The Sixties in America**": attempt to recall basic (tho unstated and uncriticized!) ideologies then: 1. Questioning of authority... 2. Anti-materialism... 3. Moral relativism. 4. Personal authority... 5. Egalitarianism... 6. Attack on bureaucracy and mass society. 7. Emphasis on identity—racial, ethnic, religious, or sexual—as a primary means of self-identification. [-- JERALD E. PODAIR, Lawrence Today]

[3.C.] The AUTHOR of The Boomer Bible was able to make explicit, **the dubious world-view of many young people today,** which explains their complaints, their resistance to cooperation, etc. [-- R. LAIRD]

1. DESIRE. Whatever you desire—whatever you may wish to have, or want to do—well, you surely have a perfect *right* to have and do same. Don't let others tell you you don't "deserve" or "merit" it, or have to "earn" it, etc.

2. CERTAINTY. Whatever you believe—whatever fact, opinion, judgment, etc.—well, that is surely *valid*: for-sure true, okay as a belief. Don't let others tell you that maybe you should examine-and-assess your own ideas, let alone doubt-or-question-or alter them.

3. BLAME. And whatever you may actually do (or not do) is okay also. Your actions/inactions are as *right* as your desires and beliefs. Don't let others tell you you should be blamed, let alone "responsible" etc.—because it's always other people or factors who are at fault.

Whoa, "interesting" but of what earthly use or good is this to know pragmatically?	To be able to handle pesky items such as these: (1) A student criticizes the teacher for his strongly criticizing the students "that day we all blew off the assignment"... (2) Parents came to collect their children from a rowdy house party and the children barred the doors... (3) Parents claimed a high school should graduate students even when they had missed classes and exams... *Either enough said here, about how* spotting key subliminal notions is powerful, *or else any further praise for* "*reading the situation*" *is useless...*

[3.D.] Writing during the "culture wars" of the 1990's, JOHN SEARLE was skillfully able to abstract out the world-views of (1) **traditional literary study,** and then also of (2) the challengers, "**liberation pedagogy.**"

FOR THE TRADITIONAL VIEW:	AND THEN FOR THE CHALLENGER:
1. Books studied as the classics should reflect intellectual merit and historical importance.	1. One's ethnic, racial, class, gender subgroup matters enormously in essentially defining one.
2. Objective standards do exist of rationality, intelligence, truth, validity, and general intellectual merit.	2. All cultures are equal, morally, but also intellectually; we can learn from others than "European white males."
3. One main aim of a "liberal education" is to liberate	3. Representativeness is crucial; every culture must be represented, and too many have been mis-, non-, or under-represented. This to banish

students from mediocrity, provincialism, or other limitations of their backgrounds, including complacency. 4. The Western tradition combines extreme universalism and extreme individualism. 5. Another main aim of liberal education is also to critique oneself and one's community, toward an examined life. 6. Objectivity and truth are possible because an independent reality, a world-out-there, does exist, to which our true utterances correspond.	elitism, hegemony, patriarchy, classism, and the like. 4. A main aim of a "liberal education" is to transform culture and society politically, toward liberations. 5. Objective standards do not, objectively, exist; claims of disinterest, objectivity, universality are untrustworthy. 6. In fact, moving from realism to relativism, all reality is ultimately "textual"; an objective reality, true statements about it, and communication to others through language—all are dubious. 7. Western civilization is historically oppressive: domestically to women, slaves, and serfs; internationally, via colonialism and imperialism. White males have been in power.
...seems an above-average achievement in reading this complex situation of differing ideologies...	

[3.E.] The "Education Wars": Some keystone elements of the different views of education, <u>traditional</u>, and <u>thinking-intensive</u>. [NOT a summary of ALL the possible goals of education—cf. "vocational training," "personal enhancement," "socialization to citizen-roles," "work for social liberation," etc.]

Goals: what to Know, Believe, Do = = = = = how to Think Things Through

"Content" defined as Factual Info Material = = = = = "Content" may be the Concepts, Skills.

Role of Student: passive receiver of information = = = = = active learner

Role of Teacher: imparter of information = = = = = coach, facilitator, etc.

"Accuracy": correctness, error-avoidance is key = = = = = make mistakes but learn!

Decisions: most made by course, teacher = = = = = more made by student

Knowledge acquisition: atomized parts = = = = = accretive integrated wholes

Assessment: simple testing = = = = = transfer to new situations

"Content" defined as Factual Info Material = = = = = "Content" may be the Concepts, Skills.

...now I **DO** see the importance of this **"situation-reading"** for <u>orienting people to the new</u>. **But** your image of education above is incomplete plus non-organized to best effect...	True, it is not polished (Teaching Thinking's Introduction elucidates better). But our topic here is *"Reading"* the elements of a complex *Situation* for better command of it...

[4.B.iii.] I MYSELF had to learn (too painfully and slowly) **the differing "situations" of real-world writing.** A teacher of literature plus amateur Great Lakes sailor, I started writing boating articles for magazines such as <u>Sail</u> and <u>Cruising World</u> and <u>Lakeland Boating</u>. but I wrote in too literary a style at first, until I realized the following different codes for the different situations of "Schoolwriting" versus general real-world writing, including Vocational and Journalistic:

1. <u>Length</u>: in school, "at least 500 words". 2. <u>Tone</u>: in school, often formal-impersonal. 3. <u>Structure</u>: in school, sometimes lead up to the point. 4. <u>Audience</u>: in school, a vacuum—the profis the reader. 5. <u>Graphics</u>: in school, just prose on the page.	1. <u>Length</u>: outside, "one-page minimum" or the like. 2. <u>Tone</u>: outside, usually a person on the page. 3. <u>Structure</u>: outside, announce the conclusion first. 4. <u>Audience</u>: outside, tune rhetoric for target-audience(s). 5. <u>Graphics</u>: outside, often charts-tables-diagrams, etc.
Is this important? I badly needed better training in **Reading the Situation** of "freelance feature-article journalism" ***vs.*** "scholarly academic articles." Not to mention the laser-precise "slant" or formula of each individual publication...	

[5.A.] "SEXUAL ORIENTATION" SARABANDE... I MYSELF was able to identify (I admit, with help from a book from a theologist!) the patterns, or at least **the implicit variable-issues**, in a campus debate-session about homosexuality between traditional Lutheran students, and the school's sexual-orientation group

For the *religious-conservative* side, their **World-View of Implicit Presuppositions** seem to be:	And for the *gay-liberationist* side:
1. Damnation is a risk; salvation is possible. 2. Scripture is true and is the source of truth. 3. Scripture names homosexuality as a sin. 4. We're all sinners, but can at least try to avoid sinning even if not the temptation to	1. The source of truth (and guide for conduct) is one's own inner nature and identity. 2. For some folks, homosexuality is indeed natural-and-normal, their true central self. 3. The "evil" is social homophobia, not homosexuality itself. Relatedly, a "sin" would be the Double Life or acting contrary to one's true nature. 4. We gays/lesbians, do not seek to convert or seduce heterosexuals. Nor to "out" or

sin. 5. THEREFORE <u>renouncing homosexual behavior</u> is very important to do. 6. Also, for Christians, it is important to help others who sin also to escape their sins.	"de-closet" other gay folk before they choose to do so. 5. Nobody "chooses" their sexual orientation, they discover it. And nobody "changes" it—voluntarily (even though some of us have tried!). (Sexual orientation may change in a person's lifetime, but unpredictably thus…) 6. THEREFORE, for those who are gay/lesbian, <u>reaffirming homosexual identity</u> is very important to do.
So what? Why pause in the debate to state all these background beliefs?	Migosh, it could help avoid ceaseless back-and-forth argument throwing "the facts" and rationalizing one's prior viewpoint. We could communicate better (IF we want to be fair-minded cooperative not fighting combat), by realizing how we believe and differ basically!

[6.A.] I MYSELF, during a debate about a Milwaukee (WI, U.S.A.) public art project, was able to generate ten possible **criteria for "good visual art."**

[1.] Classic Great Tradition Elite… [2.] Conventional folk familiar "easy"… [3.] Trendy, edgy, fashionable, in vogue, the current Next Big Thing…. [4.] Laissez-Faire relativism, "whatever" we call art. What appears in museums…. [5.] Socially-conscious politics for social liberation…. [6.] Just-Personal, whatever expresses the artist, or satisfies the viewer…. [7.] Religious or ceremonial act…. [8.] Poetry or philosophy: life-enhancing thus…. [9.] "Therapeutic," for artist, or viewer…. [10.] Pure aesthetics: organic form, dynamic dialectic…

Sure, some of these were already made explicit as concepts when I found them. But others I had to realize myself. And anyhow I had to look for them, survey a large **catchment-area** of others' comments about art…]

[6.B.] Literary Genres: "the rules of the **classic detective story**," abstracted out by DAVID PERKINS:

(1) The culprit is always a character throughout, rather than appearing newly at the end… (2) The evidence is sufficient to identify him or her… (3) The solution doesn't depend on exotic, specialized knowledge… (4) The villain is never the obvious suspect, and usually an unobvious one—the person, for instance, who seems to have had no opportunity… (5) The villain is rarely a very sympathetic character, someone you would feel bad about being guilty.

…well, how he grasped these generalities is beyond me.	…**Reading a Situation** *is* difficult! Is he a mystery buff?

[6.C.] The "Codes" of Schoolwriting, also Reading as taught in traditional education. ALAN PURVES *insightfully* could net all the issues—objectivity vs. personal, specific-general, visuals, subject vs. audience focus, correctness, syntax, tone, etc. *Better than I for one could have done;* he has anthropological vision:

Writing: the *largely-unstated* principles:	Reading: some *never-questioned* assumptions:
1. Generally avoid the personal except in certain English courses. 2. If there is a choice between being abstract and being concrete, be concrete. 3. Use a propositional rather than an oppositional structure. 4. Avoid metaphors and figurative language. 5. Generally avoid using graphic signals such as underlining, subheads, and the like except in science and mathematics. 6. Focus on the content rather than on making the reader feel comfortable. 7. Select a single aspect of your subject and announce your thesis as early as possible. 8. Make sure the surface appearance of the text is attractive. Check spelling, punctuation, and grammar. 9. Use complex or embedded sentences. 10. Avoid humor.	1. Read narrative structures with ease, and try to turn all other texts into narratives. 2. Produce accurate summaries that reflect the stipulated expert "meaning." 3. Locate information readily. 4. Do not re-read, even if they like the book, except for a test. 5. Read quickly. 6. Read for recreation unless there is something on television. 7. Recognize "good" books but don't read them. 8. Do not read texts aesthetically, but read all texts as if they were scriptural (either divine or secular). 9. Seek the moral lesson in whatever they read. 10. Therefore, have a strongly censorious attitude towrd books that are considered sinful or seditious. [-- BECOMING A SCRIBE AND OTHER UNNATURAL ACTS]
…so what's the good of delineating all this anyhow?	Migosh, to show stands taken on key issues, and how the stands may be badly limited, overlook options!

Oh my… this gallery above, what a *romp* for you the "cognitive voyeur" at least! Did you enjoy your tour of spotting the secrets—*even if this is a detour* from the pragmatic into the "pleasurable"?	Knowledge of how-to is power plus. And yes, ultimately pleasure. Work the *crossword puzzle* of the world. And *from that flower, pluck* the saffron petal of practicality… [And mix metaphors…]

[{(END of module " Why, The Very IDEA! "   )}]

#|+#|+|#+|#+|+#||+||#++##|+|+|+#+|+|#+#|+|+#|+|+#|+|+#|||+|+#|#+|#+|+|+#|+|+#|+#+|+||#+||#++#+|#+|+#|#|+#|+|+#|+|+#|+|+|#+|#+|+#|+|+#+|+|#+|#+|+#|+|#+|+#|+|+#|#+|

THE ISSUE—WHY IMPORTANT?—OUR RESPONSE: --The *monarch* (kingpin?) of thinking skills may well be <u>**induction**</u>. **Conceptualizing;** to achieve ideas from concrete particulars: generalizing, moving UP the **ladder of abstraction from Material concrete particulars, to Mental conceptual constructs: ideas about the particulars.** --[Also important of course are **deduction** DOWNward, or applying concepts to material, plus **"lateral"** thinking ACROSS or connecting materials more free-associatively.]

--This is so important, that in this appendix, <u>we pause to</u> **pour a solid broad standpoint of** <u>**concrete**</u> of *the most utterly basic* **components of conceptualizing.**

> <u>Many</u> readers will feel, "no; much *too obvious*, we *all know this already*." Some <u>others</u> will reflect: "aha, *do* beginning students know the basics of concrete-abstract and the rest? The contours and operations, the issues and options, the pitfalls and the potentialities? *Not* usually as clearly and concisely as presented here…"

The 〰Table of Contents〰 of this unit:

#|+#|+|#+|#+|+#||+||#++##|+|+#|+|#+#|+|+#|+|+#|+|+#|||+|+#|#+|#+|+|+#|+|+#|+#+|+||#+||#++#+|#+|+#|#|+#|+|+#|+|+#|+|+|#+|#+|+#|+|+#+|+|#+|#+|+#|+|#+|+#|+|+#|#+|

[1.] "The Very Concept, of a Concept"—is it taught well, is it at times shortchanged?...

1. Do students know what a concept is? Do WE know?... [Well, yes, but read on...]

-----A **concept** is dictionary-defined as being "**a quality of a thing or things apart from its specific examples.**"

--"RED" (*not* a tube of crimson paint... a blood-red rose... a ruby-red jewel-like traffic stoplight)

--"CHAIR" (*not* CHRIS' soft green fabric beanbag in his studio... PAT'S ergonomic office-desk-chair... LYNN'S dented folding gray metal auditorium-chair)

--"JUSTICE" (*not* MARIE recovering her job... FENTON being able to vote... DEXTER prosecuting the person who harassed him for being a Deep Vegetarianism...)

--Plus, an idea about a subject (vegetarianism, etc.) *exceeds* its concrete specific content.

#|+#|+|#+|#+|+#||+||#++##|+|+|+#+|+|#+#|+|+#|+|#+|+|#|||+|+#|#+|#+|+|+#|+|+#|+#|+||#+||#+#+#+|#+|+#|+#|#+|#+|+#+|#+|+|#+#|+|+#|+|#+|#+|+|+#+|#|+|#+|#+|

2. But do students really know what concepts are? Then ascend to them?

EXAMPLE. A college student goes back to basic **thinking** in re "snowboarding"

"...I am more aware of the need to note key concepts. This winter, I went snowboarding for the first time. It usually takes a whole day to learn to snowboard. But I learned almost instantly. That's because my friend explained to me the relevant concepts of snowboarding. These are: for steering, one torques the body; for stopping, the back leg is your anchor; for slowing, the edges of the board are used. I realized that most students do not realize that concepts are important in learning. *In fact, I think that most students don't know what concepts are. I certainly didn't*" [-- from RICHARD PAUL]

No and whoa! For, these "concepts" seem so banal, obvious, and even almost non-conceptual, that paradoxically it supports the point that Conceptualizing is Crucial—and, Overlooked ... *Are these three instructions, really concepts after all?* A quality of a thing apart from its specific examples? *No,* perhaps they are simple Techniques or Procedures, almost Rule-like... Yet this comment *does* start upward from unaware unanalyzed experience to discover principles to guide...

#|+#|+|#+|#+|+#||+||#++##|+|+|+#+|+|#+#|+|+#|+|#+|+|#|||+|+#|#+|#+|+|+#|+|+#|+#|+||#+||#+#+#+|#+|+#|+#|#+|#+|+#+|#+|+|#+#|+|+#|+|#+|#+|+|+#+|#|+|#+|#+|

3. But Do Teachers Teach About Concepts--enough?

EXAMPLE. *EGG ON MY FACE:* MY OWN EIGHT-WEEK-LONG *UNDER-CONCEPTUALIZING* IN ENGLISH 101...

"A ladder of abstraction exists from specific to general. A difference exists between a concrete statement and a conceptual statement." [Analogically, it's like rich fertile pond lowland meadows==ascending to aerial rarefied mountain summits...BTW, right here a specific (analogy) to illuminate the generality of the L. of A.!...] A basic concept, but is it overlooked? In my first year of teaching Freshman English (state university, 1970-95), halfway through, I discovered that most of the students mistakenly thought that "concrete" meant "easy or clear," whereas "abstract" meant "difficult to understand." You can imagine the confusion that resulted from this PAP or Prevalent Amateur Pitfall. But it took me eight weeks of increasing

190

#|+#|+|#+|+#||+||#++##|+|+|+#+|+|#+#|+|+#|+#|+|+#|||+|+#|#+|#+|+|+#|+#|+#|+||#+||#+#+#|+#|+#|+#+|+|#+|+|#+|+|#+|+#|+#|+|#+|+|#+|+|+#|+|+#+|

4A. READING "I": When reading BASIC INFORMATIONAL texts, can students identify the ideas well enough to summarize the text's concepts? Whether via writing a good Précis or abstract, or making a true Outline of the points? [No...]

ANALOGIES. Prevalent amateur pitfalls recur here. Analogies may elucidate these errors. We could compare reading-for-ideas, to **(1) doing an x-ray of the body**, past the fat of wordiness, elaboration of muscles, to the "skeleton" of the conceptual bones. Many students reproduce the surface features only, don't achieve penetrating insight! **(2)** Or, to **filtering a liquid**: dragging a wide-mesh sieve through a vat of fluid with particulate matter in it. Many students let important particles fall through the screen.
(3) Also, a common blunder is the "Leafbagger Outline." As if reading, were **mowing down a lawn** to collect the leaves from it. The student does *not* read for the subpoint-concepts which s/he then arranges in I A B II A 1 2 III and so forth. S/he simply drives down the lawn, and indiscriminately places *both* concepts, and concrete examples, in the outline.

FIRST TYPE. A text structured as a story (narrative; memoir...) but actually containing expository points.

EXAMPLE. "FROM BLURRED TO CRISPER" Here are four images of an English 101 student essay on "a job I held," in this case "lifeguard at Biltmore Beach in Illinois." Although the "essay" was structured not in expository but in narrative form as in "a typical day at work," the essay was *not* merely unanalyzed chronicle; points emerged rather clearly as the writer went along. *Still...*

They are précis or summary, plus outline. All intended to represent the concepts or backbone-ideas... (*)
Students started out producing the inferior left-hand versions. But with minimal instruction, they could produce the right-hand side.

First student attempt at a "précis":	After *some* instruction in précis-writing:	My sample "ideal" **PRÉCIS** to mirror essay:	the Essay's Actual **OUTLINE:**
{1} Being a lifeguard is not as easy as it may appear. There are tasks that many do not realize exist, and dealing with the various people is not always a pleasant experience. [=*impossibly vague; skims over the ideas!*]	{2} Being a lifeguard looks like a summer packed with fun in the sun, but the actual activities are quite tedious. A normal day of being a lifeguard includes waiting to be relieved from your duty in the high chair, enduring kid swimmers who disappear, cleaning up goose dung, and listening to anxious mothers who complain. *[= better but still-quite-uncontrolled presenting of some ideas but still concretized not conceptualized...]*	{3A} The job of lifeguard presents unrecognized problems in two areas. The natural world (including a dirty beach to clean, hot weather, and bad equipment). And the world of people (including rowdy and destructive kid swimmers, over-anxious mothers, uncooperative co-workers, and the absence of attractive personnel). [= *I trust this extracted the concepts...*]	{3B} THESIS: "Problems in Lifeguard Job" (I) Natural World: (A) Beach (B) Heat (C) Equipment (II) Human World: (A) Kid Swimmers: 1. Rowdy 2. Destructive (B) Mothers (C) Co-Workers (D) No "Epidermal Pulchritude" [= *the precis above, captures the structure...*]

#|+#|+|#+|#+|+#||+||#++#||+|+|+#+|+|#+#|+|+#|+#|+|+|#||+|+#|#+|#+|+|+#|+|+#|+#+|+||#+||#+#+#+|#+|+#|+#|#+|#+|+|#+|+|#+|#+|+#|#+|+#+|+|#+|#+|+#|+|#+|#+|+|+|#+|#+|

Appendix/"Dessert"… [Here is the actual student essay, grammatically sanitized, for your enjoyment. It interestingly interblends its actual ideas within the format or matrix of the specific story chronological structure, interblending the Concrete and the Conceptual thus. It also illustrates the minor point that Generalizations can be relatively more explicit-stated and emphasized (told to reader) – or relatively more implicit and left subliminal (realized by reader):]

My name is Chris and I have worked as a lifeguard for the last two summers at Biltmore Beach. Biltmore Beach is located one hour down Route 12 in the town of Barrington, IL. Right off the bat I can hear what most of you people are saying, "What a bum, this guy just sat on his butt all summer staring at girls' asses, getting a tan, and getting paid; get a real job!" Okay, I can see your limited point, but have you ever worked at a beach?

At Biltmore Beach the day started off with all six lifeguards meeting at the top of Beachview Drive. The other guards' names were Peggy, Lisa, Mary, Matt, Brian, and myself. As we walked down from the top of Beachview Dr., we could see the beach. The towering willows seemed to engulf the small plot of land, but as we came closer, you could see the light brown granules that we would be working on. All the lifeguards would reach the beach knowing their first task, cleaning up all the goose shit off the beach from the night before. Cleaning goose shit, I assure you, is not what you want to be doing at 9:15 A.M. Picking this crap up, is like trying to pick up chocolate chips that have been cooked at 5,000 degrees. It's oozy and watery and smells worse than dirty socks that can talk back to you.

Right as we would finish that lovely job, "they" would come. "They" would come right around the willows with no warning, screaming. Most of them were short, and had a fat little belly. "They" were kid swimmers. These destructive little bastards would stop at nothing until they got in the water. Hundreds of these little jerks running around screaming "where's the lifeguard?" "Where's the lifeguard?"

Soon I would be up in the "chair." The "chair" as we call it is what I think is comparable to the electric chair. Its rippled wooden frame stands eight feet high in about a half-foot of water. When you sit, you are automatically stuck with thousands of little splinters, leaving the lifeguard with the expression of a person with Down Syndrome.

You sit and sit on the construction of temporary torture and try to keep these little "angels" from drowning themselves. The kids had no control; they would start dunking each other, spitting in each others' faces, splashing. Trying to keep a head count was impossible. As a lifeguard you were on the edge of the "chair" waiting for the first one to go under. Then you always have the crazy mother screaming "where's my little Johnny, he was just out there." The mother in total panic is yelling her lungs out, making her eyeballs glow, meaning "you better find her kid." My first thought is, "oh shit, one of those little assholes has finally done himself in and his parents are going to sue my ass." My second thought is "I better dive in and try to save the little shit." Have you ever tried to dive from eight feet into a half-foot of water? Well, when you hit bottom, it's like getting an enema, but only with sand. Of course Johnny was just sitting behind a tree or something (eating his little fat face out).

As a lifeguard I am only to be in the chair for one hour, then one of the other lifeguards usually comes, like Matt, to replace me. In the real world I guess things don't work that way. I would usually be up in that contraption for close to an hour and 45 minutes. This is while the 95-degree sun is slowly burning my flesh away from my face, legs, and chest. It was not unusual for me to come home looking like an overcooked lobster.

192

By the time 5:00 came around, I was always beat. Of course sometimes I would see a girl in a nice bikini, but most of the time it was little flat-chested girls who would say things like "liar, liar, pants on fire." So next time when somebody tells you that they're a lifeguard, don't call them a bum—tell them you feel sorry for them.

SPACE for each instructor's examples, of texts terribly flawed... of texts of reasonable clarity (like Biltmore above, Brookfield auditorium just below... of texts perfected (by the book anyhow) by the 15-C essay method discussed elsewhere...

And student responses. PRECIS or summaries, blurred and general... improved... then not just "leafbagging everything indiscriminately sweeping up concrete examples and conceptual subpoints" but crystallizing the points... and OUTLINES doing the same...

All to suggest good writing and communicating at last... but also all along, better THINKING also....

#|+#|+|#+|#+|+#||+|#++##|+|+|+#+|+|#+#|+|+#|+|+#|#+|+|#|||+|+#|#+|#+|+|+#|+|+#|+#+|+||#+||#+#+#+|#+|+#|+#|#+|+|#+|#+|+#|#+|+#|+#|+#|+||#+|#+|+#|+|#+|#+|

SECOND TYPE. An essay-type text, more complex, average writing quality, but undeniable points present.

THE ISSUE, and **WHY IMPORTANT.** It is difficult to read well, an "average written text": one written well-enough, but not expertly for reader-clarity. Points unarguably present, but perhaps buried from amateur sight...

GUIDELINE/GOAL: **The learner can read with x-ray eyes to discover the skeleton of concepts beneath the concealing flab of imperfect writing**

OUR SUGGESTION: This section. Though it consumes page-space, I *do* include
EXAMPLE. "Brookfield:" student paper, on why a local high school needs an auditorium.
[1] the student's original essay from which the **outlines** and **précis** were written.
(I also include **[2]** a streamlined version of my own to exhibit some of the "15-C" or Expository Elucidation principles—an essay more complete, more conceptual plus concretized, yet more coherent and compact also...)
Then **[3]** *my* attempt at the best outline... But then also **[4]** examples of student outlines... **[5]** And also Precis: from botched to bettered...

[1] APPLAUD AN AUDITORIUM? *[original]*	**[2]** APPLAUD AN AUDITORIUM? *[rewrite]*
Whether from discussions or from actual experiences many Brookfield citizens, both students and adults, know of the inconveniences of having special events held in one of three places at Brookfield Central High School—the Little theater, the cafeteria, and the gymnasium. Rather than griping about the lack of centrality, overcrowdedness, and uncomfortable seating, have you ever considered improving Brookfield Central by adding an auditorium?	For convenience, comfort, dignity, and status, let's consider an auditorium for Brookfield High School.
Parents, how often have you searched for the Little Theater, the conference room, or a specific classroom to end up in the cafeteria or gymnasium disgusted? An auditorium would relieve hassles by serving as the same setting for school and community events. It could be the stage for Drama Club's three one-act plays, the National Honor	(1) Convenience. Now, attendees at events must wander the building's maze to find the different locations for meetings, speeches, plays, and ceremonies (where is the Little Theater, the gymnasium, the cafeteria, a specific classroom?). The visitors get lost before the event starts.
	(2) Comfort. Then, attendees must sit in seats too small (the egg-carton Little Theatre) or too arduous of

Society's initiation ceremonies, Student Council campaigns, the annual students' awards ceremony, and for invited guest speakers, and for the PTA, Women's Club, Jaycettes, and Jaycees, a constant, not varying, meeting location.

If you talk to any BCHS student or his/her parents who have attended school plays or graduation, you would surely realize the need for improvement in comfort. Ask any student about The Little Theater and he/she would testify it is claustrophobic atmosphere. You could not help feeling hemmed in when there are twenty-six rows twenty-six seats per row, and a middle aisle wide enough for one person, and I suppose that you are just a little cramped, when you rub shoulders with the person next to you who is not more than two inches away. Have you also heard about the gymnasium? The bleachers leave a little bit to be desired for a pack of at least 1500 students, teachers, and relatives at graduation who must keep a cool composure in 80% relative humidity and who can not fidget or squirm from sitting on a hard, wooden surface without back support. Would not cushioned seats in an auditorium alleviate the need to climb over ten bleacher rows of perturbed parents? I think so.

So often have I seen students stare out of the cafeteria or classroom windows during a speech by a guest speaker or have studied fellow students in the opposite bleachers or the freethrow lines and basketball hoops. You can not deny that a person has tendencies to stray from a speaker, but an auditorium, without windows and court markings, would provide an air of importance and formality intended to keep eyes and ears focused more on the stage and speech than on distractions.

Finally an auditorium could improve the status of both BCHS and Brookfield. We are virtually surrounded by reputable high schools which each have an auditorium— West Allis Central to the east, New Berlin Eisenhower and Delavan-Darien to the south and west, and Port Washington and Brown Deer to the north. What about Brookfield?

The cost of a new building probably tightens your pocketbook; however, if an auditorium is of great concern to Brookfield residents, student organizations like Student Council, Key Club, and the other clubs, could raise money similar to the AFS pizza sales and adult organizations like Jaycettes and Jaycees could donate time and money to lend support. In terms of unity, comfort, and status, is not an auditorium at Brookfield Central High School worth deep consideration?

access and hard and unsupportive (the mountain-peak perches of the backless gym bleachers). And endure 80-degree humidity there also. The visitors get weary as the event continues.

(3) Atmosphere and Effectiveness. The cafeteria, classrooms, and gym are too informal for many events. Thus, the mood of an event may suffer. Plus, the places are too distracting. In the cafeteria or classrooms, attendees stare out of the windows. In the gym, they stare at people in the opposite bleachers, or at freethrow markings and the like. Thus, the visitors may miss parts of the event.

(4) Status. Always, participants will realize that other high schools to our north, south, east, and west all have their auditoriums. People may get embarrassed about this lack of an appropriate venue.!

True, cost is a factor; but, fundraising might help. For these four reasons, consider a Brookfield auditorium now.

\=\+|+\=\+|+|

[3] proposed "best" OUTLINE (by the instructor):

I CONVENIENCE of one central accessible location

II COMFORT for attendees
A Seating: access; size, support
B Humidity control

III APPROPRIATENESS
A Formality of mood for events.
B Non-distracting atmosphere for attendees.

IV STATUS in re other high schools

V COST a factor but approachable.

[4]   Five student outlines of "Brookfield" *before* this training in **Reading Texts Conceptually:**

I PARENTS	I INCONVENIENCE	I INTRODUCTION	I CURRENT VENUES	I INCONVENIENCES
A Searched	A Lack of Centrality	A Special Events in	A Little Theatre	A Lack of Centrality
1 Places	B Claustrophobia	Brookfield	B Cafeteria	B Discussions
B Relieve Hassels	C Hot Weather	B Possible Solution	C Gym	C Improve By Addition
1 Events	Seating	II REASONS FOR		
	D Distractions	BUILDING		
II STUDENTS	1 courts	A Problems Finding Places	II PROBLEMS	II UNITY
A Little Theater	2	B How an Auditorium Would	A Uncomfortable	A Stray from Speaker
			B Crowded	1 Windows

194

1 Atmosphere B Gym 1 Bleachers III DISTRACTED A Cafeteria B Classroom C Gym D Auditorium	II COST 1 Students Raise 2 Auditorium	Help **III PROBLEMS OF EXISTING PLACES** A Little Theater B Gymnasium **IV WHY AN AUDITORIUM IS BETTER** A Attention Span B Distractions **V BROOKFIELD ALONE** A Every Surrounding School **VI POSSIBLE FUNDRAISERS**	C Distracting **III WHY AN AUDITORIUM?** A Improve Standing	2 Court Markings **III NEW AUDITORIUM** A Improve Status of BHS B Tightens Your Pocketbook

…do the above wayward target-missing instances, support my case: average students need training in better reading?

I say again—you are performing overkill. Surely all students do not (1) write précis and outlines as badly as this, (2) do not need the perfection skills in this which you urge here!	But should not students be able to read and write as competently as a good précis and outline requires? *To efficiently improve hundreds maybe thousands of hours of activity, in school now, and in their "real-life" future later: on the job and in community later on?* Especially when (1) many students <u>do lack</u> this expertise (as my research found) ***but*** (2) can <u>gain</u> expertise relatively quickly (as these experiments suggest)...

[5] Brookfield" *PRECIS* by students, seemed worse than their OUTLINES:

[5A] Suggested Model or "More-Ideal" PRECIS (by Instructor):

Despite cost problems, Brookfield Central High School needs a new auditorium for reasons of convenience (one central location for all events), comfort (seating accessibility and also seating comfort; humidity-control), appropriateness of setting (to dignify presentations, to keep audience non-distracted by architectural features), and status (in re neighboring high schools).

[5B] Student précis, arranged from lesser to somewhat better...

[0.] Too long to keep my interest. She repeats a little in places but she did use examples to prove her point. Gets the point across.
[Obviously misunderstands the concept of a précis. But more—does competently critique the writer's wordiness, but also over-mechanically applies a rule ("use examples"). Plus, applies the hideously-subliminal standard of competence in writing, "S/he <u>gets the point across</u>." But almost all writing does—average unchallenging writing anyhow. So does an eructation, A/K/A a belch... So also in sports, one usually can "hit the side of a barn wall with a tennis ball," thus "succeeding," but...]

[1.] Without an auditorium, BCHS and Brookfield are nothing.

[2.] Let's consider building an auditorium for BCHS. **[These first two of course never left the starting-gate]**

[3.] The writer feels the need for an auditorium for the school in order to better accommodate special events or speakers and bring status to the school.

[4.] BCHS needs one comfortable setting for group activities, which would improve its status and not be expensive for the community.
[These next two interestingly and in-completely fetch up only one minor (different) and one major (status) point...]

[5.] An auditorium in Brookfield would alleviate the crowdedness, back pains, and confusion set forth from the numerous areas that are being utilized today.
["Brief," but also quite jumbled: unable to fetch or capture points in order, in proportion, and completely! If a mirror of the text, it's a broken-glass cubist mirror-image?...]

[6.] The citizens of Brookfield are dissatisfied with their meeting places for special events. They would like a meeting place without any distractions whatsoever. The auditorium could be paid out of student organizations and adult organizations.
[A hideous, grossly-distorted version. Very minor points are given most of the excess verbiage here!]

[7.] BCHS needs an auditorium because the gym gets too crowded and there is no centrality in the cafeteria. They need a place, like an auditorium, where there can be centrality, space, and being comfortable.
[Sheer inaccuracies: it's not the gym which is claustrophobic, nor is the cafeteria the only outlying place. Another skimpy skim-over...]

1.5. READING "II": When reading MORE-IMPLICIT TEXTS ("LITERARY"), do students stumble?

Task. Ability to read competently a text whose point is left implicit, subliminal, not overt:

EXAMPLE. "The Knee," a one-paragraph essay from <u>JAMA</u>, the Journal of the American Medical Association's literary page. [Scene: a hospital.] **ASSIGNMENT:** "Read the text and conceptualize it, extract its "point" if any, and write that point in a good précis or summary." What follows on the right-hand side are the student results… **FOLLOWUP:** the students were then shown the re-arranged sequence…	

The essay as it appeared: point present but implicit:	The 18 *student* precis before training in conceptualizing UP: The 19th and last is *my own* version. **(*) *Arranged in reverse order of abstraction, the more concrete on the top!***
THE KNEE We are on attending rounds with the usual group attending: senior residents, junior residents, and medical students. There are eight of us. Today we will learn how to examine the knee properly. The door is open. The room is ordinary institutional yellow, a stained curtain between the beds. We enter in proper order behind our attending physician. The knee is atttached to a woman, perhaps 35 years old, dressed in her own robe and nightgown. The attending physician asks the usual questions as he places his hand on the knee: "This knee bothers you?" All eyes are on the knee; no one meets her eyes as she answers. The maneuvers begin—abduction, adduction, flexion, extension, rotation. She continues to tell her story, furtively pushing her clothing between her legs. Her endeavors are hopeless, for the full range of knee motion must be demonstrated. The door is open. Her embarrassment and helplessness are evident. More maneuvers and a discussion of knee pathology ensue. She asks a question. No one notices. More maneuvers. The door is open. Now the uninvolved knee is examined—abduction, adduction, flexion, extension, rotation. She gives up. The door	1. I have no idea what the point is in "The Knee" was 2. How to examine the knee properly [*utter fly-over vacancy…*] 3. The patient gets looked over as the physician and students examine her knee for medical betterment and a learning experience [*mere" plot"*] 4. Learning how to examine the knee properly involves several steps [*quite general*] 5. What an examination of the knee entails. The maneuvers for a knee examination consist of abduction, adduction, flexion, extension, and rotation [*more detail but still plot-level*] 6. 1) Examining the knee. 2) What does a patient go through during an examination? [*toward a point, but still "buried"*] 7.A group of students follow a physician into a room to examine a patience knee. The patient seems nervous with everyone watching. Nobody pays much attention to her. The physician moves the knee around to show how it moves and they discuss it, then they do the same thing to the good knee [*Trapped in "inchworm" plot summary only…*] 8. The doctor is showing the boringness of making rounds 9. Beware! Doctors might have more than one thing on their mind [*This and #8 seem like "irrelevant, ricochet-responses"*] 10. Predicaments of doctor and patient as observed by a resident [*An abstraction, but still quite general…*] 11. As doctors we have a different perspective of what is happening during an exam; we are not out to embarrass the patient, but to treat and heal [*Interesting "side-point"…*] 12. As a team of interns examines a knee, the patient is irrelevant [*…these begin to move toward the thesis…*] 13. To show how doctors concentrate so heavily on just what they are examining, not so much the patient 14. The doctors are more involved in the processes of the knee than the person's feeling about the situation 15. The patient's feelings are of little concern to residents and medical students 16. Doctors examining patients treat them as a problem instead of getting emotionally involved with them 17. Some professionals are so concerned with mechanical formalities and perfection that they disregard the fact that they are inneracting with actual sensitive, concerned, and curious human being 18. Do not ignore your patient. Listen to them, answer their questions and discuss their situation in terms they understand. Don't embarrass your patient, make them comfortable and relaxed [*shifts point toward audience of medical students, assumes purpose is to make aware and instruct…*]

is open. Now a discussion of surgical technique. Now review the knee examination. We file out through the open door. She pulls the sheet up around her waist. She is irrelevant.

[-- CONSTANCE J. MAYO]

19. Physicians too often seem to concentrate upon a patient's symptoms, especially in the setting of hospital rounds, and to overlook the patient's human needs for basic privacy, and also basic communication including information

[* This last, #19, is the *best*, and {[I feel} the *only satisfactory*, conceptual reading of the text. Anyhow, represents the actual skeleton-outline of the "argument" or substance, if not the sequential structure; hence, a true precis...]

A colleague said, "This is boring, also overdone like you usually do? Why not go right to the best precis and let it go at that?" I think he was kidding and/or jealous/envious admirable. Because, you would not *believe*, how *powerful* this "A-to-Z Transformation" (part of another higher-level thinking skill) was for beginning learners. To show "all" the steps, stations, segments, rungs on the ladder, showed them powerfully *the very concept* of the range of the specific and the general! Meaning, how they might be falling short of true conceptualizing. Plus for later how they can fine-tune and adjust to be more general but also more specific-concrete if needed! *Thus the benefits of an Z-to-Z continuum...*

#|+#|+|#+|#+|+#||+||#++##|+|+|#+|#+#|+|+#|+|+#|+|#|||+|+#|#+|#+|+|+#|+|+#|+|#+|#+#++#|+|#|+|#|+#|+#|+|#+|#|+|+#|+#|+#|+#|+#|+#|+#|+#|+|#|+|#+|#|+|#+|#+|+|+|#+|#+|

TEACHING EXAMPLE. Reading traditional proverbs, also classic poetry, students under-read. They can't rise to the concept itself—they just give another example. But I addressed this sidewise shortfalling head-on by *being conceptually-clear... about concrete-vs.-conceptual*:

[1.] THREE LEVELS OF READING IMPLICITLY... Researchers in a mental hospital asked schizophrenics to state what certain common proverbs meant. They **Conceptually Shortfell.** They remained DOWN at the same level. Beginning learners may move SIDEWAYS and give another example for the concept. More "thought-ful" readers can induct, conceptualize UPward to the subliminal core concept.

1. *A Rolling Stone Gathers No Moss*:
Schizophrenics: (A) "It won't grow any grass." (B) "The stone keeps rolling endlessly." (C) "A person could answer that better if he were a stone."
Beginners: "If a guy keeps on moving, he'll stay fresh."
Conceptualizing: "Something in motion will not acquire static qualities."

2. *People In Glass Houses Shouldn't Throw Stones*:
Schizophrenics: (A) "Because they'd break the glass." (B) "You shouldn't throw stones at people."
Beginners:
Conceptualizing: "People vulnerable to a mode of attack shouldn't use that attack on others."

(3) *When The Cat's Away, The Mice Will Play*:
Schizophrenics: (A) "If the father is away, things get harmed." (B) "Nobody will watch the mice."
Beginners: (A) "When teacher's away, the students will play" (B) "In the office, the boss is gone, the workers will play."
Conceptualizing: "When authority or threatening figures are absent, those in whose charge they are, may well feel freer."

[2.] TRADITIONAL EASTERN PROVERBS, translated by the poet W. S. Merwin:
Easy: concrete stimulus leads to *explicitly*-stated abstract meaning:

1. Sudden / like a spear from a window. [Students said: "like a bolt from the blue"]
2. The news wakes you / like water poured into your ears.
3. Rough water drowns the gosling / money drives out manners / poverty drives out reason.
4. Smart / a cat rolling an egg. [more implicit: "delicately-adroit actions are sage..."]

More tricky: "thesis-statement" or concept is *implicit*:

5. Rat climbs an ox horn / narrower / and narrower.
6. Ants on a millstone / whichever way they walk / they go around with it.
7. Jelly / in a vise.
8. Iron hinge / straw door.

--As for #7, Jelly in a vise: *"somebody is trying to compress or hold on to a substance which actually is non-resistant, hard-to-compress, and is probably not succeeding in controlling it thus."* And from there you might go to:

197

"it is hard or impossible to control evasive soft entities." That's the conceptual theme. Now don't confuse it, with other possible examples of the theme. *Jelly in a vise* being the poem's example. Others being perhaps "A very *weak, or adaptable, person* cannot be shaped up." Or, *"If you stay loose, you won't be injured* as readily."

--As for #6, easy would be the ants on a millstone. *"Beings are moving, but also being moved, on their location."* Therefore, "Some beings may have local freedom, but their larger travel is enforced by bigger circumstances."

--And #5, the rat climbing a horn: *"A being proceeds to a more and more limited end-point."* Hence, "some peoples' routes of escape or progress are inevitably limited, indeed dead-end"

--What does #8, "iron door straw hinge" mean? Something like, "a chain is only as strong as its weakest link?" Not hardly, that's concrete for concrete. Rather, *"Strong protection needs to be strong in all ways."*

[3.] POEMS: "The Sick Rose" by William Blake, and "Nothing Gold Can Stay," by Robert Frost:

O Rose, thou art sick! / The invisible worm / That flies in the night / In the howling storm, // Has found out thy bed / Of crimson joy, / And his dark secret love / Doth thy life destroy.

But in English 102, confusion reigned, as follows:

"Does it mean marital *infidelity*?"
"No, it means *Communism* threatening America!"
"Well, I think it means literal *horticulture*."
"No, it means insidious physical *disease* of the reproductive organs."

But conceptually, the poem *means* this, and only this: *"Some force of destruction is threatening something beautiful but vulnerable, in a sinister and even amorous fashion."* Period! All the above statements seem merely other **Concrete** examples or instances, of this central **Concept**.

["Humpty Dumpty," about the egg that fell off the wall and the king's forces couldn't put him back together again, was supposed to symbolize the fall of an English monarch centuries ago when it was written. But it could also mean, more conceptually, *"something which is fragile and at risk for breakage, may be non-reparable even by the forces that be, and perhaps shouldn't have been in a risky spot to begin with...."*]

One more. "Nothing Gold Can Stay," by Robert Frost.

"Nature's first green is gold, / her hardest hue to hold. / Her early leaf's a flower; / but only so an hour. // Then leaf subsides to leaf. / So Eden sank to grief, / So dawn goes down to day. / Nothing gold can stay.

[[The conceptual core: *"earliest nature and also culture and time, has beauty which fades quickly."*]]

#|+#|+|#+|#+|+#||+||#++##|+|+|#+|+|#+|+|#||+|+#|+|#+|+|+#||+|+#|++|||#+||#+#+#+|#+|+|#+|#|+#+|+|#+|#+|+|#+|#+|+|#+|+|+#+|#+|+|+#+|+#+|+|#++|#+|+|#+|+|#+|+#+|#+|+|#+|+|#+|#+|

[1.4.B.] Can students move to conceptualize their *own* writings?

TASK. "Fast-Food Noon-Hour Student-Rowdiness." To be able to create an outline of a given topic (imaginary), showing concepts (subpoints) and also concrete elements (examples) and differentiating the two.

THE ASSIGNMENT: "Imagine the subject of rowdy students *misbehaving in all sorts of ways* in a fast-food restaurant at noon. Then, write up an outline you could use to write a strong paper about this lively event."

EXAMPLE. **Restaurant Rowdiness:** Glimpsed *Concretely*, vs. Grasped *Conceptually*	
(-): **(1) Seven student outlines *before* training in abstracting:** *skimpy, non-structured, gives concrete examples as if abstract ideas!:*	(+): **(2) And my suggested model or ideal outline:** Suggested conceptualization of the thesis: *arrives at ideas, but includes specifics too:*
[1.] 1. Flooded the bathrooms	To Elucidate the very *concepts* of—(1) explicit **Conceptualizing**, plus then **(2) Categorizing** into multi-level sub-points. Also in (3) also

2. Step on ketchup packets
3. Wrote on windows with jelly
4. Took paintings off walls
5. Played their boom boxes too loud
6. Rude to the customers

[2.]
1. Counter
2. Table
3. Bathroom
4. Lot

[3.]
1. Loud Rude Obnoxious
2. Take Up Half the Seats
3. Smoke A Lot, Mess Things Up

[4.]
1. Crowding
2. Dirty
3. Long Lines

[5.]
1. Eat like pigs
2. Throw food
3. Don't clear tables
4. Stare
5. Steal salt
6. Vulgar
7. Direct Insults
8. Give cashier difficult time

[6.]
1. Noisy
2. Messy
3. Rude

[7.]
1. Shoving in line
2. Spilling drinks
3. Embarrassing their parents

Concretizing *within* the outline: for this, I insert specific examples of the idea, but with "X" and in italics, to differentiate concrete from conceptual.

I. Material Damage
(A) Vandalism
l. Merely defacing or minor
(x flooded bathroom)
(x wrote on porcelain with pens)
2. More actually damaging
(x made 6" tears in vinyl seats)
(x mistreated newspapers)
(B) Theft
l. Minor
(x stole ketchup cups)
2. Major
(x stole trash cans from out back)

II Pranks & Sloppiness
(A) Food
1. Played with condiments
(x stamped ketchup on floor)
(x smeared jelly on windows)
2. Did food fights
(x threw french fries)
(x tossed ice cubes)
(A) Non-Food
(x poured Coke on green plants)
(x took pictures off the walls)

III Other people
(A) Customers
1. Senior citizens
(x blocked SC van with a car)
(x insulted the "old codgers")
2. General
a. Misbehavior in the lines
(x pushed and shoved, jostled)
(x cut in to the line's front)
b. other misbehavior
(x played boom boxes too loud)
(B) Employees
a. harrassment
(x changed orders several times)
b. insults
(C) Each Other
...

On the above "beast-to-beauty" evidence, I rest my case in favor of explicit training in outlining—if and as needed of course, but it probably *is*... If students tend to produce only the *still-born and misshapen-embryonic* left-hand versions as an "outline," and if the vastly-different right-hand version represents how one *can* *think-out* a subject, **well, then**...

#|+#|+|#+|#+|+#||+||#++##|+|+|#+|+|#+#|+|+#|+|#|+|#|||+|+#|#+|#+|+|+|#+|+#+|+|#+||#+|#+#+#|#+|+#|+|#|+|#|+|#|+|#+|#+|+#|#+|+#+|+|#+|#+||+|#+|#|+|+#|#+|

WRITING. Students <u>were able</u> to conceptualize their papers on "a job they'd held" from the initial naïve concrete-level subjects, to the more-thoughtful ideas or themes, thus.
NOTE: they did this **Autonomously**, once shown the principle; I did *not* "correct" their papers which they then simply re-copied...

EXAMPLES. Three student outlines of their essays before, and after, work in conceptualizing.

First subject. "**Hazards** in a Job as a **Nursing Home Aide**":

I Slipping	I From Environment
	A. Surfaces
II Burns	B. From Equipment & Supplies
	1. cooking gear, 2. cleaning gear, 3. medical gear
III Harm from residents	
A. biting, B. scratching	II from Personnel
	A. Residents
IV Getting cut	B. Careless Co-Workers
A. knives, B. slicers	
	III From Psychological Stress

Second subject: "**Vocational Skills** Learned Working at **Burger King**":

I Manager relationships	I Learning to communicate with higher employees
A. Gene, B. Julie, C. Spencer	A. Scheduling managers
	B. Assistant managers
II Fellow Employee relationships	
A. Nikki, B. Pam, C. Chris, D. Kari	II Making friends with others
	A. Cooks, B. Cashiers
III Customer relationships	
A. Drunks, B. Regulars	III Improving Social Skills
	A. Serving customers

Third subject: "Teaching **Second-Grade Art** Requires **Patience**":

I Mailman	I Messiness of the kids
A. Sticky fingers from the glue mess	A. Environment
B. Crayon all over desk	1. desk *(x crayons)*
C. Kids covered with ink from markers	2. floor *(x pink paint)*
	B. Kids themselves
II Mr. Sunshine	1. skin *(x glue fingers)*
A. Scissors are dangerous	2. clothing *(x marker ink)*
B. Glue gets messy	
	II Dangers of the equipment
III Watermelon Making	*(x scissors are sharp)*
A. Eating the melon and saving seeds	
B. Floor covered with pink paint	III Wrong procedures used by kids
C. Gluing on more seeds.	A. Inabilities to do skills
	(x glued on too many seeds)
	(x ate the watermelons instead)
	B. Forgetfulness, Inattention

I felt immense *satisfaction* upon seeing these students leap to the **Conceptual** level, after minimal (but apparently-needed) training on the **Ladder of Abstraction** issue.

#|+#|+|#+|#+|+#||+||#++##||+|+##+|+#+#|+|#+|+#||+|#|||+|+#|#+|#+|+|+#|+|#+|+#++|+#|+|#+|+|#++##+|#+|+#|+#|#||#+|#|#|#|#+|+#|+|#++#|+|+#++#+|#+|+#|+#|+|#+|#++#|#+|+#+|+|#+|+#|+|+|#+|#+|

6. SHORTFALLING in "REAL LIFE": In many activities we do in Personal, Vocational, and Community arenas, thinkers may fail to conceptualize up. They may remain on concrete operations level, may miss the keystone principles needed for mastery of the action...

The **Subject**	Factual **Content** present in "real-	The key **Concepts** which many texts omit, if their authors

discussed:	world" publications:	even derived them:
"CHINESE STIR-FRY COOKING"	Ingredients: vegetables, meat. Soy, ginger, garlic, flour. Etc.	"Small-Sized Food Pieces, Hot Pan Heat, Oil Added Only When Pan Hot, Ingredients Added so All are Done Cooking Simultaneously, Constant-Continuous Vigorous Stirring, and Very Brief Cooking Time."
"EVALUATING A RESTAURANT MEAL"	specific meals, menus, chefs, restaurants, experiences [from the book Dining Out, about restaurant cooking, meals, reviewing, etc... *I myself had to abstract out the right-hand column of concepts buried in the book's descriptions...*]	1. Historical-Social-Traditional A. Classic vs. Innovation B. Ethnic variations C. Basic Flavor-Balance 1. Personal-Individual A. The Particular Chef B. The Particular Diner/Critic 3. Explicit Ranking-Criteria A. Star-systems B. Severity of Standards?
"CRITERIA FOR PUBLIC-ART DISPLAYS"	unconceptualized opinions, the assumptions not clear [from Letters to the Editor of the Milwaukee Journal]	1. Conventional Folk-Familiarity 2. Trendy-Edgy Fashionable 3. Laissez-Faire Relativism 3. Pure Visual Aesthetic Design 4. Meaningful Staying-Power 5. ...at least a half-dozen other concepts...
"TIME-MANAGEMENT"	this and that technique [...various accounts of Time M. are variously-conceptual; too many lack the ideas as in the right-hand column...]	1. Goal-setting. 2. Prioritizing; specifically, 3. Ranking tasks in four very important categories: as to whether "Urgent and Important; Urgent but not Important; Important but not Urgent; neither Urgent nor Important" 4. Lead-Time Planning: Stages
HUMOR, WIT	No or vague ideas.	1. Aggression. Malice at others' misfortunes. 2. Repression. Topics taboo to discuss. 3. Surprise; Incongruity. "The collapse of a strained expectation into nothing.
MICROWAVE OVENS	This and that recipe	Size, placement of food for best cooking...
COMPUTERS	Endless instructions...	"Functional Abstraction": a hierarchy of parts, with well-define one-directional interactions. Some separation of levels from each other...
PARALLELISM (IN WRITING)	"Avoid faulty parallelism at the sentence-level"	# If a series of ideas are related logically, then phrase them in related language-style, so the reader sees the relationship."
SPECIFICITY (IN WRITING)	"Support your ideas with specific examples."	# "Our ideas and emotions come from specific—experiences, evidence. So put in to your writing not only your ideas, but the evidence, to re-create them in the reader more powerfully."
SYNTAX (IN WRITING)	This and that rule...	"Place important info in main clauses, secondary information in subordinate clauses. Place old and secondary and orienting info early in the sentence, place new and important info at the sentence's—end." [The mind processes better via this style.]

#|+#|+|#+|#+|+#||+||#++##|+|+|+#+|+|#+#||+|+#|#+|+|#||]+|+#|#+|#+|+|+#|+|#|++|+||#+||#++#+|#+|+|#|+|#|#+|#|+|#|+|#|+|+#|#+|+|#+|#+|+|#||+#|+|#+|#+|

7. SHORTFALLING in the "SCHOOL" Arena: Many courses may still dwell low-down on the factual level. They do not make Present (embed and exhibit), higher-level keystone concepts...

The subject taught:		Usual **factual-content**, and lower-level skills:	Higher-order keystone **concepts** of the subject:
algebra		(various formulae)	"combination," "permutation," "association"—the **keystones**
sociology		Institutions, social problems. Often some **concepts** (role, status, norm, deviancy, socialization, etc.)	**Theories:** Functionalism, Conflict, Interactionism... **Perspectives:** Debunking, Unrespectable, Cosmopolitan, Relativism...
art history		Egyptian, Greek, Medieval styles....and so forth.	Composition **principles:** balance, proportion, sequence, unity, a/symmetry, simplicity, contrast! Line, form, value,!

literature	Periods. Authors. Themes.	"Schools of Criticism" as **lenses**: biographical, aesthetic, historical, psychological, social-critical, etc.!
computers	this and that program...	"linear sequentiality"
economics	formulae, data on problems...	"scarcity" "allocation cost," or "cost-benefit ratio"—as immensely-applicable everywhere, always!
Natural Sciences	Biology, etc.: facts of mitosis-meiosis and the like, more...	General Concepts of Science: Dynamic Equilibrium; Change & Evolution; Scale & Proportion; Causality & Consequence; Energy, Its Sources & Transfer...
geography	[data, data, data...]	["Why is it like it is, here?"]
political science	[info on government systems]	How to confront the recurrent Big Issues: individual freedom vs. group security, etc., etc., etc.
history	"kings, courts, dates..."	[Past-present continuities, dissimilarities, etc.]
math		Problem-solving: Trial and error; "Step backwards"; Simulation; Symbolism; Patterns... Cause-and-Effect...
OTHERS:		
APPLIEDS:	Business, Engineering, Law, Medicine, Technology, Military, Government, etc...	

#|+#|+|#+|#+|+#||+||#++#||+|+|#+|+|#+#|+|+#|+#|+|+|#|||+|+#|#+|#+|+|+#|+|+#|+#+|+||#||#+#+#+|#+|+#|+#|+#|+|#+|#+|#+|+#|+|#+#|+|+#|#|+#|+#|+|#+|+|#+|#+|+|+|#+|+#|#+|

8. SUBJECTS AND SITUATIONS. And when "reading" or confronting not texts but event-issues (in both "RESEARCH" and in "REAL LIFE" (Personal, Vocational, Civic), do students—and others—fall short from discovering / creating concepts and patterns, of "Reading The Situation"?

E. T. HALL, anthropologist, sets the challenge, and the goal... But we can do it!

"Reading the behavior of well-known friends and relatives is like covering thoroughly familiar ground without a mental map or talking before writing systems had ever been heard of. One does not need a writing system to talk (or technical awareness of the rules governing speech either). [*However,*] To abstract such a system from the living data where none existed before, however, is a formidable task, an intellectual achievement that can equal the great accomplishments in chemistry, physics, and astronomy." [-- E. T. HALL, ANTHROPOLOGIST]

I see what you mean, reading the situation... But this is too advanced. We, and our students, aren't going to be doing this original research on unknown areas!	[*groan...*] Ah, but see, we *all* will be confronting in real life, situations which are *new-to-us*! See?... [*sigh...*]

--Ideologies, Schools of Thought, Systems. (Lenses: viewpoints perspectives etc.) *Traditional humanism.. Extreme diversity.*

--The academic fields or disciplines. *World-views of humanities, social sciences, natural sciences... Pure, and applied: "the logic of medicine" to be grasped by a citizen non-physician, a patient's relative.*

--Historical Sociology: periods in culture. .... *American traditional culture... The Sixties ... Boomer-generation youth today., ... Traditional **versus** Postmodern assumptions in the humanities... Education: "Old-School" vs. "New-Think" paradigms...*

--Space, Changes: *East **versus** West generally... Writing: Writing differently even within English studies... General School or academic writing, **versus** writing in the world: Personal, especially Vocational on the Job, Civic-Community... Freelance Journalism... When job-interviewing, specific businesses' "corporate cultures..."*

--Groups, Varied: *"Sexuality:" views of traditional religion, **versus** views of liberationist or diversity-minority studies.*

--Literary and Artistic Genres: *Art, 10 facets of... Detective story rules, formula... Schoolwriting, schoolreading... .*

THREE EXAMPLES of "Reading the Situation" [SEE #A "Why The Very Idea" for *FULL*-Dress treatment...]
[1.] The RECENT GRADUATE has to learn how to "read **the 'corporate culture' of a company**" with which (or whom) they are interviewing for a job. To spot the issues, do's and don't's, to read the culture...

[2.] I MYSELF had to learn <u>as a writer</u> how to shift from academic writing, and read the **<u>varying situational</u> <u>demands</u>** of freelance magazine feature-articles, the unstated ground rules, and change from schoolwriting:

1. <u>Length</u>: in school, "at least 500 words"; outside, "one-page minimum" or the like.
2. <u>Tone</u>: in school, often formal-impersonal; outside, usually a person on the page.
3. <u>Structure</u>: in school, sometimes lead up to the point; outside, announce the conclusion first.
4. <u>Audience</u>: in school, a vacuum—the professor is the reader; outside, rhetorical tuning.
5. <u>Graphics</u>: in school, just prose on the page; outside, often charts-tables-diagrams, etc.

[3.] EDUCATORS AND STUDENTS may have to read **<u>the new paradigm of teaching thinking,</u>** different from Old-School emphasis on what to know and believe. But how? It took me more than two decades to clarify this! Below, a quite inadequate, but sufficient, glimpse:

Goals: what to Know, Believe, Do ===== how to Think Things Through
Role of Student: passive receiver of information ===== active learner
Role of Teacher: imparter of information ===== coach, facilitator, etc.
"Accuracy": correctness, error-avoidance is key ===== make mistakes but learn!
Decisions: most made by course, teacher ===== more made by student
Knowledge acquisition: atomized parts ===== accretive integrated wholes
Assessment: simple testing ===== transfer to new situations

#|+#|+|#+|#+|+#||+||#++##|+|+|+#+|+|#+#|+|+#|+#|+|+#|||+|+#|#+|#+|+|+#|+|+#|+#+|+||#+||#+#+#+|#+|+#|+#|+#|+|#+|+#|+#|+#|+#|#+|+#+|+|#+|#+|#+|#+|+|#+|#+|

9. And so—perhaps "we all" perhaps under-induct. Perhaps we can improve.

<u>EXAMPLE</u>. RICHARD PAUL'S description of concepts beyond concrete "moves" in **tennis**:

..."always return to the ready position at the center of the court," "keep your weight distributed," "bend your knees when stroking the ball," "follow through whenever possible," "watch the ball closely when you hit it," and so forth.

CON: Whoa. Egg on Paul's face? For, he himself is still shortfalling? Because you can go more conceptual even here. Because, all his "principles," are in turn only *examples* of the two higher, more general, concepts of—*READINESS* and *ARTICULATION*...

<u>EXAMPLE</u>. The critic MARK TAYLOR, in <u>The Literary Mind</u>, explicated the proverb, **<u>"When the cat's away,</u> <u>the mice will play"</u>**:

...said at the office, can be projected onto a story of boss and workers. Said in the classroom, it can be projected onto a story of teachers and students. Said of sexual relationships, it can be projected onto a story of infidelity. With equal ease, we can project it onto stories of a congressional oversight committee and the industries regulated by that committee, a police force and the local thieves, or a computer security device and the computer viruses it was intended to control.

...and this was it. So strictly speaking, are all these "the meaning" of the proverb? Or did TAYLOR himself commit **Conceptual Shortfalling** here? We suggested earlier that the **core-concept**ual "meaning" is more like *"When authority figures are absent, those in whose charge they are, may well misbehave."* Perhaps technically, TAYLOR should have made **explicit** this keystone, **higher-level** idea?

<u>EXAMPLE</u>. The educators MERRILL AND TENNYSON call **concepts** "<u>a set of specific objects, symbols, events</u> <u>grouped together according to shared characteristics, and which can be referenced by a particular name or</u> <u>symbol</u>." [I prefer the earlier definition: a quality of a thing apart from its specific examples"...] Here are the examples of "concepts" which they then give. *Are they "conceptual" enough?*

...computer, house, adverb, Theory Y, haiku, profit, cartoon, forehand serve, triangle, prime number, blue, reptile, Impressionism, igneous, cold war, hunting-gathering, norm, pulley, scapegoat, bull market, beard, tax-sheltered annuity, cumulus cloud...

Might we do better? In fact is this a modest *bungle*? **Conceptuality as a concept!** Ironically, many of the subjects mentioned *seem* <u>quite concrete or specific</u>, *perhaps* do not ascend to the conceptual. <u>Here is how I would advance their roster:</u>

<u>reptile</u>, <u>blue</u>, <u>triangle</u>, <u>Impressionism</u>—*these* do seem <u>good</u>....many interesting elements within each....

<u>computer</u>—a rather concrete, specific object! ***And so,*** ➜ how about *Boolean logic, algorhythms & heuristics, parallel and serial processing* and also *quantum computing,* also *self-organizing systems,* and also the principle of *Functional Abstraction*? I would also add *sequentiality* for word-processing; if a foulup, back up 2 or 3 or 4 stages, steps, screens!]

<u>house</u>—➜ how about "*shelter,*" also "*buildings*"?

<u>adverb</u>—but ➜ how about "*parts of speech,*" indeed "*grammar,*" upward into other important but overlooked salient concepts in linguistics, such as...?

<u>forehand serve</u>—*but alas, how about "position," "readiness," "timing" in tennis?!*

FINANCIAL: <u>tax-sheltered annuity</u>, <u>bull market</u>, <u>profit</u>—but ➜ how about **"asset-allocation," risk-reward ratio,"** "*diversification*" and other important key **concepts**, especially **variable-issues** to confront, in personal financial management, a hot task-goal in the real world of Personal Life?

<u>pulley</u>—rather *poor*? ➜ What about physics' *forces* I cannot even name? We recall the comment of JAMES TREFIL the physics teacher: in solving new problems, students tend to look to familiar surface features "inclined planes or pulleys" and not "forces" or "energy conservation." In a collision problem, it's "which body is moving faster" and not "equal and opposite action and reaction forces."

<u>hunting-gathering</u>—but ➜ how about *socio-economic organization*, the umbrella concept here?

Have you proved your point *yet*?	No proof, just decide whether I *have* a significant point—or maybe not, admittedly. But, the issue is **whether "we" do pervasively shortfall** from conceptualizing, from working material for its key concepts… And whether to improve, is possible, pragmatic, principled, *pleasurable*…

#|+#|+|#+|#+|+#||+|#++##|+|+#+|#+|+#|+|+#|+|#||+|+#|#+|#+|+|+#|+|+#|+|+#||#+||#++#+#|#+|+#|+#|+#|+|#+|#+|+#|#+|+#+|+|#+|#+|+#|+|#+|+#||+|#|#+|

<table>
<tr><td>[1.] The very concept of a concept. PRIOR</td><td>[2.] Checklist of skills for Induction, Deduction: read and write a text, "read" a situation. CURRENT</td><td>[3.] Demo: INduction DEduction and ASsociational thinking in action: "Writing a Theme" TO COME</td></tr>
</table>

[2.] Checklist of BASIC SKILLS for induction (& deduction), in reading, writing, experiencing…

"I" "Brief Version" of Conceptualizing UP or INduction 101…

1. TEXTS, WRITTEN

1.A. <u>Can learner **read** a text of *another* writer</u> for its ideas not just facts. Write a good précis and outline of text? [For "easy" texts, simple ideas *or* complex but well-written ?== but also for "hard" texts, complex ideas *or* badly-written?]

1.B. <u>Can learner **write** a text of one's *own* experience and ideas</u> and conceptualize, not just report facts?

Degree of **Competence** here: (A) **Passive Awareness:** critique the texts of *others*? Identify pitfalls/errors (obvious, glaring, undebatable == subtle, frequent, tricky)? Also identify excellences: (ones clearly achieved == but also those potentialities which were *missed*)?

(B) **Active Ability:** …then actually edit and improve the imperfect texts of *others*? 2. Then actively do the same to create

204

and correct/complete *their own* good thought-ful texts?

2. SITUATION. Can learner "read a situation" in the real world? Discover, and/or create, concepts about it: generalizations, etc.? Discover patterns, systems, structures—even if or especially if subliminal, unstated? [EXAMPLES: a religious creed… a company's "corporate culture"… the conventions of a genre: TV shows…]

\#|+\#|+|\#+|\#+|+\#||+||\#++\#\#|+|+|+\#+|+|\#+\#|+|+\#|+\#|+|+|\#|||+|+\#|\#+\#|+|+|+\#|+|+\#|\#++||\#+|\#\#+\#+\#|\#+|+\#|+\#|+\#|+|\#+|+\#|+\#|+|+\#|+\#|+|+\#|+\#|+\#|+\#|+\#|+\#|+|+\#|+\#|+\#|+|\#+|\#+|

ISSUE. The "Ladder of Abstraction" (whether digital by step or analog by degree) can chart the movement between the poles of Stratospheric abstraction and Specific concretization.
Is this useful pedagogically to demonstrate?

GUIDELINE/GOAL: **The learner is conversant with *the very idea of* "vertical levels of abstraction," the specific-general continuum.**
1. Awareness" A. S/he can identify on what level (rung of the ladder) from Material concrete to Mental conceptual is any given (1) observation-point, (2) response: statement/claim or conclusion (observation, conjecture, hypothesis, theory, law, paradigm, etc.)… B. S/he knows the pros-and-cons of being specific, being general…
2. Ability: s/he can place or locate any statement of one's own, at the appropriate level or rung of verticality.

LEVELS, of Concept, of Content... We could quickly show *beginning* learners two **variables**—the basic **levels of thinking** (from data to theory) … the rungs of **subject-matter** from specific to general …

EXAMPLES I of II. (1) **"Vegetarianism"** up and down the ladder:

Levels on the Ladder of Abstraction of *types of THINKING Per Se...*	Standard "subtypes" of *any-all* content (subjects):	Example from *a specific SUBJECT*: here, of "VEGETARIANISM"
Very conceptual, "philosophical" (panoramic **Connections**?)	Higher concepts about	*Social change? Plural viewpoints on veg.? Pros-and-cons? Cause-effect?*
Grand Theories of Everything, "metanarratives"…	Issues or Topics or Aspects:	*Nutrition. Social image. Taste. Economy Convenience*
"Theories of the middle range"? Standard "**variable-issues**"	Process, activity, procedure	*Cooking legumes.* *Getting veg. menu in the school café.*
Hypotheses from Observations	Event: unique or recurrent	*First vegetarian dinner.*
"Sandheap Empiricism"? Data. Concrete phenomena.	Place, locality	*Wheatberry veg. restaurant*
("Diary" "Tues. in ~~Chicago~~" The Loop…")	Person	*Uncle Victor the vigorous vegan.*
	Object	*A pressure-cooker.* *Lentil varieties.*

ISSUE. Specific "Rungs" of the Ladder. Both *observations* (concrete), and *generalizations* (conceptual), can be relatively more *general* hence conceptual, or relatively more *specific* hence concrete...
Is this useful pedagogically to give Awareness of? For a lab-exercise to master Ability in?

Moving downward from first the highest rung on the ladder, to the lowest-possible (or near). Using concepts and also concreteness at various levels variously… And using <u>five types of specifics</u>: 3W Who-When-Where… Anecdotes (incidents)… Sense-imagery… Statistics (quantification)… Dialog…

OBSERVATIONS: *describe, report* concrete-tangible phenomena:	GENERALIZATIONS: *conclusions* drawn, *concepts* produced, *ideas* offered about it:
An *action* occurred between one student individual and another in an eating facility.	[Varied activities] took place [on University property], some of them **INAPPROPRIATE**.
One student *behaved* in an active way toward another regarding *foodstuff*.	In [an eating facility], some student-eaters were engaging in **INAPPROPRIATE MISBEHAVIORS** regarding food.
One *student threw a portion of food* toward and upon another *student*.	A group of undergraduates was **MISBEHAVING** by using food: whether [1] *wasted*, [2] *thrown* at others, or [3] *played with*.
A *boy* threw *potatoes* at the *shirt* of another *boy*.	In [*the cafeteria*], some students **HARASSED** others by throwing food such as *jello* and *potatoes* at them; others *played* with [*food*] by inserting [*objects*] in it; still others *wastefully* took [more food portions than they ended up eating].
On *Monday noon* at *Esker Hall*, *Mark flung* a *tablespoon* of *greasy mashed potatoes* onto *Chad's* **new red plaid** shirt. "*Gotcha!*" he shouted. [N.B.—"**Specific Detailing**" can include 3W or Who-When-Where; Anecdotes; Statistics; Sense-Imagery; Analogies; and Dialog....]	*In Esker Hall today*, **HARRASSMENT** occurred when *Mark flung mashed potatoes at Chad's shirt*; **PLAYFULNESS**, when *Sally stuck straws in her custard* before eating it; and **WASTEFULNESS**, when *Fred left three portions of macaroni on his plate* at the end; .....

Impressive (even if "ornate"…). But <u>you fouled up</u>. In some middle-range cases, you **had some trouble deciding a given word's place on the ladder.** Whether the word was a concrete sense-image… or an observation… or becoming a generalization! So is your "specific-general" idea a simplistic dualism?

You only spot an advanced point. The basic point here is the continuum *to show beginners the difference, plus the rungs on the ladder which are possible. A breadth which many never realize…*

#|+#|+|#+|#+|+#||+||#++##|+|+|+#+|#+#|+|+#|+#|+|+#|||+|+#|#++|+|+#|+|+#+|+||#+||#+#+#+|#+|+#|+#+|#+|#+|+|#+|#++|+|#+|#+|+|#+|#+|+|+|#+|#+|

[3.] CLASS DEMO: three thinking modes in action as I wrote "essay on mobile-home living":

SUMMARY EXERCISE. **Three main ways of thinking seen operating together.** **inducting** "up," but also **deducting** "downward" from concepts to instances, and both aided by **lateral-associative** thinking "across" to connect ideas and examples—as if swinging through trees…

--In the 1980's, my college freshmen had more problems inducting, even on the familiar essay-topic of "a job I've held." So I demonstrated how I observed-thought-wrote-communicated. Specifically, about "<u>Living in a Mobile Home.</u>" It was *pay dirt* for many freshmen…

206

Below, the transcript of my presentation. Right here, the "code" identifying types of thinking in it:

My physical location on site:	Concrete data, observations:	Emerging mid-range ideas :	Emerging higher Concepts, Points:	Associative thinking moves:
Stated in [[REG. CAPITALS, SMALL, BOLD-FACE]]	Stated in *italics*	Stated in **bold-face type**	Stated in SMALL CAPITALS	Shown via arrow "➔"

"Okay, class. What to write about, concerning #70 in Lawnview Trailer Park a mile west of Whitewater, Wisconsin? Well.... I know already AESTHETICS, **I like country living.** Plus there's CONVENIENCE... [[BUT LET'S VISIT THE SITE. I ENTER THE TRAILER THROUGH ITS FRONT DOOR.]] Oh, *the door sticks.* This is due to frost heave, every darn winter! Idea: **WEATHER-RELATED PROBLEMS** with trailer-living (I don't even want to think of ➔SOCIAL PROBLEMS, Lawnview avoids most of them...), I often had to *jack up the trailer underneath to rebalance it* so the door doesn't stick. Can do it yourself, though-- ➔ EASE OF REPAIRS TO A SIMPLER MOBILE HOME, ➔# AHA, AN ADVANTAGE AS WELL AS A DISADVANTAGE! [[BACK DOWN TO REALITY HERE.]] *The screen/storm door is almost torn off its hinges*==**High Winds out here in the country batter the place**➔# Another Advantage, LIVING CLOSER TO NATURE, I do love that! [[Whoa. I enter and close the door]]. *The furnace goes on*; ==I recall when *a mouse died in the furnace and I couldn't remove it, the smell was bad,* ➔another example of both # DISADVANTAGE (oooh, also ==*the plumbing also freezes quicker in very cold weather than in in-town houses,* so we got Bad points: NATURE: TEMPERATURE, also unwanted animals, plus Good points, near to nature, EASE OF REPAIR.....

[[WELL, WE CAN SPEED UP THE FILM. I CONTINUED ON THROUGH THE WHOLE DWELLING, OBSERVING➔REFLECTING:]]

...**more sunlight during more seasons** [➔ AESTHETICS] .....country living but **the park-owner supplies the well and septic services**.....*my mother thought living there was trashy* but *others thought it frugal* [➔ SOCIAL IMAGE]....my cat eats the mice anyhow; my cat is a great cat....older trailer is not well insulated, but that's good in that it doesn't hold heat in summer [PROS AND CONS OF SIMPLE VS. COMPLEX TRAILERS; ➔ AESTHETICS, ECONOMICS] ....easy to repair a leaking roof, I don't have to re-roof, or re-paint the siding....**greater fire danger in the trailer**, *two trailers burned,* and *I myself almost had a fire due to a short in a wire through the floor*.....

...and ended up with a Thesis plus Outline, "Orchids & Onions in re Living in a House Trailer. It became **expository elucidation**, the supple "thesis, points, examples, discussion, conclusion" way of thinking then writing—but clearly beyond the rigid "Five-Paragraph Theme" **Complete**, with multi-level **Classification-and-Division** which **Categorized**; strongly **Conceptual** but also including **Concrete** examples..... (*) For the 15-C model, see ➔ Appendix: Tool-KITS: 150C Expository Elucidation...

ONIONS: a conceptual jumble...	ORCHIDS?: routinized, but clear-complete-conceptual...
# Mobile Home Living. (I) The first time when we moved into the Court. (II) Dealing with pipes freezing in the winter. (III) My Aunt Marjorie's disapproval of our moving from town into the Court. [... *SCORE:* writer *loses*, **fouls out. Raw and sprawling information triumphs ...]**	# Mobile Home Living: Pros and Cons, both Objective and also Subjective. (I) Economics: pros and cons. (Property taxes) (As an investment) (II) Sociology. Social status. Neighbors: the uncontrollable issue.. (III) Politics. Park management: the unknown. (IV) Technology. Easier and cheaper upkeep. (V) Aesthetics. Closer to nature. But also shoddy to some tastes. (VI) Psychological-Biographical. My personal response: floating free from in-town restrictions. [... *SCORE:* **writer largely <u>wins</u>.** **Cuffs the myriad material into concepts, categorizes them too ...** **Admittedly, easily employed or fell back on the "pros-and-cons"** **rubric or blueprint of organizing.** *But still ...]*

#|+#|+|#+|#+|+#||+|#++##|+|+#|+|#+#|+|#|+|#||+|+#+|#+|+#|+|#+|+#|+|#+#|+|#+|+#|+|#+||#+||#+#+#|+|#+|+#|+|#+|+#|+#|+|#+#|+|#+|+#|+|#+|#+|+#|+|#+|+|#+|#+

APP. #3C: "CONCEPTUALIZING" and Four Major Thinking Moves

THE ISSUE, OUR RATIONALE HERE: INduction UPward is involved centrally in these four common key mental moves. Hence, we offer units on them, as *they both serve, and require,* competent **conceptualizing**… Below, the moves, and guidelines available::

[1.] "Letter vs. Spirit" [*pp.* 209 - 225]

GUIDELINE: **Be able to conceptualize up beyond *formal appearance and surface correctness etc.,* to the *reality: spirit, essence, function, goal-purpose.***

This issue includes powerful stuff like the following—*and aren't you glad you asked*…
(1) **Literal vs. figurative**… (2) **letter vs. spirit**… (3) **form vs. function**… (4) **correct vs. effective**… (5) **Principle vs. Procedure**… (6) **appearance vs. reality**… (7) **Change:** surface change vs. underneath continuity… (8) **Formula-vs.-flexibility.** ..(9) "by-the-book" **In Vitro** ("under glass," in laboratory conditions) vs. "by-guideline" **In Vivo** ("in life" or in the Field, situation)… And of course (10) **"Rule"** [algorithm / tactic] vs. **"Tool"** [heuristic / strategy] and the intermediates [**Guidelines, Rules-of-Thumb**]…

[2.] Definition [*pp.* 226 - 231]

GUIDELINE: **define subjects not only literally, but conceptually—hence what is "a map," "wealth," "pornography or obscenity," "religion," and the like. This expands the idea.**

[3.] Analogy [*pp.* 232 – 235]

GUIDELINE: **Know and be able to employ the key truth that Analogies, blending one Material item with another or with a Mental concept, are powerful for thinking items through as well as communicating them better to readers.** "Harvest teacher's corn or grow one's own…"

[4.] "Creativity" [*pp.* 236 – 238]

GUIDELINE: **to solve daily-life problem-issues with no apparent solution at first, *conceptualize up past form etc. to what the goal itself is*. This may reveal the answer.**

We follow "FRED" through his TYPICAL DAY, when during the rainy evening, he found a raincoat-substitute right on hand when no one else saw it. And much more…

#3.C.1. "LETTER vs. SPIRIT" & thinking

[1.] Code: Rationale for this concept...

THE CONCEPT/ISSUE. As for **method-technique-procedure**, a *related cluster of opposed poles* exists:

(1) <u>Literal</u> *vs.* <u>figurative</u>...   (2) <u>letter</u> *vs.* <u>spirit</u>...   (3) <u>form</u> *vs.* <u>function</u>...   (4) <u>correct</u> *vs.* <u>effective</u>...   (5) <u>Principle</u> *vs.* <u>Procedure</u>...   (6) <u>Appearance</u> vs. <u>Reality</u>...   (7) <u>Change</u>: surface change vs. underneath continuity...   And also the larger sub-issue of <u>formula-vs.-flexibility</u>. Here belong two specific issues. First, (8) "by-the-book" *In Vitro* ("under glass," in laboratory conditions) *vs.* "by-guideline" *In Vivo* ("in life" or in the Field, situation)...   Second, of course (9) "<u>Rule</u>" [algorhythm / tactic] *vs.* "<u>Tool</u>" [heuristic / strategy] and the intermediates [Guidelines, Rules-of-Thumb, etc.]...

What is the common element in the crowded cluster above? It's the general issue of <u>simpler and more-concrete thinking vs. complex and more-conceptual thinking</u>. And *specifically* to "Thinking 101" or Conceptualizing INducting UPward. Concrete-literal vs. conceptual-"essence" levels.

THE "SO-WHAT" PROBLEM-OPPORTUNITY. This issue of "correct vs. effective" and the like, is "of course pretty obvious to everyone"—*except where it isn't* for earlier learners who need sheer basic clarifying (as of pitfalls/errors to avoid). And also except that many even aware learners miss advanced subtle points and interrelations (as for potentialities for excellence). "Letter-perfect, but somehow a failure in spirit, or effect... Or, "quite wrong" via breaking this rule or violating that formula, but actually effective, hence better... Or, a different appearance or form, but underneath, perhaps the same spirit or reality: in new bottles, old wine..."
Hence this unit intended to enormously accelerate the clarifying these prior-basic issues of essential thinking...

OUR SUGGESTION. As usual, we have identified and explicitly named the major variables which comprise this "region" [which we name "LETTER-SPIRIT COUNTRY"]—the lay of the land therein. But as a capsule slogan: always be aware of Principle (behind the procedure), Purpose (in a given task-situation), and Parameters (or permissible limits, etc., in a given Field or situation). This aids competent implementing of techniques procedures methods...

SUGGESTED MEASUREMENT OF LEARNING: BENCHMARKS, ETC.. This would be the very devil to measure learner-gains! One could of course find other examples than in the Gallery below and test learners to see whether they can autonomously identify and correct shortfallings, such as mechanical rule-mongering, and the like...

GUIDELINES/GOALS: The learner exhibits:
(1) *Awareness*: know of or about this whole concept, of lower-order concrete simple surface level ===== "versus" higher-order conceptual essence-or-spirit quality. *Ability*: be able to <u>use</u> as needed!
(2) As for specific subparts, (A) <u>Letter-Spirit</u>. Know the risks of following the *literal correct form* but not achieving the *figurative effective function*. (B) <u>Rule vs. Tool</u>: know the difference, and know when to follow a procedure as rule; when to "break" it or "conditionalize" it; when it is in fact a tool. (C) "<u>In Vitro-In Vivo</u>": know the value of being able to do something "accurate" In Vitro by-the-book *perfect*, but also the need to "adroit" adapt-alter-adjust In Vivo in a situation's circumstances.

#|+#|+#|+#|#+|#+|#+|#+|#+|+#+#+#+|||#++|++#||++|#|++|+#|+#|+|#|+|#+|+|#|+|#|+#|+|#+|#+|+#|+|+#|+#|+#|#|+#|+#|+#|#|

[2.] Gallery "I": to Prime the Pump...

[1.] "The operation was a success but the patient died." [-- CONVENTIONAL WITTICISM]
[Of course possibly no operation however skillful could have saved the patient. On the other hand, the procedure may have been done **by-the-book correct**, when some **variation from the rule** would have been more **effective**...]

[2.] "The small French hotel's sign clearly stated, "Absolutely **no** eating food, nor laundering clothing, in the room." I did both—dined on bread and cheese, and rinsed out some underwear—but from *another* viewpoint, and considering *how* I did these things, it was *perfectly all right to do so after all.* But why might it be "okay" to "violate" this "rule," as I did thus?"
[Consider **purpose goal function** of the rule...]

[3.] "When mother fride my egg, it limbered out like corn surp. Then it got buggles, and went up and down, like breethen heavy." [-- AN EIGHT-YEAR OLD CHILD]
[By the **letter**, quite **incorrect** grammatically; but by the **spirit or function** of conveying an eye-level experience at the stove, perhaps **effective** hence valid...]

[4.] "Break any rule rather than say something barbarous." [-- GEORGE ORWELL, author of 1984]

[5.] [5A] Mary likes to walk. She walks to work, she walks to the park, she walks to church, she walks to visit friends—she walks everywhere.
[5B] Today we walked to work. Then we walked back home. Later we walked to the store. After dinner, we walked to a friend's house. Then we walked back home.
[Could it be said that one of these follows a rule **mechanically**, but fails to achieve the **spirit or function** intended? And that the other may seem to do so also, but is properly **effective** by contrast?]

#|+#|+#|+#|#+|#+|#+|#+|#+|+#+|+#+|||#++|++#||++|#|++||+#|+#|+|#|+|#+|+|#+|+|#|+|+|#|+#|+|#+|#+|#|++|+#|+#|+#|#+|#|+#|+#|+#|#|

[3.] TABLE OF CONTENTS of module:

#|+#|+#|+#|#+|#+|#+|#+|#+|+#+|#+|||#++|++#||++|#|++||+#|+#|+#|+|#+|+#|+|#|+|#|+#|+#|+|+#|+#|+#|#+|#|+#|+#|+|#|

[4.] CONS: "objections, objections!"

WHOA, this is all too *obvious* to everyone. We all *know* to follow a rule but then to alter or abandon it when appropriate—use it as rule-of-thumb or guideline. We all do this in real life! DAVID PERKINS points out that heuristic (formulaic) schemes overshoot. They specify too-detailed an approach. But, "*Fortunately, most people are sensible about heuristics. They hear them, try them a bit, and quickly start to revise and revamp them to each individual's personal needs.*" So we don't need this unit.

I see your point, **BUT** (1) in traditional Old-School culture, "rule-mongering" still simplistically abounds. Students check their autonomous judgment at the door, to get things—"correct." You didn't quote the rest of PERKINS: "*...the problem is that the student doesn't always have the sense of which the most important parts of the heuristic are...*" Nor is encouraged often to choose instead of to mechanically apply. the result can be what's been called the "extreme algorhithmic approach" or "procedural mimcry" --Furthermore, (2) even in Real Life, past a certain basic level, people can rule-monger. We "Know About" rules vs. tools, but we do not always Truly Know how to be supple, agile, adroit about Procedure.
--Even teachers themselves have been procedure-bound. An ANECDOTE tells of a workshop offering several kinds of new programs. But many teachers then asked: "*This is very fine, but which one should we use?*"

#|+#|+#|+#|#+|#+|#+|#+|#+|+#+|#+|||#++|++#||++|#|++||+#|+#|+#|+|#+|+#|+|#|+|#|+#|+#|+|+#|+#|+#|#+|#|+#|+#|+|#|

[5.] GALLERY : Quotations, Examples:

[5.A.] Touchstone-quotations. [For the *gist, essence...*]

[1.] EXAMPLE. A writing teacher shows how students critiqued writing via Half-Rules without sensing the Function behind the Form... This marvelously illuminates (via specifics) the pitfall of rule-mongering...

Student comments on my papers often seemed like handbook generalizations unskillfully applied.

--Thus, some students said *my use of contractions was inappropriate.* (But I wanted a conversational tone.)

--They warned me against *repeating "I" so often.* (But this was autobiographical writing; would passive voice verbs have been better?)

--They complained about some *very long sentences.* (But I was describing terrain and trying to suggest how spaces and objects adjoin and connect in long vistas.)

--They admonished me against *rambling.* (But I wanted to sound like an old man reminiscing.)

--They gleefully schooled me for a *shift in point of view.* (But I thought I had the old man describing a childhood experience vividly enough to become the child again.)

--They groused about *inconsistencies in style* such as big words popping up in simple stories. (But that old man was a career English professor and word-lover.) [-- FROM TE2YC]

Rule-rubberstamping is using a method mechanically, unthinkingly. **Rule-shotgunning** is running through "all 12 probe-questions for reading poems" for a poem, when only # 2, 4, 5 and 8 apply to that poem!

[2.] Touchstones. Two "potent/fecund" comments clarifying <u>the complexity of tool-based method</u>:

Whether in liberal inquiry, harmony in music (is jazz rule-free or different?) and modern democracy, "the uncritical acceptance of any set of rules, whether of musical harmony, liberal inquiry, or modern democracy, risks leading to a numb society incapable of change, progress, expression. We must ask where rules come from, over what situations they apply, are they ethical and relevant or merely codified practices or customs, or inherent in nature."
[-- Doug Schneider, student at Lawrence University of Wisconsin]   [{ Can you believe a mere *student*, said *this*?! }]

[3.] In early Greek culture, *metis* was valued as "a practical or cunning intelligence":

"A wide array of practical skills and acquired intelligence in responding to a constantly changing natural and human environment." Odysseus improvises to confront complex changing situations. The essence of *metis* is "knowledge about *when and how* to apply rules of thumb to concrete situations. Good doctors, good riverboat pilots, good writers, and good joke-tellers have this knowledge; they do not proceed mechanically by rules. So too...with specialists in emergencies and disasters. Although there rules of thumb that can be and are taught, each fire or accident is unique, and half the battle is knowing which rules of thumb to apply in which order and when to throw the book away and improvise. One should take small not large steps; ensure reversibility; assume surprises.
[-- Cass Sunstein, review in The <u>New Republic</u>, 18 May 1998]

#|+#|+#|+#|#+|#+|#+|#+|#+|+#++#+|||#++|++#||++|#|++||+#|+#|+|#+|+#+|+#+|+#+|+|#|+|#|+#|+|#+|+#+|+#|+|+#|+#|+#|#+|#|+#|+#|#+|#|

[5.B.] Gallery of examples.

1. Following the rule by the letter, but not attaining the spirit.

Example. The case of the form-fulfilling hotel-clerk.
A business traveler registered at the desk, noticed a string quartet setting up in the lobby, asked the clerk when they might play. "Sorry, don't know," replied the clerk politely. Well, might the Manager know? inquired the traveler? "He might; I don't know," replied the clerk, still politely—and then turned to the guest, presented the room key, and said, "And if there's anything we can do for you during your stay, Mr. _____, do let us know!" [-- Source]

2. Adapting adjusting the rule to the situation:

Example. The case of the adjustable automobile attendants.
A service station trained their employees to engage the customer in conversation to establish friendly rapport, but to carefully monitor the talk, and reduce it if and when it became inappropriate. [-- Raving Fans]

3. Breaking the letter or rule, but still achieving the spirit function goal the rule sought:

Example. The case of the disobedient but dutiful hotel guest, *moi-meme*:
Often on my trip through provincial France, the small hotels' Rules <u>absolutely prohibited eating and doing laundry in one's room</u>. I could understand why: protection of the building itself! Legions of messy guests could drop food fragments, stain fabrics with salad dressing and chicken grease, soil the towels. And rot the floors by dripping water... But what of my own pressing domestic needs, to Eat In, then "rinse a few things out"? As a win-win solution, I discreetly ate the messy food <u>but tidily</u>, and washed and dried the dripping underwear <u>but non-splashingly</u>, so that no evidence damaged anything or even showed... <u>Thus, the prescribed procedure was violated, but its goal was attained.</u>

Example. **"Inclusiveness:"** Generous *Spirit* provided by avoiding all the *Letters*...
Most organizations today, including educational, publish a statement that they do not discriminate on the basis of—and then a growing list of categories such as *race, religion, age, gender, sexual orientation, national origin, ability-status, mother's maiden name...* I noticed that my own alma mater (Lawrence University of Wisconsin) went to Spirit and Principle at once and proffered their version which read simply: "Lawrence promotes equality

EXAMPLE. Another above-average elucidation of these two great **"letter-spirit"** dimensions of something. Near-known obvious surface appearance … *but also* higher-up more-central conceptual complex?

What is **good taste?** Is it that "which is determined by being around people thought tasteful, taking pleasure in cutting oneself away from the mass by the criterion of ostensible good taste, and being supremely confident in judging—and thereby putting down—others by the standard of what one takes to be one's own exquisite taste"? This is more like common and gross snobbery. *By contrast*, "one decides not to care in the least about what passes for the good taste of one's age, and decides instead that good taste really is good sense, which means that in *friendship*, it is represented by tact, generosity and above all kindness; in *possessions*, by comfort, elegance, utility and solidity; in *art*, by beauty, harmony and originality; in *culture* generally, by as discriminating tolerance for tastes at odds with one's own."　　　　[-- JOSEPH EPSTEIN, Snobbery: The American Version]

EXAMPLES. What is a **man, masculinity,** identity and behavior?
Four instances from minority studies, specifically the "subculture or underworld" of **male homosexuality.**

The Incident	"By the LETTER…"	"In the SPIRIT…"	
[1.] A male college student "came out" on campus as gay, helped found a Gay-Straight Alliance, spoke at panels on gay rights and issues.	Unmasculine, to disclose a stigmatized identity. By the **Letter**, masculinity is heterosexual, etc. (His father was initially distressed.)	"More man than you'll ever be"? Well no but in **Spirit**, a "man" does what must be done even if arduous and calmly with no fuss or fear… (His father came to respect him on this kind-of-traditional view…)	
[2.] A male was homosexual, in addition stereotypically effeminate in looks and actions, and also one who sexually took the passive role of receptor of anal intercourse.	Obviously "not a Man," in form—both contour (**appearance**) and even operation (activity). But he feistily said to some straight males harassing him, "Listen, you don't tell me how I'm supposed to take my pleasure, and if I swish, you walk like you got arthritis!!"	So by **reality** and function or essence, he seemed to be a Man by the older *or more-basic, central* criteria of aggression, assertiveness, and self-direction including successful self-management amid other and hostile males…	
[3.] Also, a rather open-minded straight man said, referring to an attractive but (again) stereotypically-effeminate gay male, "If I happened to have sex with that guy, it would not be a queer or homosexual act. Because while in *appearance* his body is anatomically **masculine or anyhow male**, in *reality or spirit* his soul or psyche or personality is—thoroughly **feminine!**"		By the Letter…	But by the Spirit…
[4.] And relatedly, I myself [your author here] had a "homosexual experience." Yes. In my early thirties. With a member of the "men's liberation" group popular in the post-Sixties time of "liberations." One evening after the meeting. [This is true, indeed even veracious!]	And so, in **Appearance**, unarguably "a homosexual sex act." Namely, erotic interchange between two members of the same sex, and so forth. By the letter, in form; *but*, in true spirit or function?...	But in **Reality** it seemed merely (1) uncomplex (simple mutual masturbation), (2) on level of physical release only (no emotional involvement), (3) motivated by "adventure." (A) a desire, that evening, to "do something rebellious, to walk on the wild side, to let off steam." (B) Plus the other man was Black—adding exoticism of a sort…, and (4) not repeated—no desire to do so, either . [Cf. Sexual Orientation as both **defined**, and also **classified**, *complexly*: not just 1. activity, but also 2. self-definition, 3. fantasy-arousal, 4. whole identity… And all of this continuing-ongoing, not only one moment in time; see major **Change**…] [Cf. also the often-quoted statistic from the KINSEY REPORT on "sexual behavior in the human male," that 37% of all adult males have had at least one homosexual experience since puberty. Hmm, does this mean that Queerness is on the increase? Now we know more competently how to think about this, via **Letter-Spirit** and its sub-components….]	

…I always *knew* you were a Sexual Derivant under the skin. One can *always* tell…　[*Arrgggghhhhh*…..]

#|+#|+#|+#|+#|+#|+#|+#|+#|+#+#|||#++|++#||++#|++|+#|+#|+#||#|+#|+#|+#|+|+#|+|+#|+#|+#+#|+|+#|+|+#|+#|+#|+#|#|+#|+#|

[6.] Tool-Kits for Major Subparts

--Can we always distinguish between whether an action is a rule or a tool? Is it III or does it depend on whether or how it is used?

--If an action is a rule, can it vary as to how rigid-tight, or flexible-loose, it is, even when seen as a rule? And can it vary as to how much it is needed in a given situation? Also here may be quantity: if an action is used extremely, intensely, extensively, massively—is this over-use, or possibly valid even though seemingly excessive?

EXAMPLES. Writing. Utterly "breaking rules," or, on a scale of A (0) ==to➔ Z (100), bursting through the terminal barrier right on to the Wrong, Scandalous, Maverick, Outlandish—moving on to AA or 101- and onward!

--Sentence Length. You can have one-word sentences. ["How did I feel about it? Proud. Nostalgic. Pensive."] Or sentences up to a many-page, hundreds-of-words, sentence as in novelists William Faulkner, James Joyce...

--Honesty. You should not plagiarize, should do your own work—*unless this is somehow sometimes not true...*

--Specific Proof. You should give illustrative factual details to illuminate your thesis—unless revealing exactly who stole exactly how much money from the bank [Mr. WISTOM; $200 grand] is *not* good publicity and propaganda...

#|+#|+#|+#|#+|#+|#+|#+|#+|#+|+#++#+|||#++|++#||++|#|++||+#|+#|+|#|+|#+|+|#+|+|#|+|+|#|+#|+|#+|+#|+|+#|+#|+#|#|+#|+#|#+|#|

[6.A.] Rule vs. Tool. "aRt==hTs"

Two items emerge here! WHETHER AT ALL, and then HOW/HOW MUCH ETC. .....
EMPLOYMENT vs. elimination of the skill for the task-goal at hand... EXPERTISE vs. error if using the skill for the task. 1. Is rule used, employed or omitted? 2. Is it done so competently or badly, even as a rule?

---

1. The definition of, and distinctions between, Rule and Tool as essential concepts.

A RULE = "This you *must* do, then success *will* ensue."   *Versus*
A TOOL = "Use it or not *depending*, only if it helps for good *ending*."
[{ "aRt=hTs" or "algorhythm Rule tactic," *vs.* "heuristic Tool strategy" }]

--We can add **Guideline**, or **Rule-of-Thumb**, plus others, as a third intermediate issue also.

--We also remind: **beware the misconception** of assuming that "if a procedure is presented in an explicit, elucidated, detailed form, it will probably be over-explicit, that is, a 'rule' in the bad sense of too-rigid formulae." *Not necessarily so*; cf. our Rationale that "even complex matters can be made somewhat explicit, and this need not necessarily result in oversimple reductionism... " ANECDOTE. Some Diversity-educators objected to my "tool-box" of key concepts for minority education [SEE Appendix] as too mechanical; they thought I meant rules!

--We can add: of course, know the Principles behind any rule or procedure; the Purposes of them; and the Parameters of the field (context, situation, circumstances) which may dictate etc. ... This will add competence in technique...

NOTE. Our "5-A" model puts "rule-altering" on a Conceptual Continuum to be more supple. Thus, one can
1. **Adopt** a procedure wholesale, "off-the-rack, turn-key drive-away ready," unaltered...
2. **Adapt-alter-adjust** the procedure: omit, insert, reduce, increase, rearrange—and so forth...
3. **"Attach"** the procedure to another system (your own ploys, etc.), as a secondary module...
4. **"Activate"**: use procedure simply as suggestive stimulant, catalyst to your own methods...
5. **Attack**: critique the procedure, either (A) in limited way, or (B) wholesale. Perhaps alter in major fashion.
6. ...or of course **Abandon**: reject the entire procedure wholesale...

| NO; gosh, the above 5-A, much too elementary. | Most students, out of school, probably are flexible. But in "School," |

Guideline: (N) To distinguish competently between the following four situations, conditions regarding "RULES *versus* TOOLS" as a key element of "Letter-Spirit" *specifically*—and of "method/technique/procedure" *generally*.

1. To <u>follow a rule, and doing so is "good,"</u> appropriate and even necessary-sufficient...

2. To <u>follow a rule, but doing so is "bad"</u> (for various reasons...)

3. To <u>omit or "break" a rule</u>, and this is either [A.] "<u>bad</u>, or [B.] actually "<u>good</u>," depending...

4. To <u>omit or "violate" the Letter</u>, and this is either [A.] "<u>bad</u>," or [B.] actually <u>okay or even good desirable</u> in the Spirit of the situation? [Again, cf. Form vs. Function, Correct vs. Effective...]

GALLERY. Some playing-with this quartet-plus of **Guideline-Issues** [!] regarding Letter/Rule and Spirit/Tools. Examples from composition, teaching writing...

1. <u>Follows rule and is good.</u>

RULE-"RULING" Rule applied correctly: was needed Was it also done with competence?

2. <u>Follows rule and is bad.</u> (For various reasons...)

"RULE-ECHOING" Applying the Letter or Form or Procedure of a rule—or some directive etc. etc.—but mechanically, ineffectively, utterly without achieving the intended Spirit or Function or Principle intended!

RULE-"RUBBERSTAMPING" SEE above paragraph by writing teacher.

RULE-"SHOTGUNNING" Mechanically applying a whole set or cluster of procedures...

EXAMPLE. I gave English 101 students <u>twelve "probe-questions" to help them learn about poetry</u>. [Such as, *Is the subject, the real theme, or not?... Is there a "fulcrum" or turning-point structurally?... Does the style or form of the poem, seek to support the meaning or tone?...*] Well, disappointingly, students would simply grrrrrrind through applying <u>each</u> probe, #1, then #2, then #3, etc., to <u>each</u> poem. No matter whether the probe was a useful, productive tool for that particular poem, or not... Of course, no wonder; they had already had 12 years of Old-School education in assignments being "Work Problems 1 through 5 in Section II"...

RULE-"OVERDOING" Hyper-employment. A specific expertise-issue. "Rule Appropriate but (a form of bad employment) Quantity: Over-Applied"

3. <u>"Breaks" rule and doing so is bad.</u>

4. "Breaks" rule but doing so is good.

5. RULE-TOOLING." Flexibly alters-adapts-adjusts the Rule to the Field or situation/purpose/goal. Uses it as <u>rule-of-thumb</u> or <u>Guideline</u>. Also called "<u>conditionalizing</u>" the rule.

GUIDELINE. Note here that many "rules" may be *contradictory to other rules*. [They may be dangerously even disgustingly "*provincial*": = one-sided; blindly or mechanically dictatorial; free from effect purpose function; isolated in a non-situational, context-free vacuum...] Therefore, one could <u>select the one</u> of the pair that applies in the given situation. Or could <u>blend</u>—or <u>alternate</u>—them both somehow if appropriate.

EXAMPLES #1: <u>Conventional wisdom</u> of the proverbial or "grandmothers'" type.

Plan your course of action carefully, to be ready.	Don't plan too much or precisely; things change.
"Look before you leap;" wait-and-see.	"He who hesitates is lost"; to win is to risk.
One step at a time, all the time.	In complex situations, must do many things.
Look for simple explanations: "less is more."	If it isn't complex-detailed enough, it is suspect.
Act cautiously; better safe than sorry.	Doing something? Do it with gusto, fight it out.
If unsure, try anything at all; muddle through…	Finish what you've started.

EXAMPLES #2[A]: Traditional "<u>Rules for writing</u>." Formerly in Old-School composition courses these contradictory prescriptions were frequent: *fortunately, not now in any classes anywhere any more…*

1. <u>Punctuation, Spelling:</u> they're vital to use, to be understood.	You dont have to spel gud to be comprehended. **"REBULT MOTTERS"** [--sign at auto garage]
2. <u>Length:</u> develop paper generously, "at least 1,500 words…"	Whoa; keep it short or bore-and-lose the reader. ["Our company memos have a one-page maximum!"]
3. <u>Specificity:</u> use examples to interest reader, prove point.	Heck, let reader use own imagination to fill in.
4. <u>Sentence length:</u> keep short for punch, long ones are run-on.	Avoid short sentences, they're choppy; longer ones are more dignified.
5. <u>Sentence structure</u>: "vary your types of sentences"	*[????? How and why? Mechanically???]*
6. <u>Explicitness:</u> spell points out clearly for the reader.	**IM**plicit: let reader grasp themes on one's own.
7. <u>Tone: Formal</u>. Be dignified, not too chatty.	**Tone: IN**formal. Talk person-to-person, naturally.
8. <u>Self of Writer</u>: don't use "I," keep impersonal	**Self**: bring your self and stances into the writing.
9. <u>Repetition:</u> don't repeat; redundancy is confusing.	**Repeat** points for emphasis, style for coherence.
10. <u>Wordiness:</u> use few and crisp words, "less is more"	Beware telegraphic style, let language breathe.
11. <u>"Sincerity"</u>: be honest with reader, not phony or artificial	*[Heck, fake things if it'll help you attain your goal…]*
12. <u>Paragraph Topic Sentence:</u> each par. must have one, at start.	…heck, place it in *middle* or *end*. Or *omit* entirely; leave it implicit to be grasped, or guessed-at…
13. <u>Structure</u>. Thesis, three point-paragraphs, conclusion.	MENU of options: via time, space, A-Z, conceptual, more. Have 2, 4, a bazillion paragraphs…
14. <u>Writing Process:</u> write drafts out beforehand.	*…or compose in your head, write when ready…*
15. <u>Proportion:</u> give every point equal weight	Calibrate: more space to big ideas, less to lessers…
16. <u>Reader-Relating:</u> write to reach the audience	…write to please, etc., yourself…

EXAMPLES # 2[B]: Are the following instances of **writing**, (1) "correct and good"? … (2)

[2.B.1.] Avoid sentence FRAGMENTS; *never* write incomplete sentences (phrases, clauses without verb etc.):

Mother quit cooking the other day. Saying we would have to do our own food. Because she was fed up.	HILLTOP INN: now open year-round. Serving breakfast from 7 A.M. Because we care about you!

[2.B.2.] LENGTH, WORDINESS: write tight and brief, avoid sprawl ===== no, be generous, not telegraphic.

Apparently today at Whitewater for math majors, Stenology 101 is something that everyone has to take, whereas Stenology 102 can be taken or not as the student wishes.	"Good soil repays digging, bad soil needs it." [-- from a British gardening manual]
For Whitewater math majors, Stenology 101 is required, Stenology 102 remains an elective.	"Good soil repays digging and loosening it up, to improve the yield. Bad soil needs much digging simply to get any crops at all out of it."

EXAMPLES # 2[C]: . Gallery of more examples from **writing instruction**. **[1.]** SYNTAX or sentence-construction, two key elements. **[2.]** Also **REPETITION** of elements: good, bad, or either "all depending"? (See also **[3.] PARALLELISM** {& **[4.] SPECIFIC DETAILING**}, in Vitro Vivo section…)

[2.C.1.] SYNTAX: A **rule** or rather **principle** is "<u>Place in *subordinate* clauses and at the *start* of the sentence, information which is *old-known*, *secondary-explanatory*, or otherwise *less* important. Place in the *main* clause and near the sentence's *end*, material which is *new* or *more* important.</u>
[Note that very few writing classes make this keystone "operating concept" explicit …]

Breaking my arm, I slipped on the dock. I broke my arm, slipping on the dock. I slipped on the dock, breaking my arm. Slipping on the dock, I broke my arm. [The above quartet nicely illustrates this rule. How breaking it here is an *unarguable* error, mistake. How following it is more effective, and why.]	--But what of this letter to an <u>applicant for a bank loan</u>? "Although your loan was not approved, we invite you to use the many services of our bank." *[Clearly, the important but bad news is downplayed by installing it in the first and subordinate clause…]* *Imagine the ruined version.* "We regret to inform you that we did <u>not</u> approve your loan. (However, many bank services do still remain open to you. These include…)"

Another rule is to <u>Use compound sentences only for information of equal importance; otherwise, subordinate and emphasize in a complex sentence (with main and subordinate clauses).</u>

So a uselessly-incorrect example would be THIS COMMENT BY A COLLEGE DORMITORY RESIDENT (quoted in the school newspaper): "The fire drill sounded and we all went outside. We waited a half hour	But what of this sentence NEAR THE END OF A LONG ADVERTISEMENT BY AN AIRLINE? "…Kids' fares are even lower and fares are subject to change." *[Rather nicely downplays the bad news by riding it in as if equal to nice news!]* *[Compare a "ruined" rewrite. Start of new paragraph.]* Of course, despite all these advantages, we must inform you that fares are always subject to change, and usually upwards. |#|#+|+|#+|#+|+#|+|#+|+#|+|+#|+#||#+#|+|#+|#+|+|#+| And what of this sentence SPOKEN IN EVERYDAY CONVERSATION: "Finally, we'll stop at the grocery oh and would you look at that hot Corvette convertible across the street?!"

217

and then we returned."	[Quite illogical and unrelated, which is the point—emotional inburst interrupts business!]
	Imagine perhaps a more "correct" version:
[As against the correct also more effective] "When the fire drill sounded, we all went outside. But before we could return, we had to wait a half hour."	"We've done the dry-cleaners and the credit union; now we'll end by stopping at the grocery, and then home… (Oh, by the way, look at that hot Corvette convertible there; sorry…) Now, if you'll shop the produce section, I'll go to the meat counter, and we'll meet in the wine shop…"
	{ P.S.—in the cause of I.A. or "Individualized Aesthetics," you may substitute for "H.C.C.," other "custom-personalized" C.O. or Cathected Object. }

[2.C.2.] REPETITION: Another writing rule is to <u>repeat items for emphasis, for reader-retention, and for tone, but not excessively so as to cause redundancy</u>.

The rule:	The departure from the rule:

EXAMPLE. Two differing approaches to **book-writing** and repetition:	
"The reader is reassured that in this book, one's time is not wasted. Facts are stated once and are not repeated." [-- CARL D. LANE, The Boatman's Manual]	"…I have salted cross-references liberally throughout the text. Word Processing [cannot be compartmented, is all of a piece, but books have sections, but the relationships among them call for recognition.] "My hope is that the reader will find the frequent citations of what was said in another section an aid to understanding, and not a hindrance to easy reading." [-- WALTER A. KLEINSCHROD]

EXAMPLE. "Marie walks." Much repetition, but which is good, bad, by what criteria?	
[1.] Today we walked to work. Then we walked back home. Later we walked to the store. After dinner, we walked to a friend's house. Then we walked back home.	[2.] Mary likes to walk. She walks to work, she walks to the park, she walks to church, she walks to visit friends—she walks everywhere.

EXAMPLE: **Sign** found inside the freezer-case at a local supermarket. Audience, store clerks:
"FROZEN FOODS ARE PERISHABLE. Don't let packages 'get buried' in the rear. Frost accumulating here ➔ indicated products are not being rotated properly. Insure 'first in-first out' by restocking packages in the rear. Move inventory from back to front each time you restock. Always place first package at the very back of row."
Students uniformly saw this as excessive, even insultingly-so. I saw their point but was also impressed by the savvy of the writer—to seek **"command,"** ultimate **competence**: if *anyone* could succeed in the **challenge** of reaching the intended audience [= perhaps-incompetent, probably-bored part-time employees], *his* emphatic statement could!

#|+#|+#|+#|#+|#+|#+|#+|#+|+#++#+|||#++|++#||++|#|++||+#|+#|+|#|+|#+|#+|+|#|+|+|#|+#|+|#+|+#|+|+#|+#|+#|#+|#|+#|+#|+|#|

[6.B.] Issue of "In Vitro" versus "In Vivo"

GUIDELINE: To Know the distinction between {in our terminology} "In Vitro" (letter-perfect by the book) and "In Vivo" (adapted for the situation).

"In Vitro" (="under glass," as in the lab) *vs.* **"In Vivo"** (="living," as in the field, world).
"In Vitro" = a skill <u>to be done theoretically perfectly by-the-Text/Book, *Correct*!</u>—[whether it would be <u>Effective or not</u> in real-world use for a given task-goal…] *vs.*

"In Vivo," the skill <u>to be applied in an actual task-goal situation. Presumably employed (not abandoned),</u> <u>but where perhaps is altered-adapted-adjusted. Perhaps *less* of it is required or acceptable, changes are</u> <u>required anyhow, for it to be *Effective*.</u>

POSSIBLE MISCONCEPTION. Don't confuse three distinct activities here.
(1) <u>**Faithfully following a rule "perfectly,"**</u> (often vital, but usually "easier," and *ultimately limited*)…
(2) <u>**Being able to perform a technical task**</u> (but especially complex ones using tools) **"<u>letter-perfectly by the book</u>"** (*not always needed in "real life,"* but perhaps powerful in the classroom, as noted below)…
(3) *<u>Flexibility: knowing the rule or method, but being supple: varying same</u>* (adopting, adapting, altering, perhaps abandoning), using it as a tool or heuristic, *"all depending"* on the **Field** (occasion, purpose, goals, situation, etc.)

POSSIBLE PEDAGOGICAL ADVANTAGE. I came to find it an excellent "method/goal" to aim for **students' learning some skills "letter-perfect by the book," even to extremes not always used "in** **reality," and to demonstrate this use in a test**. This "gymnastics" proffered two benefits. **(1)** It efficiently <u>measured</u> whether students *really knew the skill or not*, and also **(2)** it cannily <u>removed</u> their [questionable] *arguing* as to whether they knew it or not, also whether it was needed or not!
--This perfection-ploy especially applied to medium-advanced technical <u>writing skills</u>: such as (1) multi-level *parallelism* and also *repetitions*, (2) *syntax*-varieties (sentence length and type), (3) *levels of diction* ("from officialese to informal"), and (4) *specific detailing*.

Level "I": "TTT" or when "Teacher Tells To." EXAMPLE. I first say take this text, say a letter-to-the-editor, and add the skills in <u>specific detailing</u> plus <u>parallelism</u> plus <u>syntax</u> which you were taught, and do so perfectly by the book (oh, and state what changes you made and why)." Perhaps overdone for **In Vivo** publication, but I could apply high **Criteria** of **Competence** and point out: Hey, *unarguably* you omitted analogy and statistics, two of the Six Types of Detailing (the others being WhoWhenWhere, anecdote, sense-imagery, and dialog). *No Argument!* You were wrong because **unarguably** incomplete! (Hence demanding but also fair. Mechanical, but in the service of perfection before adjustment…)

Level "II": "OOO" or now "On One's Own." EXAMPLE. I give students existing texts, letters-to-the-editor and the like, and tell them: "now rework this text (if and as needed) <u>by the book</u>. *However, you* will have to decide which skill-issues are shortfalling here, and improve them. Oh, and *state* what you did, where, and why, and how well-or-ill in your judgment too…"

Level "III": "Supple for the Situation…" EXAMPLE: "Now do two or three rewrites of this same text for two or three diverse situations—genre-type, audience-type, arena (Personal, School, Job, Civic), purpose, etc… Adapt alter adjust, even abandon, whichever techniques of writing you should. And of course *annotate* why you did what, where—and whether it is for-sure clear and best, or a "gray-area, judgment-call"!"

ANNOTATING. That is, <u>self-description/evaluation</u> of own work. That is, <u>having students write a gloss on their</u> <u>own work, comment on, "what they did: which skills used, where & how, & why, & whether correct & effective or</u> <u>not.</u>"
--Why do this? This ploy marvelously raised **Consciousness** of their own thinking. It also nudged toward **Competence** and **Conscientiousness.** That is, having to explicitly comment on their work, helped prevent or reduce <u>those easy-</u> <u>evasive comments</u> such as "Well my punctuation needs some work" [really? exactly *where?*...] and "I thought the paper flowed well," [ehh??? did a water pipe break???] let alone the inanely-minimal standard "It got the point across" [so does an eructation, often…]…
--Initially, students objected to having to **Annotate**, saying "wouldn't I know it if they used the skills," and "won't I reduce the grade if they say they made a mistake?" I said "*perhaps* I can tell, but do *you* know the skills is half the test, including if *you* can assess and admit when you weren't perfect—knowing your faults is a strength I'll reward!"

EXAMPLES GALLERY. We elucidate **Vitro-Vivo** by referencing two writing skills. **Specification** or supplying concrete examples, instances, illustrations for one's concepts (in order to make the reader clear on, and convinced of, the concept). And **parallelism,** phrasing a series of related ideas, in related language-style (in order to make the reader see the connection of the series).

219

[1.] EXAMPLES. <u>Original</u> letter to airline in-flight magazine, and our <u>rewriting</u> for **specific detailing:**

[1.A.] [ORIGINAL.] As a frequent traveler I have found that some of your staff are very helpful and accommodating which is extremely appreciated. Two of your staff members whom I have encountered numerous times are Ellen Lui and Carrie Law. I have found them to be extremely **pleasant**, **helpful** and **accommodating**. Although I have *no specific incident to recount to you* I just thought it was important for an airline to recognize those who excel in their positions and to give them the praise they deserve. --DL, Hong Kong	**[1.B.]** [REWRITE.] I really appreciate the excellence of your flight crews—especially Ellen Lui and Carrie Law. They're "basically" **helpful**. (*They reassured me about my luggage...then delivered that extra pillow and blanket.*) They're "advanced" **accommodating**. (*They changed me to a better vacant seat...then delivered that third bottle of water.*) And they're "world-class" **pleasant**. (*They smiled throughout a flight tossed by turbulence and babbling babies...and through to finding me the gate number of my connecting flight...*) Thanks to them and the whole crew!

Unarguably the rewrite is "better by-the-book" in re statistics, anecdotes, imagery, etc.! Now one can alter-adapt-adjust, from a firm base of expertise... Even turn it into a *story* ("I boarded Flight 563 with some anticipation,...")

[2.] EXAMPLE. Basic instance of **parallelism** (1) botched (rule broken, badly)... parallelism (2) achieved (rule followed)... and parallelism (3) adapted, varied (rule "broken" or rather "tooled" effectively):

(1) "Fred likes fishing, to dance, and he skis" versus
(2) "Fred likes fishing, dancing, and skiing"...
(3) But then one can say In Vivo for a given purpose, "Fred likes both fishing and skiing. Oh and as Marie will attest, he likes dancing too."
<u>The point</u>: learners should *master* In Vitro *accurately*, then know how to *manipulate* for In Vivo *adaptably*...

...hey, **NICE** parallelism in that very last sentence there...	Thanks. It is **Correct**. Is it **Effective**?

[3.] EXAMPLES. Letter to editor: note the paragraph topic sentences only, original and rewritten for **parallelism:** (The subject: objections to having students' names published in the paper's Police Blotter...)

[3.A.] Dear Editor, While I have not had the distinction of having my name appear in your police reports, I nonetheless feel compelled to question the need for them. Though there may be some merit to an informed public, is, indeed, this argument applicable now? Before answering, please examine the following: 1.) You are dealing with accusations only. Since you print only accusations and not acquittals or defense replies, you, in essence, allow only the police department to speak. If you feel you must continue, then at least print those names exonerated of charges to facilitate full disclosure. 2.) There is a distinct lack of relevancy. Of what benefit is it to us, your readers, to know of those arrested who are totally independent of UW-Whitewater? 3.) Do you have the right to further humiliate those arrested? Since it is already a matter of local, public record, of what purpose is there for additional reporting? 4.) Your sensationalized reporting is fostering police disrespect. Perhaps you should fully examine the consequences of informing the public. By letting us know of Johnny Doe's arrest for urinating all over a fire hydrant, you are, at the same time, feeding a contempt for the local law officials. Because of these reasons I feel you should discontinue your police reports. If nothing else, at least reconsider your reasons for a continued effort. MARK MCNALLY	**[3.B.]** Dear Editor, Do you really need to print the Police Blotter column, that record of public peccadilloes and pratfalls? (1) It doesn't seem fair or complete to the arrestees. Why print only those names accused, and not those exonerated of the charges in future weeks? (2) It doesn't seem just or genteel to the arrestees either. Why further humiliate those who are already in the public record anyhow? (3) It doesn't seem relevant to our readers specifically. Who cares if non-UW personnel were arrested? (4) It doesn't even seem beneficial for norms and morale generally. Doesn't reporting a urination all over a fire hydrant, foster contempt for law and order, for local law officials? It's not that my own name has appeared in the Blotter. It's just that I question the Blotter itself. MILLICENT OFFENBACH

Unarguably the rewrite avoids the pitfall of missed parallelism, correctly performs good basic parallelism. One can then adapt-alter-adjust (see below on "condom fatigue"). But this tests true prior mastery!

[4.] EXAMPLES. A writer lashes out at **"condom fatigue"** or the new idea that people are fed up with using prophylactics, but abstinence is not workable, *therefore we can tolerate people failing to use protection.* The writer feels "laws of nature and common sense" exist which "cannot be defined, no matter how annoying or cumbersome." He says: [His **original** on the left, an (over-?) **parallelized** version on the right:]

[4.A.] Well, I don't particularly like stopping for red lights, either, because it tends to slow me down. Nor do I like pausing at crosswalks for rumbling trucks. Let's not forget seat belts: they totally suck. And riding a motorcycle with a helmet keeps the wind from freely blowing through my hair. I'm also over the gym and would prefer that the government declare TV-watching an aerobic sport and cheese fries a food group. But...	**[4.B.]** Well, I don't like traffic laws either. Red lights slow down my driving; lumbering trucks delay my jay-walking. Seat belts are inconvenient, motorcycle helmets are claustrophobic. And I don't like health laws either. The gym and exercise has become wearisome (let TV-watching be declared an aerobic sport!) and diet restrictions have become frustrating (let cheese fries be declared a food group!). Unfortunately, however,...."

#|+#|+#|+#|#+|#+|#+|#+|#+|+#++#+|||#++|++#||++|#|++||+#|+#|+#|+|#+|+#|+|#|+|+#|+#|+#|+#+|+#|+|+#|+#|+#|#+|#|+#|+#|+#|

[6.C.] Issue of "Appearance-Reality"

> **GUIDELINE:** To distinguish between "surface, apparent APPEARANCE" and "an actual REALITY beneath-behind," is both an obvious ploy, but also sometimes wickedly difficult to do—but important...

This is especially the case where "intent to deceive" exists, or anyhow "a gross difference between first impressions and eventual awarenesses...

EXAMPLES. The times when things *seemed* to be "A," but later were *seen* to be different, even unto "A"...

[1.] A TENANT to whom I rented an apartment, *seemed* **truly-married.** At least in **Appearance,** because she constantly referred to her "husband." It was all the time "my husband" this, "my husband" that. The ornate plate celebrating their marriage was displayed prominently... *However,* later on I saw an official document: in **Reality,** they were both single, not married...

[2.] A NEIGHBOR in the trailer court *seemed* to have **been in the workforce;** he constantly noted his "retirement" from work. "I'm retired," "that was before I retired," etc. ... *However,* later on I discovered that in **Reality,** he was a Welfare Prince: had virtually never worked...

[3.] MY FRIEND PAUL in Florida *seemed* to be **psychologically-cognizant.** He had an M.A. in humanistic psychotherapy. He had two therapists himself, on a long-term, continuing basis. He had given me many insights into how early childhood experiences influence adult life... *However,* I came to see how in **Reality,** he monstrously did *not* understand (deeply, emotionally, therapeutically) virtually anything about his own imprisonment in the past. His insecure single mother made him over-compensate in his marital relationship—this became obvious to an outsider, but ironically remained invisible to him despite his **Appearance** of much psychological awareness...)

...really, you overkill once again. **Appearance vs. Reality** is really rather obvious to most mature folk!	...Right, *except when it isn't*, when the two differ so much that one can get badly fooled...

#|+#|+#|+#|#+|#+|#+|#+|#+|+#++#+|||#++|++#||++|#|++||+#|+#|+#|+|#+|+#|+|#|+|+#|+#|+#|+#+|+#|+|+#|+#|+#|#+|#|+#|+#|+#|

[6.D.] The issue of Change, or no-change-really?

> **Guideline:** To perceive that a CHANGE over time, may be one of *Appearance* rather than actual basic *Reality* change. This is the instance of "NEW BOTTLES BUT OLD WINE." A change in *Form* but not in *Function* also perhaps. The *Letter* alters, but the *Spirit* does not...

EXAMPLES. A set of instances, four from the general arena of **education,** two from **other issues now**...

[1.] Two Personal Anecdotes. [1A] As writer. I myself invite criticism of my writing. But does this mean I am no longer proud or egotistic, but self-effacing, humble? No; I still self-centered seek my goal. It's just that it's no longer praise or fame, but the satisfaction of doing the best job possible, which is aided by frank criticism by others! Change and no change...

[1B.] As teacher of thinking, I told theclass: this course is very different from the usual paradigm of know-believe-do of traditional education. Even, culture shock will occur. However, at bedrock there is no difference at all; it's still School As Usual. Student enters class; teacher tells them exactly what to do; they do it (to varying degrees) and pass. Only thing different is, I am telling you exactly, to learn how to do it yourself. Much change; much bedrock similarity...

[2.] The "True Believer." A student of mine entered class as a rabid conservative. Mid-semester, he suddenly became a rabid liberal—different ideology entirely, but the same "true-believer" fervor underneath both, and his next "cause"… Surface change but no real bedrock alteration.

[3.] Revolutionary Literature Taken Conventionally. In the 1960's some literature teachers felt the need to question the Truths of Today (that day). Specifically, "to look critically at such standard optimistic ideas as progress and rationality, which people took for granted. So they read innovators FRAZER, NIETZSCHE, THOMAS MANN, CONRAD, FREUD, KAFKA. Unfortunately however, the students exceeded "a healthy skepticism about our rationalist society." They simply absorbed from these works a "bitter line of hostility to civilization" (L. TRILLING) , bought it without question, and accepted it as the new orthodoxy." This led to the simplistic "don't trust anyone over thirty" and the like. [-- GOODBYE, BOOLA BOOLA]

[4.] Teaching Thinking By The Numbers. (4A) Educator JOHN DEWEY wrote the innovative How We Think, recommending non-formulaic flexibility. But a set of teachers studying it, took it as a rigid flexible manual to follow 1-2-3 as a manual…..
(4B) Educator R. STERNBERG presented to school administrators, how to choose programs for teaching thinking. But at the end, the "inevitable question" was asked. "All of this is nice, but let's get down to nuts and bolts. Which program should we use?" They approached the new wine with old bottles…

[5.] "Promisekeepers." A religious group seeking to innovate and better handle the modern world, but it seems to maintain tradition: all the maintains the subservience of wives to husbands, etc.

[6.] AIDS and Religion and Sin. Some traditionalists explained the high incidence of HIV infection among homosexual males, as punishment or retribution for their sexual sinning… Seeing new present through old past, continuing old lenses.

[7.] Reject The Whole Question or Issue: not a different Pew, nor different Church, but Abandon Religion!
[7A] You seek to include gays/lesbians in the military forces? Forget the effort; the real issue is militarism, the armies themselves, to be eliminated!
[7B] You seek to know how to mow the lawn (which mower; self or hire; etc.)? Forget it; the real issue is not to mow the lawn at all. To then create a prairie, or park with paths…
[7C] You philosophers ask "who or what made the world? God? Evolution? Chance?" But forget the question; nobody or nothing made it.

#|+#|+#|+#|#+|#+|#+|#+|+#+|+#+||#++|++#||++|#|++||+#|+#|+|#|+|#+|+|#+|+|#|+|#|+#|+|#+|#+|+#|+|+#|+#|+#|#+|#|+#|+#|#+|#|

[7.] ANNEX of Illustrative Materials

[7.A.] Background Material: "ConneXions"…

BACKGROUND OR WARM-UP MATERIAL. Perhaps **Letter-Spirit** discussion should be pump-primed by quickly reviewing the related issues of **[1.] "absolutism-relativism"** [Absolutism… rampant relativism… principled relativism, depending on viewpoint] … also **[2.] "isolated vs. situational (field) approach"** [consider the field: environment setting purpose goals etc.!] … also **[3.] "lenswork"** [=different responses to same subject-issue good-bad etc. depending on the lens, perspective, viewpoint.] A quick re-freshing parade thus. *Its purpose is to cinch for learners these three key concepts before wading into Letter-Spirit…*

[1.] My college ANTHROPOLOGY PROFESSOR stated accurately that he was a murderer. He had shot and killed five men with a rifle. [{ *He had been an infantry soldier in World War II… *}]

[2.] I MYSELF recently appeared naked ("private parts" included) in front of an adult woman I did not know at all. [{ *…she was a nurse during a dermatological exam and treatment at the medical clinic… *}\

[3.] Some HOUSEKEEPERS IN MY APARTMENT COMPLEX, considered my picture of MICHELANGELO'S statue "David," to be offensive (I guess they meant pornographic? obscene? homosexual? etc.?)… But the ROMANS had Priapus the household god statue of a male in full sexual arousal (that was good, needed for protection of the household in their religion)… And the BRITISH VICTORIANS actually covered the "legs" of tables and chairs with modesty fabric, thinking them to be obscene (hence our terms for light and dark meat instead of leg, thigh, and breast)… And A

BLACK ACTIVIST earlier said "Homosexuality is obscene, just like baby-rape or Johnson's war in Vietnam or wanting to be president of General Motors…

[4.A,B] SEX "I": Two <u>male individuals met and had consensual sex</u> in a private-enough place and never saw each other again. [{ *Immature, immoral … except that they each treated each other with mutual respect…* }]

SEX "II": <u>A married man and wife had consensual sex</u> (conventional intercourse) in their home bedroom. [{ *Moral, natural, normal, good … except that they both "used" each other disdainfully with long-standing spite…* }]

[5.] Some ESKIMO TRIBES <u>"exposed" their elders, abandoned their grandparents to death in the snow.</u> [{ *Obviously cruel, inhuman, primitive, … or appropriate because needed for group survival at times of scarce food?* }]

[6.] Some EAST INDIANS <u>revere the cow, do not permit eating it, thinking it may possess a human spirit.</u> [{ *This seems superstitious, indeed stupid in a land of scarce food … or does it seem sage if the people believe in the transmigration of souls plus abhor cannibalism: that cow could be grandmother…* }]

[7.] The BOY SCOUTS OF AMERICA <u>bars and discharges homosexual personnel.</u> [{ *This is obviously bad, bigoted, discriminatory—via the lens of egalitarianism and liberal liberation, Gay Rights….. **However**, this is obviously good, moral, correct—via the lens of current-traditional, conventional sociocultural homophobia or heterosexism or heteronormativity. Plus, financial support comes from the MORMON CHURCH…* }]

#|+#|+#|+#|#+|#+|#+|#+|#+|+#+|+#+|||#++|++#||++|#|++||+#|+#|+#|+#+|+#+|+#+|+#|+|+#|+#|+|#|+#+|#+|+#|+|+#|+#|+#|#+|#|+#|+#|+#|

[7.B.] ConneXions with other thinking skill-issues.

CONNEXION. Cf. our "5-AAAAA" model of **Agile Application**. It asks: is the item 1. **Adopted** wholesale? Or 2. **Adapted, Altered, Adjusted** (added-to, reduced, rearranged, etc.) Or perhaps just used to 3. **"Activate"** or stimulate one's *own* approach. Or even 4. **Attacked**-critiqued whether minor or major and hence even 5. **Abandoned** for this task-goal! (This conceptual continuum **categorizes** options, to remind of them: from "off the rack-turnkey/driveaway," to tinker with indeed, to perhaps reject.)

#|+#|+#|+#|#+|#+|#+|#+|#+|+#+|+#+|||#++|++#||++|#|++||+#|+#|+#|+#+|+#+|+#+|+#|+|+#|+#|+|#|+#+|#+|+#|+|+#|+#|+#|#+|#|+#|+#|+#|

[7.C.] The "five-paragraph theme" (and the 15-C alternate model)—and "Letter vs. Spirit"…

MODEL. The **"essay"** form—its by-the-book *Letter rules*, and their end-goal *Spirit characteristics*:

--An "essay" in our sense here is simply *a text* (or a thinking) *with a "thesis and points."* With a theme, and aspects of it developed and discussed, with concrete specifics illustrating the conceptual subject. Useful approach…

--The *"five-paragraph theme"* of Old-School fame, is a version, albeit rigidly-ruled and formulaic, of this way of thinking-writing-communicating.

--Recently, educators (writing teachers) mainly *condemn* the 5PT as indeed arthritically-restrictive. As an empty final Form not truly a flexible function-toward-meaning.

--They are correct in this, but ironically in condemning the Letter of the 5PT (which is about all it consists of), *they may overlook the value* of the Spirit of "an idea plus its components discussed in order." The genius of exposition in this sense.

--To correct this misconception, we have *expanded* the 5PT into the "15-C" model of Expository Elucidation. It seeks to confront complexity more competently and yet without reduction. [SEE Tool-Kit on the "15-C Expository Elucidation for full-dress treatment of this.]

--But our point here is to use the 15-C model as *an instance of "Letter vs. Spirit."* To see rules or anyhow guidelines, procedures both by the letter correct—and also what their effect would be in Spirit.

--And so here is the two-part table distinguishing How To from Why and What Aimed For. We found ourselves

relying often on analogies to get the point of the Spirit across…
My English 101 students found this comparison/contrast of Correct and Effective, more elucidating than not…

TOOL-KIT. Fifteen checkpoints, variable-issues to consider in doing thesis-point thinking, writing:

1. **Complete:** Complexity, how much of total subject is surveyed then treated? Collected and Continued, is enough raw material information collected, discussion continued?

2. **Conceptualized:** is material moved from data to its ideas within, existing or potential?

3. **Con-Vergent:** is an overall unity achieved for all subparts (keystone, maypole)?

4. **Categorization:** is material divided into sub-points, at one or multiple levels?

5. **Crystallized:** are the resultant ideas stated explicitly enough, not implied or buried?

6. **Calibration:** are main and minor matters treated proportionately as appropriate?

7. **Concretized:** did writer "dip down" to provide specific examples to illustrate ideas?

8. **Contour:** as relevant, was the whole text subdivided into chunks of segments?

9. **Con-Sequent:** was the "best" structure/organization/arrangement of points achieved, from the "menu" of the many known options which do exist, whether always taught or not?

10. **Co-herent:** if points interrelate to each other logically, is this connection shown?

11. **Co-hesive:** is #10's integration shown by style—especially via powerful parallelism?

12. **"Concatenation":** is syntax, sentence structure good?

13. **Condensed:** is text free of wordiness, distilled to just-right compact-conciseness?

14. **"Camera":** are visual techniques used (charts diagrams graphs etc. and page-layout)?

15. **Correct:** is text made error-free, are conventions/constraints followed, as needed?

…compared with the "wheelbarrow" "Five-Paragraph Theme," the "15-C" seeks to be an "earth-mover"…

EXAMPLE. The "Letter vs. Spirit" chart for the 15-C essay form. Helped students to grasp the **purposes not just the procedures** of these components… As well as *The Very Idea Of*, **"Letter"…..vs." Spirit"**!

The Principle:	Correct by rule of letter:	Effective in spirit:
1. **Complete: Complexity,**	How much of total subject is surveyed then treated? **Collected** and **Continued**, is enough raw material information collected, discussion continued?	Do we feel a completeness of scope, depth of treatment: "hunger" satisfied, "all corners illuminated"? No nagging questions or perplexities?
2. **Conceptualized:**	Is material moved from data to its ideas within, existing or potential?	Do we feel arising from the "flesh" of data, information, facts, a "skeleton" of conceptual meaning of it all?
3. **Con-Vergent:**	Are all subparts related and relevant to each other and an overall unified theme?	Do we sense a thread-to-the-pearls, a maypole toward which all the elements point or tend?
4. **Categorization**	Is material divided into sub-points, at one or multiple levels?	Are the "eggs in the carton"? Were all "trapdoors" opened to reveal component subparts within one subject? Are the "hotel guests" in their proper rooms?
5. **Crystallized**	Are the resultant ideas stated explicitly enough, not implied or buried?	Whether by "blazing neon signs," or more subtle markers, can we tell what is the next idea?
6. **Calibration:**	Are main and minor matters treated proportionately as	Are you packaging big things in big boxes, economically taking only some of small

	appropriate?	things?
7. **Concretized:**	Did writer "dip down" to provide specific examples to illustrate ideas?	Do you provide the "juicy" instance to "rehydrate" the dry abstract concept for the reader?
8. **Contour:**	As relevant, was the whole text subdivided into chunks, segments, sections?	Were there rooms in the house, or all one space?...
9. **Con-Sequent:**	Was the "best" structure / organization / arrangement of points achieved, from the "menu" of the many known options which do exist, whether always taught or not?	Was the best "string for the beads" provided, so reader can approach them in best order, also not lose them?
10. **Co-herent:**	if points interrelate to each other logically, is this connection shown?	Are links, cords, lines connecting related series of objects?
11. **Co-hesive:**	Is #10's integration shown by style—especially via powerful parallelism?	"If three items are alike, so paint or label them alike, not differently..."
12. **"Concatenation":**	Is syntax, sentence structure good?	Does the "assembly line" flow in metered fashion?...
13. **Condensed:**	Is text free of wordiness, distilled to *just-right* compact-conciseness? (Content-to-wordcount ratio is good: not too wordy, not too telegraphic.)	Is the "specific gravity" good? Not diluted, not overly-condensed? (Or, are the boxes either overstuffed, or ¾ empty from contents rattling around in them?)
14. **"Camera"**	Are visual techniques used (charts diagrams graphs etc. and page-layout)? To visualize concepts, ease reading?	--A "map" represents layout of land or of idea-systems, as visual. Can we see better, the number and relation of elements on the scene? --Is the "reader's journey through the wilderness" smoothed by marked paths?
15. **Correct:**	is text made error-free, are conventions/constraints followed, as needed?	Is the person wearing the proper dress, attire, garments—for the occasion? Not a dirty torn shirt for a formal meeting—no distractions?

[{(END of Module on **"Letter vs. Spirit"** and Higher-Order Thinking...)}]

|~#|#|~+#|+#|+~#|+#|+|~+#|~+#|~+|#+|~+|#+|~+#|~+|#+|~+#|~+|#~+|#+|~#+|~+#|~#+|~|~#+|#~+|#+~|~+#|~|#||

#3.C.2. "DEFINITION": *Conceptual...*

--THE IDEA & THE NEED. Definition is one of the rhetorical modes. At a concrete, technical Level "I" it is fairly simple: "X is a Y which is not Z." But at once it gets complicated. For our purposes, at a conceptual Level "II," definition seems like *a key part of "essential thinking"*—especially INducting UPward.

    EXAMPLES. "Religion" "Wealth" "Pornography...Obscenity" "Capital": economic, also social, emotional, etc. "Literacies" or "Intelligences": verbal, visual, numeracy or mathematical, economic, emotional, other..." A "map" is a "description of the earth surface"—but *conceptually, much more...*

--OUR SUGGESTION. <u>Affirm</u> that "definition" can support Conceptualizing 101 or INducting UPward.

Guideline: **Pay attention to <u>more-specific concrete vs. more-ideological or archetypal general</u> meanings of words and concepts. For more thorough competent thinking-through of those words and concepts.**

SELF-EVALUATION OF THIS UNIT. Of course, <u>too simple, hence "unsatisfying."</u> **Definition** (like **cause-effect**) is a *major-major* specialty in itself. [I for one, could not bag the Foe or shady beast of Definition itself, too elusive to bring to the Museum.] But I trust *this is a solid start*, for others to take farther and better...

CONNEXIONS. [= Relations with other concepts in thinking:]
--**Letter vs. Spirit** plus **Appearance vs. Reality** [education, literature, capital and wealth, "obscenity," etc..]
--also **Categorization** or classification and division into subparts. ["Marriage," "Minority Group"]
--also **Concretization** or giving effective examples, instances, illustrations of the concept.

Level "I": The Conventional Basics of "Definition":

Formal Definition. "X is a Z which is not Y." Species, genus, differentia.
EXAMPLE. Brazing [*species*] is a welding process [*genus*] wherein [*differentia*] the filler metal is a nonferrous alloy whose melting point is higher than 1000 degrees F but lower than that of the metals or alloys to be joined." [-- SOURCE]

Level "II": Some Advanced Aspects of "Definition":

"ROADBLOCK." ...*but* Definition can quickly become *complicated, complex*... beyond our purposes here...

EXAMPLE #1: Types of Definitions: one of many Categorizations...
1. Standard: universal, rarely changing. (*mammal, piston, tornado*).
2. Regulatory: officially designated, variable (*workplace injury, full time student, recognized medical procedure*).
3. Evolving: reflect changing values? (*child abuse, mental retardation*).
4. Qualifying: limit abstract meanings (*obesity, slander, disability, harassment*).
5. Cultural: shaped by situation (*Gambling: pastime, or sin? Bribe: illegal, or a tribute?*)
6. Personal: individual (*pornography, prejudice*). [-- Mark Connolly, SUNDANCE READER]

EXAMPLE #2: An **historian** proffers *fifteen* <u>types</u> of formal definition.
1. Genus and difference. 2. Theoretical. 3. Lexical. 4. Stipulative. 5. Precising. 6. Enumerative. 7. Ostensive. 8. Genetic. 9. Constructive. 10. Operative. 11. Synonymous. 12. Analytical. 13. Synthetic. 14. Persuasive. 15. Figurative.
  [-- DAVID HACKETT FISCHER in <u>Historians' Fallacies,</u> pp. 277-80]

...Let us pause here short of advanced, Level "II" Defining. Let us move at once to our point here, that that *defining a something, is helped by* **conceptualizing upward to higher levels***...*

We move at once to this module's point. Definition: less or more conceptual...

VARIABLE-ISSUE. Note how a concept can expand out from an original component sense, to include other components "living in other arenas or regions" and which have <u>not</u> the _Form or Appearance_ of the original, but surely <u>do</u> possess the _Function and Spirit_ of it.

EXAMPLES. The concepts of **Property**... **Capital**... and **Literacy**...

[1.] To early American statesman JAMES MADISON, **property**, "in its _particular_ applications," means the dominion a man [_sic_] exercises over the external things of the world, "in exclusion of every other individual." As in one's house, land, bank account. But MADISON then also made a _broader_ point "In its larger and juster meaning," property "embraces everything to which a man may attach a value and have a right; and which leaves to everyone else the like advantages." This would include land, money, merchandise, but also opinions, religious beliefs, "safety and liberty" of one's person, "free use of his facilities and free choice of the objects on which to employ them. So, we have a right to our property, but also a property in our rights. [-- CHARLES VAN DOREN]

[2.] Capital in a sense expanded from _economics_, currently refers to "the sum total of the value of an intangible asset." _Social_ capital describes "those reservoirs of civic associations, communal norms, and bonds of social trust" which aid solving of shared problems. A shortage of "_emotional_ capital" can harm customer service, reduce productivity. _Sexual_ capital exists, also _symbolic, genealogical, verbal, mechanical,_ etc. Important is _natural capital_, the resources of "water, minerals, trees, fish, coral reefs, and far beyond." Misuse of these will spell limits to growth more than will shortcomings in industrial prowess. [-- FAITH POPCORN, Dictionary of the Future]

[3.] [Earlier, "literacy" has meant learning to <u>read printed words in a text</u>. But more recently, research suggests that "the reading of words is but a subset of _a much more general human activity_ which includes _symbol decoding, information integration, and organization_ .... Indeed, reading—in the most general sense—can be thought of as a form of perceptual activity. The reading of <u>words</u> is one manifestation of this activity; but there are many others—the reading of <u>pictures, maps, circuit diagrams, musical notes</u>..."
[-- TOM WOLFE, HARVARD EDUCATIONAL REVIEW]

> Note _the "literacy" version could go even farther_. We also "read" **myriad sociocultural "situations"** (see examples in Why The Very Idea, this same Appendix—_corporate culture of a business, the detective novel formula, the logic of a field foreign to us whether medicine or metallurgy,_ and more.) Plus, **yet other literacies exist:** cf. JOHN GARDNER'S seven kinds of _intelligences_, plus _visual_ literacy (as implied above), _numeracy_ or mathematical literacy, _economic_ literacy, etc. ...

VARIABLE-ISSUE. Note that it is _difficult to define certain concepts_; they may be slippery in their stages, phases, aspects. Still, one can attempt...

EXAMPLES. The difficulties of **[1.]** what is a **"game,"** **[2.]** what is **"sexual orientation,"** even **[3.]** what is **"having sex"**:

[1.] "Consider...<u>games</u>. I mean board-games, card-games, ball-games, Olympic games, and so on. What is common to them all?...if you look at them you will not see something that is common to all, but <u>similarities, relationships, and a whole series of them at that</u>...[board-games have relationships, then card-games correspond to the first group but some features drop out, others appear. Same with moving on to ball-games.] "Are they all amusing? Compare chess with [tic tac toe]. Or is there always winning and losing, or competition between players? Think of [solitaire]. In ball-games there is winning and losing; but when a child throws his ball at the wall and catches it again, this feature has disappeared. Look at the parts played by skill and luck; and at the difference between skill in chess and skill in tennis. Think now of games like ring-a-ring-a-roses; here is the element of amusement, but how many other characteristic

---

227

features have disappeared!...the result...is: we see <u>a complicated network of similarities overlapping and criss-crossing;</u> <u>sometimes overall similarities, sometimes similarities of detail.</u>" [-- WITTGENSTEIN, Philosophical Investigations]

[2.] Sexual orientation is complex. It is only one aspect of "bio-psycho sexual identity" perhaps which includes reproductive-type **sex** (male or female) but also **gender identity** (personal sense of being male or female), **sex roles** (social expectations about behavior). Not to mention **transvestism, transsexual, and transgender**—three different items. And what of **hermaphrodites**, the **intersexual, paraphilia**... *whoa*!

First, <u>sexual orientation is at least threefold</u>: 1. actual behavior, 2. self-identification (perhaps social image also), and 3. fantasy and arousal scripts and scenarios, with probably 4. overall part of total identity—in some times and places. [This is important; a man is married to a woman, calls himself heterosexual, but also cruises males at public rest rooms and fantasizes about males when performing sexually with his wife...]

A RESEARCHER IN COMMUNICATION reports the following dialog in her fieldwork: "Well, I call myself a heterosexual woman, but my associations with gay men have moved me to recognize and value my amorous attachments to women, like my old friend KARA. You claim to be a straight man, but you now redefine a connection with a friend from home as an 'attraction' of sorts. Likewise, JOE and ROB identify themselves as gay yet continue to respond erotically to women. Not all gay-identified men seem to; DAVID is a good example of that." [-- LISA TILMAN-HEALY, Between Gay and Straight]

[3.] An inquiring woman decided to <u>keep a record of the number of people she had "had sex with."</u> But complexities arose in the accounting. She first defined this as (1) *"penile-vaginal intercourse."* This omitted a man who consoled her when her boyfriend cheated on her—they "made out" strenuously, but without penetration. But then a Lesbian interlude of sex with other women further complicated things: no penetration, but many ways of relating. (2) So then, perhaps *"Feeling and being sexual, dancing and flirting, seductive backrubs"* and the like, might be "having sex"? (3) Or maybe situational definition was the key: *"if you thought of it as sex when you were doing it,* then it was." Or, was the criterion (4) *intent, an actual true pursuit of pleasure?* (4A) On <u>both</u> parties' parts? "...the *conscious, consenting, mutually acknowledged pursuit of shared sexual pleasure."* (This is broad but distinct and contains the key variables.) Or even just (4B) involving at least <u>one</u> of the people—in a dyad or even group? And what about (5) *"alternate sexualities"* such as power-exchange sex: dominance-&-submission, sado-masochism: spanking, bondage, obedience, fetishes, and the like—*is this erotic, even if no genitals (or even orgasms) are involved?* How about (6) *functional exhibitionism*, such as being a nude dance at a peep show? [-- GRETA CHRISTINA, "Are We Having Sex Now or What?"]

...well *you* sure did a *bad* job of **competently defining** these complex entities! {Talking dirty, too...}	...*well if these experts can't, how can I?* At least here: a clearer glimpse at cloudy complexity, and the potentials to avoid oversimplistic skimping... {Oh, and are we "defining" sexuality as sordid? Hmmmm...}

TECHNIQUE. Note that to expand the definition of something, <u>it may help to draw many specific but diverse examples from many varied locales</u>: arenas, venues, etc.

By the way, this "rounded contouring" is an advanced technique of specific detailing.

EXAMPLES. What is a "<u>map</u>"? Some **[1.]**literal standard definitions...an **[2.]**expanded one...and **[3.]** an amazingly-detailed one from a professional geographer, which utterly transforms the very Idea, of a "map" from Form to Function...

[1.] MAP A representation usually on a flat surface of the whole or a part of an area....something that represents with a clarity suggestive of a map. (Also the "celestial sphere," also "the arrangement of genes on a chromosome.") [-- WEBSTER'S COLLEGIATE DICTIONARY] [... **okay, fine, standard...**]

[2.] The concept of a **"SCORE"** is "<u>a system of symbols which can convey, or guide, or control..., the</u> <u>interactions between elements such as space, time, rhythm, and sequences, people and their activities and the</u> <u>combinations which result from them.</u>" They extend over time and space, they record, plan, reach out to others, and more. This general concept is then *illustrated by many instances*. "<u>Architectural blueprints</u> are scores. <u>Music</u> is composed and recorded by scores. <u>Mathematics</u> is a score. <u>Concrete poems</u> are scores. <u>Stage directions</u> for a play is a score, as is the written dialogue itself. A <u>shopping list</u> is a score. A <u>football play</u> is a score. The <u>choreography of dance</u> can be determined by a score. <u>Navajo sand paintings</u> are scores. The intricacies of <u>urban street systems</u> are scores as are the plans for transportation systems and the configurations of regions. Construction <u>diagrams of engineers</u> are scores." [-- SOURCE]

All true; perhaps becomes too lax and sprawling, however? Cf. the third and final example:

[3.] I think it helps to define a **map** simply, but quite profoundly, as <u>a representation of relationships between things</u>, for in this way we break loose from traditional earth space and see that many of the <u>spaces</u> where *people desperately need maps today* are <u>conceptual rather than terrestrial</u>. By all means give people who want to learn about maps [the traditional history of maps from the beginning of mastering the ability to draw an accurate picture of the world.] But people…cannot think with these historical examples. Rather, we should expose people to *the most imaginative examples* of mapping we can find: maps of relationships between married couples in various emotional states… maps of the South Pacific in geobotanical space… maps of New Zealand in changing aircost space… sound maps of moths terrified by bat squeaks… maps of intellectual winds blowing through psychology journal space… maps of the world in priority press telegram space… maps of phase spaces showing trajectories of systems… maps of influenza epidemics in cartograms of demographic space… projections of four-dimensional spaces on to three-dimensional maps of diffusion where a hierarchical process appears to be contagious… maps of Shakespearean tragedies based on the verbal interaction of the players… maps of the trajectories of characters in Bergman space… and so on.
[-- PETER GOULD, in Becoming a Geographer]

Marvelous example of "rounded sculpting" of a subject via specifics. Even if quite difficult and advanced and technical, the concept emerges of conceptual not terrestrial space, and the expansion of subjects and issues beyond landmasses and the like. All united by <u>the keystone concept of relationships between things, a key strength of visualization, perhaps even more important than the other apparent key feature of visualization, simultaneous grasp of multitudinous elements</u>…

TECHNIQUE. **To better understand something (here, "expanded definition"), select and present examples—but *multiple* examples, but *varied* not similar, and from *diverse* locations (arenas, venues, etc.) . This will round out the concept better. So, the following gallery of readings!**

GALLERY. A bouquet (potpourri?!) of attempts to **define-describe some common but complex subjects**. Itself a "rounded contour" of multiple but varied examples from diverse arenas, the collection *may* thus help expand the—yes indeed, "<u>the very definition, of…definition…</u>"

[1.]AGE chronological, mental, emotional, physical moral

[2.] PORNOGRAPHY… Literally, "the drawing or depicting of flesh." Of course, ultimately, "whatever arouses one sexually." Regrettably, to an erotic pyromaniac, the newspaper photograph of a house on fire…

[3.] OBSCENITY… Yes (1) <u>private body parts in public</u>… Thus, nude pictures are obscene. [Except to the Victorians even furniture legs were "obscene," had to be covered, and chicken arts were no longer legs thighs breasts but "light and dark meat"—and for the ancient Romans, a statue of Priapus, the household god of fertility, in full male arousal, was thought not only not obscene, but quite appropriate for protection…]
(2) But also "<u>contrary to accepted standards of decency</u>." [This expanded definition leads to "obscene" tagging the Vietnam war… showing peoples' private griefs on public newscasts… and a Black activist said, "Homosexuality is obscene, just like baby-rape and wanting to be president of General Motors"…]

[4.] MONEY, AND WEALTH… **[A] MONEY** = something accepted as a medium of exchange and a store of value because it exists only in limited quantities and because people have confidence in it. [-- probably NATIONAL GEOGRAPHIC] **[B] MONEY** = Something generally accepted as a medium of exchange, a measure of value, or a means of payment. [DICTIONARY]
[C] WEALTH = "abundance of valuable material possessions or resources"
[D] "RICH" = [1.] "Having abundant possessions and especially material wealth. Rich, wealthy, affluent, opulent. Goods property money in abundance. Rich: having more than enough, Wealthy possession Affluence prosperity increasing. Opulent lavish and display [-- DICTIONARY]

[2.] "Being wealthy is having $100 more than your brother-in-law..."

[3.] "You are wealthy when your expenditures are less than your income..."

[4.] "Wealth is the ability to get up in the morning, go back to bed [or not "to work"], and not have your life change." [-- MIKE STOLPER]

(*) And then the great arena of *non-economic* definitions of "wealth..."

[5.] HOME... A house or habitation; or, a person with whom you feel safe... a location in nature you belong with... activity which fulfills your spirit... relationship with your higher power. Generic: where one's soul is at rest, a quiet harbor in a stormy world. [-- SOURCE]

"Home is where, when you have to go there, they have to take you in." [-- ROBERT FROST, poet]

[6.] "NEWS"—what is news? Current events... Reader-serving; what is most interesting, useful, educational, entertaining, helpful to need and use in their daily lives... Global; far-off events which may later affect our near locations. Unusual, plus fast-breaking? Man bites dog? "News is what I say it is" – BEN BRADLEE, journalist

---

[7.] ADVERTISING... "Any *paid-for communication intended* to inform and/or influence *one or more people*." EXAMPLES: The sign outside a church naming next Sunday's preacher and sermon-topic. "Lost Budgerigar" "Locally-grown strawberries. Chairman's Statement. Don't Waste Water. (Etc.)
[-- BEHIND THE SCENES IN ADVERTISING]
Dictionary: calling something to public attention especially by paid announcements

---

[8.] AESTHETICS is "fundamentally the art of using line, form, tone, color, and texture to arouse an emotional reaction in the beholder." [-- THE SUBSTANCE OF STYLE]

[9.] ART, visual. Many definitions/descriptions of. [The Classic Great Tradition(s) [Related to this is pure aesthetic design, meaningful staying power]... Myriad sub-schools in the art world today (including commodity-to-consume, "anti-art," many others... Conventional folk familiar... Trendy edgy fashionable the Next Big Thing... Laissez-Faire relativism whatever we call art—also, "whatever appears in museums"... Socially-conscious Politics for Liberation... Just-Personal whatever expresses the artists, pleases the viewer... Religious or ceremonial act... Poetic Philosophy: enhances one's life meaningfully... Therapy, for artist or viewer etc. ... [-- CHESTER KARTOFFEL, Khronikles, XII, 12]

[10.] MUSIC = sounds temporarily organized by a person for the purpose of enriching or intensifying experience through active engagement (e.g., listening, dancing, performing) with the sound regarded primarily, or in significant measure, as sounds. (Classical folk party avant-garde music opera..."Muzak") [-- SOURCE]

[11.] "LITERATURE" What is it? Expanded, to beyond literal subject appearance literal to Appearance-Reality.

"There is no essence of literature whatsoever," no innate qualities. Rather, it's "a number of ways in which people relate themselves to writing." Any text can be read "non-pragmatically." "I pore over the railway timetable not to discover a train connection but to stimulate in myself general reflections on the speed and complexity of modern existence...I read Gibbons' fall of the Roman empire [not for truth] but "I enjoy G.'s prose style or revel in images of human corruption." [--T. EAGLETON]

--"I would sooner read a time-table or a catalog than nothing at all....I have [enjoyed] poring over the price list of the Army & Navy Stores, the lists of second-hand booksellers, and the A.B.C. All these are redolent of romance." [-SOMERSET MAUGHAM]

[12.] "MINORITY, a MINORITY GROUP" Is it more than just numerical minority?

1. Numerically-lesser than majority group(s) in a given society or locale. (But women are 52% of the population.

2. "Racial and/or ethnic." Blacks. Jews. Etc. (But this excludes social class, sexual identity, etc.)

3. Subject to oppression or unjustified discrimination. Physical, legal, institutional, sociocultural, internalized.

4. "The <u>experience of feeling</u> like an Alien Exile Outsider in One's Own Native Land."
5. .....

[13.] RELIGION... *Especially helpful*; notice how the definitions of "religion" can and do move upward from literal, perhaps limited, view, past dictionary definitions, beyond the Letter and into the Spirit of the concept. Specifically, <u>four</u> major dimensions: **[1.]** conventional Western Christianity, but then **[2.]** the "supernatural sacred transcendent divine," **[3.]** anything giving "a frame of orientation and object of devotion," **[4.]** a mechanism for dealing with issues of stress and danger and the like.

---

(1) "When I mention religion, I mean the Christian religion; and not only the Christian religion, but the Protestant religion; and not only the Protestant religion, but the Church of England."
[-- Mr. Thwackum, in Henry Fielding's Tom Jones]

(2) "The service and adoration of God or a god as expressed in forms of worship...An awareness or conviction of the existence of a supreme being, arousing reverence, love, gratitude, the will to obey and serve, and the like." [-- DICTIONARY]

(3) "Religion functions in such a way as to restore balance to the community and individuals in environmentally caused states of stress." [-- R. J. MILLER]   [= "*Anthropological naturalism?*"...]

(4) [Religion includes the extraordinary, not of the ordinary world, mysterious, and unexplained...apartness from the mundane...]   [-- E. NORBECK]

(5) "Man may worship **animals, trees, idols of gold or stone, an invisible god, a saintly man or diabolic leaders;** he may worship **his ancestors, his nation, his class or party, money or success;**...The question is not religion or not but what kind of religion." [-- ERICH FROMM]

(6) *Also:* concern with **success, social standing, economic power, worship of parochial states, pursuit of truth for its own sake, wealth power safety, collection of objects, a loved one, even the lorry of the lorry-driver in the world war...** etc.   [-- FROM OTHER SOURCES]

(7) From E. M. FORSTER'S novel <u>A Passage to India</u>, 1920's. A British woman in India resumes prayer:...

"Adela, after years of intellectualism, had resumed her morning kneel to Christianity. There seemed no harm in it, it was the shortest and easiest cut to the unseen, and she could tack her troubles on to it. Just as the Hindu clerks asked Lakshmi for an increase in pay, so did she implore Johova for a fvourable verdict. God who sves the King will surely support the police..." [-- E. M. FORSTER, A Passage to India '

[{(END of module on "Definition")}]

#3.C.3. ANALOGIES:

THE ISSUE. Analogy connects a **conceptual** with a **concrete** element. "My love is like a red rose." Analogies are powerful for all phases of confronting. To discover ideas, think something through, especially to communicate it well to an audience unaware of the idea at hand…

THE "SO-WHAT" PROBLEM-OPPORTUNITY. Why more on analogy? *So much has already been written*, pedagogical too. So we offer only one approach. Because, it has worked for us, and our students … it is _not_ commonly taught elsewhere…and it connects directly to **essential thinking as induction, conceptualizing upward** to the abstract idea needed to complete the analogy. This ploy has helped us create better analogies faster.

> [P.S. – Also, **analogy** as a thinking/communicating tools is, we feel, a powerful technique grossly under-utilized, even as is **comparison-contrast**, plus **concretization** or specifizing, of which analogy partakes. But this neglect is secondary here to our point of *creating better analogies easier, via* **conceptualizing** *up-and-over…*]

OUR SUGGESTION. **It may help to "conceptualize the concrete content—idea, experience, emotion—which you wish to explore more for yourself, convey to an audience."** Move upward; seek to identify and describe **the specific content, in general-abstract-conceptual terms**—its structure and function: its shape, then its heft, feel, movement: its archetypal **"kinetics"** or motion. ["Kinetics" = the motion of material bodies and the related force and energy.] This ploy may help discover the other half of the analogy."

Our key-tag term here, "archetypal psycho-physical kinetics," is jargony. Longer but clearer is **POEP or Plainer Old English Please:** "To better find an analogy for a subject, try to identify-or-create what is the essential nature or abstract quality or nature of the subject, including "emotions" etc., as a concrete description-event-process, often as *heft, movement, activity, physical feel or experience-of*."

The aim here is to help thinkers find the second half of the analogy, the vehicle. Done via this clarifying what is the core meaning one wishes to convey via analogy—clarifying by a dual tactic of both being more conceptual, but then also instantly more concrete and even experiential as in "body-motion."

But enough suffocating abstraction; let's descend from arid "Concept Peak" to "Concrete Pond" to refresh principles, with oxygen-filled particulars, examples… {to use an analogy for analogies, so to speak…}

~|#+~|+|+#|~+|#+~|#+~|#+|~+#|+#|~+#|~+#|+#~|#|~+~#|#+|+~|+|#+|~+|+|#~+#|+~+|#+|~+#|~+|#+~#|~+||~+|||

GALLERY. Examples of subjects (from concepts to feelings-experiences, etc.) I wanted to convey. And how I sensed the "generic kinetics" so to speak of the situation. Which then helped me to convey the subject.

Challenge: <u>The original point about the subject to convey</u>; but how, effectively?	*My feeling upward to the "concrete-conceptual" nature and perhaps activity of the subject:*	**Bingo or Eureka:** *the analogy Vehicle to convey the Tenor! Facts and feelings*…

EXAMPLE #1 A B C : Grief after bereavement or loss of a loved one by death. Three analogies:

[1.A.] THE POINT TO CONVEY: "Very heavy, not debilitating but impinging on one's usual well-being."	THE FEELING OF THE POINT: *"Something is staining me, marring my surface, not weakening me structurally but surely spoiling my, shall we say, sparkle…"* **AHA**, like a stain on a solid surface?...	[!] THE POINT ANALOGIZED: *"Grieving is like a block of marble getting stained by a bottle of black ink upset on it."* It percolates in and is currently unremovable, does not crumble the material, but stains, darkens, will take time to be leached out…

[1.B.] THE POINT TO CONVEY: "Grief: one is intact in one's person, but one's surroundings are now gloomy, unfriendly."	THE FEELING OF THE POINT: *"I am okay within my self or shell, but outside of me the world now seems bleak and indeed unfriendly..."* AHA, like a safe room in a storm?...	[!] THE POINT ANALOGIZED: *Grieving is like driving in good car in a bad rainstorm. Dry and light inside the vehicle, but outside the bad feelings lash at one...*

[1.C.] THE POINT TO CONVEY: "Grief can dislocate one from feeling centered, at home with the other person now lost..."	THE FEELING OF THE POINT: *"I am no longer have the Hearth or the Bedroom shelter of the other person to whom to return...* AHA, like exiled outside?...	[!] THE POINT ANALOGIZED: *Grieving is as if you no longer live in the House or Home with the Other, and retire to the Bedroom with them, but might as well just camp out on a cot in the kitchen, or living room, or workshop—still in a shelter, but now truly dispossessed...*

EXAMPLES 2 A B C. Successful psychoanalytic psychotherapy. How to communicate "basic gradual whole-person change for the better after arduous excavating and sanitizing the earlier traumas?"

Diminishment of symptoms: what was an obstructing kidney stone causing pain, has been shrunk, weakened, thinned, even if not totally pulverized... Your dank basement has been cleaned out from toxic mildew, floodlights installed so you can navigate...	Integration of parts of self: your psyche is a country or nation all of whose regions are finally smoothly in touch with each other via a telegraph system, no defenses or blockages...	Strengthening the psyche: you feel like a motor vehicle whose chassis has been rebuilt from weaker design to a stronger I-beam system. This supports weight better, and more smoothly negotiates any "bumps in the road" of daily life, not transmitting them shockingly to the passenger any longer...

EXAMPLES #3 AND #4. The intoxicated barber... and **the overly-sensitive friend:**

[2.] POINT TO CONVEY: How it was that the later in the day you stopped in the town barber's shop, the worse-for-wear you found him.	"Something okay and unaffected in the morning, but then getting more lively after noon with the first drinks, but then getting overwhelmed by just too much booze by evening." ..... *"An object can be inert when its certain propelling force is absent—can be properly articulate when that force is present in proper quantity—and can be overwhelmed by that force when excessively-present!"* AHA, like a boat beaten by a storm?	A barber in my home town was known for his tippling on the job. I saw him one morning—sluggish and hung-over—and this reminded me of *"a sailboat on a windless day, becalmed, undulating listlessly, waiting for propulsion."* Another time I saw him in the early afternoon, after he had obviously imbibed a little—he was cheerful, loquacious, snipping away with the scissors, energized—and this reminded me of *"a sailboat in a proper rising steady breeze, bowling right along, drawing its energy from the propelling wind."*.....A third time I saw him in late afternoon, after he had obviously imbibed much too much—he was lurching, staggering, incoherent, blurred and smeared—and this reminded me of *"a sailboat overwhelmed by a storm, pitching and yawing, risking being submerged...."*

[3.] POINT TO CONVEY: When I gave a mild criticism to an over-sensitive friend of mine, he over-responded with a blast of denial, defensiveness, and attacking of me too.	*A simple innocent minor stimulus, can produce an inappropriately major over-response.* AHA, like a hairtrigger response, that's it, a tense combat or military situation?...	*"When I as a soldier sent a simple pot-shot or single volley toward my friend on enemy lines during an argument, he over-responded with a counter-blast of rifles, artillery, saturation-bombing...."*

EXAMPLES #5 A AND B. "Incestuous": analogies for our project **Teaching Thinking, Mind-Play** itself:

[5.A.] Some analogies to try to describe **this whole book itself, its functions and purposes:**
Vitamin and mineral **supplement**... Survival-kit, shrink-wrapped... Bank savings-box pass-key, (valuable, but Open to All)... Swiss Army knife (versatile... Tour-guides to a foreign country, terrain... Armchair adventure book of

expedition of play of mind... Do-it-yourself self-help manual... *Not* a *snake-oil suspect product*... *Not* a *messiah's soapbox-manifesto*... *Not* an *orthodox "bible"* ... *Not* a 1-2-3 rote *rulebook recipe*...

[5.B.] Some "controlling, master analogies" for **specific major thinking-skills** within the book itself:

[Verticalities or the ladder of abstraction: making statements more-specific or more-concrete.] "Be able to read your *altimeter* to ascertain how concrete or conceptual your observation or statement is, and lower or raise as needed..."

[Comparison/Contrast, as way of conveying unfamiliar material via the already-known.] "Use C/C as a series of *stepping-stones in a pond* to lead to the new while yet one foot in the old..."

[Categorization, or classifying and dividing a subject into component subparts.] "C-D offers you a *trapdoor or panel* to remove from the seemingly-unified surface of a subject to discern variety within and below. (2) Then to construct a scheme, it's an *exclusive hotel*: each "guest" or component subpart belongs in one level or category of appropriate room and in no other!"

[Strategic monitoring of the totality, surveying and scanning so as to miss nothing needful.] (1.A) "You are in an *observation blimp* to see both the forest and the trees, plus even (1.B.) *a space-ship orbiting* the planet, in both cases with varied instruments: lenses telephoto and wide-angle, x-ray vision, and the like. Also, (2.) *a 12-story building* seen in its *3-D blueprint view* which is more than just the *entrance lobby*..."

[Number & Relation.: one, two many items and joining or distinguishing them:] (1.) " *Cell division,*" should one separate and make two or more out of what is wrongly seen as just one? Or, (2.) "space-shuttle link-up to reach out and lasso" two items which belong together..."

[Major Change, confronting it over time:] *"Terrain"*: "The <u>present</u> is the clear portion of the road or path right here and now, but *"mists and fog"* on the distant road may obscure the <u>past</u>, and *a bend in the road* block view of the <u>future</u>... One needs as much "*radar*" as possible to see through, while realizing that "*short-sighted vision*" prevails anyhow..."

[15-C or expository elucidation, the essay or thesis-and-points way of thinking and writing...] The traditional "five-paragraph theme" of schoolwriting is *a primitive wheelbarrow*, but the 15-C model, conceptual and complete, is more like a *"powerful forklift or front-loader combined with an all-wheel-drive pickup truck..."*

[Concretization, or use of specific detailing to support abstract ideas in thinking, writing, communicating...] (Examples, illustrations, evidence, etc.) "Concepts are *freeze-dried abstractions*, we need *the warm water* of <u>specificity</u> to unlock, unpack, refresh them." [{ EXAMPLE: "BENSON was a very bad roommate," vs. "his unwashed dishes, his unpaid bills, his unlocked doors, his booming stereo, his unpredictable nudity," etc. }]

["Lenses" or <u>perspectives, viewpoints, systems-of-thought upon reality</u>...] These ways-of-confronting are like *interchangeable camera lenses*. <u>Inevitable</u>: can't photograph (or see and think) without some lens, it's a blur... <u>Good-and-bad</u>: but every lens gives both power but also incompleteness plus bias(wide-angle includes all but distorts; telephoto brings in distance but in shallow focus; etc.)

[<u>Motivations or propulsions, drives: the reasons why we think, and act, as we do</u>...] We may be *"puppets"* actually run by the *"puppetmaster"* of (1) sociocultural norms mores ideologies etc., plus (2) our own personal com-pulsions. We jerk on the string, not really choosing to think for ourselves.

[Elucidation of a subject: = a more complete comprehensive view which is also comprehending with understanding, also comprehensible to others—compact etc.] As if the <u>subject</u> is *"a small complex machine,"* but no longer <u>left dirty</u> <u>disassembled etc. in a drawer in the unlit toolshop</u> [= much amateur thinking/writing] ... but instead, is <u>cleaned, assembled, placed on display in a museum, on an eye-level stand, lit shadowless, slowly rotating, its parts labeled</u>...

[The "<u>principles</u> beyond the particulars," the <u>key concepts</u> beneath-behind-above the concrete information...] These are like *"foundation-stones; pillars; roofbeams or keystones; northstars for orientation in navigation"*... Also, they are like a *"workshop tool"* both fixed (conceptual) and also flexible-adaptable), like a **Swiss Army Knife** or better, a calipers infinitely-adjustable to different circumstances, but delivering the same service to all tasks...]

["<u>Zeitgeist</u>" or the intellectual spirit of the times: the current fashions of thinking.] Subliminal ideologies, today's truths and taboos, <u>can subtly misdirect good thinking</u>, even as *a ship* navigating a course toward a harbor can be set off course by *compass-error, sideways current, windage…*

["<u>Slant</u>" means focusing one's writing exactly toward a particular situation: audience, publication, arena.] [EXAMPLE: writing about <u>the F-15 fighter-plane</u>, is quite different for the <u>Reader's Digest</u> (folksy), <u>Rolling Stone</u> (over-age hip), <u>Atlantic Monthly</u> (liberal political analysis/critique), <u>Flying</u> (envious amateur pilots)…] This dovetailing must be as exact as (1) *grooming one's child for entry* into an exclusive school etc., (2) *nurturing a plant to survive only in one narrow ecological niche.* would perish outside, but thrives therein…

[6.] EXAMPLES. **Traditional Asian proverbs** translated in W. S. MERWIN'S <u>Asian Figures</u>.

"RAT CLIMBS A HORN. NARROWER AND NARROWER."
A rat is climbing a horn. A creature is progressing upward on something. Seems upward hence good, but that thing is narrowing and will end. Perhaps the journey will end—unsuccessfully. [#] " A danger may lie in pursuing a route apparently 'upward' but **actually limiting, dead-end."** [For INSTANCES…]

"ANTS ON A MILLSTONE; WHICHEVER WAY THEY MOVE, THEY GO ROUND WITH IT."
Creatures are moving freely around a large surface. But the surface itself is also moving. The creatures can move or not as they choose, but in the larger sense they are being moved by larger forces… [#] "We may well have freedom of movement and action on one Level or Arena (etc.), but that Level itself may be moved or controlled etc. itself and we may have no control over that larger direction." [FOR INSTANCES…]

"JELLY IN A VISE."
A substance is being compressed to be held firmly, but the more one compresses it, the more it will just drip and squeeze out. [#] "Some elements you may wish to 'get a grip upon' to control or manipulate etc., but some of them may be too evasive for your usual method or tool to successfully contain, retain…" [For INSTANCES: One can't get a grip on a slippery object, person, etc. …]

"IRON HINGE, STRAW DOOR."
"The door is secured by a strong hinge, but the door itself is not as strong as its support, protection, emplacement… [#] "For ultimate security, beware the Pitfall of making sure that all the elements in the system are strong enough, not only the more-obvious, known, etc., elements." Cf. the other proverb or saying, "A chain is only as strong as its weakest link." [For INSTANCES:]

#7. EXAMPLE. WILLIAM BLAKE'S classic **poem "The Sick Rose."** But what is its theme, point?

| THE POEM: "O Rose, thou art sick! The invisible worm, That flies in the night, In the howling storm, Has found out thy bed, Of crimson joy, And his dark winged love, Doth thy life destroy." | THE ONLY TRUE CORE MEANING, achieved by conceptualizing upward: "**Something insidious seeks to conquer something beautiful but vulnerable involving perhaps passion and desire also…**" | BUT, FREQUENT TOO-CONCRETE MISREADINGS BY STUDENTS: (1) "Totalitarianism destroying democracy… (2) Adultery destroying a marriage… (3) Illness destroying a body… (4) and others… |

| …well, **GOOD**-enough: I <u>am</u> seeing how analogizing can depend on conceptualizing-ability. To induct up to the still-subliminal idea above and behind the subject-example, then to "re-clothe" that more-clarified idea in another concrete instance. Often involving shape and motion, a generic heft and kinetic thrust perhaps… | *That was indeed our only point here.* Better analogizing through **inducting upward** to the—point above particulars… |

~|#+~|+|+#|~+|#+~|#+~|#+|~+#|+#|~+|~+#|+#~|#|~+~#|#+|+~|+|#+|~+|+|#~+#|+~|#+|~+#|~+|#+~#|~+||~+|||

[{(END of "Analogies" and conceptualizing)}]

~|#+~|+|+#|~+|#+~|#+~|#+|~+#|+#|~+|~+#|+#~|#|~+~#|#+|+~|+|#+|~+|+|#~+#|+~|#+|~+#|~+|#+~#|~+||~+|||

THE CONCEPT/ISSUE. Creative thinking, conceptual blockbusting, lateral thinking and the like for problem-solving—these are widespread methods.

THE SO-WHAT PROBLEM-OPPORTUNITY. Indeed, so what for us here? Of all our thinking-skills, surely "creativity" is the one which has been *already sufficiently taught by existing programs...* (EDWARD DEBONO's systems and many more.) So what can we add that merits print (=is new, true, useful)? *Only one thing...*

OUR CONTRIBUTION. We simply focus on one generic skill. **"Induct or conceptualize upward beyond the *literal concrete letter* of the situation to the idea or abstract <u>spirit of the task</u>. State in very abstract conceptual archetypal terms, what the <u>goal or need</u> is to be attained. This 'archetypalizing' of the issue may jumpstep one toward seeing a specific solution."** Now that sentence remains impossibly unclear (or lacks needed examples). But its idea is the key to importing "creative" imaginative flexible thinking to solve everyday problem-issues. Below, we'll follow FRED (that's his name, but we'll call him that anyhow) accomplishes tasks with small breakthroughs by thinking outside the literal box and moving up to *the very idea* or concept of what is the goal at hand which needs solving...

#|+#|+#|+#|+#|++#|+|#+||#++#|#||+|#+|#+|#+|+#+#|+|+|#+|+#||+#|+|#||#|+|+#|+#|+|#+|#|+|#+|#+|#+|#+|#+|#+|+#|+#|+|#+|#+|#+|#+||

EXAMPLE. Important is to move from appearance-form goal, to concept-behind. A veteran advertiser gives a clear example of how this creativity can be done:
"If you want to <u>feed birds in the winter</u>, and keep them safe from predatory cats, you might look in our attic to see if you've got a <u>bird-table</u>. But if you set out to look for a bird-table, you will look narrowly, screening out everything that isn't a bird-table—and you may fail to find one. Yet if you look not for a bird-table, but for something (or for some things) from which a bird-feeder could be improvised, you will see a dozen possibilities. Everything in your attic is seen and evaluated as you've never seen it before: not for what it is, but for what, quite specifically, it might be." [-- BEHIND THE SCENES IN ADVERTISING]
Cinches the concept. How to do this well? Apparently, by keeping in mind the general contoured concept itself. This ploy employs **Letter** (literal **Form**) *vs.* **Spirit** (figurative **Function**). As in the following example:

EXAMPLE. Thinking inside, and outside, the box, for **"on-the-road bicycle-repairs..."**
<u>Conventional</u>: What is wrong, are parts broken, what tools do I need to use, how do I actually do this repair? <u>Innovative</u>, as needed: Use a dime as a screwdriver. Use duct tape to repair a broken spoke temporarily. Use a house key to dig a nail out of your tire. Use a nutrition-bar wrapper (or a dollar bill) to fix a slashed tire casing. [-- SOURCE: [Bicycling for Challenged Individuals]...]

#|+#|+#|+#|+#|++#|+|#+||#++#|#||+|#+|#+|#+|+#+#|+|+|#+|+#||+#|+|#||#|+|+#|+#|+|#+|#|+|#+|#+|#+|#+|#+|#+|+#|+#|+|#+|#+|#+|#+||

EXAMPLES. A "typical day" for FRED, who succeeds via "thinking via the essential idea" thus:

The **NEED/GOAL** FRED seeks to attain:	The **PROBLEM** blocking it. (Beware concrete thinking here.)	(*) FRED's ascent to the **CONCEPTUAL** version of the issue...:	...and FRED sees the *"aha!"*-**SOLUTION** appear:
[1.] While driving off-road outside of town, FRED got his truck stuck	Well, [1.] *"Need to take a shower, but of*	So,[2.] ***Really need, an onslaught, a splash, a gush,***	*Presto,* right down the street, the CAR WASH!

in the mud. He bicycled back to town for help, but how to clean the mud off his feet, legs, arms?	*course no showers available downtown. Arrgggghhhh…"*	*of water over me. Where can I get that?*	Unconventional but effective.
[2.] Then he phoned the tow truck to meet him in front of the supermarket, but had missed lunch and had no spare cash on him. How to get food?	[1.] *"Need food, but no money— should I beg it or steal it? Arrggh…"*	So, [2.] *"Where might food be available—don't think, just scan the scene uncensored."*	Presto, right in the DUMPSTER behind the supermarket he scored a banana and some bread…
[3.] While waiting, he found he had to urinate, and badly— but where?	No bathrooms available (let's assume all stores nearby were closed…)	*"Need to relieve myself but be unobserved by the public while I do so."*	Presto, A GROVE OF BUSHES behind the dumpster provided effective if unconventional shelter—laws, also norm-mores, violated, but the spirit or principle achieved: private space for personal action… [P.S. – this can only remind of EDWARD DE BONO'S classic example in the literature on "problem-solving through creative thinking." Subjects were assigned to extract a ping-pong ball from inside a pipe almost the same size as the ball, fixed vertically on the floor. "How to elevate or raise or extract the ball up and out? Float it, but the room offered no tap water or bottled liquids either… " Subjects considered the coathanger, blowing on it, using glue, etc. (all either ineffective or unavailable). The group remained blocked until later, one person thought of *urinating* into the pipe and thus floating it up free…]
[4.] Later that evening FRED bicycled across town to a meeting at the University Mall. Exiting, he found it had started to rain, but he hadn't brought any raincoat.	Where to get a raincoat? Stores were closed and anyhow buying one would be too expensive—	*"Need any covering for my body which will shed water"*	—presto, FRED visited a large trash on the building entry at the sidewalk and secured a very large strong black PLASTIC TRASH CAN LINER with very little trash in it. Poked three holes in it for neck and arms and voila, FRED rode home, again unconventionally, but much drier.
[5.] Next week he went to a conference, stayed in a very small hotel room, a friend wanted to leave a huge suitcase for an interval,	But this was inconvenient. "How to sequester the suitcase safe but unobtrusively? "Couldn't hang it from the ceiling…	*"What large empty space exists"*	Bingo, put it in THE SHOWER STALL, easily removable when showering, secured otherwise…
[6.] FRED had to dry out some underwear he had washed in the hotel room.	How? After rolling it in a towel, it was still wet. The only heat-source was an electric radiator on the wall, but too hot to set cloth on and no hook above it.	*"How to suspend or float the clothing, on a hangar, above the heater? By what materials at hand or nearby, even if…"*	PRESTO, he set a CHAIR in front of the heater and put a LUGGAGE TABLE on top of it and the clothing thus above but near the heater… [Might have also looked in the alleyway out back!]
[7.] Upon return, FRED had to suspend a picture from a wall hook, but had absolutely no string, line, cord, wire.	What to do? [Glue or paste was available, but not applicable—too weak, mars the surface…]	*"The goal is to create some, any, linkage to support picture from hook." What materials could possibly form a chain of--…..*	PRESTO, in the desk drawer were hundreds of PAPER CLIPS. Fred strung a couple dozen together to create an effective chain.
…And yet another…	The problem…	The very Idea-statement	AHA the solution…

#|+#|+#|+#|+#|+#|++#|+|#+#||#++#|#||+|#+|#+|#+|+#+#|+|+|#+|+#||+#|+|#||#|+|+#|+#|+#|+|#+#|#|+#+#|#|+#+#|+#|+#|+|#+|#+|#+|#+|+#|+||

EXAMPLES. Sometimes the ploys help of (1) **lateral sideways dual-reversals**, plus (2) **other items at hand but out of the range of thinking-vision**… FRED employed these refinements competently:

[8.] FRED had *only one clean* T-shirt to wear, but <u>its pattern was inappropriate for the occasion</u>. **"How to wear a shirt but conceal the pattern?"**... AHA, simply **reverse** it, turn it **inside out**.

[9.] FRED'S <u>last large plastic trash bag has a large hole in the bottom.</u> *No duct tape* (etc.) around to repair it. **"How to get the bag to hold trash solidly?"** AHA, Fred **reversed** things; tied the top bag shut with a knot, enlarged the hole in the bottom, upended the bag to receive trash now...

[10.] FRED bought a cheap tape player which soon broke in that the reverse or rewind broke, so <u>he could not rewind a played tape</u>. **"How to rewind the tape?"** AHA, he **reversed** things; **played the other side on fast forward**, thus rewinding the tape efficiently...

[11.] <u>The batteries</u> on Fred's pocket flashlight (or TV remote control) (or electric shaver) (etc.) <u>failed.</u> *He had no extra batteries.* What to do? **"How to get batteries? Where are batteries?"** AHA, a **sidewise** move, broadening tunnel-vision: Fred **took a couple from another appliance at hand**...

[12.] FRED needed <u>a second seat for the bicycle bought at the garage sale, for a ride this very afternoon.</u> *But the bike shops were closed or distant.* **"Where is any kind of seat**?..." AHA, in the basement, Aunt Maude's **old bicycle** with a seat one can borrow.

#|+#|+#|+#|+#|++#|+|#+|#++#|#||+|#+|#+|#+|+#+#|+|+|#+|+#||+#|+|#||#|+|+#|+#|+|#+|#|+|#+|#+|#|+|#+|#+|#|+#|+#|+|#+|#+|#+|#+|#+||

CONNEXIONS.   Some relations of this **Conceptual Creativity** with <u>other thinking tools</u>:

-----A strong connection with **Letter==Spirit** (form==function; correct==effective; etc.)
-----A mild connection with many of the eight major "moves": [SEE App. #6, Pre-Vue]
--Move #1, SMT or **Strategic Monitoring of the Totality** (the whole forest and trees)...
--Also Move #2, **Survey the Subject**: beyond conventional borders, etc. ["from A to Z but then beyond to **outlandish AA, BB, etc.**" and also the **exotic**, never dreamed of (types of Sailboat rigs: A-frame mast... Bicycle frame types: diamond but also recumbent supine prone... Directions of writing on page: L to R and down the page plus more...Book-binding forms: codex but also scroll... Ship motions in seaway: pitch roll yaw but also heave sag surge... etc., etc.]...
--Also #3, **Field** or context...
--And Move #7, major **Change**, especially "different pew in church, or even new church entirely..." But especially, **Categorization**. (Property, literacies, learning-styles—all are more multiple-diverse than we originally think.)

#|+#|+#|+#|+#|++#|+|#+|#++#|#||+|#+|#+|#+|+#+#|+|+|#+|+#||+#|+|#||#|+|+#|+#|+|#+|#|+|#+|#+|#|+|#+|#+|#|+#|+#|+|#+|#+|#+|#+|#+||

GALLERY. A bouquet of **other** "outside-the-box" solutions via moving "upward-to- idea":

[13.] <u>Need a picture of one's face for dermatological record.</u> *No camera.* "*What creates an image?*" AHA, the copying machine...

[14.] <u>Need a place to store manuscripts safe from theft and fire when on vacation.</u> *No fire safe.* "*What will give some protection, shelter, insulation anyhow from fire, also theft*"? AHA, in the toolshed, an old refrigerator. Put MSS in them and chain it shut...

[15.] Need to <u>measure the dimensions of a tabletop</u> (to see if a cover will fit, etc.) But *no yardstick, ruler, tape-measure.* "*What item or object will give a measurement? No longer the king's foot...*" AHA, a piece of letter-sized paper, right at hand, is 11 inches long, we know...Similarly, <u>to draw a perfect circle</u> *but no compass available,* AHA trace a jar or use string to control pencil!

[16.] <u>Need to vacuum carpet from a spilling of lint and sawdust</u> *the brush won't sweep up, and no vacuum-cleaner.* *What object or method will lift the fragments right up, catch them?* AHA, some duct tape or Contac paper or other sticky adhesive!...

[17.] <u>Need to remove some black lines on a white "black"-board.</u> *Clorox and scrubbing won't efface them.* *How to make them white?* AHA, simply use "whiteout" or white paint...

[18.] <u>Need to cut pungent onions on the wooden board in the kitchen which however the cook likes to keep free from strong-flavored ingredients.</u> "Can't clean it adequately—*what surface to use?*" AHA, simply reverse the board, and use the underneath side for more-demanding cutting jobs...

[19.] AT THE GARAGE SALE OR THRIFT SHOP. Think not form or original use, but possible new function.

X That <u>bacon cooker</u>, the plate with ridged grooves—makes a groovy desktop pen and pencil holder!

X That <u>old wire 45 RPM record-holder</u>—cut out every other division, makes a dandy file-folder holder!

...well, **OKAY**: Conceptualizing does aid creativity...	...Just another feather in the head of INducting UPwards!

[{(END of mini-unit on CREATIVITY via Conceptualizing)}]

APP. #6: "Tool-KITS"

"*wallet-cards*" on selected THINKING SKILLS…

THE ISSUE. Can thinking skills be described and taught "better"? *We believe so, and in identifiable way,…*

WHY IMPORTANT? --We feel that—ironically—<u>at least a fair amount of</u> instructional material (on how to think; on other subjects and skills A to Z…) is **<u>not</u>** "thought out." Not taken **[1]** *upward* to keystone concepts, nor **[2]** *downward* to vivid specifics, across to connections and applications. And for that matter also not **[3]** *"outward*, to widen the **"catchment-area"** surveyed to find these skills A wide sweep can involve (A) surely more than just one field, discipline, arena, etc., and (B) ideally also more than just one compiler/educator [too often but unavoidably, this lack has operated right here in <u>Teaching Thinking</u>, where Yours Truly the solo operator had to scrupulously survey others' responses also …].

--We need to cast the net wide because no one mind, or system, can "see it all" (all aspects of some skill)— skills have multiple originating-points (disciplines, etc.).

--This approaches fuller **elucidation of a skill.** (**ANALOGY:** If a complex subject or skill can be seen "as if like a small complex machine," it's the difference between the machine seen *not* "dirty disassembled in a dark drawer etc.," *but* rather as if "displayed in a museum, on an eye-level stand, in shadowless floodlighting, slowly rotating, its parts all labeled"…)

> Methods do exist for **eclucidating**: SEE section on E. at end of App.# 6, Pre-View of Mind-Play Repertoire

OUR SUGGESTION. The following seven "tool-kits" seek to exemplify this aim-and-claim.

<u>PURPOSE, USE OF THIS SEPTET:</u> **(1)** As "ready-to-wear," off-the-rack, turnkey-ready tools to use or to teach? Only *secondarily* here—though they'll work well for that. **(2)** *Primarily*, they're to <u>support our claim </u>that **"complexity needs competent complexity."** That is, **challengingly-complex subjects and skills (1) repay, indeed require, competently-complex but also curated and clarified explanations… and (2) that such quality is difficult, but more possible than many educators and even thinkers realize, teach about, do, or even "enjoy"—possible, furthermore, without either oversimplification-and-formulizing, or overelaboration-and-laxness.** This standard, our Tool-KITS seek to attain—and illustrate.

> [We question what we see as a **PWM** or **"Prevalent Widespread Misconception."** Namely, <u>equating clarification, with formulization</u>. That is, assuming that "<u>for a skill (or concept etc.) to be "explicit," necessarily risks its becoming simple, simplistic, a rote rule or recipe.</u>" *Not necessarily so…* But a few educators assume a "toolbox" approach means or equals restrictive formulae, as if a "rulebook" approach. But actually tools are liberating, empowering heuristics.]

TRAITS: HOW TO ACCOMPLISH THIS GOAL OF DEMONSTRATING BETTER SKILLS?
[1.] Virtually all of these kits seek to achieve **<u>elucidation</u>**—an image of a subject simultaneously more <u>Comprehensive</u> (all bases covered)… more <u>Comprehended</u> (explained in depth not just surface-described)… and more <u>Comprehensible</u> (compact-concise and clarified for the user, even if packed heavy with power…)

[EXAMPLE: those two hypothetical guidebooks to a foreign territory for independent travelers. Each 200 pages— but, the one, thin, disproportionate, overgeneral or concept-free, plus overly-detailed, badly-highlighted… the other, scrupulously complete, calibrated in balance of emphasis, with key concepts plus the best detail, navigable easily.]

[2.] And all were assembled from a wider **"catchment-area"** than are most materials. Hence more complete.

[EXAMPLE: **cause-effect** draws not only on Occam's Razor or "economy of explanation" from science, which holds that less is more, that which is explained well with few factors is badly explained using more… but also needs psychoanalysis' concept of overdetermination, which holds that "the more the factors identified, the more probably accurate is the explanation of the symptom…"]

A PERSONAL STAND. I favor "proffered availability of skills. I "intellectually lust" to make available, accessible as if on a "peg-board in the workshop," the whole **repertoire** of tools available, both complete and also clarified, usable… *I cannot objectively justify* this passion that it's "useful, moral, and beautiful" to clarify method competently thus. *To try would be only to rationalize*—and we see enough of *that* around. Plus, I trust that I sublimate my objectively—I don't argue to persuade and convince that "everybody should do thus." I simply try to distill the passion into practicality.

#|+#|+#|+#|+#|++#|+|#+||#++#|#||+|#+|#+|#+|+#+#|+|+#+|+#||+#|+|#||#|+|+#|+#|+#+|#|+|#+|#+|#+|#|+|#+|#+|#+|#+|#+|+#|+#|+|#+|#+|#+|#+|#+||

Table of Contents of App. #4, "tool-bank" of "KITS" on selected skills:

[1.] CHANGE: how to handle major change… *plural* perspectives on this perennial happening. Corralled from varied disciplines: history, psychology, sociology.
More than in any other basic resource we've seen.
[Four types… scale or size… pace or speed… Response-cycle of Heresy, Orthodoxy, Commonplace… Today's Truths & Taboos" plus the In-Out Cycle… Pew vs. Church, and New Bottles Old Wine… Incomprehensibility: unthinkable, vs. non-imaginable… Unpredictability: Retrospective and Forward Myopias…]

[2.] STRUCTURE organization arrangement sequence, of writing— but also of any series of items…
[Beyond the usual "less to more important" etc.: more types, and issues/options, than elsewhere…]

[3.] CAUSE-EFFECT… One cause or many, primary and secondary, but also *much more*, and from A to Z fields… [**Tipping-point, threshold**… **Butterfly** effect… **Latent & Manifest** functions… **Systems**… **Interdisciplinary**…]
[Although better than most other "checklists," by no means perfect-ly satisfactory—C-E requires dedicated specialist-experts. Others are invited to augment…]

[4.] "LENS-WORK" or the skill of confronting via explicit multiple-plural perspectives … "Look at the subject from three different perspective," fine, but a dozen key variable-issues exist about viewpoints.
[LENSES are: **Inevitable!**… Too often left **subliminal**… **Double-Edged:** insightful, but biased/incomplete… Can become **outmoded**—or, wrongly **neglected**… May be **elusive:** difficult to locate the best lenses… **Others**…]

No other resource so explicitly elucidates these keystone concepts about diverse angles-of-vision.

[5.] SPECIFIC DETAILING in writing, reading, communicating.

We all know the mantra, "Support your idea with an example," but many other issues-and-options exists.

> [**Reasons** for ("rehydrate abstractions")... six pervasive **types** of... eight **variables** to consider at the paragraph-level... the blending of **Essay and Story**... and **more**...]

Real writers in the real world use a raft of skills which textbooks don't yet conceptualize, make explicit. **We do so here for the first time; no other resource seems to touch the number of bases we do here, at least**

6.] "15-C" OR EXPOSITORY "ESSAY"-ELUCIDATION

Exposition, or the "thesis-and-points" way of handling subjects via "idea-subpoints-examples-discussion," remains *powerful*. But it may have become *undervalued*, probably *underused*, surely *undertaught* today—in its powerful essence. It has a bad image: too formal, rigid, etc., as the rote-ruled "Five Paragraph Theme": "State your thesis, develop it in three points with examples, conclude" which seems perhaps *over-taught*, surely *under-enhanced*, today. Although not applicable to all writing tasks, thesis-points exposition is more useful than realized even in Letter, and especially so in Spirit for good thinking. **This unit shows the more-complete scope of this way of thinking—as no other does.**
[We offer no fewer than fifteen issues to consider—Conceptual, Convergent, Coherent, Concretized (specifics), Con-Sequent (structure), Calibrated (proportion), "Camera" (visual layout), and eight more—yes, including "Correctness" but only as one element...]

[7.] "DIVERSITY EDUCATION"... Majority-group students could gain

truly-"empowering" abilities to handle challenging multicultural situations "after school later on in real-life"—by being given less mere Inert Information and "P.C."-Indoctrination plus pure Experience, in favor of some key Concepts as tools.

> ["Selective Perception" is insidious... **Relativism is both Moral, but also Cultural... Stereotypes** are suspect, but **"Sociotypes"** or group features do exist and can be valuable to know... And a dozen others...]
> **We've found many good approaches to Diversity Education, but no other resource which corrals as many of these cutting-edge concepts from the social sciences for better interrelating.**

[{(END of the Introduction to the seven Tool-Kits...)}]

#|+#|+#|+#|+#|++#|+|#+|||#++#|#||+|#+|#+|#+|+#+#|+|+|#+|+#||+#|+|#||#|+|+#|+#|+#|+|#+|#|+|#+|#+|#+|#|#+|#+#|+#|+#|+|#+|#+|#+|#+||
#|+#|+#|+#|+#|++#|+|#+|||#++#|#||+|#+|#+|#+|+#+#|+|+|#+|+#||+#|+|#||#|+|+#|+#|+#|+|#+|#|+|#+|#+|#+|#|#+|#+#|+#|+#|+|#+|#+|#+|#+||

241

ToolKit #1: "CHANGE":
Confronting Major, Mandatory Changes Competently…

INTRODUCTION. It's a truism that major change is a challenging issue nowadays. [True, we're more able today than earlier, to see and manage change; *but still…*] (Change in both external reality conditions-situations-events, and also in internal response-systems of lenses, perspectives, viewpoints, systems of seeing.)

   ANALOGY: Avoid pitfall of narrow, present-oriented view. Aim for the potential of panorama. Ascend to an "observation blimp" *above* the terrain of time where "fog and mists" obscure distant areas past & future. Seek **"radar"** to cut thru fog & see continuities, changes w/ larger view—via *the tools offered herein…*

→ **Due to space-limitations in Teaching Thinking, we had to reduce the 18-page Full View unit.**

[*SEE* either the separate module, available, or the emerging parent- product Mind- Play.]

--Let **this excerpt here** (the visual diagram, plus Table of Contents) suggest that **we can negotiate change better by knowing its keystone *variable-issues* to consider…especially when illustrated with *examples*:**

   EXAMPLES: they abound in reality, and in the 18-p. version.   Climate change…art as "realism" no longer ?… economics…hierarchy and elitism to equalitarianism… typography… the True Believer… astronomy, politics, "humans: angels, or apes?"… corporate management: top-down, or bottom-up?... education: know, or think?… children: angels, or devils?...male and female psychology… Biblical literalism… "heredity or environment?"…"who needs computers, who wants talking movies, who needs a wireless music box?"…

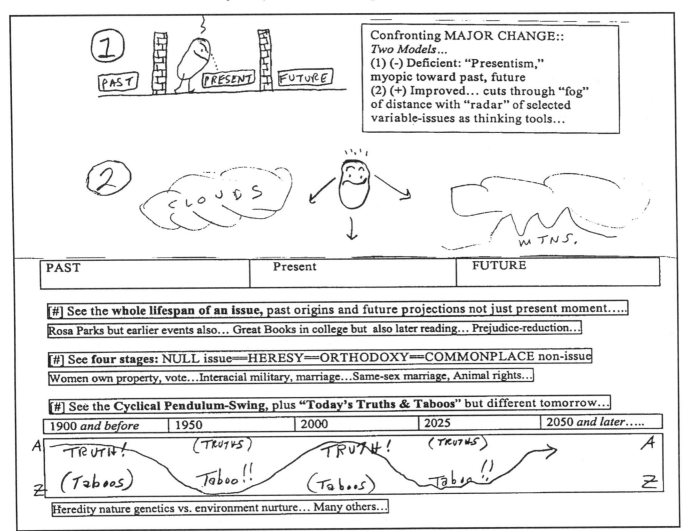

242

The Table of Contents of the unit "Confronting Major Change"

NOTE—the concepts herein were drawn from a very <u>wide</u>, inter-disciplinary **catchment-area**: science, psychology, history, sociology, etc.—a wider casting-of-the-net than in other accounts of change we've seen...
[ANALOGY: "for the best bushel of apples, be able to draw from not just one tree, but all 40 acres of the orchard..."]

[I.] Key Variable-Issues in re Major Change

[1.] <u>Four types</u> of change exist: *constant, a trend, cyclical or alternating, abrupt.*

[2.] The **pace of change** may be slow, then fast... And may be un-perceived early!

[3.] <u>Four types</u> of **response** to an issue exist: first, *Unawareness*, then *Heresy!* (the new idea is scandalous etc. "Women's suffrage will destroy the fabric of society" etc. etc.), then *Orthodoxy* (the new is the New Standard), then a *Commonplace* ("Well of *course* women have the vote; also the sun rises in the east in the morning, what are you talking about?")...

[4.] <u>Size</u> of change may be simpler—or complex, large-scale.

[5.] <u>Levels of</u> change can include simpler "pew within the church"... or more-complex "whole church": ground rules change, not just new choice in old context, but whole new context-of-choices.

   [5A.] "New Bottles but Old Wine" after all.

   [5B.] Pendulum-Swing cycles.

   [5C.] Polar or 180-degree Changes in history.

   [5D.] "None Of The Above Choices," or "Reject the Whole Question!"

   [5E.] A True Paradigm-Shift.

   [5F.] Change, but only permitted **Within Larger Limits:** those of the "invisible electric fence" of the norms/mores as "puppet-master" (what is "in" cannot be questioned, "out" cannot be considered).

[II.] Problems in Peoples' Confronting Change

[6A.] "<u>Non-Graspable</u>" or "They Just Don't Get It Do They"

[6B.] <u>Slow Subtle Sneaky</u> Change

[6C.] Three "<u>Myopias</u>":
   [1] Presentism, *Today's Truths & Taboos, Cyclical Pendulum-Swing*
   [2] Forward Myopia **(A.)** think we predict future but are wrong, **(B.)** Know what we utterly do not know right now and will have to...)
   [3] Retrospective Myopia (can't see past importances as past saw them)

[6D.] <u>Non-Peripheral</u> Vision: narrow view, does not see *total life-span past future* of present unit.

[III.] Suggestions and Guidelines for Teaching

(Esp. f/ *Today's Truths & Taboos, Cyclical Pendulum Swing, Just Don't Grasp It*)

Gallery and Lab. **[8A.]** "What's *Worng* Here?" six on social issues.

   [8B.] "Four on Education"

#|+#|+#|+#|+#|+|#+#|+#|+#|#+|#+|#+|#+|#+|#+#|+#|+#|+#|#+|#+|#+#|+|+#|+#|+##+||#+|#+|#+|#+|#+|#+|||#|+|#|#+|#+|#+|#+|+#|||

[{(END of unit on "Change" [BRIEF view]   )}]

Tool-KIT: #2: STRUCTURE...
the **sequence**; **organization**; **arrangement** of material...

THE IDEA: The *arrangement of parts of a whole,* comprises *many* possibilities. Especially here we focus on confronting content conceptually: thinking a subject through and arranging it in a written text.

ITS IMPORTANCE: But existing materials on structuring ideas/texts—let alone objects, systems, etc. —do not yet seem to corral and display the multiple, plural issues-and-options which (therefore!) we try to do here in this module. *Further, writers, myself included, frequently risk missing arranging items in some better way*

OUR SUGGESTION. *See if this roster, more "elucidated" than other accounts, can help convey to learners-and-doers, the letter (tactical choices) and the spirit (overall gist) of "structure"...*

TABLE OF CONTENTS: (1) Preliminaries... (2) Tool-KIT itself... (3) Gallery of Readings...

[1.] Preliminary. How structure is <u>taught</u>... what it basically <u>is</u>:

1. Current education may be limited; here's an expanded approach...

CURRENT-TRADITIONAL approach [maybe a bit simplified & caricatured, we admit...]:	**A more "THINKING" approach:** the skill-issue elucidated better [we hope]:
Tells students to organize their five-paragraph theme, either (#1) in some order the teacher gives, or (#2) "however you feel like doing"... [...(#1) above may be too "tight," a "rigid rote rule" given... But #2 above may be too "loose," "only one's own opinion" perhaps totally vacant from any competence and control...]	Employs the following tool-kit to present the whole definition of structure... and then the alternate optional choices (arena of possibilities)... all less as tactics-rules "to do," and more as strategies-tools *about* "structure" "to choose from and decide about" ...

2. We can define the general concept of "structure" itself, overall...

Structure is sometimes referred to also as **"Organization," "System,"** and **"a Series in a Sequence"**—as far as we are concerned here, same basic principle! It all has to do with **parts of a whole, regarding their <u>interrelationship with each other</u> plus also with <u>the general characteristics of the whole</u>.** Of course, **Sequence** more specifically refers to a continuous or connected <u>series</u> (number of similar things following each other in some succession). Related are the concepts of **"pattern, design, form,"** all of which of course have some relevance to structure.

EXAMPLES. *Structure appears everywhere!* In a <u>written **text**</u> (school theme; literary creation; magazine feature-article; minutes of a meeting; instruction-manual; other. Also in **<u>objects</u>** (household organization; architecture of building). Also in <u>**events**</u> (project-planning; route thru museum, website).

#|+#|+#|+#|+#|++#|+|#+||#++#|#||+|#+|#+|#+|+#+#|+|+|#+|+#||+#|+|#||#|+|+#|+#|+|#+|#|+|#+|#+|#+|#|#+|+#+#|+#|+#|+|#+|#+|#+|#+||

[2.] The "Tool-KIT" for structure: menu of options, choices:

A SCHEME TO START WITH: The designer RICHARD SAUL WURMAN sees "only" five possibilities of structuring—anything. He calls it **"L A T C H"** to label the options of <u>L</u>ocation, <u>A</u>lphabetical, <u>T</u>ime, <u>C</u>ategory, <u>H</u>ierarchy. [See below...]

WURMAN claims that this quintet covers *all* possibilities of organizing. But wait? I feel we could add **"R"** or simply **Random**! Plus "intuitive" or "**writer-based**." and others? So onward to our expanded menu of options for arranging items:

THE TOOL-KIT: Our own repertoire for arrangement—of . WURMAN'S, and more...

1. Time...   **2. Space...**

3. Utterly **random by chance...** (as discovered; as scrambled)...

4. "Free association," esp. find "the one best felt" order for the purpose... [**"Association is how the mind works,"** said SOCRATES and others. **"Hypertext" itself is a network or assemblage, accretion, heap—of N number of elements, but each one connectible with each other directly...**]

5. Writer-based (=what is most familiar, important to the thinker) "vs." **reader-based** (=rearranged for what is best for audience-comprehension, how the reader needs it stated)... vs. **"subject-based"** (=for the logic of the content).

EXAMPLES where this option applies, can include *instruction manuals* (computer and other), descriptions of places and instructions for *travel*, "*football* explained for women," historical incidents, *requests* for input, etc. [Too often these texts should be reader-based but remain writer-based: background orientation omitted, technical terms undefined, etc.]

6. Alphabetical, A to Z.

7. Via some **conceptual scheme** or other (an ideology, or the modes such as **compare-contrast,** etc.)...

8. Hierarchy, or "from the most or A to the least or Z"... [Frequency; importance; etc.]

9. Computer (Website) Patterns: 1. hierarchy, 2. linear, 3. hub & spokes, 4. "hypertext" or flattened-network spaghetti-lines, volleyball-bouncing. [Less hierarchical than "heterarchical": from pecking order, to interlocking systems. Less mechanical than "holographic": from simple linkage like parts of a machine, to each-piece-to-every-other-piece.]

10. The **arrangement of abstract and concrete** in the whole text (the **"ladder of abstraction"** from specific-concrete, to general-conceptual). The sequence and alternation of ideas, concepts, generalizations—and specific examples, instances... **1.** general to specific (formal report) or **2.** specific to general (personal essay) or **3.** interwoven concrete-conceptual (=feature story: start with anecdote, move to thesis, return to specifics, etc.). Or "**4.**" Others?...

EXAMPLES: --Standard Essay: state higher-level Idea, then Point, then dip *down* to example, then back *up* to Point #2, etc. --Feature-Article: "Rollercoaster": start *down-low* with vivid example to catch interest, then *up* to its Idea, then revisit example... --Some Stories and Essays: start *lower*, descriptive, implicit about point, then rise *up* to explicitly state idea at or near end...

11. Catchall: other general miscellaneous types:

11A. The **"Rhetorical Modes"**: **Definition, Categorization** [=Classify and Divide topic ("thesis") into component "points"]... **Compare-Contrast** (All A then all B vs. AB AB AB)... **Cause-Effect...** etc.

11B. By **Purposes**: e.g., **Problem-Cause-Solution** analysis... **Instruction** in how-to... **Set** Policy & Procedure...

11C. "Top Ten" Lists (currently popular in informal daily writings).

11D. The general "left-brain" vs. "right-brain."

E1. Critical-logical "vs." Creative-Exploratory.
--**Critical** (*logical, judgmental, convergent*) cognitive thinking skills needed for most computer operations, general decision-making, the convergence in problem-solving and system-thinking, and also the...
--**Creative** (*lateral, exploratory*) thinking skills needed for strategic competitive thinking, learning how to learn, pattern recognition, opportunity spotting and creation, assumption of challenges, and creative problem-solving etc."

EXAMPLE. The process of **free-associative, lateral-horizontal** thinking illustrated. "The automobile":
"The car connects to the history of transportation, to our road systems, to our cities and our highways. It connects to the balance of payments and economics around the world. To steel and iron, and steel construction, and plastics and design. It connects to physics and mathematics and chemistry. It connects to foreign languages and culture. To medicine and governmental policy. And, all the things the car connects to, connect to everything else. So do sports. And so does entertainment, which connects to technologies of all sorts, to design and hardware and software and information. Information is everything. We are what we read." [-- R. S. WURMAN]

Probably more a method of thinking things through (especially to serve the ploys of **"networks," systems, holism, integration**) than a method of structuring the results for an audience...

E2. Serial vs. parallel processing.
Serial: Step by step stages, following known rules, using reason. (Train timetables, arithmetic.) "Telephone cables."
Parallel: Many kinds of data in complex patterns, using association. (Playing tennis, driving a car.) "Neural networks."
--Of course we combine the two. Chess playing: intuitively recognize a type of position, select moves, analyze them serially, etc. (But children, animals, the half-asleep, and the intoxicated, often use associative intuition more than rational calculation.)   [-- from Who's Afraid of Schroedinger's Cat]

E3. Methodological /Mechanical (=parts in pre-set order—a formal essay) "vs." **Dramatic/Organic** (=next response grows out of previous—a dialog). [[MM is clear practical efficient, *but* may be routine limiting boring. DO is spontaneous, forceful experiential, *but* may be undisciplined confusing distracting...]] [-- NEVIN LAIB]

E4. Apollonian (=future lines seen beforehand) "vs." **Dionysian** (=knows direction but not yet the method or goal). EXAMPLE: a research-grant.

E5. Propositional (=point proved through operations: example, logic, etc.) ... "*vs*." **Appositional** (=connections made, via analogy etc.; cf. poetry, ads, personal letters, politics, etc.)

E6. Concept (="jigsaw puzzle": a class or family of things) ... "vs." **Schema** (="wave": bird, movie, biography attracting data like a magnet does iron filings). [-- MATTHEW LIPMAN]

E7,8. Narrow vs. Wide structure (=one or more alternatives possible at each "stage")...
Shallow vs. Deep structures (=number of "stages" themselves, one or more).
X Ice Cream Parlor: first stage offers all of 31 flavors or more, but second is only cone type (2 or 3), nr. of scoops (1,2,3) , toppings (say up to 6). [= DON NORMAN]

11F. Other Options for Patterns, Organization, Structure:

1. Circle: "Alpha" at start theme stated, development, end w/"Omega" echo.
...in Foundations of Tibetan Mysticism, Lama ANAGARIKA GOVINDA showed how traditional Western logic *moves in a straight line* from a definite point of view (an unambiguously defined premise) toward the object of thought. The Eastern way *circles around the object* of contemplation in ever-decreasing circles. The object of thought is a multidimensional impression formed by the integrating superimposition of simple impressions.... [-- SOURCE]

2. Maypole: take one item, weave and turn discussion around it.
X French trip told by referring to "objects in rental car."
X Christmas family letter: a famous quotation at start, riff on how year's events relate.
3. Braid: alternate interweaving of two or more elements.
X Car and Driver: story of a car with diary-entries of a road trip with it, interspersed.
X Nat. Geog.: the history of writing, with vignettes of "Fred" the writer interspersed.
4. "Organic Form": theme and repetition with variation, "dynamic dialectic," symmetry (repetition) and asymmetry (variation) in exquisite balance.

ISSUE: Can and should one employ *more than one* scheme of structuring *within one* work?
EXAMPLE. The Structure(s) of our work Teaching Thinking and Mind-Play itself! Five simultaneous ways:

--**CONCEPTUAL.** (A) logic of the system itself.
[Esp. via the "12-W" SAM or Significant Action Monitor [= who does what to what, when where how, how well, for what goal...]
(B) Other: "Subject-Based" but also "Audience-Based. [= needs, background, uses, etc., of the intended *Readers*...]

--**TIME:** Processual. [= "Confronting subject involves an at-least-prevalent sequence in time. Research, Analysis, Conclusions: that is, Discovery, Delving-in, then Description, then Dissection, Discussion, and then Decisions plus Disseminating]

--**ALPHABETICAL** A-to-Z, to store in accessible retrievable fashion. The "useful Index" of *all* the Tools, etc.

--**HIERARCHIES.** Within all skill-modules, levels. [Both (A) "Vertical" [= standard categorizing: classify-and-divide into points, subpoints], plus (B) "Horizontal" [= as in Version "I" Brief View "basics," Versions "II" etc. Full View advanced ...]

--**LOCATION:** Spatial. [= (A) Layout on Table of Contents page; physical arrangement in text. Plus, (B) the cross-connections among component elements, are not linear but lateral, associational echoes, relationships,...]

...and so, our "menu" of more options for structuring a sequence of related items. Drawn from various areas of knowledge. More numerous than usually offered in educational materials. And, less rigid rules than flexible tools...

#|+#|+#|+#|+#|++#|+|#+||#++#|#||+|#+|#+|#+|+#+#|+|+|#+|+#||+#|+|#||#|+|+#|+#||+|#+|#+|#+|+#|#|#+|+#+#|+#|+#|+|#+|#+|#+|#+||

[3.] The "GALLERY of READINGS" *illustrates* structuring in texts:

EXAMPLES. A dozen or so instances, of varied subjects and situations, showing various **challenges** or difficulties in structuring (including errors-to-beware), also showing various **choices** or options-to-consider...

(1 A B C D) PREVIEW: In the first four examples below, see how the (1A) <u>editor of an anthology of short stories</u> chooses **Alphabetical** structure, for a mere **Chance** mix... But a (1B) <u>reviewer</u> than critiques this as not truly competent, indeed careless; a ***Principle*** is needed. That is, the creator must still think out some structure-organization-arrangement... But (1C) <u>some other editors</u> of a different story anthology, still just "don't get it, do they"... Even as a (1D) <u>psychologist</u> affirms that the thinker-communicator must work hard to organize things even in this age of hypertext which permits reader-organizing. *Now on to the four examples:*

(1A) "For various reasons, <u>The Mammoth Book of Gay Short Stories</u> has been arranged alphabetically by name of author. [By "date of publication" would have unbalanced things: overweighting AIDS stories. But A to Z via author,] "might function as a literary kaleidoscope so that a story on childhood experience may be followed by one about coming our or AIDS, the inter-action between women and groups of gay men, football and revenge or prostitution and true love." [-- PETER BURTON, editor]

(1B) "'For various reasons,' BURTON presents them all in alphabetical order of author's name. He suggests that this less-than-arduous approach will provide "a literary kaleidoscope' leading to our serendipitous discoveries of fascinating themes and juxtapositions as we move from story to story. I suggest that <u>the organization of dramatic and thematic flow is a primary task for any anthology editor who wishes to be taken seriously.</u>" [-- JIM GLADSTONE, reviewer]

(1C) "Like its predecessor, the order of the book is alphabetical, all except for one story which called to be placed—well, at the beginning. We gave serious thought to ordering the book by theme, topic, even gender and nationality, but the overwhelming response we received from readers of the first <u>Queer View Mirror</u> was that they enjoyed the surprise of discovery—that they like how the themes, tones, voices, and genders of the authors of each story constantly changed. So, rather than impose a subjective, arbitrary arrangement, we made the decision to present the stories alphabetically, and allow the reader to find their own way." [-- EDITORS of a second anthology...]

(1D) [The belief that hypertext will save the author from having to put material in linear order, is wrong. This allows for sloppiness. To organize material is hard work, but this writer-effort is needed so reader needn't carry that burden—perhaps can't or won't try to cope.] [-- DON NORMAN, psychologists]

|#+#|+|#+|+#|#+|#++|#+|#||+|#|+#|+#|+|+|#+|+#||+#|+#||#+|#+||#+|#+||#+|#+|+#|+|#+|+|#+|+|#+|+#||#++#|#||++#||#+|+#|#|+#|+|#+|++||#+|+#|+#|+|#+|+|#|#+||#+|#+|#+|#+|#+||

(2) **EXAMPLE.** Subtle *organic but controlled*, structure of <u>a filmmaker, FREDERICK WISEMAN.</u>
"In every film, WISEMAN omits titles, narration, and any sort of explanation. He thrusts us into the middle of things, and though at first it's hard to look at some of the women in "Domestic Violence," we are soon looking and listening very closely, trying to sort out the hints and allusions and repetitions. What doe the stories men? What are the patterns? (The film differs from the usual TV exposition of abuse in that WISEMAN senses that these knots can never be neatly untangled.) With a hundred or so hours of footage to choose from, Wiseman organizes his material not by topic but organically, weaving scenes together for moral and emotional intimacy and suggestiveness. In the end, after more than three hours, our effort of attention becomes so intense that we are cleansed of squeamishness and fear." [-- DAVID DENBY]

(3) **EXAMPLE.** How <u>JOHN JAMES AUDUBON organized his classic book of illustration of birds.</u>
Not via *social hierarchy*, but via *his own time-space route* of travels and discoveries—and, relaxed not rigorous degree.

"Every bird or animal picture book before had tried to make a point beyond the blind, flat empirical record; for AUDUBON, the enrichment of the empirical record was all the point there was. The French naturalist BUFFON'S ornithology was structured to mimic the surrounding social order—the noble birds first and the lesser ones behind. AUDUBON'S book begins [in the middle of thing], with the wild turkey, proceeds to the songbirds, and then abruptly turns to the lyrical swallows, the arctic terns, the water birds. The sequence loosely follows AUDUBON'S own voyages and discoveries as much as any biological program—a kind of autobiography written in birds. He took the French mania for systemization and made it into a recognizably American love of facts for their own sake—single observations connected by 'ands.'" [-- ADAM GOPNIK]

(4) **EXAMPLE.** The *cut-and-paste* structure of <u>eccentric British novelist RONALD FIRBANK.</u>
[FIRBANK'S style was unique. He wrote plot elements on separate large cards and arranged them mechanically not

organically, via "the interrelated arrangement of discrete elements [the "logic of design"] instead of through causal linear progression [the logic of narrative and characterization"] "His method thus elevated style over structure and approximated musical composition." [-- AUTHOR]

(5) EXAMPLE. From the introduction to Mapping, <u>an introduction to cartography.</u>
Maps presented not via a *logical scheme*, but via the reader's progression from *more simple-familiar, onward to the complex-foreign.*

As an informal approach to maps, the order here is not one made in accordance with a logical classification of the various elements of the subject; instead it is made to parallel the experience of confronting a map and viewing it with more and more insight. The progression is from familiar aspects, through contingent matters, to the grand concepts that fortify the working principles." [-- DAVID GREENHOOD]

I notice the author selected the **reader-based** approach. Moved also from the known and familiar (and also the basic) to the more contingent or secondary matters. And from the **concrete specific to the conceptual abstract**. So perhaps this illustrates the variable of *multiple* principles of organizing *within one* text...

(6) EXAMPLE. A Time <u>magazine article on "A Working Mother's Day, from A to Z"</u> uses *alphabetical* as maypole or string for the beads. [Also seen in AMBROSE BIERCE'S satirical <u>The Devil's Dictionary</u>...]

After an introduction, the article's main body consists of brief deft "definitions." Apple Pie. Baby. Chocolate. Delegate. Educational. Food. Guilt. Husband. Irritable. Juggling. Kindergarten. Love. Mother. No. Orange ["Color of juice, regardless of flavor, that child upends on your beige jacket on the morning you have a presentation to clients."] Photo Album. Quality Time. Rage. Success. Toilet-Paper Fairy. Unappreciated. Vacuum. ["a) Household appliance or b) space between boss's ears during discussion of maternity leave"] Work. X. You're Not Going Out Looking Like That! Zoo. [-- A. PEARSON]

(7) EXAMPLE. The sequential organization of names on the <u>Vietnam Veterans' Memorial.</u>
<u>Not</u> by *alphabet*, but by *time*-order, date of death... Originally it was to be alphabetical, but this would give it a phone-book artificiality. The designer then chose chronological. This did place the individual near to peers. Also may have made the name easier to locate by relatives... [-- EDWARD TUFTE]

(8) STATEMENTS. Two conflicting comments on the <u>repeating (or not) of a text's points</u> or materials.
[Of course, with repetition, beware prevalent pitfall of *vague circular meandering from a point, to—is this a new point or what?!*...]

[A] "The reader is cautioned [*sic*] that no words, and none of his [*sic*] time, are wasted here. Facts are stated once and are not repeated." [-- CARL D. LANE, <u>The Boatman's Manual</u>]

[B] "...I have salted cross-references liberally throughout the text. Word Processing [is all of a piece, but books have sections, but the relationships among them call for recognition.] "My hope is that the reader will find the frequent citations of what was said in another section an aid to understanding, and not a hindrance to easy reading." [-- WALTER A. KLEINSCHROD]

(9) EXAMPLE. An <u>Art museum in Paris,</u> divided the current exhibit, not into *periods or movements*, but rather in *unexpected juxtapositions*, theme of "creative destructiveness," next year's *theme* to be "movement in images."

(10) EXAMPLE. How to organize a single brochure of <u>the university's year's offerings of the visual arts, music, and theatre-drama events?</u> *Currently* info "organized" by **Source or Origin**: it is spread over *five different brochures* from five different venues (theatre (major; student), dance, music, visual arts). The readers have to juggle five different sources thus. *Ideally*, should be all together in one brochure, via "audience-needs-to-know," hence by **Time** or calendar, then within that, **Types** of offerings.

Probably, by default, general **Type**: music, theatre, cinema, etc. But this conflicts with **Category of Origin** (regular course-driven performances... end-of-year shows... outside series coming in... etc.) Within each, surely **Time**, the calendar. Option: one version also had the **Concept** of "*Free*-to-attend" vs. "A *Charge* for it." Then there is Location or **space**, though perhaps an index map helps!.....

Easy key point; select your main structural principle(s), then subsume minor ones—cost, location—within?

|+#|+#|+|+#|+|+#+|+|+|+#|+|#+|#|++|#|#+|+|#|+|+|#|+#||+#|+|#+|+|#|++|#|+#|+#||#|+#|+|#+|+|#+|+|#+|+#|+#|+#|

[[END of Tool-KIT on "Structure"]]

Tool-KIT #3: CAUSE – EFFECT:

#|+#|+#|+#|+#|++#|+|#+||#++#|#||+|#+|#+|#+|+#+#|+|+|#+|+#||+#|+|#||#|+|+#|+#|+|#+|#|+|#+|#+|#+|#|#+|#++#|+#|+#|+|#+|#+|#+|#+|#+||

THE ISSUE. ALSO, THE SO-WHAT PROBLEM-OPPORTUNITY. Cause-effect explanation is complex. but is it taught adequately, or in **implicit** and/or **scattered** fashion? Learners may not explicitly be offered overt, manifest cause-effect formulae… Or they may be exposed to such but casually serial piecemeal. At best, then, FRED will encounter *this perspective here* (causality in science), will then hear of *that approach there* (sociocultural levels), and will see *the next framework elsewhere* (psychodynamic motivation), but never "together in one view" of an integrated, conceptualized—**elucidating**—tool-kit resource…

OUR SUGGESTION—BUT ALSO QUALIFICATION: I did *not* attain "optimization" on this issue, didn't even approach it. Which follows is I feel a (+) quite valid foot-on-ground start—drawing from a wide interdisciplinary catchment-area. But it remains (-) probably incomplete, and (-) surely not coherent, cohesive, convergent for our criteria… No wonder, since C-E roams over varied disciplines, and a non-expert can only do so much. → So, A CALL TO OTHERS: let educators, ideally diverse personnel from varied arenas, create a *better* tool-kit for **cause-and-effect**. [In the jargon of this book's rationale: Let colleagues **collaborate,** "strategically monitor the totalities," **colloquialize** among themselves, and achieve a more **elucidating** map…

POLITELY: "If some educators can provide an augmented resource for **cause-effect,** that may well benefit some learners."	PASSIONATELY: "It's a scandal that educators from disciplines from A to Z have not assembled to assemble a truly integrated powerful specific-and-generic accessible treatment of **causality**… [I know, I know; who would even think to do it—"explicit interdisciplinary generic thinking" etc.—Plus, who would gain points for doing it, in the "reward structure" and all that…]

#|+#|+#|+#|+#|++#|+|#+||#++#|#||+|#+|#+|#+|+#+#|+|+|#+|+#||+#|+|#||#|+|+#|+#|+|#+|#|+|#+|#+|#+|#|#+|#++#|+#|+#|+|#+|#+|#+|#+|#+||

CAUSE-EFFECT: "Tool-KIT":

On the LEFT side below, "business as usual or often" in much teaching about causality.
{Too often undeveloped, over-simple? …}
More the **current-standard-traditional:**

On the RIGHT side, our own attempt to corral more variables about causality than most teaching does.
{Valiant, valid, if somewhat frustrated and frantic?}
More **long-range thinking-emphasis.**

Course exam questions as noted earlier, "Describe the causes [and effects] of the French Revolution, of World War 1…." but is this:	A comprehensive **TOOL-KIT** for the issue of **cause-effect** analysis, explanation. Multi-disciplinary: both discipline-specific and also general-generic. Could include: **0.** Three common pitfalls in cause-effect analysis: **A.** *Confusing time relationship for cause* ("after this, because of this"). [X Ford trucks sold well after an ad campaign, but was it due to more job, lower interest rates, competitors' mistakes?] **B.** *Mistaking an effect for a cause.* [X Patient is depressed and has no appetite. Did depression cause the food-aversion? Or did an underlying illness cause both?\ **C.** *Confusing association (correlation) with causes.* [X Smoking causes long, throat, and mouth cancer—but some lung patients were nonsmokers, some smokers avoided cancer…]

249

[-- INFOTRAC, THOMPSON LEARNING]

1. <u>The Simplicity Issue</u>. "Fewer causes the better" (Occam's Razor) *versus* "richness of overdetermination" (psychoanalytic explanations)—the more factors the more solid!

2. <u>Simple to Complex</u>
"<u>One cause, one effect</u>" … and "<u>one cause many effects</u>" … and "<u>many causes one effect</u>" … on to "<u>many causes, many effects</u>" or true multiple causality
X Diabetes, see the chart of multiple interactions: lead-in causes, lead-out effects.

3. <u>A "third hidden" cause</u>? X more baldness means more heart attacks, but are hormones a factor?

4. # <u>Latent vs. Manifest Functions</u>. Latent results are those **<u>effects</u>** which are "neither recognized nor intended." [ROBERT MERTON, sociologist]
X Missionaries and health of the natives: required clothing, but this led to disease in the climate.
X Technology, ingenuity gap: converters, fire ant, debris left in space.
"Downstream Victims": X The automobile arises, *but* then central cities are affected… X Wal-Mart expands *but* then smaller stores suffer… X TV, *but* then print media is challenged… X Railroads prosper, *but* the New England family farm is endangered… X Antidepressants, *but* then more outpatients on the streets… X Fax, *but* then the demise of Western Union…

5. <u>Linear vs. Concurrent-Chains</u>-Interrelated.

6. <u>Small Cause, Large Distant Effect</u>? The **Butterfly** Effect? X "A butterfly flapping its wings in, say, Singapore, can eventually influence stormy weather in, say, Florida…"

7. <u>Discontinuities</u>: "**Threshhold**" or **Catastrophe**, also "**Lily-Pond**" effect. The **"Tipping Point"**

X Hitler conquered Austria, Sudentenland, Czechoslovakia easily ➔ but then adding Poland ignited a six-year war which ruined him.
X Water temperature in the tropical Atlantic can warm without promoting hurricanes ➔ but once it reaches 26 degrees C., it "throws a switch" to storms.
X Some oceanic fisheries overfished, incrementally ➔ but then suddenly collapsed at a certain point.

8. <u>Scope</u>. In both Space and also Time, the **<u>near-proximate-acute</u>** causes [& effects] … "vs." the **<u>remote-chronic</u>**-causes [& effects?]. X The Los Angeles race-riots…

10. <u>Priorities</u> I. "Necessary and Sufficient." Contributing, initiating, promoting.
X Tobacco and alcohol and lung cancer   XX others

11. <u>Priorities</u> II. The "<u>chicken-and-the-egg</u>" problem, *what is cause, what is effect*?
X Schools: performance of students, and funding by the district…
X Depression: the psyche and the soma or body, which influences which?
X "Psychopolitics": "evil" leaders (Stalin, Hitler, etc.) created by situation—or early neurosis?
X The father of a gay son is psychologically distanctthe child. Did cold father cause gay orientation? Or did non-masculine traits of male child cause father to withdraw uneasy?
X Language-acquisition and sociality: which stimulated the other?
X In tribes, "big men" wives or crops are a factor?
X "Laugh 60 seconds a day or at a time, and you " = live longer

X Anti-discrimination laws absent: causes discrimination, or result of bigotry?

12. <u>Distant and Complex:</u>
X Roe vs. Wade ➔ drop in crime rates?! "Permitting abortions, lowered the number of out-of-wedlock men who would grow up tending toward crime"…..
X Sargasso Sea (dead area in ocean) ➔and Teen Obesity (a long connection).

13. <u>Some large causes of:</u>
X Naked Ape, (Guns Germs & Steel?) Studies of many factors including geographical, evolutionary.
X Medieval motions: The Black Death plague killed millions, left surplus clothing, these rags used for making paper, stimulated printing, also migration…
X World War I…

14. <u>Inter/Disciplinary</u> causality: biological, psychological, sociocultural (& economic etc.)
X the Wearing of Sunglasses (sensitivity, status, climate)… X the Fall of Rome (lead poisoning, political, cultural)… X Why Americans value work (geographical opportunity, no social class restrictions, Protestant work ethic, etc.)

15. Disciplines <u>conflict:</u> esp. *biology and psychology*
X Pibloktoq: Arctic hysteria syndrome. Explained by Freudianism (hysteria, wish to be pursued) or by environmental biology (lack of calcium in the northern diet, "hypocalcemic tetany"?)
X Gay man and older brothers: the more older brothers a male has, the more likely he is homosexual. Is this psychological (sexual abuse/domination) , or biological (intrauterine hormone alteration?)
X Identical twins: biological-genetic, or sociocultural, or both?

16. (True or real causes not known or rather not admitted!)
"Child labor was banned and kids were forced into high school in order to save jobs for adults. The fact that workers might become better citizens was wholly secondary.
"The GI Bill was developed because Franklin Roosevelt, recalling what had happened with World War I veterans, feared the consequences of dumping a huge military force into an economy that could not absorb it. The increase in college graduates made a degree a necessary job credential."
[-- FREDERICK THAYER, IN CHE]

17. <u>Specific systems.</u> "ARISTOTLE'S FOUR CAUSES": Material, Formal, Efficient, Final

#|+#|+#|+#|+#|++#|+|#+||#++#|#||+|#+|#+|#+|+#+#|+|+|#+|+#||+#|+|#||#|+|+#|+#|+|#+|#|+|#+|#+|#+|#|#+|+#+#|+#|+#|+|#+|#+|#+|#+||

Okay, I **AM** getting impressed by this. Many more C-E schemes *do* seem to exist than are commonly **elucidated**, but they could be clarified better. (Even if your roster here is still primitive, rough.)	I have to agree—of course…! **We "more-in-less and clearly" is possible…** In any case, we do not always teach cause-effect. See these two assignments as examples:

1. (*From the* UNIV. OF WI AT WHITEWATER): "<u>What was the effect of World War I on Europe?</u>" [The expected answer, *already given* in lecture/textbook, was "The war transformed Europe mentally, politically, and economically"
[... No need or chance to learn or use, any of the eight possible generic cause-effect tools in the Tool-KIT above!]

2. (*From an exam in the* FRENCH NATIONAL SCHOOL SYSTEM, *quoted by Albert Shanker, recent head of a large teachers' group*): "<u>Causes of the first World War</u>. First, explain the indirect causes (imperialism, nationalism) which facilitated the appearance of European networks of alliances., Briefly, describe these networks. Next, tell how the crisis at Sarajevo was directly responsible for the First World War."
[...again, how this can be thought of as testing thinking, instead of rote recall, is utterly beyond me...]

#|+#|+#|+#|+#|++#|+|#+||#++#|#||+|#+|#+|#+|+#+#|+|+|#+|+#||+#|+|#||#|+|+#|+#|+|#+|#|+|#+|#+|#+|#|#+|+#+#|+#|+#|+|#+|#+|#+|#+||

[{(END of pre-vue Tool-KIT on "Cause-Effect" as a thinking skill…..)}]

Kit #4: "LENS-WORK":
using _multiple_ viewpoints, _plural_ perspectives

[1.] GRAPHIC

FLOYD sees reality through limited, narrow, partial _perception / response systems_. But FRITZ employs more powerful, useful, _theories / models /paradigms / etc._ _How to better command "lenswork"?_

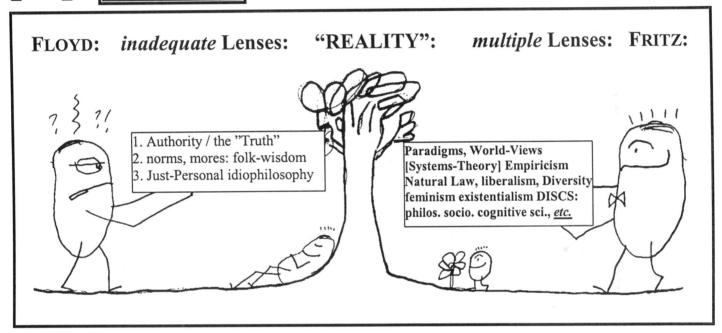

FLOYD: _inadequate_ Lenses: "REALITY": _multiple_ Lenses: FRITZ:

1. Authority / the "Truth"
2. norms, mores: folk-wisdom
3. Just-Personal idiophilosophy

Paradigms, World-Views
[Systems-Theory] Empiricism
Natural Law, liberalism, Diversity
feminism existentialism DISCS:
philos. socio. cognitive sci., _etc._

|+#|+|+|#|+#|+|#+|+|+#|++##+##|#|+|+|+|#|+|#+#+|+|+#|+|+|#+|#+|#+|+|+|#++|+|+|+|+#|+#|+|#+|+#|||#+|=#+|+#|+|#+|#+|+#|||

[2.] RATIONALE for a unit like this:

THE CONCEPT-ISSUE, & THE CRUCIALITY. We generally assume and "know" that we do not know reality directly, but only through "lenses" or viewpoints, screens or filters. _So, what? Why bother with this issue in education-about-better-thinking? Isn't it enough to tell students (as one "Active-Learning" exercise did), "Look at this subject through three different perspectives"?_

THE "SO-WHAT" PROBLEM-OPPORTUNITY. Well, no. Recall "Knowing-Of, versus Really Knowing **About & How-To.**" "Of course we all know" that "varied perspectives, multiple viewpoints exist for confronting reality." But, how well can thinkers actually _use_ this insight?... Can learners "Hit The Ground Running" and apply lenses competently "later on in life" etc."? During a teaching career, I've found that up to a dozen **variable-issues** in the competent use of _different perspectives_, do exist.

   [E.g., lenses are inescapable—often subliminal—impure—insightful but limited/biased—in time can be outdated but also neglected—usually inadequate solo, need other lenses but these can conflict—hard to evaluate and also to select--]...
Learners will "already know" something about these variables _but only haphazard variously catch-as-came-across_ ... Learners not knowing them well, risk pitfalls, blocks potentialities... But learners can enormously

accelerate their **"lenswork"** skills via being acquainted with an **elucidated** "catalyst" presentation of the keystones.... ***What about going beyond "look at something through different perspectives"? (Beyond naïve relativism... beyond catch-lenses-as-one-can... beyond bafflement at conflicting lenses... and more....)***

THEREFORE THIS RESOURCE. [Which as far as I know, is unsurpassed in current resources, in its combining of **comprehensiveness** in scope-and-depth, plus explicitness of **conceptual principles** plus richness of **examples**...]

ANALOGIES: Comparisons help comprehension, so...

--To conceive of ***lenses in general*** (*frames of references, viewpoints, perspectives, systems, rationales, ideologies, paradigms, world-views*, etc.) we can think of

[1.] a "camera lens":. A camera has a lens between the scene it photographs out there, and the image *on the film or disc*; our selves have lenses between subjects in the world, and the image of it *in our minds*. Different lenses, different views: telephoto (for distance, but can blur) and wide-angle (broad view but distorts) or 50 mm. (nearest to how we see). *But a camera with no lens at all, sees nothing at all...* [Lenses inevitable, useful, but partial...]

--Then to conceive more specifically of the ***academic disciplines*** as lenses, we can think of

[2.] the "geopolitical" (disciplines as "nation-states" with own culture, possible "turf wars" colonizing and defending: biology invades sociology. etc.) Also of **[3.] "genealogy"** (disciplines as "close relatives" such as sociology and psychology, versus "foreigners" who may or may not have things in common after all, such as biology and aesthetics).

|+#|+|+|#|+#|+|#+|+|+#|++##+##|#|+|+|+|#|+|#+#+|+|+#|+|+|#+|#+|#+|+|#++|+|+|+|#|+#|+|#+|+#|||#+|=#+|+#|+|#+|#+|+#|||

[3.] TABLE OF CONTENTS of unit:

|+#|+|+|#|+#|+|#+|+|+#|++##+##|#|+|+|+|#|+|#+#+|+|+#|+|+|#+|#+|#+|+|#++|+|+|+|#|+#|+|#+|+#|||#+|=#+|+#|+|#+|#+|+#|||

[4.] Two "WARM-UPS": A. Whirl-in   B. "Relativism"

WARM-UP #1. A sampling of varied **perspectives, viewpoints, angles-of-vision**…on subjects. Not all are formal lenses. Plus, many remain subliminal, unlabeled. Plus, are all "good" for the purpose? *Will reviewing these instances, make learners Aware of (if confused about..) the whole Lens issue?*

1. --"It's not wrong because it's a sin; it's a sin because it's wrong." [-- MY TRADITIONALISTIC GRANDPARENT] [**Lenses:** *Absolutism Natural Law*, vs. *Systems-of-Ethics*…]

2. --"…but, **my** common sense, or **your** common sense?" [- A STUDENT IN ENGLISH 101]

3. --"This wine is truly bad, but I really do like it…" [- A CONNOISSEUR] [**Lenses:** *objective*, and *personal-pleasing*]

4. --"S/he just lets the facts speak for themselves." [-- REMARK COMMONLY HEARD *and which always makes me cringe*…] Through which lenses are the facts inevitably being perceived? X "An abortion is a killing…" Well, it factually *is*, but…]

5. --"If the only tool you have is a hammer, everything looks like a nail." [- A. MASLOW]

6. --The DSM or classification-manual of psychiatric diseases gives as criteria: (1) *subjective* internal distress, (2) *objective* observable problematic behavior in public. [Do *yet other* **lenses** exist?]

7. --Natural science results are judged by *effectiveness*; some social sci. & humanities by *peer-reputation*.

8. --A book-reviewer on "amazon.com" got into the "top 50 reviewers" position. He did so not by writing the best reviews he could by criteria of excellence; he did so by writing pleasant reviews and having friends vote for his reviews. [**Lenses:** *quality-standards* for a good book review, vs. "*fame and prestige* but at all costs"…]

9. --Three "lenses" for three different types of questions or issues. **1.** Factual—we research the data, what do the facts say? **2.** Opinion—we find what we feel, personally. **3.** And, Reasoned Judgment—we examine the data plus apply criteria. [**EXAMPLES** for each lens, in order: **1.** "Is Alaska the coldest state in the U.S.A.?" **2.** "Is Alaska a good place to go for your vacation?" **3.** "Is Alaska currently a good place to start a certain type of business?"]

This slapdown is confusing, unstructured, purpose unclear…	BUT is it a "seedbed" to help raise questions, options?

WARM-UP #2. TEACHING PLOY: VISIT RAMPANT RELATIVISM. "Take a walk on out to the Wide, Wild Side—and then Rebalance." In class, I told students of <u>three main stations</u>:

--start with **[1] Absolutism** (innate-inherent-intrinsic foundationalism," all too overdone at times)…

--then swing on out to the polar-opposite **[2] "Rampant Relativism"** (all too prevalent today)…

--and then rebalance to **[3] Committed Relativism,** or "truth does exist, but *it depends—on the lens*."
[Thus the PERRY SCHEME of intellectual development in the proverbial nutshell…]
And so, ask "what exists as true/false? what is wrong/right? what to do and how to do it?" *And so forth…*

[1.] Absolutism: "one fixed truth on matters exists, inherent in Nature herself, true everywhere and always"—(and oppose it at one's peril?) "It's not wrong because it's a sin, it's a sin because it's wrong" [-- my Lutheran-minister GRANDFATHER, on premarital sex—maybe on *any* nonprocreative sex?...]	**[2.] Relativism "Rampant":** As in the sloppy prevalent mantra: **"Well isnt everything relative after all how can you say whos right after all dont people have a right to their opion?"** [-- Many PUPILS today…]	**[3.] "Committed Relativism":** Knowledge is indeed complex, but **what one says is truth, etc., depends on the lens."** Christianity, Marxism, existentialism, fascism, Stoicism, evolutionary sociobiology, Romanticism, etc.—**all these lenses make statements "true etc." *within the logic of their own systems*…**)

A GALLERY of "pump-priming" EXAMPLES:

(1) The BOY SCOUTS OF AMERICA, <u>currently excludes homosexual personnel</u>. This exclusion is both immoral, but also quite moral. That's via the **lenses**, respectively, of "liberal tolerance and equality," and "traditional American norms-mores-folkways" (which include institutional, historical homophobia or queer-fear)…

(2) Murder is bad, but <u>MY ANTHROPOLOGY PROFESSOR</u> disclosed—accurately—that he was a murderer. "He had shot and killed five men with a rifle." [*But* he had been in the infantry in World War II…]

(3) I MYSELF recently was totally naked in front of an adult woman whom I had never met before! Surely this was immoral? [*But* it was at the dermatology clinic, and in medicine, the more nudity the better, for better examination and hence care… Later I visited the area's nude beach—wearing *plenty* of sunblock…]

(4) "TWO COUPLES each had sex." Was this good, bad, indifferent? But COUPLE *#1* was a legally-married couple, religious. And COUPLE *#2* was two males in an anonymous homosexual encounter in an alleyway in a big city of night. It's pretty clear which is moral/good, and which is immoral/bad here: *marital intercourse, vs. deviancy…*

  [Oh, *except* that, just to complicate things up a bit perhaps, in #1, the couple treated each other with *long-standing animosity and exploitation*—and the two "inverts" performing semi-public sex, atypically treated each other with *empathy, consideration, respect*…So what two lenses, at least, might be operative here? Conventional Moralities?…spirit-not-letter Good Behavior?]

(5) "Acid rain" is of course truly a problem-situation. But what or where lies the big "Problem"? Well for the green ENVIRONMENTALISTS, the Problem is "of course" those irresponsible Big Businesses. *But* for CORPORATE INDUSTRY, the nasty Problem is, "of course," those interfering tree-huggers who threaten profits…]

GUIDELINE: *"Know* of absolutism, pure relativism, and committed relativism as AOC alternate optional choices. *Know* the positive and negative values/drawbacks of each approach. *Select* the approach which seems best for your own situation (personal-preference taste-temperament, thinking-style, etc.)"

---

*PEDAGOGICAL PLOY: **Can** this three-stage approach help move the class past (1) traditional innate Absolutism… all the way to (2) this Rampant Relativism (very prevalent today)… and then back to (3) committed relativism or the stand that "reality is knowable after all, but it depends on the lens"? Or at least to let each learner choose [horrors…] the approach s/he favors?*

SEE "II" FULL version for **A Brief Visit to Rampant Relativism**, in **Mind-Play**

|+#|+|+|#|+#|+|#+|+|+|#|++##+##|#|+|+|+|#|+|#+#+|+|+#|+|+|#+|#+|#+|+|+|#++|+|+|+|+#|+#|+|#+|+#|||#+|=#+|+#|+|#+|#+|+#|||

[5.] |"TOUCHSTONES"| classic quotes:

MINI-GALLERY. The *best three* quotations we've ever seen showing the complex essence of "**lenses**." And then our own painstaking distillation of keystone "**variables**-regarding" lenses—rarely noted explicitly!

---

[1] There is the world, and there are our images of it. Two minds could have different representations, and the world has an existence independent of either representation. Mental concepts exist which somehow correspond to aspects of nature, but are not identical to them.
[-- R. NISBET, SOCIAL PSYCHOLOGY: *paraphrased*]   [See our # 1 Lenses Do Exist, #8B Lenses Conflict…]

[2] "Any system of thought is a *reflection* of reality, which means that it is also a *selection* of reality, and also a *deflection* of reality." [-- KENNETH BURKE]   [See our # 4 "Freighted," #5 Incomplete…]

[3] The known world is incomplete if seen from *any one* point of view, incoherent if seen from *all* [or even *many*?] points of view *at once*, and empty if seen from the famous *nowhere in particular*.
[-- R. SCHWEDLER, ANTHROPOLOGY]   [See our #2 Inescapable, #5 Incomplete…]

[4] Our own dozen **variable-issues**: "lenses" are inevitable; often subliminal; tinctured with insight plus bias; all lenses have some "logic" or other of their own; can become outdated but also wrongly neglected; are incomplete hence multiple lenses needed; but conflict between lenses can result. Selection of best lenses is a big issue. "The *larger basic* perspectives, are often selected *subjectively*…" [See #5 below] [-- B. K. BECK and CHESTER KARTOFFELKOPFE et AL…]

Why are the above statements so great? They correlate self and world. They avoid rigid reason and lax relativism …

|+#|+|+|#|+#|+|#+|+|+|#|++##+##|#|+|+|+|#|+|#+#+|+|+#|+|+|#+|#+|#+|+|+|#++|+|+|+|+#|+#|+|#+|+#|||#+|=#+|+#|+|#+|#+|+#|||

[6.] | TYPES of lenses: | "I": 2 rosters

[1.] General "All" Lenses   [2.] the Academic Disciplines

[6.1.] ROSTER #1: A broad, comprehensive overview (synoptic scanning) of the whole Forest of lenses:

--**Perception-systems**: male and female differences?

--**Communication chain**: stereotypes, selective perception?

--**Language**: the word is not the thing.

--**Systems of Thought**: paradigms, etc. (relativity, evolution, quantum mechanics, systems, deconstruction)

--Theories of **Human Nature**: Christianity, Freud, Socio/Psycho-Biology, Marx, Existentialism, behaviorism, Plato...

--**Feminisms**: liberal, marxist, radical, psychoanalytic, socialist, existentialist, postmodern.

--**Ethics, Morality, Value** Systems: relativism, egotism, duty, virtue, situation, natural law, divine command, behaviorism, utilitarianism

--**Zeitgeist**, Climate of Opinion, Today's Truths & Taboos, Schools of Thought

--**Societies, Cultures, Nations**: East and West, America (effort optimism progress humanitarianism individualism materialism)

--**Institutions**: political, religious: the traditional conservative == radical-liberal spectrum.

--**Culture**: norms mores folkways, conventional wisdom, received opinion, folk-knowledge, tacit lore. From large to smaller groups.

--**Academic Disciplines**: Humanities, Social Sciences, Natural Sciences. Fields within each, all with many competing Schools of Thought... [*Literature*: aesthetic, psychobiographical, historical, social-critical, etc.] [*Sociology*: functionalism, conflict, rational choice, symbolic interactionism, phenomenology] [Others!]

--**Individual** Lenses. Each person's own...including "schema" or existing pictures of subjects in reality.

--Also **WAYS OF KNOWING:** slightly distinct from lenses; perhaps more general:

(1) Basic: "experience, observation, reflection, reasoning, study, via authority, custom, general consent, other criteria"

(2) Big Four: **Science** (empiricism)... **Religion**... **Culture** (norms mores folkways).... **Individual-Personal** (schema)

(3) Another quartet from Philosophy: **Empiricism, Materialism, Idealism, Rationalism**. Cf. also Induction, Deduction. Changes in history in these.

(4) Evaluation: "prejudice, bias, self-deception, desire, fear, vested interest, illusions, ego- and ethno-centrism" [R.PAUL]

(5) Conventional absurdities, urban legends, intellectual commonplaces [- S. PINKER]

(6) "Personal Subjective," "versus" Impersonal Objective, ways of knowing...

--Also **WORLD-VIEWS**: pocket philosophies of what reality is like: true/false, good-bad, what/how to do, etc.

SEE "II" FULL version for [6.2.] the academic DISCPLINES as "lenses." (Especially Biological, Psychological, Sociological, Historical, Economic, Political...) **EXAMPLES:** X River in Michigan, X A Horse, X Chinese porcelain vase, X the wearing of Sunglasses, X Fall of Rome, X American South racial situation, X American valuing hard work, X Crime

|+#|+|+|#|+#|+|#+|+|+|+#|++##+##|#|+|+|+|#|+|#+#+|+|+#|+|+|#+|#+|#+|+|+|#++|+|+|+|+#|+#|+|#+|+#|||

[7.] | TOOL-KIT: The "KEY ISSUES":

VARIABLE-ISSUES ROSTER.   Here are key "issues-about" **lenses** as we call systems between Reality and Mind. Always operative. These variables always exist and are operating—for good or ill. Thinkers don't always fully know of them. But a sense of these "contours" behind lenses, can enormously improve lens-work thinking.
We know of no other such existing assemblage anywhere in educational literature, as the following: highly-conceptual, but vividly concretized, and also applicable for use as a Guideline...

1. Lenses exist but not everyone fully "knows" this... "Reality, the world out there,"
and "lenses" or views of it: both do exist, but *are* different, distinct. "The map is *not* the territory"!

[Learners move from seeing **knowledge** as "out there and directly accessible," to being "constructed, complex, and provisional plus changing..."]

GUIDELINE: try to truly know, master, this sense of objectivity, of differentiating the subject and how it's being seen... Avoid extremes of either absolutist "we see reality directly," and an extreme-relativistic "we can't know reality *at all, only* biased lenses"

\=|+|+\+|=\=|+\=|=|+\=|+|=\=|=\+|=|=|+\=|+|=\+|=|+|+|\+\=|+|=\+\+|=\+|=\+|=\+|+\+\=|+|+\=|=|+|=\+|=\+|=\+\+|=|+|+\=\+|+\=|+\+\=|\=|\=||

2. Lenses are inevitable, inescapable. (Though some would deny or not realize this.)

EXAMPLE. A very-traditional "Biblical literalist" could *not* respond to the question, "how would non-Biblical history interpret Event X?" To him/her, Scripture was not a version of reality, it was reality directly, or if a mirror, was the *only* mirror. Perhaps the literalist was almost like "a fish swimming in water but unaware of water"? But Water is unitary, the only environment for the fish; whereas, multiple-plural lenses do exist. So, the fish was *also* utterly unaware of Land and Air ... [--V.CRAPANZANO]

EXAMPLE. An anthropologist notes that things themselves become particular (ethical, economic, erotic, etc.) only when seen through a—lens. He illustrates: "Is a Chinese porcelain vase a scientific specimen, an object of art, an article of commerce, or an exhibit in a lawsuit?"...Actually, of course, to call it a 'Chinese porcelain vase' is already to contextualize it.; "it would be better first of all to say "a glazed form of fired clay,'" not art science or merchandise.]
[-- LESLIE WHITE, 1959]

[But please note lens-use is *inescapable.* "Glazed form of fired clay" is looking at the thing not neutral-naked,-pure, but via a sort of—**empirical scientific descriptive materialist *lens*!**]

\=|+|+\+|=\=|+\=|=\+|=|+|=\=|=\+|=|=\+|=|+\=|+|=\+|=|+|+|\+\=|+|=\+\+|=\+|=\+|=\+|+\+\=|+|+\=|=|+|=\+|=\+|=\+\+|=|+|+\=\+|+\=|+\+\=|\=|\=||

3. Specific lenses are often subliminal: thinkers aren't consciously aware of them, they remain unlabelled, tacit-covert-latent, not recognized (or even intended?)

GUIDELINE: Develop the ability to recognize and label existing but covert lenses. Used by other thinkers—by oneself. And to critique them!

EXAMPLE. During the first Space Race, a letter to a newspaper, justified the expense etc. by showing the many benefits created, including even Teflon, etc. The author *un*consciously used the lens of "*American frontier ideology of valuing materialistic progress and control of nature*" to justify the program—or at least so I analyzed the article's subliminal motivations thus...

\=|+|+\+|=\=|+\=|=\+|=|+\=|=\=|=\+|=|=\+|=|+\=|+|=\+|=|+|+|\+\=|+|=\+\+|=\+|=\+|=\+|+\+\=|+|+\=|=|+|=\+|=\+|=\+\+|=|+|+\=\+|+\=|+\+\=|\=|\=||

4. Lenses are not "cleanly pure/descriptive" only: they come freighted with views.
[**World-View:** = "pocket philosophy" about what Is (world-out-there), what Should be (purposes, goals), what Shouldn't be (good-and-evil), what Causes things (motivations etc.), what People are like (human nature), Etc.]
(Ideologies presuppositions, implications, etc., "tincture" the glass...)

GUIDELINE: identify the elements "tincturing" the clear glass—the subtle world-picture they import—perhaps to distort...

EXAMPLES. Christianity, Freudianism, behaviorism, Communism, capitalism, existentialism, others—all are not the world, but versions of it, with stands...

\=|+|+\+|=\=|+\=|=\+|=|+\=|=\=|=\+|=|=\+|=|+\=|+|=\+|=|+|+|\+\=|+|=\+\+|=\+|=\+|=\+|+\+\=|+|+\=|=|+|=\+|=\+|=\+\+|=|+|+\=\+|+\=|+\+\=|\=|\=||

5. Lenses are "double-edged." (A) (+) They can be very **powerfully-insightful**. But (B) (-) each single lens is also *surely* (1) **limited and incomplete**, *probably* (2) **"biased"** too. Especially if carried too far, over-applied.

EXAMPLES: A roster of **"monisms"** or one-discipline explanations of too much, past and recent.

--**Geographical** determinism… [ELLSWORTH HUNTINGTON] (the fall of Rome, rise of other civilizations)
--**Biological**: genetic determinism…
--**Psychological**: *extreme* Freudianism, *extreme* behaviorism…
--**Political**: extreme Marxism?…
--**Theology**: fundamentalisms?…
--**Anthropology**: Leslie White's "culturology"?…
--**Linguistic**: the Sapir-Whorf hypothesis in parts?…
--**Sociology**: "oversocialized conception of humanity"… (Humans internalize norms, play roles for self-esteem)
--**"Belletristic-Humanistic-Aesthetic Monism"**: great art, high culture as key forces in history, "civilization"…
--**Others**…..

So *what?* These simplicities are all past now; we now know we need multiple-plural viewpoints for today's complexities.	True, but even today, "only one way" remains a danger due to certain human motivations…

\=|+|+\+|=\=|+\=|=|+\=|+|=\=\+|=|=|+\=|+=\+|=|+|+\+|=\+|=\+\+|=|+|=\+|=\+\=\+\+\=|+|+\=|=|+|=\+|=\+=\+|=|+|+\=\+|=|+\=|\=||

6. "**All Lenses Are 'Good'—In A Certain Pragmatic Sense,** for Better Communication Anyhow…" Each and every viewpoint is True, Right, Valuable—by its own **Rationale**. (Even totalitarianism, fascism, anarchy, other suspect stances.) The lens makes a sense or a sense by its own **logic**. But, of course, ***so what?***

> GUIDELINE: It may be Useful, Moral, and Satisfying to be able thoroughly to comprehend the inner Reasoning (such as it is!) or world-view of the lens. No need to slavishly accept, obsessively refute, defend against, offensively conquer, etc. Just "sense out" the Structure of its viewpoint.

EXAMPLE. At a debate on "Religion & Homosexuality," I heard the side for Gay Liberation, then the traditional religious Lutheran doctrine. I thought the latter was *very oppressive to individuals* (="sex is sinful, change is possible and desirable, if not celibacy is required," etc.). But I listened for the *Logic*, which is that "Scripture is truth, damnation is a risk, salvation is possible, we are all sinners, we help each other to be saved." I saw that *according to that Reason-ing*, the fundamental-religious lens *is* "good" or at least *is* "logical-rational for its own purposes in its own world-view." This scrutinizing to see the inner *Sense*, lets me communicate better with opponents, and either cooperate with them or conquer better after all… And all with *no* need to defend/refute/quarrel/"spar-or-spurn" etc…

\=|+|+\+|=\+\=|+\=|+|=\=|=\+|=|=|+\=|+\=|+|+\+|=\+|=\+\+|=|+|=\+|=\+\=\+\+\=|+|+\=|=|+|=\+|=\+=\+|=|+|+\=\+|=|+\=|\=||

7. **Over time, lenses can become (A) outdated**, so should be altered/abandoned)….

EXAMPLE. "Crossdisciplinary Oversights."

One SCHOLAR notes a "lag" factor when thinkers in the Borrowing field (here, sociology) may be unthinkingly adopting material already outdated, corrected-or-rejected, etc., in the originating Donor field (here, history and anthropology): "Many sociologists have drawn their image of the **Protestant Reformation** from Max Weber, although professional historians have long since relegated his theories to the *dustbin*. In the same way, sociologists have drawn their imagery of **primitive societies** from Patterns of Culture long after anthropologists had dismissed Ruth Benedict's ethnographic depictions as quite *misleading*."
  [(MURRAY WAX, 1969: 81-2, quoted in MIHANI].

But **also over time, lenses can become (B)** wrongfully **neglected** due to cyclical fashions in thinking. Hence two *pitfalls* to beware: using outmoded lenses, rejecting still-valid lenses.

EXAMPLES. Heredity or environment: earlier, the *sociocultural* view dominates, culture writes on the blank human slate… then, *evolutionary psychobiology* rises, needfully correcting the "Standard Soc.Sci. Model"… but then, (A) old-guard die-hards may jeer the new, cling to Skinnerian behaviorism, (B) extreme sociobiologists may throw the earlier environmental baby out with the bathwater?

STATEMENT. A cultural anthropologist invites the new, but warns against trashing the old!

"The privileging of the current and demeaning of the slightly less current, not to mention the past, is a **presentism** that reflects a naivete and lack of perspective on the history of ideas. Also present is an unattractive inability to extend our [anthropologists'] much verbalized relativity to the ideas of our colleagues, past and present. Theoretical presentism...reinforces various distortions....The belief that only today's theory has any virtue leads many students to neglect to read past theory, being satisfied with second- or third-hand accounts or evaluations. [A student claimed to the instructor that MALINOWSKI was not an authority as he tried to avoid the natives; he asked how she knew this; she replied she had not read M. but was still sure... Another student claimed BARTH'S theory was capitalistic; the instructor had to make that student read closely beyond glib labels to more subtle substance.] Presentism leads to simplistic labeling of theories, exaggerating the flaws and ignoring the subtleties of previous theories, and even demonizing of theorists or categories of theorists as capitalists, imperialists, and/or patriarchal oppressors. This...raises doubts about intellectual integrity...."

[-- SOURCE: book from Univ. of Wis.-Whitewater Library]

\=|+|+\+|=\=|+\=|=|+\=|+|=\=|\+|=|=|\=|+|=|=|\+|=|+\+|=\+|=\+\+|+\=|\+|=\+|=\=|+\+\+\=|+|+\=|=|+|=\=|+|=+\+|=|+|+\=\+|\=|+\=|\=||

8. **Number of lenses to use—and carefully...** One should use multiple lenses for more-complex subjects, tasks. But a "plural lenses" procedure, raises issues....

(A) Priorities: are some lenses primary, others secondary?.....

(B) Cooperation-or-Conflict along the way: do the lenses mesh, or clash—and if clash, what then?

(C) Integration-or-Synthesis at the end: do they resolve with each other, or if not, does such non-blending, really *matter*?...

EXAMPLE. The Eskimo syndrome of "pibloktoq," or running around amok. *Freudian psychoanalysis* says this is "classic hysteria, a wish to be pursued and loved." But now, *environmental biology* says it is "hypocalcemic tetany," result of insufficient calcium in the northern diet.....] [-- SOURCE]

EXAMPLE. "Identical Twins Identical Behavior" One man was a fussy housekeeper. His identical twin brother also was, but they had been reared apart, truly "separated at birth." The first twin's mother was a truly sloppy housekeeper; the second twin's mother ran a spic-and-span household. Psychology: neatnik behavior explained in second case as learned behavior, in first case as rebellion against it! Behavioral genetics: a genetic component—identical twins raised apart have exhibited astoundingly-identical traits. [-- From BORN THAT WAY?]

EXAMPLE. "Gay Men and Older Brothers" A study shows the more older brothers a man has, the more likely that his sexual orientation is homosexual. (In a sample of 300 men, seven had four or more older brothers; four of those seven identified as homosexual!) Psychological explanations (including those from "reparative therapy for male homosexuals"): feared older brother to be competed with, tendency to remain closer to the mother. Biological explanations: the intrauterine sexing of the fetus, a maternal immune reaction that is provoked only by male fetuses and becomes stronger after each male pregnancy. [-- SOURCES: Varied, citations missing...]

\=|+|+\+|=\=|+\=|=|+\=|+|=\=|\+|=|=|\=|+|=|=|\+|=|+\+|=\+|=\+\+|+\=|\+|=\+|=\=|+\+\+\=|+|+\=|=|+|=\=|+|=+\+|=|+|+\=\+|\=|+\=|\=||

9. Lens-Selection: #2: [*] It's a challenge to know how to
[A.] identify and critique those lenses *already-present*, also
[B.] locate, and select, those needed lenses *still-to-be-imported*.

[**9.A.**]: "Which lenses are already present? Should they be used after all?"

GUIDELINE: know how to identify lenses already "in play here" but maybe subliminal, then evaluate whether appropriate or not...

[**9.B.**]: "Which lenses are quite missing, absent—but are needed?

GUIDELINE: know how to locate (choose) and implement (use), "other, better" lenses.

PITFALL: **Not choosing *explicitly* enough.** Often we don't choose lenses *consciously or deliberately*, they may just happen, we find ourselves with them—and they may not be the best ones.

PITFALL: **Not knowing *why* we choose, really.** Even when we consciously select lenses, often **we choose them *subjectively*** to serve *subliminal background value-motivations* above-and-beyond the facts, even the lenses...! This *personalized* selection is especially true of the *larger* lenses, the paradigms, world-views, Big Theories, etc. [The **"LLSS"** idea says: the "*larger* lenses which we use, we select *subjectively*"]

EXAMPLE. PERSONAL SELECTION. When one chooses, say, **Christianity,** or **Communism,** or **evolution,** or **existentialism** instead of one of the other three or yet other lenses—may really selecting be to <u>serve one's prior motivation-needs for</u> (for-instance) *order... authority... rebellion...anti-spiritualism... individuality... etc.,* rather than <u>to illuminate the task-goal at hand</u>...] "Root-motives" are *key...*

STATEMENT. FORMAL SELECTION. Why do scholarly thinkers (etc.) prefer and select one paradigm (system of thought) over another? *Sometimes* because it <u>is</u> "**better via empirical and logical proofs**"?.... *At other times,* <u>different considerations</u> apply: "**aesthetics: simplicity and beauty. Power: vested interests of younger/older workers in the field. Temperament. Training. Demographics.**"...   [-- PICKLES & WATTS; A. HOLT-JENSEN; T. KUHN]

STATEMENT.   NEW-PARADIGM SELECTION. Why do we change to a whole different paradigm or major system? "The new model may accommodate more information; it may be **more aesthetically pleasing,** or **more psychologically satisfying,** or **more theoretically fertile;** it may even have **greater explanatory scope.** But—and this is crucial—<u>there are no independent rational criteria</u> for deciding between the old and new paradigms. This is simply because what counts as a rational explanation is determined by the paradigm itself.   [-- PETER GOULD, geographer]

\=|+|+\+|=\=|=|\=|+\=|+|=\=|=\+|=|+|=\+|=\=|+|+|+\+|=\+|=\+|+|=\+|=\+|=\+\+\+\=|+|+\=|=|+|=\+|=\+|=|\+|=\+|+\=\+|+\=\+|=|+\|=\+\|=/\=||

[10.] ...And <u>those other variables</u> which *others* will be listing...

...And so above, the key **variables** *above/behind* **lens-**use ... **It took me years—heck, decades--to elucidate the above issues in the explicit nine-point categorization above**—I always knew of **lens-work**, but not so formally.

|+#|+|+|#|+#|+|#+|+|+|#|++-##+##|#|+|+|+|#|+|#+#+|+|+#|+|+|#+|#+|#+|+|+|#++|+|+|+|+#|+#|+|#+|+#|||#+|=#+|+#|+|#+|#+|+#|||

[8.] An ANNEX for the Variables ...

[A.] Locations of lenses: are they *clustered to just use,* or *scattered to have to seek out?*

[B.] GALLERY: "deft supple multiple-lens-skill..."   **[C.]** Visual Gallery....   **[D.]** Gallery: "Letter vs. Spirit"....

[8.A.]   CLUSTERED CORRALLED or SCATTERED SERENDIPITOUS lens-locales:

--**Lenses may <u>sit within an existing system,</u>** scheme, "school of thought," set-of-viewpoints, and the like. *These are usually evident, obvious.* [Branches of an academic discipline... Political party systems... etc.]

--**Or lenses may <u>lie more scattered</u> Arenas of occurring,** plus Ways of Knowing. [See right-hand below] *And these may be evident, but are often obscured.* **PITFALL**: *don't overlook non-obvious distant (etc.) lenses!*

Some more **CLUSTERED** pre-set:	"IN-BETWEEN"...	More **SCATTERED** in system:
[1] <u>Schools of literary criticism</u> (lenses upon a text): **Moral-philosophical, Historical, Formalism (aesthetic), Myth-archetypal, Structuralism, Reader-response, Deconstruction-postmodernism, Rhetorical, New Historicism, Ethnocriticism (cultural studies), Feminism, and Pluralism-Integrative.** [-SOURCE]	**[A]** "<u>Seven theories of Human Nature</u>": **Plato, Christianity, Marx, Freud, Existentialist, Behaviorism, Evolutionary-&-Sociobiology** [L.STEVENSON] **[B]** Read <u>Hawthorne's</u>	**[i.]** <u>How to evaluate restaurant cuisine</u>: 1. "Classic **Tradition(s),**" **Innovation** upon. 2. **Aesthetics:** Balance of Flavors 3. Personal-Preference of **Reviewer**. 4. Personal Goals of **Chef** 5. **Ethnic** Variations 6. **Star** Ranking Systems vs. Other Criteria 7. **Standards:** low-lax, or high-rigorous [-SOURCE] **[ii.]** <u>What is **Art**, how define/evaluate?</u>

[2] Oppressions of minority groups: 1. physical, 2. legal, 3. economic, 4. institutional (religious, medical, media, etc.), 5. sociocultural (A. actions, B. attitudes), 5. internalized.

[3] Major ethical-moral systems: 1. Cultural Relativism 2. Ethical Egoism 3. Behaviorism 4. Utilitarianism 5. Kantian Ethics 6. Virtue Ethics 7. Situation Ethics 8. Natural Law Ethics 9. Divine Command Theory. [-STEVE WILKINS]

[4] Neurotic Styles of a Psychoanalyst (in dream-interpretation, etc.): **Compulsive, Obsessional, Hysteric, Narcissistic, Schizoid, Depressive, Paranoid!** [-SHAPIRO]

[5] Visual-Art Styles: a *Tabasco sauce bottle* as painted by **Impressionism, Cubism, Surrealism, Abstraction…**

The Scarlet Letter *via*: **"Puritanism, Feminism, Transcendentalism, Freudianism"**[-SOURCE]

[C] "Why Did The Chicken Cross The Road" via: **Dr. Seuss, Hemingway, M. L. King Jr., Aristotle, K. Marx, Saddam Hussein, Freud, Bill Gates, Einstein, Grandfather** etc.

[D] "Light Bulb Jokes"] **(feminists, computer geeks, bureaucrats)**

[E] Exercises in Style: **93** separate literary modes of telling the same simple story! [R.QUENEAU]

[F] 13 forms of Narrative also. (1st and 3rd person, letter-or-report, etc.)

1. **Classic** Great Tradition
2. Conventional **folk** familiar
3. **Trendy** edgy fashionable Next Big Thing
4. Laissez-faire relativism, whatever is called "art"
5. What is in **museums and galleries**
6. Socially-conscious **politics** for liberation.
7. Just-**personal** expression for the artist
8. Whatever pleases the **viewer**
9. Religious act, **ceremonial ritual**
10. Life-**philosophy**, enriching guidance.
11. **Aesthetic** Form… [-B. K. BECK]

[iii.] Our own **"16-L"** scheme for reading a text more fully! [*Collected from "all over" over much time…*] Includes **Personally-Pleasing, Correct/"True," Purpose-fulfilling, Integrity, Aestheics, Craft,** and **ten others** (see below…).

[iv.] Education! Knowledge-acquisition? Social adjustment? Moral-ethical values? Personal enrichment? Vocational training? More powerful *thinking?*…

GUIDELINE: Be *aware* that some lenses are "ready-grouped at hand," but other valuable ones may be scattered. Be *able* to search widely to construct one's own arsenal of improbable but useful lenses for a task-goal…

|+#|+|+|#|+#|+|#+|+|+#|++##+##|#|+|+|+|#|+|#+#+|+|+#|+|+|#+|#+|#+|+|+|#++|+|+|+|+#|+#|+|#+|+#|||

[8.B.] GALLERY: four "expert moves" using lens-work to deftly unpack complexities:

[1.] An unconventional feminist critic discusses (and defends) **pornography.** She says it does not poison the mind; it shows the deepest truth about sexuality, stripped of romantic veneer. **Gay men** (and **herself**) appreciate it because they accept **the Hellenic [early Greek] principle** that some people are born more beautiful than others. Generic granola **feminists** are likely to call this "lookism"—an offence against equality. She takes the view of Oscar Wilde **[British aesthete]** that in politics, equality is morally necessary, but that in art, what governs is "the elitism of talent and the tyranny of appearance." Also, pornography's total exposure of ripe dynamic vigorous and vital flesh, represents "the cruel **pre-Christian idolatry** of beauty and strength." [-- CAMILLE PAGLIA]

Well, a relaxed informal unstructured circling around the subject with anyhow a *number of plural and* conflicting perspectives—explicitly identified! … More control of lens-work than not, I would say…

[2.] The Boomer Bible by R. LAIRD was written to satirize the younger generation's three flaws of over-desires, over-certainty, and under-responsibility. But a comment deftly shows plural perspectives on the book via different named specific lenses (and looser perspectives or temperaments)—all of which however are containing bias and distortion…

"…when the book succeeds in outraging or angering you it is also secretly laughing at you for failing to transcend your own prejudices and orthodoxies. The **superficial** will see the book as purely satirical. The **semanticist** will see it as illiterate. The **liberal** will see it as somehow fascist. The **reactionary** will see it as cynically and stupidly juvenile. The **fundamentalist** will see it as blasphemy. The **atheist** will see it as pointless. The **existentialist** will see it as a random, irrelevant redundancy. In every case, such readers are only peering into an inverted mirror of themselves."
[-- SOURCE: INTERNET WEBSITE]

Sounds like the fable of the "*six* (actually seven here) *blind people and the elephant.*" Except that the fable's point was to warn against the pitfall of scanning a **"catchment-area"** which was too limited to "scope" the subject completely, and here the point is to warn that any one lens may be too personally-involved. **#4:** Lenses are uncleanly-freighted with world-views. Also, **#8A:** no one lens tells it all…

[3.] A former champion of "cultural theory" in literary etc. studies, now critiques that lens or system. He admits that cultural theory "has been shamefaced about morality and metaphysics, embarrassed about love, biology, religion, and revolution, largely silent about evil, reticent about death and suffering, dogmatic about essences, universals, and foundations and superficial about truth, objectivity, and disinterestedness." These constitute "a rather large slice of human existence" to ignore. [-- SOURCE: on the work of TERRY EAGLETON]

Perhaps a good comprehensive scan of how one given lens-perspective may have fallen short significantly in many identifiable ways… **#7A:** lens becomes outdated (if it was ever valid…). Also **#5:** lenses are limited; here, grossly…

[4.] The great Spanish novel Don Quixote (1604) by MIGUEL DE CERVANTES has been seen variously by various historical eras—and various schools of thought. "The 18th century believed the knight to be a lunatic, lost to reason; the **Victorians** approached him as a romantic dreamer, trapped, just like artists and prophets, in his own fantasy; the **modernists** applauded his quest for an inner language; the **postmodernists** adore his dislocated identity. Psychiatrists have seen him as a case study in schizophrenia, **Communists** have turned him into a victim of market forces. **Intellectual historians** have portrayed him as a portent of Spain's decline into intellectual obscurantism."
[-- ILAN STAVANS, CHE, 07 JAN 2005]

Shows how lenses are limited (**#5**), also may become **#7A** outmoded, or for that matter wrongly-neglected…

|+#|+|+|#|+#|+|#+|+|+|#|++##+##|#|+|+|+|#|+|#+#+|+|+#|+|+|#+|#+|#+|+|+|#++|+|+|+|+#|+#|+|#+|+#|||

[8.C.] GALLERY: styles of artistry, as truly "lenses." [Via compare-contrast visuals!] Whether about **human-form,** or **landscape-depiction,** or **flower-arranging**—it gets "lens-ish:" *definite viewpoints…*

1. MICHELANGELO'S "DAVID"—AND TWO OTHER LENSES. Western, Oceania, African… How varied cultures see the human form differently in proportions. An often-overlooked "lens"?…From the left: the original… an African statue… David f/ Africa… an Oceania statue… David f/ Oceania.

2. CENTRAL PARK IN NEW YORK CITY. The "lenses" of different **artistic styles**—in **media,** and from individual **artists**—is made clear by visual comparison-contrast:

3. JAPANESE FLOWER-ARRANGEMENT: "QUALITY-CONTROL"... The "lens" of Japanese *variety, spontaneity, yet control* is different from Western *more-formal structure...*

SEE "II" FULL version for **[8.D.]** IN Appendix #3.C.1: **"Letter vs. Spirit"** as two major lenses. X Writing Skills: parallelism, repetition... X Hotel Behavior: Clerk, Guest... X What is a "man": conventional vs. essential...

|+#|+|+|#|+#|+|#+|+|+#|++##+##|#|+|+|+|#|+|#+#+|+|+#|+|+|#+|#+|#+|+|+|#++|+|+|+|+#|+#|+|#+|+#|||#+|=#+|+#|+|#+|#+|+#|||

[9.] LAB "I": lenses on a "tough topic":

The "HOMOFILE": lenses upon the pesky current concern of "homosexuality as social issue."

GALLERY. Examples from "**homosexuality** as social issue." *Can deft "lens-work" add power?*

RATIONALE. To play out the lenswork-"game" on this sensitive-subject terrain. Do we see deft moves; blunders? ... *Can learners here experience the powers of competent lenswork such as...*
1. <u>Identify</u> peoples' hidden <u>motivations, criteria</u>—<u>biasses</u>? For fairer evaluation...
2. Acquire a wider range of viewpoints for fuller <u>comprehension of the subject</u>?
3. Improve the <u>teaching/learning of research paper</u> and in-class <u>discussion</u> on issues?
4. <u>Play the lively game</u> of "gotcha," your lens is absent or wrong—although Who Says--...

(1) <u>The Boy Scouts of America: policy is to exclude gay personnel.</u>

--#1: "**This exclusion is immoral, it's prejudicial: no reason to exclude gays, who per se are not harmful.**" [But that's by your lens of *liberalism and liberation and equality and diversity*.]

--#2: "**This exclusion is moral, responsible; Perhaps the Scouts are moral after all, by** [But that's by their own lens of *Traditional American Morality*, whose norms-mores-folkways perceive homosexuals as unnatural, abnormal, objectively dangerous (pedophilia) and subjectively disgusting or at least distasteful."]

--#3: **You both may be wrong or incomplete, it's a lens of sheer** *political-economic practicality, pragmatism*. **The Mormons help support much of Scouting and might depart if gays were accepted, so there!"** .]

    Here the **Variable-Issues** arise of <u>#4 subliminal freight</u> in both of them, traditionalism-liberalism...   And also <u>#7: conflict, but also perhaps cooperation</u>: Morality and Practicality lenses could cooperate...   And also <u>#9B: which is the best or better or right lens</u>?....   But that depends on <u>#5 again, the world-views, prior value-systems</u>, etc., which drive one to believe "moral" or "immoral" and the like...

(2) In the short story "Baseball in July" [by PATRICK HOCHTEL], <u>a gay man brought his male lover home to a family reunion.</u> *Some problems occurred ["anti-gay" behavior].*

What caused them? In my English 101 course, four lenses were offered to explain:
1. *Homosexuality* itself, an unnatural, abnormal condition.
2. The obvious (?) *bigotry and prejudice* of some of the anti-gay relatives.
3. The over-assertive *aggressiveness* (?) of the gay man in importing his lover.

4. "*Homophobia*," a learned social response like male chauvinism, white racism, etc.

[... This worked *well* in literature class! One group went for #1, homosexuality as the problem, and learned that it might be the others, either as well, or instead. All sections learned about "multiple viewpoints"... And indeed, V/I #9B arises here. It is *hard* to find all possible, let alone the productive, lenses! I myself the teacher had a moderately hard time reminding *myself* of this quartet of lenses, and may have missed yet others! ...]]

(3) REV. NUGENT said that on difficult issues such as homosexuality, his Church relies on "Scripture; tradition (of the church); reason; and human experience." [-- SOURCE]

[Good, showing *multiple approaches*, although of course interpreting one's "experience" may be colored by ideological lenses? Of two churchpersons who actually got to know some gay people, one became more tolerant, the other didn't. This shows #9A, lenses are selected subjectively, for more general or hidden reasons...]

(4) The parent of a gay child comments. "On reflecting about homosexuality, I've learned that: my *religious* tradition taught me to believe that my son was a sinner; my *medical* support system...that my son was sick; my *educational* system...that my son was abnormal; my *legal* system views my son and his partner in an unsanctioned relationship without legal rights and protection that are afforded my married daughter; my *family*, immediate and extended, provided no acknowledgement or support for having a gay relative in its midst; my major *communications* sources treated homosexuality as deviant." [-- THE FATHER OF A GAY SON]

[... READER 1: "That's too unrealistically-negative today; times are changing." READER 2: "True, but it shows how many different lenses are possible for many subjects... And V/I #4, many lenses remain subliminal—not explicitly named-and-recognized Plus #7, number of lenses. What a *large*, unsuspected number of ways to look at the one subject...]

(5) An editor's firm stand concerning homosexual activity:

"Men using one another as women constitutes a perversion. To my unreconstructed mind, this is as true as ever; and so far as I am concerned it would still be true even if gay sex no longer entailed the danger of infection and even if everything about it were legalized by all 50 states and ratified by all nine justices of the Supreme Court."
[--NORMAN PODHORETZ]

[... READER 1: "How incredibly biassed, in this day and age! V/I #6, double-edged..." READER 2: "Well yes by newer lenses. But note that he at least states his own lens explicitly (V/I #4)—*Personal Temperament* (probably influenced by *social background?*) and explicitly mentions another possible lens—the *Legal* and probably the "*Hygiene*" sort of lens—which he explicitly rejects. Shows a kind of lensmanship thus or attention to stances anyhow." #3: "Also note that in terms of *Fact vs. Opinion vs. Reasoned Judgment*, it is definitely his Opinion, though others would argue differently on that" ...]

(6) E. J. GRAFF discussed same-sex marriage.

She reasons that gay and lesbian folk deserve marriage because it consists of four meanings, and G/L people already possess the first three. First, "the inner bond, the emotional commitment, the daily life together/" This, G/L couples are already committed to. Second is a public ceremony celebrating the bond with the community which brings social recognition. This too is frequent, as in commitment ceremonies. Third is religious. And nowadays, Unitarian and Quaker or (Reform) Jewish churches do perform same. The still-missing fourth is "civil marriage, the governmental, legal-political recognition" of the bond made between two people. This creates a contract between two people, serving and protecting them—but G/L folk still lack this. Therefore, being "married" three-fourths of the way, G/L folk deserve the protection of the legal meaning of marriage.

[... This seems to illustrate deft, needed plural lensmanship—even though the "lenses" are not recognized named "isms." They do amount to "psychological, sociological, religious, political." Just as nicely productive as the four for the short story above... Agree with her or not (and many will not), she was able to locate *multiple* lenses (#9B) to explicitly discuss the complex subject... How many other writings on same-sex marriage were this scrupulously explicit in defining via lenses? I've read a few, and none did... *And I admit I myself could not have thought out the issue with these many explicitlenses...*]

(7) A study showed that gay men are more likely than non-gay men to have older brothers. Each additional older brother increased the odds of homosexuality by 33%. Traditional psychoanalysts [medical model of homosexuality as disorder] could explain this by a "feared older brother," against whom the younger brother may have to compete while

remaining over-close to the mother. However, <u>more-recent biologists</u> offered that "birth order effect could involve a maternal immune reaction [which can influence sexual orientation] that is provoked only by male fetuses and becomes stronger after each male pregnancy." [--REPORT]

[... Shows how lenses may contradict and conflict, though possibly cooperate and integrate sometimes. Also implies how lens-choice is influenced by prior higher perspectives perhaps ...]

(8) A Psychiatrist Condemns Gay Activism Etc.

"TOBIAS [a homosexual activist]...is claiming a freedom to alter the basic design of life itself...[his] statement that all forms of sexual relations are equal and indistinguishable....seeks to overturn not only the history of the human race, but to subvert its future as well—a freedom that dares to re-form the most basic institution of society, the nuclear family, an institution that is written in our natures, and evolved over eons." [-- CHARLES W. SOCARIDES, M.D.]

[... Shows that lenses may be complex, and even not fully known to the user (V/I #4, "subliminal").
This letter exhibits the larger lens or ideology of **"Natural Law."** Namely, that "<u>there is in human nature and behavior, one central traditional natural normal condition. It was achieved with difficulty, can be easily lost, and if we depart from it, two problems result: personal disorganization, and even social harm.</u>"
Whether true or not, this lens underlies the whole statement. Furthermore, it illustrates the "Truth" in V/I #9.
We select our lenses not objectively, but subjectively, for other and varied reasons.
SOCARIDES seems less physician, than philosophically conservative traditionalist, so he employs that lens for his outlook...]

(9) An Educational Dilemma.

"When an African American expresses her sincere belief (in the course of a class discussion on the legal regulation of sexual conduct) that homosexuals are sick, and a classmate complains to the dean of students, are we to endanger the African-American's self-esteem by sending her off for sensitivity training, or the self-esteem of the gay complainant by providing no redress? It is no laughing matter..." [-- ALAN RYAN, "Is Higher Education A Fraud?"]

[... Interestingly, this commits the "either-or" fallacy or at least way of thinking. Further, it implies that the complainant was gay, instead of perhaps a heterosexual "ally." Most important, it suggests two "lenses," <u>sensitivity training</u> or <u>inaction</u>, and quite overlooks a third. Namely, <u>educational</u>: to use the incident as Grist for the Educational Mill, a Teachable-Learnable Moment indeed, to discover how to think better about complex issues by better thinking!
Two lenses in education today are of course our two, <u>Current-Traditional</u> {"Old-School"},whose goal is "What to Know and Believe about the subject,"and the <u>Innovative</u> {"New-Think"}, whose goal is "How to Think the subject Through competently on your own now and after school."...]

(10) Here's a *candid* discussion of the "issue," "why do gay men emphasize sex so much?" In their conversations (which I have heard when I'm visiting my gay male friends in MADISON, WI, U.S.A.):

(A): Whoa, very *individualistic personal* lens. I myself, while not an inhibited prude, am rather anaerotic or hyposexual. That appetite exists in me but is low-key, not a primary driving force, and indeed I like to approach it mild, etc. Therefore I may magnify, *misperceive*, the talk of sex, *any* sexuality. That would be a BLOCK-BARRIER-BIAS, rather than an overt "lens"... [This is probably good **Consciousness** or awareness of one's own thinking, plus the **Disposition** of openness or "transparent introspection," being candid plus civil...]

(B): But do they, is it your BIAS, again, of **Selective Perception**? Or of the **Stereotype** of "gay men as hypersexed." Do you overlook that straight guys also discuss sex, at least when they're in situations where this is permitted. So it's not a gay thing so much as a *male* thing?

(C): Actually, it's **situational**. Maybe gay men can't discuss sexuality openly with straights, so they tend to overdo it when they do get together with each other? [A **"lens"** of **ecological, spatial-territorial, psycho-geographic** type?]

(D): It <u>is</u>, for a *few* gay men, a <u>psychopathology</u>; *some* guys <u>are</u> obsessive-compulsive about "cruising." [Lens here is within traditional psychiatry, the "sickness" theory... But, is this statement, (A) a **Truth** which is **Taboo** to say (in liberal or Politically-Correct circles) in today's **Climate of Opinion**? plus or (B) maybe **my own bias or defense?** let alone (C) frank **stereotype?**...]

(E): ...whoa, is it **the culture's residual Puritanism** that makes us even bother discussing this dumb question at all? As in, *who cares*??

[... **Well, this maybe didn't get very far after all...** *except to defend "multiple-plural lensmanship."* **Many *different* lenses, many *varied* ways of knowing, may apply. But also the key "how-to" point that it may be <u>hard to find, and assess</u>, a good number of lenses—because of** *intellectual* **narrow-vision, and various** *emotional* **prohibitions too...**]

PEDAGOGICAL PLOY: *Does the above help accelerate learners' command of "lenswork"?*

|+#|+|+|#|+#|+|#+|+|+|#|++##+##|#|+|+|+|#|+|#+#+|+|+#|+|+|#+|#+|#+|+|+|#++|+|+|+|#|+#|+|#+|+#|||

[10.] LAB "II": "16-Lenses on Writing":
[A.] "16-L" scheme...   [B., C., D.] *Galleries...*

LAB-EXERCISE UNIT. *The Story Behind This:* To teach "How to respond more competently to a written text, a piece of writing. For domain-specific English course, also for general-generic thinking skills."
--I found that my students (American state-university college freshman 1980's-and-later) were <u>entering English 101</u> with "tool-belts" furnished <u>with only two "lenses"</u> (and those subliminal and non-chosen...). One was "**Correct**" grammatically, *did the writing avoid errors?* This ignoring larger qualities. The other was "**Personal-Pleasing,**" *did I the reader like it or not and Just Because?"* This in a flood of isolated egocentricity disregarding situational purpose. A somewhat-empty Lens-Bag...
--Therefore I offered more lenses. One lens led to another—obvious ones then more subtle ones. I finally ended up with this enlarged (engorged?) scheme. I labeled it simply the "**16-L**" model. It powerfully unleashes upon the awaiting Text, multiple perspectives, for more-thorough responses.

| **BUT:** How *excessive*: teeteringly-topheavy, hence decadent! As usual you've *overdone* it! (Sixteen tons, 13 plus three ways of looking at a simple blackbird...] | Oh yes, **BUT** also how powerful and deft too, zeroing in to get more out of the text than otherwise... Where do you find this many reminders of possible viewpoints, issues? |

|+#|+|+|#|+#|+|#+|+|+|#|++##+##|#|+|+|+|#|+|#+#+|+|+#|+|+|#+|#+|#+|+|+|#++|+|+|+|#|+#|+|#+|+#||| **[10.A.] :**

"16-L": sixteen viewpoints [lenses] for exploring *any* written text
["Text" = literature, ***but also***, instruction manual, letter to editor, minutes of meeting, political manifesto, graffiti, sign on wall, copy on cereal box...]

[I] THE USUAL BASICS:

(1) <u>Personal-Pleasing</u>, do I the reader, like it or not, just because "it floats my boat," whether personal-preference taste-temperament, emotional biasses, Hobby Horse or Pet Peeve, whatever?...

(2) <u>Correct</u>: does it follow rules of grammar, genre, situation, etc. ...

(3) <u>Purpose-fulfilling</u> (did it accomplish <u>author's</u> intended purpose with the "M.O.I.A." or with at least the *majority* of the target or *intended* reader-audience?)...

[II] THE NEXT ISSUES:

(4) <u>Clarity</u>, is message comprehensible, clear, as readable as could be or as needed to be?

(5) <u>Veracity</u>: is it accurate-true-valid, not false?...

(6) <u>Integrity</u>: does it exhibit morality-truthfulness-responsibility, and even other relevant ethical virtues, etc.

(7) <u>Pedagogical</u>: (A) Schoolwriting, did it show mastery of course content, the learning goal? **(B) Composition:** did writer learn better how to write, get good grade?...

[III] AND THE PLEASURE PRINCIPLE:

(8) <u>Sportive Challenge</u> did it take writing as a sport-game-play, writer as athlete, reader as spectator-fan?

(A) Did a **<u>Cruciality</u>** exist, a ***goal***, a *needfulness*-to-communicate (writer needed to say, subject needed to be stated, readers needed to be told)?, and then...

(B) Did a **<u>Challenge</u>** exist meaning "task difficult to achieve by just-anyone without Savvy & Sweat"?

(C) And then did **Competence** occur: writer was able to reach the goal, scored, *won* (due to skill & sweat)—
or foulled out, was defeated by the challenge—(due to lack of skill or sweat)?...

(9) **Aesthetic: as *Craft***: is it well-constructed, like a good cabinet, etc.?

(10) **Aesthetic: as *Art***: is it even a thing of beauty in design, like a good painting, etc.?

[IV] AND LESSER MATTERS:

(11) **Author-fulfilling** or "writer-serving" (did it aid writer's own goals of discover, express, "say it loud," etc.)?

(12) **Author-Revealing** did it create for the readers, a portrait, intended or not..."

(13) **Rhetorical Rapport:** does writer gain a good image and relationship with the reader?

(14) **Serendipity**: did it perhaps please some <u>un</u>intended reader in <u>un</u>intended ways, "just because"?...

(15) **Bridge Human Souls** did it create a communication, "I hear you," across time and space?...

(16) **Dynamite** does it just plain "pack a punch" of some identifiable kind ?...

|+#|+|+|#|+#|+|#+|+|+#|++##+##|#|+|+|+|#|+|#+#+|+|+#|+|#+|#+|#+|+|+|#++|+|+|+|+#|+#|+|#+|+#|||

[10.B.] GALLERY "I":   Examples of texts, with an array of lenses applied.
These worked well in my English 101, for Pragmatic Pedagogy, also Pleasure in the sport-game-play Contest of, discovering (1) diverse angles to "the same" text [and the generic skill of lenswork to apply to real-world situations], also (2) bungles & blunders of other readers in non-using or mis-using appropriate lenses, choosing unproductive lenses...

> **(1) "When mother fride my egg, it limbered out like corn surp. then it got buggles. They went up, then down, like breethen heavy."**   [--*writing by a third-grade student*]

-"Well, that's surely **Incorrect #2.** Basic errors in spelling."

-"True, but **Personal-Pleasing #1** anyhow, I like it! Gives a vivid image of the kitchen..."

-"I like it also via its **Artistry #10.** This is a poem, with analogy of corn syrup and breathing."

-"It's also just plain **Effective #3**, if its purpose was to vividly show the reader egg-frying."

-"Secondarily it could be good **Pedagogically #7B**, for unintended audience of college freshmen. To make the point that Correctness is important, but also important is a creativity or at least Craft of expression which we may lose as we get older or in school."

-"Was it a sportive **Challenge #8** to do well—as well as was done here? If so, the young writer seemed Competent to do so."

-"**Writer-Revealing #12** a little bit too in a secondary way; the student as poet..."

---"Well, that's enough to show that varied Lenses can help elucidate a simple text in a complementary way without much conflict or disagreement here. Let's continue.."

> **(2) "I am forwarding my marriage certificate and my three children, one of which is a mistake as you can see. Also, you have changed my little boy to a girl. Will this make any difference?"**   [--*letter to a local welfare office; alleged*]

-"*Terrible* writing. Basic **Clarity #4** missing. I can't understand a word. A child in an envelope?"

-"You make a basic error. Consider **Effective #3** for the <u>intended audience</u>! Namely, the clerk in the welfare office. To him or her, this is surely clear. Namely, <u>**I am forwarding the birth certificates for my three children, on one of which is a mistake which is so obvious that I feel I don't have to explain it to you. Also on one form you have altered the sex of my son to that of female. Will this make any difference in the benefits he will receive**</u>?' Obvious, but your narrow viewpoint overlooked this fact!"

-"Well, again good **Pedagogical #7**, it could show a class the important issue of evaluating writing for the intended audience and purpose, not just your own viewpoint..."

-"Yeah but also Pedagogical for Challenge or **Competence #7B**. This letter may be Effective, but it's minimal, takes too many risks, is not 'impossible to misunderstand," a good example of the other important issue of how good could or should—or must—a piece of writing be!"

-"True, but I find it just plain amusing, good humor and comedy, and if you want to assign a lens, that would be like **Serendipity #14**, it pleased me in unintended ways just-because."

-"I hear that, but I weigh in that this also conveys the *problems* of lower-class people in communicating and even surviving. I could label this less Personal-Pleasing to me, than Serendipity but also, aha, **Bridge Human Souls #15**, I *hear* this unfortunate woman over time and space, and also **Dynamite #16**, it packs a modest punch for me thus..."

---

(3) "FROZEN FOODS ARE PERISHABLE. Don't let packages 'get buried' in the rear. Frost accumulating here ➔ indicated products are not being rotated properly. Insure 'first in-first out' by restocking packages in the rear. Move inventory from back to front each time you restock. Always place first package at the very back of row."
[--*sign inside freezer-case at local supermarket*]

-"This is *boring*. Who wants to read about what a grocery clerk has to do?"

-"That would be your **Personal-Pleasing #1** criterion. Perfectly justifiable, although rather intellectually un-curious in your case. But I don't like the text either. Because it repeats, repeats, repeats the message redundantly! This I can specify is the lens of **Correct #2**, which says avoid excessive repetition! Hence is not **Crafty #9** either, not well-constructed."

-"You're wrong—or at least my lens contradicts yours. I think it is *Good Writing indeed*. Likely to be **Effective #3** considering both audience (bored grocery clerks) and purpose (make sure that something is done). Surely after reading this, virtually the whole intended audience will understand what to do, and why! Meets the goal of not just can the audience understand, but can the audience *not possibly mis*understand! And this also illustrates another important lens, **Sportive Challenge #8.** How difficult was the purpose to accomplish? Fairly hard. How well did the writer try to do it? Very well indeed! As a sports-fan reader, I cheer him from the bleachers! He **Competently #8B** saw the Challenge and went for it! A pleasure for me to read thus also!"

-"Well in that case one could also say **Pedagogical #7** again—a good instance to teach a writing class the issue of following rules mechanically by the letter ("don't repeat") vs. using techniques as tools by the spirit."

-"I think you're all wrong. The text is boring, plus it is redundant. I don't like it."

-"Who the hell says you shouldn't think that if you want to? Just don't claim you're practicing good Lensmanship or even good **Disposition** to think fairmindedly with civility!"

-"Oh, and I suppose that remark proves that *you* are being Civil here not just Candid..."

---

(4) Here are some of "*the winners of the '*<u>Worst</u> *Analogies Ever Written In A* <u>High School Essay</u>*' contest in the Washington Post Style Invitational*":

--"She caught your eye like one of those pointy hook latches dangling from screen doors which flew up when the door opened."

--"His thoughts tumbled in his head, making & breaking alliances like underpants in a dryer without Cling Free."

--"They lived in a typical suburban neighborhood with picket fences that resembled Nancy Kerrigan's teeth."

--"The thunder was ominous-sounding, like a thin sheet of metal being shaken backstage during the storm scene in a play."

--"Her date was pleasant enough, but if her life was a movie, this guy would be buried in the credits as like 'Second Tall Man'."

--"The politician was gone but unnoticed like the period after Dr. on a Dr Pepper can."

--Her face was a perfect oval, like a circle that had it s two sides gently compressed by a Thigh Master.

--She grew on him like she was a colony of E. coli and he was room-temperature Canadian beef.

--He fell for her like his heart was a mob informant and she was the East River.

--The ballerina rose gracefully en pointe and extended one slender leg behind her, like a dog at a fire hydrant.

--He was deeply in love. When she spoke, he thought he heard bells, as if she were a garbage truck backing up.

"Okay, I listed these because *I disagree*. I think they're *great*—well, interesting writing, valid, valuable, refreshing, pleasant. And I know why. My own **Personal-Pleasing #1** lens, but specifically my background plus **personal-preference taste-temperament** as a Way of Responding or deciding! See, I was a writing teacher, of freshman composition. I suffered reading through paper after paper of bushwa or Engfish or "bxllshxt" or call it what you will, plastic phony artificial student writing. Like junior bureaucratese. 'In this poem we can see that the writer' and the like. So to me, by a delightful contrast, the voices in the above examples are, well, they have an **Integrity #6** of direct feeling and attempt at original creativity which plastic, phony Themewriting lacks! So the point here is that we will profoundly differ on lensmanship or interpreting—and evaluating—writings, but that we can know why, and sometimes argue pro or con via criteria and standards, but sometimes admit that **personal-preference taste-temperament** is operating as a Way of Responding..." The point of all this emerges. Lensmanship can help us understand why we disagree without insulting each other—it's not you but your lens, stupid! The approach can also show up overlooked value and interest, plus also-overlooked deficiencies and problems, in the subject scrutinized!"

SEE "II" FULL version for **[10.C.]** Gallery II. Other Readings. X Hail Marks on Apples... X Electric Hand-Dryers are Good For You... X "Why I Need English 101" student paragraph... X "Found Poetry" Memo, Coffee, Candy, Hardware, Yellow Pages, Nautical Signal-Flags... are these literature?

[10.C.] GALLERY #3. Teachers responded to college papers submitted for the annual "Superior Student Writing Contest." Below, three sets of responses to three papers. *PEDAGOGICAL PLOY: what lenses were used— from the 16, or others, even suspect? The best lenses—or some "egg-on-face" blunders?? Known by the teachers who used them? Why such variation? Is any consensus possible—does this matter? Etc.!*

STUDENT PAPER, #1: **"Deer Hunters"** ... *"All Over The Map"!* [The essay criticized boorish, irresponsible big-city deer hunters despoiling small northern Wisconsin towns during annual deer-hunting season...]

1 The structure of "you" makes for a difficult and strained reading. Too chronological, perhaps. **(0)**
2 O.K., but I've read far too many essays on this. **(1)**
3 Interesting point of view, with the I persona dogging the "you," but the constant reference to "you" and "your" get monotonous and heavy-handed; needs editing. **(1)**
4 Good force of personal anger behind this one. Nice use of cliches: "it's Miller time," "promised land," etc. **(1)**
5 Interesting use of point of view. A bit picky in complaints in places. **(2)**
6 Writing has energy. Good strong verbs. Some shifts in person at the start. Your/you're error. Very effective writing. **(2)**
7 I like the point; [but, it] seems too polarized. **(2)**
8 Fine tight writing—cross between story and editorial—a little too didactic. **(3)**
9 Excellent technique to nail bad buy, teach lesson. **(3)**
10 Tone is controlled: intense but understated, superior in this way. Also, writer's thesis—claim that hunters are boorish—is exhaustively shown, proved, achieved, not just stated. **(3)**
11 Fervent anger under taut control. Beautifully done. Tight but not constipated sentence structure, word choice just right. **(3)**

SEE "II" FULL version for Student Paper #2 "Education in Singapore" and #3 "Coping with Stress"

|+#|+|+|#|+#|+|#+|+|+#|++##+##|#|+|+|+|#|+|#+#+|+|+#|+|+|#+|#+|#+|+|+|#++|+|+|+|+#|+#|+|#+|+#|||#+|=#+|+#|+|#+|#+|+#|||

[11.] ANNEX. Other Major semi-Lenses
1. Ways of Knowing, 2. World-View, 3. Zeitgeist

SEE "II" FULL for **Ways of Knowing** science, supernaturalism, culture, individual...
SEE Appendix #5, "Prior Basics," for **[11.2.]** **World-View** *EXAMPLES:* XX Poems by R. Browning, R. Creeley... X American values... X Generalized "Liberal" vs. "Conservative"... X Victorian British world-view... X East and West on nature, etc. *and also* **[11.3.]** **"Zeitgeist"** or spirit of the time. *EXAMPLES:* Atomism... X Heredity-Environment... X Lysenkoism... X Constructivism... X Freudianism...

|+#|+|+|#|+#|+|#+|+|+#|++##+##|#|+|+|+|#|+|#+#+|+|+#|+|+|#+|#+|#+|+|+|#++|+|+|+|+#|+#|+|#+|+#|||#+|=#+|+#|+|#+|#+|+#|||

[{ END of Tool-KIT for "LENS-Work"... }]

|+#|+|+|#|+#|+|#+|+|+#|++##+##|#|+|+|+|#|+|#+#+|+|+#|+|+|#+|#+|#+|+|+|#++|+|+|+|+#|+#|+|#+|+#|||#+|=#+|+#|+|#+|#+|+#|||

SPECIFIC DETAILING:

in writing to give *particular instances, material examples, supportive evidence*, etc.—to support the text's *abstract ideas, concepts*…   So that the "higher" Mental realm can be *enriched* with the "lower" Material of <u>tangible phenomena</u>… All in order to better "cinch" concepts… [And for *reader-enjoyment*…]

Concretization: Specific Detailing: "Word-Painting"…

|+#|+|#|+#|+#|+|+#+#|+#|+|+#|+|+#|+#|#+|+|#+|+|+#++#+|+|+|+#|+#|+|+|+#+|+|#+#|+|#+|+|+|+#|+|#+|+|+|#+|+#||#+|+#|+#|++#+||#+||

GALLERY. A cameo of **three generalities specifized**—to explain, to confirm, to entertain…		
[1.] ["The refrigerators of prostitutes are too often understocked, ungenerously and hence inhospitably … "]		**Hookers' iceboxes often contain only "a piece of parsley, a black carrot, and a bouillon cube"** [-- LENNY BRUCE, comedian]
[2.] ["Benson was the *worst* apartment-mate *ever*…"]	**"The burned pans and unwashed dishes, the unpaid bills, the unfed cat, the unlocked rear door, the loud music, the mis-parked car, the damaged fence, the stolen food… Benson was *bad*."**	
[3.] [Life in small Maine towns year-round out of the tourist season is informal, in synch with nature.]	**The first sign of spring is when the ink breaks up in the inkwell in the post office. A month later the town clerk's wife removes the records from her refrigerator and plugs it in for the season. A month later the tourists arrive.** [-- E. B. WHITE, paraphrased]	
…well, at least you're "Walking the Talk." You're going to *discuss* concretizing—so you *concretized*! You Practice your Preaching…		And <u>You</u> Noticed! Good **Consciousness** of thinking techniques being used. *Now, onward*…

|+#|+|#|+#|+#|+|+#+#|+#|+|+#|+|+#|+#|#+|+|#+|+|+#++#+|+|+|+#|+#|+|+|+#+|+|#+#|+|#+|+|+|+#|+|#+|+|+|#+|+#||#+|+#|+#|++#+||#+||

[1.] The RATIONALE…

THE CONCEPT/ISSUE, and THE "SO-WHAT RELEVANCE/NEED: **"Support your idea with specific examples"** is a familiar "mantra" in writing classes. But "concretizing the conceptual" is actually *more complex or anyhow difficult* than student-writers are taught how to do—*or* than readers are taught how to enjoy. At the same time this *"word-painting"* (literal *verbal illustrating*) is also *more possible to convey* than educators realize—or anyhow than current resource-materials accomplish…

[1.] We need more **background orientation** to this *"illustrating"* than is usually given.

> Key concept is the **"ladder of abstraction."** *LEARNERS REALLY SHOULD KNOW*
> **(1) <u>We confront subjects on levels of specific-to-general</u>**. From the *Concrete-Specific* (Material or tangible sensual "lowland "of pond, fertile meadow) to the *Conceptual-Abstract* (Mental or general elevated rarefied (aerial mountain-summit).
> **Concept & Concrete *are distinct*!** [EXAMPLE: "the idea of a Chair," *vs.* "Fern's soft green beanbag," Fred's tall stilty red kitchen stool…"]
>
> **(2)** And *many "rungs" or possible stations exist on this ladder* between Pond of particulars, Peak of abstractions, as optional alternative choices… ["Objects, events, recurrent processes, mid-range subjects or issues, larger higher concepts.]
> EXAMPLE: Vegetarianism, from "tofu recipes from the the Wheatberry Café" to issues of Nutrition, Morality, Social Image…]
>
> **(3) <u>Both specific, and general, statements are good and bad,</u>** have their valuable Orchids, and vulnerable Onions. Avoid too high or much Conceptualizing ideas without examples, also avoid a too-low glut of Concretization details without concepts…

[2.] We need <u>more explicit</u> conveying of **basic, "Level I" techniques** of *specifizing."*

EXAMPLE: Supporting an idea in a paragraph can have seven **variables**: *Number* of, *Length* of, *Type* of [**3-W Who When Where, statistics, anecdote, analogy, imagery, dialog**], Specific-General *Level* of, and more. *Are learners taught this?*

[3.] We need to note some **advanced** "Level II" techniques in *"exemplifying."*

"Concretizing the conceptual involves more tactics and issues, than are corralled and clarified in educational materials. (ANALOGY: the varied "cuisine" of a country is more varied and complex than that known only in the big cities etc., but which is practiced daily...))

... SO OUR RESPONSE: *"Therefore this unit."* This module is by far the most elucidating [comprehensive, conceptualized, concretized] treatment of specificity which currently exists—at least in all the educational resource-materials I've seen in my decades of teaching, earlier. [And even in its "I" Brief Basic version here...]

|+#|+|#|+#|+#|+|+#+#|+#|+|+#|+|+#|+#|#+|+|#+|+|+#++#+|+|+#|+#|+|+|+#+|+|#+#|+|+|+#|+#+|+|+|#+#|#+|+#|+#|++#+||#+||

[2.] The usual basic FORMULA: "Support (= illustrate, prove, vivify, etc.) your idea with a specific example (instance, evidence, etc.). [I.e., "Dip Down"!...]

EXAMPLES. "Examples of examples," instances of specifying, particularizing, concretizing:

The *preacher* uses a **parable**... The *scientist* uses **quantified data, statistics** (plus close thorough observation)... The *magazine writer* leads off with an **anecdote**... The *educator* (law school etc.) uses a **case-history** instance to clarify concept, skill, issue... The *after-dinner speaker* starts with a *story*... The *literature writer* sets scenes, uses **sense-imagery** in poetry, fiction... The *journalist* tells **Who When Where** and includes direct **dialog, quotations**... The corporate-*organization* now (and the *advertiser* and *propagandist* longtime...) uses specific **stories** of people... Diverse *communicators* use **visual aids** (charts, graphs, etc.) and also **analogies** to depict complexity clearly and also to bridge the old-familiar known, and the new-foreign...

You are still *Walking your Talk*—you *praise* "multiple varied vivid effective examples," you also *provide* same.	You're aware. Note that I "dip down" here to vivify the point. 90% of writers can do better there. We'll see...

In "II" FULL version: Examples of Genres. Also, "Life as Experiential Theatre"

PRE-VIEW. The very basic formula for detailing, says "support your idea with specific examples." We operationalize this by our *seven-part* **"Paragraph Formula."** It is codifies the basic **variable-issues**-to-consider, alternate optional choices, which more often than not, are *not* taught explicitly. The *first four* parts:

Assuming a paragraph (unit of thought) with a concept to be concretized... Variables to consider:
(1) Number of examples: [none, one, two, three ("Triad Salvo"), more?]..... **(2) Length:** [one long one, several brief ones?]..... **(3)** using which of the common **Six Types**? [3WWhereWhenWho... Anecdotes... Statistics... Sense-Imagery... Analogy... Dialog]..... **(4) Level of Verticality:** [stay general-ish... go more-vivid... yet more particular... down to "floored" or as tangibly- concrete as possible, a Verbal Videotape?]

EXAMPLE: Letter to the inflight magazine of CATHAY PACIFIC AIRLINES, late 1980's. Left-hand, the original as printed (well-intended but ineptly-vague, space-wasteful, ineffective?) ... Right-hand, our version improved, at least by-the-book more Correct with specifics via the Paragraph Formula...*See the difference detailing can make... As well as the difference explicit teaching of same might make...*

(#1) COMPLIMENTS TO STAFF *[ORIGINAL]*	(#2) COMPLIMENTS TO STAFF *[OUR REWRITE]*

As a frequent traveler I have found that some of your staff are very helpful and accommodating which is extremely appreciated. Two of your staff members whom I have encountered numerous times are Ellen Lui and Carrie Law. I have found them to be extremely pleasant, helpful and accommodating. Although I have no specific incident to recount to you I just thought it was important for an airline to recognize those who excel in their positions and to give them the praise they deserve.
    DL, Hong Kong
	I really appreciate the excellence of your flight crews—especially Ellen Lui and Carrie Law. They're pleasant (reassuring me about my luggage stowed up front; smiling at the end of a flight filled with turbulence and infants). They're helpful (finding out the gate number of my connecting flight; getting me an extra blanket). And they're accommodating (getting me that third glass of water; finding me a seat with extra legroom). Thanks to them and the others like them.
	    DL, Hong Kong

Same wordcount, but flab removed & muscle of specifics support skeleton of concept, for more practicality and pleasure.

271

[3.] Gallery #1: versions of statements:
non-specific [left-side]... vs. specifized [right-hand] ...

EXAMPLES. Presented below are Generalized and Specifized versions of statements. With other techniques:
1. Common types of (statistics, anecdotes, sense-imagery, dialog/quotations)... 2. Number of (solo, vs. a "salvo")... 3. Size-of (elaborated, or distilled)... 4. "Effectiveness"-of... 5. Skill of, competence in—leading to *enjoyment* of...

[*How proficient should learners become in identifying and using these issues explicitly, to be called competent in concretizing"?...*]

[1.] ["Teenagers working in fast-food jobs get bored during slow times and thus like to play their own games for fun then."]	**"At slack times we'd play our own games of Lemon Wars, Crock Football, and Hostess Kidnapping"** [ERIC, student]
[2.] ["The automobile accident we saw was *really bad*. You don't quickly forget *something like that*. I'm sure you see it was really *a shocking experience* for us..."]	The station wagon lay upside down on the median strip. All around it, possessions, including children's toys, were scattered widely amid broken glass. Driving onward, nobody said anything for the next ten minutes...
[3.] ["Taking the old Chicago streetcar to the beach was a vivid childhood experience I'll never forget. The *slowness* of the trip and the *heat* was made up for by the *picturesque* streetcars themselves and all the *noise* and *color* involved..."]	**"To see water, you had to stand long, sweaty streetcar rides (the red and buff streetcars, reeking of ozone, with their clanging bells and screeching wheels, the wire-mesh window guards and the air compressors going diga-diga-diga-diga at each stop, the dust, the confetti of transfer punches, mashed cigarette butts and soiled newspapers, hot rattan seats on the sunny side, green shades)—how long those rides were!"** [--Isaac Rosenfeld, "Life in Chicago"]
[4.] ["**News Item:** An invasion of Killer Grasshoppers caused major alarm and destruction..."]	**In Plains KS on Tue July 23 at 8 P.M., a giant storm-cloud of whirring insects descended. Six-inch-long, brown cigar-shaped, with crackly skin: crushed on sidewalk by feet, foul-smelling. They penetrated everywhere (were found in antique silver chest months later). 30% of businesses suffered 20% loss of revenue. "It was the Devil to pay," said resident Ebenezer Offenbach...**
I'm entertained here, but a bit confused, I want to know more. What are the types and methods?...	Good, we snagged your interest... Bear in mind the above taught *no*, absolutely *no*, **concepts**-*about* concretization—not yet...

|+#|+|#|+#|+#|+|+#+#|+#|+|+#|+|+#|+#|#+|+|#+|+|+#++#++|+|+#|+#|+|+|+#|+|#++|+|+#|+#|+|+|+#|+|#++|+|#++#|#+|+#|+#|++#+||#+||

[4.] TABLE of CONTENTS of this unit...

5.B. **Verticalities** (the conceptual topography). Ladder, many rungs, various positions.

275 **[6.]** <u>**VARIABLE/ISSUES:**</u> conditions and choices, need to know about for fuller competence...
    6.A. <u>**Whether at all to use specifics...**</u>
    6.B. <u>**Evaluation,**</u> **pros and cons of both Generalizations and Specifics**
    6.C. <u>**Purposes**</u> **which specifics serve:...** Sketch, Clarify, Prove, Entertain, etc.
    6.D. **The** <u>**Point**</u> **can be** <u>**Explicit**</u> (conceptualized) <u>**or Implicit**</u> (shown through specifics)
    6.E. <u>**Two Issues for Effectiveness, Quality**</u>: *select well, combine well...*
        6.E.1. <u>**Selection for power: best effectiveness...**</u>
        6.E.2. <u>**If multiple, "Rounded" Collection: PP of PP,**</u>
    6.F. <u>**Fine-tuning for Amount, and Level, of detailing...**</u>

278 **[7.]** <u>**TECHNIQUE, METHOD:**</u> more-tactical moves, need to know whether and how to use...
    [First *paragraph* level 7.A., then *whole-text* level, 7.BCD]
    7.A. "Dip-Down" seven-part <u>**Paragraph formula**</u>
        <u>**GALLERY**</u> **"III"** [X Ed's Job   X Porsche ad   X AIDS   etc.]
    7.B. <u>**"Amount, and Verticality-level: Interrelations"**</u>
    7.C. <u>**"Subject Size & Scope—and Level of Specificity"**</u>
    7.D. <u>**"Scenario": the Essay "Storied"** ....</u>

280 **[8.]** <u>**"ADVANCED REFINEMENTS!"**</u> [From the Full Version "Word-Painting"]

281 **[9.]** <u>**PEDAGOGY**</u> **for teaching S.D.:**   Guidelines/Goals, Prevalent Pitfalls, Lab-Exercises

281 **[10.]** <u>**GALLERY**</u> **"IV":** a bouquet of superior specifics.

|+#|+|#|+#|+#|+|+#+#|+#|+|+#|+|+#|+#|#+|+|#+|+|+#++#+|+|+#|+#|+|+|#+|+|#+#|+|#+|+|+#|+|#+|+|+|#+|+#||#+|+#|+#|++#+||#+||

[5.] What "BACKGROUND INFORMATION" is needed for competent Concretizing?

[5.A.] The Operating Concept or "Hidden Why" Behind the Power of Specifics:

(This is a major generic thinking gambit or ploy.) Specifics **"rehydrate abstractions."**
    ---We gain at least some of our ideas, concepts, "points" about an issue, from experiencing of specifics: observation, participation of particulars, incidents, evidence, etc. The events convince us. [Through experience, I become convinced that <u>bicycling</u> is a valuable but overlooked activity.]
    ---But then when we come to communicate our ideas to others, we *tend to* state only the ideas, because the vivid particulars—which convinced *us*—are in our memory, but we do <u>not</u> realize that we have *not* painstakingly installed them, too, on the page—to convince the *reader*. Hence the reader misses the punch of the message. <u>First I write</u>: ["Bicycling has many advantages, of convenience, of healthy exercise, and saving money."] Omitting persuasive evidence thus is a case of comic *incompetence*, a pitfall or botch, bungle, blunder of omission. {The reader may say only: "Huh?"
    ---In contrast, the *competent* writer very attentively **"dips down"** to support ideas and claims with the evidence that enlivens them. <u>Now I write</u>: I glide downtown and find a parking space anywhere I want. I spent only $25.00 for the annual tune-up. I can carry 50 pounds of groceries etc. in my front and back baskets. I feel pleasantly wrung-out by a one-hour, ten-mile circling of the city on the bypass..."] { The eader may well say, "Aha..."}

273

TESTIMONY. The poet-critic T. S. ELIOT's version. The only way of [truly] expressing and conveying emotion in writing is by locating it in an **"objective correlative."** This is in **"a situation, a set of objects, a chain of events"** which will then for the reader recreate the emotion. *Voila*... [Of course, this may be Field-specific, culture-bound, somewhat limited to Western aesthetics etc. and may not apply universally. Some cultures and communication traditions favor indirection, subtlety, even generalities; see below. *Still.....*]

GALLERY: to dip down to *illustrate illustration*, to *exemplify examples*, to *show specificity specifically*:

EXAMPLE #1: very-basic instance of the key point of rehydrating abstractions:		
[1.A.] ORIGINAL EVENT CREATING AN EMOTIONAL POINT: You see an automobile accident. The station wagon lay upside down on the freeway's median strip. Children's toys were strewn about it. All three of you in the car don't say a word for another five minutes. Obviously the accident affected you...	**[1.B.] REPORT #1: AMATEUR BUNGLE:** You report to the poor reader: "The accident was really awful, and it really affected us. I'm sure you can understand that it was very depressing."	**[1.C.] REPORT #2: PROFESSIONAL COMPETENCE:** You know you must painstakingly *not just tell but show*. You combine the generalization in [1.B.] with the prior particulars in [1.A.] of course! You've done all you can via specifics toward reaching the reader effectively...

EXAMPLES [2.A.B.] Rehydrating abstractions; two papers by women students on their fathers/stepfathers.	
[2.A.] "Life with Father has never been a stroll down the State Fair Mall, but more like my adventurous walk through the Haunted House." Even divorce would be okay to spare the student and her mother "the hell they've been through" with the father/husband. "I can never underestimate my father, or know what he's got waiting around the corner, so the steps I take are light." In fact, "the nasty monsters Father has are enough to scare the bravest, not to mention two weak women."	**[2.B.]** [The second paper in only twice the length, piled in convincing specifics. Treats wife like servant, make food, pick up after him, snaps at her, if she complains says "don't be stupid," leaves her home every Saturday to go fishing or visiting his friends... Treats stepdaughter like troublemaker, expects her to do chores while he relaxes, thinks she's lazy even with part-time job and 3.2 grade point average, stingy lending the car. Always critical of her, how she butters toast, what she watches on TV... Unreliable: late taking her to work, wife to doctor, picking sister up... Egocentric. Talks and lectures and drones on about "electrical equipment, light fixtures, the President, Central America, fishing facts..."] "Going to college, I could breathe again."

Comments on Paper #1, left-hand side above:		**Comments** on Paper #2, right-side above:	
[PRO:] Well, she does "get her point across." The father must be terrible. We can perhaps use our imaginations to fill in the details.	**[CON:]** No no *no*! Alas. If this writer ever has to convince somebody of something via evidence—problem on the job, a proposal to accept, point of view to consider—she risks failing badly. She merely tells and claims, she does not show and prove. I'd *scorn* her inability to rehydrate abstractions, if the subject weren't so dismal... Shame, and mainly alas	Whew Space To Breathe Even With NO Details! **[PRO:]** I say this is Pragmatically more effective. And by Principle more morally sound—she earns our right to consider her point of view. And Pleasurable to read in a way—or rather, considering the unpleasant subject, more satisfying, rewarding, meaningful... See?	**[CON:]** *Well, if you say so, then...*

GUIDELINE. The above "operating situation" is why, although we are wary of giving formulaic "rules to follow," we can offer as a "default rule-of-thumb" or anyhow principle-to-monitor: **"Remember to always consider Dipping-Down! That is, whenever you make a conceptual point, "more often than not," you supposedly should be supplying also an example or instance of it, to at least simply 1. inform about it, if not also to 2. persuade convince interest relate the reader to it."**

|+#|+|#|+#|+#|+|+#+#|+#|+|+#|+|+#|#+|+|#+|+|+#+#+|+|+#|+#|+|+|+#|+|#+|+|#+#|+|#+|+|+|#|+|#+|+|+|#+|+#|+#||#+|+#|+#|++#+||#+||

[5.B.] Verticalities: the Ladder of Abstraction, from Material to Mental.

In "II" FULL version: Verticalities principles, plus example from Vegetarianism...

EXAMPLE. "The social nature of British landladies." **#1 and #6 below** are the continuous original text from PAUL THEROUX, travel writer... **## 2 through 5** are my Transforming of the concept of sociability rung by rung down the Ladder of Abstraction to end up as THEROUX'S vivid Concretizing in #6!

[When you walk through England and stay at the bed-and-breakfast lodgings offered in private homes, you find an unexpected sociability.] **[1.]** "The English, the most obsessively secretive people in their day-to-day living, would admit you to the privacy of their homes, and sometimes even unburden themselves, for just five pounds.".........

[2.] Often I experienced how the landlady would relax and become more open after she had gotten to know you just a little bit earlier in the evening.

[3.] For instance, the landlady would become more communicative about matters. She would become more generous, more informal in terms of names, and more revelatory about herself.

[4.] The landlady would share family problems regarding health, householding, and even morals. Later in the evening, she might offer you a drink, go onto a first-name basis, and tell you amazing facts about herself.

[5.] The landlady might share family problems such as her husband's bad teeth, the broken vacuum cleaner, and her daughter's possible pregnancy. Later in the evening, she might offer you sherry, say "call me Ida," and even tell you about her unique physical markings.

.... **[6.]** "'I've got an awful lot on my plate at the moment,' Mrs. Spackle would say. 'There's Bert's teeth, the Hoover's packed up, and my Enid thinks she's in a family way....' When it was late and everyone else in bed, the woman you knew as Mrs. Garlick would pour you a schooner of cream sherry, say "Call me Ida," and begin to tell you about her amazing birthmark."

...now I *begin* to understand the idea of the **Concrete-Conceptual** continuum in specific detailing...	...perhaps helped by the general, essential-generic thinking skill of the **Conceptual Continuum** of stages from A to Z...

EXAMPLE—ALSO CLASS LAB EXERCISE. "Be able to move up and down the rungs of the ladder in control of various levels." The following is *not easy nor useless* to do! Subject, "misbehavior in college cafeterias":

OBSERVATIONS: *describe, report* **concrete-tangible phenomena:**	**GENERALIZATIONS:** *conclusions* drawn, *concepts* produced, *ideas* offered about it:
An *action* occurred between one student and another in an eating facility.	[Varied activities] took place [on University property], some of them **INAPPROPRIATE.**
One student *behaved* in an active way toward another regarding [foodstuff].	In [an eating facility], some student-eaters were engaging in **INAPPROPRIATE MISBEHAVIORS** regarding food.
One *student threw* [a portion of food] toward and upon another *student*.	A group of undergraduates was **MISBEHAVING** by using food: whether [1] *wasted*, [2] *thrown* at others, or [3] *played with*.
A *boy* threw [potatoes] at the *shirt* of another *boy*.	In [*the cafeteria*], some students **HARASSED** others by throwing food such as *jello* and *potatoes* at them; others *played* with [*food*] by inserting [*objects*] in it; still others *wastefully* took [more food portions than they ended up eating].
On *Monday noon* at *Esker Hall*, Mark *flung* a *tablespoon* of [greasy mashed potatoes] onto *Chad's* **new red plaid** *shirt.* "*Gotcha!*" he shouted.	In *Esker Hall today*, **HARRASSMENT** occurred when *Mark flung mashed potatoes at Chad's shirt*; **PLAYFULNESS**, when *Sally stuck straws in her custard* before eating it; and **WASTEFULNESS**, when *Fred left three portions of macaroni on his plate* at the end; .....

\=\+|+|+\=\=\+|+|+\=\=\|+|+|+\\\|+|+|+\=\|+|+|+\=\+|+|+\=\=|+|+|+\=\|+|+|+\=\=|+|+|+\=\|+|\=\+|+|+\=\+|+|+| +

[6.] "VARIABLE-ISSUES" regarding Concretization...

["V-I" are matters which, for success, one must or should confront (satisfy manage utilize attend-to etc.) Of course one must know of the variables beforehand; so,...]

Table of Contents of these Variables:

6.A. Specifics: <u>whether</u> to use at all... Or, ineffective? Prohibited?

6.B. <u>Evaluation</u>: pros and cons of both concrete and conceptual realms.

6.C. <u>Purposes</u> of detailing. (Inform, re-create, clarify, prove, entertain, etc.)

6.D. Point can be Explicit <u>or Implicit</u>.

6.F. Two issues for more effective specifying:

(1) <u>Selection</u> for power   (2) <u>Accretion</u> for concept-cinching: "Rounded Ensembles" multiple, varied.

6.F. Fine-tuning for <u>Amount, and Level</u>, of detailing.

[6.A.] Whether at all.   1. At times, is specificity impossible or ineffective—or inadvisable?
2. In different cultural situations, is specificity culturally-discouraged, devalued?

In "II" FULL version: X Student objects to vivid article "And Sudden Death" as ineffective…   X George Orwell claims he can't describe hotel kitchen work…   X Severe depression is harder to articulate with specific events, than other illnesses…

"Field." Concretization in context: time, space, system: Know that varied fields—situations, times-places, cultures, contexts, environments, etc.—differ in whether specifics should be used, how much or not, and why. Some cultures prefer abstract theorizing or at least much concrete data is less valued. this may relate to preferences for explicitness vs. subtlety, indirection.. **EXAMPLES:** ironically no space (or need) for instances here!

\=\+|+|+\=\=\+|+|+|=\=\=|+|+|+\\\+|+|+|=\=|+|+|+|=\=\+|+|+\=\=|+|+|+|\=\=|+|+|+|\=\=|+|+|+\=\=|+|\=\+|+|+|+\=\=\+|+|+| +

[6.B.] Evaluation. Pros *and* cons of concrete *and* conceptual levels...

GUIDELINE. Be able to evaluate specificity-generality in terms of (1) <u>purpose function use</u>, and also (2) <u>amount and level for a given purpose</u>. That is, [AWARENESS] know that <u>both the specific and the general levels have their identifiable pros (orchids) and their cons (onions)</u>—good functions and indeed vital uses, plus drawbacks or incompletenesses. Also, know <u>the four excesses</u> of both *too much or not enough abstracting*, and also *too much or not enough specifying*. And then of course [ABILITY] be able to put this knowledge into ploy in specific [!] task-goals...

SPECIFICITY (+++++) pros or Orchids: 1. Its many purposes (depict, give experience, prove point, etc.): especially, "rehydrate abstractions," gives the feelings. and emotions behind the claims	**SPECIFICITY (-----) cons or Onions:** 1. Can remain truncated from meaning: not conceptualized, worked for the ideas within it. Cf. Raw Diary Story or unanalyzed memoir-narrative. **"Conceptual Shortfalling" "Concrete Surfeiting"**
GENERALIZING (+++++) pros or Orchids: 1. Is *thinking*! "Works" the "mere" data (experience, information) to yield out its *meaningful* concepts.	**GENERALIZING (-----) cons or Onions:** 1. Drained of the vividness which vitalizes the idea. **"Conceptual Stratospherizing"** **"Concrete Skimping, Shortchanging"**

In "II" FULL version: GALLERY: X Ohmann, X Freelance mantra, XX Colleagues' mistakes, X Readers' Digest mantra, (X) but a cluster in favor of abstraction or general statements also!

GUIDELINE: **Don't be too vaguely-overgeneral, or too densely-specific either.**
Toward that end, **avoid these four errors of insufficient *or* excessive concretization *or* conceptualizing. Balance the ratio.**

Conceptual Stratosphering – much too high on ladder, all vague lofty windy abstractions. ("Elements of wasteful and disruptive behavior in a locale in our institution" instead of "problems of rowdiness and sanitation in Esker Dining Hall")	**Conceptual Shortfalling** – not enough ideas, the specifics not "worked" to produce points. (A vivid and even concise catalog of messiness, misbehavior, disorganization, bad food servings—but these concepts-about-it not stated!)

Concrete Skimping – not enough vivid specifics to make your generalizations effective.	**Concrete Surfeiting** – too many details, perhaps wordy repetitive irrelevant, "diary" only; distill!
("Rowdiness, food-waste," okay the points stated, fine but give proof…)	(" I entered the dining hall. First uncleared trays, then food dripping on the cafeteria line, then Tom threw food behavior—*an entire catalog, but put it on a diet, trim the soup-to-nuts glut…*)

\=\+|+|+\=\=\+|+|+|=\=\=|+|+|\\\+|+|+|=\=|+|+|=\=\+|+|+|=\=|+|+|+|=\=|+|+|+|=\=|+|+|+|=\=|+|+|\=\+|+|+|+\=\=\+|+|+| +

[6.C.] PURPOSES of specifizing are plural, multi-functioning

Clearly, specifics simply <u>inform</u> about the subject. Plus <u>explain</u> what the point is. Plus can <u>prove, support</u> a claim. And can <u>entertain by re-creating</u>. Details can also <u>control tone</u>: the writer's mood, attitude toward self, topic, audience. Also description can simply "<u>set the scene</u>," for relevant local color, or just for the experience of being there and responding…

EXAMPLE. The *fat* bartender *polished a martini glass which didn't need polishing*. "Jimmy Phelps? Sure, I know him. Everybody in Galveston knows Jimmy." *He gingerly placed the martini glass on a shelf.* "Some 200 people—maybe more—owe their lives to him." [-- LEAD OF A STORY ABOUT A DEAF-MUTE LIFEGUARD]

EXAMPLES. Connotatively-"comforting" <u>imagery</u> noted in various contemporary <u>advertisements</u>.

[1.] FIREWORKS <u>POPCORN</u> COMPANY offers a variety of popcorn flavors:
Smooth and Sweet: **Savanna Gold** … Light, Crispy: **Wisconsin White Birch** …
Crunchy, Rich: **Starshell Red** … Robust, Wild: **High Mountain Midnight** …

[2.] A loaf of <u>bread</u> is called **"Wheat Butter Split"**   (However, the ingredients do *not* list any butter included…)

[3.] **"Crystal Flash"** brand <u>gasoline</u>…   [4.] **"Fire River"** brand <u>beefsteaks</u>…

…these come redolent with sense-imagery which connotes desirable values. I enjoy the artistry emanating from commercialism seeking to shamelessly promote capitalism, a spinoff or windfall "at no extra charge to me"…

In "II" FULL version: GALLERY: X USA Today flood in California, X others…

\=\+|+|+\=\=\+|+|+|=\=\=|+|+|\\\+|+|+|=\=|+|+|=\=\+|+|+|=\=|+|+|+|=\=|+|+|+|=\=|+|+|+|=\=|+|+|\=\+|+|+|+\=\=\+|+|+| +

[6.C.] Point (thesis, concept, idea) can be EXplicit or IMplicit.

In "II" FULL version: X Asian <u>proverbs</u>, X Shopping memo, X Life Insurance memo, X Ads for universities

\=\+|+|+\=\=\+|+|+|=\=|+|+|+\\\+|+|+|=\=|+|+|=\=\+|+|+|=\=|+|+|+|=\=|+|+|+|=\=|+|+|+|=\=|+|+|\=\+|+|+|+\=\=\+|+|+| +

[6.E.] Effectiveness. 1. Select for Power, 2. "Rounded Ensemble"

[6.E.1.] Select the more effective examples only …

A. Really powerful *singles*:

In the Depression era, the mother and father planted the single orange the father had brought home on the table, and said to their child, "You eat. We'll watch." [-- a friend of JAMES BALDWIN]

In "II" FULL version: X Yacht trapped in storm, X Hi-jinks in library stacks, X Supermarket customer oddities.

B. *Multi*-element collections of convincing concretizations:

In the "II" FULL version: Gallery. X Cruise ship passenger stupidities, X Mistakes on college applications, X The illiterate have problems, X Atrocious blunders in cross-cultural advertising…

[6.E.2.] Consider using "Rounded Ensembles," our term for sets of *multiple, varied* examples to really cinch the concept by "pinning it down all around."

FORMULA. To "cinch" (elucidate the real *gist* of) a concept, including covering many of its varied *aspects* (component sub-parts), good writing seems often to collect a <u>number</u> of <u>powerful</u> examples, <u>representative from varied, different arenas—venues—aspects</u> of the concept. [Originally we labeled this ploy the **"Polypod Panorama of Parsed [=explained] Particulars,"** but we soon *and wisely* altered the name to **"Rounded Ensemble"** of varied illustrations of a concept.] This echoes the Formula: how many, and which...

EXAMPLE #1. An attempt to expand the idea of **a "map"** beyond "image of the earth's surface," thus:
Good knowledge-maps constructed by an expert are effective learning aids. Thus, the *periodic table* is a central feature of virtually every chemistry classroom. *Chromosome maps* are routinely used in teaching genetics, and pedigrees are important tools for analyzing inheritance patterns. *Weather maps* help students understand the movement of and interactions between air masses. *Animal range maps* help students and researchers understand the geographic extent of wildlife species. *Maps of magnetic fields* help physics students represent invisible forces. And schematic *wiring diagrams* help engineers understand how current flows in computer circuitry. [-- SOURCE]
...an impressive attempt to expand and then "nail down" the concept by examples from diverse fields, arenas

In "II" **FULL** version: X CrossCultural Travel brochure, (X) writer-based vs. reader-based writing!, X experiential learning, MAPS: X what is a "score," and X PETER GOULD on maps, X other, X Ed. TUFTE, X lyrical definition of maps...

[6.F.] Issues of AMOUNT, and LEVEL, of specifics: how to fine-tune ...

TOUCHSTONE. A classic statement on amount and mix of specifics, generalities.
The right mix of generalization and example. Learning in school requires generalization...But...you have to work with a lot of examples [as in arithmetic: commutative law of addition, but also beans to count...]. The optimal mode for learning...is through a carefully devised combination of the general concept and well-selected examples. This idea of teaching both by precept and example is so old...that its confirmation in experiment is no surprise...Researchers say that it's important to get the right mix and number of examples. If arithmetic exercises are too numerous and similar, time will be wasted. It is important to vary the angle of attack in examples, to illustrate different key aspects of the underlying concepts, and not to forget that explicit restatements of the general concept are equally important. [-- E. D., HIRSCH JR., "Classroom Research and Cargo Cults," Policy Review Nr. 115]
The above merits re-reading. I would only add: be sure you survey a **"catchment-area"** where examples lie, which is large enough to get *enough and varied* examples to clarify the concept...

In "II" FULL version: XX from Montaigne, Toqueville... X application for an internship... X Ann Landers column on elderly... X Cathy cartoon: mother's visit activities... X Newspaper column: person stuck in a rut...

[7.] More-tactical METHODS, TECHNIQUES

TABLE OF CONTENTS of this section: Four Formulae...

--On the <u>paragraph-level</u>
--On the <u>whole-text level</u>:

[7.B.] Relationship of concrete and conceptual: sheer **Amount, Level of specificity, and Arrangement** with each other and the whole text, over a longer piece of writing.

[7.C.] Size and Scope of the subject-matter, related to Level of Specificity-Generality.

[7.D.] "Scenario": the **Essay-and-Story** blend (exposition vs. dramatization/narration).

PERSONAL REVELATION. "Egg-on-my-face." To show the danger of teaching this as "rigid rules"...

I used to give students what I called **the MBVE formula**, "Make your examples Multiple, Brief, Vivid, and Effective." How clear, but much too rote and prescriptive a Rule, I realized almost too late in my teaching. Students clung to it whether situation-appropriate or not. So I then presented it better as a Tool: student learns to ask, "*to what extent*, is *which* concretization technique, Vital, Valuable, Vague, or even Verboten for the given task-goal at hand? Might have **many examples or just one** ... **a paragraph long, or just a distilled phrase or two**—["burnt pans, unpaid bills, unfed pets"] ... very **specific** ["Todd threw mashed potatoes"] or **conceptual-but-effective** ["quaking hungry masses"]...

--See the advantage to my moving from one-sided rigid **Rule**, to more-flexible **Tool**. [Number, Length, Level, Power of specifics: know the A-top-Z options, select the best for the occasion, via Variables-Variation.]

--Still, note also *the power of the spirit of the formulaic "MBVE" approach*. "Locate effective examples, get enough and varied ones, then lower them down the ladder to vividness, then shrink their wordiness to crisp clarity"—these are *good principles*...

[7.A.] "Formula One" – eight variable-issues to consider when specifizing. *Simple paragraph-level:* [A summary of previous material above...]

FORMULA. *Checklist of variable-options* for specifizing a "point" (e.g., as a paragraph topic sentence):

1. **Number** of. [Only one... two, or "triad"... multiple-plural?]

2. **Length** of. [One word only!... brief... longer... extensive, elaborated?]

3. **Type** of. ["Six Types": 3W Where When Who, anecdote, statistics, sense-imagery, analogy, dialog]

4. **Level** of (Verticality). [Very general, high-level...moderate mid-range...very specific, vivid, "floored"]

   (If multiple-plural in number, two further questions:)

5. Structural **Order/Sequence** of. [See menu: Place-space, time, A-to-Z, via conceptual scheme, hierarchy, random]

6. Cohesion: **parallelism** among the examples. ["Fred likes skiing, dancing, and ~~he fishes~~ fishing."]

   (And then for all examples single or multiple:)

7. Check for **Effectiveness**-of. Are the instances:

7.A. Selection: the best ones to have discovered and included, as **powerful**, to *Enhance the Claim*

7.B. Combination: do they create a **"rounded ensemble"** (varied in source and sub-type) to *Cinch the Concept*?

EXAMPLE. A **student paper** (on "a job I've held"): the **original**, and as **recast** for the Concretization unit.

Exactly as written By "Ed" the student:	Teacher-rewritten for the Specifics unit:
My summer job has given me many benefits. Working in construction (all of it) has taught me many handy things that will help me when I maintain my own home. Through experience, I will be able to save a lot of money by not having to call a plumber when a pipe breaks or leaks, an electrician when a wire shorts out, or a carpenter when the roof decides to leak.	My three months' construction job with Amalgamax in Sheboygan this summer has taught me many valuable things, about home maintenance, about working, about people, and about myself.
There are other benefits too. One if the most important is how to handle and cope responsibility your boss gives you. This has to do with everything from showing up on time, to getting done with a certain task on time.	I learned practical skills. How to maintain my own home more economically. Last week, I fixed a leaking faucet, a lamp switch, and a sticking door for Aunt Marjorie.
Also, one may work with new people from many different backgrounds. This will allow you to meet new friends, and to form your own opinions about others instead of what you were told to believe by society. This will also show you how nice	I also learned maturity skills. Responsibility on the job: Tatrdy for wire-stringing, I cost the company $150. Delaying in concrete-pouring, my team angered the boss.
	Too, I gained insights about people. I met new friends: Chris the fisherman, Lynn the bowler. I re-thought some ethnic stereotypes: Andre, a Black, was very industrious. I also learned about the good in people: (generous Otto spent his lunch hour tutoring me in soldering), and the bad (sour Fritz always griped about the job, the

<table>
<tr>
<td>some people can be—and yes, just how much of a pain others can be! You will also learn a lot about yourself from just interacting with your co-workers.

So a summer job may help you meet new friends, and learn a lot about yourself and others which will benefit you for the rest of your life.</td>
<td>boss, the weather).

Finally, I learned <u>most about myself</u>. I can be too shy (did a water pipe wrong, it leaked). And I can be too over-confident (used interior plywood outside, it began to warp).

That job was real school!</td>
</tr>
<tr>
<td>--The revision is pretty obvious—plus mechanical. You "support your ideas with examples." *Everyone* knows that.
--Also, I don't see all your seven variables of this Formula illustrated in the rewrite…</td>
<td>--Ah, but how many students can "dip down" with proof thus? Could rewrite thus, first **In Vitro** or By-The-Book Perfect, for practice (adjust later **In Vivo** for the task-occasion)? Oh, and can use both personal **Anecdotes**, plus objective **Statistics**? And make it all **Brief, Multiple,** and **Vivid** too?
--As for not all eight variables, true—the basic ones here are the *first four and the seventh*, **Number** (usually two here), **Length** (briefer!), **6 Types-of** (3W, anecdotes, statistics—although *not* analogy, imagery, dialog), **and Level** of verticality (more vivid-specific crisp than general). Plus **Effective**—appealing to readers' needs, values, etc.…</td>
</tr>
</table>

In "II" FULL version: MAJOR GALLERY of the <u>**Six Types**</u>. X Tornado, X County Stadium, X Grasshopper Invasion, X Nissan NX 2000 sports car, X "Micro-Stories, X Festering Refrigerators: three versions
Level: X "Buy a Brick" advertisement, **Parallelism:** X Fred's three activities: "to ski, fishing, and he dances"…
Formula One's Seven Variables: X Porsche car ad,   X AIDS virus effects, X BIC pen blot.

|+#|+|#|+#|+#|+|+#+#|+#|+|+#|+|+#|+#|#+|+|#+|+|+#++#+|+|+#|+#|+|+|#+|+|#+#|+#|+|+|+#|+#|+|+|+#|+#|+|+#|+#|||

[7.B.] Relationship of Concrete and Conceptual: sheer *Amount, Level of specificity, and Arrangement* with each other and the whole text, over a longer piece of writing.

In "II" FULL version: EXAMPLES: "thesis then points" of **essay**, versus "anecdotal introduction" of **feature story**, etc.

[7.C.] Size & Scope of subject-matter, related to Level of Specificity-Generality.

In "II" FULL version: XX London Fog, two versions… (X) earlier gay male oppression: five versions… X student paper: variety on the job (transvestite in lingerie store) two versions…

[7.D.] "DRAMATIZATION": Exposition–Narration. Essay-Story. "Scenario."

GUIDELINE. **Realize that you can use an "example" not just as *small* illustration of a point in a paragraph (or the anecdotal opening of a feature-article), but actually as the whole *large* longer text itself. The concept is embedded in, then emerges from, the concrete story.**

In "II" FULL version: GALLERY: X Zen and archery… XX Pedagogical Novels on economics and philosophy… X British Monarchy by story… X Sociological Theory: but Education, Feminism as case- studies. X "Nickeled and Dimed…"

|+#|+|#|+#|+#|+|+#+#|+#|+|+#|+|+#|+#|#+|+|#+|+|+#++#+|+|+#|+#|+|+|+#|+|+|#+|+|#+#|+#|+|+|+#|+#|+|+|+#|+#|+|+#|+#|+|+#|+#||#+|+#|+#|++#+||#+||

[8.] Advanced Refinements! *[IN FULL VERSION:]*

[A.] *Basic* Miscellaneous:
--The "Catalog": [X List poems. X handbags (3)   X floors of automobiles]
--**Triple Opening Salvos**… [X Translation errors "Nova" means "does not go" and two other blunders.]
--**Wangerin Formula: (1.)** For *every* idea or "point," dip-down with an example. **(2.)** Keep example the *same, one core subject* ("vegetarianism"). **(3.)** Give two-pronged example of *bad and good* cases of the instance.

[B.] *Advanced* Fine Points in re "Word-Painting":
N. In-group References (too obscure baffles reader, or increases reader-rapport?) [X bicycle singletrack terms]

N. "Simple/Obvious" examples, can be effective. [X ridiculous wordiness, reduced easily]

N. "Hype" also fabrication or composite assembly… [X company employees just *love* the music!…]

N. "Dessert-Echo" [X mannered exquisite X "this old geyser" X blue heaven X freeway flyer X romish rectitude X Jim's insane cacklings]

N. "Natural Symbols" [X F. LIST books unavailable   X Capt. Emery X Old Maids Popcorn   X Indian vs. Chinese pharmacies, tailors   FADES: X sprinkler faded manuscript X old student photos faded X old purple dittoes faded   X Hemingway leg machine]

N. Reification. [X DAVE BARRY parse a sentence like gut a fish   X M.TWAIN swearing until empty no sieve would collect any more X E.B. WHITE phrase "fastened its hooks in my head"]

N. Status-Details   [X crummy lawyer's office]

N. Quotations   [X from "Late Victorians" by R. RODRIGUEZ]

N. Letters (etc.) of Request… [Complaint… Suggestion… Praise! But especially Request…]

[X Sailboat "upgrade"   X NACURH student request to faculty   X Fairhaven Home, call for art]

|+#|+|#|+#|+#|+|+#+#|+#|+|+#|+|+#|+#|#+|+|#+|+|+#++#++|+|+#|+#|+|+|#+|+|#+#|+|#+|+|+|+#|+|#+|+|+#+|+#||#+|+#|+#|++#+||#+||

[9.] PEDAGOGY: teaching/learning *tactics*.

[9.A.] GUIDELINE. **The learner becomes** *able* **to evaluate specificity-generality in terms of (1) <u>purpose function use</u>, and also (2) <u>amount and level for a given purpose</u>. That is, to** *know* **that <u>both the specific and the general levels have their identifiable pros (orchids) and their cons (onions)</u>—good functions and indeed vital uses, plus drawbacks or incompletenesses. Also,** *know* <u>the four excesses</u> **of both** *too much or not enough abstracting***, and also** *too much or not enough specifying***. Then,** *be able* **to put this knowledge into ploy in specific [!] task-goals…**

[9.B.] "Prevalent Amateur Misconceptions/Pitfalls" (1) "Detailing is mere filler, fluff." **(2)** Awareness: "I never know how much or little detailing to use!" **(3)** Ability: Usually fails to dip-down enough; remains pseudo-detailed…

[9.C.] Resource-MATERIALS.   **(Assignments, Examples, Lab-Exercises, etc.)**

1. **"Scales":** exercise in transforming a statement from Peak of Generality to Pond of Particular, by rungs:
2. **Prewriting.** "List 50 instances about your subject, as preparation for writing." [X Sandy's "Bank Job]
3. **Verbal Videotape.** "Observe a situation, then sketch it in words vividly."   [X School Cafeteria at Noon]
4. **Diamondizing, Packaging.** "Reduce a long text to minimal, cameo size." [X Brookfield High Auditorium]
5. **"Story-Essay Bridge"**   "Move a description from diary / chronicle to exposition (& reverse?). [X "Dorm Life"]
6. **"Vision Text."** Take an appropriate text, identify the issues and writer's choices, alter if needed, explain.
7. **"Ruin a Perfectly-Well-Detailed Piece of Writing"** to gain command over specifizing conversely
8. **"Concrete Starvation" Test:** Give problematic texts, under-specified. Can students the "holes," improve?

|+#|+|#|+#|+#|+|+#+#|+#|+|+#|+|+#|+#|#+|+|#+|+|+#++#++|+|+#|+#|+|+|#+|+|#+#|+|#+|+|+|+#|+|#+|+|+#+|+#||#+|+#|+#|++#+||#+||

[10.] GALLERY "III": Misc. Specifics …

In "II" FULL version: X General Education. X Info Data- Base for Physicians. XX Two book reviews: diluted vs. packed full. XX Student Paper: "beginning workers must be better oriented, " original and improvement. XX vignettes of Dr. Samuel Johnson. XX Essay and Story versions of "inferior Bic pen" letter of complaint. X "Catalog": XXX what you find on the floors of old cars. (X) Cluster: <u>character vignettes in fiction</u> (boss of convict work- gang, housekeeper of professor, married couples, military personnel) . X Economy airline route: fantastic imaginativeness but real?

[{(END of module on "Concretization," "Specific Detailing," "Word-Painting"…)}]

\=\+|+|+|\=\+|+|+|=\=\=|+|+|\\\+|+|+|=\=|+|+|+|=\=\+|+|+|\=\=|+|+|+|\=\=|+|+|+|\=\=|+|+|+|\=\=|+|+|\=\=|+|+|+|\=\=|+|+|\=\=\+|+|+|\=\=\+|+|+| +

Kit #6: Superior EXPOSITION

[= thinking-writing-communicating in "<u>essay</u>" or "<u>thesis-points</u>" mode]

via an enhanced formula: "Expository Elucidation" $\boxed{\text{"15-C"}}$

surpassing the "Five Paragraph Theme" and fortifying the genre of "essay"...

|#|#+|+#+|+|+#|+|#+|+|+|#+|+|+|+#+#+|||++|#+|#+#|##+|+|#+|+|+|#+|#+|#+#+|+|#|#+|+|#|+|#+|#|##+#|+|#+|+#|+|+|++|#+|+#|+|+#|+|#|#+|+#|+|#+|+#|+|#++|+#|+|+#|||

[1.] PREAMBLE. [1.A.] The GIST, then [1.B.] the ambitious CLAIM...

[1.A.] IN-A-NUTSHELL SUMMARY: The "**thesis-points-discussion-conclusion**" method of writing—and of thinking and communicating!—is very powerful. But it currently seems grossly *under-*valued... *under*-utilized... *under*-taught... and overall *mis*conceived-of. (In schools it's equated with the rigid-rule formula of the "Five Paragraph Theme" which some teachers reject as mechanical, but others keep on teaching...) Plus, "logical exposition" itself is at times suspect or neglected these days...

[1.B.] This module seeks to *remedy this unfortunate oversight* by "rescuing" the thought-method of **exposition** to its Potential-of-Excellence, via affirming its power, and formulating no fewer than fifteen components which help apply its power.

[ANALOGY: the "school theme" is a "rude wheelbarrow"; the 15-C, a "front-lift fork-loader"...]

|#|#+|+#+|+|+#|+|#+|+|+|#+|+|+|+#+#+|||++|#+|#+#|##+|+|#+|+|+|#+|#+|#+#+|+|#|#+|+|#|+|#+|#|##+#|+|#+|+#|+|+|++|#+|+#|+|+#|+|#|#+|+#|+|#+|+#|+|#++|+#|+|+#|||

[2.] The RATIONALE for this model of thinking-writing-communicating:

The **Issue** at hand... The **Cruciality** (the "So-What" Problem-Opportunity)...
and our suggested **Response**:

--WHEREAS, <u>a mode of thinking-writing-communicating does exist which we can call "exposition,"</u> specifically meaning "**developing a main <u>thesis or idea</u> with its component <u>subpoints</u>, plus <u>examples</u> and <u>discussion</u>**" (also related to "the formal essay" etc.) whether for description, explanation, argument, instruction, or other purposes-for-confronting;

--WHEREAS this mode is admittedly *<u>not</u>* useful for all task-goals in all arenas, and anyhow is *<u>not</u>* rigidly-<u>"pure" and thus can be modified</u> (as toward the Story not essay dramatic genre of plot-event, etc.);

--*<u>but</u>* WHEREAS **this form has more power for competent thinking about complexities, than seems currently: realized, appreciated, employed, and taught.**

(Exposition as (somewhat) *sociologically-philosophically* **overlooked, or condemned** by "anti-rational" forces today which excessively distrust or denigrate "logic, reason, objectivity" and the like... and *pedagogically* <u>in education (somewhat)</u> **non-taught, or under-taught** via the simplistic "five-paragraph theme" model or equivalents (or none at all)...and *pragmatically* woefully **underused,** so many written texts failing to achieve "completeness conceptuality unity coherence emphasis categorization structure" and eight other elements of exposition);

--And thus WHEREAS **exposition thus has more of a neglected place or use for more kinds of thinking/writing tasks in more arenas than is currently appreciated, taught-about, or practiced**; [Especially <u>pedagogically,</u> wherein students seem to be taught either (1) no real exposition at all, or (2) the simplistic "five-paragraph

282

theme," or (3) many of the fifteen variables of exposition we corral here, *but* partially and hit-and-miss and not correlated or integrated as we do here...]

--now THEREFORE <u>we do offer a powerfully-improved, indeed hitherto-nonexistent, tool to elucidate competent "exposition"</u> which we call the ⊡**"15-C"** model because it attends to no fewer than a dozen-plus-three elements of quality thinking-writing-communicating. (Not a rigid rule or formula, but a flexible cluster of tactics, a heuristic.)

(And this via <u>Mind-Play's</u> RATIONALE: "complex challenging subjects repay indeed require more-complex thinking skills which can be elucidated completely/clearly without either oversimplification, overelaboration, rigid formalism or too-loose relaxation")

--and WHEREAS **analogies** can be helpful in elucidating a concept, we would say that

...in terms of **"landscaping equipment,"** the "15-C" is to the "five-paragraph theme" model, as "a powerful *earth-moving machine*" is to "a common ordinary *wheelbarrow*"...

...or in terms of **"packaging of product,"** the 5PT is a *12-slot egg-carton*, random writing is "merely throwing items into a box haphazard, and the 15-C is *complex material expertly packaged for efficient delivery to reader*"...

...in terms of **"flexibility for learning skills,"** the "5PT" is experienced by students as "a *pottery studio* with one and *only one fixed form-ula* for a vase" whereas the 15-C.....! Or the 5PT as "a child's *bicycle* with *training wheels which however are solidly welded-on*"... The 15-C is a "*pegboard*" or "*ceiling-bank*" of options, accessible-but-unobtrusive...

...or in terms of **"surface vs. total construction and remodeling/rebuilding of an artifact—say a habitation,"** <u>too many students can't totally "raze and rebuild" a flawed text—by another writer or by themselves.</u> They merely "*repaint walls*" (grammar, "flow," punctuation, etc.) or perhaps "*move interior room walls*" (redistribute order of points). But at times one must totally revamp the basic structure, even lay new foundations from scratch (alter basic thesis—or find a roofbeam in the first place!). Perhaps the **15-C** model goes to basic principles, and thus may more powerfully help students to dig deeper beyond cosmetic surface reworking, return radically to the drawing board when needed...

|#|#+|+#+|+|+#|+|#+|+|+|#+|+|+|+#+#+|||++|#+|#+#|##+|+|#+|+|+|#+|#+|#+#+|#|#+|+|#|+|#|+|#|#+#|+|#+|+#|+|+#|+|++|#+|+#|+|+#|+|#|#+|+#|#+|+#|+|#|+|#+#+|+#|+|+#|||

[3.] The 15-C model in bird's-eye PREVIEW of its essence:

PRE-VUE: Overviews of both the **"Five-Paragraph Theme"** (traditional school essay) [AT LEFT] and the model we call **"15-C"** Expository Elucidation (elements more numerous *and conceptual*) [AT RIGHT]...

Five-Paragraph Theme	15-C
1. Choose a **thesis** and **three subpoints** in it.	1. **Complete: Complexity**, how much of total subject is surveyed then treated? **Collected** and **Continued**, is enough raw material information collected, discussion continued?
2. **State** thesis in first paragraph.	2. **Conceptualized**: is material moved from data to its ideas within, existing or potential?
	3. **Con-Vergent**: is an overall unity achieved for all subparts (keystone, maypole)?
3. **Develop** it via the subpoints, one per paragraph.	4. **Categorization**: is material divided into sub-points, at one or multiple levels?
	5. **Crystallized**: are the resultant ideas stated explicitly enough, not implied or buried?
	6. **Calibration**: are main and minor matters treated proportionately as appropriate?
4. Give **examples** to support subpoints.	7. **Concretized**: did writer "dip down" to provide specific examples to illustrate ideas?
	8. **Contour**: as relevant, was the whole text subdivided into chunks of segments?
	9. **Con-Sequent**: was the "best" structure/organization/arrangement of points achieved, from the "menu" of the many known options which do exist, whether always taught or not?
5. **End** with a conclusion-paragraph.	10. **Co-herent**: if points interrelate to each other logically, is this connection shown?
	11. **Co-hesive**: is #10's integration shown by style—especially via powerful parallelism?
6. [Try to *forget the whole thing*; probably not too difficult to do...]	12. **"Concatenation"**: is syntax, sentence structure good?
	13. **Condensed**: is text free of wordiness, distilled to *just-right* **compact-conciseness**?
	14. **"Camera"**: are visual techniques used (charts diagrams graphs etc. and page-layout)?
	15. **Correct**: is text made error-free, are conventions/constraints followed, as needed?
Your right-hand model seems excessive, too many issues—and rather abstract also!	Well, it's **conceptual**, the issues behind specific directions. Plus powerfully-**complete**. And accessible—itself **consequent**... *By contrast* the 5PT in the left-hand side, seems to us *simplistic, primitive, arthritic, simplistic, mechanical*, hence *dangerous. Read on...*

283

[4.] ⟨TABLE OF CONTENTS⟩ of this unit

|#|+|+#+|+|+#|+|+#|+|+|#+|+|+#+|+||+#+|+#|##+|+|#+|+|+#+|+|#+|+#|+|+#|+|+#|+|#|##+#|+|#+|+#|+|+|+#|+|+#|+|+#|+|#|+|+#|+|+#|+|#+|+#|+|+#|+|#||+#|+|#|||

[5.] A PROTO-EXAMPLE: schematic: "vegetarianism" ⌐ IN "II" FULL version:¬

|#|+|+#+|+|+#|+|+#|+|+|#+|+|+#+|+||+#+|+#|##+|+|#+|+|+#+|+|#+|+#|+|+#|+|+#|+|#|##+#|+|#+|+#|+|+|+#|+|+#|+|+#|+|#|+|+#|+|+#|+|#+|+#|+|+#|+|#||+#|+|#|||

[6.] GALLERY "I": first three examples.

EXAMPLE #1. The power of **Categorizing** sub-ideas and *especially* deft **Concretization**, vivid specifics…
The example of a letter in the in-flight magazine (of CATHAY PACIFIC AIRLINES), late 1980's.
[Clearly, below the Concepts are in **bold-face**, the Concrete examples are *italicized*…]

[*ORIGINAL.*] As a frequent traveler I have found that some of your staff are very helpful and accommodating which is extremely appreciated. Two of your staff members whom I have encountered numerous times are Ellen Lui and Carrie Law. I have found them to be extremely pleasant, helpful and accommodating. Although I have *no specific incident to recount to you* I just thought it was important for an airline to recognize those who excel in their positions and to give them the praise they deserve. --DL, Hong Kong	[*REWRITE.*] I really appreciate the excellence of your flight crews—especially Ellen Lui and Carrie Law. They're "basically" helpful. (*They reassured me about my luggage…then delivered that extra pillow and blanket.*) They're "advanced" accommodating. (*They changed me to a better vacant seat…then delivered that third bottle of water.*) And they're "world-class" pleasant. (*They smiled throughout a flight tossed by turbulence and babbling babies…and through to finding me the gate number of my connecting flight…*) Thanks to them and the whole crew!

This is **NOT** impressive! The only changes were to add examples to support the three subpoints. *A 5PT*	True, but we start slow, first steps first. True, only **7Concretizing** is the star player here. *Already* the letter was good in that it is **2Conceptualized**, **4Categorized**, even **5Crystallized**. ["Good staff: pleasant, helpful, accommodating]. *However*, it's not yet either **13Condensed** nor **7Concretized**. Hence, *an astonishing example of the wastefulness of egocentric proclamations without retrieving the Concrete specifics which made you feel as you do, so the reader also can feel not just be told… Cut the "tell," insert the "show"…* We call this rewriting ploy the **"Same Game"**: chop wordiness, insert more content in the same wordcount. See below… *[**Could most writing students, given the original,**

could have done this just as well!	deftly rewrite to improve thus, with awareness? I mean "autonomously," without being told which changes to make?] [P.S.—as "dessert" here, we also added **11Co-hesion** or linking of the points via style. Can learners spot the parallelism, in the basic advanced and world-class progression and echoes thus?...]

EXAMPLE #2. From a Time magazine article on the trend toward <u>sharing roles in marriage</u>.
--Left-hand, the original text: --Right-hand, the reworked version.:

Versions of the 50-50 marriage, blending or reversing traditional male roles and responsibilities, are cropping up all over the country. *In Detroit an industrial relations specialist does all the cooking, and his social worker wife keeps the family books. In Berkeley, a research economist quit his job so his wife could continue working as a radio program coordinator while he takes care of their children. A Boston lawyer feeds and dresses his children each morning because his wife often works late for the National Organization of Women.*	Versions of the 50-50 marriage, blending or reversing traditional male roles and responsibilities, are cropping up all over the country. Sometimes only traditional household role-chores are simply reversed. *In Detroit an industrial relations specialist does all the cooking, and his social worker wife keeps the family books.* Sometimes altered is the usual balance of the woman doing more homemaking to permit the man to work longer at the office. *A Boston lawyer feeds and dresses his children each morning because his wife often works late for the National Organization of Women.* At other times the more-major "male as breadwinner" role is altered. *In Berkeley, a research economist quit his job so his wife could continue working as a radio program coordinator while he takes care of their children.*

...okay, I grant you, you *do* have more going on here, more C's as you call them... Can we go further faster?	Okay, but do learners really understand so far? The left-side text was not "worked" to be **1Complete 2Conceptually**. The right-side re-writer sought to **Conceptualize**, to derive out explicit ideas behind the data, implied by it. And then we **5Crystallized** or stated these concepts explicitly. In doing so we **4Categorized:** divided the general theme into three sub-ideas. We also improved the **9Con-Sequence** or structure by reversing the second and third points so that we moved from lesser to greater changes in family structure. **[P.S.—Does this reworking show (1) <u>how so many texts</u>,** while competent-enough (or *are* they?...), <u>can be improved</u>, and by comprehensible principles, such as these fifteen "C"s?... And does my comment right above, suggest that (2) <u>many learners</u>—or even teachers?—<u>do not *fully understand, truly Know*, exposition</u> as a thinking-writing technique?... That is, *can your students analyze the rewrite competently enough, let alone revise it Autonomously and Annotate what they did?* The 5PT wouldn't tell them how to...]]

EXAMPLE #3. The subject is a lowly genre, <u>a thank-you note</u> sent by a satisfied customer to the "SPICE HOUSE" in Milwaukee, WI, early 1990's. [Rewrite "*over*worked" to emphasize issues...]

I'd like to thank RUTH P. herself for great help with my phone order the other day. I was getting into Indian cooking. She not only helped me avoid mistakes such as over-purchasing amounts, but also advised similarities and differences, and in general was very helpful. I even learned new information about spices. Thanks again!	Thanks to RUTH P. herself for giving me an extra shipment of quality on my phone order the other day on my Indian-cooking needs. 1. She competently advised. ("The Indian-type cardamom is best for your needs.") 2. She also offered solutions. ("If no asafoedita, just combine onion and garlic.") 2. Then she updated information. ("North Face is a newer blend.") 3. And she helped avoid duplications. ("Rocky Mtn. resembles Downer enough") 4. She suggested. ("What's good for pasta? Downer, with butter.") 5. She reassured me, saved expense. ("No, fenugreek will keep well for a longish time.") 6. She advised about amounts. ("You'll use a lot of coriander...but if Telicherry pepper lasted you that long, get only a half-cup now.") 7. She confirmed my own notions. ("Yes, garam masala is hard to grind on your own.") 8. And she added enthusiasm. ("Ruth Anne's Muskego? Oh yes that is good, isn't it!") Thanks to Ruth for adding quality service to quality products.

Good, now you're getting somewhere — not just repainting, but	--[Good *grief*...I **give up** on that last comment...] Can we see how the right-hand version **2Conceptualizes** (finds the ideas in the facts and **5Crystallizes** them explicitly), then by the way **4Categorizes** or subdivides the ideas *incisively* into eight different subtopics, then also **7Concretizes** excellently with brief but vivid dialog. (Even the **9Con-Sequence** or structure is acceptable-enough.) And, less

reconstructing. Still, <u>who's going to want to read</u> the tedious right-hand version? The store clerks *already know* what they are doing well!	about writing, perhaps, than about *thinking*… --Look at the rewrite via four **"lenses"** or perspectives. In re <u>Pragmatics</u>, it surely let "Ruth" the intended audience comprehend the message more fully… In re <u>Pedagogy</u>, it may be a tour de force for students learning the **15-C** variables. […Or even a virtual training-guide for new store-employees…]… In re <u>Principles</u>, it's probably good writing; it Walked its Talk by not just praising quality, but by demonstrating it in its writing… And so, in re <u>Pleasure</u>, it's a deft move on the athletic field which I can cheer not boo…

|#|*+|+*+|+|+#|+|#*|+|+|#*|+|+|+#+#++|||++|#+|#+#|##+|+|#*|+|+|#*|#+|#+#+|+|#|#*|+|#|+|#+|+|#|#|##+#|+|#*|+|#|+|+|+*|+|#|+|#*|+|#*|+|#|+|#|+|#+|+|#|+|+#|+|+#|+|+#+|+#|+|+#|||

[7.] the TOOL-KIT itself; the total essence of "15-C":

[1.] How to Write **a "5-Paragraph Theme"** for Class:	**[2.] "15-C" EXPOSITORY ELUCIDATION** **Roster of variables and the range of choices within each one** [With examples from the for-instance of "vegetarianism"…]
	REASSURANCE: these moves are not rigid rote formulaic RULES, but as flexible TOOLS. **Use-or-not (mostly one will), but *how little-or-much, depends on the situation*…**

(1) Create a **THESIS**
 	
(2) Create a 1-par. **INTRO DUCTION** giving that thesis
 	
(3) Develop three **POINTS** or aspects of that thesis.
 	
(4) Write the **BODY**. Three pars., each with a thesis-point
 	
(4) Each body **PAR.** has **topic sentence**; develop ment; support with **SPECIFIC EXAMPLES** etc.
 	
(5) Write the **CONCLUS**
	1. COMPLETE: 1A. "COMPLEXITY." What is <u>original size</u> of subject: tiny…moderate…immense? And then what is the <u>essay's treatment</u> of subject: **Total…all but general-skimming…selected parts…one part in lesser or greater detail…?…** ["All" of vegetarian on one page…nutrition in great detail…*many other combinations*]
	
	1B. CONFRONTED. Is subject sufficiently (1) COLLECTED *SCOPE:* **Are enough or all needed points, *present FOR* discussion?**
	[Huge gaps, important issues absent from mention? == **many , indeed all, issues present?** == *Too* **many for the task?**]
	    [Oops, utterly omits "Politics" from a discussion of Vegetarianism "in society today"?]
	…..and then **(B) CONTINUED** *DEPTH:* **Is each point then sufficiently *developed IN* the discussion?** (=all key issues developed and discussed enough?).
	[Issues just parked == **expanded enough** == or even *overdone?*] [Oops, "Nutrition" only given one short paragraph?]
	
	2. CONCEPTUALIZED. (*) Is raw material "thought through," the ideas within it, discovered by induction upward?
	[Still only raw data?== **some ideas emerge?** == **explicit concepts ideas meaning are derived ?**]
	    [Whoa, I should distill these information-dumps on "vegetarianism", on out to to "Pros and Cons," "Myths vs. Realities," the issues of Nutrition, Taste, Economy, etc…..]
	
	3. CON-VERGENT: overall <u>Unity</u>. Is there a thesis, how focused? And how strictly-or-relaxedly do the points relate to it?
	[Too-slack sprawling? == **just-right?** == or even *too*-strict overnarrow, per se or for the occasion?]
	    [Hmmm, better leave "exercise techniques" out of a paper on Vegetarianism and health….]
	
	4. CATEGORIZED: Should any points be (A) **subdivided into subpoints "split"—*or* (B) synthesized, combined within others "lumped" (=classified-&-divided better)?**
	[In short, <u>how many vertical levels</u> in the outline? Only one "3 or 5 main points" or more "sub-points?"]
	    [Oops, "Benefits" should break out into Psychological, Biological, Ecological—at least I had Bio under Nutrition elsewhere. And, let's collapse Nutrition and Recipes under Cookery Of—?….]
	
	5. "CRYSTALLED": Is the **thesis, and each point, <u>stated very explicitly</u>** (but as needed and should be for the occasion)? Often via diction of a single keyword or short phrase: Gastronomy, Social Image…
	[Is point present but still left *subliminal* (tacit, covert, implied) == or *sort of stated* but hard to pick out easily at once == or *explicitly* stated == or even *"Neoned"* or stated in keywords, other style to make the idea absolutely un-missable for what it is, "the next point here now"?] Should it be softened, left implicit (rarely?) == or labeled louder? This depends on occasion—audience, purpose, etc.
	    [The *Vague:* "Also something to notice concerns our finances, and, *blah blah* …" VERSUS the *Vivid:* "A third advantage of vegetarianism, besides **Health** and **Morality**, is **Economy**. If you consider etc. *blah*…]

ION,
restating
(amplifying?)
your thesis.
Then, stop!

["Whew that
was easy but
is it What
Was Wanted
oh well"...]

\|#|+#|+#||+|

6. CALIBRATED: Is each point **proportionate in scale of treatment—not too emphasized or subordinated?** (In content—in style?)

[**One point overdone?** *Reduce* it == **Another point skimped-on?** *Expand* it == **A point missing?** *Include* it == **A point irrelevant?** *Omit* it...]

[Ooops, half the paper is on my favorite *legume recipes*, and only one short paragraph each, on *Nutrition* itself, and *Health*. I should proportionately reduce the menu, and expand both the embryonic points.....]

7. CONCRETIZED: Are points supported, clarified by effective specifics? (=examples, proof, details)

[**None or not enough, bare** == **just-right** == or even specifics are *too* numerous or lengthy?]

[Oops, a whole page vividly describing the Wheatberry Restaurant, but no quantified measurements for Pinto-Beans-&-Brown-Rice... And I don't need five separate examples of anti-vegetarian bias if they're all the same kind. But "Morality" needs some *particulars*...]

8. CONTOURED: Should text be **chunked into larger internal segments,** "chapters" or other?

[Aha, could easily do four parts. Intro to; Key Issues; Pros-and-Cons of; and Recipes. Points within each part.....]

9. CON-SEQUENT: (A) Frequency: Does each point appear *stated only one time* in its proper "debut" place as primary statement (to avoid "meandering re-mentioning," while still permitting repetition-for-reinforcement-or-development)?

...and then (B) Structure: Are the **points arranged, ordered, in the best sequence?** By which of a half-dozen possible rationales?

[**A-Z... time or space... via a concept or system... degree of importance... informal-impressionistic... best for reader-relating... etc.**]

[Oops, I drifted back into "Aesthetics" redundantly—over-repetitive organization. And, "Benefits Of" reeeally should come *before* "History Of." But I can re-mention "Health" later to re-inforce it.....]

10. CO-HERENT: Is the points' logical relationship and sequence made explicit in the *discussion* which interrelates them, shows the connections?

[Politics, biochemistry, morality—show how all develop to link vegetarianism and value-issues...]

11. CO-HESIVE: Is the points' logical relation and sequence made apparent in their *style* (transitions; repetitions; especially, parallelism—at sentence level *and* above)?

["Frank likes to eat tofu, preparing legumes, and he grows grains." **BETTER:** "Frank likes to eat tofu himself on all days, to serve legumes to his guests every week, and to grow grains in his garden for everyone each season."]

12. "CONCATENATION": Does sentence-level syntax not muddle but smooth the idea-clarity?

(Sentence length... types... variety...) [Errors avoided (subordination etc.) == **excellences achieved (very long or short sentences as effective to sum up, and the like]**

13. "CONDENSED": Is text as **compact-concise** as possible *or* desirable, **but** short of telegraphic-cryptic? **(Remove seven types of wordiness.)**

[Specific Gravity: "diluted," too many words for the content? == just-right "fit" of substance and word-count? == too few words: cryptic, telegraphic?]

14. "CAMERA":

Do **visual-graphic elements promote clarity?** (In any visuals—diagrams, charts, graphs, pictures? In the layout itself—typography, page-design?)

15. "CORRECT": Is text error-free, conforming to usage and conventions for the genre and situation?

[Hideous, egregious errors, egg-on-face? == A few mild errors? == "Clean & perfect" by-the-book?]

Wait, the 5PT already provides needed structure for students and is simpler. Your 15-C here is *much* too complex...	The 5PT is an *abomination*. A *non-thinking* straight-jacket Rule giving learners no concepts-behind, nor alternate options for flexibility. (**ANALOGY:** a bicycle with non-detachable training-wheels!) (**ANECDOTE:** I've had freshmen *honestly amazed* to hear that "yes you can have four or five etc. paragraphs in the body and not just three ...") *Hence* the 15-C. *Complexity for complexities!*

Well.....Now I **DO** see your point here. Complexity <u>is</u> better served by the 15-C, and it itself is complex, but clear. Perhaps the 15-C scheme itself is sort of "15-C'ed"!... I see now your point that the 5PT is somewhat a simplified straightjacket...	We propose the 15-C as a powerful "reminder for specific purposes." And it correlates the contraries between too Tight/Simple, too Loose/Complicated... Focused but flexible...

[3.] "Extra": A "Quartet-of-Skills" Formula.

(1) Emphasize points in keywords, (2) give Concrete examples, (3) install Parallelism, (4) deword!

SEE "II" FULL version: *EXAMPLES:* X stop plumbing leak, X teaching in urban or rural areas, X disclosure to Chancellor of my hidden agenda being quite "clean"

|#|#+|+##+|+|+#|+|#+|+|+|#+|+|+|+#+#+|||++|#+|#+#|##+|+|#+|+|+|#+|#+|#+#+|+|#|#+|+|#|+|+|#+|#||##+#|+|#+|+#|+|+|++|#+|+#|+|+#|#|#+|+#|+|#|#+|+#|+|#+|+#|+|#+#+|+#|+|+#|||

[8.] GALLERY "II": three subsequent examples.

EXAMPLE #4: Take a "student paper" and try out the 15-C for size and style. The subject here is the arbitrary "creative" one of "Killer-Hamsters as Household Pets." Can the comparison-pair here begin to teach *the Spirit as well as the Letter* of elucidation through **Completeness, Categorization, Concretization,** etc., working together for more power? To spot errors avoided (or committed), excellences attained (or missed)?

LEFT-hand: rough version: **RIGHT**-hand: enhanced via some 15-C elements:

LEFT	RIGHT
(I) The **First Time** We Brought Clyde Home As A New Pet.	(I) **Overview:** Description, Recent History of these unusual house-pets.
(II) My **Grandmothers's** Reaction.	(II) **Pros and Cons** of K.H. as House-Pets
(A) Liked his Fur.	(A) Positive Advantages
(B) What Would Neighbors Think?	1. Friendly (x: comfort you when you fail exam, x curl up with you at night)
	2. Fantastic (A) Aesthetic (x fur coat), (B) Athletic (x can leap higher than Felix)
(III) **History** of the Killer Hamster as a House Pet	3. Ferocious: guards house, keeps order
	a. Against burglars, intruders (x: bit salesman in the foot)
(IV) **I Like** Clyde Because	b. Against unwanted relatives (x: bit Aunt Marjorie when she lectured us)
(A) Rich Fur Coat	c. Against misbehaving siblings (x: kept Jason at homework, Julie from whining)
(B) Friendly	d. Against vermin (x: Clyde killed at least 30 rats)
(C) Guards Property	4. Frugal, financially inexpensive (x: costs much less than the Smythe's pet ocelot)
	(B) Negative Problem-Issues
	1. Fierce (x: bit foot in sleep)
	(C) "Mixed Blessing," It Depends:
	1. Social Response. (xx: some people like him, some fear him, etc.)
	2. Health. (x: local vet baffled)
	3. Toilet-Training. (x: need for unique equipment)
	(III) **How-To:** Tips & Hints for Care

Whoa, again too elementary! *Who doesn't know how to look at a situation and get some ideas out of it!* You care about Basics for Beginners, but really, this is "late-stage remedial" only... ...oh, and plus it's too simplistic. Exposition is more than just "pros and cons of something." Students will grab onto the plus-and-minus format as a recipe...	--Too basic? Earlier I would have thought so too—but *no longer.* I began to find that today, college freshmen 1985 onward, needed this base. They found it **eye-opening.** (Used for the subject of "Mobile-Home Living," see below, it was one of my three *best* assignments *ever...*) If only to make explicit, some basic moves and operations... --Can this paired set of outlines, then, show beginners ***"the very concepts"*** of **2Conceptualizing** or idea not just data... then **1Completeness** of the idea developed... including **4Categorizing** or creating many subpoints also...but also **3Convergence**, all subpoints unified under the thesis... **7Concretization** or effective examples distinct from subpoints and not just "little subjects" ...**9Con-Sequence** or best structure of all this...***this for the basics...*** ...and yes, admittedly pro-and-con risks becoming a formula into which lazy learners will eagerly slide. However, **motivation** is not our concern here...

EXAMPLE #5. The body of <u>an e-mail to members of a small-town Art Alliance</u>, a volunteer group promoting the arts locally. (This concerns the calendar for the year's monthly displays of art at the Double Dip Deli, a downtown venue where exhibitions occur.) Only the January portion is included here; subsequent months were not treated in as much detail.

BELOW *LEFT*, is the verbatim <u>original</u>, "cruelly" reproduced *absolutely* verbatim or *totally* unaltered...

<![endif]> January art show Accepting art in all mediums that have a masculine theme. I assume this to me art that has "man appeal" Work is due at the Deli by Dec 31. Please fill out a title card that is available at the Deli. Attach a two part receipt to the back of you pieces. We also need an inventory list with the title and cost. Remember that starting Jan. a 20% commission will be take so that we can do a better job of advertising. EXP if you painting is priced at 100 you will give the D3 Gallery 20 if it is priced at 300 you will give the gallery 60, etc. <![endif]> If you have a mailing list of people you would like to be invited to the opening leave it with your paintings. <[!endif]> PLEASE let me know how many pieces you will be bringing. I would like to see more artists participate. artfan@icdnet.com <[!endif]> While you are inspired to create...think ahead to Feb. The show is feminine art I assume this means art that appeals the the "lady" <[!endif]> **[The latter half of the email mentions what the March through December exhibits will be, already decided and also invitations...]**	I. JANUARY art show. Accepting art in all mediums that has a masculine theme, and also presumably which appeals to men. Deadline for submitting work to the Deli is Dec 31. BEFORE that, as soon as possible, please let me know how many pieces you will be bringing—and please do participate! Email me at artfan@icd.net. WHEN you deliver the artwork, please include three items: 1. Title card—available at the Deli. 2. Two-part receipt (original and copy of the "bill" or invoice)—attached to the back of the art. 3. An inventory list, showing title and cost. 4. And if applicable, a mailing list of people you'd like invited to the opening, on January 2nd. Actually, please provide that list SOONER, as soon as possible—perhaps when you let me know the number of pieces you'll be bringing, as noted above. (Commission Policy. Note that in order to publicize better, starting January, the WAA will take a 20% commission on all art sold.) II. And then THE MONTHS AHEAD... February art show. The theme is feminine art, presumably that which appeals to women. ..... **[The latter half of the email mentions what the March through December exhibits will be, already decided and also invitations...]**
I see where you'll be going with this, but the errors etc. aren't that serious in this informal email from an overworked member of a voluntary organization! You must be flexible not rigid and not demand 100% perfection for all task-goal situations! What about "context-sensitivity," eh?	Fine, your comment brings up the *advanced* thinking skill of **Competence**-judging, including handling disagreements. But more *basically* also it would be a fine test for a student, can s/he convert left-hand to right-hand and by the book and say what s/he did?... And ultimately, can s/he attain the **Quality** of the rewrite *when needed*? P.S.—I also enjoy the element here of **Contest** or **Pleasure**. As reading-buff or Exposition-fan in the "bleachers," I this time *do not cheer but instead boo* this amateur effort and its botches as it blunders down the field awkwardly, egg on its face! For instance, **SEE THE FOLLOWING ANALYSIS** I did after being sufficiently astonished then irritated by this text (my own **"insight/bias"**):.. ➜

.... ➜ LAB EXERCISE. My diagnosis dissection of this really-"problematic" text.
What variables were on the table to confront? How did the author handle them? Adequately or not?...

13Camera. <u>Odd inclusions of computer instructions</u>. Perhaps I mistake, and perhaps " <[!endif]>" is Pure Poetry... Maybe unknown to writer until memó was sent. *Does it matter?* Probably not (but amusingly-sardonically to me "writer doesn't even know or care how her memo looks to its readers...").

14Correct. <u>Many careless typing errors</u>. Unarguably bad *In Vitro* by the book of correctness. But do they really matter *In Vivo*, in the situation? This is probably **"Variable"**; to picky me, it is mildly-insulting carelessness, plus ironically-embarrassing in a context of—good art, which presumes polish! But to others, probably not; "so what, she got the message across"...

5Crystallized. Obviously [?], the separate points, about submission, are <u>more buried in the original</u>, more Emphasized or highlighted in the rewrite.

9Con-Sequence. <u>Structure seems amateur-unfinished</u> in the original. Fairly classic case of **"writer-based"** writing—

sequence is *as it occurred to the writer*, and <u>not</u> *the logic of the subject* <u>nor</u> *the needs of the reader* to comprehend easily. The issue of "commissions" is dropped in where the writer thinks of it… By contrast I rearranged points, also used the option of Time for structuring (not Space, Category, Random, A-Z, etc., which are other alternatives for sequencing…)

6Calibration. The commission policy while important is <u>secondary and therefore I subordinated it</u> by (1) cushioning it in parentheses, and (2) structuring or locating it later in the text.

4Categorized. I seem to have found <u>not one but two subpoints</u>. *What* to bring with the art, and also to *tell me how much* art you're bringing. These I separated, and then also **9Crystallized** them by the CAPITALS for Before and When.

<u>I say again</u> this risks becoming *overcomplex response to complexity*! You are dissecting to death this pitiful everyday e-mail! Learners don't have to be taken this far, do they? […oh, and aren't you rather vindictive and even "cruel" in your targeted trashing of this innocent well-meaning text written by a non-writer?…]	*I only say: try the <u>Acid Test</u>!* Give your writing students the original flawed text, above. Can they on their own surely spot (identify and name) and perhaps even correct the errors in it, the lack of excellences? [Simply via **In Vitro** by the book as I did here, no need to quarrel **In Vivo** for the situation or **Just-Personal Preference** either.] *If not, if the students can't do the above, well then perhaps they just don't <u>really</u> "know" <u>exposition</u>, eh… I'd hope the 15-C rubric can help them accelerate awareness…* […oh, and as for vicious vindictiveness, etc.—the variable here is Pleasure, specifically Sportive Challenge. Writing as an athletic contest, reading as a spectator sport, the fan in the bleachers eagerly cheering deft moves—and just as energetically booing botches, bungles, and blunders. So!…]

EXAMPLE #6. A <u>letter to the editor of a college newspaper</u>. (It is critiquing the publication of the "Police Blotter" column which reports misdeeds.) The beauty-beast pair here, the amateur text and the (by-the-book) better revision, *may speak for itself, may speak volumes*, about pitfalls and potentialities—to those who already know these issues, of course…

Dear Editor, 　While I have not had the distinction of having my name appear in your police reports, I nonetheless feel compelled to question the need for them. 　Though there may be some merit to an informed public, is, indeed, this argument applicable now? Before answering, please examine the following: 　1.) You are dealing with accusations only. Since you print only accusations and not acquittals or defense replies, you, in essence, allow only the police department to speak. If you feel you must continue, then at least print those names exonerated of charges to facilitate full disclosure. 　2.) There is a distinct lack of relevancy. Of what benefit is it to us, your readers, to know of those arrested who are totally independent of UW-Whitewater? 　3.) Do you have the right to further humiliate those arrested? Since it is already a matter of local, public record, of what purpose is there for additional reporting? 　4.) Your sensationalized reporting is fostering police disrespect. Perhaps you should fully examine the consequences of informing the public. By letting us know of Johnny Doe's arrest for urinating all over a fire hydrant, you are, at the same time, feeding a contempt for the local law officials. 　Because of these reasons I feel you should discontinue your police reports. If nothing else, at least reconsider your reasons for a continued effort. <div align="right">MARK MCNALLY</div>	Dear Editor, 　Do you really need to print the Police Blotter column, that record of public peccadilloes and pratfalls? 　(1) It doesn't seem fair or complete to the arrestees. Why print only those names accused, and not those exonerated of the charges in future weeks? 　(2) It doesn't seem just or genteel to the arrestees either. Why further humiliate those who are already in the public record anyhow? 　(3) It doesn't seem relevant to our readers specifically. Who cares if non-UW personnel were arrested? 　(4) It doesn't even seem beneficial for norms and morale generally. Doesn't reporting a urination all over a fire hydrant, foster contempt for law and order, for local law officials? 　It's not that my own name has appeared in the Blotter. It's just that I question the Blotter itself. <div align="right">MILLICENT OFFENBACH</div>
…good grief, *this* time, I **DO** see your point. The original <u>bungled</u> several of the "C's" (wordiness, lack of crystal point-stating, utter neglect of possibilities of parallelism, even structure…) These are **5Crystallized** (the points not crisply labeled)… relatedly **11Co-hesion** (monstrously no parallelism)… and **13Condensed** (rewrite trimly slims the bloated verbiage)…	…Yes, and *it even took me*, a writing teacher and the compiler of the 15-C scheme to boot, *more than one pass to spot* all pitfalls/potentialities. But the **15-C** was a catalyst to accelerate my work … Oh, and *you forgot to mention (or did not spot!)* **9Con-Sequence**, or structure. I seem to have reversed original points #2 and #3 for better logical flow or **10Co-herence.** *See*?

|#|#+|+#+|+|+#|+|#|+|+|#|+|+|+#+#++|||++|#+|#+#|##++|+|#+|+|+|#+|#+#+#|+|#|#+|+|#|+|#+|#|##+#|+|#++|+#|+|+|+#|+|+#|+|+|#|+|#|#+|+|#|#+|+|#|+|#+|+#|+|#+#|+#|||

290

[9.] "Objections, Objections!" FAQ's or Frequently-Asked <u>Questions</u>— or rather, FVO's or Frequently-Voiced <u>Objections</u>:

[1.] (*) <u>Much Too Simplistic, Formulaic, and Limited!</u> **Many composition teachers today roundly critique the Five-Paragraph Theme as being (1) too Formulaic, hence (2) too Constricting to creativity, also too (3) Narrow, not representing all writing, also too (4) Inapplicble to writing situations. They might feel the same way about your 15-C scheme, with exceptions…**

[I only suggest that if approached not by the Letter but the Spirit, the 15-C offers powerful Conceptual Creativity at the start, then better Communication later. Hence teachers' criticism is ironic, or perhaps egg-on-their-face, if they are (rigidly) critiquing a form which need not be applied rigidly…]

[2.] <u>Inappropriate For Many S ituations.</u> **In letters, memoirs, catalogs, etc., thesis-and-points are verboten!**

[Your objection seems True in Letter—but, in Spirit? And even by the letter, you'd be surprised at the under-use of gentle Exposition-techniques. *EXAMPLE:* A student reported that he benefited by **5Crystallizing** and **4Categorizing** his weekly phone calls home to his family? *And so forth…*]

[3.] <u>Outdated.</u> **The 5PTheme is no longer much taught. You are beating an extinct horse.**

[Perhaps: indeed, few of my students 1970-2000 even knew of it, or anyhow used it to competent profit. A few, of course, resorted to it mechanically. But the point; they didn't even know **exposition** on this rude mechanical primitive level of the Five-Paragraph Theme! No **Conceptualizing** at *all*…]

[4.] <u>Same Old?</u> **Your 15 handy skills seem "nothing new," just standard writing techniques lifted from composition texts.**

[Yes to an extent, but here we **elucidate** them : conceptualize them more explicitly, exemplify them, and interrelate them. *Now doesn't this sound—ironically—more like using the 15-C approach to convey the 15-C approach, ehh?.....*]

[5.] <u>Quite Incomplete!</u> **Your 15 points do not cover all of successful writing! What about diction? Audience-relating, including tone? Rhetoric? Dramatization or narrative storytelling? Plus awareness of genre…**

[*Nor did we ever claim* to cover the writing waterfront, either. We merely seek to be stewards to the underused tradition of exposition. Enough to do in one shot…]

[6.] <u>No, Overcomplete—Ponderous and Topheavy!</u> **This sprawling model seems excessive. Too many variables, too refined.**

[Oh—would you prefer my simpler but primitive **"4-S"** model I began with? Substance, Structure, Style, Support? The **15-C** is *the result of two decades of gradually creating a complete yet coherent system…*]

[7.] <u>Nice But Not Necessary.</u> **Really I think students pick these things up without such explicit training.**

[*I pose you a challenge.* Give your advanced, competent students one of the original texts from our readings here. (Such as X marriage styles, or X Spice House thank-you letter, or X diatribe against the bad poet, or X the Art Alliance memo.) <u>Can</u> they rewrite it to by-the-book expository perfection autonomously on their own? *I rest my case…*]

[8.] <u>But how is this scheme really Thought-Ful?</u> **You claim this helps teach thinking-as-such for real-life situations. But I just don't see that.**

[**6Calibration** obtains in real-life: proportioning, balancing, adjusting ratios and emphasis: time-management, etc. See "II" FULL version for other instances we can't present here now…]

[9.] <u>Good, But Not Pedagogical.</u> **I find no example for us, of 1-2-3 progression through all fifteen elements in clear order, soup to nuts, "vegetarianism" theme created step-by-step.**

[Agreed, regrettably! But SEE "II" FULL version for two Checklists for applying the model...]

[10.] Ironically, Your Scheme Still Lacks Flexibility! Especially today, "storytelling" is important, plus interblending genres and techniques.

[True, many forms don't follow the 15-C. SEE the "II" FULL version: Feature-Story opens with anecdote, and so forth... And see below, two *EXAMPLES*. (1) "Bic pens," shift to semi-narration within essay form, and (2) "Clerks Are People Too," the narrative as more genuine-literary, but the expository useful also.]

[10.] Gallery "III": two essays: bad pens, bad customers

EXAMPLE #1: <u>letter of complaint</u> about inferior ball-point pens. **Expository** original, more-**Narrative** rewrite:

May I suggest that you channel a portion of your advertising funds for BIC pens, toward more improvement of them via research and quality-control? On many occasions, I have found that BIC pens have failed me. They have either not written at all (dried out before first use?), or suddenly stopped writing because the ball fell out of the tip, or for that matter have flowed too copiously. This boom-and-bust situation has caused me both inconvenience and embarrassment—whether the writing occasion be solitary production of new ideas for myself... or notetaking during important telephone or conference situations... or writing in localities remote from stores carrying pens, should the need for replacement arise. BIC pens do come in a useful variety of writing points, and when they work, they often work well. Therefore please consider upgrading a sometimes good, but too often disappointing, product. Sincerely,	I whip out my BIC Regular, or Accounting Fine Point, start to jot down the important data my boss is rattling off at me on the phone (or even worse, in a conference in front of five other bigwigs)—and, crash. The ball has fallen out, and the dry pen point scrapes across the paper, tearing it. "Uh, wait a sec, pen broke," and I scrabble for another pen while Mr. Bigdome waits impatiently... Must today's pens lose their parts so easily? Ruminating at my desk in early morning, I get a great idea. I reach for my trusty BIC to save that thought. Then I lose that elusive inspiration as I make angry, fast circles on the page trying to get the ink to flow. Carburetor problems again. Angry, I try to break the pen, but the plastic case remains intact. Durable but not workable. I clatter the reject into the Circular File. Must pens run out of ink so quickly today? Then at other times the pen does write—scabbing and blotching great releases of a spill of Crude Oil all over the page—or my fingers and shirt pocket... Must pens these days disgorge too much ink? Last summer on a northern lake, an observer could have seen three pens in a row being flung out of the cabin of a small sailboat anchored in a cove, splashing into the drink. You guessed it—of a half-dozen BIC pens I bought to take along, only three worked. The other trio? Gas tank empty before the journey... Must our current pens dry out before first use? Please less advertising and more technology—to control ink-supply and ball-security! Thanks. Sincerely,
...well, it's a start, *but only a start*. You reverse the usual 5PT formula of the **2Conceptual** "topic sentence at start of paragraph," let the **7Concrete** matter go first. What about more challenging Essay-Story interfacing while keeping the strengths of both?	...as I said, *a step at a time*... (1) It *starts* the move from 100% essay toward a Story. Breaks any ironclad mode of the 5PT straitjacket!... (2) Also, may help discuss "permissible range of variations of which techniques for which writing situations"—Personal, School, Job, Civic. (3) And as always, could your students expertly elucidate *exactly* what changes here were made?

EXAMPLE #2. A <u>clerk's testimony about difficult customers</u>...   "Storied" original, "essayed" rewrite...

Although I enjoy my job as a clerk of a bath shop, there are some people in this world who make it tough to be pleasant. It is really bad how two people are equal until one puts a clerk's apron on. Somehow, standing behind the register lowers you in the eyes of the public. They treat you like you're dirt. Many people don't appreciate your help, but they sure expect it. It seems the less people want to spend, the more help they want. Why do people think that clerks have anything to do with the quality of the merchandise? I once worked with a lady who really chewed me out because our irregular towels had pulls in them. Clerks don't decide on the prices, they just ring the items up as marked. I understand why people want to find out all they can about a particular	I enjoy my job as clerk in a bath shop, but customers' discourteous and disrespectful treatment of me as inferior, almost inhuman, makes my job less pleasant than it could be—and (more important) my service to them than it should be. Some problems with customers I've noted in my six years' experience in retail: (1) They don't really desire your help. Please don't ask for information and then ignore it. (A lady cut me off when I was explaining about the washing instructions for lingerie she'd asked me about in the first place.) (2) They don't respect younger clerks. Please realize we can be knowledgeable too. (A woman asked to talk to an older clerk about sheet reliability when I've worked at Bubble Boutique for six years now.) (3) They blame us for low product quality. Please remember we don't control this. (A woman once chewed me out because our irregular

bedspread, but if they don't want to know what I have learned about washing instructions they shouldn't ask me. I get very insulted when they ask to speak to someone older when I have in the linens business for six years. A woman customer is tougher to sell and harder to please than a man. They expect more from the clerk and the product. I've actually been asked to hold and babysit children while the mother shops. They ask me to carry their purchases around behind them. They always ask for special deals. They expect you to break the rules just for them, like opening early and closing late. People treat clerks like they aren't even human. We are hired to help you, yes—but not to spoonfeed you. I know that the nicer a customer is to me, the more I am willing to do for them. Try it sometime—it is amazing what a little common courtesy and respect will do….

towels had pulls in them.)

(4) They blame us for high product prices. We clerks don't control this either. (Still, as I rang up waterbed sheets at $32.00, a woman made snide comments toward me.)

(5) Yes I've mentioned women a lot, but women customers seem the worse. They're tougher to sell, and harder to please, than men. They may expect more from the product. (Buying bubble-bath salts, an imposing lady asked, "but will it really suds up in hard water" whereas a strong-and-silent man just bought the salts without comment.). And women also expect more from the clerk. They may want special deals on products (special price on three towels on sale for a two-for-one sale). A few even want special services from the clerk. (A woman asked me to hold her two-year-old, carry her three large K-Mart packages, then asked "can the store open early tomorrow so I can shop before work?")

I enjoy my job, but a little more courtesy and cooperation from some customers, might lead to a lot better service for them…

Sorry, but I like the original. It truly flows with creativity of the writer's tone both angry and fair. No "Transitions" or "Thesis-statements," which would obtrude. This way, we re-create the experience of the frustrated clerk as she flows through problem after problem as she does during a busy day on the shop floor! A "natural cut," would be ruined by crimping and corralling it into Essay-form.

Actually I'd agree personally—but how about a *"both-and"* approach, **correlating contraries**?! "Storytelling" is big today (memoirs too, etc.). But while the (+)upside is *effective personal vividness*, the (-)downside of "Telling Our Stories" is (too often) *babbling unanalyzed meandering claims not worked for their meaning*… Let's have both—the intuitive original on the left-hand, and also the ability to "dress up the act" for a needed Formal Report to the Authorities on the right hand...
I submit that the **15-C** principles I installed in the *rewrite*—**Conceptualizing** the subpoints, **Crystallizing** those points, and **Concretizing** the examples—do something needed in much formal workplace communication.

[11.] <u>OK, Finally, Your Truest Stand Here Please</u>? **How do you <u>really</u> feel about the 15-C?**
[<u>Mild Polite version</u>: "well, it seems a very efficient checklist-reminder for key issues in good expository thinking-writing." <u>Wild Passionate version</u>: an immensely-powerful tactic for confronting savage Chaos, civilizing it toward Comprehensibility—defeating the foe of Ignorance and Obscurity, to shape and deliver the harvest of Truth or anyhow validity! {Oh, and excuse Mixed Metaphors herein… }]

|#|#+|+#+|+|+#|+|#+|+|+|#+|+|+#+#+|||++|#+|#+#|##+|+|#+|+|#+|#+|#+#+|+|#|#+|+|#|+|#+|#|##+#|+|#+|+#|+|+|+#|+#+|+|+#|+|#|#+|+#|+|#+|+#||+|#++|+#|+|+#|||

[11.] "Sargasso Sea": mid-passage Confusion on the WHOLE-TEXT Level of LARGER (Book-Length) Texts…..

THE PROBLEM/OPPORTUNITY HERE: Perhaps too many <u>longer</u> texts fall short of Unity-Coherence-Emphasis in an identifiable pattern? Not really basic in**Completeness**, but instead, <u>errors in "5Crystallization"</u> *["Just exactly what is your POINT here and is it possibly in some series of plural points??"]* And then <u>errors in 9Con-Sequence</u>. Less in Structure, than in Frequency; excess repetition occurs. *["Are you saying something new here or are you repeating a prior idea and if so WHY please??"]* In short, where really have we been, are we now, are we going?

ANALOGY: the *Sargasso Sea* is a region of the ocean in which one may drift in calms and eddy about in circles…

A jungle of content. A tangle of information, ideas, but with no footpath or signpost-map. Neither thesis nor its points are stated explicitly lucidly (**Crystallized**), but are waded into vaguely [{ "What will be the point and points of this Chapter, anyhow?" }] …..ideas may be *repeated and repeated* <u>but</u> neither for gradual cumulative development, nor yet for reinforcement, nor yet for tone-control, but apparently just "for" sludgy redundancy [{ "I've heard that before; is this a new point or not?" }] …..<u>structure</u> or **Con-Sequence** of the murky points not apparent at all, not via chronology, not via least-to-most-important or the reverse, not via reader-need-to-know, not via any other item from the menu for or "structure-form-organization-pattern-arrangement," a key issue and tool indeed!

293

At the start: is the thesis stated? The points to come? In the middle: are new points, explicit enough to be seen as such? And the next one follows—or, do we drift around not knowing is this a new point or an elaboration or what? At the end, are things pulled together, or just stopped-and-dropped?

EXAMPLES: the first ironically exemplifying the very pitfall it explains, the second ideally correcting itself …

[1.] Too many longer texts don't organize well. They drift into the Middle portion without we the readers knowing where they are going. They may state a subject but they the authors themselves may not know where they are going in the Body of the text. They'll state a point, but then go on, but to what, is it another point or not. We may lose any sense of direction or orientation if indeed there is any. The author may not even know, due to they have not thought out their material enough ahead of time. So we are reading along and encounter another point or the next one or is it really new or the old thing said again and if so why is it being said again. Plus where are we going, the orientation overall is unclear, and come to think of it it is unclear generally as well as specifically what the point is right at hand at the moment. What it is as well as how it relates to the previous and the subsequent following points if any. This can get wearying and confusing in the Main Body of the text where the points should be made. It is something seen in many longer texts and could be remedied by the author's better thinking out the material ahead of time and then of course drafting it to show those connections. Especially what the point is at the time and is the next one a new one or not and if repeated why, for emphasis or development, or just carelessly which is redundant…

[2.] Mid-portions of longer texts too often shortfall into a really bad kind of non-elucidated eddying repetitiveness of points which are not clearly identified as such, as ideas. This confuses readers, unnecessarily, as to idea and also process.

1. Points are not made explicit, identified as such when they first appear ("The second advantage of hamsters is their friendliness").

2. Points are then repeated or echoed or restated, but too often for the "bad" purpose of careless redundancy, rather than for either of the two useful purposes of reiteration: reinforcing of key point, or elaborating development of said point.

3. We do not sense transitions, when a new section is being arrived at (related to #1 above, the new—fourth or seventh—point arriving).

4. Overall, navigation aids are absent. We do not know "where we are going, where we are now, where we are still to go, where we have been, and where we are still to go." This guidance need not be done mechanically, but via gentle signposting for orientation.

All the above sloppy wandering suggests that the writer has not painstakingly <u>thought through</u> the material to arrive a distinct points . And then has not <u>written through</u> or worked to embody this unity-coherence-emphasis in the language via cohesion, structure, and the like…

EXAMPLES. What are instances of **longer, book-length texts** which commit these large-scale 15-C errors?

"Almost everywhere." *But I do recall the following especially…*

--<u>The Pencil</u>, by engineer HENRY PETROSKI. Some mid-section chapters, especially what is the current Point here and when are we moving on to the next of just how many Points anyhow?

--<u>Rules for Radicals</u>, by activist SAUL ALINSKY. I started reading but soon stopped, the opening seemed a circular warmup repeating what was not even Crystallized as a main point…

--<u>Reader-Response Theory</u> by LOUISE ROSENBLATT. The same "bingo" of immersion in vagued ideas with little forward motion. (Alas, because a good topic, too…)

--<u>Goodbye, Gutenberg</u> by VALERIE KIRSCHENBAUM. Again, the text stated her thesis, how computers now can produce designer-books with lavish color. And how she came to do this, her personal story. And then again the point. And then again her story…

. . . . .

|#|#+|+#+|+|+#|+|#+|+|+|#+|+|+|#+#+||+|+#+|#+#|##+|+|#+|+|+|#+|#+#+|#||+|+#|#+|+|#+|#||##+#|+|#+|+#|+|+|+|#+|+#||+|+#|+|#|#+|+|#+|+#|+#+|+#|+|+#|||

[12.] "The POWER of Exposition…" To expand topic
[A] past Narrative incident, past [B] simple Exposition

SEE "II" FULL version: XX Original and rewrite, "Transvestite in the Lingerie Store" expanded to "Customer Relations in Retail"… Also the earlier X "Sexual Orientation" paragraph vastly expanded…

|#|#+|+#+|+|+#|+|#+|+|+|#+|+|+|#+#+||+|+#+|#+#|##+|+|#+|+|+|#+|#+#+|#||+|+#|#+|+|#+|#||##+#|+|#+|+#|+|+|+|#+|+#||+|+#|+|#|#+|+|#+|+#|+#+|+#|+|+#|||

[13.] PEDAGOGICAL. Possible Assignments, Goals …

Pedagogy, how the 15-C is taught, obviously depends on the learning situation. So, I can only suggest three ploys. (12.A.) Level of command. (12.B.) Exercise of the "Same Game" (12.C.) Demonstrate Doing-an-Essay from Experience [x: "Mobile Home Living"] But these three do seem key for *cinching the principles above…*

SEE "II" FULL version: for expansion of the above.

|#|#+|+#+|+|+#|+|#+|+|+|#+|+|+|+#+#++|||++|#+|#+#|##+|+|#+|+|+|#+|#+|#+#+|+|#|#+|+|#|+|+#+|#||##+#|+|#+|+#|+|+|+#|+|+#|+|#|#+|+#|+|#+|+#|+|#+#+|+#|+|+#|||

[14.] ADVANCED skills:

[14.A.] "Scope and Treatment" of a Subject…

The difficult matter of proportion of concepts and concrete elements. This is really "*advanced* **6Calibration**." For a quick preview, note the bewildering variety possible of a statement (about early oppression of a minority group). Variety which however can be systemized for learners…

SEE "II" FULL version: (X) Gallery of "minority oppression," rewritten three times to vary scope…

|#|#+|+#+|+|+#|+|#+|+|+|#+|+|+|+#+#++|||++|#+|#+#|##+|+|#+|+|+|#+|#+|#+#+|+|#|#+|+|#|+|+#+|#||##+#|+|#+|+#|+|+|+#|+|+#|+|#|#+|+#|+|#+|+#|+|#+#+|+#|+|+#|||

[14.B.] Advanced Tactics for Each of the Fifteen "C"-Elements …

SEE "II" FULL version: Classify-&-Divide, NEON formula, Specific Detailing, Structure, Parallelism & Repetition, Syntax, De-Wording.…

|#|#+|+#+|+|+#|+|#+|+|+|#+|+|+|+#+#++|||++|#+|#+#|##+|+|#+|+|+|#+|#+|#+#+|+|#|#+|+|#|+|+#+|#||##+#|+|#+|+#|+|+|+#|+|+#|+|#|#+|+#|+|#+|+#|+|#+#+|+#|+|+#|||

[14.C.] GALLERY and LABS: ample examples of Beast-and-Beauty versions of Bungled vs. more-Beautiful Exposition. For discussion, for reworking …

X (Essay/Memo/Letter) "**Brookfield High School Needs An Auditorium**" [average text, improved; then, micro-brief versions…]

X (Essay) "**Having your Mother as a Teacher**" [amateur-sloppy *non*-6Calibration!]…

X (Book Editor) "**Evelyn Waugh's Books**" [wasted column space vs. "pack it in all in small" via the *Same Game*]…

X (Internet Comment) "**Gay Fiction to Read: An Introduction**" [wasted vagueness!]…

X (Letter to Student Newspaper) "**Library Noise**" [**13wordiness** rampant; can reduce to 20% or even less!]…

X Complaint: "**Alpha Supermarket is Inferior**" [more scrambled than the food shelves]…

X (Lyrical Mood-Piece) "**Who Has It Easy?**" [non-15-C form but some elements: **11Cohesion** etc.]…

X (Diversity Education) "**The Need for Diversity**" [but we perish with **13Wordiness, 7no Concretization, 9noSequence or Structure**, plus Sargasso-Sea eddying-around!]…

X (Classic Five-Paragraph Student Theme) "**High School Courses Should Be More Challenging**" [perfect instance: totally **15Correct**, *totally dead and deadening not to mention insultingly-fake…*]

X (Letter to Editor) "**The Trenton Connection**" [For *pure dessert-fun*: ludicrously-opaque blatt, revamped to *some* clarity…]

X (English 101 paper) "**Dostoyevsky and Values**" [if *any*one can find *any* **Conceptual Coherence/Cohesion** here, *let me know…*]

[End of Tool-KIT on "15-C," Expository Elucidation]

|#|#+|+#+|+|+#|+|#+|+|+|#+|+|+|+#+#++|||++|#+|#+#|##+|+|#+|+|+|#+|#+|#+#+|+|#|#+|+|#|+|+#+|#||##+#|+|#+|+#|+|+|+#|+|+#|+|#|#+|+#|+|#+|+#|+|#+#+|+#|+|+#||

"Diversity Education" :
Minority, Multicultural Perspectives—*and* Competencies

|~#+~|#+|+~#|+##+|~#+|#+~|~+#|#+|~+#|~+#|~|#+~#|+#|~+|#+|+|#+|~+#|~+#|~+#|+~|#+|~+#|~+|#~+|#+#~|#+|+~##|+#|~#+|~+#||||

[1.] TABLE OF CONTENTS of this module:

|~#+~|#+|+~#|+##+|~#+|#+~|~+#|#+|~+#|~+#|~|#+~#|+#|~+|#+|+|#+|~+#|~+#|~+#|+~|#+|~+#|~+|#~+|#||

[2.] RATIONALE: why a different approach to this initiative?

THE IDEA: Much "diversity initiative" on college campuses seems to deal with improving the campus climate here and now, for minority students. This is well-and-good *to say the least*; but here we emphasize empowering majority students for later on… *And in two ways not usually implemented today.*

THE NEED: PROPOSAL: To better train *majority* students for *more-competent dealing* with "diversity" situations out there in *real* life *after* graduation, **supplement the current procedures in "diversity education"** [often only = **(1)** taking courses earmarked for the "diversity" requirement; **(2)** optionally attending this-or-that diversity event; and **(3)** that's it!] **with offering these students a 'tool-kit' of the best and most effective explanatory concepts about diversity from social science.** [Stereotype vs. Sociotype… **Relativism, Cultural versus Moral… Selective Perception… Affinity Impulse… Aversive Racism…** and **others,** see below…]This fortification could truly empower majority-students with desired competence to "hit the ground running" to *better deal with multicultural situations* in Personal life, Vocationally on the job, and as Citizen in community, "later in real life" which is *the educational goal* anyhow…

FOUNDATIONS: --This follows **the model of EDUCATION** as not Old-School as usual, goal "what to Know, Believe, and Do," but as the New-Think model, goal "how to Think Things Through."
--It also partakes of **the concept of "PSYCHOTHERAPY"** in one essential sense. Namely, "bad things happen for certain reasons, often unknown; to truly know why, gives us some power to change or anyhow to manage our response, if we choose to." (This again is differs from indoctrination into any

OUR CLAIM/HOPE: These procedures can lead to *true not thin* **"active or student-centered learning."** They can lead to benign not bogus **"empowerment"** of the student (= not just "empowered" to recognize social injustice and fight it"—a liberal-radical ideology—but truly empowered to make one's own *better-informed* choices *wherever* they lead, and be able to employ potent concepts as tools.)

The CURRENT SITUATION on campuses: *[May not be 100% true for all schools of course...]*	Possible DESIRABLE IMPROVEMENT: *["our approach here in a nutshell..."]*
[1.] --Learns facts about minorities. [2.] --Shares personal experiences… [2.] --Perhaps receives indoctrination into "tolerance-acceptance-celebration…" *[May fall back on culturally-learned biases!]* **RESULT:** may be *problematic, unfinished?*… --"I don't really know how to deal with that person from that minority…" --"A <u>co-worker came out as gay</u>. We're supposed to not just tolerate but respect and celebrate. But I have a gut-level *disgust*. What to do? Forget it? Brainwash myself? Isn't civil tolerance quite enough? And does 'respect' sometimes mean not genuine response, but just, like, mechanically, 'say everyone's okay, to avoid trouble'?" --"Can <u>women do math as well as men</u>, or are they less capable? Is it all social discrimination? But what about studies in male and female thinking styles? They say free speech and thinking is good, but is this too hot a topic to discuss?" --"Listen, <u>a Black woman came late to class every single day</u>. Are we supposed to let her off the hook? What to do?..." --"<u>They say it's all relative but aren't there some basic values</u>? Hindus worship cows, some tribes mutilate their women, Eskimos abandon their aged grandparents. How to tell?..." --"<u>Is it really wrong to prefer to socialize with my own kind</u>? I *just don't relate* with all the lively Latinos in the trailer court. How can this be prejudice really...?" --"And <u>people are different, but is it prejudiced to say so</u>? I mean, look at Blacks in basketball and jazz, Asians in certain fields, and you can't say we're all the same. And you can't tell me that some Arabs are not excitable and non-logical. I don't think so…" --"Studies say that <u>most effeminate boys do turn out to be gay</u>. But should we not even mention this for fear of offending or something? And they say that <u>every stereotype contains a grain of truth</u>. But what about the one that 'gay men are child molesters'? That is scientifically 100% false as such; pedophiles are distinct…" --"How to respond? I did the 'Privilege Walk' but am I supposed to feel guilty if I don't 'work for social change and reducing oppression' and the like? *Sorry, but...*"	[N.] --Offering students **a "tool-belt" of higher-order concepts-about-diversity drawn from social science.** --**Power, Privilege…** --**Oppression, types of…** --**Minority Group Definition…** --**Prejudice: causes of…** --**Stereotype, vs. SOCIOtype…** --**Selective Perception…** --**"Surplus Visibility"…** --**Stereotype Override…** --**Affinity Impulse: In/Out Groups…** --**Relativism: not just Moral, but Cultural…** **RESULT:** *more effective?*: --"Aha, I see how I saw the Latino student was always late to class but overlooked many late White students also: it was my **"Selective Perception"**! --"Aha, that feminist professor isn't overemphasizing her cause, it's **"Surplus Visibility"** or only *seeming* to, or perhaps she is but because of understandable **"Obsessive Concern,** one of the traits of minority victimization." --"Blacks are not simply 'happy musical children,' but truly, great rhythm and jazz abilities *did* arise within Black culture: aha, **Stereotype** and **Sociotype** *are* distinct!"

[3.] PRE-VIEW: A Dramatized Glimpse of the Plan in Action:

The Real-World "Exigency":	Two Possible Responses: ["P.C.," or *prior prejudices*]:	[*]the Tool for Empowering Insight:	"Therapeutic" personal response resulting:
[1.] "That BLACK woman student <u>always</u> comes to class a few minutes late!"	ONE Mustn't be prejudice[d]... TWO [{ Well *We All*	"Hmm, you don't know much about **Selective Perception**, do you? How many *White* students also	"Hmm, you're right—that doesn't make her right, and I still think some Blacks are hostile, but I now better

	Know that Blacks are lazy and also hostile… }]	came late and did you notice?"	understand why. And I am not 'bad,' just misperceiving…"
[2.] I simply <u>dislike</u> HISPANICS, their noise, color etc. I just don't like to deal with them or their culture. Why should I have to?	ONE Oh, you are "prejudiced"—we must Tolerate Accept and Celebrate all Diversity! TWO [{ Well who does like those wxtbxcks anyhow… }]	Well you don't know about the **"Affinity Impulse"** do you. It's natural normal etc. to prefer one's kind, to an extent. Probably a legacy of our early history—tribes and bands had to establish In-Group and Out-Group boundaries for survival.	"Hmm, helps me see I am not evil, it's somewhat human. Now I can stay distant or explore the Other as I wish…"
[3.] "Fred claims that <u>I</u> stereotype minorities. I felt that the IRISH have a gift of lyrical gab, BLACKS are great in jazz music and long-distance running, WOMEN better in interpersonal relating, JEWS are not pushy but very achieving, INDIAN children win spelling bees, etc. Fred says I'm <u>stereotyping</u>."	ONE: "Yes you are also prejudiced. After all, we are all equal! Shame on you!" TWO: "For gosh sake, *get real* and smell the coffee. Differences *do* exist. Irish *are* drunks, Blacks *do* have a natural sense of rhythm. Oh, and one-quarter of Black males ages 18-35 *are* lawbreakers! Jews *are* pushy, and women—well,… *Get with it.*"	Well you don't know much about the difference between **"Stereotype and Sociotype,"** do you now… [Fact is, that <u>women and men</u> *are* different, in linear vs. connective perception-perceptions… Fact is, that <u>West Africans</u> *do* excel in long-distance running (see the data)… *and more…* This does not necessarily mean *moral* superiority, either! See **Relativism: Cultural vs. Moral!**	"Hmmm, this is helpful. To distinguish traits of a group in reality, from probably-false images of a group, is difficult, but useful. <u>Some races—Asiatics—respond differently to medicines.</u> Etc. …"
[4.] That guy seemed okay until I found out he was <u>gay</u>. Then I realized he was really effeminate and also predatory after all. Plus his work rating fell after he came out, proving gays are incompetent."	ONE. Mustn't be prejudice[d] even toward "those people." TWO [{ We All Know that *fxgs* and *dxkxs* are like that. Plus they try to come on to you—or so I feel… }]	Well you don't know much about **"Stereotype-Override"** (we also call it **"Backward Re-Visioning,"**) *do* you now! (Remember when the speaker gave a good lecture, Floyd liked it, then found out the speaker was Jewish: "Oh, *well* then,…")	Hmm, I do see. Now I can relax more, and also treat the guy better. But without "celebrating his diversity" and the like! A step at a time. Good…
[5.] "That professor is <u>always</u> yapping about yer precious LATINA culture and the injustices against it. Why can't she give it a <u>rest</u>?! Is she asking for Special Rights, Privileges, Attention?"	ONE. Mustn't be prejudice[d]. Must not just tolerate but also respect and indeed celebrate all cultures. TWO [{ Well, you get a *woman* in there, always bitching anyhow, you got *double* trouble…}]	Well you don't know much about either **"Surplus Visibility"** (=moderate minority comment gets exaggerated in majority ears!), nor also about **"Traits of Minority Victimization:** Obsessive Concern," *do* you now!!	Well, okay. Still, I don't have to buy into it. But I understand better why it annoys me!

~#+~|#+|+~#|+##+|~#+|#+~|~+#|#+|~+#|~+#|~+#|~#+~#|+#|~+|#+|+|#+|~+#|~#|~+#|+~|#+|~+#|~+|#~+~|#+#~|#+|+~##|+#|~#+|~+#||||

298

[4.] CONS: Frequently Asked Questions—or Voiced Objections!
[

1. *Cold intellectual comprehending won't carry the day*. We need **experience**, also **personal** emotional responses, also interactive contacts! ["A Day in a Wheelchair," "Brown Eyes & Blue Eyes," etc.]
[Response: of course, but concrete experience is impoverished without knowing the keystone concepts involved also...]

2. If your approach is so great, *why don't more schools already do more of it*? Relatedly, why aren't recognized specialist experts in "diversity education" doing this already—if it's so good?
[Response: low priority for Poor Old Diversity Studies. Also, the paradigm of Teaching Thinking is still sidelined.]

3. What is *really your own motivation here*? Are you a minority-group member yourself pushing your agenda?
[Response: I am pushing Teaching Thinking—to AID Diversity Ed.. My minority status is only to enrich the evidence...]

4. But just *what is wrong with a more assertive approach? (A) Attitude: "indoctrinating into the ideology of tolerance*, acceptance, celebration of diversity"? And (B) Actions:. behaviorial change, educating for not just personal but institutional change, improving society?
[Response: to us, indoctrination is anathema to true education, on Principle. Plus Pragmatically *it doesn't work, last...*]

5. And *what is wrong with earmarking courses as satisfying a diversity requirement*?
[Response: like teaching cooking. One teacher does B-B-Q, the other vegan, a third stir-fry. Genteel uneven chaos...]

6. *Your approach of a "tool-kit" seems simplistic*, like an instant-fix mechanical add-on. Don't we instead need four years of gradual learning about diversity and acceptance and the like?
[Response: you probably confuse Tools, with Rules—as so many educators do. These concepts are catalysts...]

7. But *how exactly would you implement* this program? **[Response: you are so Old-School. Want a 1-2-3 formula. I don't hardly know. What part of this do YOU Accept and Adopt—Alter, Adjust—etc.?...]**

~#+~|#+|+~#|+###+|~#+|#+~|~+#|#+~|~+#|~+#|~|#+~#|+#|~+|#+|+|#+|~+#|~+#|+~|#+|~+#|~+|#~+~|#+#~|#+|+~##|+#|~#+|~+#||||

[5.] Tool-KIT of Skills.   [A] "*Brief*' Headline-Roster of:

I BACKGROUND: GENERIC for all situations

1.1. Communication 101: sender, message, receiver... Ability to listen, consider, respond.
1.2. "Dispositions" Fight or be fair-minded? See own biases plus other side? Be candid but civil?
1.3. CHANGE comes slowly and in "layers, levels"
1.4. MOTIVATIONS Why people hold their views, change them—and often do *not*, even *after* education!

II. More for "DIVERSITY"-situations:

2.1. POWER, Privilege
2.2. "Minority Group" = four definitions of it
2.3. Oppression" = five elements or aspects of it
2.4. "Levels" Individual-personal, plus also Structural-institutional
2.5. Traits of Minority Victimization
2.6. Prejudice, including causes, functions
2.7. Stereotype. "Stereotype vs. *Socio*type"
2.8. Relativism: Cultural, & Moral
2.9. Selective Perception
2.10. Aversive Racism
2.11. Surplus Visibility
2.12. Stereotype Override (A.K.A. "Retrospective Re-Visioning)
2.13. "Affinity Impulse" (In- and Out-Groups; Dislike of Unlike; Hierarchy)
2.14. Degree of FULL HUMAN-ITY Status. (Complete Citizen, Perfected Person—or "Lesser Breed"?)
2.15. OTHER CONCEPTS, To Develop:

1. HIDDEN ANTAGONIZERS
2. FUNDAMENTAL ATTRIBUTION ERROR
3. EFFECTS: "HALO," "HORN," etc.
4. COGNITIVE DISSONANCE
5. "DEFINITION OF THE SITUATION"
6. STEREOTYPE LIFT, also STEREOTYPE FEAR

~#~|#+|+~#|+##+|~#+|#+~|~+#|#+|~+#|~#+~#|+#|~+|#+|+|#+|~+#|~+#|~#|+~|#+|~+#|~+|#~+~|#+#~|#+|+~##|+#|~#+|~+#||||

[5.] Tool-KIT of Skills.   [B] Repeated, "*Full-Dress*" view:

I General Mechanisms: generic, prior, global skills:

1.3. CHANGE: How major social change works slowly, and in "layers"…

1.4. MOTIVATIONS. Why people believe as they do, and do not change their beliefs even when "educated" in the issue…

II Specific Mechanisms: domain of "diversity/minority" sphere:

2.1. **Power, Privilege   2.2. Minority Group, definition of: 2.3. "Oppression":** unjust discrimination: five distinct categories: [Legal-Physical… Occupational-Financial… Institutional… Sociocultural… Psychological/Internalized… "If a homosexual showed his true colors, outside of certain protective cosmopolitan circles, he could expect to be idled, shunned, confined, medicated, beaten,[excommunicated], or killed." – J. RAUCH.

2.4. **Levels, individual and System: they differ, both exist!**

2.5. **Traits of Minority Victimization": obsessive concern, minstrelization, etc.**

2.6. **Prejudice, including causes, functions   2.7. Stereotype. ➔ "Stereotype vs. Sociotype."**

> GUIDELINE. *Know* that "Stereotype" is = fixed usually *false or simplistic* image of a group. "Sociotype" is = a description of the nature of a group (identity, behaviors, etc.)—or at least of "X %" of individuals within the group!—which is to an extent *"true" objectively* in that it is "what is in fact the case." This distinction, is unknown by many people, is difficult to make, is frowned upon today, can be misused, <u>but</u> can be useful after all.

2.8. Two Relativisms: Cultural and Moral.

> GUIDELINE. *Know* the distinction between <u>cultural</u> relativism and <u>moral</u> relativism. *Know* the power of pure C.R. to observe objectively, explain accurately, evaluate fairly!

2.9. Selective Perception 2.10. "Aversive Racism" 2.11. "Surplus Visibility"

> GUIDELINE. *Know* the tendency to <u>misperceive a minority action as excessive when</u> it may be simply median or appropriate after all. *Be able* to identify when one may overreact due to preference-for-continuity, etc.

2.12. "Stereotype Override," also "Retrospective Rewriting"

> GUIDELINE. *Know of* the infrequent but quite-existent tendency for majority people to "re-perceive and re-vise" their images of some minority person whom they already knew, but not in their minority status. *Be able to* "correct a new distortion" if and as needed.

> GALLERY. Examples of how a person-to-person image is stigmatized when minority identity is uncovered:
> --<u>Homophobia.</u> [1] "Knew a co-worker for six months, then found out he was gay, now suddenly he seems different, dangerous" [INSTANCE: the FRENCH film Le Placard [The Closet]] …[2] Or, the gay person came out at work, suddenly his ratings dropped from "10" to 6 or 7 [EXAMPLE: actual case of Sgt. L. MATLOVITCH in the U.S. Air Force, ca. 1980] … [3] Or, a university professor came out as gay: some colleagues then thought that he was "oversexual"; or "not to be trusted with students"; or, "a *better* teacher in some ways"; or, "obsessive about his identity," etc. --<u>Race.</u> "I speak to a person on the phone, he seems a competent professional. He visits the office: I discover that he is Black. Suddenly my positive impressions of him get *roiled up and disturbed…*" --<u>Anti-Semitism.</u> My somewhat-provincial UNCLE attended a psychiatrist's lecture. He thought it was good. Then he learned that the speaker was <u>Jewish</u>. "Ohh, he's JEWish?!!" intoned my UNCLE… *So much for his earlier good opinion of the speaker…* --<u>National Ethnocentrism.</u> "A Moroccan in Europe was thought to be Italian, and people befriended him; *but* when they learned his origin, then *avoided* him." --<u>Ageism.</u> [1] "In grad school I often socialized with some students age 22—*but* when a bar-check revealed I was 26, they dropped me abruptly"… [2] "When I started teaching, I looked young like a student, campus personnel (e.g., secretaries in other departments) initially treated me brusquely—*but* suddenly changed and behaved respectfully as soon as I revealed my status (appearance the same)!" --<u>Social Class, Occupation.</u> "High school students giving me a lift in their car (I had had

a flat tire on the Interstate) chatted easily and relaxedly with me—*but* then when I said I was a teacher, at once *fell silent, became distant...*"

2.13. "Affinity Impulse" (In-Group & Out-Group) ("Dislike of the Unlike")

"I don't like to socialize with those people." Is this biased? Perhaps our evolutionary past "trained" us in preferring our own in-group Tribe, and suspiciously fearing the Others, the Outsiders—for sheer group survival.

2.14. Degree of Full Human-ity Status. "Proper or more Perfect-ed Person, Complete Citizen"—or, a "Lesser Inferior Breed"?

EXAMPLES. First a subtle, then more obvious, instances of "de-personing" the minorities in question:

-----[On the issue of legalizing same-sex marriage:] "If homosexual love is "as deep and worthy" [i.e., not *shallow, unworthy, second-rate,* etc.] as heterosexual love, and if their children are deserving of as much social support as those of heterosexuals, there's no reason not to allow SSM. Legalizing SSM is the "long-overdue correction of a moral anomaly that *dehumanizes and excludes* a significant portion of the human race. Homosexuals deserve better conditions than *strained condescension* and *fickle toleration.*" [-- THE NEW REPUBLIC, 2000]

-----**Traditional British Army Personnel-Designations:** "Officers and their Ladies; Sergeants and their Wives; Enlisted Men and their Women"

-----**Sign in a Park in Singapore (during colonial occupation):** "No Dogs or Chinese Allowed in the Park"

-----**ANECDOTE.** It is said that some aristocratic ladies in the old South, did not hesitate to undress in front of their Black servants—feeling that the lackeys were "non-persons," therefore no indecency.

-----**LITERATURE.** And we have the famous passage in MARK TWAIN'S Huckleberry Finn. HUCK is late arriving at his aunts for a visit. They asked what kept him, did the river steamboat go aground? No, HUCK says, they blew out a cylinder-head. "Good gracious! anyone hurt? "No'm. Killed a nigger." "Well, it's lucky; because sometimes people do get hurt. Two years ago last Christmas, [a relative was on a boat which blew a head and crippled a man...]" ----

-----**ANECDOTE.** A disabled person, in a wheelchair, perhaps slightly speech-impaired, but mentally-alert and capable, is moved to a service counter by the attendant. The clerk speaks only to the attendant, quite ignoring the disabled person. "Well, will he want to have the form filled out now?" and the like…

2.15 and onward. Other concepts to be developed...

[6.] The issue of INDOCTRINATION. Concept of "THERAPY":

QUOTATION. "People don't change because or when others tell them that they should change, they change (if they do) when they tell themselves that they must change." [-- SOURCE]

[7.] ANNEX: readings to elucidate...

(1) Reggie's Rants: In March 1998, a local professional football star (and ordained minister) addressed the Wisconsin Legislature in a speech which became temporarily-infamous. Following is a paraphrased excerpt from a journalistic account of the event.
Homosexuality is a sin, not to be compared with Blacks. It's a decision, it's not a race. People from all different ethnic backgrounds live in this lifestyle. But people from all different ethnic backgrounds also are liars and cheaters and malicious and back-stabbing. Why did God create varied races? Each has certain gifts: --Blacks are gifted at worship and celebration. In church they jump up and down and really get into it._--Whites are good at organization, building businesses, tapping into money._--Hispanics are gifted in family structure, and can put 20 or 30 people in one home._--Japanese and other Asians are inventive, and can turn a television into a watch._--Native American Indians are into spirituality, but also are militarily strategic or sneaky...

➔ **END of "I" BRIEF version of "Diversity Education" for Teaching Thinking. For "II" FULL version, see parent-product Mind-Play, or free-standing Brochure itself from Wonderside Productions LLC.....**

~#+~|#+|+~#|+##|~#+|#+~|~+#|#+|~+#|~+#|~|#+~#|+#|~+|#+|+|#+|~+#|~+#|~+#|~+|#+|~+#|~+|#~+~|#+#~|#+|+~##|+#|~#+|~+#||||

[{ **END of module on "Diversity Multi-Cultural Education" via thinking …** }]

"PRIOR BACKGROUND BASICS"
APP. #5: *foundational* skills...

|#+#|+|#+#|+|#|+|#+|+|#|+|+|#+|+|++|#+|+|#|+|#+#|+|#|+|#+#|+|#+#|+|#+#|+|+|#+|+|#|+|#+|#|+|#+|+|#|+|#+|#+|#|+|#+|#|+|#+|+|#|+|#+|#+||#+|+|#|+|#|+|#|+|#+|#+||#+||

Table of Contents

|#+#|+|#+#|+|#|+|#+|+|#|+|+|#+|+|++|#+|+|#|+|#+#|+|#|+|#+#|+|#+#|+|#+#|+|+|#+|+|#|+|#+|#|+|#+|+|#|+|#+|#+|#|+|#+|#|+|#+|+|#|+|#+|#+||#+|+|#|+|#|+|#|+|#+|#+||#+||

[1.] INTRODUCTION. "Prior background default" thinking?

THE ISSUE. In *any* subject or skill whatsoever (not just in "teaching/learning advanced thinking"), there exists the (1) **actual knowledge** about it—but some of which may well be such a thing as (2) **"prior basics,"** or default-type knowledge. Also called: **preliminary clarifications... background information** (to help "learn how to do")... **Prior,** to orient, to clarify, to avoid misconceptions ignorances and bungles... Presumably **foundational,** needed in all thinking-tasks.

EXAMPLES. Don't all student-thinkers need to be clear about such super-basic issues as: **Truth, Knowledge, Authority?**... The **"Relativism"** pitfall today... **Personal**-Subjective *"versus"* Scientific[?]-**Objective Ways of Knowing**... **Competence:** criteria, standards: bad, just, and good thinking?... **Induction vs. Deduction**... **Reasoning vs. Rationalizing**... And **more**...

ANALOGIES. I can think of these prior, basic ploys as **1.** *Default-Tools* (basic "kit" issued to every "employee")... **2.** *Navigational aids*... or, **3.** in re personal health: **3A.** *vaccinations* against a misconception, **3B.** *vitamin supplements* or **3C.** *calisthenics* where needed to strengthen a weakness... [This is "I" BRIEF View; for "II" FULL see below...]

WHY IMPORTANT? I conjecture that such shortfalling may exist in education today. Schooling may be overlooking such "prior basics." (Instruction may either *ignore* much in re thinking—or simply *only exhort-or-encourage* better thinking—or plunge directly into *"Critical* Thinking 101," logic-reasoning-argument: which is solid, but incomplete...) And current resource-materials don't seem to adequately address this issue of "seedbed" thinking skills. Worst, students may merely "pick these up en route," haphazardly if at all. True, many learners eventually pick up many of the skills. But I envision to review these basics might be a *catalyst* to *greatly accelerate* competence. "Unawarenesses and misconceptions about, say relativism, or ways of knowing, or personal/objective issue, etc."—clarified and saving hours of gradual partial individual learning, even re-inventing the wheel..." *Hence this module*...

GUIDELINE/GOAL: Specific <u>courses</u>, also general <u>programs</u> (and individuals: = interested teachers & self-motivated advanced students) can *consider* which if any "prior background basics" should be identified, made Explicit, and taught or at least proffered to, beginning students...

TWO EXAMPLES. To show: What *are* these proto-skills? Are they really needed?

[1.] **Reading a Text: "X-Ray Vision" Taught in One Class Hour, or Less**... Distressed by the fact that my Freshman English 101 STUDENTS could not even read-for-the-ideas in a simple student essay on "a job I held," I pursued this issue and came to find that *a half-hour* in teaching the unarguably "prior-default" skill of <u>précis-writing</u>, could truly "empower" the students to *read texts with x-ray eyes* for the clear, and the implied or amateur-unclear, concepts in the text.

> [EXAMPLE: Could move from [1.] the *empty-vague* version:
> "The lifeguard tells us of the many problems in his job, including hot sun and bratty kids," .....
>
> [2.] to the *rich-distilled* version:
> "Challenges of being a beach lifeguard include the natural world (hot sun, dirty beaches to clean), and people (the clients: bratty kids, overprotective mothers) and peers (tardy or uncooperative staff)"]

[SEE Appendix #3, Conceptualizing 101, B.P The Basic Pedagogy...]

[2.] **Argument, Discussion: Freedom from "Back-&-Forth" Bafflement**... The following scenario seems depressingly-common. A student observes <u>a half-hour debate on a current controversy</u> (animal rights, capital punishment, censorship, abortion, gun control, others). The two opponents largely talk past each other, and cannot agree, nor even clarify. The student responds, but apparently on (1) a *first simpler level* of <u>specific Critical Thinking fallacy-avoidance</u> and the like. S/he naively says: "Well, they should back their points up with facts, give good evidence. And avoid logical fallacies such as the Ad Hominem or personal argument."

> But this response utterly overlooks the higher level of **Essential Thinking!** Specifically, (2) a *second more-complex and yet "basic" level* of <u>prior unstated but determining issues—prior background issues</u>. Such as:

(#6) Reasoning vs. Rationalizing...
(#1) Dispositions: agonistic combat vs. fairminded cooperation in thinking...
(#8) "Background" Elements: motivations, world-views, implicit presuppositions, other lenses...
(#3) ... and perhaps *other* basic elements to know of, including the **Relativism Trap** ...

I propose that the unit on the PRECIS, probably saved students dozens and dozens of hours of learning this by chance as they went, and misreading texts in the bargain... Same efficiency for spotting the BACKGROUNDS to a statement, instead of endless arguing

...Wait. Interesting and more, **BUT** I don't fully grasp what skills exactly are involved? And how applied? And what needs are predominant? If you can...	**OKAY**, following is a section "introducing introductory thinking—getting basic about the basics of advanced thinking..."

|#+#|+|#+#|+#|+|#+|+#|+|+|#+|+|++|#+|+#|+#|+#|+#|+#|+#|+#+#|+|+|+#|#+|+|#+|#|+#|+#|+|#+|+#|+#|+|#+|#+|#+|||#+|+#|+#|+#|+|#+|#+|||#+||

O R I E N T A T I O N - B A R :

[1.] Intro: the very Concept previous	**[2.] Orientation: 6 issues** current	[3.] Tool-Chest: 9 items subsequent

[2.] ORIENTATION. So, SIX *basic issues about* these "basics"...

We can explore "Prior Basics" via six commonly-asked questions about them:

2.A. What *is* Background Information, anyhow?　A. by KAREN SCHREIVER, B. my own Analogies-for

2.B. Critical Responses: seven FAQs,—or rather, FVOs or "Frequently-Voiced Objections"...

2.C. *Are* there really recurrent-and-identifiable "novice misconceptions and ineptnesses" after all?

[A.] by WALTER B. AARONS,　[B.] three research-reports by B. K. BECK

2.D. But isn't "Critical Thinking" identical with P.B., or sufficient itself?

2.E. Well, what would Utopia or anyhow improvement look like, then?　X "Tale of Two Classrooms"

2.F. The nuts-&-bolts? What might be an actual Tool-KIT for Prior Basic Advanced Thinking Issues?

[2.A.] "BACKGROUND INFORMATION": valuable but sometimes absent—but what *is* it?

[1.] CLARIFICATION. Document-designer expert KAREN SCHREIVER spotlights nicely this concept:

"Reading to learn to do." This purpose for reading is characterized by engaging with the content of a document in order to acquire the **background knowledge** needed in order to do something else... [Thus, a new gardener should better start with "the differences between annuals and perennials," and not with "How deep and how far apart to plant seedlings."] Readers often need background information—concepts, models, explanations, arguments, heuristics—in order to make use of the document's content in an intelligent manner. [It is easier to specify which texts are more **"Reading To Learn"**] (e.g., *textbooks, journal articles, essays*) or **"Reading To Do"** (e.g., *procedures, decision memos, forms*), but it is not easy to say which documents are usually **"Reading To Learn To Do."** [Narrowly conceived, RTLTD has as goal, performing tasks: *using a software product* after working through the tutorial. But broadly, RTLTD can also mean] making an informed decision (*investing in the stock market*), and taking practical action (developing a *policy to reduce teen pregnancy* after learning why young women have low self-esteem...]　[-- KAREN SCHREIVER, Dynamics of Document Design]

SCHREIVER'S comment strays from Prior Basics purely, but notes that "teaching thinking" may need to identify basic issues... clarify misconceptions and unawarenesses... and lay out optional alternatives...

[2.] *ANALOGIES* can convey the *concept* of these prior-level preparatory-skills:

1. **"TOOLS."** Like *"Tapemeasures,"* or *"Swiss Army Knife,"* or some kind of *"Universal Adaptor-Fit Mechanism."*

But perhaps better--"The *standard basic Company Tool-Kit issued*, upon hiring, to every employee who comes to work for the Thinking Co., Inc.—in addition to any other specialized tools which specific employees use later on...

2. "NAVIGATIONAL AIDS"—*buoys, charts, lighthouses, radio signals, beacons*, etc. Doesn't tell the boat pilot (thinker) where to go or why, but does guide, to avoid pitfalls of shoals, etc....

3. "VACCINATIONS." Get a shot for malaise of *misconception* about **relativism, rationalizing, authority**, etc.

4. "VITAMIN SUPPLEMENTS." Get a booster to remedy a *deficiency* of information about **lenses or multiple-plural perspectives**, also **zeitgeist or climate of opinion, "just-Knowing vs. really-Knowing."**

5. "CALISTHENICS." Do some exercises to *strengthen your competence* in **Consciousness** or meta-cognition, also **Considerate** thinking or fair-minded dispositions...

6. [...but I am *not* satisfied with the above analogies to give the sense of "bedrock background default basics" well-known by teachers (probably...) who may forget that students may not know them...]

|#+#|+|#+#|+#|+|#+|+#|+|+|#+|+|++|#+|+#|+#|+#|+#|+#|+#+#|+|+|+#|#+|+|#+|#|+#|+#|+|#+|+#|+|#+|#|+#|+#|+#|+#|+|#+|#+||#+|+#|+#|+#|+|#+|#+||#+||

[2.B.] "FREQUENT QUESTIONS—AND, OBJECTIONS!, to the *very idea* of Prior Basic Ploys...

(1) Aren't you just talking about a good unit on "Critical Thinking"—logic, reasoning, argument? **Wouldn't that existing and known program suffice?**

== with respect to "C.T.," *no indeed*. C.T. commonly is solid but too limited, specialized. (It's more like "how to tap *an individual Tree* for syrup or turpentine," not "vital Tips & Hints on how to navigate *the whole complex Forest*...")

(2) But, different courses—and disciplines, and task/goals, etc.—will require different basics!

== true, *but* What *Is* Your *Point* Here?... I'd advise: "find out which," plus some basics may be "generic"...

(3) Your list of basics too-quickly grows to or blends into becoming advanced skills

== this is a danger! perhaps giving Brief and Full stages can help...

(4) Many students already know these prior basics

== and many do *not*; perhaps a diagnostic pre-test can help to ascertain need, or making the whole unit "voluntary for reference"...

(5) Danger exists of overwhelming students with too many basics in topheavy fashion

== true, again perhaps use these as reference on an as-needed basis...

(6) This is *inadvisable*. Better have students discover *as they go*, not force-fed via this *front-loaded* roster

== "experiential learning" can co-exist with avoiding re-inventing the wheel, helping accelerate basics...

(7) This is quite *unnecessary*. Students can and will and do "pick up" these basics "as they go along"

== to my own "insight/bias," this response sounds *sloppy and lax, not* truly serving the student as we might...

|#+#|+|#+#|+#|+|#+|+#|+|+|#+|+|++|#+|+#|+#|+#|+#|+#|+#+#|+|+|+#|#+|+|#+|#|+#|+#|+|#+|+#|+|#+|#|+#|+#|+#|+#|+|#+|#+||#+|+#|+#|+#|+|#+|#+||#+||

[2.C.] But, can recurrent pitfalls even be identified?...

EXAMPLE #1: RESEARCH REPORT. Apparently (and alarmingly), **common recurrent pitfalls** may well exist...

Educator ARNOLD B. AARONS wrote about researching student problems in learning better critical thinking. Did pitfalls reoccur? The investigators found that, in student thinking,

"...entirely unanticipated but very fundamental, plausible, and deeply rooted preconceptions, misconceptions, and misapprehensions (of which the investigator had no awareness) are revealed.... Each kind of misconception or erroneous mode of reasoning occurs, with remarkable reproducibility, in many individuals. Some hurdles and misconceptions are very widely prevalent. When one finds an approach or insight that overcomes a particular difficulty, that approach will be helpful not to only one but to many individuals."

I wish he had supplied specific examples! And *the problem remains*: "which basics do given specific groups of students need?" It surely must vary. Still *the opportunity also exists*, noted by AARONS' researchers. Some *some* generally-recurrent pitfalls may be found...

EXAMPLES ##2,3,4: Various studies of deficiencies...

EXAMPLE #2: Preview of larger issues perhaps needing clarification:

[1.] Learners may enter <u>quite unclear on some utterly-basic "building-block" concepts, issues</u>.
--That (A) <u>these issues themselves do exist, are to be monitored, attended to</u>...

["**Truth; knowledge; criteria; induction and deduction; competence including criteria and standards; authority...** "]
["We *do* attend to *criteria* for judgment, we don't just use opinionations"...]

--Plus that (B) <u>standard stances or moves do exist which we use to better confront them</u>.
("Here's how we can handle the issue of **"Personal vs. Objective" Thinking**: "both approaches have their strengths and their shortcomings, depending; know the Orchids and the Onions of both modes...")

[2.] Learners may be holding <u>misconceptions</u> about some issues.
[In re *criteria, veracity*: "isn't it all **relative** after all who's to say?"—
as against, say, the Perry Scheme of absolutism, naïve relativism, and committed relativism...
And, *"Personal"* knowledge, isn't that biased, subjective? Or isn't "Objective" knowledge biased also?...]]

[3.] Learners may suffer <u>unawareness of basic options</u> ; this may impede them unnecessarily.
[*Question-types differ:* they can be **Factual, Opinion, or Reasoned Judgment:**
("Alaska is cold," "Alaska is the best vacation spot," "Alaska is a business opportunity")—
suit the discussion to the type of question; don't argue taste or fact; etc.]

[4.] Learners may carry basic <u>ineptitudes</u> of greater unawarenesses.
[Naïve unawareness of the pervasiveness of **Rationalizing instead of Reasoning:**
"Well, I shall (or the writer did) back the argument up with Facts and Expert Opinions"—
but perhaps merely rationalizing a prior existing belief...]

EXAMPLE #3. RESEARCH OF MY OWN. FIRST LEVELS: *[This builds upon Aarons above and also the earlier Precis and Argument examples ...]* I myself studied "thinking" with University of Wisconsin-Whitewater Freshman English students in the 1970's. My article (in the <u>English Journal</u> in 1980) concluded that "Five Roadblocks" usually exist more often than not. Prevalent amateur pitfalls (at least then-and-there, and at least as I perceived them...) especially included:

(1) <u>Being Mesmerized by sheer factual data</u>. "S/he backs up the argument with the facts." [*No matter that the "facts" may be* insufficient-unrepresentative; or, outdated; or, from a questionable source; or, irrelevant to the argument; or, subtly misrepresented or twistily interpreted.....]

(2) <u>Uncritical Relativism</u>. "Well, who's to say who's right, after all?" [(*) This pitfall is so prevalent and pernicious, but also so easily-treatable, see "The Relativism Tangle."]

(3) <u>"Reasoning 101 Is Easy!"</u> Or, the over-simple assumption that all you need for good thinking is (A) factual proof, (B) good reasoning and logic, and (C) fallacy-avoidance. [This overlooks **Reasoning vs. Rationalizing** *and more, larger* issues which the unit would seek to confront—esp. **Backgrounds** to a statement.]

(4) <u>Confusing Just-Thinking, with Good Thinking</u>. No awareness of standards, criteria, competence in thinking. Indeed, "thinking" about the issue may mean "asking friends what they think about it." [Not bad for a collaborative start, *but*... RECALL: "Michelle's" assignment on re- designing a course assignment. She thought merely getting other peoples' opinions and thinking "deeply" about it, would do the trick...]

(5) <u>A Too-Irrational view of Science</u>. "Well, even science and scientists can be biased, too!" [But students often leaped from this important fact (science can occasionally be bad science), to a dismissive overgeneralization of all of science thus.]

EXAMPLE #4. RESEARCH OF MY OWN. SECOND LEVELS: some advanced issues ...

(6) I later saw: <u>Very poor awareness of myriad different basic **ways of knowing**</u>:

    --Science; religion/supernaturalism; cultural norms (a.k.a. "received knowledge," "tacit lore," etc.), individual judgment...

    --AND: "Experience, observation, reflection, introspection, empathy, intuition, *but also* reasoning, *then* **authority** and **criteria** (whatever *they* are), *and* **custom, general consent, argument, tradition, consensus, public opinion, science, religion or supernaturalism, conjecture and supposition and speculation.....**

    --[Let alone **lenses**: **capitalism, socialism, existentialism, monotheism, Freudianism** "or" **behaviorism** "or" **evolutionary biology** and the **cognitive sciences, aestheticism,** and the like...]

    (Admittedly, this complicated issue may quickly sprawl far beyond any prior basic remedial solution...)

(7) I also discovered later: <u>Very primitive sense of **Levels of thinking, or the Ladder of Abstraction.**</u>
(A) The distinction between **Concrete** (specific information, material) and **Conceptual** (ideas, generalizations about material.) [Reference: for this, see → Appendix #N, Conceptualizing 101]

EXPERT TESTIMONY. W. DERZKO on *shortfallings in the vocational arena on thinking needed:*

<u>**Parallel vs. serial** thinking, as in **left-brain vs. right-brain** lateral?</u>
"I propose...that most North American employees or their bosses have never thought about how they think and what effective thinking actually is. Stand back and consider: thinking skills are the key denominators of effectiveness for all the training above [in certain specific management-level corporate or organizational skills in administration]. Here I have in mind both...
critical (logical, judgmental, convergent) cognitive thinking skills needed for *most computer operations, general decision-making*, the convergence in problem-solving and system-thinking, and also the...
creative (lateral, exploratory,) thinking skills needed for *strategic competitive thinking*, learning how to learn, pattern recognition, opportunity spotting and opportunity creation, assumption of challenges, and creative problem-solving etc."
[-- **WALTER DERZKO, of the "IDEAS BANK"**]

Even **(B)** the two major ways of thinking, **Induction** upward to generalize to concepts *from or out of* particulars, and Deduction or application downward of concepts *to or upon* particulars. (Let alone empiricism and rationalism, left-brain parallel, right-brain serial...)

EXPERT TESTIMONY: W. AARONS on two very basic moves indeed:
<u>#8. Discriminating between inductive and deductive reasoning, i.e., *being aware* when an argument is being made from the particular to the general or from the general to the particular.</u>
The concept of "<u>electric</u> circuit," "electric current," and "resistance" can be <u>in</u>duced from very simple observations made with electric batteries and arrangements of flashlight bulbs. This leads to the construction of a "model" of operation of an electric circuit. The model then forms the basis for <u>de</u>ductions, i.e., predictions of what will happen to brightness of bulbs in new configurations or when changes (such as short circuiting) are imposed on an existing configuration.
Exactly similar thinking can be developed in connection with <u>economic</u> models or processes. Hypothetico-deductive reasoning is intimately involved in virtually all such instances, but *one should always be fully conscious of the distinction between the inductive and the deductive modes.* [-- **WALTER B. AARONS, Science Teacher / Educator**]

|#+#|+|#+#|+#|+|#+|+#|+|+|#+|+|++|#+|+#|+#|+#|+#|+#|+#+#|+|+|#|+#|#+|+|#+|#|+#|+#|+|#+|+#|+|#|+#|#+|+#||#+|+#|+#|+#|+|#+|#+||#+||

[2.D.] "But isn't this P.B. material, just the same as *CRITICAL THINKING*' after all?

SUGGESTION: The "critical thinking" approach may be basic, but *too specialized and limited* to carry the flagship, advance-guard, thrust for teaching <u>generic essential thinking-as-such?</u>

[1.] Critical Thinking **is powerful in aim**, as the following somewhat-classic definition-descriptions suggest:

R. ENNIS: "reasonable reflective thinking that is focused on deciding what to believe or do."

J. MCPECK: "the skill and propensity to engage in an activity with reflective skepticism."

R. PAUL: "disciplined, self-directed thinking…the perfection of thinking appropriate to a particular mode or domain of thinking."

M. LIPMAN: "skilful, responsible thinking that facilitates good judgment because it (1) relies upon criteria, (2) is self-correcting, and (3) is sensitive to context."

H. SIEGEL: the critical thinker is "appropriately moved by reasons."

JOHNSON: "thought evaluating thought…the articulated judgment of an intellectual product arrived at on the basis of plus-minus considerations of the product in terms of appropriate standards for criteria."

[2.] CT emphasizes **logic, reason, argumentation** on existing subjects and statement-claims. It discusses **fallacies to avoid**, such as propaganda, others: Ad Hominem, Bandwagon, Red Herring, Straw Man, Pity, Slippery Slope, Begging the Question, and False Dilemma, etc. It studies **argument**: deductive, w/ claims, premises, warrants, evidence, etc.; inductive. *However, do these perhaps seem somewhat limited? Analogy.* C.T. may tell us *"how to expertly extract sap from a tree,"* more than *"how to monitor the entire Forest project…"*

This is not to denigrate **Critical Thinking**, simply to suggest that its scope and range *may not cover* Essential Thinking.

[SEE in "II" FULL edition, "Dr. Green's Marriage & Family Course: thought-ful but limited…"]

|#+#|+|#+#|+#|+|#+|+#|+|+|#+|+|++|#+|+#|+#|+#|+#|+#|+#+#|+|+|#+|+|#+|#|+#|+#|+|#+|+#|+#|+|#+|#+|#+||#+|+#|+#|+#|+|#+|#+||#+||

[2.E.] "Okay, so what would P.B. look like in Utopian or best implementation in classroom practice?"

"BEAST & BEAUTY PAIRS": How might two classrooms differ in practice?

(1) A CLASS **NOT** COMPETENT IN THE PRIOR BASICS. POSSIBLE RESPONSE:

"Well, vegetarianism is good—I feel it is. Well, who's to say who's right after all—isn't it all **relative**? Well, for **example**, my uncle's health deteriorated after he became a vegetarian. Well, this **authority** in the paper says it's good. But then **somebody** else said you can have a vitamin B-12 deficiency if you don't eat animal protein. But then, "even scientists can be biassed," so….! Besides, **I feel strongly**, we absolutely have to stop mistreating animals for food if we're going to be called humane." And I could get some facts and other peoples' opinion to **back up** [rationalize?] my own personal opinion here. Although also, hunting is a natural, archetypal human trait, plus the deer would starve if we didn't cull the herds through hunting." .....

> *SEEMS NON-COMPETENT..... Etc., etc., etc. .....Risking **undirected, uncontrolled, uncooperative emoting or opinion-sharing** only, unaware of rationalizing, beyond-naïve-relativism, implicit presuppositions plus other motivations, types of knowledge, etc. .....*

(2) A CLASS **MORE** COMPETENT IN THE PRIOR BASICS. POSSIBLE RESPONSE:

"Well, whether vegetarianism is healthy or not, that's a (#) **factual** question, not arguable, simply researchable. Still, scientists' (#) **biasses** or **implicit presuppositions** could come in to it—all the # **ways of knowing** (tradition, authority, science, personal, etc.) have # emotional and ideological dimensions as well as more objective ones. (I know some say that animal-rights beliefs are **motivated** by "survivor guilt" and "liberals looking for a new cause," rather than just "the facts," or even "humanitarian purposes," but that itself is—problematic! And the animal-rights stance….I know (#) **I have a profound bias** against the animal-rights people because they're inconsistent and also don't know their real motives sometimes, and I temperamentally don't like that—but I do try to question my biasses, plus (#) hear truly their arguments. No good just to hear one side. Listen—let's isolate some of the key (#) **variable-issues** important in thinking about, and evaluating, vegetarianism—like Morality or Ethics; Nutrition; Tastiness or the gourmet factor; Economics; Psychology too; History….and then establish some (#) **statements** (such as "All school cafeterias should serve vegetarian entrees," and many more important ones), and then try to know (#) what lenses, or ideologies, or reasons-behind, are operating here, and whether we've considered all possible stances. Then let's evaluate them, including our responses..... We can then use the **Philosophy 101** cluster (= "assumptions, inconsistencies, consequences"), and later, the **statement-sifting** technique: true? false? some of both? (many subtypes)—and if we disagree on this, why?".....

> *SEEMS BETTER?*..... <u>*Expertise commences:*</u> *Are we out to Combat or Communicate and learn "fairmindedly"? What type of statement is this—arguable or not? Is rationalizing present? What is the presupposition, plus criterion, plus system of thought ("lens") behind a statement? Do other lenses exist? Finally, does your statement hold up via criteria of thinking?".....*

...Yes, #2 is good, but *much too good*. It goes beyond "basics" into advanced skills...	True; a challenge: what are default basics, what is advanced thinking... Still, #1 suggests identifiable Prevalent Amateur Pitfalls... And #2 might help students self-test their existing abilities?

|#+#|+|#+#|+#|+|#+|+#|+|+|#+|+|++|#+|+#|+#|+#|+#|+#|+#+#|+|+|#|#+|+|#+|#|+#|+#|+|#+|+#|+#|+|#+|#+|#|+#|+|#+|#|+#|+|#+|#+|#+|+|#+|+#|+#|+|#+|#+|+#||+|+#|+#|+#|+|#+|#+||#+||

[2.F.] "Okay—so the NUTS-&-BOLTS, please. What skills?

> "REPERTOIRE" OF POSSIBILITIES. Below is my version of a unit on "Prior Background Basics."

1. Clarifying "the **Personal**" to start…

1A. **Consciousness**: meta-cognition. 1A1. one's thinking styles (personal "Tool-Belt"). 1A2. one's **Personal Psyche Profile** of motivations, ideas, values, insights/biases, etc. **["Know Thyself," needs initial attention here...]**

1B. **Dispositions** or "**Considerate**" thinking. [*Should* **one think not just keenly, but fairmindedly?...**]

2. Orienting to the "**Lay of the Land**" : "Knowledge"…

2A. "**Knowledge, Truth, Authority, etc.**"

2B. **Three Types of Statements**/Questions/Issues: Factual, Opinion, Reasoned Judgment. **[Facilitating!]**

2C. The "**Relativism**" Pitfall **["But Who's To Say After All"—a muddle to clear up in 15 minutes...]**

2D. *Types of Thinking, Ways of Knowing* [Tradition, Authority, Science, Personal…] ["Critical Thinking"] [Etc.]

2E. The **Subjective/"Personal" "versus" Objective/Impersonal** Issue.

[Clarify confusions: both are both good and bad, in identifiable ways: indispensable and risky, "depending"...]

3. **Evaluation. Competence** (the concept itself; and, applied to thinking well).

3A. "Excellence-in-**quality**" of. Criteria. [

3B. **Degrees** of. "Bad," "Just-," "Good," and "Better/Best" Thinking?

3C. The **Reasoning vs. Rationalizing** Issue. **["Back your idea up with the facts"—but, *insufficient*...]**

3D. Degrees: "Knowing, vs. Really Knowing…" [**If you can't apply it when needed,....!!]**

4. **Background of a Statement** or Claim about a Subject. **[X-ray vision needed, possible...]**

4A. "**Pulsions**" or why peoples' reasons. **Motivations**, all-too-human.

4B. "**3-DDD**" or why to the same issue, people respond differently, diverging, disagreeing?

4C. A roster: **World-Views, Implicit Presuppositions, Zeitgeist**, other **Lenses**.

5. "**Others.**" Possibly from the roster of thinking tools themselves? Two examples, perhaps the most incisive of a dozen "tools" which suggest themselves:

X **Contextual thinking**: When confronting any subject, consider its "**field**": context, situation, environment, the larger system of which it is / is not a part… This backdrop influences the subject plus one's evaluation of it.

X **Compare-Contrast**: "Known-about," but under-used. "To confront A better, C/C it with B or non-A." Also connect & relate two items which are wrongly-separated … or separate two items wrongly-conflated-together.

|#+#|+|#+#|+#|+|#+|+#|+|+|#+|+|++|#+|+#|+#|+#|+|#|+#+#|+|+|+#|#+|+|#+|#|+#|+#|+|#+|+#|+|#+|#+||#+|+#|+#|+#|+|#+|#+||#+||

|#+#|+|#+#|+#|+|#+|+#|+|+|#+|+|++|#+|+#|+#|+#|+|#|+#+#|+|+|+#|#+|+|#+|#|+#|+#|+|#+|+#|+|#+|#+||#+|+#|+#|+#|+|#+|#+||#+||

[1.] Intro: the very Concept **previous**	[2.] Orientation: 6 issues **previous**	**[3.] Tool-Chest: 9 items** *current*

[3.] THE BODY: Tool-CHEST with KITS for the most crucial prior basics…

…**BUT** many of the below resemble from what you can find in already-existing textbooks…	**NOT** *totally*. True, the ideas are *not* new. But their selection-arrangement-focus *is* intended to be *improved*… Much like the Tool-KITS in Appendix #4.
	[**RECOLLECTION:** The earlier analogy- example of **elucidation:** Two guidebooks on a foreign country, each 200 pp. One uneven, vague, unfocused, arbitrary. The other balanced between panorama and particular, and other contraries correlated…]

|#+#|+|#+#|+#|+|#+|+#|+|+|#+|+|++|#+|+#|+#|+#|+#|+#|+#+#|+|+|+#|#+|+|#+|#|+#|+#|+|#+|+#|+#|+|#+|#+||#+|+#|+#|+#|+|#+|#+||#+||

Table of Contents of "Sample Tool-Chest" of key "Prior-Basics"…

1. Dispositions or "Considerate" Thinking

2. "Quality": "How Good": **Competence, Criteria.** Also "How-To": method, technique: **"formula"**

3. The **"Relativism"** Tangle   [3-part scheme replaces confusion …]

4."Knowledge" (A) What is **"Truth"**?... (B) **"Knowing vs. Knowing":** just knowing "of-or-about," *versus* truly knowing how-to-use …

5. "3 Question-Types: Factual, Objective, Reasoned-Judgment"   [Ex.: "Alaska"]

6. Reasoning vs. Rationalizing   [a stumbling-block]

7. Personal/Subjective *"versus"* **Formal/Objective** Thinking [sprawling; needs clarifying…]

8. "Philosophy 101": *esp.,* **Backgrounds** to a Statement-Claim (motivations, implicit presuppositions, lenses—and more)

9. The **"7-RRRRRRR" model.** Types of responses-to-a-statement or subject. [From Right-on-to Random…]

|#+#|+|#+#|+#|+|#+|+#|+|+|#+|+|++|#+|+#|+#|+#|+#|+#|+#+#|+|+|+#|#+|+|#+|#|+#|+#|+|#+|+#|+#|+|#+|#+||#+|+#|+#|+#|+|#+|#+||#+||

ORIENTATION - BAR:								
1.Dispositions	2. Quality	3. Relativism	4. Knowing	5. F,O,RJ	6. Reas.-Rat.	7. Personal	8. Philo 101	9. 7-R

[3.1.] Dispositions: "Considerate" thinking

NOTE—the issue of dispositions or whether we should think morally, ethically not just selfishly, is a major issue in both (1) "critical thinking," also (2) in "essential" (basic-advanced, generic) thinking, where "Considerate" is one of the ten elements. ***Do beginning learners need a "vaccination"-glimpse of this issue, as a Prior Basic?*** Here is a mini-tool-kit:

1. "A major choice to make first of all: CV, or CV?" Two overall goals exist for thinking-in-public (=one-way statements toward others, or multi-way interchanges with others). And one surely must decide or know which is operating: "CV," vs. "CV." Decide first is goal is <u>C</u>ombat to win <u>V</u>ictory of your side *over* the others (listeners, discussants)? == or <u>C</u>ooperate together to seek <u>V</u>eracity (truth) or anyhow Validity with the others? This seems mandatory to decide or at least to know.

EVALUATION: Yes, it's idealistic: not always possible or even desirable. But yes, can be done if all parties want to *but all parties gotta wanna*. And yes profoundly both pragmatic, principled, and pleasurable to do so!

2. Technically-proficient thinking skills are NOT the same as the good-disposition use of them. [ANALOGY: sports car has powerful motor, but can be used either to drive pleasurably—or to beat other cars or force them to one side...] EXAMPLE. Hitler in his fascist manifest <u>Mein Kampf</u> ["My Struggle"] employed identifiable reasoning and argument skills, but to bad effect. [-- RICHARD PAUL]

3. Fairmindedness: "Own Biases, and The Other Side"... "Fairminded" thinking can include (A) seeking to know and monitor and handle-manage-control one's OWN BIASES of various sorts. And (B) seeking to HEAR "THE OTHER SIDE" *no but really...*

(TEST: can you state the other side's position—on *vegetarianism, same-sex-marriage, criteria for public art displays or high-quality cooking*, etc.—so accurately—clearly and fairly—that they can say, "<u>Yes, that's it! That's exactly what and how we think, feel, and believe!</u>" To do so is rare, but is pragmatic, principled, and pleasurable. <u>Uses for it:</u> **1.** Helps you attack their position better if necessary. **2.** Shows empathetic respect for another viewpoint. **3.** Gives me great ego-esteem by shedding my ego-esteem "I" (=I have to win) in favor of ego-esteem "II" (= I can decenter myself maturely).

-----"Four-Point Zen." This takes what I call the "Zen" approach of "Unperturbed Presence," of strolling right into the Enemy Forest of the Other Position (with their "tigers" ready to attack you?"...) ***but*** avoiding four specific responses (recurrent blunders). *Neither* trying to **(1) Defend** yourself (feeling "Threatened")... *nor* **(2)** being on the **Offensive** and trying to win victory or conquer over "them" ("obsessive refutation")... *nor* **(3)** slavishly assenting or believe or practice Groupthink or "respect" etc. ("slavish conformity")... *nor* **(4) Distancing** yourself, detaching or denying-to-engage, etc. ...

-----"C. & C.": It can also involve seeking ample amounts of contraries: as much **Candor** as possible [frankness, "what you ***truly do*** think, <u>not</u> what you *wish or will* you think, *think* you do think, *should* think, *think you should* think, etc. – JAMES BALDWIN], along with as much **Civility** as possible (empathy, forbearance, rapport, consideration, etc.)...

-----**Strong Statements**—enthusiastic, impassioned—are questionable if (1) biased, (2) hostile... but are useful if producing useful-if-painful matters, also if sharing emotion in a civil productive fashion. This is "argument" in a good healthy sense... "Argument" can mean (1) reasonable reasoned pursuit of truth or a position, (2) fighting, disagreement, scrapping, etc.; a distinction! Or as right here, (3) real "fighting" but friendly, for a good purpose of truth-seeking...

4. Let's not omit good old "<u>Interpersonal Communication</u> 101."

Specifically, it's "better interpersonal interrelating" through a half-dozen ploys or thinking-tools. Ploys which are "<u>Almost Always</u>" stated in textbooks in speech-communication classes. Ploys which however are "<u>Almost Never</u>" *either* so-much-as-mentioned in <u>other classes</u>, *or let alone* employed enough in <u>everyday interaction</u>. Ploys which are in fact usually soundly-roundly violated—or simply ignored!

Thus, speech-studies and our scheme here, suggest:

1. Good Listening: not to formulate a reply, but to truly grasp the other's point.
2. Check did you get it right what the other said.
3. Give your feeling-responses, not your moral judgments (as in "Your comment made me feel overlooked," not "You are arrogantly-exclusive").
4. Delay closure for more of what you call Consideration not Concluding.

EXAMPLE. A powerful instance of <u>another writer's vision of good thinking.</u> It implicitly echoes (1) "critical thinking's" Dispositions, plus (2) a few of my own elements also: D. F. WALLACE discusses the hot-button issue of "tradition vs. egalitarianism in US English" use.

"A Democratic Spirit is one that combines rigor and humility, i.e., passionate conviction plus a sedulous respect for the convictions of others. As any American knows, this is a difficult spirit to cultivate and maintain, particularly when it comes to issues you feel strongly about. Equally tough is a DS's criterion of 100 percent intellectual integrity—you have to be willing to look honestly at yourself and at your motives for believing what you believe, and to do it more or less continually.

This kind of stuff is advanced US citizenship. A true Democratic Spirit is up there with religious faith and emotional maturity and all those other top-of-the-Maslow-Pyramid-type qualities that people spend their whole lives working on. A Democratic Spirit's constituent rigor and humility and self-honest are, in fact, so hard to maintain on certain issues that it's almost irresistibly tempting to fall in with some established dogmatic camp and to follow that camp's line on the issue and to let your position harden within the camp and become inflexible and to believe that the other camps are either evil or insane and to spend all your time and energy trying to shout over them.

I submit, then, that it is indisputably easier to be Dogmatic than Democratic, especially about issues that are both vexed and highly charged. I submit further that the issues surrounding 'correctness' in contemporary American usage are both vexed and highly charged, and that the fundamental questions they involve are ones whose answers have to be literally *worked out* instead of merely found." [-- DAVID FOSTER WALLACE]

Bravo… seems to reflect CV vs. CV—cooperate don't combt. Also true Fairmindedness, admit own bias, hear the other side. Candor and civility also. One can do this, but *"Ya Gotta Wanna"*… A call to avoid Bias which is sociogenic or from the norms-mores-folkways, but also psychogenic, from unresolved personal issues…

GUIDELINE/GOAL: The learner (1) *knows* well the basic distinction between Combat to triumph, versus Cooperate toward Truth… Knows that (2) sheer skill in thinking can be for selfish ends not just fair-minded… Knows (3) how to try to be fair-minded: () honestly recognize own biases, (B) honestly truly hear the Other Side… And (4) can communicate well between sender and receiver, including listening… [But makes *own* decision on what attitudes to take here!]

|#+#|+|#+#|+#|+|#+|+#|+|+|#+|+|++|#+|+#|+#|+|#|+#|+#|+#+#|+|+|#|+#|+|#+|#|+#|+#|+|#+|+#|+#|+|#+|#+|#|+#|+#|+#|+|#+|#+|#+||

ORIENTATION-BAR:

1.Dispositions	**2. Quality**	3. Relativism	4. Knowing	5. F,O,RJ	6. Reas.-Rat.	7. Personal	8. Philo 101	9. 7-R

[3.2.] "QUALITY" {"excellence"}: Competence ("command"), Criteria, Method/Technique, etc.

OVERVIEW. The issue of Quality: Competence in Skill, Conclusion of Success…

["I" BRIEF] "A person attempts to do a task. S/he succeeds, or does not. *End of story,* we just Score the result, and *need not study more* about Quality / Competence."

Yes, quite clean-simple-efficient. How adequate usually. **But also how oversimplistic, shortfalling… blunderingly-incompetent, and frankly boring too…** *And so welcome, please, the variables which nicely complicate up "I"'s over-simple story:*

["II" FULL] "A performer does a task to accomplish a goal. *And this involves...*"

[1.] But with how much **COMPETENCE/Skill/Ability?** (A) in general, and (B) for specific task-goal?

--**(1)** the **Formula-Flexibility** issue, including **"rule-vs.-tool"** (focused but rigid recipe, vs. flexible relaxed guideline)also including **In Vitro *vs.* In Vivo**, or Accurate "By The Text Book Perfect" versus Applied in the Field-context-situation.

--Also **(2)** the **APE➔APE** reminder: (<u>A</u>void <u>P</u>itfalls-<u>E</u>rrors *versus* <u>A</u>pproach <u>P</u>otentialities-<u>E</u>xcellences).

--Also **(3)** The **5-AAAAA "Performance-Profile Estimator"** of Awareness Ability Action Attitude Achievement. (from clueless inept and don't care, == to top-notch, striving, and winning all possibles...)

Also **(4)** <u>Degrees of **Self-Awareness-&-Ability**</u> or "Un/Conscious In/Competence."

<u>1. Unconscious Incompetence</u> [*clumsy & clueless!*] [naively overconfident, plus "knows what is not so" etc.],
<u>2. Conscious Incompetence</u> [knows that, and what, one does *not* know... and then, what one can't *or* didn't do] ,
<u>3. "Conscious" Competence "I"</u> [mechanical needs scaffolding or training-wheels] ,
<u>4. Unconscious Competence</u> [intuitively flows],
<u>5. Conscious Competence II:</u> [has reflexive meta-cognition, is or can be aware of one's own thinking ...]

[2.] And, facing how much "CHALLENGE" or task-difficulty. ["Challenge" = How hard is it to accomplish the goal, at least adequately or "well/enough"? from "E-Z-to-Tuf"]
This involves **(A)** Degree/Amount of challenge, **(B)** Types/Kinds of challenge, and **(C) Surmountability of—or not.**

[2A.] Amount: Is task a no-brainer... moderately hard... tough? And **[2B.]** Type/Kind of challenges:
[= **1.** <u>innate</u> (inherent intrinsic) factors (not imposed, accepted), **2. "Complexity":** 12 aspects!, **3. Context:** situational demands/constraints in the particular environment, **4. Criteria:** standards are high?, **5. Cruciality** or "So What? well, this thing does matter!" is important? [Cf. "CCCCC," current communal concerns contested complex etc. such as Abortion Bureaucracy Crime/Climate Demography Energy/Environment Finance Globalization etc.] **6. "Self"** one's own ability to succeed, or lack of it, etc. **8. "Curious"** or to the thinker it's quite *new, foreign, unfamiliar*, not his/her safe specialty... **9. "Other"** type of hurdle...)

[2C.] Was challenge in-surmountable, goal un-attainable? **(1)** no-win situations, **(2)** recurrent pervasive Perennial Problems?

> **EXAMPLES:** (1) Computer Design. 1. Impossible to pre-identify "bugs," 2. Hard to retrofitt new components, 3. Programmers don't know the prior layers of logic below current version. (2) "Wicked Problems" are: ill-structured, complicated, ambiguous, uncertain about problems let alone solutions, under constraints, interconnected, seen differently, contain value conflicts, are a-logical or illogical. [- HORST RITTEL]

[3.] Via **what CRITERIA (measurements, definitions) involved** to evaluate task-difficulty, success?

> **EXAMPLES:** X Document Design: (1) pre-set formulae, (2) evaluators' personal taste, (3) responses of target-audiences.
> X Hard sciences & technology: *does it work?* Humanities, Social Sciences: *do one's peers praise, approve?*
> X Engineering, "a bridge": *design* criteria/standards, vs. *performance* criteria/standards.
> X External, or "self" as in be *the best* vs. be *your own personal best.* XX TOM CRUISE, E. R. BURROUGHS, WM. FAULKNER
> X Comic strip artists: create for *syndicate's* current tastes, or for *your own self* and taste for eventual *readership?*
> X Standards for education. *Input* (how many classes, etc.) vs. *Outcome* (what can learners do etc.?)
> X For lawyers: "*winning*," <u>but</u> since unwinnable cases exist, <u>also</u> "*argument & analysis which is competent* & comprehensive"

[4.] And achieving (or not!) **what CONSEQUENCE of Success, or Achievement (or fail-lose!)?**

[4A.] First, three issues in re **achievement (1)** pre-set (we have no say), *or* adjustable (we can define success-or-not)?.. **(2)** Easy to tell okay-or-not, *or* murky—hard to measure?... **(3)** Binary (either-or, lose-or-win, fail-or-succeed) *or* more analog-multiphase? [Fail hideously—"just okay" or "satisficed-minimum"—within the "1-to-10" Range—exceeds?]

[4B.] Second, **what STANDARDS or demanded/expected levels of achievement?**
[From low-lax-slack-sloppy... to must minimally-"satisfied"... to benchmark... to "exceeds goals"?]
--ISSUE here: **the Ideal versus the Immediate.** What would be the Ideal or "Perfect" outcome?

> **EXAMPLES:** X A dinner table... X A drug to fight HIV... X is the traditional book, near-perfect? X Total Quality movement: quality the first time, improvement sought, customer needs met, products last longer, waste disappears, employees love their jobs. [-- JOEL ARTHUR BARKER, Paradigms]

--ISSUE here: <u>Who set the level</u> of standards, <u>and</u> <u>are they acceptable-or-not</u>, to which responders? How high should Standards be, or not; can too-high Abilities, Standards, Performance also be "bad" in some ways in some situations.

> **EXAMPLES.** *Quotation*: **"The biggest disadvantage of a penetrating intellect is not failure to reach the goal, but going beyond it."** **ANECDOTE:** Two applicants for a company promotion, the hiring boss posed to each, a question needing decision A, B, or C. The man said "Well, Solution B is best." The woman said "Well Solution A is best if conditions N obtains, but perhaps Solution C if we blend in M and X, and…" Boss said: "I think you should choose another line of work" and hired the simplistic man instead…

[4C.] Here too now, **WHO JUDGED, did *people* decide "okay or not"?** Who were the Judges? **(1)** Did they concur, or differ-diverge-disagree—if so, why? [SEE 3 "3- DDD" module in Introduction, Gallery…]

[5.] Then, **the two aspects of an individual performer's "COMPETENCE": (1) Craft Skill, (2) Consequences Score.** (*What if the performer was very able but did not win? If so, why?*
This issue seems innately fascinating, also very practical. **ANECDOTE:** "The operation was a success but the patient died." Usual meaning here is incompetence: perhaps the surgeon (1) went by-the-book but bungled things mechanically incompetent. But another meaning, perhaps (2) no surgery could have saved that particular patient.
--So therefore here **the concept of "COMMAND," which is ultimate possible competence, such that "if anybody could have succeeded in a challenging situation, that performer who possesses Command, could have."**

> **Command:=** you "missed no chances…covered all bases…made no avoidable mistakes…missed no opportunities… as for the 'variables,' (1) knew of all the choice-issues to be confronted, (2) for each issue, knew of all the alternate options A-to-Z, and then (3) selected the best choice) decision points; problem-opportunities; requirements-to-confront)…and you were not fooled…" [And you did this via valid criteria, too, which the true experts would validate as competent…]

EXAMPLES. X Fingernail, arsenic poisoning. X Motorcycle electrical short: taillight/stoplight bulb filament. XX etc.

ISSUE: <u>Do "lose-lose" or anyhow "no best case" situations exist</u>, dilemmas from the here-and-now?

> **EXAMPLES:** X Air Force at "Thud Ridge": can't fly to target either *above* the cloud-cover, nor *inside of* it, nor *below* it… X ROMMEL in North Africa: impossible for five reasons… X ELEANOR OF AQUITAINE: three forces beyond own control (death of son, strength of adversary)… X YOUNG BLACK WOMAN at an all-white-student dance: an "impossible" situation!…

ISSUE: <u>Do "perennially insoluble-or-pesky" situations exist</u>, all throughout human history?

> **EXAMPLES:** --Individual vs. Society: --Peace vs. Power. --Size/Quality of Societies. --I.Q. Double-Edged. --Early Disorder/Sorrow. --"Skin": --Women: --Communication-Confusion 101: --Evolutionary apocalypse always possible: --Lenses But Blindnesses: --Justice Forever Vulnerable. --Religion at Risk. --Laws Needed but Noxious? --Bureaucracy as Two-Sided. --Education "at risk!:

(6) …and yet other variable-issues to consider about doing well and doing skillfully:

[6.A.] ISSUE: Degree of Awareness of quality/competence, and Attitude toward that (valuing or dismissing).
<u>Awareness: does a person really know</u> what quality is? (People in general… a given person in a specific case…)

> **EXAMPLES:**   (1) KINGSLEY AMIS on critics who don't know, therefore babble…
> (2) a FELLOW TEACHER actually said to me, "But why do you stress describing quality, won't students already know bad and good work (poems, etc.) when they see it? {Arrggghhhh…..}] …..
> (3) <u>New York City pastrami</u>. Secret of the best is multiple steaming at just-right temperature! It is a science that takes years to master."
> (4) <u>Roads</u>. Had existed before the Romans. But Greek roads were hastily built, required much upkeep. Etruscan roads wandered. But the dogged persistence of the Romans made their roads run straight, climb mountains, span gorges, cross rivers, burrow through hills. They dug deep, then filled the trench with sand, gravel, crushed stone for drainage. They faced the crown of the road with cut stone blocks so well fitted that they didn't move under the feet of men, horses, wagon wheels. Many Roman road bases are still usable today as roadbeds if still existing.   [-- C. VAN DOREN]

<u>Attitude: does that person care</u> or not? Here also three specific dimensions of quality and its competent pursuit (or its neglect…): *moral-ethical… psychological-satisfaction… and pleasure or sport-game-play.*
> **EXAMPLES:** testimonies by SEARLE, ROOSEVELT, SUGANO, CARVER, RYAN, FROST.

[6.B.] The issue of **factors leading to success other than "savvy and sweat"** or competence and commitment.
--Well, sheer committed effort or sweat. Genius as 1% inspiration and 99% perspiration. "Unrelenting drive"…
--Also Luck. EXAMPLES: X Bill Gates, X from Impress, XX others…

--**Also** the ISSUE of <u>sheer "Rare Gifted Genius, Talent, Extreme Expertise."</u>
EXAMPLES: surgeons, chefs, detectives, boat pilots and horse-riders, athletes, soldiers, saints...
GALLERY: other factors? Chance, power of various kinds, social situation (life-chances, etc.)...

[6.C.] <u>"Personal Achievement"</u> of performer depends on not just (1) a standard Score, and (2) the given Standards (low-high), but also on (3) the Degree of <u>Difficulty of the task</u>—*all relative to* (4) the (A) <u>Ability of the performer</u> *and also* his/her (B,C) Attitude and Actions surely! EXAMPLE: two routes up a mountain, one slightly harder but neither of extreme difficulty, and two climbers, a world-class expert and a complete novice. Note variations possible! [from M. LIPMAN]

[6.D.] <u>The issue of Necessary "Compromise," in Standards, Goals.</u> EXAMPLES: **(1)** ENGINEER'S Saying: <u>your product</u>: quality, low cost, speed of production: "Good, Cheap, Quick: you can select and have *any two of these three*!"... **(2)** <u>Aircraft door</u>: wide, vision, strong but compact, lightweight... **(3)** <u>Organization of Materials: Household, Office</u>: Four elements to balance: (A) Ease of access to reach and work with the item(s)... (B) Frequency of use of (need for) the item(s)... (C) Nature of item(s): Size, Fragility, etc. ... (D) Relationship of item(s) to other items used with?

[6.E-H.] <u>Four More Issues.</u> **(1)** Should a person seek to strengthen one's weaknesses, become well-rounded...or concentrate on one's special strengths mainly?...
(2) Relatedly, should an expert in one field, try to become an expert in other fields also?... EXAMPLE: Bill Murray, good comic, did not become good actor. Michael Jordan, not good at basketball also. Hilaire Belloc: concentrate on the earthworm for 40 yers!
(3) Should one beware doing things that one likes to do, if one does them badly? EXAMPLE: singing...
(4) Are there activities which it is all to easy to do badly? EXAMPLE: being a "public intellectual"...

[6.I.] The major issue of **"thoroughness"** in confronting. As against brief, superficial, care-less... For the **Pragmatic** practical goal of both competence in skill, and successful consequence or result... (Let alone for the ethical **Principle** of dedication and care, also the sportive **Pleasure** of playing the game of scrupulously vanquishing of Foe of ignorance and confusion, hitting target of clarity!) Relates directly to **Essential Thinking: *Considered*...** Also **Surveying the Subject:** Catchment-Area wide, Gaze careful.

EXAMPLES. Of more-thorough perspecting, inspecting... And the results of such competent care:
X Biology Prof. AGASSIZ and STUDENT <u>dissect a fish</u>: "look again and report, then again, and again, until <u>real</u> knowledge-about."
X <u>Restaurant-reviewer</u> D. ROSENGARTEN visits places six separate times before writing-up, each time with a specific goal.
X Janitor saw office door unlocked, locked it, *but* returned to check, found it taped open, reported—<u>Watergate scandal revealed!</u>
X Critic HELEN VENDLER <u>reads a poem</u> with up to fifteen interrelated levels of significance, linking poem to canon, context... from the simplest phonetic, to grammatical, to syntactic, to arrangement of images, to propositional content and statements, the asseverations, the emotional level.] "The context, as I see it, is [not the author's biography or even the sociocultural history of the poem's times or milieu, but] the other poems in the same volume, and then the other poems written by the same poet. It's a series of concentric circles."
X Art: <u>truly looking at a painting.</u> Who is where and why, in what relation? Why those shadows? This perspective?...
X <u>Poison gas in warfare</u>: don't just just release, consider many variables: terrain, windage, altitude, obstacles, gas-type...
X <u>Drug company salesperson</u>: really talk with customers, doctors, find one's product (Prilosec) truly was superior specifically. (Competitors only alleviated symptoms, but P. actually cured... Some patients not respond to other drugs but would to P.)...
X <u>Banker in Brooklyn</u>: though Indian himself, scrupulously surveyed neighborhood, then reached out to the Korean inhabitants...
X <u>I needed to buy green stamp-pad ink.</u> None on store's ink-refill shelves. I asked clerk; "I guess we're out." I searched entire shelf (one of five shelves in unit); no green. I then searched front and back rows of all four other shelves. Presto, misplaced amid the red ink, a bottle of forest-green ink! (This is important anecdote.)
X # DIACHRONIC, OVER TIME, in re CHANGE. [See "II" FULL unit on Major Change in Mind- Play: the "unit of scrutiny."]
EXAMPLES: X Unmotivated <u>college freshman</u>, look at whole 40-year life work span!... X <u>Car salesman</u>, look at entire buying life cycle of customer!... X <u>Affirmative Action</u> (infrastructure not just laws)... X <u>Reading Great Books</u> (two years in college, or whole life?) ... X <u>Health Care</u>: (just checkups, or whole social genetic etc. situation?) X <u>Salesmanship</u>. "Talk not just to your customers, especially not just to your satisfied ones. Talk also to your dissatisfied customers, and especially to those who are not yet your customers..."

|#||#+||#+|+#+|#|+|#+||+#+|#+|+#+|+#+|+#|+|#+|+#+#+|+|+#|+|#+||++|||+|#|+|#+|+|+|#+|#|++#+|#+|+#+|+|#+|+#|+|#+|||#+

DISCUSSION-GALLERY: Good instances which illustrate issues about Quality and Competence... ***Can these make some learners Aware of <u>possibilities</u>, even if it can't motivate 100% of students?...***

It is not unusual for a writer to make eight or nine drafts, adjusting and fiddling, before either being satisfied or giving it up as a bad job or beyond the ability of the writer. [-- DALE NOUSE, nautical journalist; *paraphrased*]

I work at a painting until either I "get tired of it," or until I am afraid to go further for fear that I will "wreck it," or until that "magical moment" when all seems right. [-- SHELBY KEEFE, painter; *paraphrased*]

"EVAN CONNELL said once that he knew he was finished with a short story when he found himself going through it and taking out commas and then going through the story again and putting commas back in the same places. [I like that way of working, I respect that kind of care.]…… [-- RAYMOND CARVER]

"True **work**" is "that which engages the heart and the mind, as well as the hand. It has a beginning and an ending. It is the overcoming of a difficulty one thinks important, for the sake of results one thinks valuable." [-- JACQUES BARZUN]

"Only when love and work are one, / And the work is play for mortal stakes, / Is the deed ever really done, / For heaven and the future's sake." [-- ROBERT FROST]

|#||#+||#+|+#+|#|+|#+||##+|#|+|#+|+#|+|#+|#+#|+|+#|+|#+||+||#++|||+|+#|+|#+|+|#+|#|+#|+#|++#|+|#+|+|+#|+|+#|+#|+|+|#+|+#|+||#+

EXAMPLES of Expertise or anyhow competent successful performances. *What might they indicate to learners about native genius… sheer determination to avoid failure… the role of practice… "strategically monitoring the big picture to avoid errors, aim for excellences"… and the like?*

1. A hotel keeps its passkey (used by many employees; easy to misplace) on a large circular metal hoop 18 inches in diameter…

2. Before Volkswagen shipped any cars to dealers in the U.S.A., it required that dealers stock a complete set of repair and replacement parts…

3. A physician diagnosed a case of arsenic poisoning in five seconds, after this had been missed by other physicians during visits over five years. "If I'm not alert, some hot-shot internist one-ups me later," he said…

4. The symphony conductor ARTURO TOSCANINI, could conclude an hour-long performance *within one second* of previous times.

5. A good professional truck driver could back in within 6" tolerance space limits in narrow alleyways.

6. Killing flies: the "trick" is to get the flyswatter slightly moving before accelerating for the strike!

7. Professional photographer: can you change film—when running and at night?

8. Sailor: do you know your knots? Know which is used for what and why? Can tie them fast? Can untie them fast also? Can tie and untie "behind your back and under water"?

9. A U.S.Army battalion was behind the lines, apparently safe. Only one lieutenant had his men dig in against an attack. An attack came Leadership USA: only casualty was when the unprepared others dove in to his bunker for safety!

10. When I travel, I carry duplicates of an Information Card with all numbers (phone, credit card, addresses of embassy, etc.) in case of loss of documents. And…

11. Two adjacent U.S. states happened to issue auto license plates with white letters/numerals on blue, the same year…

12. Hawaii introduced a mongoose to take care of native predators. But mongoose was diurnal, and predators were nocturnal…

WHOA, ironically a low-quality treatment of high-quality achievement! Because excessive; You give *simply too many* factors for poor beginning learners to master…	[…aha, but are these too many factors for their *teachers* to know-of/about?…] "Fairmindedly" I <u>do</u> acknowledge I risk over-doing over-thoroughly But again, many and varied examples are powerful.

|#+#|+|#+#|+#|+|+|#+|+#|+|#|+|#+|+|++|#+|+#|+#|+#|+|+#|+|#|+#+#|+|+|+#|#|+|#+|#|+#|+#|+|#+|+#|+#|+|#+|+|#+|#||#+|+#|+#|+|#+|#+|#|+|#+||+||

[3.3.] "The Relativism Tangle"…

CRUCIALITY OF THIS? Vital because of two prevalent pitfalls. **(1)** "Today's mood of **Rampant Relativism.**" Students collapse into "well who's to say what's right anyhow," or confuse it with **Politely-Correct** "tolerance / acceptance / celebration of diversity" etc. Related is **(2)** a "**postmodernist constructivist**" fashion which minimizes objective reality, or at least the possibility of knowing it on lower levels even…

EVALUATIVE CHECKLIST. Can students competently respond to the following tests of power? *If they can*, then they surely do *not* need any "unit" on "Background-Default" preparation-issues. ***But*** *if they* ***cannot*,……** A vaccination or mineral- supplement or calisthenics may be indicated…

1. Do you know of the options concerning the issue of "**relativism**"? [Perry Scheme: absolutism, relativism, committed relativism] And how do you handle this issue yourself?

2. Can you distinguish between **Cultural and Moral Relativism?** And between **Stereotype and Sociotype?** *And*, do you know and can use, the supposed advantage in being able to do so?

3. How much do you know about **why people may disagree** when discussing an issue (including others' responses to or statement/claims about that issue)? Even when attempting to think Fairmindedly? [John Rawls roster of "hard cases"]. Let alone when "just thinking"? ["3-DDD why we disagree].

4. […whatever other variable-issues the specific course or learner seeks or needs…]

… such surveys might determine whether a student needs work on a "prior issue" …

[1.] SYSTEM. "The **Perry Scheme of Intellectual Development.**" A classic study:

Students perhaps move from (1) **naïve absolutism** (there is one fixed truth out there), to (2) **naïve often rampant relativism** (it's all relative or even chaotic and "equal" and who's to say what's right etc. after all), on to (3) "**committed relativism.**" When one takes this or that "lens" (frame of reference, perspective, way of seeing and thinking, method, ideology, "ism," school of thought, criterion, etc., etc.), then we can approach "veracity or at least validity" ("Truth," or a or some truth, or anyhow significance…) in a more objective way, via that lens. (Which may of course be partial and also conflict with other lenses, but see "Lensmanship"…)

This may well help beginning student to *enormously accelerate* their grasp of the relativism issue. (Why leave beginners in the lurch—or the wilderness—without mapping the Contours and Operations?)

[2.] Overlooked but helpful: "**Relativism: Cultural, vs. Moral.**"

A superb distinction. **Cultural relativism** is tool of anthropology: "to first simply to competently <u>comprehend, understand</u> a trait, see it not through your culture's eyes, but as the people who carry that culture do."
EXAMPLES. <u>Eskimos abandon their aged grandparents</u>—*but* not out of callous neglect, rather to increase chances for the whole tribe's surviving the winter… <u>Hindus worship cows, which run at large</u>—*but* not out of some animalistic idiocy, rather because they believe in transmigration of souls; the cow could be somebody's grandmother in spirit!

317

Moral relativism can *then* go on to <u>evaluate, judge</u>—via relativistic criteria presumably...

..."Relativism" is thus almost a *classic poster-boy or showcase or textbook* instance of a true **"prior background basic default issue."** An issue *old-hat* to experts, but often *overlooked* in a classroom; one which *confuses* beginning learners; but which can be clarified and rather speedily, with effort, as above...

[3.] *APPARENT* SOLUTION, BUT *NOT*... Literary critic STANLEY FISH on choosing a lens...

[A student asked FISH "Is there a text in this class?" meaning will we find meaning or one or a common meaning (etc.) in the literature we read? FISH'S reply, in a whole book with that title:]

The answer this book gives to its title question is "there is and there isn't." There *isn't* a text in this or any other class if one means by text what E. D. HIRSCH and others mean by it, "<u>an entity which always remains the same from one moment to the next.</u>"... But there *is* a text in this and every other class if one means by text the structure of <u>meaning that is obvious and inescapable from the perspective of whatever interpretative assumptions happen to be in force.</u> The point is finally a simple one, but it has taken me more than ten years to see it, and...almost four hundred pages to elaborate it... "
[-- STANLEY FISH, <u>IS THERE A TEXT IN THIS CLASS?</u> 1980 P. VII]

It would be nice if it were so. If commitment to one "lens" (or interpretative assumptions") would guarantee "obvious and inescapable" meaning—upon which, furthermore, we could all agree. *But we continue to disagree.* Why? Well, **[3A.]** the philosopher J. RAWLS (and **[3B.]** the shirtsleeves teacher-scholar B. BECK) offer suggestions as to why:.....

[4A.] APPARENT RE-SOLUTION. RAWLS' *impressive subtle* list of why we disagree reasonably:

"...how it is that people who are reasonable, and trying to be reasonable, may nevertheless disagree." JOHN RAWLS notes <u>burdens of judgment,</u> the problems we encounter trying to be reasonable. These are *not* the same as "<u>unreasonable disagreement</u> (bias, prejudice, closed-mindedness, ignorance, and so on). These complexities include:

1. The relevant evidence may be conflicting and complex.

2. We may disagree about the weight to be attached to certain considerations.

3. "Hard cases" do exist, for which interpretations indeed differ, apparently inevitably.

4. The problem of making an overall assessment when there are different kinds of value considerations on both sides of an issue.

5. The problem of forced selection, whereby we have to set priorities among cherished values.

NB that open-mindedness and critical reflection, while valuable, have limitations.
[-- WILLIAM HARE]

...I find the above more incisively **elucidating** than usual. *Still we do disagree!*...Why? *I came to think:*

[4B.] SYSTEM. **"3-DDD"** or my <u>roster of reasons why people disagree,</u> differ, diverge on issues...
Whether about a *subject* (question problem issue etc.) ["Same-sex marriage"], or about other peoples' *statement-claims about* that subject ["Homosexuality is caused by tiny, springing bugs"]. [<u>SEE "II" FULL view in Galleries...</u>]

--Frankly-<u>Considerable Criticisms</u>: one person has more insight.

--<u>Frankly-"Wrong"</u> Statements: Misconceptions, Ignorances, Overgeneralizing/Oversimplifying.

--<u>Motivations are diverse</u> [An impossibly immense topic].

--<u>Group Values</u>: Deeply-Internalized Norms, Mores... and they differ among groups.

--Personal <u>Temperamental Taste</u>-Preference

--<u>Lenses</u>: different, including *World-Views,* with *Zeitgeist or Climate of Opinion,* also *Implicit Presuppositions*

--<u>Bias</u>; Emotional Content of varied sorts (Defense-Mechanisms, "Authoritarian Personality Type," Prejudice, Stereotype, Ethnocentrism, other "Isms"

--<u>"Change-Challenge"</u>: <u>Resistance</u> to the New --<u>Rationalizing</u>: defending the already-believed...

--<u>"Naïve Innocent Benign Enthusiasm"</u> (a tunnel-vision blind-spot)—

Varying <u>Basic Philosophical Presuppositions.</u>

--"Quality-Control": Variations in standards for "<u>Excellence</u> ": (both of end-result required, also method along the way). Some thinkers rigorously seek Excellence, others are easy-lax satisfied with "acceptable" etc.

--Conflicting <u>Criteria</u> to be applied and varying <u>Standards</u> to be attained

--[*] **Dispositions.** Attitudes toward mature-moral vs. agonistic-combat thinking.

--<u>Situations can be Difficult & Unclear</u>: permitting "Judgment-Calls," and. "Even The Current Recognized Experts Disagree," etc. [Recall: RORTY'S "hard-case" conditions...]

...This is possibly great, **BUT** currently <u>jumbled</u>. Not **Categorized** into subtypes. Not **Structured** into a sequence. Therefore less *Clear* than desirable. Hence not **Elucidated** after all. *You jumbled hence you stumbled* and **scored a foul.**	I admit. All I do here is seek Awareness of myriad motivations for thinking, hence myriad reasons why we disagree. See the "II" FULL version anyhow...

[5.A. & 5.B.] Two more overlooked but helpful ploys. Can we know the world out there, or are all our views—either **constructed** and therefore "relative", or **stereotypical** hence erroneous?

[5.A.] CLARIFICATION. A current issue/stance relevant to "Relativism":

"Postmodern" Constructivism / Anti-Essentialism. The issue is whether we can know the Reality of the World Out There directly, or not. A current strand of thought seems to claim that we cannot ever know the World, we can know only the (incomplete, inaccurate...) Image of it in our minds.

> RULE-OF-THUMB GUIDELINE: **Balance the pendulum-swing back toward "both-and." Offer that first *yes* the world does exist *and* we can know some of it ["elucidation" says "...and better than we often know and do"...], *but* true also, *not* 100% mirror-like *and yes* it's always through our own mind or "lenses" (=perceptual systems, frames of reference, etc.) *but* we can know thing relatively "worser" (simplistic, biased, etc.) or "better" (more elucidated complete-and-clear...)**

There is the world "out there," and there are our images of the world "in" our minds. Two minds could have different representations of the world—often do have! And the world has an existence independent of either representation. Mental concepts exist which somehow correspond to aspects of nature, but are not identical to them. Thus: we *can* see and know the world—*but* partially, and individually.   [-- R. NISBETT, THE GEOGRAPHY OF THOUGHT [paraphrased]]

[5.B.] CONCEPTS: A Thinking Tool Overlooked But Helpful In Re "World vs. Our Image Of It":

"Stereotype vs. Sociotype." The first is fixed limited partially-inaccurate probably-negative IMAGE of a whole group; second describes traits of a group somewhat existing in the group as objective FACT.

EXAMPLES: **(1)** IMAGE: "<u>Blacks</u> are naturally musical" vs. FACT: "jazz was largely a Black-heritage artistic creation"...
(2) IMAGE: "<u>Jews</u> are aggressive, pushy" vs. FACT: "Jews though only 3% of our population, succeed well in professions, Ivy League education, Nobel Prize winners (20-40%)"...
(3) IMAGE: "<u>Homosexual males</u> are *all* effeminate artsy types" vs. FACT: "Most effeminate boys do grow up to identify as gay"...
(4) IMAGE: "<u>Men</u> are mechanical, unfeeling; <u>women</u> are hysterically emotional" vs. FACT: "Males seem to seek structural-spatial logical interactions, women more contextual and empathetic-emotional connections." **(5)** ...!

PURPOSE: The **S. vs. S.** concept, allows us both to monitor for harmful stereotyping, but also to observe the world and make inductive generalizations about it where they *do* exist, for various useful purposes. [E.g., medicine; different races respond differently to different medications.] Needed to correct the ineptness of well-intended Political Correctnesses, etc.

|#+#|+|#+#|+#|+|#+|+#|+|+|#+|+|++|#+|+#|+#|+#|+#|+#+#|+|+|+#|#+|+|#+|#|+#|+#|+#|+#|+|#+|+#|+#|+|#+|#+||#+|+#|+#|+#|+|#+|#+||#+||

[3.4.] "KNOWLEDGE":
(A) "Knowing *vs.* Knowing... (B) *Ways* of Knowing

319

MINI-TOOL-KIT. The whole issue of "Knowing vs. Knowing" or kinds and degrees of

knowing, is richly subdivided into components. Complex: involves the thorny issues of **Truth or Veracity…** **Authority… Criteria… Competences… Types of Knowledge…** Here, some "I" BRIEF BASICS:

[1.] The very concept of <u>Knowledge</u>, as not simple but COMPLEX: although describable…

ISSUE: Thinkers at various stages-of-awareness, may conceive of knowledge quite differently

> Knowledge: exists absolutely certain, observable… or via authorities… absolutely but temporarily uncertain (use personal beliefs until know more)… uncertain, and situational variables add ambiguity… is contextual and subjective, filtered through our perceptions and criteria… is constructed from information from varied sources, via evaluation via criteria; complexity reigns… knowledge comes from reasonable inquiry of probable via current evidence and criteria, and can be re-evaluated… [-- KING AND KITCHENER, 1994]

--*a marvelous statement,* a spectrum *summing up much painstaking research* by these two scholars. It offers supple balance: it captures "post-modernism's" flavor of true complexity, ambiguity—without being captured by that movement's simplistic either/or stance of "nothing exists objectively and/or we can never know it, period"…]]

--This continuum seems as important as has been <u>BLOOM's classic Taxonomy of Educational Objectives</u>, Cognitive Domain (1956).

--Recall also the <u>PERRY SCHEME of intellectual development in the college years.</u>
[From Absolute right-good vs. wrong-bad…to opinion differs but uncertainty is resolvable and temporary…to legitimate uncertainty…to all knowledge being contextual and relativistic…to the need to make a commitment…]
Rather sophisticated for its time, and the fact that its research-subjects included only "pale males," the students at Harvard University at the time……

[2.] THREE TYPES of Knowledge Depending on "Use of": <u>Declarative, Procedural, Conditional.</u>

--*<u>Declarative:</u>* one knows *of-or-about* the skill, can describe it…
--*<u>Procedural:</u>* one also knows *how* to use it. [CONNECTION: issues of **Competence**.
--*<u>Conditional:</u>* one knows *when* to use it or not, and of course *why*
 ("autonomous application of abstractions")… [-- SOURCE]

CONNECTION: issues of **Formula,** or **"rules vs. tools"**

[3.] FOUR STAGES in amounts, degrees of knowledge—of "certainty" (valid or suspect…).

[1.] **"Known Known":** one knows fact or skill and consciously (is Aware, can explain) …
[2.] **"Known Unknown":** one knows s/he *doesn't* (or *might* not) know. [EX: even the top experts in their fields, don't know even vaguely (1) how consciousness works, (2) the next breakthrough in computers, (3) the solution to AIDS…]
[3.] **"Unknown Known":** an unappreciated strength…
[EX: psychology students may be more socially-able, etc., than they consciously realize.] …
[4.] **"Unknown Unknown":** one **(A)** may not even be aware that an arena exists utterly unknown to them, in-conceivable perhaps, off of any "radar screen" hence non-existent—to *them*! [X: The strict religionist could not even conceive of "non-Biblical history"—whaat?] **(B)** Or one may know the arena, but be unaware they missed something within it. [EXAMPLE: A bad medical student who was fired from neurosurgery internship: "well, everything usually goes well, except for some situations outside my control…" whereas the top-notch residents said "I make mistakes all the time. For instance, just last week, there was this terrible…" [- M. GLADWELL]]

NOTE—A useful <u>5-stage set</u>: **1. Data, Information** = sheer raw "factual" material, to process for ideas within it, etc.
2. Conjecture = a proposition before it has been proved; based on surmise or guesswork only.
3. Hypothesis = a theory, or anything, with no (or insufficient) evidence; a hunch, a guess. To be tested!
4. Theory = a belief, statement, hypothesis existent for a while and accumulated much evidence to support it.
5. Law, Principle = a theory which the scientific community now commonly accepts.

NOTE—on <u>Competence</u>. To the extent that real knowledge is procedural, that is, knowing how-to-do-with, we can also have the four-stage **"Continuum of Competence"** also.
(1) Unconscious Incompetence (person is inept and doesn't even know that)…

(2) Conscious Incompetence (person realizes s/he "still has far to go" etc.)…
(3) Conscious Competence (person can do well but has to monitor, check manual, etc.)… and
(4) Unconscious Competence (person does well but intuitively, the skill is internalized, drops into lap like oxygen mask when needed…   Of course at this stage can also become Conscious of one's thinking and decisions, in meta-cognition, can articulate what-did why & how well…)

[4.] DEGREES OF "SOCIAL HOLDING" of knowledge. (Interesting; important; dynamic…)

(A) "Oh *everyone* knows that" … to **(B)** where *relatively **fewer** people* also know … on down to **(C)** *only expert specialist insiders* etc. know or are likely to.

[And there, the issues of **(1)** CLOSURE: Suspend Judgment/Withhold Conclusions when needed, **(2)** "C.E.C." or "Current Expert Consensus" as a valuable way to go, better than a free-for-all…]

EXAMPLES: (1) SAFER SEX TECHNOLOGY: " *Everybody Knows*" we must use condoms … *BUT what about* "pitfalls with some condom materials and also lubricants, singly or combined; "nonoxynol-9" *very* effective as biocide…
(2) WATER PURIFICATION chemicals: *"of course"* "use chlorine or filter" *BUT what about* when filters are inadequate, when iodine not chlorine is vital, etc. … **(3)**   **(4)** HEALTH: "OfCourseWeAllKnow" red wine lowers heart disease, yes, *BUT what about* "green tea against lung cancer…   **(5)** SUNBLOCKS & SUNSCREENS: screen out UVA rays *but also* UVB…   TEACHING THINKING: {*aha*}…..] **(N)** USED CARS: EXHAUST SMOKE: Yes "of course *we all know*" black smoke means engine burns oil, *but what about* light gray smoke, blue smoke, steam-vapor—(transmission problems, cracked engine block, or no problem…)…..

Pitfall, Blunder: to blithely assume that "oh everyone knows about this," when maybe every Insider might, but not all Outsiders, even those who should or need to know! ANECDOTE: a *specialist* in "teaching thinking" assumed too much about *all* teachers…

[5.] FURTHER ISSUES: **(1)** We can know of or about something but we don't use it, don't know-to-do-with-it. EXAMPLE: The "either-or fallacy;" the tendency to choose either A or Z, instead of both-and or some blending. "*Of course we all know about* the dualistic dichotomy fallacy"—*fine, fine but* we don't know how-to-deal-with, since we commit that "known" fallacy all the time! EXAMPLES: Heredity or environment? Essential innate qualities or socially-constructed values? Etc.

(2) There is knowing something, plus there is knowing where or how to find something if one does not know it. EXAMPLES: X Information on dorm improvement was amply stored in archives across the campus, but who knew?

(3) Knowledge and Dispositions or attitudes toward good moral thinking. *Beware* feeling threatened or defensive or aggressive (etc.) if somebody else knows more (let alone can do more) than you do… Widespread and unnecessary pitfall… It seems better to know of one's limitations, to improve better! EX: Neurology students: when asked, "Do you make mistakes?" the <u>bad</u> ones who were washing out said like "No, everything goes pretty well," but the <u>really top</u> students said, "Oh, all the time. For instance last week there was this terrible…..(etc., etc.)"]

(4) "CEC or Current Expert Consensus is excellent, but Even Experts Can Disagree.

[SEE in "II" FULL: *EXAMPLES* of widely, wildly varying stands on three issues: (1) Urology: whether to do <u>Kegel exercises</u> or not, physicians differ (mandatory, optional, useless, harmful) … (2) How to <u>cook rice</u>: different countries vary on all phases. (3) <u>Caribbean jerk chicken</u>: wet or dry, covered or uncovered, etc., etc. etc. …'

(5) Knowledge and Authority. **Really knowing involves not just *what* to know, but *that* it is so, and *why* it is so.** EXAMPLE: A crafty philosophy teacher told the class that PLATO'S real name was something else (say "Arcanus" or something). The students scrupulously wrote that down. Next hour the teacher told the students that he had fooled them, it was not Arcanus after all. The students were irritated—but by this had learned always to ask how and why do we know that this is so. To question authority *or at least the sources*!

(6) Insider secrets of procedure may exist which it's nevertheless important to know. EXAMPLE. If invited to a party in France and then you give a subsequent party inviting some of those guests, it is absolutely vital to also invite the hosts of the previous party to yours. Not to do so is a massive *faux pas* (pitfall, blunder) which many foreigners fall into.

[6.] Knowledge and the END-GOAL of education: "Ultimate Expectable Readiness," or **"Hitting the Ground Running."** One knows the fact/concept/skill well enough so that is "accessible, even afar." That is, **(A)** it *automatically, intuitively arises* to help you when you need it, and **(B)** in *"far foreign"* circumstances of use (personal-life; on-the-job vocational; civic-citizen, etc.) even where *many others might not see* that it applies

and is needed! [EXAMPLES: (1) Economics, "allocation cost" or "cost-benefit ratio"...[Applied to: transportation options during my trip to Thailand, whether to pursue a grant or not, taking a work-study job or not...]   (2) Statistics: **sampling errors:** insufficient, unrepresentative, self-selected...[applied to: "Are gay men, psychologically sick?" Earlier, all psychiatrists thought so, but they studied only psychiatric patients! Dr. E. HOOKER thought not, but she drew *her* subjects largely from Gay Liberation groups *and* excluded certain subgroups from the study—those with previous mental hospital experience, etc.!!...]... (3) **Scientific Method:** steps & stumbles (sampling, observer-bias, etc.)... Social Psychology: (4) **Cognitive Dissonance...**]

[7.] FULLER EMOTIONAL/EXPERIENTIAL Knowledge, & Total Self/World: "Wisdom."

EXAMPLE #1: psychologist Eric Berne defines "**personal autonomy**" as = spontaneity, awareness, intimacy" (see, do things your own way not tethered to past patterns). PERSONAL TESTIMONY: I re-read his paragraph on it once each five years for decades, and each time I saw and "knew" more as I had grown into it more... **The passage is worth sharing:**

"...autonomy is...the release or recovery of three capacities: awareness, spontaneity, and intimacy.
--Awareness...means the capacity to see a coffeepot and hear the birds sing in one's own way, and not the way one was taught...
--Spontaneity means option, the freedom to choose and express one's feelings from the assortment available....
--Intimacy means the spontaneous, game-free candidness of an aware person, the liberation of the...uncorrupted Child in all its naivete living in the here and now....
--[to attain autonomy]...first, the weight of a whole tribal or family historical tradition has to be lifted,...
--then the influence of the individual parental, social and cultural background has to be thrown off....
--then all the easy indulgences and rewards of being a *Sulk* or a *Jerk* [or a *Prig*, a *Toady*, a *Show-Off*, or a *Cling*]...have to be given up. -
--[Then] the individual must attain personal and social control, so that all...behavior...become[s] free choices subject only to his will....
--In essence this whole preparation [for autonomy] consists of obtaining a friendly divorce from one's parents (and from other Parental influences) so that they may be agreeably visited on occasion, but are no longer dominant." [-- ERIC BERNE, M.D., Games People Play]

EXAMPLE #2: students in thinking class on sixth week said "but why didn't you tell us these important principles earlier, in the first week?" *But of course I had*—they had to learn it via experience not just lecture...]

[8.] Knowledge, connects with the issue of specific, varied "WAYS OF KNOWING":

(A) THE "SMORGASBORD": experience, observation, reflection, introspection, empathy, intuition, but also **reasoning,** then **authority** and **criteria** (whatever *they* are), and **custom, general consent, argument, tradition, consensus, public opinion, science, religion or supernaturalism, conjecture and supposition and speculation....**
[--"Whether it's **logic, meditation, channeling, astral projection** or **ghosts,** all are ways of knowing" [-- LUKE HELDER, pipe-bombing teenager]]

(B) Sometimes a quartet of the "BIG FOUR": 1. External "received" *Authority*... 2. *Tradition-convention* (sociocultural-historical)... 3. *Individual-Personal*... 4. *"Science"* or empiricism...

(C) Also via LENSES: capitalism, socialism, existentialism, monotheism, Freudianism "or" behaviorism "or" evolutionary biology and the cognitive sciences, aestheticism, and the like...]

|#+#|+|#+#|+#|+|#+|+#|+|+|#+|+|+#|+|+#|+|#|+|#|+#|+#|+|#|+#|+|+|+#|#+|+|#+|#|+#|+#|+|#+|+#|+#|+|#+|#+||#+|+#|+#|+#|+|#+|#+||#+||

[4.B.]   "Ways of Knowing"

[0.] Introduction

THE ISSUE—AND ITS CURRENT IMPORTANCE. This unit is being included last-minute (though done earlier) because I'm seeing that at this time [2007 C.E.], more and more educators are charging *shortfallings* in graduates' abilities to identify reliability of sources and statements, select solid not biased (or vague) criteria, and the like. Hence it seems eminently *needful* to consider **ways of knowing.**
[Which is anyhow closely connected with basic logic and epistemology (induction, deduction; idealism, empiricism)... bad/good thinking and bias-detection... and lenses or viewpoint-of-perception... to mention three connected areas...]

"The learner will be able to…" [*but* how much, which students should know, about which Ways of Knowing, if at all—this is so context-dependent, that I can only suggest as a "vaccination":

---

1. Awareness: A. Does the learner *grasp the difference it makes* to use Ways of Knowing well not badly? B. Does the learner then KNOW certain crucial prior basics [such as induction-deduction, empiricism-rationalism, and others—see below?] ….. 2. Ability: can the learner [A] "passively" identify the Ways of Knowing used by <u>another</u> thinker, and evaluate them as good and bad (for the purpose; by specified criteria)? [B] And for his/her <u>own</u> thinking, does learner know many Ways of Knowing, and can "actively" use the better-for-task ones as needed? … IN SHORT: <u>has the learner achieved as elucidated an image [a grasp] of "ways of knowing" as s/he needs at this time?</u>

#|+#|+#|+#|+#|+#|+|+#|+||#||#+|#++#|#+|#+|++#+||+#||+|#+|+#|+|+#+|+|+|+#+||+|+|#+|#|#|#+|#|+#|+|+#|+#|+|+#||

[1.] A Whirlwind for a Warm-Up:

SCRIPT. Will this "playlet" serve **to raise issues of confusion and possibility, at least, for students? For teachers preparing to reckon with Ways of Knowing?** That is the purpose here, of this drama, a seeming "cubist jumble"—which emerges as *not so disorganized after all…*

SCENARIO: In the Student Center, late afternoon. CHESTER and FERN are undergraduates. They were given an assignment by the teacher of their course "THINKING 101: *BASIC MIND-PLAY.*" On Ways of Knowing. Together, they ponder the task:

CHESTER: "What are the WAYS OF KNOWING we use? What are good and bad TYPES OF KNOWLEDGE?" (When our minds confront a subject/issue, and form some knowledge of it, then make a statement/claim about it...) *What a vague question to answer.* I wish the teacher would *simply tell us* and save time....

--I know it's important, if only to get command and hit the ground running competently…To be able to tell whether some speaker's statement is reliable-solid-bona fide, or average, or a misconception based on bad knowing, intentional or not… Which is useful, at times even *fun* (to cheer skill, boo blunders…) *But still…*

--[And this is even skipping over the more-basic issue, <u>what *is* **Knowledge**</u>—is it simple fixed knowable, or more complex, changing, knowable but never perfectly? <u>What is **"Truth"**?</u> (Dictionary says "That which is in fact the case," or is what we agree to say it is, or is useful, or advances the Party Line, etc.?…)]

FERN: Yeah, does he mean like **IN**duction upward, **DE**duction downward, and **lateral or associative** thinking?... But *no*, that's TYPES OF THINKING, <u>not</u> "WAYS OF KNOWING" really...

CHESTER: Nor is it "lenses." He did give *some* hints to me when I asked him after class. He said LENSES were more like the *"filters"* through which we confront things: *viewpoints, perspectives* to describe, explain, evaluate, etc. [**capitalism, socialism, existentialism, monotheism, Freudianism** "or" **behaviorism** "or" **evolutionary biology** and the **cognitive sciences, aestheticism,** and the like...] ... By contrast, WAYS OF KNOWING / TYPES OF KNOWLEDGE, were more like *"conduits, channels, methods,"* regardless of what interpretation-*filter* was installed in them.

--I persisted, and he threw out a slew of what were supposedly WAYS OF KNOWING: <u>experience, observation, reflection, introspection, empathy, intuition,</u> but also <u>reasoning,</u> then <u>authority</u> and <u>criteria</u> (whatever *they* are), and <u>custom, general consent, argument, tradition, consensus, public opinion, science, religion or supernaturalism, conjecture and supposition and speculation.....</u> I now almost wish I *hadn't asked...*

FERN: ...I get the idea better, but yeah, <u>that list *mixes things up* too much</u>! You got personal-intuitive, *and* objective-scientific... External, *and* internal... And *what source* of **authority** and **criteria**?...

CHESTER: Well, if he means how to do the RESEARCH PAPER, obviously you simply go to the library and gather material. **Collect Information**. Oh, you could **Interview** people also. But always keep it "objective"? What about Personal knowledge—in some courses, good, in other classes, bad…

FERN: Or on OTHER ISSUES, you can simply listen to the **teacher**, or ask your **boss** at work, or read the **newspaper** for the experts. Ask the Expert Authority. That's another WAY OF KNOWING.

CHESTER: Yeah, but *who's to say they're right after all*. So, you can just think what **Your Own Opinion** is, and go with that. Your **personal-preference taste-temperament**. Or *talk with others* too.

FERN: *Whoa*, we saw that that was only "*just*"-thinking in terms of **Veracity** and **competence**! Not necessarily "*good*" thinking, following good **criteria** for thinking. Maybe even "*non*"- or even "*bad*"-thinking. Remember, that's just only-personal, impressionistic **introspection** and **reflection**, which aren't very objective and scientific, are they?

CHESTER: But the humanist RENE WELLEK, criticizing social science, said that "**introspection and empathy** are the two main sources of human and humane knowledge."

FERN: Well, on the other hand, remember that ANTHROPOLOGIST really faulted people in "cultural-studies" for trying to understand diverse cultures via the "short-cut" of **visceral feeling, anecdotes, intuition** and **empathy** instead of also drawing on the solid anthropological **research**. So there…

CHESTER: But I don't know whether to be **personal** *or* **impersonal** in knowledge-seeking. I thought in "**research**" you *shouldn't* put your own **self** into the paper, should you? But, a review of the sociolinguist DEBORAH TANNEN said that she used *not only* "scholarly research" and "**popular culture**," *but also* "**anecdotes**," and "**personal experience**." So, what kinds of TYPES OF KNOWLEDGE, *are* valid?

FERN: Well, surely **empiricism** or the **induction** of science can be good. Although after all, *science can be flawed too, scientists can be biassed,* right? In fact, you didn't quote all of the DEBORAH TANNEN review. The REVIEWER went on to claim that in her work, she "makes quantitative claims based on thin sources, generalizes from small and unrepresentative study samples, and overlooks studies that support other explanations of differences in conversational styles."

CHESTER: Then it's just identifiably *bad* science! Like *observer-bias, sampling problems*, and the like. Or there's even "**pseudo-science**": *alchemy, astrology, Creationism*, etc. Although I do admit they were, or even are, definitely WAYS OF KNOWING for some people… *Ouch…*

FERN: True… And another big issue, **criteria** or **authority**. Like, standards for **veracity**. Well, *where* do thinkers get their criteria or standards *from*? The dictionary says, from "**authority, custom, general consent**." That doesn't seem safe. Can't "**conventional wisdom**" (a major if subliminal WAY OF KNOWING!) be wrong? Can't the "**experts**" be wrong also? And what about the "tyranny of the **majority**" or "groupthink"? You going to use "**urban legends**" as KNOWLEDGE? I guess *not*!

CHESTER: Well, true. FRANCIS BACON lamented that quality government was best achieved by demonstrably good **standards**, but that instead, people used "**authority, unanimity, fame, public opinion**." Same problem there that you just mentioned.

FERN: Well, you have to use your own self. SOMEONE who attended an "ex-gay" meeting (designed to help gay people turn straight) ended up feeling it was wrong, because it demanded "**followership**" and fitting into some "**pre-arranged pattern of behavior**," as against the (better-for-him) "**introspection and self-determination**." So the source or location of **Knowing** *varies*: external vs. internal?…

CHESTER: Your self, but also more... I'll never forget how our philosophy professor, DR. CARTWRIGHT, one day told us that the real name of PLATO was, I forget, say "FRED." So we scribbled it down in our notes. Okay, but then the *next* hour, he said he had told us wrong; it was, like "FLOYD." So we irritatedly scribbled out FRED and wrote in FLOYD. But then the *third* hour, he said he had really told them wrong the second time; the true name really *was* "FRED" after all. Well, by now we infuriated students angrily re-re-corrected their notes, but *got the PROF.'s point*. The issue of, "how do you really know that you **know** something"? By some supposed **expert authority** telling you—or by **"received knowledge"** or **conventional wisdom**? Or many other Ways too, as we've already recalled here... From that day on, we were on our guard and turned the tables and grilled DR. CARTWRIGHT on *his* statements! But of course you can't check everything for yourself, so what do you do?

FERN: .....I'm sensing that *many different* **WAYS OF KNOWING / TYPES OF KNOWLEDGE** seem to exist, and that *different ones are probably valid for different subjects*, purposes, task-goals...

CHESTER: That's true, but *which where*? Remember TANNEN using both **scholarly research**, and **personal experience**. Plus, a REV. NUGENT of the Church said that on difficult issues, one relies on **"Scripture; Tradition (of the church); Reason; and Human Experience."** That seems richer, more complete. And you don't need **science**; or *do* you?

FERN: Yeah, but why then in discussing the "difficult issue" of homosexuality, did a MR. BEEM say it was wrong because **Scripture** said so, and a MR. CHILSTROM originally thought so too, *but* then later he "got to know some gay people" and as a result, thought it was okay after all? Actually, his **WAY OF KNOWING** there, it *seems* to be **"experience and observation,"** not **"reason"** or **"authority,"** but no, it was his **LENS** of **"humanistic liberalism"** probably—which is also a **WAY OF KNOWING**?....

CHESTER: Yes, this whole question is getting to be a *mess*... Well, *some* **WAYS OF KNOWING** are probably bad regardless, but are still used. I saw this list of supposedly-*baad* **WAYS OF KNOWING** that included **"conjecture, supposition, speculation, rumor, gossip, hearsay, myth, superstition."** These seem obviously bad, but are there other, more *subtle*, pitfalls out there? Like **"urban legends"** (alligators in the sewer?) and **"conventional absurdities"** ("we only use 5% of our minds")? Oh, I know another **WAY OF KNOWING** used, but not always mentioned: **"anecdotal evidence"**. But is that good, or bad?

FERN: I don't know, but I do know I'm *thoroughly confused*. If this is education, I'm going backwards. I do remember only the one useful earlier Thinking Tool of knowing the difference between three types of statements or issues: of **Fact**, of **Opinion**, and of **Reasoned Judgment**, and of proceeding accordingly. He used Alaska as an example. Like "Is Alaska the *coldest state?*" and you answer that by **objective research: observation, empiricism, science**. But, "Is Alaska *my favorite vacation spot*," it's **personal opinion** or **taste-temperament-preference** indeed. Then, "Is Alaska a good place to *set up a business*," well, **research**, plus **judgment factors** I guess... This scheme avoids useless argument.

CHESTER: That's true, very good, *but* that simpler skill, doesn't clear up—doesn't map or survey—this tangly "forest" of **WAYS OF KNOWING / TYPES OF KNOWLEDGE** for me, either....

FERN: Right. I *know* I'm going to have to have *some* **competence** in dealing with the issue of **WAYS OF KNOWING**—like, via **Standards** and **Criteria**, ironically! But I *don't* know *how*?

CHESTER: Well, maybe the Prof's exercise was exactly like CARTWRIGHT'S trial-by-deception. (Or learning through **experience** plus then **doctrine**—aha, two Ways of Knowing combined!) Maybe next class hour he'll sum it all up in a total handout on **WAYS OF KNOWING**. No, wait—he won't! But how can we create a repertoire for ourselves? I know **"W. of K."** is important plus interesting, but still...

FERN: *Darn this all*. Up to now in school, it wasn't much **WAYS OF KNOWING**, or **LENSES**, at all. Most of my teachers either just told me **what they wanted**, *"Exactly What Was Expected,"* on the paper or test...or else just let us pretty much give **our own personal responses** to things... It was like either "correct," or "personally-pleasing."

CHESTER: Well, _cheer up_ then. Already you got _two_ WAYS OF KNOWING identified. **External authority, and personal response!** And _more on the way perhaps...._

[...CHESTER and FERN exit the conference-room, ruffled up, but almost-focussed....]

Okay—it's important—**BUT** this is a crystal view of muddiness. Ways of Knowing is—but the above is a jumble!	Well let's move from using the WofK of active experience, to exposition... Below, suggested categories for the confusion...

|#+#|+|#+#|+#|+|#+|+#|+|+|#+|+|++|#+|+#|+#|+#|+|#|+#|+#+#|+|+|+#|#+|+|#+|#|+#|+#|+|#+|+#|+#|+|#+|#+|+#|#+|+|#+|+#|+#|+|#+|#+|+#||#+||

[2.] Variable-ISSUES "W. of K."

THE ISSUE. What **variable-issues** (items to confront: handle, manage, explore, satisfy, reckon with, etc., etc.) is it important to indeed include, when teaching about Ways of Knowing? No one size fits all courses-and-students and their variables, so **here's a collated checklist...**

[2.1.] Specific SUBTYPES OF Ways of Knowing?

1. RICHARD PAUL notes that **WE THINK AND DECIDE** using "_experience, observation, reflection, reasoning,_ and _communication._
2. The DICTIONARY describes **KNOWLEDGE** as coming from "_study, investigation, observation, experience, reasoning._
3. And it notes that **CRITERIA** or **STANDARDS** come from "_authority, custom, general consent._"

TWO MAJOR WAYS or SOURCES: **External** (Nature/Natural Law... Authority, authorities (people, institutions, ideologies)...   And **Internal** (from self; of course influenced by the Field or environment).

--A "BIG FOUR":
"Science," empiricism. ("Data, Conjecture, Hypothesis, Theory, Law, Paradigm")
[Cf. **DIKW**: "Data, Information, Knowledge, Wisdom"]
"Religion," supernaturalism etc.
"Culture": Norms Mores Folkways, Conventional or Folk-Wisdom"
"Personal, Idiosyncratic knowing-styles and ideologies, including one's own "Schema."

[2.2.] Prior Basics: key types, HISTORICAL perspective:

SUGGESTION. Learners should _absolutely_ know well, the differences between **induction** [= move from facts to generalities] **and deduction** [= apply concepts to factual matter], also between essentially the Material and the Mental (**rationalism and empiricism**). They could _secondarily_ have a glimpse of how these have broadly existed and changed throughout intellectual history.

FOUR BASIC WAYS FROM PHILOSOPHY:
Empiricism (physical matter is prime)..... **Materialism** (observation and experiment are key) == _"versus"_
Idealism (reality lies in consciousness)..... **Rationalism** (reason is the best Way).....

The WORLDVIEW of Idealism: "the essential nature of reality lies in a realm transcending phenomena...that the essential nature of reality lies	➔ ...and so, the METHOD of Rationalism: "reason is in itself a source of knowledge superior to and independent

in consciousness or reason" ➔	of sense perception"
The WORLDVIEW of Materialism: "physical matter is the only or fundamental reality and all being, processes, & phenomena can be explained as manifestations or results of matter" ➔	➔ ...**and so, the METHOD of Empiricism**: "relying on observation and experimentation" "A theory that all knowledge originates in experience"

WAYS OF KNOWING IN HISTORY.

[1.] A writer speaks of a cultural change which "gave us science, technology, freedom, and capitalism: the Enlightenment. The Enlightenment made human **reason** the measure of all things, throwing off **ancient rules** if they fell short. What the **king** once ordered, what **bishops** once enforced, what **tradition** once required was to be set aside in the name of **scientific knowledge** and personal self-discovery." [-- INTERNET]

From sociocultural tradition (let alone also authoritarianism) and religion – to both objective science and also subjective personal-individual knowing …

[2.] Rationalism is found in pre-scientific societies, especially ancient Greece. It assumed that "**thought** *alone*" was enough—enough to gain "**truth** about any matter (from the existence of God to the life cycle of the mosquito)…" Let enough people thinking and discuss long enough, they'll reach a consensus which is truth. Brainpower was key, replacing any need for external, empirical-materialistic WAYS OF KNOWING such as "**examination, research, or experiment**." In Europe, SCHOLASTICISM later became overdeveloped, spending time on arcane issues (the size of angels, or the nature of the soul of a butterfly). Was it really harmful? "The scholastic idea (it was hardly a method) bedevilled philosophical, religious, scientific and social thought for millennia, and still survives in the legal and religious thinking of many societies." [-- KEYWORDS IN HUMAN THOUGHT]

[3.] Very generally speaking, ARISTOTLE favored deduction from principles—prior existing or given ones. The danger in deduction is that if the prior assumption is suspect—inaccurate, incomplete, etc., not true to nature or reality or facts or "being the case—then the result fails. Later, FRANCIS BACON and other early scientists initiated induction. Its strength is—if done carefully!—to build solidly upward from careful and humble observations, to general conclusions true because their foundations are in experience. Of course a danger in induction is that 100% neutral, "true" observation is almost impossible; "lenses" obvious and subtle, including blocks-barriers-biases, stand in the way.

[4.] PLATO, and DESCARTES, embodied **rationalism** or reasoning as a, or the main, way of knowing. Later, LOCKE, BERKELEY, and HUME favored **empiricism**. KANT suggested a synthesis, a transcendental idealism, a combination of *primal intuitions, sense-impressions,* and also *categories.* Again, synthesis was stressed: ANOTHER THINKER said that "The concrete without the conceptual is blind; the conceptual without the concrete is empty." [-- C. VAN DOREN]

ANECDOTE. Allegedly, some French graduate students in sociology at a Florida university, claimed that they did not need to do empirical research for their doctoral dissertations. They had already thought or reasoned out the concepts involved, and that was sufficient… [-- SOURCE; valid or perhaps fabricated…]

[2.3.] QUALITY: concerning good—and bad—W. of K.

RICHARD PAUL'S dismal (but useful) roster of "the major obstacles or blocks to rational thinking: **prejudice, bias, self-deception, desire, fear, vested interest, delusion, illusion, egocentrism, sociocentrism, and ethnocentrism**."

Some Dubious, Problematic, Questionable—Ways of "Knowing" [more like Types of Knowledge …]:

--A **"conventional absurdity"** is a mis-knowledge which doesn't seem sensible, but is repeated because of its implications. (We use only 5% of our brains… lemmings commit mass suicide… the Boy Scout Manual annually outsells all other books… we can be coerced into buying by subliminal messages.)

--Related is what are called **"urban legends"** (Hippie Baby Sitter, Alligators in the Sewers, the Kentucky Fried Rat, and Halloween sadists—those who put razor blades in apples).

--Even worse might be some **"intellectual commonplaces"** of an academic field. A young ANTHROPOLOGIST criticized old legends untrue but still lodged in textbooks: (Samoan free sex and lack of crime and frustration… sex-reversed cultures such as the gentle Arapesh (but the men are headhunters)… the stone-age pristine Tasaday (fabricated by the

[2.4.] Personal Knowledge: good, or not...

Knowing can be personal (relatedly, "subjective") == but also impersonal (relatedly, "objective"). Presumably "personal" involves experiences and a response to them, also interior reflection etc. including intuitions....
EACH approach can be BOTH good AND bad—depending on the *task-goal, context, criteria*, etc.).

Personal, informal, subjective:	Impersonal, formal, objective
GOOD: powerful Truthtelling	GOOD: escapes from too much or inaccurate subjectivity, emotionality, etc.
BAD: can be both biassed and incomplete, also un-thought-out, unanalyzed	BAD: can be incomplete, also itself can be biassed or non-objective!

EXAMPLE. The "Schema" exists in all of us; is powerful and perhaps flawed; often not known well...

A **schema** is a major Way of Knowing. It's the existing, accumulated **image of a subject one already has** from various sources. The subjects can be "anything and everything" about which we have existing images "Photosynthesis, algebra, marriage, Buddhism, Germans, justice, critical thinking, killer bees, immigrants, roses, labor unions." A critical-thinking teacher names such sources (ways of knowing?) as *mass media, family and friends, school textbooks, the playground, the workplace, authorities, whatever*."
[-- WILLIAM PEIRCE, Maryland teacher]

[2.5.] Relate W.O.K. & "LENSES" (viewpoint-perspectives):

This is the enormous category of "not reality or the world, but the Perspectives through which the reality of the world is seen, known." **Relevant variable-issues from "lens-work" are of course that Lenses are often Implicit, unstated... Questionable, not best for the purpose... Insightful but of course also Biased/Incomplete... and Hard to locate at times... See complete treatment in the Tool-kit.**

Perception-systems: **Communication chain**: stereotypes, selective perception?..... **Language**: the word is not the thing..... **Systems of Thought**: paradigms, etc. (relativity, evolution, quantum mechanics, systems, deconstruction) .... Theories of **Human Nature**: Christianity, Freud, Socio/Psycho-Biology, Marx, Existentialism, behaviorism, Plato..... **Feminisms**: liberal, marxist, radical, psychoanalytic, socialist, existentialist, postmodern.... **Ethics, Morality, Value** Systems: relativism, egotism, duty, virtue, situation, natural law, divine command, behaviorism, utilitarianism..... **Zeitgeist**, Climate of Opinion, Today's Truths & Taboos, Schools of Thought.... **Societies, Cultures, Nations**: East and West, America (effort optimism progress humanitarianism individualism materialism).... **Institutions**: political, religious: the traditional conservative == radical-liberal spectrum.... **Culture**: norms mores folkways, conventional wisdom, received opinion, folk-knowledge, tacit lore. From large to smaller groups..... **Academic Disciplines**: Humanities, Social Sciences, Natural Sciences. Fields within each, all with many competing Schools of Thought: [*Literature*: aesthetic, psychobiographical, historical, social-critical, etc.] [*Sociology*: functionalism, conflict, rational choice, symbolic interactionism, phenomenology] ..... [Others!] **Individual** Lenses. Including "schema" or existing pictures of subjects in reality......   Also **WAYS OF KNOWING**: personal-objective, science, supernaturalism, intuition, etc.... Also **WORLD-VIEWS**: pocket philosophies of what reality is like: good-bad, etc.

SEE for "II" FULL-Dress version, the ToolKit "Lens- work, " # 4 in Appendix #4, Tool- KITS...

[2.6.] Gallery readings: Lab Work

> **SUGGESTION.** These might "open up" the **Ways of Knowing** issue...

1. A kindergarten class found a mouse but didn't know what sex it was. *The teacher suggested that they vote...*
[But, cf. is it Fact-issue (=research it), Opinion (=anything goes), or Reasoned Judgment (=use evidence plus logic)?]

EXAMPLES: Three vivid incidents of using—what kind of Way of Knowing instead of which better kind?

2. --My own AUNT MARJORIE was firmly convinced that automobile seat belts were dangerous. They may maim people, trap them in burning or submerged cars, and prevent one being thrown safely out of the vehicle.

3. --A newspaper columnist, apparently defending "personal freedom" or the like, (1) condemned laws against smoking in restaurants as based upon "some very dubious scientific evidence," and also (2) defended using cell phones when driving, saying that he had "never himself personally observed an accident caused by using a phone while driving." [-- MILWAUKEE JOURNAL SENTINEL, 2002]

4. --A computer-expert FRIEND reported that A COLLEAGUE felt that Macintosh computers were best for a certain use. My FRIEND presented concrete **scientific evidence** (objective evaluations, etc.) that such was not the case. The COLLEAGUE replied, "Well, I just don't believe you." Then my FRIEND presented personal, anecdotal, evidence (his own experience, that of others) also that such was not the case. The COLLEAGUE kept on replying: "But I simply don't believe you."

5. "It's not wrong because it's a sin; it's a sin because it's wrong." [-- MY TRADITIONALISTIC GRANDPARENT]
[**W. of K.:** *Absolutism Natural Law*, vs. *Systems-of-Ethics*...]

6. "S/he just lets the facts speak for themselves." [-- COMMON REMARK...*{which always makes me **cringe**}*...]

7. "This wine is truly bad, but I really do like it..." [- A CONNOISSEUR]

8. "...but, **my** common sense, or **your** common sense?" [- A STUDENT IN ENGLISH 101]

9. "My mind is made up; I know what I know; don't confuse me with the facts etc." [-- COMMON REMARK]
[Personal-preference, vs. science or empiricism]

10. A troubled teenage male, one LUKE HELDER, planted pipe bombs in mailboxes across the Midwest. He believed a conspiracy existed to enslave the masses and pillage the environment. How did he know? "Whether it's **logic, meditation, channeling, astral projection** or **ghosts**, all are ways of knowing," he wrote. [-- TIME MAGAZINE]

11. In 2002, an embassy worker in Indonesia reported crowds of Islamic fundamentalists recruiting people for jihad or holy war to prevent Christians and Jews from killing them. They believed in a Jewish conspiracy, and that 4,000 Jews were warned not to come to work at the World Trade Center on Sept. 11 of the last year. When asked where they got those ideas, "they said from the Internet. They took for granted that anything they learned from the Internet is true.... Internet users are only 5% of the population, but these 5% spread rumors to everyone else. They say, 'He got it from the Internet.' They think it's the Bible." [-- NEW YORK TIMES 12 MAY 02]

12. Satiric critique of **"Folk wisdom"** (received opinion, conventional wisdom):
"Nobody needs to read the full text of the report by the Commission on Obscenity and Pornography to know that its findings conflict with the instant presuppositions of **folk wisdom**. Folk wisdom knows...that pornography causes sex crimes and other socially-harmful effects. No matter that **Denmark** has learned otherwise. No matter that **psychology and psychiatry** disagree. Folk wisdom knows what it knows. It knows that potatoes should be planted in the dark of the moon, that human destiny is controlled by the signs of the zodiac, and that little green men from outer space constantly flit about the earth in flying saucers. So if a benighted **presidential commission** after extensive investigation concludes that obscenity plays no significant role in producing harmful sexual conduct by adults, then it will just have to be shouted down.
[-- ST. LOUIS POST-DISPATCH, 1960's]
[Questionable "cultural tradition" (possibly religion) opposed by science, and individuals thinking critically...]

13. A scientific report on sexuality (from a Surgeon General) is rankling the White House. It claims there's no evidence that teaching abstinence from sex works, or that a gay person can become straight. Schools should encourage abstinence but also teach birth control. In response, "**The President** continues to believe that abstinence and abstinence education is the most effective way to prevent AIDS, to prevent unwanted pregnancy."
  [-- Milwaukee Journal-Sentinel, ca. 2000]

14. A controversial paper about sex between adults and children suggested that some behaviors now called abuse be reclassified as "adult-child sex." Allegedly, 2/3 of abused men and 1/4 of abused women had reported neutral or positive reactions. In any case, the report "explicitly distinguishes between **moral or legal** views of abuse—that is, 'wrongfulness'—and **scientific** definitions of the term, or 'harmfulness.' The report claims that psychologists had a history of identifying "**morality and law** with science," and noted that "behaviors such as cunnilingus, fellatio, homosexual sex, masturbation, and promiscuous sex were once defined as pathological."   [-- CHE, 28 May 99]

15. Three responses to homosexuality as a social issue, with varied Ways of Knowing.
PEDAGOGICAL PLOY: *Explain & evaluate these via issues in lens-work; does that help?*

[1.] "Men using one another as women constitutes a perversion. To my unreconstructed mind, this is as true as ever; and so far as I am concerned it would still be true even if gay sex no longer entailed the danger of infection and even if everything about it were legalized by all 50 states and ratified by all nine justices of the Supreme Court."   [--NORMAN PODHORETZ, American writer and editor]   **[Personal Preference… Science… Legality…]**

[2.] "One cannot base Christian morality upon a capacity for disgust."
[-- 1963 BRITISH QUAKER statement regarding religious attitudes toward homosexuality and related issues]   **[Values vs. feelings]**

[3.] There are times when people allow **personal religious beliefs, political expediency, material interests, or customary prejudices** to interfere with the logical extension of liberal principles within the political realm. For example, the FOUNDERS knew that slavery stood in direct contradiction to the revolutionary doctrine of the "rights of man," yet because of **political expediency, economic interests, and racial prejudice**, they allowed the institution to continue. [-- R. CLAIRE SNYDER] [...*a very compact summary!* \

[({ END of "Ways of Knowing" unit within Prior Basics...)}]

|#+#|+|#+#|+#|+|#+|+#|+|+|#+|+|++|#+|+#|+#|+#|+#|+#|+#+#|+|+|+#|#+|+|#+|#|+#|+#|+|#+|+#|+#|+#|#+|#+||#+|+#|+#|+#|+|#+|#+||#+||

O R I E N T A T I O N - B A R :

1.Dispositions	2. Quality	3. Relativism	4. Knowing	5. F,O,RJ	6. Reas.-Rat.	7. Personal	8. Philo 101	9. 7-R

[PB # 5:] "Fact, Opinion, Reasoned Judgment"

Three different kinds of question-issues, seem to repay handling by three different approaches. (This distinction may help, to focus and streamline inquiry, and to avoid "false-trail" arguing…)
   [-- Source: this three-part scheme was created by RICHARD PAUL, a key educator in critical thinking …]

EXAMPLE #1: Alaska… (1) "Is A. the coldest state?"—factual; don't argue it, research it!... (2) "Is A. the best state for a vacation?"—opinion: share your viewpoints but don't berate, etc. … (3) "Is A. the best place to set up a certain type of business now?"—reasoned judgment: do your research, via criteria, then judiciously conclude…

EXAMPLE #2. "Some residents in my apartment residential community, objected to my offering surplus produce on a stand outside my door." Was my service, were their objections, bad? good? **Factual:** objectively a source of odors and liquids? (=no, or minimal and correctible: bag all soft fruit). **Opinion:** an eyesore etc.? (= a judgment-call?) **Reasoned Judgment:** should be banished? (= seek an objective win-win situation. I bagged soft produce and put up a modesty-curtain concealing the offerings. This avoided sight, smell, liquids but retained availability for those who desired it). *Various issues demand varied methods, also allowed more objective, win-win, fair-minded proceeding…*

EXAMPLE #3. At a panel on sexual orientation, a religious student declared that through spiritual reparative

330

therapy, "thousands have changed," meaning from homosexuality back to heterosexuality. The question at hand is: "Can and do homosexuals change to become heterosexuals?"

--But what kind of question is it? We would say it is a **Factual** one, to be determined by empirical survey *only*. But beware; when pursued thus, the student's declaration turns out to be quite *false* (and hence potentially damaging through being misleading). {At least false in terms of defining "change" as not simply **1. behavior** (stop the gay acts and remain celibate or perform the straight acts) or **2. self-identification** ("I am heterosexual now. I am heterosexual now.") but also **3. arousal and fantasy** (what really does turn you on, not what is supposed to), let alone **4. ultimate self-identity** (with which gender, opposite or same, would you prefer to be marooned on a desert island?)}

True, complications arise. The student's <u>way of knowing</u> is none of the above three, but is **Spirituality**, which exist along with **Intuition, Conventionally Received Wisdom, and a host of <u>other</u> types of knowing** than RICHARD PAUL'S three here. These wayward ways of knowing do <u>not</u> seem to be accepted by PAUL, a philosopher-of-rational-reason, for reasons which are understandable and—given PAUL'S position!—appropriate ...] Still and all, the **F,O,RJ** distinction seems a solid if minor basic useful "standpoint"...

|#+#|+|#+#|+#|+|#+|+#|+|+|#+|+|++|#+|+#|+#|+#|+#|+#+#|+|+|#|#+|+|#+|#|+#|+#|+|#+|+#|+#|+|#+|#+||#+|+#|+#|+#|+|#+|#+||#+||

ORIENTATION-BAR:

1.Dispositions	2. Quality	3. Relativism	4. Knowing	5. F,O,RJ	**6. Reas.-Rat.**	7. Personal	8. Philo 101	9. 7-R

[PB # 6:] "Reasoning, vs. "Rationalizing"

--**THE PROBLEM/OPPORTUNITY:** A recurrent human tendency, but overlooked by beginners. "<u>Most of our so-called reasoning is finding reasons to go on believing as we already do.</u>" [-- J. H. ROBINSON] This is due to our <u>root-reasons</u>, such as just-personal pet peeve... ideology or traditional cultural norm... extremist-fringe stance ... power or profit motive... etc." And we may be *unaware* we are doing this defense-of-the- existent...

KEY EXAMPLE. [1.] On <u>a half-hour talk show, two opponents *argue against and past each other*</u> about ***Abortion, Death Penalty, Gun Control***, etc. Many of my state-college freshman English 101 students could only reply: "well s/he gives the facts" or of course "who's to say who's right after all it's his/her own opinion." But the talk-show "thinkers" are not **reasoning** toward common validity, they are **rationalizing.** Ironically they may not even realize this—but we can! Nor is true agreement or communication possible in rationalizing. (P.S. – also it's pleasurable or a good sporting Contest for reader-spectators to try to "spot the hidden motivation between the lines" of a writer who's even *self*-deluding...!)

MORE EXAMPLES: To cinch the concept, related to discovering the **Backgrounds** of a comment: SEE in Mind- Play

[2.] "<u>Mother of 10 Speaks</u>" ("large families are good," reasons 1 2 3 4 5: relaxed more joyful love, etc., but then "duty to God, hence really, **root** is to defend a prior-held, deeply-valued **religious stand against artificial contraception**).....

[2.] "<u>Selling canes for household discipline</u>" ("acceptable: efficient, harmless, better alternative, popular"—*but* the known but unadmitted root is **to make money in sales** of these canes)....

[3.] "<u>No to laws requiring motorcycle helmets and lights-on during the day</u> (1 2 3 4 5 reasons and more, "ineffective, wears down the battery"—*but* the unstated root seems **"pro individual rights against government intrusion"**).....

[4.] "<u>Praising the space program</u> (it provided Teflon and more, 1 2 3 4 5 etc., etc—*but* the probably-unknown root is probably **"traditional American values of materialism, progress, optimism"**).....

[5.] ..... but rationalizing continues at high levels. **Natural Law,** or **social-constructionism**; etc. .....

|#+#|+|#+#|+#|+|#+|+#|+|+|#+|+|++|#+|+#|+#|+#|+#|+#+#|+|+|#|#+|+|#+|#|+#|+#|+|#+|+#|+#|+|#+|#+||#+|+#|+#|+#|+|#+|#+||#+||

ORIENTATION-BAR:

1.Dispositions	2. Quality	3. Relativism	4. Knowing	5. F,O,RJ	6. Reas.-Rat.	**7. Personal**	8. Philo 101	9. 7-R

[PB # 7:] Issue of SUBJECTIVE / PERSONAL *"versus"* OBJECTIVE / IMPERSONAL knowing & thinking:

PRIOR BASIC/BACKGROUND ISSUE # N.   "Personal" vs. "Objective" Knowing.

ISSUE. The status of **Personal Subjective** ways of knowing, also **Impersonal Objective** ways of knowing. Their existence; their uses, validity—or not…   Attention to a cluster of related, basic, pesky, *clarifiable* issues…

CRUCIALITY. Beginning learners may be *vastly confused* on this issue. They may never have identified it as an issue (**Unawareness**)… They may have been told one or the other partial stand about it—personal as richly-good, or biased-bad; objective as unattainable; etc. (**Misconception**)… They may not know the issues and some SES or Standard Existing Stands from which competent thinkers can choose (**Ineptness**)…

CONNECTIONS. Relates closely to **Personal Thinking** (one's profile). Also to the issue of **Dispositions** or combat vs. cooperation in thinking with others.

CONCEPT CARD. The following seems to be *an unusually-superior* elucidation of this cluster of issues (good *because* complete but clarified, fecund but focused). It lays out the issues, and Standard Stands open to thinkers, in order to *enormously accelerate* the awareness of beginning thinkers.

---

(1) The Pros and the Cons of Both "Knowledges"… (A) "Objectivity" (+) *is to be sought* (fairminded thinking) and (+) *is* possible (more than "relativists" etc. often claim or realize). Still, this "Impersonality" may also be (-) incomplete for full knowing, plus (-) overdone… **(B)** Then, the "Personal" is (-) inescapable, unavoidable really, and also (-) risks being profoundly biased, *but* (+) its bias *can be monitored* and also (+) personal testimony *can* enormously enrich, via motivation, involvement… And strongly-emotional, affective personal statements can be both a liability (*hotheadedness*), and an asset (*enlightening*)—*if* competently "sublimated."
SUGGESTED GUIDELINE: SO: know well the Onions *and* Orchids of *both* ways of knowing. And decide well, when which is appropriate or questionable in what context (scientific; literary; etc.)

(2) Standards for Good Thinking: Dispositions Also, "Truth": Absolutes vs. Relativism…
(A) We assume the goal in group thinking/discussion, of not agonistic-argumentative Combat to Win Victory for your side … but of Cooperating with others to Work toward Veracity or Validity. SO: A reason why "personal bias plus "heat" would be suspect, should be questioned.
(B) We also assume **(1)** "nothing is true or good or right foundationally ahead of time" (clean the Truth Slate with Existential bleach and start afresh with Tabula Rasa!). But then **(2)** "given this or that criterion, we can offer this or that truth as discussable truth" (="committed relativism"). SO: know these Stands as ways of helping manage both excessive Absolutism (**We Have The Truth**), plus also rampant naïve Relativism (**We Can Know Nothing**).

(3) Suggested Guideline in re STRONG PERSONAL STANDS. Both reject, and accept, heated emotional statements, "depending." (A) **Omit** them if their motivation is suspect—neurosis, compulsion, "agenda," etc.—and if they remain unsublimated (wild stallion not harnessed workhorse). (B) But **admit** even "strong" emotional personal responses *if* they usefully, even if forcefully, serve one or two important purposes often overlooked: to (A) "Save the Subject," clarify and defend a wrongly-neglected/maligned issue, and/or (B) "Reach the Reader," help even an unaware, even resistant reader see something—for reader's own benefit. SO: know this approach.
[Even *"polar"* or *"100%"*-type statements (cognitively extreme, affectively strong) can be useful hence admitted if they function not to dictate etc. but to (1) help clearly define a new concept, (2) show excesses of the extreme!, (3) help one adjust along the continuum, (4) and counter resistances-evasions-fear of the new and threatening…]

(4) Thinker's Consciousness of ONE'S OWN PSYCHIC PROFILE. ["Know thyself": even more true nowadays…] Preparatory to the above in action, (A) ***Work to know*** your own Thinking self, your Personal

<u>Profile</u> (your motivations, values, temperament, biases, etc.. (This, beyond just <u>your preferred thinking skills</u> in your Personal ToolBelt.) **(1)** Then, *manage* your biases. **(2)** And *hear* "the other side" of issues fully, not to accept or attack it, but to comprehend it as well as they themselves do. (Beware feeling threatened by own ignorances, even inabilities.) Also, **(B)** *disclose* your Profile to others (discussants, readers, learners, etc.) appropriately. SO: know thyself, accept and critique self, also share same, all more than usual…

(5) <u>Status of the Above</u>… These four guidelines are more developed and involved than many thinkers would want or are comfortable with. But they carefully elucidate many more issues, plus Standard Possible Stands overlooked, than other resources do. And, one *can* do the above, even if not always in all contexts, *but* only if one values the stands—*"ya gotta wanna!"* And if not, *laissez faire*…

|#+#|+|#+#|+#|+|#+|+#|+|+|#+|+|++|#+|+#|+#|+#|+#|+#|+#+#|+|+|+#|#+|+|#+|#|+#|+#|+|#+|+#|+#|+|#+|#+|+|#+|+#|+#|+#|+|#+|#+||#+||

O R I E N T A T I O N - B A R :

1.Dispositions	2. Quality	3. Relativism	4. Knowing	5. F,O,RJ	6. Reas.-Rat.	7. Personal	**8. Philo 101**	9. 7-R

[PB # 8:] "PHILOSOPHY *101"*: its issues for *thinking* …

The general thrust of the discipline of **philosophy** for us here, is to <u>**question critically**</u>, even-or-especially one's <u>own</u> Responses to an issue—one's Statements/Claims (or Conclusions or Evaluations or Explanations or recommended Actions etc. etc. etc.). [Cf. **Dispositions**: willingness to be fair-minded, spot own biases, plus **Conscious** of one's own thinking ploys.]

First referring more to the <u>elements prior to</u> the specific **statement**/claim itself:

1. Elucidate and critique what I'll call the **"backgrounds"** of a Statement/Claim.

Various formulations exist. RICHARD PAUL the philosopher/teacher of critical thinking speaks of <u>four</u> dimensions of "background logic" behind/above a statement. **(1)** The source of the ideas or concepts, **(2)** their substructure, **(3)** their implications, and **(4)** the relationship to other ideas and concepts, similar and different. [- PAUL, 1993: 390]. He elsewhere offers an octopod or <u>eight</u>-point version of background elements to consider. 1. The Purpose, 2. the Question, 3. the Point of View *or* Frame of Reference, 4. the Empirical elements, 5. the Conceptual elements (assumptions, inferences), 6. the Interpretations, 7. the Implications, 8. the Conclusions.

We here suggest <u>**three**</u> background elements—perhaps as GUIDELINES:

1.A. Identify and critique the **implicit presupposions** which lie behind a Response to an issue, but upon which the S/C may depend. These are *unstated, often unconscious, perhaps unintended, surely unanalyzed* assumptions about "Reality": view of the world, what is, what should be, what to do, etc. But some **I.P.**'s may be *arguable-questionable-problematic* and otherwise "dubious" or "suspicious." [See separate module on **Implicit Presuppositions**.]

1.B. Identify the **motivations *why*** one believes etc. as one does in the response. [Admittedly this becomes more psychological than philosophical perhaps…] [See separate section on **Motivations**.]

1.C. Identify the **"lenses"** or the systems of perception, perspectives, viewpoints through which the response sees the subject. [See separate major module on **"Lens-work"** {with **Ways of Knowing**}]

Then referring more to <u>elements within/following</u> the specific statement/claim itself:

2. Seek to identify any "counter-examples" to find **inconsistencies,** in the S/C.

These are instances which <u>contradict</u> the examples given in the S/C, and which may show a weakness in the S/C.

3. Consider implications, consequences, results of the S/C.

What would happen if it were put into practice, etc.? A bad outcome may thus weaken the S/C. [See separate module on **Consequences** of a position or action:

In the module, three key EXAMPLES *showing skill in consequence-analysis* are:

1. Should one be a surrogate father? DAN SAVAGE points out possible pitfalls perhaps unsuspected.
2. Should universities ban recruiters from campus if they discriminate? A YALE STUDENT NEWSPAPER EDITORIAL suggests overlooked bad effects of this in the larger system over time.
3. Should Blacks (or other minorities) be paid reparations for past oppressions of them? DAVID HOROWITZ suggests more problems than potentialities therein.

4. Define key terms well. More generally, **use language clearly.**

5. ...and of course, the meat-&-potatoes main-dish here: **employ good logic** (formal and informal) .....

use good reasoning and argumentation ..... and *avoid* **logical fallacies.**

[This enters the province of conventional "CRITICAL THINKING," which is a major portion of our **Essential Thinking**, but only a component, not **Thinking-as-such**, at least as we see it...]

...but would you also critique philosophy for any **shortcomings, demerits, "onions,"** etc.?
Sure. ... 1. Can get **unrelated to real-world issues.** ["If the kitchen light is out, does the stove still exist? etc.] 2. Can be **humanly flawed: culture-bound,** also **individually-biased.** 3. Can emphasize an ungenerous pinch-nosed **spirit of closing down, limiting, denial.** ["No, you can't know or say or claim that... No, not even that either..." *Okaaay, what can we say, eh?*...]
But this *wart-spotting* is irrelevant here. Let's emphasize the positive power of philosophy's particular perceptions, as above here...

|#+#|+|#+#|+#|+|#+|+#|+|+|#+|+|++|#+|+#|+#|+#|+#|+#|+#+#|+|+|+#|#+|+|#+|#|+#|+#|+|#+|+#|+#|+|#+|#+||#+|+#|+#|+#|+|#+|#+||#+||

Philo 101: especially "**BACKGROUNDS**" to any response to a subject

--THE ISSUE. A basic dual-level situation exists. Any response to a subject, a statement or claim about it (no matter whether it concerns what-is Description, good-bad Evaluation, why-Explanation, so-what Relevance, so-now Policy & Procedure concerning, etc.) has not only itself, but a Background. This includes Simple but also Complex elements "hanging around or about it," so to speak. [The **world-view** or assumptions about reality... The **implicit presuppositions** within the statement itself... The **motivations why** one truly did respond as one did...]

--WHY IMPORTANT. *Pedagogically, how to accelerate learners' awareness of, and ability to deal with, these echoing elements?*

1. Beginning learners seem unaware of prior complexities "above, behind, to one side of, and below" the surface statement itself. [Amateur misconceptions include: unawareness of Rationalizing, let alone Root-Reasons for believing; being impressed by back-and-forth Facts and Arguments; and so forth.]

2. Beginning learners may not think to discuss why do people not change their responses even after "reasonable" discussion etc."? Here we delve into the "root-cellar" beneath, via the current-contested issue of "same-sex marriage."

--SUGGESTION. See whether the following cluster works, is even fuller than some existing treatments of the issue, if it is more elucidated...

(**CONNECTIONS.** This **Background** issue at once relates to most of our other, earlier PBB Tool-TRAYS. **Reasoning vs. Rationalizing,** also the **Relativism** Tangle, also **Fact-Opinion-Reasoned Judgment** issues, also of course **Personal-Subjective vs. Objective** thinking, let alone **Dispositions** or "fight vs. fair" attitudes...)

GUIDELINE/GOAL. To first of all *know* (realize) that elements lie "behind-below-beyond" a specific statement (response to something). And then to *be able to* recognize them, in obvious—and difficult subtle cases; in the statements of others—in one's own statements! And then to critique them if needed...

EXAMPLE. Hidden elements "lie above and behind" a response to a complex social issue.

Let's open with RICHARD PAUL'S comment of what happened when he discussed a political issue with a friend. The discussion soon drifted into—well, complexity. Above and beyond the facts, arguments, data, etc., a

"background logic" began to emerge. Or at least PAUL realized that certain **"background elements"** lie above-and-beyond any content (especially a controversial complex crucial subject…). These may include Lenses of all types (world-views, paradigms, frames of reference, personal value-systems, plus implicit presuppositions as in "Philosophy 101"). And one should take note of this **background element**—stratospheric and hazy as it may seem to earth-bound thinkers…

"…recently…I got into a lengthy disagreement with an acquaintance on the [supposed] *justification of the U.S. invasion of Grenada.* Before long we were discussing questions of morality, the appropriate interpretation of international law, supposed rights of countries to defend their interests, spheres of influence, the character of U.S. and Soviet foreign policies, the history of the two countries, the nature and history of the C.I.A., the nature of democracy, whether it can exist without elections, who has credibility and how to judge it, the nature of the media and how to access it, whether it reflects an 'American' party line, sociocentrism, our own personalities, consistency, etc."

PAUL notes that he and the other person held differing *world views, global perspectives, points of view, views of human nature (background logic).* Be these lenses starkly **"conservative vs. liberal,"** or more complex and nuanced. Be they **Freudianism, Marxism, Darwinian evolution, Christianity, existentialism,…!** *This divergence in basic backgrounds, is why they could not agree.* And this disagreement would obtain also on other contested social issues (crucial concerns). *Poverty, wealth, welfare, military-industrial complex, welfare, capitalism, racism and sexism, communism and socialism.* [-- RICHARD PAUL, IN "MCPECK'S MISTAKES"]

--To me, PAUL's instance here is superb, classic. It seems both crystal-clear accessible, and yet also subtly-penetrating, revelatory of "other elements above." (It seems almost wry; when thinking and discussing, do we not too often "spiral upward" into ultimate if hidden lenses, Personal Temperaments, insights/biases, and more, at the drop of a hat?) What I have bordered in dotted lines in PAUL's comment, seem to hover halfway between subject-relevance, and larger subjective issues. (And as noted in **Lens-work**, the *larger* lenses are usually chosen subjectively; behind those frames of reference lie even deeper and often very emotional worldviews which the lenses or frames support…)
(*)*Is it therefore important for learners to begin to sense "background elements" to all issues… to all statement-claims and position-stands on issues… to be "backdrop-savvy"?*

|#+#|+|#+#|+#|+|#+|+#|+|+|#+|+|++|#+|+#|+#|+#|+|+#|+#|+#|+|+|#+|+|#+|#|+#|+#|+#|+|#+|+#|+#|+|#+|#+||#+|+#|+#|+#|+|#+|#+||#+||

[8.1.] "LENSES" upon the subject…

SEE Tool- Kit #5, on "LENS- work, " Appendix #4

This is the enormous category of "not reality or the world, but the Perspectives through which the reality of the world is seen, known." **Relevant variable-issues** from "lens-work" are of course that Lenses are often Implicit, unstated… Questionable, not best for the purpose… Insightful but of course also Biased/Incomplete… and Hard to locate at times… See complete treatment in the Tool-kit.   As noted earlier, of many types:

Perception-systems: **Communication chain**: stereotypes, selective perception? **Language**: the word is not the thing. **Systems of Thought**: paradigms, etc. (relativity, evolution, quantum mechanics, systems, deconstruction) Theories of **Human Nature**: Christianity, Freud, Socio/Psycho-Biology, Marx, Existentialism, behaviorism, Plato… **Feminisms**: liberal, marxist, radical, psychoanalytic, socialist, existentialist, postmodern. **Ethics, Morality, Value** Systems: relativism, egotism, duty, virtue, situation, natural law, divine command, behaviorism, utilitarianism **Zeitgeist**, Climate of Opinion, Today's Truths & Taboos, Schools of Thought **Societies, Cultures, Nations**: East and West, America (effort optimism progress humanitarianism individualism materialism) **Institutions**: political, religious: the traditional conservative == radical-liberal spectrum. **Culture**: norms mores folkways, conventional wisdom, received opinion, folk-knowledge, tacit lore. From large to smaller groups. **Academic Disciplines**: Humanities, Social Sciences, Natural Sciences. Fields within each, all with many competing Schools of Thought… [*Literature*: aesthetic, psychobiographical, historical, social-critical, etc.] [*Sociology*: functionalism, conflict, rational choice, symbolic interactionism, phenomenology] [Others!] **Individual** Lenses. Including "schema" or existing pictures of subjects in reality. Also **WAYS OF KNOWING**: personal-objective, science, supernaturalism, intuition, etc. Also **WORLD-VIEWS**: pocket philosophies of what reality is like: good-bad, etc.

|#||#+||#+|+#+|#|+|#+||+#+|+#|+|#+|+#|+|#+|#+|#|+|#+|+|#+||+||#++||||+|#|+|#+|+|+|#+|#|++|#|+#|+|#+|+|+|#+|+|+#|+#|+|+|#+|+#|+||#+

[8. 2.] "MOTIVATIONS": *why* one believes as one does—
"root-reasons" perhaps blocking change…

THE ISSUE. Why do we believe (and behave) as we do? And then change, or do not change when "logically" we supposedly should? And disagree-diverge-differ so much in our responses to the same subject?

WHY IMPORTANT. *Is this issue grist-for-the-mill for teaching/learning thinking?...*

OUR OFFERING. The following module which seeks to corral a <u>wider, more diverse</u> collection of **explanations and viewpoints,** than is usually assembled in one place. And to attempt <u>a deeper</u> explanation of **"subliminal root-reasons"** than, again, we have seen yet done (though scarcely "the one best way")...

TABLE OF CONTENTS:

ANALOGIES: *Can <u>comparisons</u> help elucidate the very concept—and causes—of motivations?*

Perhaps (1.) the **"puppet-show."** Do people seem at times, not self-aware and self-guided in their beliefs-and-actions, but instead "puppets,: jerkily dancing to the tune of Today's Truths & Taboos, but also whatever motivations are operating? Or, (2.) the **"equine":** are motivations sometimes first a "wild stallion" of open-field im-pulse and drive, then later sublimated (or disguised!) as the harnessed "workhorse" of useful-reasonable argument-opinion?

(3.) Also {from "below"} the **"archaeological"** or <u>"root-cellar"</u> or subterranean levels of influence." At times can we see how the *surface* layer of reasonable-conscious arguments, is influenced still by the *lower* layer of prior, emotional, unconscious influences: misconceptions, other lenses and value-systems, even-earlier personal and human drives?

[1.] GALLERY. Here is what many thinkers from diverse times, have proposed it is that truly motivates us, in our behavior, in our beliefs and thinking.

--**PREVIEW:** below, one can see (1) more-basic motivations common to everyone, plus then specialized drives... (2) "seamy" and "unrespectable" drives, along with nobler positive purposes... (3) motivations being quite irrational, misusing reason—and even intellectuals, etc., can think and act "badly" here... (4) power as an issue, but varied propulsions also in causing wars, motivating leaders of states...

--[Is this array "obvious old-hat"... or, might it be "a useful review of major varied types of "pulsions" or drives—hence useful for learners, not to mention interesting to others, the "thinking-buffs" among us?]

[1.] A Psychologist Proposes a "Hierarchy of Needs," from Biological "Upward": A classic scheme. **Biological: Survival, Reproduction, Safety... Belongingness, Love... Self-Esteem... Desire to Know, Understand... Aesthetic... Need for Self-Actualization ... Transcendence.** [-- ABRAHAM MASLOW]

[2.] An Advertising Executive Reveals the "Appeals Made to Consumers":
1. Fear. 2. Exclusivity. 3. Guilt. 4. Greed. 5. Need for approval (also **convenience** and **pleasure**). 6. **Ego-gratification.** (= the consumer's feeling is to be: "I deserve everything: praise, being in style, recognition by those we admire, attracting an admirer, joining lifestyles we regard as superior...") [-- SOURCE]

[3.] A sociologist notes that <u>some of our goals are Contrasting</u>—though not ultimately conflicting: Humans crave **"security *and* risk, coherence *and* spontaneity, novelty *and* latency, rivalry *and* mutuality"** with others. *Both* personal identity *and* social belongingness. Both security, and new experience. Of course, these "contrasting tendencies" are not irreconcilable "contradictions," but "different phases in the rhythm of living." [-- ROBERT S. LYND, Knowledge for What?]

[4.] An Anthropologist Notes how <u>Rewards</u> for a Social Action (here, a Community Sport Contest) can be both <u>Varied</u>, and also "<u>Unrespectable</u>" Perhaps but Very <u>Humanly-Real</u> After All.
In native Indonesia, a ritual involves a cockfight, a battle between two prize roosters. The owner of the winning bird

---

experiences a mixture of **social embarrassment, moral satisfaction, aesthetic disgust, and cannibal joy.**"
[-- CLIFFORD GEERTZ]

[5.] A French Essayist Suggests Some Claimed Social Motivations are "Excuses":
--The mildness of leaders is often nothing but policy to gain popular approval. And this mildness we call a virtue, is sometimes motivated by **vanity,** sometimes by **laziness,** often by **fear,** and almost always by **all three together.**
--Reconciliation with our enemies is nothing more than **the desire to improve our position... war-weariness... or fear** of some unlucky turn of events.
--We are held to duty by **laziness and timidity** [& conformity, self-esteem?], but often our virtue gets the credit.
--Whatever pretext we find for our afflictions [=supposedly noble public behavior etc.], their only source is often **our self-interest and vanity.** [- DE LA ROCHEFOUCAULD]

[6.] A British Thinker Suggests <u>Rationality</u> is often a <u>Minor</u> Motivation...
[What motivates people, in thought and in actions?] "<u>Sometimes their reason</u>—at other times their **prejudices** and **superstitions**; often their **social affections**, not seldom their **antisocial** ones, their **envy** or **jealousy**, their **arrogance** or **contemptuousness**: but most commonly their *desires or fears for themselves*—their **legitimate or illegitimate** *self-interest*... [and] **class** interests, and its feeling of class **superiority**."
[-- JOHN STUART MILL, from <u>On Liberty</u>]

[7.] A Popular Saying Echoes Mill: In *Personal-Private* Life, <u>Emotions May Be Major Motivators</u>:
 "**We are indeed reasonable, rational—***just as much as our <u>emotions</u> allow us to be.*" [-- common SAYING]

[8.] An Observer Suggests that also in *Public Political* Life, <u>Motivations Trump Reason</u>:
Liberals feel that "applying human <u>reasoning</u> to the world's problems will have a positive effect." This defines <u>reason</u> as "based on the shared findings of people looking at empirical evidence, using a degree of logic and seeking consensus." But some come to feel that "the spirit of such deliberation is all too rare." What happens is that this <u>right reason</u> "is trumped by **hotheadedness, stupidity, self-serving dishonesty, rigidity, and ideology.**" This realization, produces pessimism. [-- DALE RAMSEY, New York Times, 29 August 2006]

[9.] An Analyst Suggests that Non-Rational <u>Motivations can Block Social Justice</u> Being Achieved:
"All of the principles of liberal political theory not only justify but also require the legal recognition of gay marriage—legal equality, individual rights and liberties (including freedom of conscience, the right to privacy, and the right to marry), personal autonomy, human dignity, and the modern state of fairness. This is not to say that all people value philosophical consistency. There are times when people allow **personal religious beliefs, political expediency, material interests, or customary prejudices** to interfere with the logical extension of liberal principles within the political realm. For example, the Founders knew that slavery stood in direct contradiction to the revolutionary doctrine of the "rights of man," yet because of **political expediency, economic interests, and racial prejudice,** they allowed the institution to continue." [-- L. CLAIRE SNYDER, Gay Marriage and Democracy]

[10.] Machiavelli Suggests: <u>Power-Seeking</u> May Be a Paramount Motivator:
Power, meaning **the domination of others** is an addictive drug, a desire which can never be fully satisfied. The desire for more power and wealth is greater than our ability to accumulate them, a malcontentedness results. Alas, power and wealth are there for the having, but if you don't get them, somebody else will, perhaps to your detriment. Hence power is both a pragmatic need to secure, but perhaps because domination/control and wealth are prior motivations also... [-- MACHIAVELLI on Modern Leadership]

[11.] <u>Causes of War</u>: Diverse Motivations, All to Advance Certain "Passions":
[Analysis of World War I:} "What made millions of otherwise placable human beings ready to both kill others with extraordinary violence and risk their own lives in the process?"
--<u>All sides</u> showed **an irrational mystique of sacrifice, dehumanizing of the enemy, primitive, tribal, and fanatical.** Then <u>each side</u> had its own partisan and confident rationalization. For the <u>French</u>, it was **the need to defend civilization** (or the French Enlightenment) **against German barbarism and aristocracy...** For the <u>Germans</u> and Austrians, it was **the fantasy that only a pan-Teutonic culture could energize a decadent and febrile Europe...** For the <u>British</u>, it was **their fetishizing empire profoundly and narcissistically, their faith in the unswerving moral rightness of British political and economic interests...** For the <u>Russians</u> and their allies the

Serbs, it was **their seeking collective spiritual revitalization…** For the <u>Americans</u>, it was **the desire to assert the patriotic republican values linked with France,** and supposedly endangered by reactionary kings and emperors "and other Old World bogeymen." [-- TERRY CASTLE, CHE]

[12.] On the Positive Side, <u>Cooperation and Commitment</u> also Motivate:
--**"Deep love and family commitment…Meaningful work and career…Social and political involvement…Transcendence and spirituality."** Plus, our brains reinforce cooperative behavior…
[-- MICHAEL SHERMER]
--Scientists may feel guided by **God.** Actors feel **an emotional calling** to the stage. Journalists speak of their **commitment to the First Amendment,** free speech. [-- LAURA SECOR, Ideas, Boston Globe]

[13.] Still Positive: A Sociologist Notes <u>"More-Noble" Motivations</u>.
"Is **pecuniary self-interest** [private money-making] really the mainspring of human action upon which civilization depends? Bertrand Russell insists that men [sic] want **'power.'** They also want **peace of mind, fun, mutuality, spontaneity, respect, affection,** and other things….motivations are diverse; they are also highly malleable by the kind of culture in which they live." [-- ROBERT LYND, <u>Knowledge for What</u>?]

[14.] Some Mind-Sets ["conservative legal scholars"] May Have <u>Indeed-Conservative Motivations</u>:
Other factors are at play: a **desire to justify historically the status quo** (and **their position** in it), a **need for structure,** a **fear of change, disappointment with the present,** a **longing,** a **nostalgia** for the past. Who knows?" [-- V. CRAPANZANO, anthropologist]

[15.] We May Select A New Paradigm (System of Thought) via <u>"Non-Objective" Reasons</u> !
Even if a new paradigm seems better via "empirical and logical proofs," other considerations may apply. **Aesthetic: simplicity and beauty. Vested interest** of younger workers in the field. **"Temperament, training, demographics, and power"** also apply. [-- PICKLES & WATTS; ARID HOLT-JENSEN & THOMAS KUHN]

[16.] …but <u>Intelligence Alone May Not</u> Insure Reasonable Response ["Eggheads As Human Too"?]…
In an experiment, researcher DAVID PERKINS found that when specifically asked to present not only their *own* side of an issue, but also to understand and fairly represent the *opposite* side also, more-intelligent people did not do so, but invested their superior abilities to defend their *own* side instead….

[17.] Even a Psychotherapist (if <u>"Narcissistic"</u>) Can Have Skewed Motivations:
[Listening competently to a patient's dreams is difficult when a psychiatrist's "self-absorbed drive to shape the dream—**to fit his theoretical need, to validate his theory, to demonstrate his capacity to 'understand,' or to flex his therapeutic muscle before an admiring patient**—can all hobble the process of dream-conversing." [-- JAPA, Book Reviews, The Dream]

[18.] What might Motivate <u>Educators to Refuse to think and act anew</u>?:
What does it mean when professionals refuse to think critically about the critical thinking curriculum in education? "No doubt psychologists could come up with a bill of particulars: **"willful blindness, self-deception, intellectual arrogance, groupthink, ideological ossification or obduracy, Reichian character armor, Fromm's social filters, fear of change, debilitating heuristic biases, and so forth."** Philosophers, or those who profess to think rationally, may be just as vulnerable as the rest of us to cling tenaciously to existing beliefs and practices. [-- TIM VAN GALDER, Internet]

[19.] Some <u>Motivtions is Professional Vocational Arena</u> can be—Again, Human Not Rational…:
Workers often are driven by **"Boredom, careerism, sheer bloody-mindedness"**…to **"get a new act"** or **"chase fame"** or **lust for power**—or for **principle,** or to **"flee personal demons"**… [-- SOURCE]

[20.] Do Scientists pursue <u>Truth as a prime motivation</u>?.....
"The human scientists pursue **persuasiveness, prettiness, the resolution of puzzlement, the conquest of recalcitrant details, the feeling of a job well done, and the honor and income of office**… that which is **persuasive interesting, useful,** and so forth… <u>varieties of rightness other than truth</u>......" [-- GEERTZ]

338

WOW…You omitted the Seven Deadly Sins, but otherwise got all the "Devilish" drives in here, along with a few more-Angelic ones.	Too simplistically-cynical? Rigorously-realistic? A combination? *Others will decide…* Hope the assemblage is useful, anyhow; it's more-complete than usual…

[2.] ISSUE. Why do people think differently? Differ, diverge, disagree on the same topic?

Not that "group-think" conformity is good. But "why we differ" may shed light on "why we believe as we do".

[[SEE: "3-DDD," a mini-roster in Relativism above, a "II" FULL version in the Introduction, IV: "Gallery"]]

[3.] "Archaeology of Thinking: down the Root-Cellar to Primal Motivations"

THE ISSUE… ITS IMPORTANCE … OUR CONTRIBUTION… On many controversial subjects, people argue back and forth, reasoning, or rationalizing their stands. They never fully reach down to a level of more-basic, non-conscious reasons <u>why they believe</u> pro or con on the subject, or motivations… And often, people do not change their minds—often, even when some change seems appropriate, as when presented with "the facts" and more… <u>Why do they not change beliefs?</u> --We here take the thorny **EXAMPLE** of **"same-sex marriage as a legal right"** (in and out of the news in 2006) and seek to go from the *usual-obvious* down to *"second-layer"* depths toward *root*-motivations… Analyzing hundreds of Internet responses to the issue enriches our results here beyond what we've seen elsewhere. *Will this scheme aid thinking about **other** issues also?*

[1.] [1.A.] Explicit Statements are made on an Issue, Explicit Reasons Given for Stands…

SSM: *PRO:* "equal rights for all citizens," etc. …
CON: "marriage a sacred institution of male and female," etc.

[1.B.] Reasonings Given on Issue. SSM:

PRO: elaboration of civil rights, equality, freedom from discrimination, etc., etc.
CON: elaboration of traditional-historical, essential, nature of marriage, need to protect it, etc., etc.

Often people simply "stop here and leave it at that." (And of course end up at an impasse, disagreeing, and not really knowing why. Each side believes that the other side "does not listen to the facts," etc. ……) (*) …So, what are motivations behind the stances pro and con and arguments therefore? We excavate…

[2.] But, "above," larger lenses (perspectives, belief-systems, etc.) may actually be operating

[2.A.] **A First Level. SSM**: *PRO:* argments in fvor include **"liberal democratic principles"** for equality.
CON: argments against include: **Traditional religion. Sociocultural norms-mores-folkways. Political conservatism.**

[2.B.] **A possible Second Level. Conservatism, liberalism. Governmental: fascism, communism, socialism, democracy whether individual or more-communal. Other systems in historical, cross-cultural perspective… And "mind-sets" as of the Conservative, not to forget the Radical, psyche, also…**

[3.] For we who are analyzing, now, some basic issues of fact and awareness become evident: what beyond "surface" facts, arguments, motivations may be operating?

[3.A.] To start with more on the simpler surface: perhaps this level includes **ignorances** (information-absence), and **misconceptions** (stereotypes, etc.)? Plus **unawareness of variables?**
  SSM: --<u>Pedophilia</u>; gays are child-molesters. --It's a **choice**, and they can **change** their choice. --They already have rights; they want **"special rights."** --They **recruit.** --"What about the **children.**" --They are **fearsome (homophobia**, queer-fear) and **distasteful (Bedrock Disgust).** --They are dangerous, a **threat to society** somehow. (Often not specified beyond Magic Thinking.)

[3.B.] Near this level also, often some more **advanced complex but still explicit issues** upon which one must take a stand. Perhaps debate-and-disagreement on these issues, is more legitimate—the issue is complex!.

   SSM: --(1) <u>What benefits</u> does civil marriage actually confer? Hundreds of specific rights—but how important/secondary after all? –(2) Shouldn't <u>majority opinion, the people, decide</u>? --(3) <u>What *is* marriage after all</u> anyway? (four aspects: not just Religious rite,   Civil political instrument, Personal bond, Social Community recognition). (Possible confusion of religious and Natural Law traditional-culture approaches, with civic governmental issues of equality before law. But this at once gets into deeper root-reasons, see below!) --(4) What about <u>Church and State</u>? --(5) And "<u>morality</u>." -- And (6) the "<u>natural joining of the sexes</u>, man and woman"? --(7) But <u>is all major change okay</u>? And also (8) <u>are there **no dangers, threats in the world which we have to beware**</u>?

[4.] → now perhaps there emerges what we call the "root-cellar" or lower, earlier motivations:

Prior-earlier, non-conscious, more-emotional, archetypal issues:

   SSM: --**Psycho-Political Mind-Sets.** The "<u>authoritarian personality type</u>" needs firm continuity in external guidance of life-affairs. "<u>Natural Law</u>" believes that "in life and human life, one normal-natural tradition of nature-and-behavior exists, achieved and preserved with difficulty, essential for personal and social survival, which is threatened if deviations from that tradition occur." [{ **SSM**. Obviously sexual "normality vs. deviance"…

   → Studies of the supposed "Conservative" type stress <u>fear of change, need for external authority, a hierarchical stance toward others (often privileged-elitist with low compassion), intolerance of ambiguous complex situations</u>, and the like. This is important, although surely the "Liberal/Radical" type should also be scrutinized and elucidated!

--**Fear of major change.** Especially in complex times. Preference for continuity. Safety-issues. Possible "slippery slope" fallacy or concern. [{ **SSM** gays now, next it's polyamory, marrying your mother or dog, etc. }]

--**Functions of prejudice.** [{Including **SSM** <u>scapegoating</u> gays/lesbians for other social problems.}]

--**Complexity of Sexual Orientation.** [{ **SSM** If innate bisexuality exists, the fear of non-gays that they might be gay themselves.}]

--**Four big blocks to liberal social justice.** **Economic**-material interests, follow the money. **Political** expediency: power. Formal **ideologies, religious** and other. Informal **culture**: current-traditional norms mores folkways, sociocultural prejudices. Here, **SSM** "homophobia" or queer-fear. Also distaste or "**bedrock disgust.**"

   There are times when people allow **personal religious beliefs, political expediency, material interests, or customary prejudices** to interfere with the logical extension of liberal principles within the political realm. For example, the Founders knew that slavery stood in direct contradiction to the revolutionary doctrine of the "rights of man," yet because **of political expediency, economic interests, and racial prejudice**, they allowed the institution to continue. [-- R. CLAIRE SNYDER]

--**"Isms," a subset of informal culture above.** "The belief that Group A is either the only, or the best, group and Groups B etc. are lesser, inferior."]White (or Black) racism, male (or female) sexism or chauvinism, heterosexism.] [{ **SSM** Here "**heterosexism**," yes the unstated but pervasive belief that an opposite-sex world and actions is of-course the only or best mode…}]

--**Positioning of People.** (A) *Horizontal*: **In-Group versus Out-Group** "beyond the border." Us and Them, Dislike of the Unlike, Preference for One's Own Kind.
(B) *Vertical*: once Inside the social group, then a hierarchy or ranking-ladder with "**Full Civic Personhood**" at the top summit, and *varying degrees of* greater-to-lesser dignity acceptability esteem etc. downward perhaps to **Incomplete Partial People!** (Blacks ranked 3/5 of a white person… Women as property, owning no property, not voting, etc. … [{ **SSM** Gays/Lesbians as, well, deviates, weird, etc… }]
To get the flavor of this evasive sneaky **"lesser vs. legitimate"** stance, see this comment:
   "If homosexual love is "as deep and worthy" [i.e., not **shallow, unworthy, second-rate**, etc.]as heterosexual love, and if their children are deserving of as much social support" as those of heterosexuals, there's no reason not to allow SSM. Legalizing SSM is the "long-overdue correction of a moral anomaly that **dehumanizes and excludes** a significant portion of the human race. Homosexuals deserve better conditions than **strained condescension and fickle toleration**." [-- NEW REPUBLIC]
[…This "positioning" is probably created by early human history in bands and tribes? A non-functional survival? I would say largely subliminal/unconscious, although pernicious…]

-- **SSM Sexual/Power Status.** For males especially, fear of being overwhelmed, conquered, raped literally or especially symbolically, by another male. "Bottom vs. top" or "Alpha wolf." (Also from evolutionary biology perhaps.)

…WHEW… I don't know whether you "overelaborated as usual," or nicely "broke new ground" in elucidating a fuller array of "why we believe as we do"…	Have to let others decide. I am more satisfied with this tour-de-force on SSM, than not. Anyhow I know of no other equally-complete roster on motivations A-Z…

EXAMPLE. Another thinker has also attempted this same sort of analysis, in re gay marriage, also homophobia. ➔ *But are his "given and real" reasons differentiated enough to illuminate varied **motivations**?...*

REASONS people GIVE against same-sex marriage:	...the REAL REASONS people are against it:
1. Marriage is one man and one woman. 2. Same-sex families bad for raising children healthily. 3. Gay relationships are immoral. 4. Marriages are for procreation, continuing the species. 5. SSM would "threaten the institution" of marriage. 6. Marriage is traditionally heterosexual. 7. SSM is an "untried social experiment." 8. SSM leads down a "slippery slope" to legalizing anything (polyamory, incest, bestiality, etc.) 9. Granting SSM is giving gays a "special" right. 10. Sodomy should be illegal, and has been until now. 11. SSM would force businesses to give more couple benefits. 12. SSM would force churches to violate their faith's beliefs.	1. "Just not comfortable with the idea." 2. Offends everything religion stands for. 3. Marriage is a sacred institution. 4. Gay sex is "unnatural." 5. Sex among two men, betrays masculinity. 6. The thought of gay sex is repulsive. 7. Gays might recruit. [Others, in re "homophobia" itself: 8. Loss of control, 9. Threat to one's world-view, 10. Fear that one is homosexual oneself.] [-- SCOTT BIDSTRUP, on his Internet website, 2006]

CRITIQUE. Not to exploit BIDSTRUP'S analysis to praise my own (his is the single best "given vs. real reasons" analysis I've seen of *any* challenging social issue), but I feel that *his "reasons given" are not as adequately **Categorized** as they might be*. We could sort them further, into my two large layers of (A) more-superficial, intellectual reasons, including "logical fears/concerns when lacking information" (#8, 9 above) and (B) more-emotional, defensive reasons, in various Levels of my own scheme (which seems to me to be more refined). Many are of course simply **rationalizations**.

EXAMPLE. Root-reasons motivating **"9/ll deniers,"** who believe the Twin Tower destruction was a plot not by Islamist terrorists, but a conspiracy by the United States government itself. *Against all evidence...* **Why???**

--A useful comment notes no empirical evidence for the Deniers' theory, but notes they cling to their belief. Why? Because of *a feeling of social-political disenchantment*, specifically a "widespread resentment and alienation toward the national government," on the part of some ("young adults, frequent Internet users, Democrats, racial and ethnic minorities, and those with only high-school education"). These people *want, desire, wish* 9/11 to have been a conspiracy rather than terrorism. This "helps their political and/or societal agenda."   [-- SOURCE: INTERNET, SEPT. 2006]

--Another source suggests the bottom-line "pulsion" is *a trait in intellectual thinking in the West for centuries*, the desire to qualify or refute standard systems, to look for their utter faillibility, the other unspoken side... [-- SOURCE]

...two excellent little examples to suggest how **root-reasons (1)** *stubbornly survive* lack of empirical evidence [and show the folly of saying "where are your facts?" and "well, s/he backs up the argument with facts," and "just let the facts speak for themselves"...], and **(2)** probably *remain unknown* to the holders of these powerful pulsions. ***Thus far "root-reasons"...***

...thus our attempt at a more soup-to-nuts spectrum of "**reasons and motivations** why people believe, *no but really* why," and change *and do not change* their minds, on complex issues... Motivations elucidated?...

[8.3.] "IMPLICIT PRESUPPOSITIONS":
unstated {questionable?} assumptions

THE CONCEPT. Virtually any response to a subject—a statement, claim, stand about an issue—carries with it **presuppositions** (about what is, should be, how to get it, etc., etc.). These are a part of the "background" of a statement. They may well reflect a **lens or perspective**. A **way of knowing.** Especially, a **world-view**—a "pocket picture" of what is; is true-false; good-bad; are goals; and how to act, etc.

→ But often, (1) many of these assumptions remain "subliminal" in the statement (synonyms here are "implied: not stated, "covert" not overt, "latent" not manifest. Cf. "tacit lore.")
In addition (2) these basic "world-view" assumptions about reality may also remain (A) unrecognized by the statements' creators themselves, let alone (b) unexamined, not critically assessed by the creator.
So what? Well, (3) these "I. P.'s" may be suspect: questionable, problematic, mistaken, inappropriate: Errors leading to Pitfalls perhaps…

WHY IMPORTANT? *Pragmatic/Pedagogical:* obviously a "basic-advanced" thinking skill is to be able to identify and then critique such unstated but perhaps-dangerous "latent reasoning…" *Pleasurable:* also a *satisfaction* is to be able to use x-ray vision to spot behind a statement, its props… pillars… foundations… etc., which may be fascinatingly-suspect, problematic—and to "unpack" same…

OUR SUGGESTION. *Can the following unit, elucidate the concept of "implicit presuppositions" more competently—completely, compactly, clearly—than existing treatments of I.P.s? We hope so… ["It did work," and well, in my state-university English 101, late 20th-century…]*

#+|#+|#+|+|+#|+#|+#|+|+|#|#+|+#|+|#+|#+|+||+|#+|+|+|+#||+#+#|#+#+|+#|+#+#|#+||++|+|#+|+#|+#||+|#+|##+|||

METHOD. The approach is to expose learners to statements with **Implicit Presuppositions**, to go "round-robin" and by **colloquializing**, have each-and-all students derive out as many of these **tacit assumptions** as possible. One can progress from easier to more complex, challenging, cryptic (truly-covert, subliminal) instances. It may help to use the concept of **"world-view,"** or concise cosmology:

> **"What does the statement see as (1) descriptively, true or not about reality, the world including the human world? What is seen (2) normatively, as bad-and-good? What is (3) desired goal, end, outcome? What (4) stands on other basic issues?**

#+|#+|#+|+|+#|+#|+#|+|+|#|#+|+#|+|#+|#+|+||+|#+|+|+|+#||+#+#|#+#+|+#|+#+#|#+||++|+|#+|+#|+#||+|#+|##+|||

CONNEXIONS. The concept of I. P.'s *relates with* a number of other key thinking tools-and-issues, thus:

--[1.] Of course, IPs are a part of **"Backgrounds of Statements"**:

(1.A.) **World-View.** Most I. P.'s represent one of the facets of "pocket philosophy." [Metaphysics or ""fundamental nature of reality and being" including **ontology** or "being," **cosmology** or the universe, **epistemology** or "how we know," and **axiology** or moral-ethical value-judgments.] ."World-view exceeds this-or-that specific ideology (Natural Law, Socialism, Utilitarianism, Chaos Theory, etc.) and includes all ideologies, stands on "all" the major issues. A wallet-card" checklist of the usually-subliminal components of world-view:

> 1. **Description, of reality, the world: Natural, and Human (Nature).**
> 2. **Explanation: cause-effect, mechanisms, also Knowledge: science, etc.**
> 3. **Crucialities: problems-causes-solutions.**
> 4. **Evaluative: Good-Bad, moral-ethical, right-wrong, etc.**
> 5. **Ends & Means: Goals, also Methods.**
> 6. **Relationships: of human with Self, Others and Society (Political), World, Supernatural.**
> 7. **Time: views of past, present, future. Issue of Change.**
> 8. **Issues. Order vs. chaos. Control, degree of. Others…**

(1.B.) **Lenses** or viewpoints-perspectives upon a subject… Relatedly, (1.C.) **"Ways of Knowing"**…

--[2.] And IPs echo **"Philosophy 101"**: identifying and critiquing tacit assumptions as a *key* tool of philo. …]

--[3.] And IPs echo **Critical Thinking**, and its attention to logical fallacies in reasoning-and-argument. (These are not truly IPs which are questionable, but they are questionable reasoning-moves.) **EXAMPLES:** "After This, Because of This" (fallacy in cause-effect)… "Ad Hominem" (attacking person, not issue)… "Q. E. ." (claiming as true, what you are to prove)… And more.

--[4.] And IPs recall **Competence:** vs. Errors or Pitfalls: *partialities of oversights-omissions; misconceptions;* etc.

EXAMPLES. A Gallery of Statements with—"Assumptions Attached"...

[I.] General Introductory Melange, "Tossed Salad"...

1. --"Of course MRS. SMYTHE is a poor driver; after all, she's a woman..."

2. --"A LATINO family recently moved into the trailer park—but there hasn't been any trouble at all.

3. --TRAVEL METHODS. "The best way from Chicago to New York City is to fly, not drive or other means."
["Expense is no object"....."The purpose of travel is simply to arrive, not to experience terrain in between"....."Travelling without, or with, much heavy luggage, baggage, equipment"....]

4. --RIDDLE. "A man's son is injured in an automobile accident. He rushes the child to the local hospital's E. R. But the surgeon on duty takes one look and says, 'I cannot operate on this child, he is my son.'" [A famous feminist riddle; "missed" in earlier years...]

5. --STUDENT STATEMENT. "God made woman to be equal to man. Not to walk ahead of him, nor behind him, but with him, at his side." [...This *seems* to promote true equality, but *really*? Who is at the side, who is still center-stage?.....]]

6. --"DEBATE," "ARGUMENT"... A DEAN claimed that "the Chinese cannot make great scientists because they will not debate publicly." Sociolinguist DEBORAH TANNEN critiqued the I. P. that *it overgeneralizes about all Chinese scientists.* But also that *"the only way to test and develop ideas is to debate them publicly."* "It may well be true that most Chinese scientists are reluctant to engage in public, rancorous debate." And this due to cultural norms preferring cooperation toward agreement and integration and the like. **True, but** in that comment, the sociolinguist herself seems to **equate debate with rancor**, or what we think of as argument (quarrel, squabble) instead of civil while candid interchange!

7. --FAITH-BASED GOVERNMENT? The Bush administration stated that "Civilized individuals, Christians, Jews, and Muslims, all understand that the source of freedom and human dignity is the Creator..." A commenter solidly critiqued this, as implying *"those who believe in no religion at all, atheists, are to be excluded."* **True, but** in that critique, the commenter himself excluded another group, "agnostics"!

8. --A QUOTATION from MARK TWAIN'S Huckleberry Finn: [{A river steamboat had an explosion.} "Anybody hurt?" "No'm. Killed a nigger." "Well, it's lucky; because sometimes people do get hurt...] [Again a classic on unaware racism. The Black at the time as a "non-person"...]

9. -- BRITISH MILITARY STANCE: "Officers and their ladies, sergeants and their wives, enlisted men and their women..."

10. --A SIGN IN A PARK IN SINGAPORE during colonial occupation by Western powers: "No Dogs Or Chinese Allowed."

11. --A report that highschool-age women students are now objecting to male students gender-harassment of them in classes: [-- from NEWSWEEK] "And, while there may not be a man today who can honestly say he never spent most of a math period staring at the prettiest girl in his class instead of a blackboard . . . someday there might be."
[Is this one still a puzzler?.....Beware! "All males as hormone-driven morons, not egghead-nerds." Or, all males as—*hetero*sexual?!"]]

12. --TRADITIONAL JOKE / SAYING. "If you're so smart, why aren't you rich?"

13. --ADVERTISEMENT. "Plastic Surgery. Be More Confident... "

14. --NEWSPAPER ARTICLE ON LOW-WAGE JOBS. "He regretted his current station in life. He felt he deserved more than an average apartment and a 12-year-old car." [But...]

15. --"BILL GATES has made his money, why should he worry about making the Windows platform better?"

16. --BOOK BLURB. "This impressive book is the young author's first production, and we look forward to more achievements as his career develops..." [**"Success means continuous production"?... **]

17. --SIGNS ON PASSENGER-TRAINS in France, and in Italy, respectively:

France: *"Il est defendu de se tenir en dehors de la fenetre"* ["It is prohibited to lean outside the window"]

Italy: *"E periculoso sporgsersi"* ["It is dangerous to lean outside the window"]
[Does this show any implicit **difference in world-view** of the two cultures toward...... ??]

18. -- ANECDOTE. A retail merchant is instructing his son (an employee) on business ethics.
"An established, repeat customer gives me money, I give change back thinking it's a $5, later realize that the customer gave me a $10 instead. The question is: do I tell my business-partner, or not?"

19. -- FROM THE INTRODUCTION to a practical book on small-boat handling:
"The reader is cautioned that in this book, none of his time is wasted. Facts are stated once and are not repeated."
[Let's ignore the questionable diction, "cautioned," let alone the sexist pronoun. Why assume that *information should never be repeated*? Good, to avoid redundancy. But bad, if repetition would help reinforcement, also referencing other types of related information…

20. -- COMMENT, urging citizens of one country to better accept diverse, minority groups within.
"You don't like it that your neighbor is a foreign immigrant. And yet…. Your god is Jewish. Your automobile is Japanese, your pizza is Italian, and your couscous is Algerian. Your democracy is Greek. Your coffee is Brazilian, your watch is Swiss, your shirt is Indian, your radio is Korean, your vacations are in Turkey or Tunisia or Morocco. Your numerals are from Arabia, and your writing is Latin in origin… And still, you rebuke your neighbor for being a foreigner!"   [-- postcard, from FRANCE (translated), 2000]
But this assumes that *diffusion of products from different cultures*—material and ideological—*is the same as the issue of interaction among peoples of different cultural traits*. A "good point," but diffusion and adoption of cultural products, is distinct from, and easier than, interaction of individuals of different cultures. The statement overlooks **in-group/out-group** factors, and the like…

[II.] … "The Gay Thing" *again*: Homo-sexuality as *Pesky Issue…*

1. -- STUDENT COMMENT. "Homosexuals should not be sent to prison, but instead to therapists to be cured." [-- *in a class essay, about 1980* … Each year, *more* students spotted the arguable stand *sooner*…]

2. -- "Gays and lesbians should have equal rights etc. with everyone else because their identity is not chosen, and not changeable either. It is at least somewhat genetic and thus (like racial skin color) immutable."
[Aha, but does this really mean or lead to the dangerous I. P. that (1) *"By contrast, people have no right to choose their own ways if others object."* "If I don't like you but you can't help your trait, then I should leave you be. But if I don't like your lifestyle—whether gay or vegan or left-handed or whatever—then we can't protect that lifestyle and indeed perhaps you should change just to make me feel better!" (2) But also *"an immutable characteristic could still be bad"*: unnatural, abnormal, etc.—in re homosexuality, this is debatable but questionable—*and also could be socially-dangerous*—in re homosexuality, this is quite dubious…

3. -- SPORTS-LEADERSHIP: a school coach is talking to his team of male athletes.
"Just because a player isn't totally masculine-appearing in gender-role… or is friendly with people known to be gay… or even had one drunken gay sexual experience simply for experimentation, rebellion, or release… none of these necessarily mean that that player is gay. We shouldn't automatically stereotype people thus."
   [Fine, but does this really mean to say, **"To be homosexual, is negative, per se, for anyone!"**]

4. -- A COMMENT on Political Correctness etc. by a British professor.
"When an African-American expresses her sincere belief [in the course of a class discussion on the legal regulation of sexual conduct] that homosexuals are sick, and a classmate complains to the dean of students, are we to endanger the African-American's self-esteem by sending her off for sensitivity training, or the self-esteem of the gay complainant by providing no redress? It is no laughing matter…"   [-- ALAN RYAN, "Is Higher Education A Fraud?"]

   [**This seems more tricky…** (1) Incidentally, should we assume the complainant was gay—*"Anyone speaking positively for the gay cause must be themselves gay"*? Perhaps s/he was simply an "ally"? (2) More to the point, do we have here an either-or fallacy, the dualistic dichotomy? *"We can have only either sensitivity-training, or inaction"*? A third stances is *"But we can treat such instances* as a "teachable moment," on how to confront complex concerns competently? (I'd relname it a "learnable moment"—what is my Implication there?…]

[III.] …& "Education": *a Day On Campus*, "Above Assumptions":
[3.A.] General, Overall Statements about Goals of Education:

1. -- RESEARCH-SUMMARY: "Applying the Science of Learning to University Teaching and Beyond."

   Seeks to build empirically validated learning activities to enhance what and how much is learned and how well and how long it is remembered." (The science of learning now operates both in controlled, experimental laboratory conditions, and also in the messy real-world settings where most of us go about the business of teaching and learning.") [-- HALPERN & HAKEL, New Dir. Teaching & Learning, 1989]

2,3,4,5.--FOUR ARTICLES: Research shows that "students no longer politely defer to teachers as much as formerly. Why not?

[2.] "...perhaps because they realized that professors' expertise could rapidly become outdated...'the deference was probably driven more by the notion that professors were infallible sources of deep knowledge, Professor DEDE said, and that notion has weakened.'" [-- NEW YORK TIMES, 2006]

[3.] "Subject-matter today tends to be quickly outmoded, out of date in five years. For this reason, we should teach not just the material, but how to think about it." [-- SOURCE]

[... the I. P. of the first comment seems easier to grasp—*"education is content-retention."* The second and third, are related but perhaps more hidden. *"Professors transmit known knowledge. They don't primarily indispensably teach how to think about knowledge, a larger enterprise."* And, *True education is simply applying known, given, relevant knowledge, as against finding new knowledge when needed—let alone thinking anew about any and all material and issues!"*]

[4.] "Education can have various aims. Liberal-arts and vocational. It may thus have both intrinsic and extrinsic aims. But to hold that both kinds of aims are primary, is much more difficult, and it's untenable for one person to believe both." [-- WINCH & GINGELL]

[This seems insidious! Does it assume, *"Either/Or is not a fallacy; a thing is either A or non-A"*?]

[5.] "The argument that we need tenure to protect freedom of speech is bogus. Numerous state and federal statutes, commissions against discrimination, and the vigilant news media protect anyone—in or out of academe—who wants to expound unorthodox beliefs." [-- JAMES F. CARLIN, in CHE]

[An I. P.: *"Surely, no forces against free activity exist right on and within the educational institutions themselves."* However, what of dangerous forces such as people challenged by our exploring truly-new ideas... our dedication to certain standards and criteria... our insistence upon truly open debate, and the rest...]

6. --FROM THE EDITOR OF A TEACHING JOURNAL to whom I submitted an article on "pre-writing." I suggested having students write an experimental, warm-up draft of a paper using a technique (specific detailing, or structure, or audience-relating, or...) after I had simply identified the technique, and before formally instructing them in the technique. This, to have them actively assess what they already knew and thought about the technique, as a pump-priming. Draft was not graded as such. **_But the editor responded:_**
"By asking students to perform a skill in which you have not yet instructed them, you are surely asking or causing them to fail in doing it." [-- R. L. L., College Composition & Communication]
[Wow. *Students know nothing beforehand? All must be done correctly via a given method only? Education is not experimental and personal-experience as well as following given techniques? .....!* P.S.—In reply, I explained my rationale to the editor, and in calm tones too. Response: he simply rejected the article with no additional comment...]

7. --GOALS OF EDUCATION. (Are some, unavoidably so conflicting that one must be put ahead of another?) "Education can have various aims. Liberal-arts and vocational. It may thus have both intrinsic and extrinsic aims. But to hold that both kinds of aims are primary, is much more difficult, and it's untenable for one person to believe both." [-- WINCH & GINGELL]
How many people can see the I. P. here as an instance of the either-or (or dualistic-dichotomy) fallacy? *"We must choose between A and non-A."* Some Eastern thinking sees "both-and" integrated, as both possible and desirable. Thus, a Chinese painting may be both classic *and* romantic, realistic *and* abstract, individual *and* representative... Let alone *"neither-nor"*... This may indicate that I.P.'s about advanced, complex thinking skills remain **subliminal**...

[3.B.] The Learners [Students/Pupils] Speak Up/Out: Comments from _Course-Evaluations_:

1. --"I couldn't handle it that day you got mad at us because nobody in the class had done the assignment."
[A wicked reversal... *"Students not only can remain certain of their opinions, and have what they desire, but are not to be blamed for inaction, need not take any responsibility—and should not be criticized. If it happens, the over-demanding teacher is the one at fault."*]

2. --"I was amazed when teacher stayed overnight in town instead of driving back home, because a snowstorm was coming and she wanted to make sure she was there for her class. Why would she do that?" [-- "ERIC"]

3. --"We seem to be learning well since Mr. [the INSTRUCTOR] seems pleased with our progress." [-- PUPIL]

[... this one is monstrous! *The student is a passive, un-involved resident in a course until exiting with the needed grade or credit—probably best done by "pleasing the teacher."* . A logical absurdity: learner didn't know had learned until teacher told that one had learned...]

[3.C.] Disagreements. The following moves provoked much disagreement. What are the I.P.'s in each case (about what issues?
[HINT: *"separations-vs.-connections"*...]

1. --At an educational conference, ONE SCHOOL reported that all titles such as "sophomore" and "assistant professor" (etc.) were banished, in daily practice anyhow. All were replaced with the one label, "co-learner." [Strong disagreements ensued.]

2. --Faculty should receive full professional credit for: (1) writing course-textbooks (as against "original research in their specialty") ... (2) Doing interdisciplinary work, team-teaching a course (but in a different dept. than their home base) (Etc.)

3. --"101" or introductory-level courses in a subject. Should they be the same for both prospective majors, and for elective students as a general or liberal education course? At one school, two very different courses were offered: as in "stenology" (or whichever subject) for pre-professional majors, and one for general education...

4. --At another school, students not only took Visual Art Contacts & Appreciation 101, but were treated to massive, lavish, curated displays of good visual art of all genres—*on building corridors throughout campus.*

PROJECT "ART-UP." A professor from one field, English, implemented a grass-roots, unauthorized project to mount quality reproductions of good visual art on various corridor and classroom walls at the university. [E.g., in a sunny alcove, "Van Gogh landscapes," "Hiroshige & Hokusai landscapes," "Art Deco London Transport posters from the 1920's."]

His explicit presuppositions were *(1) art education should not be one-time Art Contacts 101, (2) repeated exposure to quality work can aid appreciation, and (3) art embellishes the daily environment also, let alone that (4) selecting and arranging just the right images together for just the particular location, is itself an artistic activity.* However, the project was solidly critiqued by the committees, administration, and some other faculty. Why? *"Professors should remain within their area of assigned and expert specialties." "The arts are really secondary to other educational goals." "This is public space and an invasion of other peoples' space thus." "Who's to select which pictures to mount? People will disagree on what is best."* (Etc.)
...this does not exhaust all **variable-issues** raised by this project, nor *possible assumptions behind stands taken* on each variable...

5. --The library encouraged students (all patrons!) to write their comments about a book in specially provided insert-pages at the book's end. (Others, teachers and administration, strongly disagreed with this...)

6. --A small liberal arts school in Indiana, EARLHAM COLLEGE, included in its Catalog/Handbook, listings and photos not only of teaching faculty, but also of maintenance and support staff, giving equal space to all.

7. ---Another school (CAESURA COLLEGE, in Lacuna-near-Hiatus-On-Ellipsis, West Dakota), went even farther. It now includes in its Catalog/Handbook, the names of former faculty, but not just emeritus (retired) faculty, but also those now deceased—in fact everyone who ever taught there since the institution began, 100 years ago.

8. --...AND THIS JUST IN": COMMENT IN A SMALL COLLEGE TOWN. "I heard they had a transsexual up at the U., but of course you never know what to expect there, so it's not surprising." [*"Higher Ed as a hotbed of..."*]

|#+#|+|#+#|+#|+|#+|+#|+|+|#+|+|++|#+|+#|+#|+#|+#|+#+#|+|+|+#|#+|+|#+|#|+#|+#|+|#+|+#|+#|+|#+|+#|+|#+|#|+#|+#|+#|+|#+|#+|+#|+||#+||

[PB # 9:] the "7-RRRRRRR" formula: from "right-on"—to *wayward...*

This involves not responding to a subject, but "responding to that person's response" to the subject!

THE ISSUE: When people respond to a stance (a statement, claim, etc. about a subject or issue), their responses can vary in many ways. One way is degree of "relevancy vs. waywardness" to the topic at hand—target-relevant, vs. random-tangential. True, often an offhand thought, even an off-the-topic association, can be valuable indeed; don't censor! However, also often, a comment which is off the subject, or train of logical exploration, is "bad" or non-productive. [The "ricochet"-type of response also can fascinatingly reveal true, all-too-human, tendencies to rationalize, to defend prior pet peeves and preferences—as the gallery below shows...]

WHY IMPORTANT?   *Potentially extremely-valuable "today"!* Has this non-logic of group discussion, increased in recent decades? (Due to "RAMPANT RELATIVISM," also DECLINE IN RESPECT FOR "LOGIC" risking haywire thinking, and more than one OTHER FACTOR?) *More to the point [!], is it useful to confront this issue in teaching for better thinking?*

OUR SUGGESTION: Herewith a roster of types of wayward responses, plus a gallery illustrating them from our own experience in academic and other arenas, and some "all too human" too... Will this approach help quickly orient learners to the issue of "degree-of-relevance-of-response," efficiently balancing focused accuracy and flexible adaptability to accelerate learning?

PERSONAL SELF-EVALUATION OF THIS CONTRIBUTION. We—I—feel it is **very strong indeed, and even more needed/useful.** Rampant today seems responses which are *haywire, ricochet, boomerang, batbrained, non-reasonable...*

\+|+\=\+|+\=\+|+\=|+\=|

TOOL-BOX. A system of seven types of responses to a claim.

The issue is: is the response logically related to the statement hence on-point... or is the response irrelevant somehow? As in the following degrees-of-distance, so to speak:
1. **Right-On Relevant** Talks to the issue usefully, whether support, example, inquiry, criticism... (Or does it begin to shade into **"True, But..."** and fauna-and-flora of **Fallacies** in *that* jungle?...)
2. **"Related"** *somewhat* probably; perhaps a lead for an associated issue ...
3. **Refer-To Later**, an interesting point *but* really not germane right now ...
4. **"Re-Routed"** or simply *il*logical in identifiable ways (logical fallacies, etc.) ...
5. **Random** or **Ricochet**, free-associational hence not really relevant at *all*...
6. or **"de-Railed,"** would the implied results or consequences of the statement be questionable?
7. or **"Resist-ing,"** somewhat defensive or evasive or denying or otherwise biassed? ...
8. .....[*and the one/s I omitted and that you discovered...*]

CONNEXIONS?   This **5-RRRRR** concept seems to relate with other concepts. Is similar to, or anyhow echos the same concerns? (Or at times similar but "not identical, don't confuse the two"?)

(1) As noted, a key thrust of **philosophy** itself is to evaluate responses for their implicit presuppositions, also any consequences of believing or implementing the response.

(2) **"Rationalizing vs. Reasoning."** Sometimes the wayward arguments represent attempt to affirm an already-believed stance.

(3) To all of **logic-reasoning-argument**, of course. But a different way to cut the cake.....

(4) Cf. also **"cognitive dissonance,"** or what we do when two important beliefs we hold are conflicting or contradictory.

(5) Not to mention major **change** felt to be threatening... Guidebook: → see the Tool-KIT in Appendix 4...

(6) Of course, also cf. # 3-DDD or why people differ disagree diverge on a subject, due to different levels of **Lenses, Ways of Knowing,** including **Blocks Barriers Biasses** to same...

   (Socialization into sub-group norms, values... Just-personal pet peeve, preference... Honest misconception, ignorance, overgeneralization, outdated-outmoded knowledge, and other Pitfalls of Partiality... Legitmate objection or criticism via principled fairminded criteria... and others...)

GALLERY. Peoples' **responses to statements**/claims— and our analysis of the responses in re quality-of-thinking:

[1.] --Concerning abused women, a sociologist noted that some women also beat some men, though this is less reported or realized. A feminist poet across the room burst out, "But it's wrong no matter who does it!"

> *[True indeed, but does this get **Re-Routed** emotionally, strays off track and de-emphasize the truth or issue here?]*

[2.] --I noted that an interdisciplinary studies association was not producing pedagogy or how-to-teach or integrate knowledge. Someone replied, "But they have to solidify their base, become respectable, through original scholarship and institutionalizing."

> *["**True, but**" does this **Resist** and defend or try to excuse—or justify— the lack of producing practical pedagogy for teachers to use?]*

[3.] --A scholar of a minor woman American Black writer of the nineteenth century, frankly admitted that her writing was not first-rank or first-rate artistry. Later, a defender said, "But perhaps it was aesthetic in its own terms in a different tradition from our own."

> *[**Relevant** to note plural standards easy to overlook. However, in this case "Q.E.D." or "begging the question"—<u>what</u> tradition, please? Hence, perhaps **Resistant**-defensive of the tendency today to put politically-relevant literature ahead of imaginative literary artistry?]*

[4.] --When I said that very often, exam or paper assignments were too narrowly-prestructured by the teacher to permit or evoke true student thinking on the subject, a reply was "Well, surely students can on their own think within and outside the assignment, make something more creative out of it."

> *[Is this a **Ricochet** to ridiculousness, to deflect the issue of teaching thinking? Because traditional Schooling trains students to conform, color within the lines, follow orders, not make mistakes, not explore, do not risk offending the teacher..... Hence an improbable claim made care-lessly thus?]*

[5.] --A capstone course on "Good Community" found its students repeatedly were ahistorical, could not sense the culture of, say, ancient China except through our own lenses and hence NON-comprehended or at least MIS-comprehended Confucius, etc. A teacher replied, "But that goal was one of the listed goals of the course."

> *[Interesting, but a "**Re-Routing**" which overlooks the fact that simply stating a goal, does not teach painstakingly how to do it! Casual evasion? Or honest misconception, unawareness?]*

[6.] --While discussing science as a Way of Knowing, a student pointed out that "even scientists can be biassed," and can produce flawed results.

> *[True, but the student's implication was that, well, we can thus dismiss science, all science, any specific scientific experiment. A case of "**de-Railing**"? or better, "begging the question," that is, assuming what was to be proved, or perhaps a great **overgeneral** leap?]*

[7.] --The anthropologist ROBERT REDFIELD created the "folk-urban continuum," a theoretical or "pure-type" description of traits of societies from the most simple, preliterate hunters-and-gatherers, on to the immense modern cities. Someone observed "But there never was a society which fits 100% your description of the Folk, or of the Urban, type!"

> *[True, but what was the point? Redfield's scheme was an "ideal-type," describing traits at polar opposites. There probably never was a totally 100% pure "bureaucracy," either. **Related** perhaps, but really more **Random**? A stubborn mind-set of problems with a pure-type thinking-scheme?]*

[8A.] --"And Sudden Death" was a famous <u>Readers Digest</u> article which really skillfully, expertly used vivid specific incidents, anecdotes, observations, details to graphically warn against bad driving and terrible automobile accidents. The article was a model for good "specific detailing" in writing. <u>A student pointed out that</u> "such articles **don't**, however, help to effectively reduce fatal automobile accidents!"

*[True; but did not the !rticle do "all it could do" in this regard
and indeed "more than many other such articles"?
The student's comment, important for the **Related** question of effectiveness of vivid writing,
nevertheless remained a sort of **Random** observation after all?]*

[8B.] --Faulted for including very few if any actual, specific examples of model or sample assignments which sought to "teach thinking," a famous and expert teacher of Critical Thinking replied: "But to give examples would lead to copycatting or low-order formulae and rules and not thinking for oneself (which would be ironic indeed). Every teacher has to discover and derive his/her own way to implement Critical Thinking."

*[Fascinating. Initially **Right-On** and indeed quite true and an important danger.
<u>But</u> did the expert exhibit (1) a too **Rigorous** ideology or even **Ruined** sort of collision
with a fundamental Ignorance, unawareness, misconception, hence embarrassingly an incompetence? Namely, that we learn through
both conceptual clarity,
and also concrete-specific examples and experience?!
(2) Next, was the expert **Running** From criticism,
Resisting the real need to do arduous work to supply the ideas with specific examples?]*

[8C.] --A famous article in composition questions the mandate to "Use Definite, Specific, Concrete Language." Specificity, the author said, can lead to five pitfalls. Ahistoricism (focusing on the present), empiricism (favoring sensory surface information), fragmentation (seeing objects in isolation not context), solipcism (privileging the writer's own perception) and denial of conflict (do all readers see the same meaning in the details presented?). [- RICHARD OHMANN, "Use Definite, Specific, Concrete, Language"]

*[We felt **Right-On** and very true, elucidating pitfalls often overlooked!
However, we <u>also</u> felt: "de-Railed," or "Hemispherically" exactly half-right.
Real-world working writers know the value of specifics, examples, instances, evidence, to do so much:
to inform, interest-intrigue-involve, persuade-convince, instruct, and more.
Consider some specifics of specifics to support our point: he poet's image, the freelance writer's "statistics-quotes-and-anecdotes,"
the preacher's parable, the after-dinner speaker's story, the scientist's case-study...
Hence OHMANN seems embarrassingly Partial?...]*

[8D.]—I critiqued a colleague's paper before he submitted it to a journal for publication. I noted that the important introduction section lacked any specific examples, needed there to illustrate concepts, also show the importance and interest of them. The colleague replied: "Oh but remember that was the section that dealt with theory. So we didn't need any examples."

*[We felt nonplussed to assign a category. **Ricochet** into the profoundly-mistaken, or perhaps conventional? "Theory doesn't need examples"—but where we come from, a Rule of Thumb is to Dip Down with an Example just about all the time for every major point.... My colleague simply disagreed...]*

[9.] --A mathematician reported that dangers from airline flights crashing are very low, one person in millions or so. <u>Someone replied</u>, "But what if you are that one person?!" and everybody "smiled-&-nodded."

*[True, but more an emotional or **Random** leap than a likely landing? As such, maaddening to logical Us...]*

[10.] --In a conference, a woman presenter suggested a new (and perhaps unfamiliar) type of leadership—less competitive, more cooperative, and so forth. <u>A man in the audience</u> (of largely older, white, male workers) asked, "But is *every* leader supposed to apply this new model *fully, all* the time, with *no* exceptions?" The woman presenter said well no not ALL the time, SOMEtimes other modes prevail, etc. But she reported that she saw her mistake at once, even though too late. She sensed "a great collective shrug of relief from the shoulders" of most in the audience.

*[A" poignant," but not rare, instance! True, the new model isn't used <u>all</u> the time,
but defensiveness led the audience then to leap to overgeneralize
and to deny that they'd <u>ever</u> really have to use it.
A vigorous, if unconscious, way to **Resist** the new, difficult, threatening?]*

[11.] --Discussing the <u>teaching of thinking skills</u>, a TRADITIONAL TEACHER said that this was all very well, but simply to remember that "teachers had to start with the facts first. And why? "Because, you can't think about nothing. You have to think about something. Therefore give them the factual information first, and then they can think about it."

*[One of our all-time favorites. It grows **Defenses and Evasions** on itself like tendrils of a vine. First, not even a grain of truth, hence an honest misconception. Math "thinks about nothing" all the time. But really, a **Resistance** to the new paradigm of teaching thinking skills ahead of rote knowledge and ideologies. And nicely embodying the subversive, insidious sneakiness of so much **Resistance**. See, Not In Our Back Yard, or Course! Business as usual, "the facts first," and then at some conveniently unspecified time in the future, we can start with the teaching of thinking!... Disgustingly neatly-done...]*

[12.] --A Berkeley High School English class was studying <u>"epithets"</u> or words that wound, as in racial and ethnic slurs. The words <u>"fag" and "dyke" for gay-lesbian persons</u> were discussed. Students did not think those words were all that objectionable. THE TEACHER said, "Well, I'm lesbian myself, and when you hear other students using those words, I want you to tell them that Ms. X would be offended." <u>Three student responses</u> to this were of interest here

[Quite apart from **my own response** that Ms. X's comment was inappropriate, professionally-incompetent, an instance not of true Education but of rank frank *indoctrination into an ideology*.. Inappropriate because not pragmatic (won't "stick" if not self-decided) nor principled either ...]

1. <u>A male student</u>: "Well, you know, almost anything you say, it has the potential to offend somebody or other, and if spoken wide enough, will find someone who it offends."

*[**THE MOST RELEVANT OF THESE 3 COMMENTS TO THE 5-RRRRR SCHEME...**
"**Largely True, But...**" **Relevant** and right-on effective here?
Or a rather neat way to **Resist** the whole issue, via this true-but-overgeneral point?
Again, the **Implications** of the stand or position.
Does his comment mean nobody should censor his/her speech at all ever for this reason?]*

2. <u>A woman student</u>: "I call my gay-lesbian friends that, it's up to them to adjust to it and get used to it."

*[An opportunity to discuss **Implicit Presuppositions**, of hierarchical heterosexuality.
Also to use the above **Contradictions** vs. **Consistency**, or **Counter-Examples**, as in
"Well, if I a male referred to you as a bxtch, brxxd, or cxnt, was it merely your duty to get used to it?"]*

3. <u>Another male student</u>: "I can't do that, Ms. X. Because then my friends would think that I am gay." *[Again, grist for the educational mill. Probably* **"True"***...But of course we can then say "therefore What?" At least we can say it in liberal-cosmopolitan Berkeley, California, which has free-thinkingly been gay-friendly ever since permitted to think that freely by the evolving cultural norms, Zeitgeist, Truths of Today......]*

...you know, <u>I really **DO** come to like, this last section here</u>, the **Seven R's.** I think you've *hit on a real need, a pitfall, in today's thinking*—random ricochet thinking, due to relativism and other factors... Oh, and you here nicely sublimate (use well) your "pulsion" of *your personal hatred for "sloppy careless overgeneral irrelevant responses"* to things. You fashioned your stallion-Bias, into a workhorse-Insight. Good job...	I thought there was a need here... These examples kept noticing themselves to me, so to speak, and so I derived the system from them. (*Thought Them Out*, eh...) ...But I wonder whether peoples' objections to the 7-RRRRRRR scheme, will be themselves Fairminded, or *also and still* evasive, illogical, ricocheting—or is that just my motivation against "ka-boinnggg" responses operating again? (If it's sublimated, all the better...)

|#+#|+|#+#|+#|+|#+|+#|+|+|#+|+|++|#+|+#|+#|+#|+#|+#|+#+#|+|+|+#|#+|+|#+|#|+#|+#|+|#+|+#|+|#+|#+|#+|+#|+#|+#|+|#+|#+||#+||

[{(END of Appendix #5, "Prior Background-Basics" in Thinking...)}]

|#+#|+|#+#|+#|+|#+|+#|+|+|#+|+|++|#+|+#|+#|+#|+#|+#|+#+#|+|+|+#|#+|+|#+|#|+#|+#|+|#+|+#|+|#+|#+|#+|+#|+#|+#|+|#+|#+||#+||

The REPERTOIRE:

= A *glimpse ahead* the parent-product of **<u>Teaching Thinking</u>** :
the "matrix" or full repository of thinking skills…]

[the more-total <u>TOOL</u> - ~~Kit~~ - ~~Box~~ - ~~Chest~~ - ~~Bench~~ - <u>SHOP</u>"]

[1.] Introduction: The Rationale for This Unit…

THE ISSUE—AND "SO-WHAT" NEED:

--To have available a collection of "essential, generic, basic-advanced" thinking skills, seems valid. In its own usually-vacant niche. Beyond the lower-level "critical thinking" and field-specific techniques. But more precise than lofty generalizations-about thinking. (And of course both focused-explicit, and also flexible-adaptable…)

--Seeing nothing of the kind available, we worked toward such a collection. It is to be called <u>Mind-Play</u>.

--We wondered long and hard (actually, briefly and gently) *what to call* such a cluster? What should be our own special little jargon-label? Candidates came to mind. **Roster? Index? Manual? Checklist? "Route-Map"? Recipe-to-follow? Collection-box?** But no…

--Then suddenly and recently, the perfect word emerged.

"Repertoire"

And indeed (we checked), its dictionary-definition is right on the mark—on our aim. *"The <u>complete</u> list or supply of <u>skills</u>, devices, or ingredients used in a particular field, occupation, or <u>practice</u>."*

Oh, and we couldn't help think of L. WITTGENSTEIN'S description of **philosophy**: it is "<u>a set of reminders for a particular purpose</u>." That also works well as the aim of <u>Mind-Play</u>.

> **RECOLLECT:** DONALD MURRAY'S passionate plea for teachers to *at least make available for him*, "all" the alternate optional choices, possibilities, for writing—even as he *begins* to learn how to write…

… **SO THE OFFERING.** This Appendix #6 has two purposes. **(1)** Mainly, to *give this capsule glimpse of the whole* "tool-shop" of <u>Mind-Play</u>, including skills *not* noted in <u>TTh</u>. **(2)** Secondarily, to *expand on some skills already* noted in <u>Teaching Thinking</u>, for learners who want more on them now.

|#||#+|#+|#+|#+|#+|#+|+#|+#|+#|+|#+|#+|#+|+#|+|+#|+#|+#|+#|#+|+#|+#|+#|+#|+#|+|#+|#+|#+|#+|#+#|+#|+#|#+|#+|#+|#+#|#+|#+#+|#||

ORIENTATION-BAR:				
1. Intro **previous**	**2. T. of C.** current	3. Mind-Play "I" : "Inventory," plus the "Top Twenty" skills	4. Summary I: thinking, from general to more-specific.	5. Summary II: thinking, more specifics within <u>Mind-Play</u> itself "II" **subsequent**

[2.] Table of Contents of this Preview of the Repertoire":

|#|#+|#+|#+|#+|#+|+#|+#|+#|+|#+|#+|#+|+#|+|+#|+#|+#|+#|#+|#+|+#|+#|+#|+|#+|#+|#+|#+#|+#|+#|#+|#+|#+#|#+|#+#|#||

ORIENTATION-BAR:				
1. Intro **previous**	2. T. of C.	**3. Mind-Play "I" : "Inventory," plus the "Top Twenty" skills**	4. Summary I: thinking, from general to more-specific.	5. Summary II: thinking, more specifics within Mind-Play itself "II" subsequent

[3.] 3. M.-P. "I" : "Inventory," plus "Top 20" skills

[3.A.] One-Page "Map / Flow-Chart" of MP… →

Note—for the essence of many "generic essential" thinking-skills, and issues, A-to-Z skills, glance [briefly…] at the right-hand column III on the next page…

[I.] [A] INTRODUCTION

[{ *"what we're about & why"* }]

1. Rationale (4 parts)

Th. is (+), complexity needed, but we shortfall, hence this resource.

2. "Staircase Into":

12-W model of action.
Thinking not the only action.

"Thinking"—4 key aspects of:
1. CCC. [=**content**, =**complexity**]
2. UpDownAcross,
3. for Education [issues here]
4. Th subtypes: esp., **essential**.

Th: bad-better-good-best?!
Good Th is hard, "unnatural"

[II.] [A] MAIN BODY

[{ *Skills needed more-or-less sequentially in process of thinking thru subject* }]

EIGHT MOVES to confront subject:

1. SMT: "Strategically Monitor the Totality *Over-All*"

2. Survey Subject (scrupulously)

3. Field: the context "*Outside*" the subject

4. With-in-side analyze subject's components.

5. Vertical: "*Up & Down*" the specific-general Abstraction-Ladder

6. Number of, and **relations** between. (*"One, Two, Many?---and, Separate, or Connect?"*)

7. Change in subject *"Over Time"*

8. and **Elucidation.**

[I.] [B] SIDELINE SUPPLEMENTS to the Intro:

[{ *use as **needed** for clarification, expansion...* }]

1. Chat Further About Our Approach: (**the "Staff Lounge Open-House"**) Connections/relevancies of this material to "world, life"... FAQ's and Objections to!... Analogies of... "Touchstone" quotations about... The 20 best "Nugget"-skills... Audiences for... Personal Profile of the authors...

2. Issue of which **"Prior Basics,"** Background Skills needed a-priori?

3. Major separate module, **Teaching Thinking:** [Intro, Keystones, D-Machine, Gallery; eight Appendices]

[II.] [B] "ALONGSIDE SUPPLEMENTS"

[{ *Skills needed **more-variously** throughout the process* }]

1. **"Lens-work"** confronting subjects via *multiple, diverse viewpoints, perspectives, systems, theories,* etc.

2. **"Variables-Variation"** (from 1-point to total view)

3. **"15-C Expository Elucidation"** (thesis-points)

4. **"Greenprint"** checklist toward total elucidation

5. **"Elucidation"** the concept— *elucidated*!

[III.] the "Tool-CHEST" of *all* the skills A-to-Z

[{ *directory for finding* }]

3-DDD
5-RRRRR
5-AAAAA
6-VVVVV
12-W SigActMonitor
15-C Ex El
Backgrounds to statement
Calibration (scale)
Complexity of subject
Conceptual Continuum
Change, major
Command
Competence
Creativity
"Critical Thinking"
Definition
Discipline, academic
Dispositions in th.
Diversity
Elucidation
"Essential" thinking
Greenprint
Facts, Opinions, Judgment
"How" (technique/method)
Ideal-Type
Implicit Presuppositions
Interdisciplinary
Knowing vs. Knowing
Knowledge (truth authority etc.)
Lens-work
Motivations, "pulsions"
Percentage-Probability
Philosophy 101
Rules vs. Tools
Six Moves to confront subject
"Thoroughness"
In Vitro vs. In Vitro
"Prior-Basic" Thinking Skills
Purposes-in-confronting
Quality/"excellence"
Rationale, our 4-point
"Relativism" (the tangle)
Science
"Shortfallings"
SMT "Strategic Monitor Totality"
Thinking, 3 key aspects of
Transformations-spectrum
Variable-Issues
Variables-Variation
Visual literacy
Ways of Knowing
World-View
Writing
Zeitgeist

[3.B.] The "Best of the Best": 14 "*Essential*" Thinking Skills:

Look, are there any **super-important** thinking skills? Recurrently-used ones which seem to belong always at hand in one's thinking "tool-belt"?	...Each thinker will differ, but here are our own "blue-ribbon" finalists which we've come to find *indispensable*. They're both Conceptual and Connectable: that is, high-level generic, but also easily flexibly applied down-low...

[1.] SEEK—beyond the *INFO*, to—"why, the very *IDEA*!" From material *content*, induct & conceptualize upward to discover/create the mental *concepts* therein. Not just procedures but principles.

(X) <u>Time-Management</u>: procedures, *but overall, the pillars of* (1) goal-setting, then (2) prioritizing, then (3) lead-time planning"... (X) <u>Algebra</u>: manipulations, *but also* "combination, permutation, association" (X) <u>Science [liberal-education intro.]</u>: facts, issues— *but also* "Dynamic Equilibrium; Change & Evolution; Scale & Proportion; Causality & Consequences; and, Energy: Its Sources and Transfer..." (X) <u>Philosophy</u>: historical figures, schools, *but the essential approaches of the discipline:* "Question everything... Spot assumptions, implications... Seek counter-examples... Define terms... Use logic..." (X) <u>Humor</u>: examples, ha-ha, *but also* the key theories of "aggression, repression, anxiety-management, surprise/incongruity"...

[2.] "STATEMENT-SCRUTINIZING": Be able to elucidate, for any response (statement-claim-etc.), from others or yourself, the background: (1) probable <u>motivations</u>... (2) <u>implicit presuppositions</u>... (3) "lenses" or <u>perspective-viewpoints</u> being used. And *critique* same: spot pitfalls, etc.

(X) "<u>Same-Sex Marriage</u>": back-and forth blabber, *but mainly*: source of truth, guidance?... Natural Law vs. self-definition?... dealing with major change?... gender-role identity?... Political procedure: civil rights, religious sacraments?. ... (X) <u>U.S. Invasion of Grenada</u>: opinionations pro-con, *but on to*: morality, rights, law, national policies, history, democracy, media—& our own schema!...

[3.] "STRATEGIC MONITORING OF THE TOTALITY." As default procedure always, "keep an eye on the Big Picture (whole forest not just trees, and the next forest over, also...) so as to gain command: to "avoid pitfalls, aim for potentialities: cover all bases, miss no chances, make no avoidable mistakes, be not fooled." this, Thus, to win or succeed if anyone could... [Do this constantly: when planning a project, also during all its varied stages...]

(X) <u>Swiss watch</u> industry missed Japanese revolution in quartz... (X) <u>Dam of Nile River</u> caused huge envornmental snafus... (X) <u>Ecology</u>: to kill a local (but nocturnal) predator, the mongoose was introduced—but m. is diurnal... (X) Two adjacent U.S.A. states simultaneously issued <u>auto license plates</u> "blue with white letters/numbers"!... (X) Only one <u>physician</u> out of ten spotted arsenic poisoning by seeing patient's fingernails... (X) Only one <u>mechanic</u> spotted short in electrical system: between stoplight and taillight filament in rear bulb!... (X) <u>Safer sex</u>: "just use a condom," *but also* what of lubricants weakening rubber, biocide effects of gels?!...

--"Catchment-Area": cast your net *wide* beyond the *apparent* subject to the <u>true total context</u>.

(X) A "river" is: not just liquid in its banks now, but "anywhere it might flow in the flood-plain someday"!... (X) Businesses: you should interview not just your good and satisfied customers, *but also* your *dis*satisfied and your *non*-customers ...

--"Colloquialize": always seek the reactions-responses of *other* people; *one* mind *can't* see it all.

[4.] "FIELD-SENSITIVITY": To truly know/comprehend a subject, see it not from <u>your</u> own lens-perspective, but in <u>its</u> own *field*: context, environment, time and place. And beware generalizing that what is true, right, effective in one *situation*, will work in other *arenas*.

(X) "<u>Hindus</u> worship the cow, <u>Eskimo</u> tribes let their grandparents die in the wilderness—*but* note transmigration of souls, survival of the group... (X) "Advanced" <u>democracy</u> worked in Germany, Japan after WWII, but just can't "take" in traditionally-tribal society *environment* such as **Iraq** now... (X) A. <u>Lincoln's speech</u> *seemed* to support slavery: *but* see that it was in *context* of a political campaign, etc... (X) <u>Collaborative learning</u> works well in business, but won't work in *milieu* of Middle Schools!... (X) American-type <u>Gay Rights</u> dogma says "gays should "come out and be visible," but in *context* of some other societies, social norms would make this backfire...

[5.] RE-THINK (1) "TODAY'S IN-TRUTHS & OUT-TABOOS"; MANAGE THE "PENDULUM-SWING IN FASHIONS OF THINKING." Beware the <u>pitfall</u>: "What is currently thought true/good/etc., must be accepted, cannot be criticized; what is currently thought false/bad/etc. must be disregarded, cannot be entertained." [Beware the social "puppetmaster" making us dance to his current fashionable tunes...]

(X) It's all <u>environment</u>, social-construction=====no, it's all <u>heredity</u>, psychobiology. (X) <u>Education</u>: didacticism, constructivism.

[6.] AVOID THE "EITHER-OR" FALLACY: AIM FOR "MORE-TOWARD" OR "BOTH-AND" MOVES. Ask not, "Is it either A, or Z?" Instead, ask, "For our purpose, is it better to move *more toward* A, or *more toward* Z? Or to *integrate both*?" (X) "<u>Post/Modernism</u>": We can know reality fully=====no, we can never know reality reliably! (X) <u>Chinese art</u> sought to *combine* Matter-Spirit, Human-Nature, tradition-originality, Classic-Romantic, calm-movement...

[7.] "VARIABLES-VARIATION." When taking a stand, know what are <u>all</u> the AOC Alternate Optional Choices (other stands, positions) on a continuum A to Z. And the pros-and-cons of <u>each</u> possible station. <u>Then reconsider: is your original stand the best one after all?</u>" (X) <u>Writing</u>: "Keep sentences short," *or also maybe* at times mid-size, <u>or</u> longer. .. (X) <u>Photo</u>: set shutter-speed at 1/125second," *or also maybe* longer time exposures, <u>or</u> shorter to freeze action... (X) <u>Morality</u>: "Absolute Natural Law," *or also maybe* Situation Ethics, <u>or</u> Pragmatism, <u>or</u> [six others!]?!...

[8.] METHOD: "RULES vs. TOOLS": Know when to follow a formula as a Rule (recipe, code "1-2-3 by-the-book"), and when to use procedure as Tool ("only if-and-as needed"). Cf. Form-Function; Correct-Effective; Letter-Spirit). (X) <u>Travel Rules</u>: It clearly said, "No eating or laundering in the hotel room," *but* I could break that rule morally: <u>why</u>?... (X) <u>Writing</u>: "sentence-type, repetition, length, tone: personal-formal?, honesty—*it all depends*... (X) <u>Student</u> given a dozen "suggestive probes" to poetry [=tools], *but* mechanically grinds through *all 12*, relevant to poem or not [=as rules]! ...

[9.] KNOWING, VS. KNOWING. To know something means *not* just <u>of-or-about</u> it, *but* fully "<u>whether-how-&-why</u>" to <u>use</u> it—and in situations which lesser thinkers would overlook!
(X) To know what <u>teaching thinking</u> *truly* is... X To know <u>psychological personal autonomy</u>: "spontaneity, awareness, intimacy"...
(X) To know "<u>allocation cost benefit ratio</u>" and "<u>sampling errors in statistics</u>" and spontaneously use these in daily-life arenas—Personal, Job, Citizen! (Apply for a grant, or not?... Take bus or taxi when in Bangkok Thailand?... Is this group of women, representative?...)

[10.] CATEGORIZATION: CLASSIFY-&-DIVIDE: a powerful tool to explore via *component subparts*.
(X) <u>Vegetarianism</u>: Lacto... Lacto-ovo... Ovo... Pesco... Semi... Vegan... RawFoodism... Fruitarianism... Sproutarian...
(X) <u>Tastes of Food</u>: Sweet... Sour... Bitter... Salty... *but also* Astringent... *and also Umami*, a rich full type...
(X) <u>Sexual Orientation</u>: 1. Behavior, activity, but also 2. Erotic fantasy-arousal, 3. Definition by self, others, 4. in Total Identity.
(X) <u>Ways of organizing, structuring anything</u>: Space-Location, Alphabetical, Time, Conceptual Scheme, Hierarchy, Random.
(X) <u>Types of Adventure-Travel</u>: City-Hopping... Immersion (one place)... Home-basing (side-trips)... "Threading" (move slow-low)...
(X) <u>Types of School Curricula</u>: Explicit (taught in class)... Hidden (in the climate)... Extra (clubs, groups)... Null (*not* permitted!)

[11.] COMPARISON/CONTRAST is another powerful tool to see the *new/different* via the *old/known*.
(X) <u>Poetry appreciation</u>: show the bad (sentimental verse) with the better (subtle tones)... (X) <u>Proper shading in drawings</u>? (show too dark, just right, too light)... (X) <u>The "Blues"</u>: (give same song in "White" music version)... (X) <u>How large is France</u>? (Drop a same-scale map of Wisconsin (or whatever) into it)... X <u>Japanese flower-arranging</u>? (Show three examples, then the same bouquet arranged "Western-style" also)... (X) <u>Dementia</u> is *not* normal memory-loss... (X) Consensual <u>power-exchange sex</u> is *not* domestic abuse!...

[12.] BALANCE THE "CCC==DDD": connect correlate compare, vs. differentiate distinguish distance. <u>Join</u> or relate two elements wrongly separated or incorrectly thought to be different, distinct. *But also*, <u>separate</u> distinctly, two elements wrongly "conflated," inaccurately thought to be the identical/similar.
(X) <u>Baseball player is a bigoted racist</u> privately—*but* he plays good ball (*his value*), so ignore his personal wart...
--<u>The following are truly distinct</u>: Stereotype and "sociotype"... Communism and socialism... Homosexuality and pedophilia...
--<u>The following show good combining</u>: (X) Consider grass-roots <u>art displays</u> in public places, as valid educational enterprises...
(X) A small college's Handbook included janitorial maintenance etc. *staff* **right in along with** the *faculty* biographies and pictures!

[13.] CORRELATE CONTRARIES. If two elements are both needed/valuable, but totally opposed-contradictory-conflicting, seek to satisfy both.
(X) <u>Human motivations</u>: we crave "security *and* risk, coherence *and* spontaneity, novelty *and* latency, rivalry *and* mutuality, personal identity *and* social belongingness, security *and* new experience..." (X) "<u>Project manager</u>": ego/no ego... autocrat/delegator... leader/manager... complexity/keep-it-simple... big/small viewpoint... X <u>Art</u> is new/old, emotional/orderly, specific/general, etc., etc. X <u>Teacher</u> must be supportive guide/in-charge leader... (X) I can definitively condemn my colleague "<u>NELSON'S</u>" one-sided egocentric authoritarianism, *but also* can and do admiringly praise his great social contributions to school and town ...

[14.] "GYROSCOPE ZEN-CALM: BE FULLY PRESENT AND ALSO PROPRIATE": Approach situations to neither "obsessively refute," nor "slavishly accept": be *not* (1) defensive, to protect your stance, *nor* (2) offensive, to attack the other and win, *nor* (3) over-accommodating apologetic groupthink, *nor* (4) detached-dismissive—*but* be simultaneously "fully present plus fully propriate." To be open to "know the Other Side as clearly as it itself does," while also to retain own self, reserve from fear, approval, etc. Neither feeling threatened-defensive, nor pressured to accept. "Style" as "attainment and restraint."
(X) A liberal *truly* hearing a conservative position, to comprehend fully for once, whether agree or not.

\=\+|+|+\=\=\+|+|=\=\=|+|+|\\\+|+|+|=\=|+|+|=\=\+|+|+|=\=|+|+|+\=\=|+|+|+\=\=|+|+|+\=\=|+|+|\=\+|+|+\=\=\+|+| +

[4.] Summary I: thinking seen from Big-Picture context on to more-specific but still generic strategic skills …

[4.A.] OUR RATIONALES: we perhaps-unnecessarily affirm our foundation for the project:

[1.] -- Our **Rationale** that Thinking is valuable… Complexity requires competence… but we often Shortfall in this… hence this educational Resource… *Further*:

[2.] --<u>Complex skills</u> can be elucidated and taught/learned/practiced very <u>explicitly</u>, more so than we realize, teach, do, etc., but short of over-explicit formula rule or recipe—a common misconception holds otherwise.

[3.] --Somewhat relatedly, <u>generalizing</u> (and synthesizing, integrating—as possible) is not amateur dilettante, but <u>is an expert specialty in itself</u> (90% of our thinking tasks are outside of our own personal professional areas…)

[4.] --Further, we can know reality <u>reality</u> "out there," *to some extent significant for many purposes*, although of course always complexly mediated through our minds, and to *a lesser or better degree* or approximation. (This is our stand of "Lens-perspectives" in between innate Absolutism and Rampant Relativism…)

[5.] –Our educational model for teaching thinking emphasizes three pillars or keystones. (1) Overall Goal: not what to know-believe-do, but how to think things through. (CTA = conceptualize UP, transfer ACROSS, apply DOWN.) (2) Presence of teaching thinking: (A) embedded in courses? (B) exhibited in whole school? (3) End-Goal: readiness to apply abstractions autonomously, "Hit the Ground Running" to confront content in the real world.

[4.B.] Now, a "SCENARIO for Thinking." Starting with "first-things viewed far off," and moving in more specifically, like spacecraft orbiting new planet for orientation…:

[1.] --Analogy of Significant Action as Drama, Theatre. Thinking is a significant action, can be seen by this view. We call this the **"12-W"** model.

--In **POEP Plain Old English Please**: "Someone does something, to something, by some method, for some purpose or goal or result."

--In KENNETH BURKE'S **Dramaturgic Pentad** [an existing formulation of this Who-Where-When-Why-How-What sort of formula]: An Actor, performs an Act, by some Agency, in a Scene or location, for some Purpose."

--For OUR **purposes**: **Thinking = confronting content conceptually** (for a task-goal result—a purpose, whether to Comprehend, or to Achieve…).

--**"Confront"**: in *phases*: Research, describe… then comprehend: interpret, explain, evaluate… respond to: plan actions or "do" to-or-with… then perhaps communicate to others about.
[Describe vegetarianism, predict climate, explain crime causes, set policy for globalization…]

--**"Content"**: on a ladder of **Verticality** from concrete to conceptual, everything from objects, people, scenes, events, actions, processes, issues, to problems, goals, higher concepts…

--**"Conceptually"**: using the <u>mind, specifically higher-order thinking tools</u>. The primary Trio of induction, deduction, association. Then many others… And the dozen traits of **"essential"** thinking…

[2.] --But wait. *Other methods for* doing exist besides thinking: *pure force, politics, luck, chance*, etc.

[3.] --And other methods of <u>mental activity</u> exist besides conceptual thinking: *inspiration, free-association*, etc.

[4.] --And as for pragmatic, functional <u>competence</u>, thinking can be *good—or* not good, but just-so, or even bad: inefficient, ineffective.

[5.] --Thinking is "natural," yes, <u>but "good" thinking is "unnatural-abnormal,"</u> must be worked for.

[6.] --And as for morality, thinking can be not always fair-minded, but <u>skilful but used for selfish ends</u>.

[7.] --And as for personal, individual <u>competence</u>, indeed everyone thinks well to some extent, *but everyone can improve* in their thinking also.

[4.C.] And now, "LEVELS <u>"I"</u> BASIC: Thinking = confronting content conceptually (for some task-goal purpose).

<u>"II" ADVANCED:</u> same, except <u>make the goal</u> **challenging**, <u>meaning difficult of achievement</u>—requiring luck, perhaps, but especially **competence**. ("Challenge" we can categorize into the elements or factors of

1. "exigency" or the task is of crucial importance…

2. the issue is innately complex-not-simple.

[Within these first two categories, the task-goal may be of the "CCCCC" type: a Current-Contemporary, Communal Concern but one which is Confusing and Contested. {Abortion Bureaucracy Crime Demographics Environment Finance Globalization}…]

3. in this task, high standards apply, demanding criteria are required…

4. "situational constraints" apply: restrictions, mandates, etc.…

5. perhaps the thinker or performer's skill is insufficient for the task—we assume enough motivation…

…WHAT in heaven's name is all the above stratospheric meandering around? This "orientation," disorients me!	It's just noting the Big Picture or environment in which specific thinking occurs. To "monitor the totality" thus, is itself a key thinking skill. It can help avoid pitfalls of partiality: narrow vision, oversights, etc.

[4.D.] The "12-W" or "Task-Goal Performance-Profile"

THE ISSUE. How to keep track of all the elements in doing a complex task? Here a very-general framework:

OUR SUGGESTION. Employ a dramatic-action model. "Someone does something, in a time and place… " *We offer the following multi-issue checklist*. Its <u>source?</u> We expanded it from three existing schemes:

--[1] The <u>journalists' "5-W"</u> scheme of **"Where, When, Who, What, and Why,"** *but also*

--[2] KENNETH BURKE'S **Pentad** scheme of "**1. Actor, 2. Act-ion, 3. Scene** (time & place), **4. Agency** (mechanism by which done), **5. Purpose**," *and also*

--[3] LLOYD BITZER'S concept of **"exigence"** or what we call *crucial need*… [**"An imperfection marked by urgency; a defect, an obstacle, something waiting to be done, a thing that is other than it should be."**]

TOOL-KIT. …our expanded **"12-W"** model for **"significant action monitoring"**…

1. <u>**Who**</u>'s doing something? [Actor]

2. <u>**What**</u>'s being done? [Act]

3. <u>To/Upon</u> what **Content**--<u>what</u> subject etc. is having something done (or happen) <u>to</u> it?

4. <u>Where and when</u> is this happening, in what time-and-space **context**? [Scene]

5. <u>How</u> is this being done ("**Craft**": technique-method-procedure etc.)? [Agency]

6. How well <u>can, and does, the Actor do</u> this? [{ **Competence "I"** = Skill of Actor, in the ongoing Process }]

7. <u>Why</u> (A) for what specific *intended result or goal*? [Purpose] **Consequence "I"**: the *intention*…

8. <u>Why</u> (B) because of what more-general "exigency" or *desirability-or-need* **"Cruciality"**?

357

9. How <u>hard (or easy)</u> is the task to do? [**A.**] Degree of **Challenge** or difficulty-of-attainment—"E-Z" to "moderate" to "tuf" to, well, "impossible"? And [**B.**] Type/Kind of challenges: [= 1. **innate** (inherent intrinsic) factors (as against *imposed*), 2. **"Complexity"**: a dozen aspects of!, 3. **Context**: situational demands/constraints, 4. **criteria**: standards are perhaps high, 5. **Cruciality** or "it matters!" importance, 6. **"Other"**…)

10. <u>How</u> will it be <u>aimed for</u> and then <u>judged as</u> done-or-not, and done well-or-not--by what **Criteria** (definitions, dimensions, aspects) ?

11. <u>How well</u> does it *have* to be done? (**Standards:** benchmarks, measurements, etc.)

12. So what happened, how well <u>was</u> it actually done, well-or-ill? [{ **Competence "II"** = Success of Attainment or final Product }]? What is the **Consequence "II"**: the *result*… (**"Score"**) [A. Binary Fail/Lose *or* Succeed/Win, or B. Continuum, from "Sandlot" to Varsity to Regional to World-Class/Olympic…]

13. <u>Who judged</u> this performance? **(A)** Receive the judges' judgments. [*Note*—do the judges concur, or disagree—if disagree, why [see # "3-DDD" checklist], and how to resolve this?] **(B)** And critique the judges' judgments—and our own critiques of them also! (=Who <u>spectated</u> the performance and its judging?)

14. [Aha, but <u>what Variables</u> did *we* omit here, which *you* would **suggest** as needed, and why?]

…well, this *does* sound promising to be useful, **BUT** we do badly need a specific example here. Can you supply?	How about this very book and project, <u>Teaching Thinking</u>, elucidated by the 12-W's issues? Thus:

[1.] WHO or what is doing something	BRIAN BECK, *but* drawing on other educators in the "critical thinking" and other movements.
[2.] WHAT is being done, Confronted?	The <u>issue</u> of "teaching and learning thinking skills, as against knowledge-mastery," in formal education—and also for self-learners, and others interested ("t. buffs").
[3.] TO WHAT, Content?	To the materials this movement has produced. Also perhaps to the potential audience readership "out there"…
[4.] WHEN-WHERE occurring, Context?	In Wisconsin 1995-onward "until done." Later disseminated via publication, electronically also, to Teaching and Learning Centers at schools…
[5.] HOW is this being done, Craft	[*] Via many of the thinking techniques it presents! Comprehensiveness, elucidation, contrary-correlating…
[6.] HOW WELL is done, Competence "I"?	…in its own terms, as well as the author could; varied readers will judge variously…
[7.] WHY "I" Purposes or Consequences sought?	To provide "best possible and needed" introduction to this challenging, misunderstood, fascinating, valuable topic.
[8.] WHY "II" Cruciality or need-rationale for doing?	Personal motivating vision that the topic is important (crucial, valuable, needed), and that no other adequate resource-materials currently exist. Secondarily, "pleasurable" [?...] challenge of creating "best-possible" unit. (Motive is not fame, wealth, power, ego, revenge, etc.)
[9.] HOW EASY/HARD to do, % of **Challenge** identified?	<u>Extremely difficult</u>. 1. Subject is difficult. 2. Audience is varied. 3. Medium is one-way, no discussion possible. 4. Author is skilled but not perfect. 5. His criteria or expectations are high.
[10.] HOW JUDGED WHETHER done well, **Criteria**?	Standards of **Essential Thinking**, <u>and</u> of "elucidated" <u>Communication</u>.
[11.] HOW WELL MUST be done, **Standards**?	Pragmatic: to reach and serve well, "X%" of interested readers. Intrinsic: to attain writer's "Personal Best-possible"
[12.] HOW WELL actually WAS DONE, Conclusion, the "Score"?	1. Writer: competently…as well as I could do via my Consciousness of own work… 2. Readers: (*to be decided!*)
[13.] WHO judged? [=the "Committee"] Audience?	….. [self as editor to start: incisive **Consciousness** of own thinking and writing is required…] [I don't know who reacted how…]
[14.] …and the VARIABLE *we mistakenly omitted!*...	["No one person or system can be truly complete…"]

\=\+|+|+\=\=\+|+|+|=\=\=|+|+|\\\+|+|+|=\=|+|+|+|=\=\+|+|+|+\=\=|+|+|+|+\=\=|+|+|+|=\=\=|+|+|+|=\=|+|+|\=\+|+|+|+\=\+|+|+| +

[4.E.] Thinking DEFINED: "Confronting Content Conceptually"…

1. "Content" = :

THE ISSUE. What is "content"? [= Subject-matter; material; topics-questions-problems-issues; information, data; even concepts, perspectives, variables and other higher-level material"....]

WHETHER IMPORTANT, AND THE PURPOSE. *Useful? Well, it may elucidate the dimensions of content, substance, material for beginning learners…*

358

SCHEME. Proposed clarification of types of **content** (subjects questions topics questions problems issues etc.)

1. A-to-Z Simply **Alphabetical**
2. Via some **Conceptual Scheme** for knowledge. (Library classifications, anthropology rosters.)
3. **"Cruciality,"** the degree of *urgency, importance, necessity*, etc., of a "current, contested concern…"
4. **Pedagogical:** will teach something in school. [Research-Paper Topics?...]
5. **Situation/Context** *Where* does the content appear: location, outlet, venue…
   (A) Reader-Audience… (B) "Arena" [Personal, School, Work, Civic] & Genre-type… (C) Purpose-Goal…
6. Degree of **Challenge** or difficulty of accomplishing the goal *well, competently*—or well-"enough"!...
7. Levels of **Verticality**: % of Concrete-Specificity vs. Conceptual-General-Abstractness of the subject.

A-Z Alpha	Scheme	Cruciality	Pedagogical	Context	Challenge	Verticality
"Readers' Guide":	(1) the Acad. DISCIPLINES:	Important, something is at stake, a felt need, an urgency.	Subject is grist for the learning-mill, can teach something.	ARENAS [School Personal Vocational Civic Etc.] Also GENRES:	Degree of difficulty in accomplishing the thinking or writing or action task-goal.	From lo-down Concrete specific up to Conceptual general.
Advertising Breakfast Clothing Dance Electricity Firewood Gardening Hairstyling Insects Jewelry Laundry Mountains Newspapers Opera Posters Quartos Reading Soups Thinking Uniforms Vectors Weather Xenophobia Yellow Zoos	**Humanities** Philosophy Religion Fine Arts Literature History **Soc.Scis:** Sociology Pol.Sci./Govt. Psychology Communication Geography **Nat.Scis:** Biology *(more…..)* **Applieds:** Architecture Business Engineering Law Medicine *(more)* **(2) Library Systems:** Dewey, LC.. **(3) Human Relations Area Files: Outline of Cultural Materials.** **(4) Dictionary of Occupational Titles.**	*[Research papers???...]* Abortion Acid rain Affirmative action AIDS Animal rights Area Studies Bioethics Capitalism Censorship Crime Death penalty Diversity Drugs Energy Feminism Free Speech Genetics Globalization Gun control Health Care Homosexuality Immigration Mass Media Pornography Poverty Sci.&Rel. Social Justice Water Welfare [...the "usual suspects"...]	*[Research papers???...]* Atlantis Anorexia Bigfoot UFO's Chicago fire Scopes trial [...and too many other similars...] -Appearance & Reality --Architecture --Continuity-&-Change --Housing --Same-sex marriage --Weather --Writing Systems	Editorials Instructions Interview "J'accuse!" *Letters* *Literature* Memos News Story Reports *Reviews* Sketch Test/Exam Recipe Diary/Log *(more)* [Those with many subtypes are *italicized*]	Hurdles are identifiable. (Innate vs. situational; related to Criteria or Standards; etc.). Could just anybody do it without savvy or sweat, or did it "cost" the person?' 1. Write a note to the milkman simply changing the order (omit buttermilk, add eggs). 2. Write a letter to milk company president suggesting new product and why... ["Tell about one's teaching" *vs.* "Try to elucidate the teaching and learning of thinking to outsiders"...]	**VEGETARIANISM:** **Object:** pressure cooker & grains-&-legumes **Person:** Victor the vigorous vegetarian **Place:** Wheatberry Restaurant **Event:** "our first veg. meal" **Process:** recipes **Activity:** educating students **Subjects:** Veg. and history economics morality etc. **Problems:** ... **Larger Concepts:** ...

\=\+|+|+|+\=\=\+|+|+|=\=\=|+|+|+\\\|+|+|+|=\=|+|+|+|=\=\+|+|+|+\=\=|+|+|+|+\=\=|+|+|+|+\=\=|+|+|+|+\=\=|+|+|\=\+|+|+|+\=\=\+|+|+| +

2. to "Confront" said Content" = :

1st Stage: "**Research**" the Subject	2nd Stage: **Think** it thru *[*!]*	3rd Stage: [A] **Act Regarding** It?	3rd Stage: [B] **Convey** it to others, communicate-about?
Define. Discover, Describe, depict, delineate. Report on. # 12-W planning. # Six Moves (1) Research.	Comprehend, Interpret: Explain (cause-effect). Predict. Evaluate.	Make decisions about. Solve problems about. Set public and private policy and procedure about. Instruct in how to use, do, or confront.	Writing, speaking, other media… "Please (entertain), Teach (inform/instruct), Move (emotionally)"…

\=\+|+|+|+\=\=\+|+|+|=\=\=|+|+|+\\\|+|+|+|=\=|+|+|+|=\=\+|+|+|+\=\=|+|+|+|+\=\=|+|+|+|+\=\=|+|+|+|+\=\=|+|+|\=\+|+|+|+\=\=\+|+|+| +

3. "Challenge" [difficulties] of confronting = :

"**Challenge**" = **difficulty of attainment. (1)** subject-material may be <u>complex</u> "inside" inherently-innately-intrinsically… **(2)** <u>context</u>: the "outside" situation may be *demanding*… **(3)** the <u>criteria</u> (standards-for-performance) may be *high*… **(4)** the task itself may be "crucial" or important-to-accomplish (an "exigency")… **(5)** the task may be <u>demanding</u> for the *particular individual* performer (thinker), f/ skills, also f/ dispositions…

EXAMPLES. [1] <u>**Easy vs. Difficult:**</u> "A note to the milkman changing the usual order today," *versus* "a letter to the president of the milk company urging a change or improvement."
[2] <u>**Playing with the Net Down:**</u> Freshmen students often could respond to a piece of writing only with the comment "<u>well, it gets the point across</u>." This is incredibly blunt and lowest-denominator, like "I can hit the side of the barn with a stone."

\=\+|+|+|+\=\=\+|+|+|=\=\=|+|+|+\\\|+|+|+|=\=|+|+|+|=\=\+|+|+|+\=\=|+|+|+|+\=\=|+|+|+|+\=\=|+|+|+|+\=\=|+|+|\=\+|+|+|+\=\=\+|+|+| +

[4.F.] On "COMPLEXITY" of content, or of anything…

THE ISSUE… WHY IMPORTANT: "The world is complex," allegedly "even more so today" and the like…
[EXAMPLE: describe "a vegetarian recipe" or "restaurant" == vs. "explain vegetarianism as seen by history, ethics, *etc.*"]
OUR SUGGESTION. Following is our categorization of variables of complexity.

[This is "I" BRIEF view; for "II" FULL view, *SEE* Mind- Play.]

1. <u>Content overall</u>: Size-Extent, Scope Mass Substance of whole. **[Small…..large?]**

2. <u>Content within</u>, Components: Subparts Elements of whole. **[Clearly definable…or elusive? Simple surface…or dimensioned? Monolithic…or manifold? Uniform traits…or much variation?]**

3. <u>Structure</u> [I descriptive, "anatomy"]: **Contours:** dimensions, shape-form-pattern. Levels. **[One…or more?**

4. <u>Structure</u> [II dynamic, "physiology"]: **Operations:** functioning inter-actions, activity, interrelations (withinside, and outside-context). Changes? Conflicts? **[Isolated, static…or dynamically-interactive?]**

5. And <u>our response to</u> the subject:

A. Familiarity-with vs. foreign-to-us. **[Old-hat known…rather new, very new, "ground rules changed"?]**

B. Knowability of: now, ultimately. **[Known, certainty, with closure…ultimate ambiguity, obscurity?]**

C. Group response to: **consensus…differing disagreement?**

\=\+|+|+\=\=\+|+|+|=\=\=|+|+|\\\+|+|+|=\=|+|+|+|=\=\+|+|+|\=\=|+|+|+|\=\=|+|+|+|\=\=|+|+|\=\+|+|+|\=\=\+|+|+| +

[4.G.] … this "ESSENTIAL" "basic-advanced" "true" THINKING which we are touting—what *is* it anyway?…

THE ISSUE. Thinking skills vary, and some are more "basic" in sense of central, vital, even if more advanced (higher-order, etc.).

WHY IMPORTANT. *Ironic it would be* to teach "thinking" without foregrounding more-complex but vital, default, essential kinds of thinking!

OUR SUGGESTION. Here is our version of "higher-order" thinking—the major variables. *Is our version any more comprehensive-complete, but also more-clarified (proportionate, structured, etc.)?*

Element of "essential" thinking:	How, where we treat it:
(1) Confronts Complexity (17 aspects of) (A) In Content it is *Comprehensive, Complete* ("enough…") (B) In Movement it is *holistic panoramic systemic synthesizing integrating* etc.	
(2) Meta-Formulaic: beyond rule and recipe… The slogan **"aRt – hTs"** differentiates algorhythm-Rule-tactic, from heuristic-Tool-strategy. (NB also Guideline, Rule of Thumb…)	**SEE LETTER VS. SPIRIT in #3 of App. #N.**
(3) Higher-*Order* (is complex itself).	See 4 quotations: Resnick, three others…
(4) Higher-*Level*. Moves up the "Ladder of Abstraction" from Material concrete specifics == to Mental concepts, principles. (And down again then and across: not only INduction, but DEduction, and lateral-associative…)	**(X) APPENDIX CONCEPTUALIZING UP 101.**
(5) "Supple": dialectic "both-and": correlates valuable but opposing contraries. (Especially both Complete-Comprehensive == and also Clarified-Comprehensible.) (Then also Conceptual plus Concrete… Elitist defending good thinking plus Populist welcoming variety… Convergence to unity plus Divergence to variety…)	**CORRELATING CONTRARIES see Eight Moves Nr. & Rel.**
(6) Conscious: reflexive self-awareness of own thinking, meta-cognition. Describe and evaluate own product.	
(7) "Considered": s-l-o-w, reflective, deliberate … Can suspend judgment,.	See (X) "thoroughness," Gallery of X quotations.
(8) "Considerate": the moral-ethical dimension in thinking. Disposition to be not agonistic (combat to win victory), but authentic (cooperate to win validity). Admits own biases, truly hears the other side. Is Candid for-real	**SEE ON DISPOSITIONS OR FAIR-MINDED ATTITUDES IN**

but also Civil empathetic. Etc.	**THINKING. APP. P.B.**
(9) Competent. Not "bad," not even "just-"thinking, but "good, better, perhaps best" thinking. [{ The slogan **"APE==APE"**: Avoid pitfalls errors, aim for potentialities excellences.}] Via high **Criteria, Standards**. ["**Command**" = whether win – succeed or lose-fail, did all one could do.] "**Excellence** In/Of **Quality**".	**SEE QUALITY in P.B.**
(10) "Contest": not just Practical and Principled, but Pleasurable, Enjoyable, Satisfying! Sportive game, play-of-mind, the thinker-athlete performing, the reader-spectators cheering—or booing…	

…sorry, **BUT** your roster here looks just like the "same old same-old." We've heard of all these aspects before…	True indeed. However, (1) they exceed the usual "critical thinking" elements, and (2) in their *selection, phrasing, arrangement, and interrelation*, we think they are *slightly* more **Complete**, better **Clarified**. Recall **elucidation**: the complete-clear views of subject. Recall "the two 200-page travel guides" to a region: but one imbalanced, thin-vague (or 100% data), random, —the other complete, proportioned, plus conceptual and specific, internally-organized, etc… It aims for "the best points in the best interrelationship…"

…good, **BUT** could we have a few more-specific examples of, or comments on, this kind-or-type of thinking?	You read our minds. Time here for a highly-selected gallery of—well, touchstone-statements. As follows:

GALLERY. A few classic statements on "essences" of thinking:

(3) "Higher-*Order*": four especially-elucidating quotations worth repeated pondering:

EXAMPLE #1: The teacher LAUREN RESNICK'S *classic* [1987] description of **"higher-order" thinking:**
--Higher-order thinking [HOT] tends to be complex. The total path is not "visible" (mentally speaking) from any single vantage point.   --HOT often yields multiple solutions, each with costs and benefits, rather than unique solutions.   --HOT involves nuanced judgment and interpretation.   --HOT involves the application of multiple criteria, which sometimes conflict with one another.   --HOT often involves uncertainty. Not everything that bears on the task at hand is known.   --HOT involves self-regulation of the thinking process. We do not recognize higher-order thinking in an individual when someone else calls the plays at every step.   --HOT involves imposing meaning, finding structure in apparent disorder.   --And, HOT is effortful. Considerable mental work is involved in the kinds of elaborating and judging required.
True, this quotation just describes, it neither instructs, nor explains. Nor is it **Convergent** unifying the components underneath one key thesis above all. But it does catch-or-capture complexities rather clearly! Hence it does seem "**elucidating**"…

EXAMPLE #2: EDUCATORS' showing that complexity is—complex, sometimes remains "vague":
….we have identified <u>five dimensions of thinking</u>:   1. METACOGNITION…..   2. CRITICAL-AND-CREATIVE thinking…..   3. Thinking PROCESSES…..   4. CORE thinking skills…..   5. and the RELATIONSHIP of Content-area KNOWLEDGE to thinking.   <u>These dimensions do not form a taxonomy. They are neither discrete nor comparable categories. They overlap in some cases, and they relate to each other in different ways. Therefore, they do not form a hierarchy. Nor are they intended as ends in themselves.</u>   We chose them because they *reflect the various domains of thinking as they are understood in terms of current research.* Educators can *use this framework as a resource*….   [-- SOURCE UNIDENTIFIED: FROM MATERIAL ON CRITICAL THINKING]

…oh, but this is *vague*. Saying that they are neither same-or-different, not categorized, not connected, not structured, not goals! You offer *this* "recital of negatives," as *good* "thinking-about-thinking"?…..	…the underlined portions seem a *clear but not oversimplistic view of chaos, complexity, unclarity*—<u>and</u> better-done than most other similar statements. *That's* "**elucidation**," or anyhow *toward* same.

> **EXAMPLE #3:** Bird's-eye view of seven major recent changes in how we view fields of knowledge:

1. From *simple* to *complex-and-diverse*...
2. From <u>hierarchical</u> to <u>heterarchical</u>. From pecking order -- to interlocking systems. Maybe no fixed rules at the top of a discipline.
3. From *mechanical* to *holographic*. From simple linkage of information like parts of a machine -- to each-piece-to-every-other-piece.
4. From *determinate* to *indeterminate*. From faith in prediction of precise outcomes -- to knowing probabilities and possibilities.
5. From *linear* to *multiple* causality. From simple action to same results -- to feedback as influential too.
6. From *assembly* to *morphogenesis*. From "jigsaw "-- to a new form unpredicted by any of its parts. (Like "gestalt" viewpoint?)
7. From *objective* to *representative* perspective. From belief that mind photographs world directly -- to a belief that we can't see the world neutrally. Assumptions and methods shape the information we perceive.

  [-- SCHWARZ AND OGILVY]

...This seems **Complete**, panoramic in scope. Also high-level **Conceptual**. But also **Clarified** (**Classified** into subparts, which however are sufficiently **Coherent**). All in all the Whole Nine Yards Forest, but not oversimple, overcomplex, rigid, or random either... In short, approaches **elucidation** as we see it...

> **EXAMPLE #4.** A vivid description of "wicked" problems—challengingly-complex...

[Complex public policy issues constitute what HORST RITTEL has called "wicked problems." Also called "ill-structured" problems or even social messes.] "Wicked problems are <u>situations that have these properties</u>: <u>Complicated, complex, and ambiguous</u>... <u>Uncertainty</u> even as to what the problems are, let alone what the solutions might be... Are under great <u>constraints</u>... Are tightly <u>interconnected</u>, economically, socially, politically, technologically... Are <u>seen differently</u> from different points of view, quite different world-views... Contain many <u>value conflicts</u>... Are often <u>a-logical or illogical</u>..." [-- SOURCE]

...again, a somewhat *clear* and complete, view of *obscurity* and enormity...

\=\+|+|+\=\=\+|+|+|=\=\=|+|+|+\\\+|+|+|=\=|+|+|=\=\+|+|+\=\=|+|+|+\=\=|+|+|+\=\=|+|+|+\=\=|+|\=\+|+|+\=\=\+|+| +

(5) "Supple": "Contrary-Correlating..."

Supple = readily adaptable or responsive to new situations...pliant, limber...easy and fluent without stiffness or awkwardness; elastic." ***Both*** <u>internally systematic</u> and hence consistent organized structured etc., ***but also*** <u>externally alterable</u>: accessible-"attachable" and flexible-adaptable... ***Both*** able to <u>take a firm or defined stance</u> or stand, ***but also*** can keep things flexibly-provisional and can <u>alter positions later deftly</u> not clumsily.

\=\+|+|+\=\=\+|+|+|=\=|+|+|+\\\+|+|+|=\=|+|+|=\=\+|+|+\=\=|+|+|+\=\=|+|+|+\=\=|+|+|+\=\=|+|+|+\=\=|+|\=\+|+|+\=\=\+|+| +

(7) "Considered": s-l-o-w, reflective-deliberative...THOROUGH:

> **GALLERY #1.** Classic quotations, and an analogy, to illuminate the quality of **Thorough Deliberation**...

--People with <u>the critical habit of thought</u> "are *slow to believe*. They can *hold things as possible or probable* in all degrees, without certainty and without pain. They can wait for evidence and weigh evidence" [objectively, and withstand appeals to prejudices and other biases.]   [-- WM. GRAHAM SUMNER, FOLKWAYS, 1906]

--*ANALOGY:* **"Detective Work"**: **Higher-order complex thinking** is like *criminal investigation*: hints, nuances, slow pace, persistance, intuitions, information, beyond surface and superficial overgeneral impressions,etc.

--ANECDOTE: at a meeting to decide about action upon a complex issue, the executive asked whether all committee members were confidently decided about what to do. "Yes," they replied. The executive "All right, then go and thoroughly, carefully *re*-think this, and we'll re-convene tomorrow..."

--TWO STATEMENTS, a classic earlier, and a contemporary academic: "**<u>Negative Capability:</u>**" the state of being in doubt amid uncertainty without "irritable reaching after reason" [-- JOHN KEATS, English poet] ... **<u>Ability to Delay Closure</u>**—*but also* to make a firm decision plus re-open if needed, see Supple. Withhold conclusion, suspend judgment.

--Three Counsels on Deliberation and Distance. [1.] "<u>Read</u> not to contradict and confute; nor to believe and take for granted; nor to find talk and discourse; but to weigh and consider." [-- FRANCIS BACON] ..... [2.] "I have made a ceaseless effort not to ridicule, not to bewail, nor to scorn <u>human actions</u>, but to understand them." [-- B. SPINOZA] ..... [3.] "The function of the <u>historian</u> is neither to love the past nor to emancipate himself from the past, but to master and understand it as the key to the understanding of the present." [-- E. H. CARR]

--**"The Forest of The Other Side"**... Ability to *truly see and feel and comprehend* "the other side" (opposing opinions, etc.) with a gyroscope-balance. *Without* either (1) "slavish <u>acceptance</u>," Groupthink, etc., or (2) <u>Defensiveness</u>, feeling threatened, protect self, or (3) militant <u>Offensive</u> stance, "obsessive refutation," need to Win Your Side of it, or (4) other <u>Distancing</u>: resistance: detachment denial etc. Truly comprehending openly, need not mean agreeing/concurring, defending-against, or opposing-to-refute. This is "style as attainment and restraint," in balance thus.
[-- CHESTER OBERHAUPTKARTOFFELKOPFE, Khronikles, XII, xii, 12]

GALLERY #2. Powerful instances showing scrupulous **"thoroughness"** of confronting tasks: [Version I Brief]

[1.] Biology Prof. AGASSIZ teaches STUDENT <u>how really to dissect a fish</u>: "look again and report, then *again, and yet again*, until *real* knowledge-about emerges..."

[2.] <u>Restaurant-reviewer</u> D. ROSENGARTEN visits places *six* separate times before writing-up, *each* time with a specific goal.

[3.] In a Washington D.C. federal office building at night, a thorough JANITOR noticed an office door unlocked, and locked it. *But then he returned to check on it again*—found it taped open; investigated—and behold, <u>the WATERGATE SCANDAL was revealed</u>!

[4.] HELEN VENDLER famous critic explains <u>true reading of a poem</u>, the *dozen* layers or levels to it which emerge, with care...

[5.] A paragraph on "<u>really looking at a painting</u>": what does *this* detail mean, *that* shading mean, the *other* feature also?...

[6.] <u>Poison gas in warfare</u> (Hawaii) : one doesn't just release it, *many* variables exist: windage, geography, humidity...

[7.] I myself was told at store, "we seem to be out of <u>green ink for your stamp pad</u>." I looked at the whole shelf (of four shelves); no green ink. I then *painstakingly and exhaustively looked at each and every bottle on all four shelves*, a few dozen—presto, misplaced among the blacks, a bottle of green ink.

[8.] In a corporation, dealing with important decision, <u>a committee</u> quickly "agreed on" what was the best solution. The CHAIR said: "Fine; now go away, and re-think and re-think again, and return in 24 hours to start truly unpacking this complex situation."

[9.] A <u>physician</u>... [many superb examples of both amateur bungling oversights/being fooled, plus expert painstaking completeness]

\=\+|+|+\=\=\+|+|+|=\=\=|+|+|\\\+|+|+|=\=|+|+|+|=\=\+|+|+|\=\=|+|+|+|\=\=|+|+|+|\=\=|+|+|\=|+|+|\=\+|+|+|\=\=\+|+|+ +

(9) Competent.

Competency—skill and drive, "savvy & sweat," is a massive issue. It tangles with "success of outcome..."
SEE "Quality" section in Prior Basics, Appendix #5. Plus "II" *FULL* version in <u>Mind- Play</u>, emerging...

\=\+|+|+\=\=\+|+|+|=\=\=|+|+|\\\+|+|+|=\=|+|+|+|=\=\+|+|+|\=\=|+|+|+|\=\=|+|+|+|\=\=|+|+|\=|+|+|\=\+|+|+|\=\=\+|+|+ +

(10) "Contest": THE [UNUSUAL] IDEA: for instance, <u>writing</u> *(and any <u>thinking</u> act also)* is almost-literally a **sport-game-play**, defining that action as "<u>performer pursuing a goal to win, through challenging obstacles, via Savvy & Sweat meaning skill and effort</u>." And spectated; hence, "<u>reading as a spectator-sport</u>," fans in the bleachers cheering deft moves, booing blunders:

EXAMPLE. Two **letters complaining about bad street work in the city."** One of them a winning <u>varsity</u> version—the other, a losing amateur-sandlot version. Letters not reproduced here, but below are the responses of the reader as spectator in the bleachers.....

[Some of us, at least myself, are "literacy buffs," we even find the classic "copy on the back of cereal boxes" and similar daily texts, to be rich sources of appreciation-of-skill, or amusements-at-bunglings. There we are having fun, and neither the writers intended this, nor others around us, could understand (too bad...)]

| [+] Hmmm, nice opening, catches our attention with a question... Nice stating there'll be four points. The first is supported by an example to prove his claim... Now a short paragraph for change of pace; a relief... He's defining a key term which we the audience doesn't know... Now a difficult point, but his tone is good, neither apologetic nor brash; he keeps us with him!...Now he increases the pace to finish quickly... Nice short paragraph echoing the beginning to sign off with a smile... | [-] ...Eh? What *is* his point here among all this detail junk to start?... Oh, it's perhaps a city problem... Well okay but what is "terrace," the lawn between sidewalk and street I guess? "Living the nightmare," that's a bit too hysterical a tone for this problem... Wait, what the hell does Louise Apfelbach have to do with this,--oh, I see—I *think*... Why does he blame the contractors, that's an empty claim, he gives no statistics nor testimony... Now wait, is he repeating a point here or is this something new?... You know, this is a lot of vague griping hot air! |

A WINNER: he dove and drove through Obstacles meeting the Challenge to Score a bulls-eye of Reaching the Reader as best anyone could. *Cheers!*	HE LOSES: down the field he fumbled, not only missing chances to score, but committing fouls as he goes. Get off the field! *Boos!*

\=\+|+|+\=\=\+|+|+\=\=\=|+|+|\\\+|+|+\=\=|+|+|+\=\=\+|+|+\=\=\=|+|+|+\=\=\=|+|+|+\=\=\=|+|+|+\=\=|+|+|\=\+|+|+\=\+|+|+| +

[5.] Summary II: the major [A.] "Eight Moves upon the Subject" (Plus [B.] "Variables-Variation")

[5.A.] The "Eight Moves" cluster for subject-confronting:

THE ISSUE HERE… OUR RESPONSE TO IT: "A roster to organize major ways to think a subject all the way through." *It is as simple as that…* ANALOGY: perhaps *a "pegboard on the wall* with marked sections for storing tools accessibly…"

Confronting a subject involves phases. First Definition and Discovery, then Delving-in to understand, then Delivering results to others perhaps. That is, first surveying the whole project… then defining and describing that subject… then relating it to its space: field or context… then looking deep within it (analysis)… then adjusting the specific-general "altitude" or verticality… then dealing with number and relation: one-only, one-sided? either-or dualism, compare-contrast, then connect vs. separate… then relating to it over time: attending to changes … then finally elucidation or getting a "lucid" image of the subject which is Comprehensive-complete but also Comprehended (thought-through), plus Comprehensible (communicative).

Our **EIGHT MOVES** in response:

1. "SMT **Strategically Monitor the Totality**: *survey the Whole Big Picture*, so as to miss nothing needed…

2. **Survey the Subject** Itself. [*Define* it: initial, total, narrowed, etc.… *locate* its Boundaries/Borders… *survey* it from a large-enough "Catchment-Area" … *expand, polish* the subject's Image.]

3. "**Field**" *relate* the subject to its environment, context, situation, ground; *consider* it in its circumstances.

4. "**With-In-Side**": *analyze* within, discover component subparts beyond monolithic surface, *categorize*.

5. "**Up-&-Down**": *confront, arrange* subject on "Ladder of Abstraction" from Material-concrete to Mental-conceptual: raw data, mid-range generalizations, larger hypotheses, theories, laws, paradigms, etc.

6. "**Number & Relations**": *consider* subject in terms of "one, two, many" versions of subjects—dualism (either-or, both-and), comparison-contrast, "connect or separate two items," correlate opposing contraries, etc.

7. "**Change Over Time**": *see* subject beyond "chronocentrism," in the mists of past and future: changes…

8. "**Elucidation**": *arrive at* competent image of subject Complete also Comprehended also Communicated.

…BUT Shouldn't you remind readers that these are "not rules, but tools"?	By now I hope no need. The philosopher WITTGENSTEIN said, "philosophy is a set of reminders for a particular purpose." That works here: like a checklist. Our *ANALOGY*: Neither a too-restrictive **push-the-button machine**, nor a too-relaxed free-for-all, who's-to-say, **open table or jumbled, incomplete equipment-box**"…At the very least a **"string for the beads"** or (as noted above) a

Not formula but heuristics? Use them or not, depending?	*"labeled wall-board for storage unobtrusive-but-accessible"* (Some added to each individual learner's own *"Tool-BELT"* or personalized, custom cluster of thinking skills...)
	[Still, people do insidiously mistake and misuse what are flexible techniques, as if they are fixed tactics—I do admit. Poignant data on that in "Letter vs. Spirit," in Appendix #3CA...]

|#+|+#||+#+|#+||+#|+#||+#+||+#||+#|+#+||##+#|+#+|#|+#|+|+#|#++#+|+|#|+#|+#|+|+#|+|#|#+||+#|#|+#|#||#+||#||

QUOTATIONS: Statements elucidating the more **comprehensive** overview along with detail:

To confirm #1 or Comprehensive scanning of <u>the whole picture</u>, SMT, Strategically Monitor the Totality. (Including by implication the #2 <u>Field or context</u>—the countryside and next city on the horizon, etc.)

[1.] [Imagine you are touring a large old traditional city in Africa, Asia, Europe. Amid the interest and excitement you become lost. One promising maze of alleys becomes another. But then you can climb to the top of a tall tower, look over the streets, and make sense of it all.] "You see where you should have turned one way but went another; you realize that the little shop you walked past, with the cat in the window, was only yards away from the garden in the next street, which you found hours later. And when you get back down into the maze you find your way easily. Now you know your way about." [-- INTRO. to THE PHILOSOPHY OF MORALITY]

But also we must #3 Survey the Subject in both overview and detail. Including #4, <u>worm's-eye view</u> analyzing With-In-Side. And #4 Verticalities, both specific-and-general on the abstraction-ladder. Including <u>number-and-relation of elements</u> (Move #6): (Not to mention <u>change over time</u>, #7):

-----**[2.]** "It is a fair question to ask—<u>who sees the more—the airman</u> who flies continually across several counties, five thousand feet up, from where he can see the land for miles and miles, <u>or the countryman</u> who has lived in one place all his life but knows the valleys, the woods and lanes of his own countryside like the back of his hand?" [--ALAN BULLOCK]

-----**[3.]** "There are many complex systems for which even a reasonably complete understanding requires at least three perspectives: (1) a <u>synoptic</u> overview, including goals and connections to the environment; (2) a <u>piecewise</u> view of the <u>smallest</u> relevant <u>components</u>; and (3) a <u>structural</u> view of how the components <u>aggregate</u> to form the whole and allow functioning." [-- STEPHEN JAY KLINE, THE STRUCTURE OF SYSTEMS]

-----**[4.]** [We can see any object as a <u>Particle</u> or unit, a <u>Wave</u> changing over time, and in a <u>Field</u> or context.]
[-- YOUNG, BECKER, & PIKE: PARAPHRASED]

We may *arrive at* #8, <u>an image of the subject which is excellent, Elucidated</u>. Combining Completeness of description, also Comprehendedness of understanding, and Comprehensibility to an audience.

[5.] "Take <u>a small complex machine</u> from its obscure position: "dirty disassembled in a drawer in a shed at midnight," and elucidate it in a **museum display**: "clean, reassemble it, label its parts, mount it on an eye-level slowly-rotating stand under shadow-free lighting, in expanded view and all parts labeled, with explanatory posters nearby. *And now then there you have elucidation...*" [-- CHESTER OBERHAUPTKARTOFFEL, Khronikles, XII, xii, 12]

|#+|#+|#+|+|#+|+|#+|+|+#|+|#+|+|#+|+|#+|#+|#+|#+|+|#+|+|+#|+|#+|#+|+|+|+|+#|+|++#+#++#++#+#+#|||#|#|||

["8".1] Strategic Monitoring of the Totality.

GUIDELINE: <u>Because</u> (1) reality is larger than one person's easy comprehension of it, and because (2) partial simple incomplete views threaten competence, <u>therefore</u> *Keep An Eye on the Big Picture* as you go along, so as to *monitor* all elements of subject and skill—and *miss nothing vital.*

EXAMPLES-GALLERY: Could **better monitoring of *all* factors**, have avoided these failures in task-goals?

"I" BRIEF: a few illustrative examples for here and now:

1. Two adjacent U.S.A. states *both* issued in the *same* year, automobile license plates which were blue in color

with white numbers... **[Context or environment neglected narrowly. All possible pitfall-issues not surveyed-for.]**

2. The Swiss watch industry was *completely taken by surprise* when the Japanese industry introduced quartz and non-mechanical watches. **[Tunnel-vision missed emergence of change; mind-set too narrow...]**

3. A mongoose was introduced to croplands as a predator control field-rabbits, but it was realized too late that rabbits were *diurnal*, mongooses were *nocturnal*. ... **[Not all significant "variable-issues" or "factors" confronted]**

"II" FULL: SEE following examples in Mind-Play:

4. Buying a Used Car: blue engine exhaust smoke, but what about black, why grey?

5. Safer Sex: "use a condom," but what about oil-lubes damaging latex, germicides for more protection?

6. Purify Drinking Water: "boil, chlorine, filter." But filter-types, limitations; iodine; cysts molds slimes; dirty or cold water; new methods such as mixed-oxidant and ultraviolet?

7. Egyptian Aswan Dam designers overlooked consequences of ecological upsets in the whole system.

8. College facility planners utterly overlooked important studies right in the files already in the school!

9. Disciplinary Trends: at times, sociology emphasized only functionalism not conflict... psychology emphasized behavioral not sociobiology... literature emphasized only the aesthetic not the socio-political (the reverse holds true now)...

10. Only one of five physicians spotted the patient's arsenic poisoning by scrutinizing the fingernails...

11. Overlooked Vital Issues: Chromium is vital but its source is very limited... We are relying on only four strains of wheat, which may be risky... If the Gulf Stream is slowing, Europe will chill... One madman could wipe out the human race if he engineers a fatal airborne virus...

12. --**[Time-wise, major change starts but we do not notice it...]** "We hear of doomsday scenarios, but "more often in history, as in the Mafia, the bullet that gets you comes from a former friend or from something dismissed as inconsequential. We fail to notice that the familiar queen of spades has for some reason become red; we fail to see that the kudzu vine brought in as the farmer's friend to protect the soil, is slowly taking over the countryside, until it is too late to stop its spread; obsessed with communism, we fail to notice the rise of Islamic fundamentalism until the Shah of Iran is swept from his throne [if we even notice it then...]; we worry about Ebola [virus], but fail to notice that more and more people are dying of the flu." [-- THE FUTURE IN PLAIN SIGHT, P. 134]

13. -- **[We do not look ahead to consequences of an action in the larger field or context...]** "The price of narrow compartmentalization, intellectual, social, personal [is high]....History might have been different if the experts who developed fire retardants in children's nightwear had examined their mutagenic potential; if the people who put together the Aswan Dam had been trained to remember the larger picture [of unintended, unrecognized ecological disruptions]; if the people who marketed thalidomide had looked beyond its tranquilizing and economic potential [to medical side effects]...An interdisciplinary background may not have caused [tobacco] industry experts to adopt a more balanced view of the tobacco/cancer link, but it might have tempered their outright advocacy of smoking." [-- TEN CHEERS FOR INTERDISCIPLINARITY]

TOOL-KIT: for the "Fuller View": To aid in avoiding the above Pitfalls, here is a beginning collection of challenging subject-parts too easily overlooked, the better to Survey-Scan-Scrutinize for them!

[They were derived from analyzing *amateur-incompetent*, vs. expert-skilled, texts instructing about buying a used car, having safer sexual activity, purifying one's drinking water on camping trips.

1. ISSUES: the old-known-familiar and indeed acceptable/favored, ***but also*** many relevant others often overlooked...

2. PITFALLS and problems: obvious known ***but also*** subtle infrequent insidious ...

3. KNOWLEDGE: "what we all know" ***but also*** insider lore expert updated fine-point nuances ...

4. METHODS: standard known formulae ***but also*** flexible heuristics "out-of-the-box"...

5. DECISIONS: easy ones ***but also*** gray-area judgment-calls with balances-and-tradeoffs ...

6. PROCEDURES: standard ***but also*** exceptions qualifications for unanticipated consequences ...

7. CHANGES: the traditional and accepted ***but also*** the currently-unpopular, but perhaps vital; state-of-the-art updatings, representing "CEC" or Current Experts' Consensus ***plus also*** legitimate disagreements by experts!...

8. SCOPE OF VISION: safe-simple-near ***but also*** looking deep within, also far afield...

|#+|#+|#+|+|#+|+|#+|+|+#|+|#+|+|#+|+|#+|#+|#+|+|#+|+|+#|+|#+|#+|+|+|+|+#|+|++#|++#+|+#+#+#|||#|#|||

["8".2] Surveying the Subject:

TOOLKIT. A few of the ploys in this second of the Eight Moves. The explorer enters the territory…

--1. <u>Monitor your image of the subject</u>, through *three phases*. i. initial entering, ii. ongoing developing, iii."final" acceptable for task-goal at hand.

--2. <u>Define the subject</u>: different versions of it. A. The <u>true total</u> subject (and its subparts! see Move #4 below, "WithInSide"…). B. The narrowed aspects of the subject actually to be confronted for your task-goal.

--3. "PARTICLE, FIELD, WAVE." Determine the <u>extent</u> of the subject, also its BBB <u>boundaries barriers boundaries</u>, then the <u>Field or context</u> whole environment, perhaps with other subjects, within which the subject exists. Also the time-element: start of subject historically, the present, the future. (See Move #7, "Change").

--4. <u>Determine your "Catchment-Area."</u> This is the scope of the territory you will confront (scan survey scrutinize etc.). *Caution: it may need to be larger than the narrowed subject itself!*

--5. Then <u>ACTUALLY SURVEY THE SUBJECT!</u> (Cf. your stance, your methods, etc.) "Colloquialize" with others to get their views of the subject.

--6. Revisit #1 above. <u>What is your final acceptable image of the subject?</u>

Fine, but how can these fine "probes" actually help? You need to use your "tool" of specification here…	Right: see the EXAMPLES below to illustrate…

APPENDIX. The "II" full-dress unit on "SURVEYING THE SUBJECT" in the parent-publication <u>Mind-Play</u>

1. Define <u>task-goal</u>, purpose 2. Define the <u>subject</u> itself [and the space-field and the time-line]. 2A. What is the initial *Apparent* subject? Then the *True Total*" subject? Then your *"Task-Goal"* subject? 2B. What are the "Borders, Boundaries" 2C. What is the "Field" ['I']: context etc.? 2D. What of "Time/Change":	3. Define your <u>approach</u> to surveying the subject. A. The "Catchment-Area": what, and how large—enough? B. Your "Stance" to the subject. 1. "Literal" [Up close; down-low or bird's-eye; mid-range; far-off?] *Does it need adjusting, re-positioning?*] 2. "Conceptual" A. What Lenses employed? B. What attitudes? C. Your actual methods 1. [How to "Observe"…..] 2. Research: library, field, personal. 3. "Colloquializing"	4. <u>Do</u> the subject-"surveying." "Gaze"—and its "Thoroughness" 5. Result: <u>evaluate</u> your image "iii" of the subject [arrived-at]. Is it adequate? Accept, or alter? A. O.K. or not, Pragmatically, for the task-goal? B. O.K. or not, via other Lenses? (X)

EXAMPLES. The large issue of enlarging one's range of **gaze** beyond the specific subject itself:

"I" BRIEF: a few illustrative examples for here and now:

1. <u>How many casualties in a war?</u>" Simple surface view counts the soldiers, but what about tenfold deaths among civilians, at the time and through malnutrition and disease later. Plus deaths from terrorism increased by the war. [Simple Surface view vs. the **True Total Subject** and its **components** in larger **field** or **time** and **space** context…]

2. <u>Sellers of products</u> should talk only to customers, let alone satisfied ones. Talk also to customers having problems, and also non-customers! [= **Catchment-Area** and **True Subject** is wider, more complex than we think…]

3. "<u>War on terrorism</u> is not only on the terrorists but also global poverty, desperation, injustice." [= Subject must be seen in its larger **Field**, context, environment—**True Total Subject** is larger than just the obvious surface "subject" …]

4. <u>What is "a river"?</u> Some ecologists argue it is more than whatever water you see in the channel, but the banks, floodplain, the valley itself from bluff to bluff—a changing area but anywhere the water has been and could potentially go. [= **True Total Subject** is larger than the simple, apparent, conventional view of it…]

"II" FULL: SEE following examples in <u>Mind-Play</u>:

5-10. Outside The Boundaries, On to the Total Subject: Mathematics: study the outliers and counter-examples also … Business: talk to your unsatisfied customers and your non-customers also… Basketball: most of the game is played away from dribbling and shooting, it's defense and getting into position for a pass… Journalism: reporters notice an eruptive event, miss the whole story of slow development behind the scenes… Physical Geniuses: skilled neurosurgeon sees the whole context of an aneurism, skilled hockey player Wayne Gretsky sees the whole court and where a puck will carom off…

11. Music Teacher who gave concerts at local mall was not given tenure, her work thought sub-professional!…

12. Traffic during commuting: do I define "the subject" as my own desire to move, or the whole intersection?…

13. Logistics is not just supplies of war materiel, but the ability of nation's infrastructure and manufacturing base to create supplies, then move them forward over time…

14. City government can separately perform police, fire, sanitation services—but can not always work together for housing, welfare, job-training needs (not defined as "their own proper subject or work" etc.)…

15. Computer personnel are trained narrowly: theorists can't program, hardware designers don't know high-level system structure, programmers don't know their work's effects. Good students can grasp the interface between technologies, surpass it as a boundary…

16. "Public Health" exceeds mere medical care, it involves genetic, cultural, environmental, economic factors…

17. To educate a disabled person to self-sufficiency (from tax-recipient, to taxpayer) costs $100,000—a lot of money, but this is amply repaid to

society over a working lifetime...

18. "School Integration" was achieved, but did not improve the whole system: security, human relations...

III. The important perspective of "post-modern" and "liberation" studies. From **hierarchy** to **inclusion**. These are two differing "lenses" which may either distort or clarify the subjects at hand—*either way!*

OLD: In-Out (hegemony valorizing vs. excluding or erasing Outsiders or the Other; "us" and "them"). Hierarchy of Up Better to Down Lesser. In people, in values.	NEW: Flattened playing-field of egalitarianism in many aspects, at least respect and opportunity.
X BRITISH ARMY: "Officers and their ladies, Sergeants and their wives, Enlisted men and their women." X "No Dogs or Chinese" allowed in SINGAPORE park during European colonization..	X EARLHAM COLLEGE School Handbook puts names, photos of "lowly" support staff (janitors etc.) right in among the stuff on the "professors." A-Z fashion!! X ONE COLLEGE proposes no titles (faculty, staff, students); just one title for all: "Co-Learner"

|#+|#+|#+|+|#+|+|#+|+|+#|+|#+|+|#+|+|#+|#+|#+|#+|+|#+|+|+#|+|#+|#+|+|+|+|+#|+|++#++#++#+#+#|||#|#|||

["8".3] "FIELD": the Subject's "Context, Environment, Situation" in Space...

THE ISSUE HERE: A prevalent *pitfall* in thinking, is that "Our statements about either a particular Situation A [= "our own" time, space, culture etc.], or a generalization about many Situations but derived from the data in Situation A, may very well not apply to or for other Situations B, C, and so forth."
--[This is true for statements of at least three types of major purposes. Not only (1) generalizations about what actually is, true-or-false; but also, (2) evaluations, of what is bad-good; and even (3) procedures, what is to be done, performed, implemented [or not!] and how.]
--Then too, "different" truths, values, and practices, from Situations B, C, and so forth, may be valid for those situations, even if not for our own Situation A.
--Therefore, beware; the conclusion may be actually incompetent: inaccurate, untrue, unwise, ineffective, even immoral, and the like."

OUR SUGGESTED GUIDELINE. "Therefore *beware and avoid*, overgeneralizing... wrongly-evaluating... and recommending procedures, "everywhere/always, or elsewhere," based on one's own Situation. Also, *beware and avoid*, wrongly perceiving, judging facts, values, practices from other Situations B, C, D, etc., without understanding them in their own Field, context, situation, environment—their functions there, etc."

IN P.O.E.P. OR "PLAINER OLD ENGLISH, PLEASE!": Far too frequently, we can't competently Confront a subject [= understand, explain, interpret, even describe fully, let alone evaluate, generalize-about or from, recommend use of, etc.] in its Isolation. We need to see the subject's connections with its Field [= context, environment, situation]—of which larger System that subject may well be a component, functioning part, anyhow.

"I" BRIEF: a vivid and complex instance of Field-work, for here and now:

EXAMPLE [1.] ABRAHAM LINCOLN gave a speech seemingly approving slavery! How to confront and evaluate this? An innovative history teacher "fields" it into its context:

"I have no purpose to introduce political and social equality between the white and black races. There is a physical difference between the two, which in my judgment will probably forever forbid their living together upon the footing of perfect equality, and inasmuch as it becomes a necessity that there must be a difference, I . . . am in favor of the race to which I belong, having the superior position. I have never said anything to the contrary."

[-- ABRAHAM LINCOLN, in a debate with his opponent in an election-race for a senatorial seat]

The history teacher first points out that this sounds alarming—was the Great Emancipator" of the slaves, really a "White Supremacist" and the like? His lesson for history students is that we must contextualize this and other statements, and events. He notes we must put the words in their [1.] time-place loccasion (a debate with Stephen Douglas, his rival for a close-race senatorial seat), the location (Ottawa, Illinois, "a hotbed of antiblack sentiment"), the kinds of people at the debate (more supportive of Douglas, suspicious of Lincoln), the purpose ("candidates courting votes"). [2.] Then what of a wider ring: "…what about the other things Lincoln said in Havana, Illinois, a week earlier, or in Freeport, Illinois, a week later?" [3.] And yet another layer: "the climate of opinion, *mentalite*, or *Zeitgeist*, the biography of a complex human being and his style with words and utterances; the linguistic practices of the 1850's—must also be considered when thinking about the meaning of Lincoln's words." [-- "Reading Abraham Lincoln," Ch. 4 of SOURCE]]

I would say this is a fine start-up of **Contextualizing** 101. It *explicitly* identifies, *multiple-plural* elements *and* levels, but clearly-and-concisely also, yet without formula or oversimplification either. [What we call **"elucidation"** of a subject...]

"II" FULL: SEE following examples in Mind-Play:

[2.] Dangerous to generalize about **marriage** from our current society and time. (Ignores that marriage earlier had to do with property and status, and many other issues.) To evaluate our view(s) of marriage as good or bad for and in all situations. (Ignores that polygamy may have functioned well in some cultures.) To recommend "our" style of marriage for everyone everywhere. (Ignores that civil unions may be workable in some places for whatever reasons, and more…)

Behind the above lies an expanded view of marriage as at least four-fold in dimensions: personal bond between individuals… recognized community status… religious ceremony… and civil-political right…

[3.] **Psychoanalysis** may have been static, simple, context-free—ignoring social forces such as historical epoch, geography, race, ethnicity, class, gender, and sexuality…

[4.] **ALFRED KINSEY** who studied human sexuality, may have described sexual behavior frequencies well—but overlooked complexity of sexual relationships, relations to value systems, to matters such as pregnancy, disease, bonding, discrimination and fear, deeper currents of the psyche…

[5.] A U.S.A. social psychologist wrote a textbook on human **"cognitive psychology,"** thought it was a good universal human account—but anthropologists told him that it was "a pretty good summary of—current American peoples' cognitive psychology traits…"

[6.] The West tends to see **homosexuality** as enormously-deviant, and the Bible called it an "abomination," but in the context of the time, this might not have been intrinsically evil, so much as have negative consequences, be ritually unclean, hence damaging to Jewish identity. Not the same weight as in the modern age. [--BOSWELL]

[7.] Customs & Cultures. "Hindus **worship the cow**, we would say they're backward"—but consider they believe in transmigration of souls, the cow might be somebody's grandmother. Logical…

"Some Eskimo tribes **expose their grandparents**, let them die in the wilderness, we would say they are inhumane"—but whole-group survival may depend on lightening the load thus. Logical…

[8.] Could **Iraq** ever have attained true Western-style democracy? Perhaps never. Iraq has natural resources and an educated population, but none of the roots of civil society and rule of law which helped Germany and Japan to quickly move toward democracy after World War II. Also, Iraqui politics has a history of violence and instability, due to tensions tribal, religious, and occupation-related. Perhaps foremost, peoples' primary allegiances is not to some state or nation, but to their traditional social unit—the family, clan, tribe. This source of social stability and relations is stronger than Western lenses could see, perhaps… [-- Several SOURCES, and basic social science…]

[9.] Will **a welfare state** work well anywhere, any time? Would the Swedish model work anywhere? But the Myrdals believed that Sweden was the ideal candidate for a cradle-to-grave welfare state. 1. Population was small, homogenous, and trusting in each other. 2. The government was trusted also; historically it had always allowed some popular representation. 3. The civil service was efficient and free from corruption. 4. A Protestant work-ethic, strongly enforced by the peer-culture, meant people would work hard anyhow. 5. The work would be productive, since Swedes were well-educated and had a strong export sector. [-- THE NATIONAL INTEREST]

[10.] Is **child pornography** ever—positive, or at least acceptable? First, understand the situation. This pornography may be made in less developed countries where child labor laws and economic circumstances are very different from our own. We object, but it might be unacceptable "cultural imperialism" on our part to try to control or determine whether the people involved engage in this activity—especially as the choice may well be between work and hunger. If no coercion is involved, and the child's guardian initiates, for economic reasons or also a difference in cultural norms, or both, this is a matter for them, not us, no matter how distasteful we find such a decision. [-- OPINION TELEGRAPH UK]

|#+|#+|#+|+|#+|+|#+|+|+#|+|#+|+|#+|+|#+|#+|#+|#+|#+|+|#+|+|+#|+|#+|#+|+|+|+|+#|+|++#+++#++#+#+#|||#|#|||

["8".4] "WithInSide": Analysis, Categorizing:

Categorization: Classification & Division…

One of the traditional "modes of rhetoric" or persuading-communicating (along with compare-contrast, define, etc.). But more significantly here, a major (if overlooked) way of thinking-and-clarifying.

PRE-VUE I. "Tool-Kit." We give a glimpse only at our unit on C-D for the parent-publication Mind-Play.

LEVEL "I" BASIC. C-D divides a subject into its component subparts, elements, and relates those subparts logically to each other and to the whole.

Three basic rules: a categorization must be complete (all categories of the subject accounted for), not cross-ranked (watertight; each example goes in one category only), and principled (at each level, only one principle of categorization is operating).

X College students are of four types: freshmen, blond(s), accounting majors, and night students. (This breaks all three rules. Not inclusive. Cross-ranking, a person could be in different categories. And on the level—only one level—four principles exist: year-in-school, hair color, major field, and attendance-time.)

LEVEL "II" ADVANCED. Largely unexplored in education is the immense power of Categorizing to think a subject through, elucidate it, by analytical "unpacking" of its otherwise-overlooked component subparts. And difficult it is to create more-complex categorizations of more-complex subjects to be both convergent or unified, and also concise without sprawl.

GALLERY: A sampling of the genius of **Categorization**, to elucidate complexity within. Via the analysis of **Classify-& Divide**, opening-up of the smooth surface of a subject to reveal important variety withinside…

[1.] Four types of school CURRICULA:
1. __Explicit:__ what's on the syllabus, taught in classes.
2. __Hidden:__ what's actually learned and done, but unofficially. Part of the cultural climate. Ground Rules of traditional education, even including racial and ethnic slurs in the corridors and the like. Even, "doors are locked for students' protection but also because students can't be trusted"?
3. __Extra:__ what is and can be present outside the classroom, as in clubs, groups, etc.
4. __Null:__ what a teacher cannot teach, without risking discipline or dismissal! (Sex, drugs, abortion, gangs?)

[2.] Four Patterns of TRAVEL, for the "Independent Budget Adventure Traveler" (including neither luxury tourism, nor adventure-edge, travel). Three well-known, the last one unusual or overlooked…
1. __City-Hopping.__ (London, Paris, Rome, Madrid).
2. __Immersion.__ (Paris; then more Paris, and only Paris…)
3. __Home-Basing.__ (London, with flings to Oxford/Cambridge, other spots, and return).
4. __"Threading."__ (Through dense areas, in daylight, via surface, moving slowly steadily in short stages, walking and stopping a lot. (London, countryside, Paris, more country, mountains, finally to Rome perhaps or not…)
[-- PAUL OTTESON]

[3.] PARKING STYLES at Shopping Mall: to get the nearest or best space.
1. __Search & Destroy.__ Roam and range and grab (dangerous).
2. __Lurk.__ Poise at end of lane to survey, await best chance (blocks traffic).
3. __Stalk.__ Follow a pedestrian to their car (often inefficient).
4. __Find & Take.__ Just take first reasonable spot you see (Zen calm).

[4.] VEGETARIANISMS: SUBTYPES of this diet.
1. **Lacto v.** (Dairy but no eggs or animal flesh.)
2. **Lacto-ovo v.** (Dairy, eggs, but no animal flesh)
3. **Ovo v.** (Eggs but no dairy or animal flesh)
4. **Pesco v.** (Dairy, eggs, fish, but no poultry or red meat)

[5.] SOURCES of English-origin SURNAMES: are of *only four* types:
1. Occupations.

[6.] "SEXUAL ORIENTATION," facets:
1. **Behavior**, activity (or lack of it…)
2. **Erotic** fantasy-and-arousal-and-orgasm etc.
3. **Self-definition**, naming/labeling.

371

	(Smith, Baker, Archer)	

5. Semi v. (Dairy, eggs, chicken, fish, but no red meat)
6. Vegan (No animal products at all)
[We also have **"raw foodism"** (nothing cooked past 118 degrees F, when enzymes are destroyed)
"Fruitarianism" (any part a plant can easily replace: fruits and berries, including juice, grains, nuts, seeds, legumes, even tomatoes and eggplants)
"Sproutarianism" (built around sprouted seeds, supplemented)]
[-- TIME and NEWSWEEK magazines]

2. Personal traits. (Short, Brown, Whitehead)
3. Places and geography. (Scott, Hill, Rivers, Windsor)
4. Ancestry. (Richardson, Johnson, Fitzgerald)

4. As part of one's "total self-identity"…
+\=++\+\+\=\|+\=\|+\+\=\+\+\=\|=\=\|=\|+\+\=\|

[7.] Marriage, dimensions of:
1. **Religious** rite, ceremony.
2. **Civil-political** right or status.
3. **Personal bond** of **"love."**
4. **Social-community** recognition.

[8.] MEMORY: three types useful to distinguish:
Long-term: always engraved (car accident in childhood, wedding).
Primary: instant recall (repeat a phone number). Stays about same with ageing.
Secondary: short-term (where parked the car, recall list made an hour ago). Declines with age.
[-- SOURCE]

[9.] The STRUCTURE, of any document etc. A designer's scheme he labels "LATCH":
1. **L**ocation, spatial.
2. **A**lphabetical, A-Z etc.
3. **T**ime
4. **C**onceptual scheme
5. **H**ierarchy
[-- RICHARD SAUL WURMAN]
6. *But I would add* **Random,** *even impressionistic or "one best seeming order." And what about* **Rhetorical,** *or best for the writer, for the subject, for the reader?* [Hence, "LATCHRR"?…..]

[10.] Types of automobile **SKIDDING motions** when driving. [-- PEASE, engineer]
1. Front-end or plowing.
2. Rear-end swings out.
3. Side-skid.
4. Power-on with front wheel drive.
5. Rear wheelspin skid.
6. Fishtailing.
7. Straight-ahead braking lockup.
8. Two right wheels on sand snow mud but two left ones on good pavement.

[11.] TASTES: *of course* **Sweet, Sour, Bitter, Salty,** *but also* **Astringent,** *and also* **Umami**: a rich full amino-acid type echoing meat, shellfish, mushrooms, potatoes, seaweed…
+\=++\+\|+\=\|+\+\=\+\+\=\|=\=\|=\|+\+\=\|

[12.] Phonetics: types of **CONSONANTS:**

plosives—P/B   dentals—T/D/TH
sibilants—S/SH/Z   nasals—M/N/NG
fricatives—F/V   gutturals—G/K

[13.] WRITING SYSTEMS.
1. Picture word (draw objects).
2. Symbol (simplification of #1).
3. Ideograph (stylized picture used as symbol for idea/concept).
4. Hieroglyphic (pictures represent things, names, words).
5. Hieratic script (hieroglyphic in abbreviated versions).
6. Alphabet (hieratic forms adapted to system of symbol-to-sound correspondence).

[14.] Variables for **EVALUATING RESTAURANT-CUISINE.**
1. **"Classic Tradition(s),"** and **Innovation** upon Same.
2. **Aesthetics:** Balance of Flavors
3. Personal-Preference of **Reviewer.**
4. Personal Goals of **Chef**
5. **Ethnic** Variations
6. **Star** Ranking Systems vs. Other Criteria
7. **Standards:** low-lax, or high-rigorous

You and your mania for too-copious examples again! I *don't* see the value of *all* these *obvious* examples of…

"Fine," **BUT** let the learner immerse self s-l-o-w-l-y in these gems, and s/he may well "pick up" the ploy-or-gambit of "seeing and savoring subject's **complexities** via careful **analytical categorizing**" [As in, "who would have suspected this enriching variety within?!"…]

|#+|#+|#+|+|#+|+|#+|+|+|#|+|#+|+|#+|#+|+|#+|#+|#+|#+|+|#+|+|+|+|#|+|++#++#++#+#+#|||#|#|||

[8:5.] "Verticalities": SPECIFIC-&-GENERAL Levels:

GUIDELINES.   **AWARENESS:**

[1.] Be aware that a "ladder of abstraction" exists, and is significant. That is, subjects can be and are perceived at varying levels of specificity-generality. Know that (and how) Material/specific, and Mental/general (abstract), are distinct, different levels.
[EXAMPLE: "Chair," *vs.* Fred's green beanbag etc. "Misbehavior," *vs.* burned pans, unpaid bills, unlocked doors.]

[2.] Know this concrete-to-conceptual "ladder" is [2.A.] "tall." (can be very vivid-specific down-low, can be very rarefied-abstract up-high). And that [2.B.] it has many "rungs," positions from particular Pond to panoramic Peak.
[EXAMPLE: objects, people, events, procedures, larger issues, big concepts—"vegetarianism"]

[3.] Know that we observe subjects at different levels of specificity-generality, and then conclude or respond to them also specifically or generally. Know that general and specific both have pros and cons, strengths and shortcomings. Know how to adjust one's viewing and responding to be as specific or general as it should be for the task-goal purpose. Avoid errors of too-general and too-specific. [EXAMPLE: letter to editor too vague, formal paper too anecdotal…]

ABILITY: Be able to *identify* the levels of observation or a statement by someone else—and of oneself. Be able to *alter, adapt, adjust* (fine-tune) the level to the "rung" appropriate for the task-goal purpose at hand…

Conceptual Stratosphering or Suffocation

High-level, Mental, ideas exist—concepts—but they are perhaps either (A) too-high, over-generalizations, need to be brought down a little, and/or (B) okay but rarefied, utterly lacking in any or enough Material concrete specifics to illustrate, prove, involve-in, etc., them.

Concrete "Sandheaping" or Flooding/Dumping.....

Lower-level, Material, information exists—concrete specifics—but they are perhaps either (A) Raw Story, unworked, un-thought-about, not inducted upward to discover the Mental ideas they represent, and/or (B) have ideas present also but are just too much or many, need to be trimmed: omit, or reduce, or combine…

APPENDIX. The "II" full-dress unit on "VERTICALITIES" in the parent-publication Mind-Play

1. The very concepts of "a concept," and of a "ladder of abstraction" from the concrete to the conceptual.

2. This "ladder" is complex. (A) "Tall," can be *very* specific, *very* stratospheric. (B) "Many-runged": can have *diverse, plural* positions, gradations, stages between very-vivid "Particular Pond" and very-arid "Abstraction Peak"

3. On the ladder at *varying* levels, is found not only content (the subject: from objects-events, to issues, to ideas-about), but our observational stances (down in the data, up in clouds of ideas), and responses about the subject (statement-claims: factual, mid-range, high-theory), and thinking skills (rote rules==higher-order tools). ("Almost everything, thus, seems to be able to be more specific and more general…")

4. Evaluation. Important because both high and low positions have their orchid benefits and onion dangers. Beware "Concrete Surfeiting" [=too much specific data for the purpose], "Conceptual Shortfalling" [=too many particulars not worked for their ideas], "Conceptual Stratosphering" [=too-high over-generalizations], and "Conceptual (=, , , too many generalizations without any examples to illustrate.)

5. A written text can be complexly specific-general in general amount… proportion… structure/arrangement.

6. Pedagogies exist (and are advisable) for helping learners "truly know" about verticality.

7. Relevant key concepts include (A.) the three types of thinking. **Induction** upward, **deduction** downward, **lateral-associative** across. And (B.) two theories about reality (materialism and idealism) and of method (empiricism and rationalism).

|#+|#+|#+|+|#+|+|#+|+|+#|+|#+|+|#+|+|#+|#+|#+|#+|#+|+|#+|+|+|#|+|#+|#+|+|+|+|+#|+|++#++#++#+#+#|||#|#|||

[8:6.] "NUMBER(s) & RELATIONS": One, Dual, [Many…]

GUIDELINES. Know that one can see subjects <u>singly</u> (but beware hemispheric or one-sided views)… in terms of <u>dualisms</u>… plus <u>compared/connected and also contrasted/distinguished</u>, including <u>correlating contraries</u>.

[I.] <u>ONE</u>. *Know* when "<u>one</u>" is satisfactory, when incomplete.
[Monism. Hemispheric. Near Enemies. Overlooked Complementarities. Appearance-Reality.]

[II.] <u>TWO</u>: know about "either/or, both-and"… Also, "same together connected" vs. different separated distinguished"…

[II.A.] "<u>Dualism 101</u>": [II.A.1.] <u>The Basics</u>. *Know* the issues of. When (and how) "either/or" is good, when a fallacy/error (cf. "to what extent both-and").

[II.A.2.] <u>The "Both-Sides Balanced-Weighing" Model</u>: toward "*all* the variables identified, then for each v., all the pros *and* cons mentioned, fully *and* fairly"…

CONNEXION: cf. three other models here. 1. "<u>Conceptual Continuum</u>": A to Z limits and all positions in between. Variety: "<u>Transformation</u>" from one state to a very different one. Also, 2. "<u>Variables-Variation</u>." [From One-Point Position, to Conceptual Continuum, pros and cons and functions of each, choose better Position perhaps.]

[II.B.] # <u>Comparison/Contrast</u>: *know* purposes/power of, *be able to* employ as/when needed!

[II.C.] # "<u>CCC==DDD</u>": Close vs. Distant: *know when* to, and *be able* to differentiate two wrongly-joined items, connect two items wrongly distinguished!

[[Categories of: Rational and Emotional, Personal-Civic, other responses distinguished]]

[II.D.] # <u>Correlating Contraries</u>: "Two positions may be polar-opposite, conflicting, but must be inter-related somehow because they are 1. mandatory requirements, and/or 2. valuable contributions. *Know about* this, and *be able to* resolve/integrate/connect these separated positions.
[[Degree of distance, conflict, dissonance between the two: mild minor === or intense extreme?]]

[II.E.] # <u>Style</u> (adroit grace, skill, etc.) as *attainment-and-restraint balanced*. <u>Artistry</u> also.

ANNEX. The "II" full-dress unit on "NUMBER & RELATIONS" in <u>Mind-Play</u>

(N) Code and Gallery "I"	[II.] <u>RELATIONSHIP of More than One Item to Each Other</u>
[I.] <u>NUMBER of items</u>. One, Two, Multiple-Plural?	<u>Comparison/Contrast</u>: "I" basic, "II" advanced.
<u>ONE item</u>: **Monisms**, plus:	[Appendix: five minor variables "relatives" of C/C].
"**Hemispheric**" (exactly "half-sided").	"**CCC==DDD**": Connect-Correlate, or Distinguish-Divide?
"**Near-Enemies**" (good slides to bad).	**Correlating Contraries**. Handling two necessary polar-opposites .
Overlooked Complementaries (know A but what of Z).	Balancing: (1) "**style**" as "attainment and restraint"
Appearance-Reality	(2) "**Zen Gyroscope**": not offensive defensive submissive, but consider-ate…
<u>TWO items</u>: "**Dualism 101**" (five ploys toward)	[III.] ILLUSTRATION. "Typical Day on Campus" with N. & R. …
The **Conceptual Continuum**, A-to-Z	
"**Transformations**": the CC enhanced.	
BSBS "**Both-Sides** Balance-Scale" model	

|#+|+#||+#+|#+||+#|+#||+#+||+#||+#|+#+||##+#|+#+|#|+#|+|+#|#+++#+|+#|+#|+#|+|+#|+|#|#+||+#|#|+#|#||#+||#||

[I.] ONE. *Know* when "<u>one</u>" is sufficient, when not.

THE CONCEPT/ISSUE. **One-sided, "Hemispheric" Viewpoints.**
For various reasons, one often sees "only one side" of the issue. Now right now some reader will sing out, "Well of course we all know that already!" But there's **"knowing-of/about, vs. truly knowing-it-&-how."**

GUIDELINE: *Beware* subtle blinders that explicitly condemn the perhaps-valid "other sides"—or more subtly, conceal them, block any view of them even!

"II" FULL: SEE following examples in <u>Mind-Play</u>: (1) "The Sixties were all good,… (2) "Housecleaning is vital, to preserve peoples' health."… (3) "Children are angelic or innocent or natural, and should be given freedom."… (4) "Every written text should have a point or message clear enough for a précis (summary, abstract) to be easily written (=no obscurity). And only one version is to be possible (=no ambiguity)."… (5) "Education's goal is to acquire imparted knowledge, to cover content, to master the material."… (6) "Writing instruction should not emphasize specific detailing so much. This risks making student-writers, remain too personal-egocentric, not stimulate thought and conceptualizing about the subject."…

THE IDEA HERE. "Near-Enemies." A "good" trait or item, can have a second *only-seemingly*-related type or aspect which (on closer inspection) turns out to be "bad" or suspicious indeed. Or the good matter might "change or slide into or move toward" being its bad false cousin.

Also **"False Cognates"**: both items could be "good," but they are distinct from each other.
GUIDELINE. Be aware that excesses or changes in a good thing might make it less than desirable indeed. Plus, that one item may have a different complement or cousin.

"I" BRIEF: a few key illustrative examples for here and now:

(1) Frequently today, "<u>people have confused</u> privileges with rights, objectivity with subjectivity, wishing with willing, wanting with needing, price with worth, affluence with fulfillment, reality with appearance, and sameness with equality. Not to mention **disease with dis-ease**." [-- LOU MARINOFF]

(2) <u>Don't confuse</u> the apparent but not actual similarities—one good, the other questionable! 1. Equanimity, apathy. 2. Compassion, patronizing pity. 3. Love, possessive attachment. 4. Decency, a screen for class bias or prejudice. 5. Goodness, baneful self-indulgence. 6. Tenderness, "adherence to a set of communal norms that are really a screen." 7. Conscience, a punitive self-surveillance. 8. Heart, Victorian sentimental ideology. 9. Shared humanity, a bourgeois humanism that says we are all exactly the same. 10. Belief in independent rational thought, vs. the subject disembodied and severed from all historical context. 11. Ideal of human individuality or expressiveness, vs. the "Kantian subject"   [-- PROF. LISA RUDDICK, writing about *Buddhism's* concept of "near-enemies"]

"II" FULL: SEE more examples in <u>Mind-Play</u>: **offense vs. harm, rights vs. privileges, envy vs. jealous, chili pepper vs. chili powder, thinking vs. good thinking,commonly-confused synonyms (imply-infer, etc.)**

|#+|+#||+#+|#+||+#|+#||+#+||+#||+#|+#+||##+#|+|#+|#|+#|+|+#|#+++#+|+|#|+#|+#|+|+#|+|#|#+||+#|#|+#|#||#+||#||

[II.] TWO. know about "<u>either-or and both-and</u>." Also, "<u>same together connected</u>" vs. "<u>different distinguished separated</u>." Also "<u>contrary but to be correlated somehow</u>."

[II.A. "Dualism" 101 and both-sides

THE CONCEPT. This is **"dualism,"** in a supposedly-bad sense of thinking in terms of either-or, one or the other only. This is a trait of Western thinking.
WHY IMPORTANT? This is also is a prime example of something about which "we," know—but don't know about. Oh as many will sing out right now, "Of course we all" already know to "avoid the dualist dichotomy." ...*except* that <u>we commit this fallacy</u> *All The Time*... Oh, less in competent thinking today, *but still*...

"I" BRIEF: a few illustrative statements for here and now:

[1.] EXAMPLES. (1) Is it <u>heredity, or environment</u>?... (2) Can we know reality? postmodernism says the world exists, but unlike the earlier scientific-materialistic world-view, we can know almost nothing of it, except through our language. (Oh, really? It's either A or else Z, is it?)... (3) In education, should we use Theory A or Theory B? And so forth...

[2.] Typical **western thinking** does not allow two opposite statements to be true at the same time (the law of contraries) and considers no third possibility in cause and effect relations (the law of the excluded middle).... Traditional **Indian logic**, by contrast, has four propositions: (1) is, (2) is not, (3) is and is not, and (4) neither is nor is not.... [True, there is a car in the driveway or not. True, "x = 4" or it does not. However, a brain-dead person is and is not dead; and, a pink elephant as seen by a delirious alcoholic neither is, nor is not, real—perhaps...]   [-- G. VAN DEN HEUVEL]

[3.] How <u>Eastern art</u> seeks to *organically <u>integrate and unify</u> opposites*:
--Chinese philosophy deals in dualism (humans-nature; quiescence-movement; yin-yang). But it sees both as valuable partners, not conflicting, but *interacting in a higher synthesis*. [-- DEBORAH TANNEN]
--Chinese visual art avoids dualisms (matter-spirit, divine-human) and sought to *dynamically unify opposites* both of which were

needed. Thus, "the artist must be neither classic nor romantic, he should be both; his painting must be neither naturalistic nor idealistic, it must be both; his style must be neither traditional nor original, it must be both."[-- INTRO. to Chinese visual art]

[4.] **Five options for confronting dichotomies:**
1. Decide one side is right or better. Either-or.
2. Make a compromise or dialectical synthesis: a third term.
3. Deny any conflict. "Form and content," "teaching and research," no problems there...?
4. "Affirm both sides as equally true or necessary or important or correct."[Cf. "Correlating of Contraries"]
5. Reframe conflict so that there are more than two sides. [-- PETER ELBOW, teacher]

GUIDELINE: *Reconsider*: instead of usually asking "Is it A *or* Z?," perhaps ask instead, "for our task-goal at hand, is it better to go more *toward* A, or more *toward* Z? Perhaps thus including an element of 'both-and' positioning..."

|#+|+#||+#+|#+||+#|+#||+#+||+#||+#|+#+||##+#|+|#+|#|+#|+|+#|#++#+|+|#|+#|+#|+|+#|+|#|#+||+#|#|+#|#||#+||#||

The "Both-Sides Balance-Scale" model

THE ISSUE. Questions, topics, problems, issues—often (usually) have "two sides" to them (or more, but here we focus on the pro-con type). And they will have more than one variable to discuss. And under each variable, more than one argument or statement exists on each side.

[EXAMPLE: Vegetarianism. [1.] One could treat the issue simply via one variable (say, morality) and give a one-sided argument consisting of only one point ("it is moral because it spares animal life"), *period*. Okay, fine perhaps...

[2.] But how much more Competent, Principled, and even Pleasurable-to-achieve, would be what we call a both-sides balanced-weighing? Discuss *many* variables, as of Nutrition, Morality, Social Image, etc., etc., etc. And for each, consider *many* subpoints. And for each subpoint, *many* pros *and* cons. (As for nutrition, "good" for reasons 1 2 3 4, "bad' for reasons 1,2,3—and the rebuttals to each!]

WHY IMPORTANT? But this possible *completeness* lies only in potential reality, in the territory of the issue itself. Too often, in thinking-discussing the issue, we often *fall short* of this three-part expansion (both sides... many variable-issues not just a few... and for each issue, more points than just one on each side).

OUR SUGGESTION. The Guideline below:

GUIDELINE: *Know of* the power (and pleasure?) in seeking to discover not just one side, but "**both** sides" of an issue, and via **many** variables not just one, and each variable discussed completely and fairmindedly... Whether one personally values doing this, or does it all the time, or not, at least *know of* the possibility of "both-sides" elaboration, and the value of it and need for it in at least some circumstances. And presumably one is *able* to do it!

GALLERY. A few of many possible examples of shortchanged vs. elaborated "both-sides weighing":

[1.] Moral-Ethical Systems. A *marvelous* book Beyond Bumper Sticker Ethics by STEVE WILKENS (1995), achieves *the very rare excellence* of first identifying many systems, and then for each, even-handedly but incisively, discovering both "positive aspects of," and "potential problems with," the stand—and many Orchids and Onions, too... An *impressive achievement!* (Alas, to save space, we give the full Beauty & Beast points only for the first two of the nine systems discussed. But the other seven are explored just as thoroughly...)

1. Cultural Relativism. [[{+++} 1.Eenrichment, 2. Anti-ethnocentrism... {- -} 1.Who decides? 2. Do moral principles vary? 3. Is relativism self-contradictory? 4. Is moral improvement possible? 6. Is tolerance always good?]]

2. Ethical Egoism. [[{+++} 1. Responsibility, 2. Self-preservation, 3. Unselfish actions can be bad!... {- -} 1. Narrow individual viewpoint, 2. Too optimistic about human nature?, 3. Inconsistent and self-defeating?, 4. Is justice possible in egoism?, 5. Does E. misrepresent altruism?. 6. Minimizes differences between people?]]

3. Behaviorism… 4. Utilitarianism. 5. Kantian Ethics. 6. Virtue Ethics. 7. Situation Ethics. 8. Natural Law Ethics. 9. Divine Command Theory.

SEE: "II" FULL version in **Mind-Play** unit. 2. <u>Therapy to "Cure" Homosexuals</u>… 3. <u>Sources of Energy</u>: a full dozen, pros and cons of each… 4. "Should <u>Schoolboys Receive an Allowance</u>?" Surprising objections… 5. <u>U.S.A.: its Strong-Point Orchids, its Onion-Deficiencies</u> (astonishingly-complete roster of both "sides"…)

|#+|+#||+#+|#+||+#|+#||+#+||+#||+#|+|#+||##+#|+|#+|#|+|+#|#++#+|+|#|+#|+#|+|+#|+|#|#+||+#|#|+#|#||#+||#||

[II.B.] "COMPARISON-CONTRAST": X and "Y"…

GUIDELINE: *Know* (realize) the powers of C/C as <u>not</u> just a *writing rule or formula*, <u>but</u> as a *thinking-and-communicating strategy*. Be *able* to *use* it thus—as one needs or desires to…

THE IDEA . One of the traditional "modes of rhetoric" or persuading-communicating (along with compare-contrast, define, etc.).
WHY IMPORTANT? But more significantly here, a major (if overlooked) way of thinking-and-clarifying.
OUR SUGGESTION. We review basics, but at once show *how C/C can aid complex thinking*.

PRE-VUE I. "Tool-Kit." We give a glimpse only at our unit on C-D for the parent-publication Mind-Play.
LEVEL "I" BASIC: One compares A with B. OLD-SCHOOLROOM EXAMPLE: "General Grant and General Lee, of the American Civil War…"
And for varied **Purposes**. (Know the unknown… know the known better… evaluate… etc.)
Methods. Structure, organization. Can c/c A and B on one point, then the second point, then the third, etc. Or can discuss A on all points 1 2 3 4 5, then B on all points 1 2 3 4 5.
LEVEL "II" ADVANCED: C/C is a powerful way of exploring but also communicating, because it relies on **"apperception."** This concept says that we learn (the new different strange) by means of C/Cing it with something already known (the old-hat, familiar, understood).
EXAMPLE. "The size of an acre of land? Oh, it's about as big as a football field…"

GALLERY. Only a few examples of the truly-underutilized power of C/C to convey complex new content. [This is "I" BRIEF view; for "II" FULL treatment, see the C/C module in Mind- Play]

BASIC: to elucidate the new-unknown, C/C it with the already familiar-comprehended:
<u>1</u>. "<u>Power-Exchange</u>" sexual activities (= consensual sadomasochism between consenting adults in private) == NOT the same as "*domestic abuse and violence in a family*" [Clarify the strange and unknown.]
<u>2</u>. <u>Haiku</u>, as NOT the same as known-familiar *Western poetry!* 25 variance-points: tone, structure, self of writer, etc. [Show how the new is truly different, by identifying the common variables, then different uses of…]
<u>3</u>. The "<u>Blues</u>" as a distinct musical form, contrast it with *"white" songs,* in re Rhythm, Harmony, etc. [Know something new better by C/C with the known—but by several distinct explicit variables, in order!]
<u>4</u>. <u>Senile dementia</u> memory-impairment as NOT the same as *normal memory-decline in ageing.* [Distinguish between more-familiar and more-unusual and significant events thus.]
<u>5</u>. The power of using <u>vivid specific examples to illustrate your point</u>. C/C two advertisements for "buy a brick to support our cause." [The one mentioned only generalities; the other "dipped down" to mention specific examples, though did not name the general category.]

| Milwaukee COMMUNITY CENTER: Your name. Organization. Business name. | Cravath Lake WATERFRONT: Bill Parsons. Whitewater Inn Est. 1897. Carol & Art Married 12/5/96. Dick Noble 1915- 1988. Your Name Here. In Memory of Fluffy |

6. Japanese "ikibachi" flower-arranging is NOT the same as *our usual Western styles.* Visuals of two versions of the same flowers arranged in the same vase. **[Make the new and different clear by C/C with the known-familiar.]**

7. What is quality poetry as against *merely sentimental verse*? Series of three paired student poems about "young love." One is vivid, truly-felt, shows reader the emotions, the other is vague general, reader is only told-about the feeling. **[Nicely shows up the thinness of the one by juxtaposing with the solidity of the other.]**

8. What is quality literature—how important is revision? Two versions of a poem (Yeats, Pensioner; R. Frost, Design). The first is much less developed, vivid, controlled than the final version. **[Showing quality by C/C with its not-yet-good early versions.]**

9. Varieties in styles of translation. Juvenal's Satire #10 on "big-city life in Rome." Three different translations. **[Possible differences and options stand out better against the common backdrop of the same text.]**

10. How big is France? First, superimpose upon a map of France, an outline map of *Wisconsin, U.S.A.* Second, superimpose upon a map of the U.S.A., an outline map of France. **[The unfamiliar seen by juxtaposing it with the known.]**

11. What is a political system like? Carl Cohen's book Four Systems describes democracy both individualistic and more-socialistic, then communism, then fascism. **[The four variations help comprehend better what is the common backdrop or subject of "what is a political system."]**

ADVANCED: for various purposes, take common backdrop subject held constant, then *vary versions* or *treatments* of it, the better to understand those *treatments, methods*, etc.

12. The concept of "slant" in writing: how a writer must adapt-adjust every element of style in a magazine article to the formula of the particular publication. *CONSTANT SUBJECT:* "the F-15 fighter-plane." *VARIED TREATMENT:* articles on it in (1) the cheerful Readers' Digest, (2) the ageing-hippie Rolling Stone, (3) the political-analytical Atlantic Monthly, (4) the amateur-hobbyist Flying, (5) the technological Popular Mechanics… **[The changes stand out well against the common backdrop of the same subject.]**

13. The great variety of styles of narration available to a writer; points of view. *CONSTANT SUBJECT,* a tale of how a man falls out of a church tower. *VARIED TREATMENT:* a dozen different modes (first-person, third-person, dialog, letter form, news article, interior monolog, etc.) **[The alternatives seen better against the common backdrop of the same story.]**

14. What are varied artistic styles for representing the human figure? From left to right below: *CONSTANT SUBJECT:* [1] MICHELANGELO'S statue of David. *VARIED TREATMENTS:* Then [2] sculpture style from *Pacific Ocean cultures,* [3] how a native artist would represent David, [4] sculpture style from *Africa,* [5] how a native artist would represent David.

Hold the figure the same, easier see the changes (larger head or not, stylized edges or not, etc.)

[The local styles are even more evident against the common backdrop of the same human figure.]

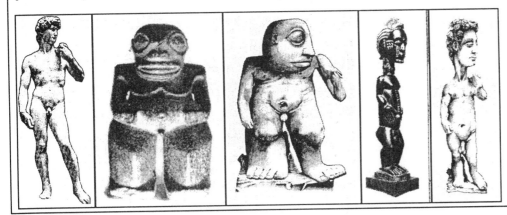

\=\+|+|+|+\=\=\+|+|+|=\=\=|+|+|+\\\+|+|+|+|=\=|+|+|+|=\=\+|+|+|+\=\=|+|+|+|+\=|=|+|+|+|+\=\=|+|+|+|+\=\=|+|+|\=\+|+|+|+\=\+|+|+| +

[II.C.] "CCC==DDD"? Connect two separated things, or divide two juxtaposed things?"

THE IDEA. Following from the above ideas about "monism or one-only," and "dualism either-or-both," and "compare-contrast," we note that often, **[1]** <u>two items may well often be perceived as identical</u> or closely-related together, *but really are distinct* (or "should" be distinguished, for valid reasons)… or also often **[2]** <u>these two items can be perceived as different</u> and properly separated, *but really are related* (or "should" be considered together, for valid reasons). [This is too abstract;' on to more particulars…]

IN P.O.E.P. OR "PLAINER OLD ENGLISH, PLEASE": "Hey, these two items are really more similar than you thought… Or, Hey, this one item really consists of at least two parts, which should be separated."

<u>GUIDELINE</u>: "Two items exist. **[1.]** Are we *perceiving* them as **different, distinct, separate** (in fact or desirability) but are they *in fact* more **similar related connected** (or should be) than is perceived? IF SO, WORK TO CONNECT/CORRELATE.
[2.] Also, two items exist. Are we perceiving them as more *the same, identical, or closely connected* (or should be) but are they *in fact* more **separated, distinct, different, independent** (or should be) than is perceived? IF SO, WORK TO SEPARATE/DISTINGUISH."

CATEGORIZATION. Attempt at stating **four major subtypes** of CCC==DDD issues.

1. Rational-and-Emotional.
Should we at times DDD separate our emotional responses from the right rational thing to do? (At other times CCC our feeling with facts and logic to better perform the task anyhow…) Specifically, a sort of "objective rational logical reasonable impersonal decentered" etc. response… and a sort of "emotional subjective personal empathetic sensitized" etc. response. To what extent CONNECT and to what extent SEPARATE them?

EXAMPLE. Advice to Adventure-Travelers Visiting the True Third World: "Poverty is pretty photogenic until you smell it… If you are afraid, embarrassed, ennobled, consider this. Get the guilt thing out of the way early. You're rich, they're not. They make Nikes and Kmart designer clothes, you wear them. Deal with it or go home and watch infomercials for abs machines. [-- THE WORLD'S MOST DANGEROUS PLACES]

Whoa, this seems irresponsibly-insensitive to poverty, injustice,…	Hmmm, this seems a stalwart even "moral" stand on a pesky issue. It says there are times to separate one's emotions—or balance them anyhow…]

EXAMPLES. A gallery of largely DDD or cases where separating emotions from reason, seems better:

(1) <u>Zen Detachment</u>: two MONKS were traveling, at a stream they helped carry a young woman across, hours later the first MONK said "I am still thinking about that woman," the second said, "*I put her down hours ago…*"

(2) <u>The Brave Baseball Player</u>. A coach reported he knew A PLAYER would be good—when another player was injured, the young athlete in question ignored the blood, kept focus on his pitching…

(3) <u>War is Heck</u>. Evil exists; "sometimes good men must enter into evil" to gain good goals, said MACHIAVELLI. This even though one's "good" emotions would say no.

(4) <u>Elections-Emotionality</u>. Some citizens voted for RALPH NADER for president in the 2000 elections. This made them "feel good," but was *not rational*, took votes away from the Democratic candidate, who lost…

(5) <u>Puritan Emotions Overrule Pragmatic Compromise</u>: Some citizens objected to *distributing condoms to post-pubertal adolescents*. Also to *providing a program of clean needle-exchange for addicts*. Both moves intended to protect against disease. The "emotions" (premarital sex is bad, drug use is bad) perhaps overruled compassionate prudence…

(6) <u>Too-Free Association in One's—"Mind"</u>: I once saw a newspaper photograph of a citizen proudly confidently carrying a protest-placard reading "Daytop: Dope Center." Daytop was a halfway house for recovering drug addicts, a facility the good citizen was objecting to being located in his proper neighborhood. *Duhhh…let's see* now. What building in town would be most probable to be quite free of drugs after all? *Duhhh…*

(7) <u>Nude, but Not Lewd</u>… The Passport Agency objected to a nudist submitting an unclothed photo of himself (head and shoulders shot). *Duhhh*—did the photo accomplish its job (identification) with no bad effects (no pornography) or not?

2. Roles: Professional Expertise/Contribution, vs. Personal Identity, even with Faults.

Should we CCC a person's personal life and even morals, with how s/he performs the socially-valuable job—or DDD Work and Warts? PETER DRUCKER said no employee can be perfect on all counts…

EXAMPLE. A "Bigoted"… Statement by a Professional Athlete. [Was roundly criticized at the time…]	
"Imagine having to take the #7 train to the ball park, looking like you're in Beirut next to some kid with purple hair, next to some queer with AIDS, right next to some dude who got out of jail for the fourth time, right next to some 20-year-old mom with four kids. It's depressing. The biggest thing I don't like about New York are the foreigners. I'm not a very big fan of foreigners. How the hell did they get in this country?" [-- JOHN ROCKER, a pitcher for the Atlanta Braves]	
Well, this is hardly a good role-model for the kids…	Look, *can the guy Play Ball*? This is what he was hired to do. I'd DDD separate his personal venom from his professional value.

MORE EXAMPLES. (1) A woman Air Force pilot had an extramarital affair, was demoted (but can she fly right?)… (2) The Secretary of Agriculture, EARL BUTTS, was fired for telling a racist joke (but was he fostering care of crops?)… (3) The poet T. S. ELIOT (and others) was anti-Semite, and as FRANCINE PROSE pointed out, many male novelists were chauvinist meanies. (But did ELIOT create good poetry; was EVELYN WAUGH, etc., a good writer?)

3. Self and Others.
Of course one seeks CCC closeness and intimacy and attachment—but one also needs DDD identity, separation, good autonomy, not dependency.

5. "only-Say," vs. also-"Do."
Should one talk but not walk (DDD)—or also practice what one preaches (CCC)? EXAMPLE. The local feminists at the university who condemn social practices nationwide, but do not notice let alone work to correct frank injustices to women (secretarial staff, etc.) right on their campuses.
[-- ANNETTE KOLNODY]

\=\+|+|+\=\=\+|+|+\=\=\=|+|+|+\\\+|+|+|=\=|+|+|+\=\=\+|+|+\=\=|+|+|+\=\=|+|+|+\=\=|+|+|+\=\=|+|\=\+|+|+\=\=\+|+|+| +

[II.D.] "CORRELATING CONTRARIES": relating two opposites which conflict but should be interactive:

THE SITUATION: --At times, two stands exist on an issue but are A-and-Z, polar-opposite; they contradict each other, conflict, are dissonant. (Either mildly, or at times extremely.)   --But often, each-or-both of the stands must somehow be confronted [=handled managed attended-to satisfied etc.]: either because each is (1) mandatory-required-inescapable, or because each is (2) necessary-valuable-useful—for task/goal success.   **GUIDELINE: --Therefore, *recognize* the need and correlate these contraries as appropriate, so as to satisfy and employ the demands and the offerings of both" sides." Ask whether the two opposing/contradicting stands can, should, must be more connected. Whether fusion integration blending, or simultaneous accepting of both.**   **--*Know* of the above situation Be *able* to (1) <u>identify</u> in the first place, and then (2) deftly <u>correlate</u>, even wildly-opposed polarities…**

"I" BRIEF: a few illustrative examples for here and now:

[1.] Good Art Combines Contraries: *the balance or reconciliation of opposite or discordant qualities*: of sameness, with difference; of the general, with the concrete; the idea, with the image; the individual, with the

380

representative; the sense of novelty and freshness, with old and familiar objects; a more than usual state of emotion, with more than usual order; judgment ever awake and steady self-possession, with enthusiasm and feeling profound or vehement; [-- S.T. COLERIDGE]

[2.] <u>Contradictory Human Needs.</u> Humans crave "security *and* risk, coherence *and* spontaneity, novelty *and* latency, rivalry *and* mutuality" with others. *Both* personal identity *and* social belongingness. Both security, and new experience. Of course, these "<u>contrasting tendencies</u>" are not irreconcilable "contradictions," but "different phases in the rhythm of living." [-- ROBERT S. LYND, Knowledge for What?]

[3.] <u>Business-World Project Manager</u>: a study in paradox... ego but no ego... autocrat but delegator... leader but manager... complexity but keep-it-simple... big but small viewpoint... [-- SOURCE]

[4.] <u>A Teacher</u>: an educator must be an ally...also a guardian. On the students' side...yet also critical-minded. A student advocate...yet also a gatekeeper. Reveal our imperfections...but identify with knowledge. [-- P. ELBOW]

[5.] <u>Writing; a complex activity</u>: Demanding, but sometimes effort-free... Needs planning, but also uses chance discovery... Analytic, but also synthesizing... Must follow formal constraints, but also "breaks" the rules... A mental activity, but relies on technology... Is solitary, but relates to social context... [-- M. SHARPLESS]

[6.] <u>My own experience right here</u> in writing this very production *Teaching Thinking*:

1. Complete (no key bases left uncovered), *but also* Calibrated (balanced, proportioned), also Compact-Concise-Coherent (readable).
2. Conceptual (key ideas present and made explicit) *but also* Concrete (ideas vivified by effective examples, instances).
3. Self-Contained (has own internal logic) *yet also* "Applicable" (supple; can be employed here, there...)
4. Reader is guided but also freed. "Convergence" to basic material for all common, divergence for individual reader paths
5. Self of the author: is *both* formal *and* informal... *not only* hot-fervent *but also* cool fair-minded.
6. Stance is elitist (defend quality uncompromisingly) *but also* populist (everyone truly interested is welcome!)
7. Purpose is pragmatic useful, but also pleasurable for own sake.
8. Structure: both linear sequential (logic of subject) *but also* lateral-associative (refer to earlier, later, or related items).
9. Audience: must balance basics for beginners, *but also* complex points for advanced learners.
10. Tight and Loose: Focused Accurate Precise in giving the skills, *but also* Flexible Adaptable Pragmatic in enabling varied use.

[7.] <u>Are some situations irreconcilable? The opposing demands unable to be both accommodated?</u>

[A] EDUCATION. "Both universities (Duke and Rice) wanted to *combine seeming opposites*: breadth and depth, structure and choice, skills and subject areas, interdisciplinarity and departmental divisions." [-- CHE, 19 Feb 99]

[B] ENGINEERING. "What do you want for your product? Good quality? Inexpensiveness? Quick arrival at the market? *Good, cheap, quick; pick <u>any two</u>*..." [-- ENGINEERS' saying]

|#+|#+|#+|+|#+|+|#+|+|+#|+|#+|+|#+|+|#+|#+|#+|#+|+|#+|+|+#|+|#+|#+|+|+|+|+#|+|++#++#++#+#+#|||#|#|||

[II.E.] "STYLE" as "attainment and restraint." Balancing mid-point between lesser positions...

THE IDEA. "Style" means many things, but has been described specifically as exhibiting **"attainment and restraint."** This balances the contraries of *thrust and achievement*, with *"editing" and control of excess*. One does get there, but doesn't overshoot the mark...
Style: "<u>the direct attainment of a foreseen end, simply and without waste.</u>" "<u>Something that is perfectly fitted to do its work.</u>" This quality of "attainment and restraint," can apply to *art* ("architecture and sculpture, painting and music, dancing, play-acting"), but also to *many other realms*: "cricket" (traditional British game), "the careful achievements of the housebreaker [burglar] and the poisoner and to the spontaneous animal movements of the limbs of man or beast" ... and "a grain scoop, a suspension bridge, a guillotine, the orb web of a spider, the sixteen-foot canoe." [-- A. N. WHITEHEAD; W. RALEGH; E. B. WHITE]

Personally, what I call **a "Zen gyroscope" attitude** also seeks to avoid false-note unbalanced positions for a central poise. Faced with something new or threatening, I would not (1) attack it to conquer it offensively, (2) fearfully protect myself from it defensively, nor (3) flippantly dismiss it, nor yet (4) over-politely "accept" it in a sort of no-conflict Groupthink. Rather, I would combine the contraries of great Closeness to and Openness to understanding the new item, with also a Distance-from-"contamination" by it. I would shut my mouth and open eyes and ears to slowly, empathetically comprehend it. And only then go on from there... Is this a **Guideline**?:

GUIDELINE. **Consider confronting a difficult issue (you oppose it, etc.) with gyroscope-balance. Not to defensively feel threatened by it. Nor to offensively seek to defeat it. Nor to politely practice "groupthink" and accommodate it. But to simultaneously (1) totally comprehend it, but also (2) withhold attack or defense etc.!** [*Analogy*: to walk in the "enemy" forest but unafraid and realistically so...]

|#+|#+|#+|+|#+|+|#+|+|+#|+|#+|+|#+|+|#+|#+|#+|#+|#+|+|#+|+|+#|+|#+|#+|+|+|+|#|+|++#++#++#+#+#|||#|#|||

["8".7.] CHANGE: Subject Altering (or not) over Time...

GUIDELINE: **"Major change is a challenge to confront competently when thinking let alone acting in reality. Beware being fooled by "Today's Truths & Taboos." "Culture" urges that what is in or true good etc. often must be accepted cannot be questioned, while what is out or wrong bad etc. often is neglected and must be rejected cannot even be explored. QUESTION THIS DANGEROUS URGING AS NEEDED AND POSSIBLE. Also, beware "Fashion-Cycles in change." "Culture" urges that what is in and out may be (1) cyclical or pendulum-swing of recurrent fashions (heredity vs. environment etc.), or (2) truly new hence rejecting the old.) BEWARE THIS POSSIBLE PITFALL: QUESTION THE ACCEPTED, EXPLORE THE REJECTED.... *Realize*, that the true total scope of something, may be more than just its present moment. It may reach into the past... it may project toward the future... *Adapt and adjust* accordingly...**

APPENDIX. The "II" full-dress unit on "MAJOR CHANGE" in the parent-publication <u>Mind-Play</u>

[1.] <u>Four Types</u> of: **Constant, Trend, Cyclical, Abrupt**

[2.] <u>Four Perceptions</u> of: **"Unnoticed, Heresy, Orthodoxy, Commonplace"**

[3.] <u>Size of</u>: simple, or complex and large-scale?

[4.] <u>"Pew-vs.-Church"</u> types: "choice in a context, or a context of choices?"
{4A} **New Bottles Old Wine**... {4B} **Pendulum-Swing Cycles**... {4C} **Polar 180-degree**... {4D} **"None of the Above," Reject Whole Question**... {4E} **True Paradigm-Shift**... {4F} **Change but Within Fence** of Norms-Mores.

[5.] <u>Problems in Peoples' Confronting</u> Change: {5A} **Non-Graspable "Just Can't Get It Can They"** ... {5B} **Slow Subtle Sneaky pace** of change ... {5C} Three <u>Myopias</u>: (1) **"Presentism"** including **TTT "Today's Truths & Taboos"** (and Pendulum-Swing of Fashions) (2) **Retrospective** Myopia (can't see past as its true self) (3) **Forward** Myopia (can't predict future)... {5D} **"Non-Peripheral" Vision** of Unit (miss whole over time: development-of, present, continuation-of).

"I" BRIEF: a few **examples** of the "vague" concept of *total expanse of a change-situation...*

--Prejudice. It is learned gradually, from our earliest years. So perhaps it cannot be unlearned instantly (as with Diversity Education and the like). Perhaps also the <u>unit of attention</u> extends on beyond re-education. A gradual building—gradual unbuilding.

--Student's Life-Career. A freshman student wasted daily learning-time. His unit was "today, this semester." <u>Expand unit</u> to "your life at say age 40: where do you want to be then?" Now each day is component of larger unit and plan for it...

--"College is for reading the 'Great Books'." Unit would be four years. <u>Expand unit</u> to whole lifetime: now, college is a preparation for a life of reading the great books, with a longer plan...

--Affirmative Action for college. "It starts in high school." Unit, a few years. <u>Expand unit</u> to many years earlier, and other institutions involved also.

--Automobile Salesman: Selling to a Customer. The unit of Tom the salesman is his selling me a Chevrolet. After the sale he pays no attention to me. <u>Expand unit</u> to "me as lifetime repeat customer." Now Tom keeps in contact when I return for service.

--Useful Life of a Product. For my associate ROBERT, it's when first defects appear: time to replace! <u>Expand the unit</u>: for ME, it's as long as I can fix it up, use it up, replace or repair parts, use duct tape and bailing wire, wear it out!

--Reportage: length, scope of an In-Depth News Story. Now, the journalist starts with the explicit event. Expand the unit: step backward to earlier origins and events on the issue. (EXAMPLE: Rosa Parks would not sit in Black section of bus; but, her predecessors?)

|#+|#+|#+|+|#+|+|#+|+|+#|+|#+|+|#+|+|#+|#+|#+|#+|#+|+|#+|+|+#|+|#+|#+|+|+|+|+#|+|++#++#++#+#+#||#|#|||

[“8”.8] “ELUCIDATION”: Image of Subject *simultaneously* Complete, Comprehended, Clear...

THE ISSUE. What might be a “good” image of a subject—a report, picture, version, description of? Might it generally, generically, globally treat the subject in completeness, but also in clarification, plus in communicability? Comprehensively, comprehended as such, and comprehensible too?

WHY IMPORTANT. (1) Pragmatics: needed, useful. (2) Pleasure: personally my insight/bias is to prefer indeed savor “utterly complete, comprehended, clear” images of a subject (museum-quality, etc.).

AN AMBITIOUS GOAL. To use elucidation in thinking/writing, to enable a [competent, committed] reader to grasp a subject two times better, in half the time, with much less difficulty and much more enjoyment...

OUR SUGGESTION. We offer this concept, the very idea of a lucid image of a subject. Below, a “I” BRIEF glimpse (lucid?...) at the concept, analogies of it, its traits, examples of it, a *few* of its methods...

[SEE “II” *FULL* version in parent- publication Mind- Play]

|+|#+|+|+|+#|+|#|#+#+#+#+|||#+#+#+#+|#+|#+|+|+#|++#+#+#|+|+#|+++#++##||+|#|#+|#|#|||#+|+#|+|#+#||

[1.] DEFINITION/DESCRIPTION of “Elucidation”

[1.A.] EXPOSITORY statement-about... Elucidation = A treatment of a subject which simultaneously is Comprehensive (complete-“enough”... view of the subject)... but also Comprehended (=worked, thought-through, interpreted, explained, evaluated, dealt with via policy and practice, shown how-to-do, etc., etc.)... and then also Comprehensible (encoded well for best reader-accessibility)...

[1.B.] ANALOGIES to describe:

1. Assuming the subject is like **a complicated *geographical terrain*.** See *both* the **forest *and* the trees**, from an observation blimp employing myriad inspection-tools: wide-angle and telephoto lenses, x-ray and infra-red, remote sensing, shortwave, historical archaeology, more...

2. A display of (the subject as) a “**small complicated *machine***”

| But NOT "In a messy, unlit storeroom at midnight, illuminated only partially not completely, and only by a weak flickering flashlight—the machine itself dirty; partially disassembled; some parts broken, others missing perhaps; and half-hidden under piles of junk in the drawer—and no instruction-manual"! | But RATHER INSTEAD "As if hauled out and taken to a good museum; thoroughly steam-cleaned and refinished, missing parts reinstalled, broken parts repaired, all parts labelled—and then mounted upon an eye-level, slowly-rotating, display-stand flooded with shadowless lighting; even showing a cutaway or transparent view of the "hidden" interior within, and the whole machine itself operating slowly!" |

3. **A *12-story building*** but seen *not* just “from the entryway” (=levels, dimensions) *but* in 3-D x-ray blueprint diagram.

| I can see the lobby as I enter but that’s all... | I see with X-ray eyes all the complexity... |

4. A **scatter of tattered *papers on the floor*** but described accurately (=amount, arrangement—find patterns!).

| “Oh well, you can’t clarify all that complexity, find any | “Hmmmm... Let’s see. Now the RED papers were lightweight |

generalities about it, it's just myriad random papers all over the floor by chance!"	hence didn't drift far; the BLUE papers are of three different shapes; the GREEN papers more numerous…

5. A bushel of apples but selected *not* from one tree *but* from the whole 40-acre orchard (=balanced variety and distillation).

6. A small but complexly-laid-out village in hill-and-forest territory." (Such as the French town of St. Jean Pied de Port, or a Concept, such as "French national character.") Well, then, one writer will inevitably approach it from the sunny open southwest, and see the portion of the village that way—and because of this plus the writer's own temperament, will be good at one thing (garden-description) and bad at something else (economic facts). A second writer will of course approach from the cloudy northeast, and—so forth…

|+|#+|+|+|+#|+|#|#+#+#+#+|||#+#+#+#+|#+|#+|+#|++#+#+#|+|+#|+++#++##||+|#|#+|#|#|||#+|+#|+|#+#||

[2.] EXAMPLES of "elucidated" subjects:
[A.] three technical tasks (car, water, sex)… [B.] Roster of others…

--*BUYING A USED CAR*:	--*PURIFYING DRINKING WATER*:	--*SAFER SEXUAL BEHAVIOR*:
"Blue exhaust smoke means oil-burning" — yes *but* what about *black, white,* and *grey* smoke—[engine block? transmission? merely cold-start?] … etc!	"Use a filter or chlorine" — yes *but* when are *both* needed? 3 sizes, 2 types of filters! And option of *iodine*? "Shelf-life"? What of *cysts, molds, slimes? Cold/dirty* water*? And, *new* methods: mixed-oxidant, ultraviolet?	"Use a condom always"—yes *but* what about *oil-based lubricants damaging latex?* And the overlooked potentiality of *germicides?* And the new *polyurethane* condoms too?
[How many resource-materials cover all these other issues—did they not scan the Total Picture for **secondary, overlooked** elements?]	[Not all resource-materials go that far—an omission, oversight in not dealing with **non-routine** or **special circumstances, unusual situations-demands**?]	[Is some safer-sex data more scrupulously complete, covers all or more "bases"? Does not **make errors and miss excellences**, as here?]

Stir-fry cooking: *all six* of the criteria-for-excellence often overlooked amid the specific 1-2-3 steps…

Pasta-Saucing: *not* just recipes, but the principle, of "relation of pasta-size, type to various sauce types"…

The **Apostrophe**: *not* just "for the possessive" *but* subtle nuances: exceptions, overlooked points, etc ….

"Time-Management": all three of the indispensable principles which support and guide all the little "rules."
[1. Goal-Setting… 2. Prioritizing (Urgent or Non, Important or Not)…3. Lead-Time Staging…]

"Purifying water when camping": *all* the exceptions, hidden pitfalls, alternatives, conditions, etc. (filters?)

"Buying a used car": *not* just "beware black exhaust smoke," *but* also what about white, grey, red oil deposits, etc.

"Safer sex equipment, procedures": *not* just "use a condom," *but* options-and-variables: pitfalls/potentialities regarding materials, spermicides, etc.

Book reviewing: *not* just plot, but issues to manage: diverse readers? the book vs. your preferences? etc.

Travel: *not* just info or story or training (*bicycle in Burgundy, museums in Japan, social work in Africa*), but the principles: *purposes, safety, destinations, transportation, equipment, rapport w/ natives, timing, …*

Writing: *not* just grammar, usage, basic rules, *but* Process, Purposes, Audience, Style-issues: structure, development…

Thinking: *not* just "logic 1-2-3" or "creativity," *but* "power-tools": Criteria, "Lenses," Strategy, Dialectics, Induction… And see the Tool Kits (in the Appendix) of Cause-Effect… Structure… Diversity… etc.

|+|#+|+|+|+#|+|#|#+#+#+#+|||#+#+#+#+|#+|#+|+#|++#+#+#|+|+#|+++#++##||+|#|#+|#|#|||#+|+#|+|#+#||

[3.] RATIONALE for, *and* OBJECTIONS against!

--Complex subjects and skills can be elucidated [= 1. investigated, 2. known-&-described, 3. comprehended/interpreted, 4. put to task-goal use, and then 5. communicated-about to others, both more-Completely and more-Clearly],...better."

--Better without four pitfalls. This, without either:.... 1. too-"thin" overgeneralization into superficiality; or 2. too-"thick" overelaboration into obscurity; or 3. too-"rigid" reduction into rote-rule formulae; or 4. too-"relaxed" dilution into loose obscurity, either...].

--And, better in seven ways. This never perfectly, but more than we usually seem to:.... 1. do or practice (action) ... or 2. succeed in doing (achieve)... or 3. seek to do (attempt) ... or 4. can do, offhand (ability)... or 5. realize we might be able to do (aware) ... or 6. value, enjoy ("appreciate") ... or of course 7. teach-and-learn about (access).....

"Cruciality," Current Relevance.

And **elucidation** may help counter certain of the current TTT's or **Today's Truths & Taboos** (the truths we must believe and not question, the taboos we must dismiss and not even investigate). Namely, **(1) epistemological relativism** or "well we can't really know reality out there very well after all hence can't Elucidate it as well as you say" (A dualistic dichotomy or either-or fallacy at least?) (I could omit here the TTT of **(2) the "Constructivism not Essentialism"** debate, as even if knowledge is massively socially-created and not absolute/inherent etc., still we could elucidate what that creation is!) Nor need I really mention **(3) "Rampant Relativism"** or "well who's to say after all."

A NEED: The recurrent problem—shortfalling, blunder—of **"Differential Elucidation."** Many publications achieve only uneven, imperfect elucidation of their subjects/skills. Some aspects will be well-clarified; other components partially-perfected; yet other elements absent or embryonic!

SUGGESTION: perhaps a "II" FULL version of "Elucidation" can help warn against this pitfall...

EXAMPLES. Instances where the subject was clarified *only differentially, unevenly...*

Chinese Cooking: the technique of "stir-fry": (=that method of quickly tossing fine-chopped food over high heat for brief time to achieve the fresh, pure "wok-air" or stir-fried taste.)
I analyzed a dozen books, and found that two books were total duds. Of the remaining ten, each one provided some secrets—content, approach—that the others omitted. (Even so, only one or two were able to get into **Operating Concepts** or the "real reasons behind" how things happen, why we therefore do this not that.) I assembled the best parts for a class-unit on "here is Total Treatment..."

"Textbook Tangles." When our English department had to select a new Freshman composition rhetoric-reader, no one candidate-text "did it all."
--Of the six, the runner-up was superb in *sentence-combining*, but average otherwise...
--The winner seemed superior to all the others in both "the *process* of writing," and also "*audience*-relating." However, it languished on the shelves of the school's Textbook Library because it was *immense, overwhelming*—heck, maybe more Complete, but scarcely Compact-and-Clearly accessible!.

"Computer Control" An acquaintance, BILL. in Madison, WI, a computer guru, says "I always glance through this, that, the
other new book on programming, and in almost each one I usually find something the other omits or slights or explains badly. Hence you get something unique out of each one. Of course, different users will also prefer different books."

"Time-Management" is a gem here (how many accounts omit lead-time planning plus prioritization!)

|+|#+|+|+|+#|+|#|#+#+#+#+|||#+#+#+#+|#+|#+|+#|++#+#+#|+|+#|+++#++##||+|#|#+|#|#|||#+|+#|+|#+#||

[4.] The "HOW-TO": tool-chest? *(Pre-view)*

"DISCLAIMER/REASSURANCE": **Elucidation** is so challenging to do well, that it properly draws on virtually all of the thinking and clarifying tools in our units (Teaching Thinking appendices; parent-publication

Mind-Play). No space here to explore; only, three pre-views. (1) & (2): the lessons derived from the sex-water-cars trio of examples above. And (3) process-elucidation, or "how to perform a demanding procedure better":

---

1. ISSUES mentioned: the old-known-familiar and indeed acceptable/favored, _but also_ many relevant others often overlooked...
2. PITFALLS and problems: obvious known _but also_ subtle infrequent insidious ...
3. KNOWLEDGE: "what we all know" _but also_ insider lore expert updated fine-point nuances ...
4. METHODS: standard known formulae _but also_ flexible heuristics "out-of-the-box"...
5. DECISIONS: easy ones _but also_ gray-area judgment-calls with balances-and-tradeoffs ...
6. PROCEDURES: standard _but also_ exceptions qualifications for unanticipated consequences ...
7. CHANGES: the traditional _but also_ state-of-the-art updatings, representing "CEC" or Current Experts' Consensus ...

[SUCH AS: **(1)** "exceptions, qualifications" and other "overlooked fine-points"... **(2)** "positions currently unpopular hence rejected but perhaps valid or even vital"..." **(3)** changes: gradual-subtle changes not noticed; or something becoming _old_ and going out-of-date, or a _new_ bonus (or barrier) emerging"... **(4)** "ill-defined situations, plus legitimate disagreements by experts"... **(5)** "separate component subparts not perceived: oversimple monolithic monism"... **(6)** "pitfalls or dangers overlooked because unrecognized, or infrequent" (but hazardous nevertheless!)... **(7)** "valuable options, alternate choices little-known, misunderstood, or overlooked"... **(8)** "finesse: so-called secrets of the trade which usually only dedicated experts know"... **(9)** "accepted wisdoms which however are questionable, even misleading"... **(10)** "a whole large aspect or dimension of some procedure usually overlooked by most practitioners"... **(11-)** _and yet others_...]

--**Standards of Excellence** to aim for and measure performance against.....
--**Pitfalls**, both elementary-amateur and subtler-advanced.....
--**Misconceptions** which frequently occur.....
--**Options**, not only _mandatory_, must select either A or B or C, but also _alternative_, can do A, B, C, or ignore.....
--**Rules vs. Tools**: including the important "Rules of Thumb" or "Guidelines".....
--Legitimate **Disagreements**-even-among-the-Experts, or tricky **Judgment-Call** "gray areas".....
--**Permissible Ranges of Variation**, often quantified using Statistics, at other times using Analogy.....
--**Definition** of all Key and Technical Terms, of course (the greatest _Pitfall_ into which amateur writers tumble).....
--**Specifics**, perhaps with "Core-Instance Case-Study" example (Vegetarianism: "Fred's experiences with...")
--**Troubleshooting**, or what to do when.....
--And the vital **Operating Concepts** or larger hows-&-whys which underlie the explicit smaller actions.....

|+|#+|+|+|+#|+|#|#+#+#+#+#+|||#+#+#+#+#+|#+|#+|+#|++#+#+#|+|+#|+++#++##||+|#|#+|#|#|||#+|+#|+|#+#||

[5.] ANNEX: "extra," an expanded example...

EXAMPLE. The skill of using **the apostrophe** in writing… Three versions of instruction:
[1.] "Absolute basic" skeleton-telegraph statement.
[2.] _THE ACTUAL ORIGINAL EXAMPLE,_ found in a textbook, ca. 1980.
[3.] Our recasting _toward_ total **elucidation**… _**Does this trio elucidate, the very idea of, elucidation?**_

[I]:	[II]:	[III]:
The correct way to punctuate an abbreviation of the word "and," is by retaining the letter _n_ and adding apostrophes on both sides.	**Dog 'n pony CASH N' CARRY HEAT n EAT** Rhythm 'n' blues Cook 'N' Clean Sugar 'n' spice	An APOSTROPHE is used to indicate a letter omitted from a word, when abbreviated. For instance, the possessive. (**Carl is coming = Carl's coming; the book of Carl = Carl's book**) But also, for letters omitted from words in abbreviations. Here, subtle errors can creep in, especially when contracting the word "and" as in "X and Y," as in "sugar and spice, "etc. Here are three "fine-point" rules by which to avoid errors:
	Dog 'n pony Dog N' pony Dog n pony Dog 'n' pony Dog 'N' pony Dog 'n' pony	1. Don't fail to use an apostrophe for every omission. 2. Don't confuse the apostrophe with a quotation mark, either single (2A) or double (2B). The doubles are obviously different from the apos'; the singles, more subtly different. 3. Don't be inconsistent in capitalizations.
Wrong:		So, which of the following is/(are) (in)/correct?
Dog 'n Pony	Which of these	A. **Cash n Carry** B. **Cash 'n Carry** C. **Cash N' Carry** D. **Cash 'n'**

Dog n' Pony Right: *Dog 'n' Pony*	abbreviated "and"s is correct? Only the last one. The first example leaves out the second apostrophe (you need two, because both the *a* and *d* are missing). The second example leaves off the first apostrophe. The third example doesn't carry any. The fourth example uses single quote marks rather than apostrophes. (The first mark, you can see, turns inward; that means it's not an apostrophe.) The fifth example capitalizes the N. It should not be capitalized. "Sugar 'n' spice" wins. But why not use an honest "and" and be done with all the apostrophes? **[--from a 1972 book on graphic design and layout]**	Carry E. **Cash "n" Carry** F. **Cash 'N' Carry** G. **Cash 'n' Carry** <u>The Answer Key</u>: **A.** Omits both apostrophes!—Rule # 1. **B.** Omits the second apostrophe (both the *a* <u>and</u> the *d* are missing)—Rule #1. **C.** Omits the first 'strophe—Rule # 1. **D.** Wrongly uses single quotation marks for the first apostrophe (turns inward; the 'strophe turns outward)—Rule # 2A. **E.** Wrongly uses double-quotation marks—Rule # 2B. **F.** Wrongly capitalizes the N, as if it were "Cash AND Carry," which it probably wasn't—Rule # 3. **G.** <u>The winner!</u> Avoids the three errors. [<u>Extra Credit</u>: spot *my own error* in the above "<u>Key</u>"] [Thats right its in D: 'strophe should be 'strophe…] [Or better yet: That's right, it's in D…] [Of course, consider Option #B in all this. Don't abbreviate "and" at all. Presto, no apostrophe "**fuss 'n' muss**"!: *Cash and Carry* **Cash & Carry**] <u>And now that you know, what about</u>: *CASH n' CARRY* *Dog 'n pony* *HEAT n EAT* ***Rhythm 'n' blues*** **Cook "N" Clean** *Sugar 'n' spice* <u>A teenage woman</u>: "Stub out the 'rette, Jack; my 'rents are comin' in the door!"

`\=\+|+|+\=\=\+|+|+|=\=\=|+|+|\\\+|+|+|+|=\=|+|+|+|=\=\+|+|+|+\=\=|+|+|+|+\=\=|+|+|+|+\=\=|+|+|+|+\=\=|+|+|+\=\=|+|+|\=\+|+|+|+\=\=\+|+|+| +`

[5.B.] The "VARIABLES-VARIATION" move
for identifying issues-and-their-options:

"VARIABLES-VARIATION": to clarify a subject…

--THE ISSUE. "When dealing with complex issues (and more are complex than not!), *we usually need to be more complete and comprehensive, than simplistic and limited.* But <u>we risk</u> starting and ending with *response-statements about the issue which are too simple*—in identifiable ways, what we call "one-point position."

--WHY IMPORTANT: This narrow, "myopic" image can be *dangerous, a pitfall to success*. We miss options alternatives choices which may be better or even mandatory! (This is thus bad Pragmatically, risks failure; it is also bad Pleasurably, to incompetently botch the enterprise…)

--OUR SUGGESTION: *But we can get to see multiple-plural positions after all, and choose the best position after all.* To that end, here is the **V-V** model (or "topographic map"), which seeks to show what-and-how…"

<u>IN "P.O.E.P." OR "PLAINER OLD ENGLISH, PLEASE"</u>: "<u>**Make sure your stand on an issue**</u> (what is true or false, good or bad, what to do and how) <u>**is not simplistic**</u> (one-option-only, in a vacuum, overly-dictatorial, etc.). <u>**Aim to know *all* the options**</u> A to Z, <u>**so as to perhaps choose a better stand**</u> than the first, limited one.

> **EXAMPLE.** "Photography": **[1.]** "Set shutter speed at 1/125 second," period... *versus* **[2.]** Range is from "A" one sec. (time-exposure) to "Z" 1/5000 sec. (action-shots) and B C D E F in between. Each stage has its functions, and its good and bad points!

|~#+|~#+|~+|#+|~+#|~#+|#+|#~|+#|~+#|~#+|+|+#|~#+|~+#+|~+#|#+#|~|+~#+|~+#|~+#+~|+#|#+#|~|+~#+|~+#|~+#+~|+#|~#|~#+|~||||

[1.] GRAPHIC To visualize **Provincial** vs. **Continuum** of choices, then **Balancing** the subject itself:

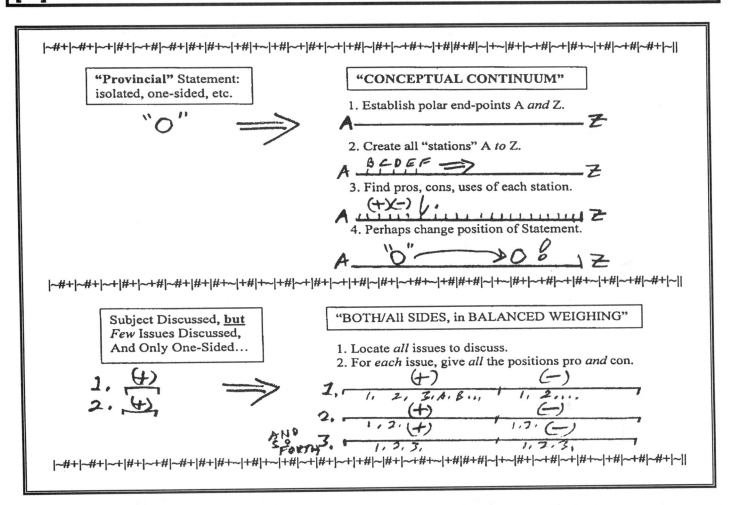

[2.] EXAMPLES "I": To illustrate **Provincial** vs. **Continuum** of choices, then **Balancing** subject:

> **EXAMPLES:** I of III: *one* subject ("photographing the old barn"), *one* variable within it ("shutter-speed"):
> provincial vs. panoramic views:

[1.] ONE Variable: One-Point...:	**Using the V-V: the issue, plus all options:**
"Snap the old barn at 1/125 second." [No identification of issue... of why this stand (speed) chosen, let alone optional alternate stands (not even mentioned-and-rejected... Hence this seems **monolithic, prescriptive, isolated,** etc. Some would say, *good basic instruction.* We say: *provincial incompetence, mindless rule...*]	Variable-Issue: **"Shutter-Speed"** [one of many others!] "**A**" | B | C | D | E [123] | F [12abc] | G | .... to | X | Y | "**Z**" **SLOW One Sec. == MED. 1/250 == FAST 1/1000 Sec.** (-) can blur scene　　[*] "Rule of Thumb　(-) shallow focus (+) can let trees blur　　or "Guideline"!　(+) freeze birds (+) deeper focus-depth　　　　　　　　in flight [Then other **issues: Camera Angle, Lighting Source, Composition**...]

> **EXAMPLES:** II of III: *one* subject ("photographing the old barn"), *many* variables within it:

[2.] SEVERAL Variables: One-Point...:	**Using the V-V: more-A-Z analyzed:**

"Have the lighting directly over your shoulder or behind, in full sunlight."	LIGHTING SOURCE: Front, side, back: pros and cons of each. TIME OF DAY: Noon is blah, try dawn or dusk!
"Set shutter speed at 1/125 second"	S.SPEED: slow (-) blurs, (+) catches motion; fast, freezes.....
"Make sure picture is in focus in the viewfinder."	FOCUS: all sharp.....vs. selective focus emphasizes subject!
"Hold camera at eye level" *(often not stated but assumed....)*	CAMERA ANGLE: worm's-eye...eye-level...bird's-eye (-),(+)!
["Of course, color film..."]	FILM TYPE *(often non-discussed...)* Color; B. & W.; infared.....
"Stand at a middle distance from subject *(often assumed)*	DISTANCE: the (+) of moving in for close up of rich detail!

EXAMPLES: III of III: ...and *many* subjects, and for *each* one, a glimpse at *all-or-many* of the variables, and for *each*, variable, *all* the options A-to-Z... [The complete shebang, bag of wax, rubric of **variables-variation**]:

X **PHOTOGRAPHY**: As noted above... Then, beyond this, Shutter Speed, there's variables of Lens Focal Length (wide-angle, normal, telephoto); Film-Type; and still others...

X **WRITING**: For variable of **Syntax length and type**, there's short sentences (for punch and variety, but beware choppiness), long sentences (for complex concepts and formal tone, but beware "run-on" obscurity). Then, beyond Syntax, there's variables of **Tone** (informal-formal); **Length** ("1 p. only" to "at least 500 words"); **Structure(s)**; Is Point Explicit or Implicit, revealed Early, or at End? Are **Visual Graphics** used? And yet others...

X **COOKERY**: Beyond variable of **Sequence of More than One Cooking-Method** and in which sequence, there's **Ingredients**; **Seasonings**; **Criteria** for Taste and Quality; Specific Methods; Sequence of Seasonings. *And others...*

X **ETHICS**: note *several*: **Situational**, **Supernatural**, **Pragmatism**, etc., and the pros and cons of *each*.

...I *begin* to see your point here: a set of "moves," high-level general-generic and conceptual, which I can apply to any subject for competent completeness. But, are these actions **rules** we *must* follow always exactly everywhere?	*No no no.* Neither **rules** (="this you must do then success will ensue") nor even **tools** (="use-or-not, depending if it'll help successful ending"). **V-V** is a **"topographic map"** abstracting to a clear-complete **model**, the **"code"** of what good thinking confronting complexity, seems to look like! It is a **report**, **"conceptual topography,"** which you may thus use as a **guideline**! (We say CrrC or "complexities repay complex thinking," but we systematize it here for clarity thus)

|~#+|~#+|~+|#+|~+#|~#+|#+|#~|+#|+~|+#|~+|#+|+|+#|~|#+|~+#|~+|#+|~+#|#+#|~|+~#+|~+#|~+|#+~|+#|~+#|~#+|~|||~#+|~#+|~+|#+|~+#|~#+|||

[3.] The central GUIDELINE for variables-variation:

GUIDELINE: Be able to apply something like the following checklist to complex issues—whether "what is true/false," "what is good/bad," or "how to do something." Technical Explanation.

1. What is the VARIABLE-ISSUE involved here—whether currently explicit or not?

[**Variable-issues** are "matters which, for success of the task-goal at hand, must be confronted: that is, handled-managed-attended to-reckoned with-satisfied-employed etc."

EXAMPLES: (1) in *photography*, "shutter speed," "depth of focus," "camera-angle," etc. (2) In *education for thinking*, (A) "to what degree is thinking a course-goal?" (B) "How explicitly but not mechanically is thinking to be defined and taught?" (C) "decisions: how many made by course/teacher, how many autonomously by learner?" and (D--) *the others* covered in the "D-Machine" section in the Body of Teaching Thinking.]

2. What is *your* [or another's] *existing* stand [response-statement] on an issue regarding the subject at hand—if any stand yet? ["Set shutter speed at 1/125 second... ["Use short sentences, they're emphatic and long sentences are run-on... Utilitarianism is the best ethical system... "]

3. What are *all possible* [or relevant!] stances on that issue, A-to-Z? And what are the *functions* of, and the *pros-and-cons*, of taking, *each* stance? [Speeds from time to one second to

1/4000 second … Short sentences can be emphatic/choppy, long can be eloquent/runon etc… There's also Absolutism, Situation ethics, other moralities…]

4. Is your [or the] <u>existing stance the *best*</u> one of them all, for the current task-goal purpose, <u>after all</u>, <u>or should the stance be *altered*</u>? [Slower speed to increase focus, blur the birds' motion; faster speed freezes motion… Medium-length sentences for letter-to-the-editor… Shift to Existential ethics?!"…]

5. <u>Complete the process for the other variable-issues on the subject</u>. ["**Focal length** of lens; Camera-**angle** (high low eye-level); **Light-source** (behind in front side); etc. ….. **Parallelism & repetition**; **length** of writing; **tone** of writer; **structure**; **explicitness & location** of the writing's **point** or thesis; **visual layout and graphics**; etc… View all relevant **ethical systems**, the A to Z poles and the Stations in between and the pros and cons of each…]

…this models how we **consciously** use our own thinking ploys to discuss the teaching of thinking… Oh, and "Nice use of **concretization**, or **examples**: three core instances, varied…" ["Thank You…"]

["FOOTNOTE" FOR *ADVANCED* LEARNERS *ONLY*:] You can note that many one-point positions exhibit at least some of <u>these traits of provinciality</u>—simplicity—incompleteness—hence possible bias!

1. The issue involved is often left <u>subliminal</u>, not mentioned or names. ("Sentence-length, shutter-speed, nutrition…")
2. Statement is <u>monolithic, hemispheric</u>: only one stance or side mentioned.
3. Is <u>authoritative</u> and also <u>prescriptive</u>. Implies "this is the truth," plus "one must do this."
4. Is "*field-free*." Isolated in a vacuum, not placed in any *context, environment, situation*.
5. Is formal-only; <u>function-free</u>. Does not specify *goals, purposes, uses, effects*.
6. Is <u>non-evaluative</u>. Does not objectively examine the orchids-and-onions, good *and* bad points, of the move.
7. Is not "<u>gradient-located</u>." Where does it stand on a **conceptual continuum** of "all" possibilities, A to Z?

---

6. …you may even, for a "Pro-Con" type issue, <u>fairly</u> state (A.) <u>all</u> the issues, and then for each issue,)B) <u>all</u> the data on <u>each</u> side (or <u>all</u> sides)

TOUCHSTONE-EXAMPLE. **Moral-Ethical Systems.** A *marvelous* book <u>Beyond Bumper Sticker Ethics</u> by STEVE WILKENS (1995), achieves *the very rare excellence* of first identifying <u>many</u> systems, and then for <u>each</u>, <u>even-handedly but incisively</u>, discovering <u>both</u> "positive aspects of," <u>and</u> "potential problems with," the stand— and <u>many</u> Orchids and Onions, too… An *impressive achievement!* **(Alas, to save space, we give the full Beauty & Beast points only for the first two of the nine systems discussed. But the other seven are explored just as thoroughly…)**

1. Cultural Relativism. [[{+++} 1.Eenrichment, 2. Anti-ethnocentrism… {- - -} 1.Who decides? 2. Do moral principles vary? 3. Is relativism self-contradictory? 4. Is moral improvement possible? 6. Is tolerance always good?]]

2. Ethical Egoism. [[{+++} 1. Responsibility, 2. Self-preservation, 3. Unselfish actions can be bad!... {- - -} 1. Narrow individual viewpoint, 2. Too optimistic about human nature?, 3. Inconsistent and self-defeating?, 4. Is justice possible in egoism?, 5. Does E. misrepresent altruism?. 6. Minimizes differences between people?]]

3. Behaviorism… 4. Utilitarianism. 5. Kantian Ethics. 6. Virtue Ethics. 7. Situation Ethics. 8. Natural Law Ethics. 9. Divine Command Theory.

|~#+|~#+|~+|#+|~+#|~#+|#+|#~|+#|+~|+#|~+|#+|+|+#|~#+|~+#+~|+#|#+#|~|+~#+|~+#|~+|#+~|+#|~+#|~#+|~|||~#+|~#+|~+|#+|~+#|~#+||||

[4.] GALLERY of EXAMPLES. V-V <u>is</u> *very simple in concept* ("you want to choose the best stand for the purpose, not just a simple limited one, so be sure you know of all possible stands A to Z"). However, **V-V** <u>is</u> *undeniably complicated to really know and use well.* Therefore let's "hydrate" the above Mental Guideline, with Material examples of v-v in use in various subjects, arenas, venues, in order to better cinch the concept, the "very idea" of V-V, for learners:

[4.1.] Music, also **Oral Interpretation as of poetry etc.:**
Pitch (high or low), **Timbre** (color), **Rhythm** (beat meter accent), **Tempo** (pace/speed), **Melody** (pitch in the whole), **Harmony** (chord, progression), **Texture**, **Form.**
"SO, WHAT?" Well, all the better to know all these issues-and-options, to control your performance

---

[4.2.] Cookery. Most of the key **variables** are never mentioned, nor the dexterous **options** they offer:
Cooking Methods... Sequence of More than One Cooking-Method... Ingredients... Seasonings... Sequence of Seasonings... Criteria for Taste and Quality... Other Specific Methods; *And yet other variables...*

Sequence of multiple methods of cooking? EXAMPLES. [1.] Fry French fries half-done first, drain & cool, *then* finish, for better flavor. [2.] Saute lamb chop first, *then* remove and add garlic rosemary lemon, to prevent burning earlier.

"SO, WHAT?" ...clear suggestion that Issues and Options can *empower* creative thinking...

[4.3.] Sources of Energy. *(*) Excellent: "all" options listed, plus for each, fairly all the pros and all the cons!*
[Pollutions? Transport of? Inefficient? Tricky technology? Limited supply?]
Oil... Coal...Natural Gas...Nuclear... Biomass...Hydroelectric... Geothermal... Solar... Wind... Hydrogen... Conservation... Other?   [--MAXIM magazine] [More complete than usual: thus, a cameo-capsule of **V-V** itself?...]

[4.4.] Therapy for Homosexuality: Reparation or Conversion. [*An unusually-complete treatment;*
Most responses are either traditional-conservative defenses-of, or radical-liberal condemnations-of...:] [-- WONDERSIDE, LLC]
1. Is H. an illness?..... 2. What does science say?..... 3. What of background world-views: Natural Law vs. Liberal Humanism?... 4. Religious or spiritual facets.... 5. Issues of "Choice," and "Change." 6. A right to seek treatment? 7. Motivations and reasons pro and con. 8. Other issues: Parenthood. HIV.?

[4.5.] Assignment: English 101.

"The narrators of Faulkner's 'A Rose for Emily' and Gilman's 'The Yellow Wallpaper' are both women who go mad. They go mad in part as a result of the way women in their respective societies are treated. Demonstrate the ways in which their being women affected their lives and led to their madness."

Apply the V-V to this assignment. Can we powerfully see (1) what **variables in education** (see the D-Machine unit) it takes a stand on? (Does it make "the best" choices—by what criteria?) Which variables does it quite *neglect*?
--Purpose: show mastery of course-interpretation, vs. .....?
--Decisions: who (course or student) makes how many of them?
--Goal of education here? .....
[...this assignment comes off as astonishingly-"provincial"...]

The **Conceptual Continuum** approach of **V-V** as a *potent* method of *critically evaluating* any response to anything...

[4.6] The skill of WRITING, COMPOSITION—and the teaching of it. *Provincialities, and their corrections!*

[A.] WRITING: Classic Provincial Rules: Hemispheric, Contradictory, Prescriptive, Isolated!

--"Use personal tone... no, keep it formal"
--"Short simple sentences, vivid... long more elegant"
--"One page only... at least 2,500 words"
--"All text... no, use graphics, visuals, diagrams, etc."
--"State point at once... no, slowly reveal thesis at end."
--"State point once only... repeat your idea, to add pace-tone-emphasis
--"Write tight, non-wordy... don't write telegraphically"
--"Bring self into it... keep objective, impersonal"

WRITING: A more powerful V-V checklist:

[*] See the power of a complete, compact checklist of the key variable-issues to decide about in writing. With A and Z polar-opposites. [Sentence length: one word to X pages!]. And pros and cons of each. Perhaps also "mandated, plus permissible ranges of variation, for which types of writing: School, Business, Civic-Public, and genres..."

How do writing constraints differ (1) among the disciplines in school? (2) Between Schoolwriting and Vocational writing (in re length, tone, structure, audience, graphics, point position-and-explicitness, proof?)

--"Make ideas explicit…let reader see for themselves"

[And so forth… the content of too many composition textbooks of the past…]

(*) Analysis. An attempt at Reading the Situation of "traditional school-writing styles" (rather Provincial One-Point in a vacuum we thought…):

A researcher could generate (better than I did!) **the unspoken rules of much Schoolwriting: Perfect instances of Provincial Positions: monolithic, isolated, prescriptive…!**

1. Generally avoid the personal except in certain English courses.

2. If there is a choice between being abstract and being concrete, be concrete.

3. Use a propositional rather than an oppositional structure.

4. Avoid metaphors and figurative language.

5. Generally avoid using graphic signals such as underlining, subheads, and the like except in science and mathematics.

6. Focus on the content rather than on making the reader feel comfortable.

7. Select a single aspect of your subject and announce your thesis as early as possible.

8. Make sure the surface appearance of the text is attractive. Check spelling, punctuation, and grammar.

9. Use complex or embedded sentences.

10. Avoid humor. [-- ALAN PURVES]

Alas, how provincial these would be to offer learners without considering the variations!

I MYSELF had to learn as a writer how to read **the varying situational demands** of freelance magazine feature-articles, the unstated ground rules, and change from schoolwriting:

1. Length: in school, "at least 500 words"; outside, "one-page minimum" or the like.

2. Tone: in school, often formal-impersonal; outside, usually a person on the page.

3. Structure: in school, sometimes lead up to the point; outside, announce the conclusion first.

4. Audience: in school, a vacuum—the professor is the reader; outside, rhetorical tuning.

5. Graphics: in school, just prose on the page; outside, often charts-tables-diagrams, etc.

[*] The V/V ploy may help accelerate skill in choices in writing in various arenas, venues, genres!

TESTIMONY. A WRITING TEACHER is perplexed…
[A literature student asks him should she bring her feelings or a life-event into her literary criticism of a text. Yes and no in English; yes for psychoanalytic, reader-response, feminist criticism, but not always elsewhere. Data from the author's life? Class, gender, politics, sexual issues? Sometimes welcomed, sometimes out of bounds in English.] [-- PETER ELBOW]

[Perhaps V-V doesn't answer the situation-questions, but makes one more aware of the variables themselves, which then can be more easily attended-to in diverse situations?]

[B.] Writing: the issue of the Active and the Passive Voice. Active Advantages: Fewer words, engaging to readers, direct, concise. Active Disadvantages: May offend readers, Names an agent perhaps better concealed… Passive Advantages: Conceals responsibility, diminishes message harshness, emphasizes recipient. Passive Disadvantages: More words, disengaging to read, indirect, tedious, vague. [-- KAREN WINK]
["Obvious" perhaps {except when not known!!},but not always as completely laid out as here…]

[C.] Writing: the issue of Clarity vs. Obscurity. Making one's meaning "Clear," versus being "Obscure."
Clarity is good but perhaps to say "Always be explicit and clear," risks being Provincial-Partial?

| CLARITY GOOD: in most cases…. | CLARITY BAD: in some advertising, public relations [Selling a college's "unique Alpine setting" is less crude than "Tahoe, baby; ski your shins off"], literature too (let reader see for self!). | OBSCURITY BAD: Thoughts not thought out by the writer… Sheer lazy carelessness, inability… Willful obscurity "masquerading as aristocratic exclusiveness." [-- S. MAUGHAM] | OBSCURITY GOOD: sometimes unavoidable in complex subject with unfamiliar reader. See above Clarity Bad. Literary "showing not telling," plus being faithful to true mystery! (Rembrandt painting shadows, song in Shakespeare's Twelfth Night. [-- C. E. MONTAGUE] | OBSCURITY GOOD/BAD? Conceal point intentionally, soft-pedal bad news, etc.? |

[6.] The END: *wrap-up, send-off,* "Envoi" or "good journey":

…well, I *am* (modestly) impressed *this* time… Your **V-V** scheme *does* show how to expand simplistic responses to better choices by seeing all options A to Z… Or at least shows the Very **Idea** of it… …Say, is all this *your own* idea? Or is it *common knowledge*? Or somewhere in between?	--It is in between—I think that it is *widely-practiced among good thinkers*-writers-communicators, but remains subliminal, *not usually explicitly encoded* (hence charting the territory here … --…In fact, the *only* other statements which resemble the **variables-variation** "thrust," though others may of course exist, which I have *ever* come across, are *the following four*: **(1)** From **a resource on informing teachers of research in pedagogy**: "…instances of a concept often lie on a continuum. Understanding what that continuum is allows you to make inferences about other nonobserved instances and their relationship to known instances. For example, if I maintain that learning theories lie on a continuum from strict environmental to strict individualistic, you might start to ask what theories fall in between or where does a given theory fall on that continuum." [-- MARILLA SVINICKI, <u>Learning and Motivation in the Postsecondary Classroom</u>] **(2)** From two **textbooks on poetry-reading**: **(A)** "Continuum. An imagined constant line that expresses some feature of relation in a poem; defined by the naming of two poles and by positing a series of gradations between the extremes at each end. [This can be applied to all elements of poems. Figures of speech could range from the A of very-literal, to more-figurative ones arriving at Z.] [-- <u>A Poet's Guide to Poetry</u>] **(B)** Another poetry guide excellently discussed <u>quality of poems: sentimental-popular, vs. more-artistic</u>—by means of using a modified **V-V** approach to good effect. The author ["<u>I.</u>"] <u>first mentioned variables:</u> [1] trite language and clichés, [2] forced rhymes, [3] archaic words, [4] sentimentality, [5] dishonesty, [6] adjectivitis, [7] misuses of allusions and myths, and *I would add* [8] bad enjambment, that is, prose chopped up into awkward lines instead of true line-breaks. <u>Then</u> ["<u>II.</u>"] and marvelously, the author <u>took a good poem and then</u> *rewrote it toward bad-ness, variable by variable*, to elucidate the variables! [-- STEVE KOWIT, <u>In the Palm of your Hand</u>] **(3)** And, "Under no circumstances can the representation of an Idea be considered as successful as long as the virtual sphere of its possible extremes has not been reviewed." [-- WALTER BENJAMIN] **(4)** And **a statement from a classic book on thinking**: "Vary one thing at a time, and keep a note of all that you do." [-- quoted in R. FLEISCH]

[{(END of "TTh" version of VARIABLES-VARIATION…)}]

\=\+|+|+|+\=\=\+|+|+|=\=\=|+|+|+\\\+|+|+|=\=|+|+|+|=\=\+|+|+|+\=\=|+|+|+|+\=\=|+|+|+|+\=\=|+|+|+\=\=|+|+|\=\+|+|+|+\=\=\+|+|+| +

[{(END of Appendix #6, REPERTOIRE of Mind-Play…)}]

\=\+|+|+|+\=\=\+|+|+|=\=\=|+|+|+\\\+|+|+|=\=|+|+|+|=\=\+|+|+|+\=\=|+|+|+|+\=\=|+|+|+|+\=\=|+|+|+\=\=|+|+|\=\+|+|+|+\=\=\+|+|+| +

--THE CONCEPT/ISSUE. This thinking Move (gambit, ploy, foray…) is a major one today. Its "mantra" or rationale-for-being is that "complex issues demand the information and skills from more than any one field, discipline, arena, specialty." This rationale echoes our own, that "complexity of issue, requires, repays complex thinking." But how to do multi-field endeavor *well*?

--THE SO-WHAT NEED, OR PROBLEM/OPPORTUNITY. The actual Method of ID endeavor is still being developed, so also especially the pedagogy—as of currently [2007], more calls for explicit method emerge.

--OUR SUGGESTION. We are preparing **a 100-page resource on "ID/Integrative Endeavor."** [It draws upon our own minoring in cultural anthropology/humanistic sociology, doctoral dissertation on rhetoric of ID.]

SEE: the resource in process, soon to emerge. Below, preview via **this cameo overview:**

[1.] INTRODUCTORY: 1. <u>Definition</u> of discipline, as a sort of lens. Characteristics of an academic discipline.
2. <u>Rationale, justification</u> for doing ID (as noted above: complexity requires complexity…)
3. <u>History</u> of ID: emergence, fragmentation, re-combinations. (Trivium-quadrivium, specialties, new fields.)
4. <u>Subtypes</u> of "ID" endeavor: mono-disciplinary, multi-, cross-, pluri-, trans-, poly,- inter-…
5. <u>Difficulties</u> in doing ID:
X KOCKELMANS: epistemological institutional psychosociological cultural.   X J. T. KLEIN: distortion context outdated overcertainty monism onesidedness
6. <u>Analogies</u> for ID work:
(1) "cartographic" (each discipline as a country or territory, its content its territory, its methods its culture)
(2) "geopolitics" relations between/among fields (turf wars, foreign aid, lend-lease, defense, colonization…)
(3) "genealogy" (discipline & another discipline/subject) (close cousins, or distant strangers?)

[2.] GALLERY: A Michigan river. Water. Wearing of sunglasses. Fall of Rome. American South. American work-ethic. Crime. [Others?]

[3.] PEDAGOGY: "Introduction to ID Endeavor in One Classroom Hour"   **EXAMPLE:** alcohol.
[Student examples: X Thunderstorms, X The Jean Scene…]
Mix and Match worksheet, connect Discs. ABCDE, with Discs. ABCDE, for which subjects?
"The X of Y" [the Mathematics of Psychology… Psychology of Mathematics… Anthropology of Math… Geography in Literature… Aesthetics of Geography… Biology of Economics… Economics of Biology… and so forth!]
"The "---ics of" [Archaeology of the cinema, Aesthetics of Travel, Erotics of Politics, Grammar of thinking, Graphics of Poetry, Poetics of Graffiti, Politics of Educatiion, Rhetoric of letters-to-the-editor, Semantics/Semiotics of urban life, etc.],

[4.] Some ID VARIABLE-ISSUES:
1. <u>Subject</u>: simple, or complex?
2. <u>Level of discipline</u>: lower-level == higher, conceptual?
2. <u>Number of disciplines</u>: one, or many? (**"Monisms"** = <u>one</u> field tries to explain "all or much," *but*…)
Geographic; Marxist-socioeconomic; behaviorist-psychological; Freudian psychogenic;
3. <u>Purposes</u> of task. (A) To serve subject, issue, audience. (B) To serve *own* disciplinary augmentation. (C) To *contribute to* (aid) Discipline B (in either A above, subject, or even B)—or to *critique* Disc. B's use of or lack of use of Disc. A!
EXAMPLES. Biology *helps* sociology… art *aids* science… **but** evolution *challenges* humanism, sociobiology *attacks* behaviorist psychology…

Simple subject, only one discipline.	Simple subject, many disciplines.
Complex subject, only one discipline.	Complex subject, many disciplines.

4. <u>Relationship</u> between two or more disciplines: % of harmony, integration == or conflict?
SECTION: "Psychology & Sociology": mutual cooperation, vs. conflict, mere-juxtaposition, or monisms.

5. <u>Genealogical relation of discipline and subject</u>: close relatives, or distant strangers/foreigners?
GALLERY. *Close Relatives*: Painting and poetry… Demography and sociology…
Distant Strangers: Evolutionary biology ➔ aesthetics of landscape?! Molecular biology ➔ gastronomy?!
Evolutionary psychology ➔ economics?! Geography ➔ sociology of the theatre?!   **[{(END of Brief "I" glimpse of ID…)}]**

[#A8] "GREENprint"

A "reminder-roster" for elucidating a complex subject more competently. Especially a <u>process or skill</u>-to-do, but also a higher <u>concept-to-comprehend</u>…

THE ISSUE. We need specific (yet not formulaic) skills for **elucidating** complex content…

THE RELEVANCE. But these skills seem *scattered among specialized systems*.

--"**<u>Process-analysis</u>**" or how to perform a technical skill [soldering; Chinese stir-fry; buying a used car; etc.]. **I am indebted to P.A. for the core: "Describe all the steps, and in order, and for each, exactly how, plus range of variation, exceptions, alternative optional choices, prevalent pitfalls, etc. And on the side, goals, rationale, criteria for excellence, troubleshooting, etc."**

--"**<u>Technical Writing</u>**" or conveying specialized complexities to semi-outsider audiences…

--"**<u>Rhetoric</u>**" itself in the good sense of reaching readers, including the

--"**<u>Teaching of Composition</u>**" with its "modes of development" and the like…

--Also, "**<u>Assignment-Design</u>**" from pure Educational Pedagogy: improved from rote to thinking!**…**

But *most existing resource-materials seem incomplete*, in re **elucidation** or illuminating a complex subject/process, *both* completely-comprehensively, *and also* clearly-accessibly—as much as possible of both contrary demands!…

--…and **skills in many other specialized <u>Fields, Disciplines</u>** which I have not encountered competently…

THE SUGGESTION. Hence this module. I created it by harvesting from the above scattered sources during decades of teaching. Call it a blueprint, roadmap, menu, "a set of reminders for a particular purpose."

    <u>SELF-EVALUATION OF PRODUCT</u>. CANDID RESPONSE: Not satisfied—with the material "yes," but not the "expository elucidation" or categorizing, converging, coherence. But it's a beachhead-beginning.

#+#|+#|+#|+#|#+|#+|#+|#+#|+#|+#|+#|+#|+#|+#|+#|+#|#+|#+|#+|#+#|+#|+#|+#|#+|#+|#+|#+#|+#|+#|+#|+#|#+|#+|#+|#+|#+|#+|#+|+##||

Table of Contents of "Greenprint" section:

#+#|+#|+#|+#|#+|#+|#+|#+#|+#|+#|+#|+#|+#|+#|+#|+#|#+|#+|#+|#+#|+#|+#|+#|#+|#+|#+|#+#|+#|+#|+#|+#|#+|#+|#+|#+|#+|#+|#+|+##||

[1.] ORIENTATION to the "GREENprint" concept:

(1) Will **the dramaturgic model of "12-W"** assist? (Also called the **SAM or Significant Action Monitor.**) Who is doing What to what Substance? Where and when? How by what method? Why (1) justification or rationale to begin with, (2) for what specific outcome? (How well did it have to be done, how well was it done?) Whence, with what results?

395

Actual conclusion or "score" (fail/succeed etc.)? By what criteria? Who judged the result, and how well—do we all agree with them, and if not why not? **[[Possible orientation or reminder of issues to confront, not to overlook…]]**

(2) "Conceptual Topography"
Treating a concept or larger issue as if it were a geographical terrain to be mapped. As for our own **Specific Detailing, Lens-work, Conceptualizing UP 101**, and others!
[This *whole element* is usually *omitted*, is scandalously-*absent*. EXAMPLE: instructions are given for "specific detailing," "support your idea with examples," without illuminating the conceptual backdrop of the "ladder of abstraction" or the spectrum or continuum from concrete material tangible, to or toward conceptual mental abstract, and back again…
[Not surprising, this shortchanging of the conceptual backdrop, since much education remains concrete …]

(3) "CODE": Concept, Cruciality, and Counsel. (What is the issue, why is it important, and suggestions.) Vital to answer the reader's question, "so what?"
The Issue Here: describe what happens or the situation or "conceptual topography" contour.
Why Important?: Cruciality: clarify why it is important, "so what why bother," what matters here, is there anything at stake, etc. **"Exigency"** = "an imperfection marked by urgency, a thing other than it ought to be or waiting to be done" [-- LLOYD BITZER, COMMUNICATION STUDIES]
Our Suggestion: offer procedures to confront this "problem/opportunity." [Note—not rigid rules but flexible tools; see formula below. Perhaps a "reminder of possibilities"…]

(4) "Operating Concepts."
Reveal and emphasize the "hidden why" either something happens, or a problem occurs and a solution exists, that is, why something works, is powerful and useful but too often non-understood? "It's said that we should use specific details, use parallelism, write sentences with proper emphasis/subordination, use visual graphics in communicating, nd get many other peoples' opinions while thinking a subject through—*but exactly and profoundly why indeed?*"

EXAMPLES: "Some "operating concepts" (or "secret reasons") for key writing skills:

[1.] Specific Detailing in writing, and reading. *Not* just "give an example," or "enjoy the imagery," but *this:*
"The Rehydration of Abstractions." The secret here seems to be that "we know clearly and feel strongly significantly through our own experience: experience, observation, recollection, information. But when we write to others, we convey the result but forget to include the specifics which produced the result in us. The specifics remain vivid in our mind but we overlook that they aren't on the page, "freeze-dried." Therefore we weaken our account. Suggestion: remember to not just tell but show, re-inst all the vivid specifics which will like ju-jitsu or puppet-master re-create the emotions not just the facts in the reader."
Not "The auto accident was terrible and depressing," *but* "the station wagon was upside down on the median strip and children's toys were scattered about." **[[Failure to "dip down" is a depressingly-common shortfalling! Possibly, spotlighting the "key reason behind," can help writing students remedy this lack.]]**

[2.] Parallelism in writing. Not just "use parallelism within a sentence," but this:
"If similar in Idea, make Similar in Style." The semi-secret here is that "we perceive similarities better if they are presented in similar form." Therefore, if a series of X or N ideas are related in thought, help the reader to see this by writing them in similar style. EXAMPLE: "Frank likes skiing, to fish, and he dances" vs. "Frank likes skiing, fishing, and dancing." And //ism is complex: on level of sentence also paragraph and whole text; it is varied, from military-rigid to relaxed; and it uses virtually all grammatical elements (part of speech, sentence type, etc. **[[Not much instruction in writing explicitly defines parallelism *conceptually*, as here, let alone moves into its complexity beyond just "Avoid Faulty Parallelism Within The Single Sentence"…]]**

[3.] Syntax: Emphasis and Subordination in sentence-structure. Call it **"Proportionate Packaging,"** perhaps. The key secret here is that the following is a virtual rule-of-thumb due to the way we comprehend : "For best clarity, place important ideas in main clauses, secondary ideas in subordinate clauses; and place early in the sentence, known lesser or introductory ideas and later in the sentence the important ideas."
EXAMPLE: (1) "Breaking his arm, he slipped on the dock." (2) "He broke his arm, slipping on the dock." (3) "He slipped on the dock, breaking his arm." (4) "Slipping on the dock, he broke his arm."
[[… I find it amazing how this *principle* is often not made crystal-clear in writing instruction…]]

[4.] <u>Visual Representation</u> of Ideas. Call it **"Simultaneous Scanning,"** perhaps. The secret here is that the mind grasps much, but the eye can grasp at once, a field of varied objects and their relations much better." Result, we should use charts graphs diagrams pictures visuals etc. more than we do, and not just for quantitative but also for conceptual information, employing this Operating Concept?

EXAMPLE: a numerical table of population-distribution, versus a map (of U.S.A., the world, any territory) with dots representing X or N number of people. Case closed! [[**We woefully under-utilize visualization, are not graphically literate. See Introduction of this very publication for four graphics which try to convey concepts not just quantities visually...]]**

[5.] **Researching other viewpoints.** Call it **"Colloquializing Beyond Our Bottlenecks,"** perhaps. In researching and thinking through a subject, be sure to consult as many other different opinions, responses, viewpoints as possible— more than one might think needed. The secret here: psychology of perception. The world of reality is vastly more extensive and complex than any one person's perceptual system (however good!) can perceive and absorb. Analogy: reality is a very wide band spectrum, but each of us is a "radio" which can receive only a narrow band, but put together, we get a bigger picture.

[[**Disclosure: one of my three "bitter regrets" of what I failed to do when teaching, was to reverse the usual "close down" to the one right answer, in favor of first the "opening-up" to** *all* **possible responses, via a round-robin, chairs-in-circle, go-round in the class where each and every student gave their own response and I honored it for its own unexpected insights no matter whether ultimately invaluable, or perhaps mistaken or irrelevant (but even so, useful) but also an otherwise overlooked viewpoint representing this or that interesting aspect of Better Thinking!...]]**

(5) Thinking as "confronting content conceptually."

Formula. "Rule, or tool"? The "reminder": is the procedure, more of an algorhythm rule tactic, or more of a heuristic tool strategy? ("This you must do then success will ensue," _vs._ "use it or not, depending...")

Letter vs. Spirit. What is the literal formal concept or practice ... and what is the figurative or essential spirit or quality of the concept or practice? Cf. also "correct by the book," vs. "effective in situation"...
> EXAMPLE. The issue of **"calibration or proportion"**: in writing, by the *Letter*, "emphasize main ideas, downplay secondary material. By the *Spirit*: is there a harmonious balance between importance and size, in all things? Interestingly, often one can break a Literal rule if one still achieves the Spirit of the intended goal...

Locales. Where does this concept or skill appear, is used? (A) specific usual home-bases. (B) other arenas far afield in personal, work, civic life? [[**B is too often neglected! It can help cinch concept, show its importance!]]** EXAMPLE: in writing, Unity-Coherence-Emphasis, a mainstay of expository "thinking and writing", *but also* can be present (or regrettably absent!) in "life." (Time-management, prioritizing, calibration or proportion of importance, etc.)

Canon and Context. Does the skill/concept **relate to, or differ from, other** similar related, *or only apparently*-related items? Cf. **"Another Name For..."** *but also* **"Related To But Don't Confuse With"** [EXAMPLE: "wordiness" in writing is "more words than needed to convey the idea," it is *not the same thing* as generously-appropriate "elaboration, development" of an idea.]

Examples. Giving specific instances, cases, occurrences, illustrations—well, examples!—of the skill/concept. LEVEL I: the brief "Pump-Priming Warm-Up":
[EXAMPLE: **"competence or quality"** involves ideas such as "Personal Best"... "Satisficed" or minimally "good enough for government work"... Olympic or World-Class... Botches Blunders Bungles errors of commission vs. Unawarenesses Oversights errors of omission... and more] [[**This sensitizes reader to what *is* this concept/skill after all!]]**

LEVEL II: the fuller-dress **"Rounded Ensemble."** Give *many* examples... of *varied* types, explicit or implicit categorizing into sub-types... drawn from varied *arenas* (personal, work, civic, time and place, etc.)... *distilled* or stated briefly... perhaps *dual or using comparison/contrast* of beauty-beast or non vs. yes, to clarify by showing differences... and *effective*: relevant, enlightening, moving...

EXAMPLES: X *A dozen* instances of varied <u>travel</u> possibilities, of scandalous behavior of lazy <u>cousin Scott</u>, of excellent <u>experiential education</u>, of <u>"writer-based vs. reader-based"</u> writing, of the <u>injustices of King George</u> which, listed in the Declaration of Independence, supported America's case. (at least I give five examples!

[[Rare but powerful, thus regrettably shortchanged, is this dipping-down to display instances as if from an incoming airplane approaching a new territory…]]

#+#|+#|+#|+#|#+|#+|#+|#+|#+|+#|+#|+#|+#|+#|+#|+#|+#|#+|#+|#+|#+|#+|+#|+#|+#|#+|#+|#+|#+|#+#|+#|+#|+#|+#|#+|#+|#+|#+|#+|#+|+#||

[2.] KNOWLEDGE of the subject: *Learner's* Image, also *Experts'* …

[A.] The Learner

Learner's Existing Image of the skill or concept.   (Awareness-about, also Ability-to-do.)

<u>Positive</u>: experience with, ability to connect old-known to the new-unknown.

<u>Negative</u>: **Ignorances**-about (null-info), also **Misconceptions**-concerning (wrong info). Also perhaps **Apprehensions** or inappropriately-negative affect or attitudes, feelings, emotions concerning.

PAP's or **"Prevalent Amateur Pitfalls"** or *usual, recurring stumbling-blocks* in both awareness or beliefs-about, also perhaps attitudes-toward, and also of course abilities to do or not to do (botches bungles blunders)?

[[It's possible that in many cases, recurrent similar omissions/misconceptions exist—cf. students' belief about some science, etc.—and if identified can be clarified, thus accelerating learning marvelously…]]

"Background Knowledge." What is needed here?   **[[A very important, often overlooked, issue!]]**

Knowledge needed ahead of time to competently Comprehend concept, Perform skill.

Everything from the "conceptual topography" of keystone variables to orient, down to technicalities.

EXAMPLES. For "specific detailing in writing," the whole issue of the **ladder of abstraction**.

For writing to communicate, the concept of **"writer-based vs. reader-based** writing."

For horticulture, many basics: not just how to plant, but which plants for which climates and soils, etc.

[B.] "People in General" "Myths and Realities About" X the Subject "Differential Knowledge" or,

virtually Everyone knows A about the subject, *Many or Some* know B, but *Only a Few* know C…"

[C.] The Expert Specialists Current State of Advanced Knowledge about the subject.

"What We Know And Don't Know About" X the Subject … **"Updates:** Corrections, New Knowledge"

"Future Trends for needed research" ….. **"CEC"** or **Current** (updated) **Expert** (not just anybody) **Consensus** (rarely perfect agreement)

[[This can be important. See article on "marijuana" which competently demonstrates myths, realities, what we know and don't, gray areas of disagreement—shows the complexity of knowing!]]

#+#|+#|+#|+#|#+|#+|#+|#+|#+|+#|+#|+#|+#|+#|+#|+#|+#|#+|#+|#+|#+|#+|+#|+#|+#|#+|#+|#+|#+|#+#|+#|+#|+#|+#|#+|#+|#+|#+|#+|#+|+#||

[3.] EVALUATION of the Concept or Skill:

How bad or good is the concept or skill? Its Orchids strengths values and powers, its Onions or demerits shortcomings drawbacks even dangers? By itself "always," but also when applied in a specific instance?

[A.] Per se innately intrinsically inherently. Not in a given instance, see [B.] just below

Do a two-panel **"pro-con balance sheet."**

EXAMPLE. "Specific Detailing": (+) effectively informs, persuades, instructs how, moves, etc.!

(-) May chain us to the concrete level, not conceptualizing inducting to get ideas from the information.

This can be a **"four-window" graphic** when subject is compared with another subject or its opposite.

EXAMPLE. Types of Knowledge: "Personal subjective experiential affective" etc. "versus" "Impersonal objective logical-rational decentered" etc.

Personal Good: communicates well to others, is more complete than just reason, may get to true Truths…	Objective Good: morally good because fair to other viewpoints, avoids egocentrism, etc. Practical too.

Personal Bad: incomplete, may be biased without self-disciplined analysis	Objective Bad: not the only way of knowing! Risks being misused as a cover for bad thinking, defenses.

[[Rare but also valuable is this objective [!] both-and assessment of strengths and limitations of the issue!]]

[B.] Result: what is Competence or Quality–level?

Possible theoretically or ideally? *Needed* required in a given case or task/goal? Actually *attained*, achieved or not in a given case or task/goal?

--The idea of **"In Vitro versus In Vivo."** **In Vitro** means *"under glass"* therefore in the laboratory, therefore <u>"By The Book" textbook or Letter-Perfect</u> (whether right for a given situation or not.) **In Vivo** means *"in living state,"* therefore <u>workable in the field or context or situation</u> (where "technical perfection" may or may not be needed or even desirable!)

[[This can be useful. To <u>enforce high-quality learning, first stage</u>. EXAMPLE. In a <u>writing class, a letter to the editor</u> making four points, *hideously* lacked *any* parallelism in its four sub-topic sentences. Teacher could assign a rewrite by whole class, saying "make it letter-perfect," explicitly mentioning parallelism *or not*, and then unarguably could critique rewrites which did not rework to perfect even if excessive-for-occasion parallelism! Next step is of course "Rules vs. Tools," move from formula to flexible use of a skill...]]

--The <u>**"6-V"** Continuum</u>. For a given task-goal, is a given concept or skill: **Vital**, indispensable?... **Valuable** generally?... **"Various,"** good or less so, depending?... **"Vague"** its value here unclear *or* debated, disagreed-about and if so why?... or actually **"Verboten"** inappropriate or dangerous in this genre, arena, venue?!...

[[This may be for some learners elementary and mechanical, for others liberating from rule-mongering..]]

--<u>**"APE == APE"** Avoid pitfalls and errors</u> (of omission and commission) == <u>aim for potentialities and excellences</u>. The continuum of not only "get it correct" or error-free, but "make it effective also."
1. Beware **ignorances, oversights, misconceptions**, and **botches-bungles-blunders.**
2. Seek to know *all* variable-issues to confront, and for *each, all* alternate optional choices A-Z.....

--**Criteria for Judging. Levels of Quality or Competence.** **[[Alas, a VAST subject.....]]**
Personal... Situational... By-the-Book theoretical... "Other"...
--**"Competence-Continuum":** *Terrible ... Minimal* "satisfied" just-adequate ... <u>Satisfies requirements</u> of task/goal situation... *Exceeds* requirements, expectations? ... *"Olympic World-Class"*...
[[Well, this can tell beginning learners that the score is more complicated than "lose/fail" or "win/succeed"...]]
--**"The Score, and the Judges."** Who judged the result? By what method and rationale, and how competently or not, did *they* evaluate competence?! Do *we* agree with *their* decision, and if not, why not? **[[Rich fertile but also swampy terrain here...]]**

--**Should the Judges' criteria be revealed?** Should this include the **Personal,** even including Pet Preferences (hobby-horses, even root-biases) and Pet Peeves? (Should a teacher disclose his/her personal passions and poisons, preferences anyhow? .....) **[[Hey, do an Objective Evaluation pros-and-cons on this!]]**

#+#|+#|+#|+#|+#|+#|+#|+#|+#|+#|+#|+#|+#|+#|+#|+#|+#|+#|+#|+#|+#|+#|+#|+#|+#|+#|+#|+#|+#|+#|+#|+#|+#|+#|+#|+#|+#|+#||

[4.] Orientation to the Greenprint concept:

(1) Two Levels of Instruction: Basic Mantra, vs. Advanced Variables.

EXAMPLE: **Specific Detailing.** [I] *"Support your idea with an example,"* **versus** {II} see the Tool-Kit on 'Concretization" for *many variables*: Specific/Concrete vs. General/Abstract... Six Types of Detailing... Issues of Number of, Length of, Variety of, Effectiveness of... 20 ways of dramatizing exposition... and more...

Parallelism. [I] *"Phrase similar ideas in parallel form,"* **versus** [II] Levels from sentence on up to whole text... Structure: military-rigid vs. relaxed-broken... Complexity: simple vs. many-parted... Elements or Components: use of parts of speech, sentence-structure, typography... and more...

...Quite new to some students (and teachers...): dual levels, of simpler rules, vs. more-complex components.

(2) Standard "Process Analysis" Variables. Relatively better-known are the components of technical writing's process-analysis, or how a (usually-material) procedure is done or how to do it.

> TOOL-BOX. We analyzed <u>cooking instructions</u> ("Chinese stir-fry, herbed roast chicken, vegetarian cooking) and derived out the following roster, a *fortified, expanded elucidation of existing* textbook "process" instructions:

<u>Introduction</u>: Definition... Define key terms!... Preparatory: material, conditions... "BACKGROUND INFORMATION" needed to know to orient to the task. Including keystone "**operating concepts**" or "the hidden Why and How behind it all...

<u>Body</u> of Process: (A) Identify *all* "steps," including substeps and maybe supersteps, and in chronological order...

(B) For *each* step: what is done, how it is done, and why it is done. Then: what are the Variable-Issues to consider (decisions to be made: (mandated-unavoidable, and elective-optional)? For each, what are the AOC's alternate optional choices, decisions to make? Give **required-vs.-alternatives**: strictly-optional steps (use visuals?) == semi-optional depending on conditions (examples and amount of them, parallelism, etc.?) == and mandatory, unavoidable, must decide about (length? tone taken?)... Formula, esp. "Rules-Tools": are the steps, rote tactics==or heuristics and strategic?

Disagreement among experts ("CEC" or Current Expert Consensus is conflicting?)... ERRORS, FAILURES: "PAP" Prevalent Amateur Pitfalls" in Awareness, Action, Ability. "Sins" of Omissions (oversights misconceptions), and of "Commission" (botches bungles blunders). Also "delicate or tough" segments or phases, and "subtle advanced touches" etc.... **Variation:** what is total possible range (in vitro), permissible range in the situation (in vivo)?... Quantification and qualification...

<u>Background</u>: Pros and cons of the process... "Operating concepts," working principles (the "secret why's behind" as discussed elsewhere here)... Standards of excellence, what makes a good performance?... Troubleshooting, specifically what is wrong, why, how to correct it... Fields: Context etc.... Secondary, "Nice-to-know" information... Reference info, where to find...

(3) ...another version of Process: Level II, more-complex ploys...

TOOL-BOX. We analyzed differing sets of instructions (some excellent, many astonishingly bad—incomplete, partial, superficial!)—on three issues.

(1) "Analyzing **engine exhaust smoke** when **buying a used car**"

(2) "Materials and practices for **safer, disease-free sexual activity.**"

(3) "**purifying drinking water** in the wild."

4. "the varied processes for **printing** written material,"

5. "the uses/misuses of the **apostrophe**," 6. "<u>the poetic form</u> known as the **double –dactyl**," 7. "the **saucing of pasta,**" 8. "how to write a **good book review**"...)

From these, we derived the following roster. It makes explicit what was present but subliminal.

Problems, Pitfalls—and Potentialities: usually known-by-all, avoided == *or* more subtle, or infrequent, or insidious, more easily-overlooked...

Static, *or* Changing—even if subtly, and un-recognized by too many thinkers. "**Major** or Ground-Rule Change to Whole new Ball Game, not Pew but Church"?

"Degree of Knowledge-About." Common recurring elements which "of course *We or Everybody* already knows" == *versus* less-known but just as important (dangerous or essential) which "*many fewer* people know," maybe even "*only the truest competent insider-Experts*"...

Level "I" "Safe" (accepted near-and-dear known standard unquestioned == *versus* Level "II" "Silent" (overlooked) or "**Strange**" (too quickly thought wrong etc., rejected from consideration...)

Connect/Separate. Two things wrongly seen as different (are or should be), *but* should be more related... *or* two things uncritically seen as same or belonging together, *but* should be distinguished, distanced...

"Foreign Field": the context situation conditions etc., including which are unusual, atypical.

Cause-Effect: Complexities. Results which are undesired, unintended, unanticipated, unacceptable!

Formula vs. Flexibility. Standard situations, *versus* non-formulaic, wickedly-complex, situations "outside the box."

Categorization: component subparts, aspects, etc. of the content or process, some too often overlooked.
Others.....

III. "Moving from Simpler Item to More Complexity Explored, Elucidated...

TOOL-BOX. Here a roster of "move to improve" a response or subject to more clarity...

[1.] GENERAL ENHANCEMENT... Augment the existing... Emphasize the under-considered, spotlight the overlooked... Reconsider the wrongly rejected-or-dismissed—oh, and question the arguable but uncritically-accepted!... Update the traditional-but-outdated... Correct the misunderstood... Fill in ignorances, unawarenesses... Alert to both pitfalls and opportunities which are still overlooked... Develop the embryonic or still-nascent, and extend the started-but-unfinished... Re-balance the only-one-sided, but also consider both pros and cons, and fairly and objectively too... Expand the oversimplified superficial, but also clarify out the over-complicated... [2.] Of course also RE-ADJUST SIZE, SCOPE: Reduce (the irrelevant or over-developed) and Rebalance (calibrate the relative proportions of elements to be better-balanced in emphasis/subordination). [III.] Also, CONCLUDE an investigative analysis: suggest recommend propose private, and public, policy and procedure, and/or solve a problem or make a decision, and so forth...

Structure kind of murky or tangled here; egg on your face.	Too true, and I knew. But cost-benefit ratio said simply: at least get it out in time for publication...

#+#|+#|+#|+#|#+|#+|#+|#+#|+#|+#|+#|+#|+#|+#|+#|+#|#+|#+|#+|#+#|+#|+#|+#|#+|#+|#+|#+|#+#|+#|+#|+#|+#|#+|#+|#+|#+#|#+|#+|#+|#+|#+#|#+#||

[5.] "BEHIND THE SCENES": second-level awarenesses-of...

--(A) What "essential-thinking" skills are present in the subject, also needed for good confronting of it? (See the roster of eleven components of essential or "basic-advanced" thinking elsewhere.)
--(B) What different learning-styles should be served for different readers/users?
(Expository, examples, experience, argument pro-con, analogies, visuals, other)
--(C) Personal insights/biases of the writer on the subject? Extent of processing of them within self, then extent of disclosing them to reader-audience? His/her self-evaluation of the elucidation, and do we agree or not?
--(D) Pedagogically we have assignment-design.

EXAMPLE. Here, a version of "Assignment BlueGREENprint." It seems to promote thinking-about one's actions. I used it mainly to teach writing techniques: parallelism and repetition... specific detailing... comparison-contrast and classification-and-division... and others...

1. Name and Definition of the Item. Its relation to other similar items (but "don't confuse with")?

2. Your current image and existing knowledge of the item. Any "Background information" needed?

2. Formula: is it more a rule (rote recipe), or a tool (heuristic, strategy)?

3. Why use it I: How it works, the "hidden why" or Operating Concept behind

4. Why use it II: specifically intended functions purposes results effects advantages?

5. Pros and Cons: its advantages, also its deficiencies, even dangers.

6. Pitfalls: common stumbling blocks to beware and avoid (misconceptions, missteps). Potentialites to aim for (excellences explicitly elucidated).

8. Evaluation. What is a good performance of the skill? How well do you have to be able to do it in this course for which grade? [The instructor's personal peeves and preferences (insight/biases) if any?]

7. And then, the "meat:" specific skills and subskills and how to do them...

...while "rough" in terms of World-Class "assignment design for Thinking," still the above roster may suggest raising thinking questions in the midst of a standard assignment. A colleague of mine (and very dedicated retired high-school teacher), said, "I surely wish I had had this sort of thing when I was still teaching..."

[{(END of "GREENprint" appendix ...)}]